Liberals in the
Russian Revolution

THE CONSTITUTIONAL DEMOCRATIC PARTY, 1917-1921

By William G. Rosenberg

PRINCETON, NEW JERSEY
PRINCETON UNIVERSITY PRESS

Copyright © 1974 by Princeton University Press
All Rights Reserved

Published by Princeton University Press, Princeton and London

Library of Congress Cataloging in Publication data will
be found on the last printed page of this book

This book has been composed in Linotype Baskerville

Printed in the United States of America by
Princeton University Press, Princeton, New Jersey

To Elie

A NUMBER of friends and colleagues encouraged me during the preparation of this study, offering sharp and incisive criticism, rather than simply benign approval. I am enormously grateful for their help. Doubtless I have failed to write the book each would have liked; but the present volume is far stronger than it otherwise would have been because of their investment.

Peter Filene, Alexander Rabinowitch, Israel Getzler, and Andrew Rossos read early versions of a number of chapters, and focused their criticisms on style as well as substance. Roman Szporluk offered counsel on the Ukraine. Ronald Suny and Michael Hittle patiently read an earlier version of the entire manuscript, as did Terence Emmons and Barbara Ringwald, indicating both directly and indirectly their sense of shortcomings. Richard D. Mann raised a number of important questions about the Kadets as a social group, and was very patient and supportive despite the obvious limitations of my work as social psychology. Nathan Smith and Peter Kenez generously and repeatedly shared their own expertise on both the revolutionary period and the Kadet party, offering sources as well as suggestions, and a great deal of encouragement. I am much in their debt. Loren Graham helped push me into a very much needed revision of the manuscript at a time when I might otherwise have avoided it.

I am particularly indebted to Sam Bass Warner, Jr., who offered a flood of comments and criticisms in a much appreciated effort to make the book more intelligible to a general reader; and to Leopold Haimson, who was far more generous than I think I deserved with his time, his knowledge, and his remarkable capacity for critical analysis. I join a growing number of historians who are deeply in his debt, and take particular pleasure in expressing my appreciation.

This investigation was also generously supported by a number of institutions. The Social Science Research Council of the American Council of Learned Societies and the Center for Russian Studies at the University of Michigan enabled me to make two trips to the Soviet Union; and under the directorship of Morris Bornstein and Alfred G. Meyer, the Russian Center at Michigan also provided other much needed and appreciated support. The Foreign Area Training Fellowship Program supported me when part of this book was being prepared as a doctoral dissertation. Two fellowships and a summer research grant from the Horace H. Rackham School of Graduate

Studies at the University of Michigan provided time for research and writing, some of which was spent at the Russian Research Center, Harvard University. Harvard was also generous with its facilities and funds when an earlier version of Chapters 9 through 15 was being prepared as a doctoral dissertation under the supervision of Professor Richard Pipes. The Russian Institute at Columbia was exceptionally generous and kind in providing me an opportunity both to complete my dissertation and begin my study of Kadet politics in 1917, and also in sponsoring the present publication. I doubt whether Alexander Dallin and others associated with the Institute when I was there realize how important their initial support was to me, or how much I still appreciate it.

I am also very grateful to the library staffs at the University of Michigan, the Hoover Institution, Harvard University, Yivo Institute, Columbia University, the New York Public Library, the Library of Congress, the Bibliothèque de Documentation Internationale Contemporaine, and the state libraries of Moscow and Leningrad, where most of my research was completed. The professional expertise of Peter Kudrik and Joseph Placek at Michigan greatly eased the burdens of locating and obtaining sources. I am also particularly anxious to thank Mr. Lev Magerovsky of the Archive of Russian and East European Culture at Columbia, who helped me through the mass of materials he attends so carefully, and Mrs. Arline Paul of the Hoover Institution and her former associate, Mrs. Marina Tynkov. Their assistance was invaluable.

The editors of the University of Chicago Press, the University of Missouri Press, *Soviet Studies*, and the *Cahiers du Monde Russe et Soviétique* have allowed me to republish some material which previously appeared in somewhat different versions. The maps on pp. 10 and 382 are reproduced from R. H. Ullman, *Anglo-Soviet Relations*, Princeton, 1968, Vol. II, with the permission of the author. Most of the typing was done expertly by Colleen Glazer, Janet Fisk, Jeanette Ranta, Lou Ann Lenio, and Carla Robinson.

Finally, I wish to mention my family. My six-year-old son Peter has complained regularly about my wasting paper, and is fully convinced, despite a measure of filial pride, that there are too many books in the house already. (Once when I showed him something I had written in the library he looked at me in embarrassment and promised he wouldn't tell.) Doubtless his judgment is sound, both in terms of scholarship and ecology, and I ask his forbearance. Sarah, my four-year-old daughter, can't believe I like to sit so long in my study. She and her friends wonder what I really do. Recently she has come to appreciate the magic of my new electric typewriter, however, and now guesses it is all right. I will ignore her condescension, and thank her for her interest in my margins. My wife Elie long ago emancipated herself from my labors. It took her far less time to do so, in fact, than it took me to respect her for it. One very happy consequence of the time I have spent on this volume, therefore, is that I can now fully champion the difference between the editor-typist-babysitter-assistant and the truly supportive spouse. I'm very grateful for my good fortune.

W.G.R.
Ann Arbor, Michigan
March, 1973

ABBREVIATIONS OF FREQUENTLY CITED JOURNALS

ARR	*Arkhiv Russkoi Revoliutsii*
GMNCS	*Golos Minuvshago na Chuzhoi Storone*
Ist. SSSR	*Istoriia SSSR*
IZ	*Istoricheskie Zapiski*
KL	*Krasnaia Letopis'*
LR	*Letopis' Revoliutsii*
NCS	*Na Chuzhoi Storone*
NZ	*Novyi Zhurnal*
PR	*Proletarskaia Revoliutsiia*
SEER	*Slavonic and East European Review*
SR	*Slavic Review*
SZ	*Sovremennye Zapiski*
VE	*Vestnik Evropy*
VI	*Voprosy Istorii*
VPNS	*Vestnik Partii Narodnoi Svobody*

CONTENTS

PART FOUR. EPILOGUE: THE EMIGRATION

LIST OF TABLES AND MAPS

TABLES

MAPS

Liberals in the Russian Revolution

WITH a few obvious exceptions, I have used the Library of Congress transliteration system in this book, without diacritical marks. Names of individuals in the text are also spelled without apostrophes. Familiar names like Kerensky appear in their common English form.

The old (Julian) calendar was used in Russia until February 1, 1918, after which both the Julian and Gregorian (or Western) systems were employed, depending on which part of the country one happened to be in. For 1917 I use dates conventional to the time (and thus the Bolsheviks assume power in October, not November). For the civil war period, I use both dates wherever possible. Where there might be some confusion in footnote references to newspapers or periodical literature, publication numbers are given.

A N ENORMOUS number of books and articles have been published on the Russian revolution in the last fifty years, but it might be said that a great deal has been written with little knowledge. With several notable exceptions,[1] much of the literature has until recently focused on the "inner meaning" or "ultimate" significance of events, rather than any real comprehension of what happened or why, on exposing "conspiracies" and "lusts" for power, rather than understanding the drama of political and social conflict, or the quest for radical change. Many crucial episodes of the 1917-1921 period, as well as the structure and scope of the revolutionary process as a whole, have largely remained obscure.

Recently, several excellent detailed studies have clarified the picture somewhat, although in some cases more questions have been raised than answered. Particularly important have been the investigations of Alexander Rabinowitch, Oliver Radkey, Peter Kenez, Ronald Suny, and Rex Wade in the United States, George Katkov in England, Marc Ferro in France, and Eduard Burdzhalov, Pavel Volobuev, Leonid Spirin, and Luka Gaponenko in the Soviet Union.[2] One great value of these works, moreover, has been that they all generally avoid attempts at broad synthesis, and concentrate instead on investigating specific problems, laying the foundation from which a thorough understanding of the revolutionary period as a whole can eventually emerge. In the meantime, we still have much to learn about such problems as the revolution as a social (as distinct from political) process, its development in the provinces, the form or composition

[1] Although written almost forty years ago, William H. Chamberlin's *The Russian Revolution*, 2 vols., New York, 1935, still remains in many ways the best single survey of the 1917-1921 period. One should also note E. H. Carr's well-known three volumes on *The Bolshevik Revolution, 1917-1923*, New York, 1951-53, part of his general *History of Soviet Russia*.

[2] Alexander Rabinowitch, *Prelude to Revolution*, Bloomington, Ind., 1968; Oliver Radkey, *The Agrarian Foes of Bolshevism*, New York, 1958, and *Sickle Under the Hammer*, New York, 1963; Peter Kenez, *Civil War in South Russia, 1918*, Berkeley, 1971; Ronald Suny, *The Baku Commune, 1917-1918*, Princeton, 1972; Rex A. Wade, *The Russian Search for Peace*, Stanford, 1969; Marc Ferro, *La Révolution de 1917*, Paris, 1967; George Katkov, *Russia 1917. The February Revolution*, London, 1967; Eduard Burdzhalov, *Vtoraia russkaia revoliutsiia*, 2 vols., Moscow, 1967-71; Pavel Volobuev, *Proletariat i burzhuaziia Rossii v 1917 godu*, Moscow, 1964, and *Ekonomicheskaia politika vremennogo pravitel'stva*, Moscow, 1962; Leonid Spirin, *Klassy i partii v grazhdanskoi voine v Rossii*, Moscow, 1968; Luka Gaponenko, *Rabochii klass Rossii v 1917 godu*, Moscow, 1970.

of crucial local organizations and groups, the influence of such factors as wage levels or socioeconomic status on urban political affiliation, and even the politics and behavior of leading political elements like the Mensheviks or the liberals.

The present book focuses on the group many Russians thought would lead their country through the revolution into the ranks of Western European democracies, the Constitutional Democrats, or Kadets.[3] As political history, it examines the values, programs, organization, and tactics of Russia's most prominent liberal party at the time of its greatest crisis. As a study of the Russian revolution and civil war, it probes the strengths and weaknesses of the one political group whose policies did more to influence the outcome of events than any other political organization besides the Bolsheviks. Throughout, my effort has been to examine Russian liberal politics in terms of their relationship to revolutionary social forces, although it should perhaps be stressed that much remains to be done before we can understand these forces clearly, and that this is a political rather than social analysis, a study of the party, rather than the broad social milieu in which Kadets operated. Investigating the revolution "from below," as it were, is a task I have reserved for future labors.

The role of the Kadets in the revolution and civil war has not yet been examined closely for a number of reasons, most of which in one way or another have affected the outcome of my own research. One is that political historians have generally found satisfaction in dealing with movements which "succeed," either to champion the "victors" or to warn against the challenge they represent. As Michael Karpovich pointed out in a seminal article many years ago, the general attitude toward the Kadets has been: "Why should one pay much attention to a political trend which could not achieve any lasting results, and which suffered such a crushing defeat?" Karpovich's own answer, which deserves repeating here, is that the historical process does not know any ultimate results, any final defeats or victories; and that the importance of historical phenomena should be assessed in terms of the time in which they occurred.[4] To this I would add that since all revolutionary movements meet resistance, the success of even the "victors" can be fully understood only by comprehending the behavior of their adversaries. While the Kadets indeed failed, partly for reasons of their own making, partly not, comprehending their weakness is no less im-

[3] Called "Kadets" from the combination of the Russian initials "K" and "D" from Constitutional Democrat.

[4] Michael Karpovich, "Two Types of Russian Liberalism: Maklakov and Miliukov," in *Continuity and Change in Russian and Soviet Thought*, ed. E. J. Simmons, Cambridge, Mass., 1955, p. 130.

portant to understanding the Russian revolution than is an awareness of the sources of Bolshevik strength. At the same time, however, the general disinterest of historians has meant that there is little one can lean on in terms of the party's prerevolutionary history as a basis for exploring their behavior in 1917. Early party disputes, organizational and tactical problems, and even personal relationships may well have affected the Kadets in the revolution and civil war to a greater degree than I am aware; and when the party's history in the Duma years is written, some of my own conclusions and observations may well have to be modified.

Another reason why the Kadets have been avoided lies in the very complexity of the 1917-1921 period itself. In the eight months alone from the abdication of the tsar until the Bolsheviks assumed power, Russia had four different Provisional Government ministries. Each had its own distinctive policies and attitudes, and each must be understood in conjunction with other complicated developments: the disintegration of Russia's economy; the cohesion of her social classes and the process of social polarization; the collapse of the army and its changing goals and composition, to name an obvious few. The civil war was even worse. The Ukraine had some six or seven different governments from 1917 until 1921, depending on how one counts; South Russia had four or five; Siberia had a score. Everywhere social movements and military efforts rose and fell in a bewildering and complicated pattern.

This complexity has clearly added to the length of my study, but it has also forced some limitations. I have not, in the main, attempted to paint a broad picture even in the realm of Russian politics. My goal has been much more specifically to investigate the Kadet dimension of the revolution and civil war, and in this way contribute to what I hope will soon emerge as a general and thoroughly comprehensible tableau.

In this connection I might also mention problems of conceptualization. When writing of liberals and even the revolution as a whole, historians and other authors have frequently used Western concepts which seem precise, but whose application to the Russian context (or any greatly different cultural setting, for that matter), is often quite tenuous. With respect to the Kadets—or the Party of People's Freedom, as they were sometimes officially known—one of the most troublesome is "liberalism" itself. "Liberal" certainly should be applied to the Kadets in the general sense. Venerating legal principles and a rule of law, holding individual civil liberties as precious values in themselves, seeking *political* democracy in the main, rather than *social* democracy or class leveling, Kadets represented in Russia what can generally be regarded as basic European liberal traditions. Also, like liberals elsewhere, most Kadets soon abandoned an early flirtation with radicalism, and came to fear the elimination of recognized authority just as they abhorred abuse of power, seeking reform from within established structures even while urging that those structures be over-hauled. Kadets themselves, moreover, insisted that they were ideolog-ically allied to their Western European liberal counterparts.

Yet "liberalism" cannot be clearly defined in the context of the Russian revolution and civil war, nor applied with easy consistency. Neither, in fact, can "party," which rarely referred in the period to a tightly knit Leninist-type political organization. Indeed, some Kadets in 1917 and the civil war years even believed that "parties" were not appropriate political forms for Russia, that they were socially and politically disruptive in a period when Russia needed unity and social peace. And in the civil war, many who insisted they were liberal be-came closely involved in politics of crude reaction, despite their own continued Kadet affiliation. Thus the Kadets cannot really be treated or understood as a coherent liberal party if one takes a narrow view of these terms; and in the pages which follow, they are used quite loosely.

There is also the problem of sources. The tendentious quality of many Soviet publications is matched by émigré memoirs, and volumes of materials compiled in the West which mislead through omission. More important, archives for this period remain largely closed to Western scholars in the Soviet Union, while Kadet party materials elsewhere deal almost entirely with the civil war and emigration. The result for a study of this sort is both the necessity of some imbalance, and the frustrating need to leave a number of important questions un-answered, such as, for example, the actual social composition of Kadet leadership in both urban areas and the provinces, and the real social base of party support in different regions. Lacking detailed member-ship lists or other similar records, I have found myself limited on these and other matters to educated guesses, some of which I can make with more confidence than others. Indeed, I initially intended to con-centrate my analysis on the civil war and emigration alone, where the Kadet documentation, at least, is relatively complete. But the critical turning point in the party's history was February, not October, 1917, and to concentrate on the latter period alone would have been to dis-tort the liberals' experience in the revolutionary period as a whole. Here, consequently, one can only hope that refinements can be added as more materials become accessible.

Finally, there is the problem of bias. It is difficult to treat any aspect of an event like the Russian revolution with the detachment expected of professional historians, and as I have already suggested, most students until recently have generally been reluctant to try. (The very mention of the Kadets in the revolution and civil war among Russian historians invariably brings either a wistful "if only . . ." response, or immediate disdain. I once mentioned my study casually in the Hoover Library to a distinguished older scholar and was immediately subjected to a fifteen-minute harangue about the "imbecility" of Kadet tactics!) But perhaps the solution here is freely to admit one's prejudices, and to accept the notion that no historian is ever fully objective, whatever the topic of study. Moreover, history as mere fact is little more than chronicle; without judgment, which operates in the ordering of events as well as their analysis, and which invariably stems from bias, it also teaches little.

My own goals and biases can be briefly laid out. My principal effort has been to seek a closer understanding of the revolutionary process in Russia by focusing on the role played by the Kadets in structuring events between 1917 and 1921, and to analyze Kadet politics not only in terms of Russia's general conditions, but also by considering the programmatic and tactical alternatives which were open to them. While I support the notion that some form of revolutionary upheaval was both certain and desirable for Russia during the first two decades of the twentieth century, I reject the idea that the outcome of events was somehow preordained. Even the Bolshevik assumption of power in October was by no means a guarantee that Soviet Russia would survive; indeed, all indications at the time pointed to the contrary, from the ongoing problems of war, military discipline, and food supply, to the general orientation of Russia's vast numbers of land-hungry peasants. Without detracting from Lenin's own profound appreciation of these difficulties or his ability to overcome them, I hope to show how the behavior of the Kadets themselves very much influenced the development of events.

This is not to maintain in the larger sense that Bolshevik success was not historically warranted, or that liberals alone were *primarily* responsible for Russia's destiny. On the contrary, I hope to indicate that it was the socialists who were generally attuned to popular aspiration in the 1917-1921 period, rather than the liberals, and who deserved political power even on the liberals' own constitutional democratic principles. Nor is it to fix blame or otherwise vulgarize a massive suffering, or even to demand that the Kadets be a group or party other than what they were. But it is to argue that from the abdication of the tsar in early March 1917 until the final defeat of the White armies in Siberia and South Russia, Kadet behavior must be assessed in terms both of the party's actual and potential relationship to the success of radical change in Russia, their commitment to social as well as political reforms, and their willingness to yield political power themselves in the interests of peaceful social transformation and the revolution's success. And in these terms, as the reader will see, I have found myself in the course of my work becoming increasingly more critical of both liberal politics, which in many ways violated the principles Kadets ostensibly supported, and many of the values on which the party's efforts as a whole were structured.

This bias is offset, however, by a genuine sympathy for the plight of many individual party leaders. Like their socialist counterparts, both moderate and radical, many liberals did indeed recognize the enormous potential for social betterment which the revolution unfolded, and found themselves desperately anxious to see it survive. Studying the Kadet party is not to investigate a monolithic group. Indeed, the Constitutional Democrats rarely if ever presented a united front. ("There exists an opinion that wherever there are two Kadets, there is a right-wing Kadet and a left-wing Kadet," one party leader wrote in reviewing his colleagues in 1921.)[5] Even within the Kadet Central Committee itself, as will become clear, both ideological and tactical commitments were often quite diverse. And in addition to those who feared democratic freedoms and the struggle for rapid social equalization, there were others who saw the revolution as a great social and political opportunity. Eventually, some Kadets even tried to work for Russia under Lenin and Stalin, serving in various administrative posts until the 1930s. For these party leaders in particular I have a great sense of compassion.

There is, of course, an enormous danger in a historian's reading back his own values into the subject he studies, and this is not my design. The past rarely provides answers to contemporary problems, and those who approach history in these terms are almost always frustrated. But the historian's mirror can be set to illuminate certain questions about social and political development which transcend chronological context, questions such as the relationship between ideology and practice, the problem of who should determine policy and define "national interest," the nature and desirability of stable political authority in contexts of social inequity, the limitations of intellectual elites in politics, or the limitations of coercive authority in societies where those who exercise power pursue markedly different goals from those they rule. And focusing on these issues has certainly been my intention. While the Kadet experience in the Russian revolution will provide no general answers, my hope is that the questions it prompts can be usefully asked of other more contemporary contexts.

[5] K. N. Sokolov, *Pravlenie generala Denikina*, Sofia, 1921, p. 52.

PART ONE

KADETS BEFORE THE REVOLUTION

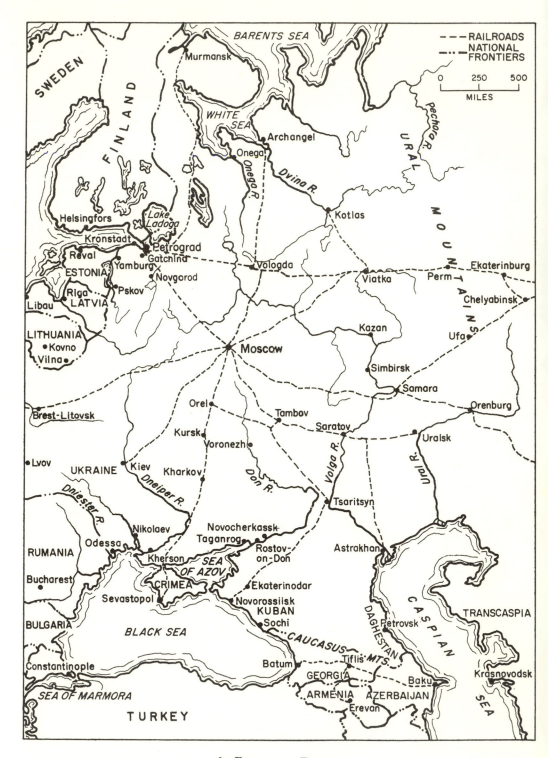

SWEDEN

BARENTS SEA

Murmansk

FINLAND

WHITE SEA

Archangel

Onega

Onega R.

Dvina R.

Pechora R.

URAL MOUNTAINS

Lake Ladoga

Helsingfors

Kronstadt

Reval

Petrograd

Yamburg

Gatchina

Novgorod

ESTONIA

Pskov

Riga

Libau

LATVIA

LITHUANIA

Kovno

Vilna

Vologda

Kotlas

Viatka

Perm

Ekaterinburg

Chelyabinsk

Ufa

Kazan

Moscow

Simbirsk

Samara

Brest-Litovsk

Orel

Tambov

Saratov

Orenburg

Kursk

Voronezh

Uralsk

Lvov

UKRAINE

Kiev

Kharkov

Dneiper R.

Don R.

Volga R.

Ural R.

Tsaritsyn

Nikolaev

Novocherkassk

Taganrog

Dniester R.

Odessa

Rostov-on-Don

Astrakhan

RUMANIA

Kherson

SEA OF AZOV

CRIMEA

Bucharest

Sevastopol

Ekaterinodar

Novorossiisk

KUBAN

Sochi

CASPIAN

BULGARIA

BLACK SEA

CAUCASUS MTS.

DAGHESTAN

Petrovsk

TRANSCASPIA

Constantinople

Batum

Tiflis

GEORGIA

Baku

Krasnovodsk

SEA OF MARMORA

ARMENIA

AZERBAIJAN

SEA

Erevan

TURKEY

Legend:
- - - RAILROADS
-··- NATIONAL FRONTIERS

0   250   500
MILES

1. EUROPEAN RUSSIA

CHAPTER ONE

Program, Organization, and Politics

THROUGHOUT the long winter of 1917, supplies of food and other essential goods grew increasingly scarce in Petrograd. Two and a half years of war were taking their toll. Production lines moved fitfully, transport was a shambles. Grain stored in the countryside began to rot. The staggering lists of casualties (which by now numbered well over five million killed, wounded, and captured) included many of Russia's most skilled workers and industrious peasants. Their indiscriminate drafting in the first months of the war was but one of a long series of blunders by a government whose ineptitude had by now alienated virtually every sector of Russian society.

Toward the end of February, lines in front of Petrograd food stores began to grow longer. There were rumors that the city's grain supply was nearly exhausted. Angry Petrograders shuffled their feet against the cold, waiting long hours for their rations, and muttering with their neighbors about the authorities.

On February 22 word spread that the government had reduced the available ration of bread. The same day, some 50,000 workers from the vast Putilov steelworks found themselves locked from their shops in a dispute over wages. The combination brought angry men and women into the streets.

The following morning, "International Women's Day," menacing crowds formed around the food stores. While at first there were only scattered political demonstrations, the actions of a few ignited the crowds. Within hours, Petrograd was a sea of red flags. The fearful and vastly outnumbered police were reluctant to assert their authority.

The next afternoon throngs moved up and down the main Petrograd boulevards. Police officials making a belated attempt to impose order met strong resistance. Shots were fired; pillaging occurred; more political banners appeared. In offices and apartments, government officials met anxiously in hurried consultations.

On Saturday, February 25, virtually all of Petrograd shut down in a vast general strike. Students, shopkeepers, and professional people joined thousands of workers in the streets. Deliveries ceased, trams stopped running, industry ground to a halt. Red banners demanding an end to the autocracy filled the city. Most important, soldiers and

11

cossacks of the Petrograd garrison showed signs of sympathy for the demonstrators. Who could object to comrades demanding political freedom and bread? In an episode soon on everyone's lips, cossacks attacked the police at Znamenskaia Square when a detachment tried to arrest some protest leaders. The melee left a police captain dead, several injured, and government authority weakened throughout the city.

Sunday dawned with heavily armed patrols on the streets. The morning was quiet. For a time the authorities were sure the situation was under control. As demonstrators began to form again in the afternoon, troops were ordered to open fire. In response, however, the demonstrators did not attack the soldiers as they had the police, but begged them to join their comrades from the factories. Crowds also rushed to the barracks, demanding that units be recalled. The troops were quickly convinced. War-weary, underfed, bitter over the army's harsh discipline, worried about "marching orders" to the front, their hearts were with those in the streets. One by one the units "went over."

As the news spread, much of Petrograd turned into open rebellion. The Volynskii regiment joined the mutineers on the morning of February 27, followed soon by other detachments. Shooting could now be heard throughout the city. The arsenal and railroad stations were occupied; telegraph lines were cut; armed soldiers and workers rushed in every direction. With looting, arson, and by now the complete disappearance of police from the streets, tsarist officials, panic-stricken, watched as the revolution burst forth.

Gathering in the wings of the Tauride Palace, meanwhile, was a small group of Russian liberals, leaders of the Constitutional Democratic party. Nervous and apprehensive, but hopeful at the same time that events could be controlled, they considered themselves rightful heirs to the falling mantle of tsarist authority.

KADET VALUES AND PROGRAM

For almost thirteen years, Kadet leaders had struggled to bring liberal rule to Russia. In the salons and apartments of Moscow, in provincial town assemblies, in the Duma chambers of St. Petersburg, they labored both to "educate Russia toward parliamentary government and a rule of law," and persuade reluctant tsarist officials that progress involved dismantling old institutions. Their struggle "was not only for a democratic constitution but also for a 'democratic ethos.'"[1]

---

[1] N. Astrov, untitled MS document on the early views of Kadet party leaders in the Panina Archive, gp. 1, fold. 3, p. 1.

Concern for ethos as well as practical politics defined the essence of the Kadet movement on the eve of the revolution. Above all, the party was not a tightly knit monolithic group in the Bolshevik mold, but a loose association as much concerned with cultural matters as with social and political affairs. In Petrograd, Paul Miliukov and the party's Duma delegates immersed themselves in legislative politics; but elsewhere, many Kadets preferred not to think of themselves as political activists in any sense, stressing instead what they called their *nadpartiinost'*, their desire to transcend narrow partisanship, and work simply toward the general goal of broad liberal development.

Organizational looseness had naturally contributed over the years to a broad diversity among Kadets on questions of political strategy and tactics, and also of social orientation, familiar to anyone who has studied Russia in the last years of the old regime. Often it seemed as if groups of Kadets had more in common with other political parties than with their own Kadet colleagues. Yet all Kadets, despite their differences, were committed to the party's general program. They also shared a common underlying system of values, which not only differentiated them in the prerevolutionary period from most other groups, but also, as we shall see, gave them cohesion in the revolution and civil war, despite new conflicts and differences.

First among Kadet values, and one reason for the presumption of party leaders in February 1917, was a broad nationalism. Kadets were not narrow sectarians. Their fundamental commitment, at least in theory, was to the welfare of Russian society as a whole, rather than to the advancement of any particular social class or socioeconomic interest:

> The Kadet party—The Party of People's Freedom—is distinguished from all other parties in that it struggles for all citizens, and not for one particular social class. For example, our party struggles not only for workers and peasants, but for the welfare and prosperity of all classes, of the entire Russian state. . . . The Party of People's Freedom will not ignore the freedom of anyone; but it works to preserve the interests and rights of all, and also the interests of the state as a whole. In other words, the Party of People's Freedom has a non-class [*vseklassovyi*] character, neither bourgeois nor proletarian, but national [*vsenarodnyi*].[2]

This national, non-class orientation (which differentiated Kadets from English liberals, with whom they otherwise liked to identify) stemmed originally from two principal sources: the "helping hand"

[2] N. O. Losskii, *Chego khochet partiia narodnoi svobody (Konstitutsionno-demokraticheskaia)?*, Petrograd, 1905 and 1917, p. 6.

disposition of the zemstvo movement, where many Kadets had gained their first exposure to social and political problems; and the general perspective of the nineteenth century intelligentsia, which considered selflessness a supreme virtue. Kadets generally thought themselves heirs to these traditions. Like their predecessors among the Westerners, they sought to lift Russia as a whole into the leading ranks of progressive European nations, constantly looking beyond politics in the narrow, partisan sense.

These feelings were undoubtedly strongest among Kadets at the time of the party's formation in 1905, and for reasons which will become clear, diminished in intensity for a number of party leaders in the aftermath of Russia's first revolutionary experience. It may well be argued, in fact, that by 1914 the core of the party considered itself as representing Russia's developing professional middle class, a posture which suited its social base, as we shall see, and which also oriented many party leaders away from mass interests as a widening gap developed between privileged Russia and its worker-peasant mass. Yet as the passage just quoted testifies (having been published as the official statement of the party's position in both 1905 and 1917), Kadets still remained theoretically committed on the eve of 1917 to the role assumed earlier by liberal members of the intelligentsia, that is, as the defenders of general rather than particularistic interests, as arbiters among Russia's social classes, and representatives of none.

Closely related among Kadet values was a veneration of Russia as a state—an orientation in which the economic and political well-being of Russian citizens was translated into the well-being of "Russia" as an abstract entity, blurring divisions between Russia's domestic and international interests. Most Kadets believed with Herbert Spenser that the world was an arena of competitive national struggle; and like others before and since, they feared Russia would be "beaten for her backwardness." Opposition to tsarist authority was thus synonymous with advancing state power; and progress in part for Kadets could be measured by Russia's ability to defend her international position.

In this regard, the outcome of the World War was obviously of crucial importance. Even for philosophical pacifists like Paul Miliukov, there could be no question about Kadet patriotism: "No matter what our attitude toward the government's domestic policy, our first duty was to preserve the unity and integrity of our country," he later recalled, "and to defend its position as a world power."[3] As we shall see, the proper definition of Russia's world position was to become a source of great conflict in 1917, particularly between Kadets and socialist

[3] P. Miliukov, *Vospominaniia*, 2 vols., New York, 1955, II, 190.

internationalists. But the concept of a strong, integral Russian state would prove among the party's most enduring beliefs.

Also, despite their differences, Kadets maintained a strong, almost absolute, commitment to a rule of law, a rule to which "all shall be subordinated, without exception, and first and foremost the representatives of state power."[4] Law was society's only means for insuring personal freedom; it protected one set of interests from encroachment by another. Most Kadets accepted the views of Boris Chicherin, Russia's first consistent liberal writer and philosopher, as well as those of Western European thinkers like Comte and Mill. The primary function of government was to regulate social behavior in such a way as to protect the private welfare of all citizens. Class struggle represented a "harmful and destructive egoism," which weakened the state as a whole. An ideal constitutional system would prevent the domination of one social group over another; a rule of law would prevent arbitrary behavior on the part both of private individuals and state officials.[5]

These nationalist, *rechtsstaat* commitments structured much of the party's prerevolutionary politics, and would greatly influence Kadet behavior in 1917 and the civil war. They also lay at the heart of the party's official program, to which all party members subscribed, whether oriented toward the right or the left. While specific details of the program were never regarded with paramount importance, and as A. S. Izgoev described it, most Kadets viewed their party as a "living organism" rather than a "mechanical union," whose "soul" mattered more than planks in a public document,[6] the program defined the party's basic position on major social and political questions. Equally important, it was also the focal point of criticism for most of the Kadets' adversaries.

The program's dominant orientation, in contrast to the approach both of Social Democrats (SDs) and Socialist Revolutionaries (SRs), was a concern for political rather than social change. The Kadet party's primary goal was to secure "fundamental civil liberties" for all Russians as individual citizens, freedom of conscience, religion, the press, assembly, movement, domicile, and petition, and the end of any restrictions based on class, nationality, or religion. Thus, twelve of the sixteen legislative projects initiated in the First Duma were Kadet civil liberties bills; and almost all of these projects were reintroduced in the Second, Third, and particularly the Fourth Duma, where they were presented in demonstrable opposition to the program of Prime Minis-

[4] F. Rodichev, "Iz vospominanii," *SZ*, No. 43, 1933, p. 290.

[5] S. Iablonovskii, *Kto zavoeval' svobodu*, Moscow, 1917, p. 14 (publication of the Kadet Central Committee).

[6] A. S. Izgoev, *Nashi politicheskiia partii*, Petrograd, 1917, p. 3.

ter Kokovtsev. Virtually without exception, Kadets felt the realization of these goals was *sine qua non* to Russian state progress.

To defend civil liberties, and to channel Russian state authority in a progressive, Western European direction, the Kadet program demanded a system of constitutional monarchism and parliamentary government. Ministers were to be responsible to a legislature elected on the basis of a universal, direct, equal, and secret ballot. No "regulation, decree, ukase, directive, or document" was to have any legal force, "regardless of what it is called or by whom it is issued" unless approved by "the people's representatives" (Article 16). This commitment would cause trouble for Kadets in 1917, when party leaders would attempt to invest legislative and executive powers in the Provisional Government before the convocation of a national constituent assembly. But before the revolution, it differentiated Kadets from the Octobrists and parties to their right, who accepted the Manifesto of October 1905 as the end of Russian autocracy and the constitutional foundation of a new order.[7]

The Kadet program also demanded a broad extension of local self-government, a logical position for those who had grown up with the zemstvo movement and were active in the affairs of city management. It supported democratic elections for local government bodies, and argued that their jurisdiction should extend to all areas of local administration, including the police. In Duma speeches and the press, Kadet spokesmen leveled some of their sharpest attacks on tsarist officials who interfered with local assemblies, particularly during the Third and Fourth Duma election campaigns, and during the war, when officials began to hamper the activities of the so-called public organizations. Interference of this sort was evidence of a "deep moral rot" in Russian society, against which Kadets had to direct the fullest energies of their struggle.[8] Here, too, the freedom of "legitimate" government organs from arbitrary interference would prove a major source of contention in 1917, this time, however, from soviets and ad hoc committees, rather than state officials.

To many Kadets, finally, the non-class, national character of their commitment found fullest expression in those sections of the party's program treating financial matters, land reform, labor legislation, and social issues. Here the party officially adopted the view of its

[7] The Manifesto and subsequent decrees restricted Russia's Duma to simply initiating, rather than promulgating, legislation and left ultimate law-giving powers in the hands of the tsar and his appointed ministers. See the English translation of the Fundamental Laws in B. Dmytryshyn, *Imperial Russia*, New York, 1967, pp. 316-24.

[8] F. F. Kokoshkin to I. I. Petrunkevich, Oct. 11, 1912, in the Panina Archive, pack. 1, fold. 6.

organizational precursor, the Union of Liberation: the harmonious and progressive development of Russia as a whole required the satisfaction of all vital social interests in such a way as to protect the equity rights of all social groups. Worker and peasant interests could not be advanced at the expense of the gentry and bourgeoisie, while Russia's upper classes could not exploit her workers and peasants. From the first Kadet congress onward, party representatives supported the abolition of indirect taxes on necessities, and the establishment of a progressive (but nonconfiscatory) tax on incomes, estates, and inheritance. They also advocated an eight-hour working day "in principle," the organization of trade unions, prohibition of night work, and compulsory government health and old-age insurance (though not in a manner which would weaken Russian economic productivity). And on the explosive issue of land reform, while Kadets, as we shall see, had serious differences about particulars, all party members desired in theory a substantial increase in the amount of land held by working peasants, which was to come not only through the distribution of monastic and state territories, but also through the "expropriation" of land held by private owners with just compensation at "equitable (not market) prices" (Article 36).

Conclusions — Most importantly opposition they generated

Most Kadets regarded these values and commitments as a source of party strength on the eve of the 1917 revolution. As "national liberals" they felt well suited to lead Russia into a new political era, preserving social harmony and defending national interests against foreign encroachment. Yet in several respects, the Kadets' very *nadklassnost'* had become more a cause of political weakness over the years than a source of strength, particularly in terms of the party's competitive position with other political groups. By purporting to defend all social interests while also advocating thoroughgoing political reform, Kadets worked their way into a classical dilemma of political moderates: they opened themselves to criticism from conservatives, who accused them of wanting more radical measures than their European liberal counterparts, even though Russia was far behind other constitutional powers in terms of political culture; and from radicals, who considered their methods conservative and their basic social commitments vague, who accused them of distrusting Russia's masses in their great concern for social order and stability, and who saw them as becoming the core of a genuine, urban middle class, with "bourgeois" values and politics which undercut their theoretical "above-class" posture.

There was, in fact, justification to both types of criticism. After 1905 most Kadets actually did not have much confidence in Russia's workers and peasants. Under the pressure of events they initially supported a universal franchise. But most expected the peasants to vote conservatively in early elections, and were shocked and frightened by the display of rural radicalism in late 1905 and 1906. Thereafter, one of the party's principal objectives was to "educate and lift the dark masses" to a point where democracy and universal suffrage would be effective in Russia, rather than simply to extend the franchise, a posture which clearly suggested a privileged, rather than a non-class perspective.[9] Many, and perhaps most, doubted that time had arrived by 1917.

Also, few Kadets disagreed with the party's official support for a constitutional monarchy, rather than a republic. Most felt the dynasty had to be preserved as a means of maintaining traditional patterns of social order and obedience. With the outbreak of the war, a number of prominent Kadet leaders had even backed away from the notion of a ministry responsible to parliament, supporting, as Miliukov said, a responsible ministry "in a moral, but not political, sense."[10] Moreover, on the question of whether Russia's legislature should be unicameral or bicameral, the program permitted "differences of opinion" (Article 14). Yet a unicameral system was likely to be completely democratic, while a bicameral one was likely to preserve limited suffrage for its upper house; the party as a whole was hedging on the question of representative democracy, and in this way supporting a position that was implicitly class-oriented.

Also, the Kadet program supported autonomy rather than independence for Poland, and postponed further measures on Finland until "future agreements" (Articles 25 and 26), thus calling into question the party's commitment to the principle of national self-determination. In the Second and particularly the Third Duma, Kadet delegates spoke out forcefully against repressive government policies in Finland; and party leaders like Maxim Vinaver and D. S. Pasmanik were champions of equal rights for Jews. But with few exceptions, Kadets firmly supported the notion of a united, indivisible Russian empire; they vigorously opposed federalism, or any similar state structure which might weaken the empire as a whole. To some extent, therefore, the rights of Ukrainians, Georgians, and other national minorities were subordinated in Kadet practice to those of Great Russians, a posture of internal imperialism which had long

[9] Discussions and resolution of the Kadet Central Committee, Dec. 10, 1905, in the Miliukov Archive, bx. 8131, sec. 13, fold. 11. See also B. Grave, ed., "Kadety v 1905-1906 gg.," *KA*, No. 46, 1931, pp. 45-53, and the discussion in E. Chermenskii, *Burzhuaziia i tsarizm v revoliutsii 1905-1907 gg.*, Moscow, 1939, pt. 3.

[10] P. Miliukov, *Taktika fraktsii narodnoi svobody vo vremia voiny*, Petrograd, 1916, p. 15.

characterized the tsarist regime itself, and which would cause Kadet leaders no end of difficulty in 1917, even within the ranks of their own party.

Kadets were scored for even greater vagueness in the years before the revolution on social and economic questions. While their program officially supported various workers' demands, including an eight-hour day in industry, Kadet Duma representatives concentrated largely on lesser questions such as the normalization of contracts and the extension of paid vacations.[11] Officially, moreover, an eight-hour day was to be introduced "gradually" in most industries (Article 44); and in print, Kadets on occasion referred to this commitment as an ideal, rather than a practical possibility.[12] From the left, consequently, they were attacked for their adherence to the concept of property, the right to inheritance, and especially the sanctity of private wealth. But groups to their right often regarded them as dangerous social levelers, particularly in terms of the notion of "expropriating" private estates.

Finally, the party as a whole remained vague on preserving the agrarian commune, and even on the question of private property in land. Kadet spokesmen supported in principle the government's efforts after 1906 to improve the condition of the peasantry; but most opposed the Stolypin reforms as giving insufficient attention to the wishes of peasants themselves, and because they were introduced outside Duma channels. And while most Kadets also believed firmly in the principle of private ownership, they refused to make a "fetish" of this, as A. S. Izgoev wrote in the official party journal;[13] and they recognized the commitment of many peasants to communal forms of agricultural ownership and production. Here, too, consequently, the party lacked firmness on issues to which revolutionary Russia would soon assign great importance.

The price for vagueness on all these matters was a confusion in what might be called the party's identity. To conservative spokesmen like the Octobrist leader Dmitri Shipov, the Kadets were dangerously radical, "striving to enlist the popular masses into a political struggle in such a way as to have a threatening meaning and disastrous consequence for the life of the country."[14] But to many Social Democrats and other leftists, as well as to many workers and peasants, the party

[11] K-D Partiia, *III gosudarstvennaia duma: Otchet fraktsii narodnoi svobody*, 5 vols., St. Petersburg, 1908-12, I, 5-10; K-D Partiia, *Tret'ia gosudarstvennaia duma. Materialy dlia otsenki eia deiatel'nosti*, St. Petersburg, 1912, passim, but esp. pp. iii-vii.

[12] E.g., E. I. Kedrin in *Birzhevyia Vedomosti*, Nov. 24, 1905.

[13] A. S. Izgoev, "O burzhuaznosti," *VPNS*, No. 1, May 11, 1917, p. 9.

[14] D. Shipov, *Vospominaniia i dumy o perezhitom*, Moscow, 1918, p. 396.

was "bourgeois," despite its proclaimed *nadklassnost'*: it preserved the privileges of upper-class, *tsenzovaia* Russia by defending social stability and order, and gradual, rather than rapid, social change.

LEADERSHIP AND SOCIAL COMPOSITION *Were the Kadets a bourgeois party.*

Were the Kadets a bourgeois party? The question has relevance not only for the historiography of Russian liberalism (particularly Soviet historiography), but also for Kadet politics in 1917, when socialists used the label with devastating effect to discredit Kadets among urban workers and peasants. The answer must be equivocal. We can reach some conclusions in terms of the social composition of Kadet leadership. But the problem becomes more complicated when we examine the party's social environment and its prerevolutionary electoral constituency.

In their writings and speeches, Kadets always denied that their party could be considered bourgeois in terms of its social composition. "Ours was a party of doctors, lawyers, and professors," ran a typical description. "The more learned a man, the more professional education he had, the more chance to find him in the ranks of the Kadets."[15] That there was considerable justification for this view can be seen in the social composition of the Kadet Central Committee, the party's highest governing body. Of the 26 members elected to its ranks at the first Kadet congress in 1905, 9 were attorneys and 9 were professors (of whom 3 were professors of law). Not a single member could properly be considered a representative of Russia's trading or commercial circles.

A similar pattern emerged in the Committee elected in 1907, which served virtually unchanged until just before the revolution. While the total number of Committee members increased from 26 to 40, the number of attorneys rose from 9 to 14, and professors, from 9 to 13 (including now 6 professors of law or legal history). There were also 2 medical doctors, 3 professional editors or writers, and 3 who could be classified as statisticians or economists; only 1 member of the Committee—M. G. Komissarov, who owned a large glass factory—was, properly speaking, a manufacturer or tradesman. If the Central Committee has to be classified in terms of social composition in the prerevolutionary period, it might best be considered professional and intellectual. A better characterization might be that used by Alexander Kerensky, who considered the Kadets a "faculty of politicians."[16]

[15] K. Miloradovich, *Chernaia kritika* (*O K-Dakh i o bol'shevikakh*), Petrograd, 1918, pp. 3-4. See also A. A. Kizevetter, ed., *Napadki na partiiu narodnoi svobody i vozrazheniia na nikh*, Moscow, 1906, esp. p. 7.

[16] Interview with A. F. Kerensky, Palo Alto, Calif., November 1964.

The "dean" of this faculty was one of Russia's most brilliant and best known historians, Paul Miliukov. Fifty-six years old as the revolution broke out, Miliukov had already written an encyclopedic study of Peter the Great's economic reforms, as well as a monumental three-volume work on Russian culture, which examined virtually every phase of Russia's historical development. For twelve years he had also edited the party's unofficial daily newspaper, *Rech'*, and had lectured both in Russia and abroad. He had also led the party's Duma delegation, masterminding overall Kadet strategy. Erudite, energetic, arrogant, Miliukov was considered by some a "master of tactlessness" and by others "a man who thinks only according to a set point of view."[17] But few doubted he was one of Russia's ablest and best informed politicians.

Miliukov's closest associates on the Central Committee in St. Petersburg were Vladimir Nabokov, Ivan Petrunkevich, Paul Gronskii, Fedor Rodichev, and Maxim Vinaver, all of whom had legal backgrounds. Nabokov in addition was a co-editor of *Rech'* (and the father of the famous novelist and poet); Gronskii taught law at St. Petersburg University; and Rodichev, the party's "Cassandra," was one of Russia's leading orators. In Moscow, Kadets were also lawyers and publicists. Fedor Kokoshkin, generally regarded with Petrunkevich, Vinaver, and Miliukov as a "prime mover" of the party's internal life,[18] was on the juridical faculty of Moscow University and also an editor of *Russkiia Vedomosti*, a leading Moscow daily. Vasili Maklakov, a future ambassador to France, had gained an international reputation from his work as a defense lawyer in the famous Beilis ritual murder trial. Nicholas Astrov and Nicholas Kishkin, a jurist and a physician, were leading activists in the affairs of city government, both sharing the Kadet hallmarks of erudition and arrogance.

Kadet professional bias was also prominent in provincial party figures, though information on social composition here is more difficult to obtain. In Odessa, the Kadet organizers were Sergei Shtern and Sergei Gutnik, both of whom had legal backgrounds (and both of whom, along with Maxim Vinaver, were leading members of Russia's Jewish community). In Kiev, the party committee was chaired by Dmitri Grigorovich-Barskii, a lawyer, vice-president of the Kievan Society of Social Organizations, and president of the local juridical association. Elsewhere the pattern was similar. Victor Pepeliaev, who was prominent among Siberian Kadets (and destined to figure heavily

17 I. V. Gessen, "Reminiscences," MS translation of Gessen memoirs, Stanford, 193?, chap. 9, p. 17; Pr. S. P. Mansyrev, "Moi vospominaniia o gosudarstvennoi dume," *Istorik i Sovremennik*, II, 1922, pp. 18-19.

18 R. Vinavera, "Vospominaniia," MS in the Hoover Institution, 1944, p. 62.

in the party's civil war history) taught at a Tomsk gymnasium. Alexander Klafton, who led the Samara Kadets (and in 1919 was to become one of Admiral Kolchak's closest advisers) had a background in medicine. In Novgorod, when 52 persons were named as Kadet candidates to the Constituent Assembly in 1917, only 1 was listed as a banker and only 2 as members of commerce, industry, or trade; in Tiflis, 5 of 28 candidates were lawyers, 4 were teachers, and only 1 or 2 were involved in commerce.[19]

Lower down in the party ranks the proportion of professionals and intellectuals was still impressive, though somewhat less large. When the Central Committee asked provincial organizations in 1906 for information on the occupations of their membership, replies from thirteen groups indicated that members of the "free professions" constituted about 21 percent. An additional 13.7 percent were listed as state officials of some sort, while 14.5 percent were labeled as factory or apartment owners, and some 6.6 percent as gentry landlords.[20] According to a critical evaluation, rank-and-file Kadets were the "urban intellectual type" who were "quite poorly informed about the peasant and rural elements of the population, and also quite uninterested in them."[21] According to the Kadets themselves, the majority of party members were "scientific workers, judicial figures, zemstvo personnel, and members of local government administrations."[22] In several important ways, however, the Kadets' professional orientation was less important to the party's politics in the 1917-1921 period than what sociologists would call the party's affect, its social milieu and relations. This, in turn, was closely related to the decentralized basis of Kadet party organization.

The basic Kadet political unit was the local "club," where members met for social as well as political activities, and where they generally held meetings, often using the English word to describe them. How local clubs organized was essentially up to local party sympathizers. A typical group might form simply because ten or twelve persons came together and decided they supported the party's program. There were no formal requirements for admission, nor even many directives from the Central Committee on questions of program or tactics, a situation which occasionally confused and annoyed local party figures, but in any case reinforced their autonomy.[23]

In the early months of the party's existence, local Kadet groups

---

[19] *Novgorodskaia Zhizn'*, July 11, 1917; *Narodnaia Svoboda* (Tiflis), Oct. 14, 1917.
[20] Chermenskii, p. 305.   [21] Mansyrev, p. 17.
[22] N. I. Astrov et al., eds., *Pamiati pogibshikh*, Paris, 1929, p. 6.
[23] P. P. Dmitrenko, "Vospominaniia," MS in the Columbia Russian Archive, n.d., pp. 93-105. Dmitrenko for a time was a Kadet party organizer in St. Petersburg.

sprang up in remarkable numbers all over Russia. The party's official journal listed some 140 different Kadet organizations in 1906, not including the many district groups in Moscow and St. Petersburg or the various student committees. Yet few of these groups were situated in workers' districts, or were specifically designed in cities and towns to attract other than middle-class professional elements, particularly after the First Duma period. In most urban areas, Kadet clubs were set up in offices or apartments; and although all elements of the population were welcome (and in some cases party figures even hoped and expected that workers would join), the club structure itself reflected a middle-class or professional middle-class orientation. As we shall see, moreover, this bias increased very markedly after the electoral reform of 1907, despite the efforts of some party radicals, largely as a result of election returns.

In the provinces, most Kadet groups were formed around local zemstvos or committees of the earlier Union of Liberation. Here Kadets at first hoped to establish close contacts with Russia's peasantry, particularly before the First Duma elections; and their representatives to party congresses frequently expressed radical viewpoints, especially on the land question. Yet despite the fact that most landlords disagreed with the party's land program, it soon became clear that Kadets in the countryside were very much a part of gentry society, at least in milieu. Provincial clubs were not peasant organizations; and in reaching to the peasants, Kadets in the provinces stretched across clear social lines, just as populists and "third element" zemstvo workers had done in the nineteenth century, and just as their party colleagues were doing toward workers in the cities. In the process, moreover, as we shall see, they more frequently encountered suspicion and hostility than support.

Social ties between Kadet professionals and privileged Russia were even closer in Russia's cities than they were in the countryside. This was particularly true in Moscow. Astrov, Maklakov, and other leading Moscow Kadets (especially Prince D. I. Shakhovskoi and Princes Peter and Paul Dolgorukov) were members of Russia's oldest families. Their drawing rooms were frequently the scenes of large social gatherings, in which guests opposing the party's political orientation often outnumbered Kadets. In 1906 and 1907, the political interests of Moscow Kadets was quite high. It was here that the Central Committee first met, and more than half of that body's initial members were Moscow party figures. But after the collapse of the First Duma, many leading Muscovites were barred from extensive political involvement as a result of their signing the famous Vyborg Manifesto. The Central Committee shifted to St. Petersburg, with Moscow Kadets becoming a distinct minority of its membership. And in the years following Stolypin's "coup d'état" in 1907, when political activity in Russia ebbed generally, most Kadets in Moscow drifted away from politics. They immersed themselves instead in "bourgeois" social organizations like the Unions of Zemstvos and Towns, where contacts extended far beyond party lines.

Only in St. Petersburg, in fact, in the years before the revolution, did Kadets maintain a clearly political orientation. It was here that party leaders were engaged almost constantly in problems of Duma legislation and party strategy; and it was here as well that Miliukov attempted to keep the Central Committee functioning as a link to other party elements, though with diminishing success. By 1911, the Petersburg Kadets had contact with fewer than fifty provincial party organizations, and these largely through provincial members of the Kadets' Duma delegation, or through those members of the Central Committee—almost half between 1907 and 1916—who had country estates. Party leaders themselves worried in Petersburg about the Kadets' general "lifelessness," particularly before the elections to the Fourth Duma in 1912. And in Moscow, the isolation and independence of the Petersburg contingent, as well as their preoccupation with high politics rather than general social concerns, was increasingly resented.[24]

On the eve of the revolution, consequently, Kadets were (and always had been) led by professionals and intellectuals, "a professors' party" in Miliukov's own characterization, which drew to its ranks "the most conscious political elements of the Russian intelligentsia."[25] And in their role as the party of Russia's leading intellectual strata, Kadets saw an additional reason to consider themselves the best equipped of all groups to direct Russia's social and political modernization. Yet not only did the party as a whole have very little political cohesion; its leadership also reflected a social milieu which was alien to millions of workers and peasants, many of whom would have to follow party banners in 1917 if Kadets were to play a leading political role in conditions of democracy and popular representation. The difficult task of Kadet "professors" would be to breach a deep social cleavage with strong historical roots.

Constituency

To what extent had Kadets overcome this cleavage before the 1917 revolution? To put the question another way, could the Kadets prop-

[24] Kokoshkin to Petrunkevich, Sept. 23, 1910, Oct. 7 and 20, 1911, in the Panina Archive, pack. 1, fold. 6.
[25] Miliukov, *Vospominaniia*, I, 352.

erly be considered a bourgeois party in terms of their popular constituency? Evidence is sparse, but an answer can be suggested on the basis of electoral returns to the State Dumas and through an examination of the party's electoral activities.

These activities in the 1905-1906 period were more comprehensive and energetic than any of Russia's other political groups. Kadets hoped to build a massive popular base, extending through all elements of the population. They were also determined to take full advantage of the concessions Nicholas had made toward constitutional rule, as if convinced their own commitment and involvement was itself a mark of Russia's readiness for parliamentary government. Special courses were set up for party "agitators," whose task was to go among the population explaining constitutional government and Russia's complicated electoral mechanism, as well as the Kadets' own program. Lecture tours were arranged for prominent party spokesmen. A prodigious amount of energy and money was spent on publications. In almost two dozen cities, Kadets began issuing their own local newspapers. According to Central Committee figures, some party pamphlets ran into printings of 80,000 and 90,000 copies, with one, addressed to the peasants, running as high as 300,000.[26]

In most cases, the early Kadet appeal was general, rather than partisan or sectarian, reflecting the party's strong initial commitment to *nadklassnost'*. It was also moderate in tone. Much has been written about Kadet radicalism in the early Duma period, and about the party's "opening to the left," which many have argued compromised its ability to cooperate with the government and undermined the First and Second Dumas. Yet most Kadet leaders felt by January 1906 that Russia was leery of political extremism. While generally reluctant to attack SRs and SDs (whom most Kadets still very much regarded as allies), the party as a whole disassociated itself from radical tactics in a deliberate effort to amass the broadest possible constituency, stressing instead a commitment to broad social progress through legal reform.[27] At the same time, most Kadet pamphlets simply explained in easy terms the rudiments of representative government and civil liberties, describing generally how Kadets hoped to serve Russia. ("The Kadet party is a big union," one pamphlet stated, for example, "organized to obtain some improvements and changes in government.")[28]

In this regard, Kadets in the First Duma period made little effort at formal political association with any of Russia's partisan bourgeois

---

[26] K-D partiia, *Otchet tsentral'nago komiteta konstitutsionno-demokraticheskoi partii*, St. Petersburg, 1907, pp. 84-86.

[27] Dmitrenko, pp. 100-115.

[28] *Krest'ianam o konstitutsionno-demokraticheskoi partii*, Moscow, 1906, p. 3.

groups; and they, in turn, showed no special inclination to associate formally with the Kadets. Historically, Russia's leading commercial and industrial groups had depended on the government for various economic supports; and while many recognized the need for political changes in 1905, particularly in terms of a more effective state bureaucracy, most were far more concerned with worker radicalism, and the threat to social and economic security posed by a democratic republic.

Ties between financial and industrial circles and the state were particularly close in St. Petersburg. In the summer of 1905, a council had been formed here to unite various local Congresses of Representatives of Industry and Trade. By 1906 it had 48 principal and 100 associate members. Its goal, in contrast to the Kadets', was to defend and protect commercial interests, and to encourage support for the regime. Here and there throughout Russia, local congresses fielded their own slates for the early Duma elections, though most soon merged their energies with the Octobrists, who shared their aversion to social leveling and political democracy, as well as to the spread of an eight-hour day and the expropriation of landed estates.

In Moscow, where trade-industrial life had historically been dominated by twenty-five or thirty "leading families," commercial groups had traditionally been more independent of the central regime than their Petersburg counterparts, as well as somewhat more progressive. Here a number of younger bourgeois representatives established their own political organization in 1905, entering in the Duma elections candidates who supported political democracy, universal suffrage, and general civil liberties. These Progressists, as they came to be called, had much in common with many Moscow Kadets, particularly in terms of their social environment. But they distinguished themselves from Miliukov and his colleagues by rejecting the notion of *nadklass-nost'* and actively defending bourgeois goals.

In the First Duma elections, however, this organizational independence of bourgeois groups did not seem to affect the Kadets. Helped by their own extensive party network (as well as the decision of many radical socialist groups to boycott the Duma in protest against limitations on the franchise), Miliukov and his colleagues scored an impressive victory. Electoral procedures were enormously complicated. In the countryside, the general pattern consisted of indirect elections through three basic curiae (or classes): peasants, landowners, and city-town dwellers (with workers constituting a fourth curia in certain specified areas). Basically, eligible voters elected representatives (or electors) to assemblies for each curia. These in turn selected electors to a provincial assembly, which then elected Duma delegates. Because the elections were indirect, and also because in many cases voters cast their ballots for slates of electors, rather than for individuals, it is difficult to interpret returns precisely. The data itself is also incomplete. Nevertheless, Kadet strengths and weaknesses are clearly visible.

Strength lay in provincial cities and towns. The party here secured almost 39 percent of the electors to the assemblies of this curia in 1906, a remarkable achievement. Kadets were especially strong in the towns of Vladimir, Kaluga, Kursk, Perm, and Khárkov provinces, as well as in the provinces of Moscow and St. Petersburg.

But both landlord and peasant disaffection from the party was also quite apparent. Incomplete data suggests that only about 11 percent of the electors chosen to the landowners assemblies were Kadets. More disappointing, the party secured only about 4 percent representation in the peasant assemblies, despite a strong effort among provincial Kadet committees to win peasant support. Most votes in these curia went to prominent local figures without specific party commitments.

Success in provincial towns was matched by comparable victories in the twenty-six cities with separate Duma representation. In Voronezh, Kursk, Nizhni-Novgorod, Odessa, Samara, Saratov, St. Petersburg, and Moscow, every elector chosen to the city assembly was a Kadet. In Kiev, 68 of 80 electors were party members; in Kazan, 67 of 81; in Riga, 70 of 80; in Iaroslavl, 73 of 80. Only in Ekaterinoslav, Kishenev, and Tula, of the cities in European Russia, did Kadets fail to elect more than 50 percent of the membership to city assemblies. And with these assemblies electing 1 Duma deputy each (with the exception of St. Petersburg, Moscow, and Warsaw, which chose 6, 4, and 2, respectively), Kadet strength in urban areas became the party's major source of actual Duma representation.

But the greatest Kadet success was in Moscow and St. Petersburg (a fact which gratified the party's central leadership, but also caused some inflated hopes about the government's possible responsiveness to party demands). In each of the twelve election districts in St. Petersburg, Kadet electors received more than 57 percent of the vote in 1906. In the Peterburgskii, Vyborgskii, Kazanskii, Admiralteiskii, and Moskovskii districts, they received 70 percent, 67 percent, 64 percent, 63 percent, and 63 percent, respectvely. In the Spasskii district they received 62 percent; in the Kolomenskii, 61 percent; and in the Narvskii and Rozhdestvenskii districts, 59 percent each. City-wide, the total was 61 percent. In Moscow, the pattern was similar. The Kadet total here was 63 percent. Party electors received more than 60 percent of the vote in eleven of the city's seventeen districts, and more than 65 percent in eight. Kadets thus emerged clearly in the spring of 1906 as the major political party of virtually all Russia's cities and towns.[29]

To hold this position, which brought the party about 35 percent of the delegates to the First Duma, Kadets had to stave off competition from bourgeois groups on the right, like the Trade-Industrialists, and from socialist parties on the left, which began in the summer of 1906 to make a concerted drive for representation in the Second Duma. The left proved especially troublesome. After the dissolution of the First Duma, Kadets led delegates in issuing the famous Vyborg Manifesto, appealing to peasants and workers not to pay taxes or cooperate with the military draft until the Duma reconvened. Most party members signed the appeal, in large measure because they expected a new wave of revolutionary disorders; they hoped to divert violent energies into the channels of passive resistance.[30] But the Manifesto was resented in the provinces as likely to provoke repressive detachments from the regime, as well as reprisals from reactionary groups like the Black Hundreds. And in the cities, Social Democratic agitators entering the electoral process for the first time sowed a similar distrust for Kadets among urban workers.[31] Meanwhile, large sectors of the urban and town bourgeoisie began to resent Kadets for abetting the radicals. In some towns this led to a shift among party supporters to the right; in others, it prompted the organization of new local bourgeois groupings.

In many parts of Russia Kadets tried to meet this new competition both by reaffirming the party's commitment to peaceful transformation, and by demonstratively including workers and peasant representatives on local slates for the Second Duma elections. The fourth Kadet congress in September 1906, for example, effectively disavowed the Vyborg appeal. It adopted a strategy of "slow assault" rather than open confrontation with the regime, taking as the party's official slogan "preserve the Duma."[32] At the same time, in local city committees like the one in St. Petersburg, where pressures were growing for elec-

[29] Results compiled from *Rech'*, Mar. 22, 1906; *Russkiia Vedomosti*, Mar. 23, 1906; *VPNS*, No. 6, Apr. 11, 1906, pp. 441-70; *VPNS*, No. 7, Apr. 19, 1906, pp. 545-46.

[30] M. Vinaver, *Istoriia vyborgskogo vozzvaniia*, Petrograd, 1917, pp. 10ff; *Delo o vyborgskom vozzvaniia. Otchet o zasedanii osobago prisutsviia S-Peterburgskoi sudebnoi palaty*, St. Petersburg, 1908, pp. 16-17 (Kokoskin testimony). The Vyborg debates appear in A. Sergeev, ed., "Pervaia gosudarstvennaia duma v Vyborge," *KA*, No. 57, 1933, pp. 85-99.

[31] Central Committee discussions on the response to Vyborg, Miliukov Archive, bx. 8122, gp. 2, sec. 5, fold. 15. See also Grave, "Kadety," *KA*, Nos. 47-48, 1931, pp. 112-39, and Vinavera, p. 55.

[32] *Rech'*, Sept. 29, 1906.

toral alliances with the socialists, Kadets added "genuine" workers and "leftists" to their slates, a step taken, according to Miliukov, "to calm our electors who very much want us to form a bloc with the left."[33]

But when the Second Duma results were in, the reduction in Kadet constituent support was apparent, particularly in major cities. In Vilno, 47 of the city's 80 electors were now from right-wing parties; in Kiev, 41 of 82. In Samara, where all electors were Kadets in the First Duma balloting, Octobrists now returned 45 electors as opposed to the Kadets' 35; and in Tula, 45 as opposed to the Kadets' 31. Left parties also made significant gains at Kadet expense. Socialist groups returned 66 electors in Ekaterinoslav, compared to the Kadets' 15; and 74 in Saratov, as opposed to the Kadets' 6.

Similar patterns emerged in Moscow and St. Petersburg. From receiving 61 percent of the vote in the First Duma elections, Kadet electors in St. Petersburg now gained only 42.6 percent. Electors from left parties secured 24 percent, and in one district, the Vyborgskii, outvoted Kadets 45 percent to 33 percent. Kadets failed to gain a majority in any St. Petersburg district in the 1907 elections, slipping from 61 percent to 35 percent in the Kolomenskii, from 58 percent to 34 percent in the Vasilevskii-Ostrovskii, and from 70 percent to 38 percent in the Peterburgskii. And in each of these districts, votes lost by Kadets were gained by the left. In Moscow, the party's city-wide strength dropped from 63 percent of electoral seats to 54 percent, the majority of these losses also going to the left. Party support here also dropped in every district, ranging from 2 or 3 percentage points in the Gorodskii, Tverskii, and Iakimanskii areas, to more than 18 percent in the Meshchanskii. Overall, the left parties in Moscow gained 13 percent of the city's electoral seats.

The only areas in which Kadet support held steady in the Second Duma elections were in the city-town and peasant curiae of the provinces. But peasant support for the party remained quite meager (103 electors out of 2,258 with 91 percent of all seats accounted for); and in the city-town curiae, left parties now secured 24 percent of the electoral seats while the Kadets held steady at 39 percent, thus emerging as a serious competitive force. Kadet delegate strength consequently dropped in the Second Duma from 184 to 99. Social Democrats increased from 17 to 65, Octobrists from 38 to 54, SRs from 2 to 37, and moderate socialists from 85 to 120.[34]

[33] D. Protopopov, ed., *Ocherk deiatel'nosti S. Peterburgskoi gorodskoi gruppy partii narodnoi svobody*, St. Petersburg, 1908, p. 14.

[34] Results compiled from *VPNS*, No. 6, Feb. 8, 1907, pp. 410-14, 435-36; No. 8, Feb. 22, 1907, p. 529; *Rech'*, Feb. 6, 1907 (suppl.). See also Alfred Levin, *The Second Duma*, New Haven, 1940, pp. 66-67.

By the spring of 1907, consequently, it was clear that Kadets could not develop the mass constituency they had hoped for at the time of the party's formation. Russia was polarizing, with left- and right-wing parties both growing at Kadet expense. Moreover, this pattern continued virtually unaltered until the revolution. Exact generalization is impossible, since changes in the electoral law in June 1907 heavily weighted subsequent balloting in favor of gentry and propertied urban elements. According to the new statute, all but six of Russia's major cities lost the right to direct representation; and in these six, a "first" curia was established for large property and a "second" for others. Elsewhere, new curiae were set up for landlords, wealthy town inhabitants, peasants, and poorer town dwellers, with voter strength in the first two categories outweighing that of the latter two. Nonetheless, it was clear in elections to the Third and Fourth Dumas that parties to the right of the Kadets had consolidated their support among the gentry, wealthier peasants, and upper bourgeoisie; and parties to the Kadets' left had made new inroads among workers and poorer peasants. The liberal center was still being squeezed; and in the process, many party figures began to think of themselves more as representatives of Russia's professional middle class than as reflecting the interests of all classes equally.

In the peasant curia in the countryside, for example, left-wing parties elected more than four times the number of Kadet electors in the Third Duma voting, while rightist groups elected more than seven times their number. Kadets showed strength among peasant voters only in Voronezh, Samara, and Ufa provinces, all areas in which the party's more radical provincial committees were still active. Among landowners, parties of the right (including the Octobrists) amassed almost fifteen times the number of Kadet electors. And the Kadets secured fewer electors in both these rural curiae than did the moderate bourgeois Progressists, who were forthright in their defense of private property and the opposition to forced expropriation, and who were making a deliberate effort in this period to win the support of landlord electors. The strength of Russia's already weak Kadet center in the countryside was thus also being fragmented. In 1912, Kadets obtained only 9 percent of all electoral seats outside Russia's six largest cities.[35]

The only firm area of Kadet strength after 1907 remained the "second curia" of cities and towns, whose voters were composed of males owning property of less than 300 rubles (1,000 rubles in towns

[35] Results compiled from *VPNS*, Nos. 43-44, Nov. 8, 1907, pp. 1863-90; *Rech'*, Oct. 19, 1907, Oct. 9, 1912, Oct. 27, 1912; *Russkiia Vedomosti*, Oct. 19, 1907, Oct. 20, 1912.

over 20,000); owners of small commercial and industrial enterprises; persons paying tenants' rates or taxes; persons occupying private lodgings in their own name; and salaried employees in state and local government—all clearly "bourgeois" groups even in a broad usage of the term. Among these elements, Kadets secured approximately 40 percent of the electors in both the Third and Fourth Duma elections, virtually the same as in 1906-1907. Kadet strength also held firm in Moscow and Petersburg, even increasing somewhat in the Fourth Duma vote at the expense of the Octobrists, although still strongly challenged by the left.[36]

What all of this data suggests is that the Kadets entered the revolution of 1917 not only as a party of intellectuals and professors, but also with a substantial following only among bourgeois and professional elements in Russia's cities and towns. The party's theoretical *nadklassnost'* remained, but in practical terms, as many party leaders undoubtedly recognized, the Kadets could not, in fact, gain a massive electoral following which transcended class lines. This lack of support also contributed to a drastic weakening of the party's organizational network, particularly in the provinces. From a membership of more than 100,000 in 1906, Kadet ranks had probably dropped to several thousand active workers or less by February 1917. More important, Kadet strength even in cities and towns was seriously challenged by a strong socialist left, whose position could only improve in 1917 as workers and peasants became fully franchised.

Thus on the eve of the revolution, Kadets faced an enormously difficult task of building a following large enough to maintain the party in power in conditions of open democracy. Russia's general condition of economic underdevelopment (with its relatively small urban middle class), the strength and potential radicalism of both peasant and proletarian elements, and the general disaffection from party principles of landed gentry and the industrial bourgeoisie—all of these factors posed difficult choices even for those Kadets who were content to consider themselves as representatives of Russia's professional elements, rather than "the interests and rights of all." The party could possibly hold its own by seeking closer ties with left-wing groups; or else with the Progressists and more sectarian bourgeois parties. As we shall see, close contacts were already established on a local level by 1917 in both directions. But moving either way involved compromise to basic party principles, as well as some effort to change the party's social composition and milieu. The crucial question in this regard, consequently, was whether the revolution would make

[36] *Ibid.*

Kadets more flexible or more rigid, whether the party in practice could make itself into something more than the representative of Russia's professional middle classes, and whether, in any case, the Constitutional Democratic movement could survive as a party in an open electoral arena.

QUESTIONS OF TACTICS AND PARTY UNITY

For eleven years, these problems of constituency, social composition, and even the party's underlying values and program had led to an endless debate within Kadet ranks about the propriety of different political tactics. Basic disagreements had existed from 1905 onward concerning the political "maturity" of the Russian people, the degree to which the party should cooperate with the government, alliances with other groups, and even the desirability of further changes in the established order. If Kadet ranks lacked cohesion on the eve of the revolution, if the party was a loose political association rather than a tightly knit, structured organization, one of the basic reasons was its inability over the years to develop a generally acceptable, coordinated strategy for social change.

From its beginning, the party had always had a sizable contingent of left-leaning militants, pressing for closer associations with mass movements and parties on the left. A number were former radical members of the Union of Liberation (though many from this group had broken with liberalism in 1905, and joined the SDs); and particularly in the early years, many were from the provinces (though the literature of prerevolutionary liberalism has often exaggerated the urban-rural distinction in this regard). Their characteristic mark was a readiness to attack the established order, and to identify with mass protests and popular demands.

This group in the fall of 1905 had pressed the party as a whole to support the tactic of general strikes. Shortly afterward, at the second Kadet congress in 1906, left Kadets had urged their colleagues to boycott the Duma along with the militant socialists, in protest over the restrictive Duma electoral law. And just before the opening of the First Duma itself, they had launched a frontal assault on Miliukov and the Central Committee leadership for being "too diplomatic" with the government. This militance continued, moreover, after the collapse of the "radical" First Duma, and the failure of the Vyborg Manifesto. At the fourth Kadet congress in September 1906, twenty-four delegates presented a petition condemning the party for not implementing a more forceful policy of resistance. ("They are calling us to Canossa," Michael Mandelshtam, a leading leftist from Moscow had declared, "and I say we won't go!")[37] Even as late as the fall of 1907, after Stolypin's "coup" had further weakened the representative base of Russia's already limited constitutional system, a resolution was introduced by twenty Kadets at the fifth party congress which again charged the Central Committee with "lack of firmness." Constantly during these early months, left-wing party leaders sought closer tactical alliances with SDs and SRs; and it was this group which proposed that the party adopt a more radical agrarian policy than forced expropriation with compensation, urging instead a comprehensive nationalization of agriculture and the establishment of a national land fund.[38]

The actual extent of the Kadet left is difficult to measure. A reasonable guess for the 1905-1907 period would put them at approximately one-third of the active party membership, judging by different votes at the early party congresses. But the collapse of mass revolutionary activity after 1906, combined with a failure of workers and peasants to rally behind the party's banners, led by the start of the Third Duma to a reduction in both their numbers and militance, and also, as we have seen, to a drastic reduction in the actual number of provincial party organizations.

Yet with forceful spokesmen like Michael Mandelshtam from Moscow, Nicholas Nekrasov from Tomsk, and A. M. Koliubakin from Novgorod, left Kadets continued to have active spokesmen in both the Duma delegation and the Central Committee. Toward the end of the Third Duma, they revived the notion of a close alliance with left parties, again hoping to force political changes in Russia by building a massive, radical electoral base. (A new "Union of Liberation" was Nekrasov's description of their goal.)[39] And even after this idea was rejected by the Central Committee, Nekrasov and others maintained that the regime could be pressured into change only by mass movements, rather than by persuasion "from above." Left Kadets wanted full civil liberties and the establishment of a democratic, genuinely representative state administration. With confidence in the political "maturity" of the Russian people, they found the dangers of elemental mass anarchism less threatening for Russia's future than the con-

---

[37] *Rech'*, Sept. 29, 1906.

[38] *VPNS*, No. 47, Dec. 2, 1907, cols. 241-60; No. 49, Dec. 18, 1907, cols. 2133-64; A. A. Kornilov, "Agrarnye zakonoproekty partii narodnoi svobody v sviazi s istoriei eia agrarnoi programmy," in N. Astrov et al., *Zakonodatel'nye proekty i predpolozheniia partii narodnoi svobody, 1905-1907 gg.*, St. Petersburg, 1907, pp. 363-73.

[39] I. I. Petrunkevich to his son, Sept. 13, 1911, in the A. I. Petrunkevich Collection. It is possible that the new Kadet orientation was related to the growth of Russian masonry. E. D. Kuskova, at least, in a letter published in Gregory Aronson's memoirs, speaks in a manner very similar to Nekrasov about a new liberation movement. See G. Aronson, *Rossiia nakanune revoliutsii*, New York, 1962, pp. 138-41. See also A. Avrekh, *Stolypin i tret'ia duma*, Moscow, 1968, pp. 430ff.

tinuation of autocratic paternalism. Above all, they remained expressly political in temper of mind and outlook. When the Fourth Duma elections showed a great proportional increase in SD strength, their notion of a left-liberal alliance was greatly reinforced.

It was precisely this emphasis on politics, however, and the confidence of left Kadets in the Russian people, that those generally regarded as the party's "right" found so objectionable. Kadets like Peter Struve, Vasili Maklakov, Ariadna Tyrkova, A. S. Izgoev, and Paul Novgorodtsev, were of a very different mind and temperament from men like Nekrasov and Koliubakin. Though committed to constitutionalism, civil liberties, and a rule of law, they regarded 1905 as the climax, rather than the beginning of the liberals' political struggle. In their view, the real danger for Russia's future development was not from the regime, but from efforts to "intoxicate simpleminded and ignorant working men and peasants with demagogic promises."[40] The essence of social order was authority, legally structured and administered. Mass oppositional politics not only weakened authority, but also detracted from the more pressing need of developing social consciousness and political "maturity." "A constitutional order is impossible while the country lacks social strata capable of understanding the tasks of governmental authority," Vasili Maklakov wrote, for example: "For a constitutional order, the support simply of a small separate group is not enough."[41] The liberals' primary function in Russia, consequently, was to engage in practical (*delovaia*) work at social improvement and political development, which would gradually (and only eventually) allow the full flowering of a representative constitutionalism.

Though present at party congresses in 1905 and 1906, this viewpoint remained generally muted within Kadet ranks in the early, "radical," months of Russia's constitutional experiment. It began to develop strongly only in the aftermath of the First and Second Dumas, when the unproductive nature of political activism seemed apparent. By the Third Duma, right Kadets were defending Stolypin's land policies as a means of pacifying the country (while their colleagues were condemning them as a misuse of state power and a violation of peasant wishes); and by 1911 and 1912, they had very close ties with the Octobrists, and openly defended "bourgeois" interests, particularly in the countryside. Struve, Novgorodtsev, Maklakov, and others were as cognizant as their militant colleagues of the dangers of bureaucratic arbitrariness and abuse of law; at one point in 1910 Maklakov himself

---

[40] A. Tyrkova, *From Liberty to Brest-Litovsk*, London, 1919, p. 88.
[41] V. Maklakov, *Vlast' i obshchestvennost' na zakate staroi Rossii*, Paris, 1938, p. 452.

even demanded a "revolution" in state administration.[42] But the conservatives wanted to underscore the monarchist character of the party, reexamine the Kadets' Duma proposals in a "patriotic spirit," formally approve the regime's agrarian measures, and rework nationality questions to align Kadets more closely with nationalist parties on the right. They opposed full democracy as "premature," and even challenged the notion that the Kadet party should be anything more than a loose political association. They venerated instead their *nadpartiinost'*, standing "above" partisan politics and expressly political concerns, while in practice supported policies which perpetuated class divisions and the economic well-being of privileged society.[43]

Although there were prominent exceptions, it was this view over the years which had come to dominate the party's branch in Moscow, reinforcing (and being reinforced by) the already existing tendency here toward close social relations with figures not active in Kadet party affairs. It was in Moscow, for example, that right Kadets like Struve and Izgoev joined in the publication of *Vekhi,* a volume of essays highly critical of the radical intelligentsia. It was here, too, that closer ties began to develop in the years after Stolypin's coup between Kadet intellectuals and representatives of Moscow's more progressive bourgeois circles, like P. P. Riabushinskii, A. I. Konovalov, S. N. Tretiakov, and S. A. Smirnov (some of whom in 1917 would join the party's ranks). Before the start of the First World War, Riabushinskii and his colleagues were not anxious for the government to go much beyond the bounds of the October Manifesto in terms of political reform. But they wanted to consolidate bourgeois pressure for administrative change, refraining from what they regarded as the Kadets' "revolutionary" phraseology, and avoiding what they regarded as Miliukov's "groundless dreams" of ministerial portfolios.[44]

By 1907 Riabushinskii and others had already thought of merging left Octobrists with right Kadets into one purely bourgeois party, a tactic which appealed to Moscow conservatives as a means of taking full advantage of the liberals' constituent strength in cities and towns, while also balancing any further growth of the left. Kadet professionals and intellectuals would be associated with moderate Trade-Industrialists and Progressists in a "healthy," practical alliance for social progress.[45] The Central Committee in St. Petersburg rejected this idea as contrary to the party's *nadklassnost'* and leading inevitably to a split

[42] Gosudarstvennaia Duma, *Stenograficheskie otchety. Tretii sozyv,* St. Petersburg, 1911, III, 1774-91.

[43] See esp. *Russkiia Vedomosti,* Sept. 27, Oct. 6, 1912; Avrekh, *Stolypin,* pp. 459-60.

[44] V. Ia. Laverychev, *Po tu storonu barrikad,* Moscow, 1967, p. 63.

[45] *Ibid.,* pp. 61-62.

with the party's left. But it remained popular in Moscow, where, toward the end of 1911, local Central Committee members worked out actual electoral blocs with Progressists and some Octobrists. Though the Progressists themselves began to swing toward more militant tactics after the Fourth Duma balloting, moving rapidly away from men like Maklakov and closer to less conservative Moscow Kadets like Nicholas Kishkin and Nicholas Astrov, the notion of a general, practical union between Kadets and progressive Trade-Industrialists remained strong. By 1913, Kadets in Saratov, Samara, Astrakhan, Iaroslavl, Voronezh, and other cities had followed their Moscow colleagues in holding "unification meetings"; Ariadna Tyrkova had begun to publish a right-wing Kadet journal, *Russkaia Molva*, expressly to counter what she and others thought was the "dangerous leftism" of *Rech'*; and Miliukov himself thought the party might finally split in two.[46]

The threat of a break was especially troubling to the party's titular chief. Over the years, Miliukov strove constantly to keep disputes from leading to an open party split. Perhaps the most politically oriented of all liberal leaders, his desire for unity was quite deliberate. Only a united liberal center, he believed, could lead Russia to "a peaceful solution to the prolonged conflict between crown and country."[47] With a volatile and potentially anarchistic peasantry, with a militant proletariat, and with an autocratic administration that in many instances was openly repressive and reactionary, Russia seemed to be struggling on the brink of violent upheaval and civil war. A united liberal, *nadklassnaia* intelligentsia exercising political authority could conceivably overcome these dangers, directing as well the process of Russia's rapid social and economic modernization.

Miliukov's vehicles in his efforts were the Central Committee group in St. Petersburg, and the party's Duma delegation, the former acting to iron over internal party disputes, and the latter as the instrument for enacting progressive, liberal legislation. All tactical and organizational lines ran through the Petersburg Central Committee. Radical views were expressed by provincial delegates like Koliubakin and Nekrasov; conservative viewpoints came from Maklakov, Struve and Tyrkova. As the dominant voice of the party's center, Miliukov smoothed disputes by championing broad autonomy for local com-

[46] *Ibid.*, p. 102; unpubl. memoirs of A. V. Tyrkova in the Tyrkova-Williams Archive, chap. 28, pp. 740-42; "Testimony" given by Miliukov to B. Nicolaevsky in 1927, in the Nicolaevsky personal archives, graciously provided to me by A. M. Bourguina.

[47] S. A. Smirnov, "P. N. Miliukov," in Smirnov et al., *P. N. Miliukov. Sbornik materialov*, Paris, 1929, p. 12.

mittees or else by referring disputatious issues to special commissions. He also encouraged minority reports which were not binding on the Committee as a whole, and generally assuaged those who threatened party splits by permitting "the maximum possible disagreement within the limits of a single party."[48] While not actually himself a Duma member until 1907, Miliukov was also involved in all major party decisions in the Duma delegation, along with his closest supporters and collaborators, Maxim Vinaver and Fedor Kokoshkin. "My share," he later recalled, "consisted in determining the middle position of a meeting, and working out a conciliatory formula."[49]

In the early years of the party, conciliation had generally meant accommodation with the Kadet left. Miliukov and his Central Committee colleagues hoped in the First Duma period that the party could build a mass electoral base, pressuring the regime in this way to recognize the validity and popularity of the Kadet program. Before the Vyborg Manifesto, he and others were also convinced that popular revolution had not yet run its course. The party's task, consequently, was also to prevent peasant and worker support from shifting to militant left-wing parties, to say to the masses, as a Kadet Duma delegate expressed it, "Believe in us. We are struggling for you. Stay peaceful and calm."[50] This involved a strategy of verbal confrontation with the government, in which the party leaders vented their anger over the restrictive nature of the Fundamental Laws, the continued absence of basic civil liberties, and the government's general lack of commitment to parliamentary rule. A radical Duma posture was also intended to preserve the party's massive popular support, even if radical socialists abandoned their Duma boycott and entered future elections.

But after Vyborg, as Miliukov and other Committee members recognized the degree to which they had overestimated the popular mood, conciliation came increasingly to mean accommodation with the government and a concerted effort to use available parliamentary means. It was largely at the direction of Miliukov, Vinaver, and Kokoshkin that Kadets adopted the policy of "orderly siege" in the Second Duma, and replaced verbal confrontation with "businesslike" activity, avoiding situations which could lead to the Duma's dissolution. And it was they as well who largely determined that the party should work energetically even in the electorally restricted Third and Fourth Dumas. The more it became clear that the party's electoral base was

[48] Miliukov, *Vospominaniia*, I, 307.

[49] Quoted in T. Riha, *A Russian European: Paul Miliukov in Russian Politics*, Notre Dame, Ind., 1969, p. 119.

[50] Gos. Duma, *Steno. otchety. Pervyi sozyv*, St. Petersburg, 1906, I, 1984-85.

narrowing, the more Miliukov and his Petersburg colleagues came to regard government concessions and appointments as the likely way to power.

By 1908 or 1909, consequently, the party's Duma delegation had become the focal point of Kadet political activity. By now one of Miliukov's primary goals was to build government confidence in the party. Though Kadets were still regarded as leading, even dangerous, oppositionists, Miliukov and his Petersburg colleagues hoped they would eventually secure government respect on the basis of their political experience and expertise. In official party literature, they vigorously defended the party's accomplishments in the Third Duma sessions; and even in 1912 and 1913, when the intransigence of Prime Minister Kokovtsev pushed Miliukov and the Duma delegation into a much sharper oppositional posture, the Kadet leader still hoped the regime would eventually come around.[51]

Now, however, party unity became more important than ever. Unable to develop a mass base, Kadets had to rely on their position as the most progressive strata of privileged, *tsenzovyaia* Russia to win government confidence and secure leading administrative positions. Even the extent of the party's organizational network no longer mattered very much. Kadets could not be voted into power; it was only in St. Petersburg that the party could have a substantial political impact. But even without much practical party meaning, Kadet unity was necessary if the regime was ever to recognize the party's national importance.

Miliukov's greatest fear in these circumstances was that the government's own blundering would precipitate a "premature" revolution, in which the Kadets themselves would be swept aside.

The War and "Patriotic Anxiety"

The outbreak of World War I had had a complicated impact on the Kadet movement. First and foremost it had strengthened the nationalist commitments of virtually all party members, reinforcing the traditional liberal desire to protect and defend Russian state interests. To Miliukov and others, both the causes of the war and Russia's new national objectives were comprehensible in Spenserian terms. Like other powers, Germany "naturally" strove for "power and domination." Her guilt was not in these aspirations, but in the fact that she had resorted to force, overstepping the legitimate bounds of international competition. There was no question in these circumstances

[51] K-D Partiia, *Tret'ia gosudarstvennaia duma. Materialy*, passim, but esp. the introduction; see also Miliukov, "Testimony."

that Russia's own international position had to be protected. All Russians had to unite behind the regime, taking as their goals the preservation of their country "one and indivisible" and the maintenance of her position "in the ranks of world powers."[52]

At the same time, the war had accentuated differences between politically oriented party members like Miliukov and the Kadets in St. Petersburg, and their more socially oriented, *nadpartiinye* colleagues, many of whom were in Moscow. And among those involved in politics, it raised the question of whether reforms now generally recognized as necessary for military victory might better be obtained from "above" or "below," by cooperating with the regime, in other words, or striking out again to ally with massive popular dissidence and revolutionary left-wing parties. How one answered this latter question, finally, determined for Kadets how important their own party organization had to be during the war. For those who wanted a return to the revolutionary "liberationist" strategy of 1905, a revitalization of local committees was an essential means of coordinating mass movements; for those who continued to rely on the Duma, party organization remained more or less unimportant.

In Miliukov's view, as well as in that of Vinaver, Nabokov, Kokoshkin, and other leading members of the Central Committee in St. Petersburg, the war brought new hopes that the government would finally recognize the Kadet party's potential government role. Pressing military needs would inevitably lead to political changes; and the natural course of reform would lead to liberal ministerial appointments.[53] Given this likelihood, the Duma remained the crucial locus of Kadet political activity. Mass tactics would disrupt Russia's military effort; the introduction of universal suffrage or other constitutional changes would lead only to further internal polarization. Now more than ever Miliukov and his centrist colleagues believed a Kadet ministry was vital to Russia's future development. But the war had also made it more important that the party's road to power lie in "bureaucratic changes from above."[54]

These were the views Miliukov presented to his Central Committee colleagues in the summer and fall of 1914, and which structured party activity when the Duma reconvened in February 1915. They also underlay the formation of the so-called Progressive Bloc, which Miliukov engineered the following summer. A loose association of liberal and conservative Duma leaders in support of a broad program

[52] P. Miliukov, *Pochemu i zachem my voiuem?*, Petrograd, 1917, p. 30; Gos. Duma, *Steno. otchety. Chetvertyi sozyv*, St. Petersburg, 1914, special sess. July 26, pp. 24-26.
[53] V. Obolenskii, "Vospominaniia," MS, lent by Prof. Nathan Smith, n.d., pp. 390-93; Miliukov, *Pochemu*, pp. 30ff.
[54] Miliukov, *Taktika*, pp. 22-24.

of administrative reform, the Bloc was designed to increase the Duma's involvement in state affairs and pave the way towards a moderate liberal cabinet. It was also a means to coordinate relations between public organizations and the bureaucracy, prompting changes in government personnel and procedures by the sheer weight of its collective prestige, rather than by frontal assault.

Ministers enjoying the nation's confidence were required for these ends, but structural change was not. Neither was a strategy which pitted one social interest against another, or even one party against another. Miliukov specifically rejected the idea of having the Bloc demand a ministry responsible to parliament, as called for in the Kadet program, rather than one "of confidence" appointed by the tsar; and not one of the proposals offered in the Bloc's program demanded basic changes in Russia's political system. Instead, Kadets supporting the Bloc committed themselves to the idea that progress could be obtained through cooperation with established authority, not through radical reforms or the tactics of mass pressure.[55]

Most Kadets in 1915 found the Progressive Bloc an acceptable Duma strategy (though Tyrkova and one or two right-wing members worried that even it was too much an expression of disloyalty to the regime).[56] Initially, however, the main concern of party members outside the Duma delegation was not so much with politics as with organizing Russian society and industry in support of the war, a task in which questions of political strategy and affiliation had little relevance. The focal points here were the Unions of Zemstvos and Towns, set up with the highest government approval shortly after the war began, and the War Industries Committees, which emerged out of a conference of Trade-Industrialists in the spring of 1915 to meet urgent needs of production and supply. Within months of the war's outbreak, prominent Kadets like Nicholas Astrov, Nicholas Kishkin, Michael Chelnokov, and others were playing leading roles in each of these groups, especially in Moscow, where activities were centered. In the process, their already close relations with Trade-Industrialist and Progressist figures like P. P. Riabushinskii and A. I. Konovalov became more intimate.

Rapidly, however, even the "nonpartisan" social organizations became a center of political concerns. As major military defeats provoked serious economic and social problems, and as the government's own ineptitude contributed to the crisis, public leaders like Chelnokov

55 *Ibid.*, pp. 15-23; A. Kornilov, *Parliamentskii blok*, Moscow, 1915, pp. 13-16. See also B. Grave, ed., *K istorii klassovoi bor'by v Rossii*, Moscow-Leningrad, 1926, pp. 279-86; *Rech'*, Aug. 25-27, 1915.

56 Tyrkova, *From Liberty*, chap. 1.

felt themselves "forced to interfere, from the instinct of self-preservation and statesmanship." "We did not want to occupy ourselves with politics," he told the Fourth All-Russian Congress of the Union of Cities in 1916, "but we had to do it."[57] As a consequence, even "non-political" Kadets had to address themselves both to questions of strategy and tactics and to the types of political changes that Russia needed for victory. And here the public organizations rapidly developed the same differences of viewpoint that existed among the Kadets.

On one hand, Maklakov, Chelnokov, Novgorodtsev, and others felt that the public groups should emulate and support the Progressive Bloc, avoiding frontal confrontations and seeking only administrative, rather than constitutional, reforms. But Astrov, Kishkin, and the Progressists under Riabushinskii and Konovalov took a much more militant approach. In their view, the Progressive Bloc was inadequate. Russia faced not only a prolonged economic and military crisis, but also a rising revolutionary wave. Basic political changes were needed. The Duma and the regime itself had to become more representative, bridging the gap between privileged society and Russia's masses, particularly if workers and peasants were to be kept from the destructive influence of political extremists. The goal of Kadets and Progressists, consequently, was to strengthen ties not with conservative parties, as Miliukov and the Progressive Bloc were doing, but with left-wing groups and mass movements, though not necessarily within party frameworks. As Riabushinskii told one gathering in August 1915, "All social elements should begin to work toward the complete seizure of executive and legislative power."[58]

This growing political militance of the public organizations naturally reinforced the left faction within the Kadet party itself, both in Moscow and St. Petersburg, and also in the provinces. It also stimulated a resurgence of party activism. Miliukov's acquiescent strategy had already become a major bone of contention at Central Committee meetings in January 1915, even among those who supported a policy of postponing anti-government criticism; when the Kadet leader presented his arguments in favor of the Progressive Bloc to special party conferences in June and July of 1915, Moscow and provincial delegates like Nekrasov, Lev Krol, and A. I. Petrovskii angrily demanded a strategy with more political muscle.[59]

The practical import of the Progressive Bloc in terms of Kadet

[57] B. Grave, ed., *Burzhuaziia nakanune fevral'skoi revoliutsii*, Moscow-Leningrad, 1927, p. 88.

[58] *Ibid.*, p. 21.

[59] N. Lapin, ed., "Kadety v dni galitsiiskogo razgroma," *KA*, No. 59, 1933, pp. 111-44; Grave, *K istorii*, pp. 265-79.

politics was that it committed the party as a whole to a nonpartisan reform coalition, which basically supported an anachronistic system of government. The Bloc not only depended entirely for success on the acquiescence of those very persons whose outlook and behavior it was trying to change; it also meant a minimal role for the Kadet party itself as a political organization. It was this which infuriated Nekrasov, Krol, and other party radicals. In their view, Kadets should move once again, as they had in 1905, toward a broad union with "allies on the left," both among parties and the people at large.[60]

Moreover, when the regime responded to the Progressive Bloc's demands in the late summer of 1915 by dismissing the Duma, rather than by changing the ministry (despite the fact that several ministers supported the Bloc's demands and its membership included figures of unimpeachable loyalty to the autocracy), Kadet militants rapidly increased in numbers and influence. Encouraged by an outbreak of protest strikes among Petersburg workers, some left Kadets even suggested that liberals should now encourage strikes themselves, perhaps involving the public organizations.[61] This was generally rejected as too damaging to the war effort; but even Moscow Kadets like Paul Dolgorukov, who were hardly flaming radicals, now attacked Miliukov's politics broadside, accusing him and the Progressive Bloc of compromising Kadet principles and thwarting party goals. The time had come, they argued, to cultivate new relations with soldiers, workers, and peasants, seeking allies for a direct struggle with the regime. In the process, the Kadets as a party had again to build up a massive national following, as they had in 1905, and be ready to assume state power even if universal elections came to Russia.[62]

Thus by 1916 tsarist police agents could write long, detailed reports about the fragmentation in Kadet party ranks.[63] On the left were partisan Kadet militants, working both in local party committees and the public organizations for a "new healthy authority in the country, capable of carrying the war to an end, doing away once and for all with the old order, and creating a new life on the basis of a new constitution, or even a democratic republic." Then there were more moderate Kadets in both the social organizations and the party's Duma and Central Committee groups, who wanted to transform the State Duma into Russia's sole governmental organ, creating a "new regime built on the principles of contemporary European parliamentarianism,"

[60] Obolenskii MS, pp. 425-26; Lapin, pp. 127-44; Mansyrev, III, 13-14; Grave, *Burzhuaziia*, pp. 61-62.

[61] Grave, *Burzhuaziia*, pp. 38-39, 52-54, 56, 63-65.

[62] *Ibid.*, pp. 68-70.

[63] E.g., Grave, *Burzhuaziia*, pp. 65ff; *K istorii*, pp. 300ff.

but not on the basis of mass tactics or partisan political struggle. There were also the "centrists," who thought of themselves more explicitly as representing Russia's professional middle classes, and whose goal was not to break relations with the government, but to support the Progressive Bloc, and create "a strong authoritative nucleus" of legislative leaders in the Duma. Finally, there were right Kadets, fearful of partisan politics and militant tactics, and anxious for Kadets to dedicate their energies entirely toward improving conditions at the front.[64] In February 1916, when pressure from Moscow and provincial party figures forced Miliukov and the Central Committee in Petrograd to call the first Kadet congress since 1907, delegates could not develop any coherent party line. Hearing Mandelshtam describe the Progressive Bloc as "hopelessly compromising the party in the eyes not only of broad democratic circles, but also of the liberal intelligentsia," they voted 46 to 27 in favor of "rapprochement" with the left (with 14 abstentions). Delegates seemed generally to agree with Nekrasov and other leftists, who saw revolution as "inevitable," and urged the party to prevent it from assuming "an unorganized, chaotic, senseless form of rebellion" by attempting to play a leading political role.[65] But one day later, after rebuttals by Miliukov and Shingarev, the vote was 73 to 14 in favor of continuing support for the Progressive Bloc.[66] These tactics were not necessarily mutually exclusive, but they were also not compatible, both because left-wing spokesmen constantly ridiculed the Bloc in the press and the Duma and because, while the Bloc stood for cooperation with the existing regime, rapprochement with the left meant allying with radicals and encouraging mass dissidence.

Shortly after the party congress, moreover, Kadets found themselves working directly against each other at the congresses of zemstvo and city unions. Nekrasov, Astrov, and other militants saw these organizations as a possible base for a new radical union movement. "It is senseless to play with the government in a subtle diplomatic game," Nekrasov argued to one group in March 1916, for example. "We must clearly, at once, state our demands in a definite manner. And having stated them, we must not wait until the government deigns to receive them, but struggle to create such an organization as will force their acceptance."[67] Before exactly the same group, however, Miliukov warned that anti-government activities would be extremely dangerous for social stability, and might even "prove to be the spark that ignites a great conflagration."[68] And in his mind, at least, there

[64] Grave, *Burzhuaziia*, pp. 176-77.
[65] *Rech'*, Feb. 23, 1916; Grave, *Burzhuaziia*, pp. 81-82.
[66] *Rech'*, Feb. 24, 1916. [67] Grave, *Burzhuaziia*, pp. 94-95.
[68] *Ibid.*, p. 90.

was no doubt that revolution would prove disastrous: "I know that a revolution in Russia will definitely lead us to defeat," he told the Duma in March. "If I were told that organizing Russia for victory meant organizing for revolution I would say: better leave her as she is, unorganized, for the duration of the war."[69]

KADETS ON THE EVE OF REVOLUTION

While Kadets argued, Russia's economic and political situation deteriorated. Shortages of food and essential goods were growing; prices were increasing; and with more than twelve million men in uniform, critical industries by 1916 were experiencing acute manpower needs, with transport in some areas virtually at a standstill. Most important, social unrest itself was rapidly increasing; and the government's ineffective response consisted largely of replacing one incompetent administrator with another. One estimate is that more than 1,400 strikes occurred in 1916 alone, involving more than a million workers.[70] In the same space of time, Nicholas appointed no less than four prime ministers. All of this indicated even to right-wing Kadets that drastic changes were in order. Maklakov himself warned that Russia was "tinder dry"; it was simply inconceivable that Nicholas would not recognize that the existing system had to be altered.[71]

Yet few Kadets fully reckoned with the tsar's political insensitivity, even on the eve of the revolution. Regarding each new barrage of criticism with resentment, Nicholas thought those who challenged the government were necessarily disloyal. When attacks came from "legitimate" sources like the Duma or the Zemstvo Union, his fear was not his own isolation from responsible public figures, but the danger that "oppositionists" might rally the country as a whole against him, as they had in 1905. The lesson of Russia's past was that revolutions occurred when elements of opposition had the freedom to meet and organize, not when popular disaffection reached massive proportions, or public institutions proved unworkable.

Thus when Paul Miliukov fired his famous salvo in the Duma on November 1, 1916, accusing the regime of "stupidity or treason," the government responded by trying to prevent the Duma and public organizations from becoming bases of oppositional activity, not by granting concessions. The Zemstvo Union was forbidden to hold its December 1916 conference in Moscow; activities of the War Industries

---

[69] Gos. Duma, *Steno. otchety. Chetvertyi sozyv*, St. Petersburg, 1916, IV, col. 2795.
[70] M. G. Fleer, ed., *Rabochee dvizhenie v gody voiny*, Moscow, 1925, pp. 6-7.
[71] M. Paleologue, *An Ambassador's Memoirs*, 3 vols., London, 1923-25, III, 216. See also Miliukov, *Vospominaniia*, II, 272-81, and Grave, *Burzhuaziia*, p. 73.

Committees were curtailed; and on December 17, the Duma was recessed until February. If the crisis deepened, the government reasoned, Russia at least would not have a parliamentary center capable of leading resistance.

Many thought it likely in these circumstances that Kadets would plot against the regime, or conspire with more deliberate revolutionaries to mobilize popular dissent. The tsarist police were so sure of this, in fact, that their agents literally flooded liberal meetings in the first weeks of 1917. Yet the step from criticism to practical action was one the Kadets were unable to make in an organized way. Each alternative course seemed dangerous. Provincial figures bitterly criticized Miliukov for continuing in the Progressive Bloc, and "ruining" the party's reputation in the eyes of the people. Expecting the Fifth Duma elections in 1917 to go to the left, they saw the party "committing suicide" by following Miliukov's policies.[72] Yet Miliukov and his supporters still felt that Russia's and the party's future lay not in popular support, but in transfer of power from above. Miliukov's model was now a "dictatorship enjoying the confidence of the public" on the style of Briand's rule in France or Lloyd George's "popular and responsible 'dictatorship'" in England.[73] At the same time, however, when rumors circulated about plots against the tsar, Kadets in Petrograd decided a palace coup would generate too much high-level dissidence.[74] Yet when Nekrasov urged open support for mass demonstrations, the rebuttal was that this would seriously damage the war effort. Early in February 1917, in fact, when the government arrested the Workers Group of the War Industries Committee to frustrate a mass march in support of the Duma, Miliukov and the Kadets urged Petrograders to stay home and "be calm."[75]

While recognizing that Russia "stood on the eve of open conflict," Kadets thus could not develop a coordinated party strategy. Many even continued to minimize the importance of the party itself, devoting energies instead to the broadly nonpartisan public organizations. Kadets remained committed to the program they had worked out in 1905, and particularly to its underlying system of values; nationalism, a rule of law, constitutional government, and at least in theoretical terms, *nadklassnost'*. And there was near unanimity on the necessity of continuing the war to full victory. Yet the steadily deteriorating political situation heightened liberal differences, rather than strength-

[72] Grave, *Burzhuaziia*, pp. 145-46.   [73] Editorial in *Rech'*, Nov. 27, 1916.
[74] "V ianvare i fevrale 1917 g.," *Byloe*, No. 13 (7), 1918, pp. 96-97; Grave, *Burzhuaziia*, pp. 163-64; Obolenskii MS, pp. 422-24.
[75] Obolenskii MS, pp. 423-24; *Rech'*, Feb. 10, 1917. See also the description of this episode in V. Zenzinov, "Fevral'skie dni," *NZ*, No. 34, 1953, pp. 193-94.

ening party cohesion. When tsarist police failed to uncover any coordinated Kadet plans, they camouflaged their surprise by insisting that party leaders were taking "special pains" not to disclose them.[76] But the fact was that the most articulate liberal critics of the old regime had no clear plans or even organizational coherence. They sat instead as anxious but passive observers to the developing drama, still hoping against hope that the government would come to its senses and call them to power.

[76] E.g., "Fevral'skaia revoliutsiia i okhrannoe otdelenie," *Byloe*, No. 1 (29), 1918, pp. 168-74; Grave, *Burzhuaziia*, pp. 161-63.

PART TWO

1917

CHAPTER TWO

The Transfer of Power

THE MORNING of February 27, 1917, dawned clear and frosty in St. Petersburg. Fresh snow had fallen in the night. Streets and rooftops glistened with special brilliance. The Kadet Central Committee was scheduled to meet at 10 o'clock on the question of Lithuanian autonomy. Shortly before it convened, news arrived of an emergency session of the State Duma. Kadet delegates made their way instead to the Tauride Palace.

Almost to a man, their mood was in marked contrast to the weather. With the rioting and shooting of the past few days, Petrograd was finally in the state of crisis Miliukov and his Duma colleagues had been working months to avoid. The question was no longer simply one of administrative reform, but of the very preservation of state authority. The angry mood of the crowd "shocked" and "worried" Paul Dolgorukov. Vladimir Nabokov was "gloomy." Peter Iurenev was "anxious." Fedor Rodichev, who ten years before had publicly called the tsar's prime minister a "hangman," shouted "Long Live Nicholas!" when he first saw jeering workers and soldiers. Even Paul Miliukov, consummate politician that he was, felt uncertain about what to do. Worried about "dark forces" of sabotage lurking behind the unrest, he felt events were "unclear." The regime might still take decisive action to restore order; he and his colleagues would have to wait before making decisions. Of all Kadet leaders in Petrograd, Nicholas Nekrasov, the stalwart leftist from Tomsk, was practically alone in thinking events could be used at once for Russia's betterment.[1]

Of immediate concern was the prorogation of the State Duma. From the moment disorders had begun four days before, Kadets and other parliamentary leaders had attempted to assert the Duma's authority, hoping the regime would appoint a new cabinet in accordance with the wishes and program of the Progressive Bloc. Their

[1] Fedor Rodichev, "Vospominaniia o 1917," MS in the Hoover Institution, 1924, p. 1; Paul Dolgorukov, *Velikaia razrukha*, Madrid, 1964, pp. 11-15; Vladimir Nabokov, "Vremennoe pravitel'stvo," *ARR*, I, 1922, p. 12; Peter Iurenev, Discussion with Kadets in Prague on the February revolution, in *Posledniia Novosti*, Mar. 25, 1924; Paul Miliukov, *Istoriia vtoroi russkoi revolutsii*, 3 pts., Sofia, 1921-23, pt. 1, p. 77.

aim, according to *Rech'* on February 25, was "not to remain in the wake of events, but to *prevent* and *direct* them," an attitude of caution and restraint which seemed to impress everyone but the government.[2] The same afternoon, a special meeting of the Progressive Bloc had determined to press for the cabinet's resignation.[3] Even Nekrasov met on February 26 with Rittikh and Pokrovskii, the two "liberal" members of the Council of Ministers, to demand a responsible cabinet subject to parliamentary recall.[4] But while some ministers supported the Bloc's new demands, the government's official response, learned by the Duma's Council of Elders late on the evening of the 26th, was to prorogue the Duma, implementing the emergency plans of December 1916. It was to hear the dismissal edict on February 27 that Duma delegates had been summoned to the Tauride Palace.

The Duma's prorogation further confused the situation. As the delegates gathered (the Kadets grouping around Miliukov and quietly talking among themselves), the predominant fear in everyone's mind was the outbreak of civil war. Whether garrison troops fought Petrograd workers, or mutinied and clashed instead with soldiers from the front, the result could only be disastrous for Russia's war effort. Somehow further conflict had to be avoided. When the Duma delegates heard the prorogation edict, they consequently moved into a "private" conference for further discussions.

Options were limited. Duma leaders had no control either of the streets or the government; they could not issue orders to the Petrograd Military Commander, or legally pass emergency legislation. There was also no guarantee of popular support from the country at large if they placed themselves at the head of rebellious workers and peasants in Petrograd; and from the government's perspective, their acts would be openly treasonous. On the other hand, if they yielded to the prorogation decree and disbanded, events would be left in the hands of the garrison and the mob.

Nekrasov on the Kadet left urged the creation of a revolutionary directorate under the liberal General Manikovskii, a tactic which could capitalize on Petrograd unrest to force basic political reforms, but could also minimize the possibility of the army's crushing the rebellion by force, assuming Manikovskii had the approval and support of the high command.[5] However, two provincial Kadets, Nicholas

[2] *Rech'*, Feb. 25, 1917, italics added.

[3] *Kak sovershilas' velikaia russkaia revoliutsiia*, Petrograd, 1917, pp. 1-6.

[4] Testimony of Alexander Protopopov, in P. E. Shchegolev, ed., *Padenie tsarskogo rezhima*, 7 vols., Moscow-Leningrad, 1924-27, VI, 100; *Izvestiia Revoliutsionnoi Nedeli*, Feb. 27, 1917.

[5] Unofficial transcript of the conference published in *Volia Rossii*, Mar. 15, 1921. Whether Nekrasov regarded a directorate under Manikovskii as a replacement cabi-

Volkov and M. S. Adzhemov, urged instead that the Duma itself take power, arguing that unrest could be curbed if Petrograd saw the country's elected representatives taking action. Rodichev, Dolgorukov, and the Kadets' more conservative delegates, meanwhile, rejected any unilateral Duma action as "illegal." Instead they argued for a new cabinet responsible to the Duma but appointed by the tsar, a tactic probably supported by a majority of Duma delegates, and urged by Duma President Michael Rodzianko, who fired telegrams to this effect on the afternoon of the 27th to both Nicholas and the army command.[6] Miliukov, finally, remained uncharacteristically indecisive. Since the Duma was not a democratic or even broadly representative body, the Kadet leader doubted that independent action on its part would gain widespread support. Yet reforms were necessary if Russia was to win the war, and perhaps now was the opportunity. Everything depended on the government's response, and on whether the rioting increased or subsided. For the time being, the Duma would do best to "wait and see."[7]

While Kadets and their Duma colleagues debated, however, events were moving rapidly. Revolutions leave little time for reticence. By early afternoon on the 27th Petrograd was again filled with demonstrators. Word came of the first garrison defections; shortly afterward, shots could be heard even from inside the Duma chambers. Meanwhile, a revolutionary council of workers' and soldiers' representatives, the Petrograd Soviet, was organizing in rooms adjacent to the Duma's in the Tauride Palace, modeling its actions on the famous revolutionary Soviet of 1905. While there is little in the surviving sources to indicate exactly how delegates to the new organization were elected, scores of noisy and enthusiastic representatives began streaming to the Tauride from all parts of the city, soldiers bursting in with news of more troops "joining the people against the cursed autocracy," socialist intellectuals jubilantly swearing "to serve the people's cause to the last drop of blood."[8] As it seemed about to take full control of the

---

net for the Council of Ministers or simply as a temporary expedient to restore order is unclear. See the discussion in S. P. Mel'gunov, *Martovskie dni 1917 goda*, Paris, 1961, pp. 26-27; and Pr. S. P. Mansyrev, "Moi vospominaniia o gosudarstvennoi dume," *Istorik i Sovremennik*, III, 1922, pp. 39-44.

[6] Robert P. Browder and Alexander F. Kerensky, eds., *The Russian Provisional Government 1917*, 3 vols., Stanford, 1961, I, 42-43, 83; see also the discussion in George Katkov, *Russia 1917. The February Revolution*, London, 1967, pp. 289-90.

[7] *Volia Rossii*, Mar. 15, 1921.

[8] The best account is still probably Nicholas Sukhanov's *Zapiski o revoliutsii*, 7 vols., Berlin, 1922-23, esp. vol. 1. Also invaluable are the memoirs of Vladimir Zenzinov, "Fevral'skie dni," *NZ*, No. 34, 1953, pp. 188-211, and No. 35, 1953, pp. 208-40.

situation, the Soviet's whole mood and atmosphere created an almost irresistible—one might almost say physical—pressure to take action.

This pressure culminated, finally, in the behavior of rebellious troops themselves, many of whom soon began pledging their "full support and loyalty" not only to the Soviet, but also to the Duma. Few in the Duma leadership group had any desire for martyrdom, either in the cause of authority or on the barricades of revolution; and the fact that rank-and-file soldiers turned to them enthusiastically surprised a number of Kadets and their colleagues alike. But because they did, Duma leaders were implicated in the rebellion whether they wanted to be or not. And under these pressures, the "private conference" of Duma representatives finally directed its Council of Elders to act.

Late in the evening on the 27th, a special "Temporary Duma Committee" declared itself in power. Its members included Miliukov and Nekrasov from among the Kadets, and its official title was "Committee of State Representatives for the Reestablishment of Order in the Capital and for Relations with Persons and Institutions," as cautious and reluctant an appellation as ever assumed by any revolutionary body. Willingly or not, the Committee declared its intention of "forming a new government corresponding to the desires of the population and capable of commanding its confidence." And it appealed to the city for calm.[9]

MILIUKOV AND THE FORMATION OF THE PROVISIONAL GOVERNMENT

The formation of the Temporary Duma Committee brought the question of state power into clear focus. Was the new regime to reflect the mood and aspiration of Petrograd workers and soldiers, to seek social as well as political transformation, and to be revolutionary in fact as well as in name? Or was it to carry on the basic tasks of its tsarist predecessor, only with more efficiency and, presumably, more success?

From the Petrograd Kadets' perspective, three closely related goals had to be met, all of which, on inspection, can be seen as designed to consolidate and control Russia's "revolutionary situation," rather than extend it: the end of mass unrest and the restoration of order in Petrograd; support from the army and the avoidance at all costs of civil war; and the implementation of those reforms which were capable of resolving Russia's general administrative and economic

[9] *Izvestiia Revoliutsionnoi Nedeli*, Feb. 28, 1917.

crisis. Most Kadets thus believed the alternatives for a new regime were limited. The capability to end mass unrest required a government which masses of dissident workers and soldiers felt would to some extent represent their interests. This clearly ruled out a military regime, a government of the right, or even a liberal dictatorship. The need for the army's support meant that the new regime had to maintain reasonably close ties with the old order, particularly on the question of Russia's commitments in the war, which limited its radicalism. Finally, the satisfaction of complex supply and distribution problems meant enlisting the support both of qualified administrative personnel and Russia's industrial bourgeoisie, whose managerial and technical expertise was essential to economic efficiency. In particular, practical competence would have to be assured if Russia was now to devote her full resources to defeating the Germans, the principal grounds on which most in the Duma justified their participation in the rebellion. This meant that, at its core, the new regime had to be liberal or at least nonpartisan, which of course corresponded to the Kadets' own theoretical orientation.

For most Central Committee members in Petrograd, the logical course in these circumstances was to invest full power in the Duma (and thus Miliukov's Progressive Bloc coalition, which many assumed the Kadet leader could control). Though elected on a limited franchise, Russia's parliament still represented a number of the country's most talented political leaders, particularly from among the Kadets, whose influence was far greater than their numerical strength. It was also a bulwark against any move on the city by the army's high command. Its leaders had worked closely with the general staff in the past, and it represented institutional continuity with the old regime. Who could accuse Russia's entire national parliament of sedition?

Whether the monarchy should be preserved, provided the Duma created a new "responsible ministry," was apparently of little concern. Right Kadets like the staid academician S. F. Oldenburg thought it should, but the Central Committee as a whole inclined to the opinion that the "monarchy factually did not exist," and that it was "undesirable and pointless to fight for its resurrection."[10] Consequently, while Miliukov and Nekrasov sat with the Temporary Duma Committee in the Tauride Palace, the Central Committee itself sent representatives throughout the city to address troop units and help take control of state institutions in the Duma's name. Paul Gronskii "seized" the telegraph agency; Vasili Maklakov and Moïsei Adzhemov "secured" the Ministry of Justice; Victor Pepeliaev, Ivan Demidov,

[10] V. A. Obolenskii, "Vospominaniia," MS, n.d., p. 443.

and Vasili Stepanov set out for Tsarskoe Selo and Kronstadt to establish contact with their garrisons. While those in the streets shouted "Down with Nicholas!" the slogan of the Kadet Central Committee was "Long Live the Duma!"[11]

This outlook coincided neatly with that of many members of the Duma itself, particularly its ambitious president, Nicholas Rodzianko. For most of February 28, Rodzianko spent his time cultivating support for a cabinet responsible to the Duma, headed by himself. Apparently he was persuasive. A number of generals were soon convinced that, while the Petrograd situation was potentially catastrophic for the war effort, a Duma with full powers had a good chance of bringing it under control. From staff headquarters in Mogilev on March 1, General Alekseev sent the tsar an urgent telegram, insisting that the Duma be supported. He also requested the appointment of a responsible ministry, with Rodzianko as prime minister. Other army leaders cabled similar views, while General N. V. Ruzskii, an aide-de-camp, stood by in Pskov to argue in person. Rodzianko, meanwhile, also planned to meet Nicholas in Pskov, expecting that the tsar would confirm both his own appointment as premier and the ministerial reform. When Nicholas and his entourage arrived late in the afternoon of March 1, General Ruzskii met him before dinner. The two talked for most of the evening. Around 11 p.m., Alekseev's telegram arrived, apparently ending any argument. Ruzskii then communicated with Rodzianko by telegraph, reporting the tsar's consent to a responsible ministry. He also indicated that a manifesto to this effect had been drafted.[12]

Meanwhile, Miliukov and other members of the Temporary Duma Committee were negotiating in the Tauride Palace with representatives of the Petrograd Soviet. Regarded by the left as the "spirit and backbone" of liberal Russia and " 'boss' of all bourgeois elements," the Kadet leader himself was a focal point of these talks, independently of his party's Central Committee. His principal concern was to create a strong but nonpartisan national regime, capable of preserving Russia's national interests rather than satisfying class demands or implementing social reforms. Insofar as a revolution could be supported in wartime, it was only as a means of rationalizing the country's

[11] Discussion of these and other Kadet activities on February 28 and March 1 are most fully reported in *Kak sovershilas'*, which seems, though anonymous, to have been written by party members. Reports on the Central Committee's support for the Duma and views on the monarchy appear in Obolenskii MS, p. 443; Rodichev MS, p. 11; and the article by M. M. Ichas, "27 i 28 fevralia 1917 g., *Poslednaia Novosti*, Mar. 12, 1927.

[12] Browder and Kerensky, pp. 91-93. This sequence is discussed fully by Katkov, pp. 317ff.

state structure to further the military effort. This required an authoritative government of statesmen, not of bickering politicians.

The crucial consideration for Miliukov was the establishment of firm state authority, which seemed to depend on two factors: support from the Soviet, whose leaders clearly exercised whatever control there was over rebellious Petrograd; and sanction from existing state authority, namely the tsar, whose endorsement was necessary to invest the new government with "legal" power and to secure the support of the army. With these concerns in mind, Miliukov quickly came to the conclusion, in contrast to his colleagues on the Kadet Central Committee, that the Duma could not become the basis for a responsible government under Rodzianko. The evidence here is hard to sort out. There is some indication that Miliukov had actually lost faith in a political role for the Duma some months before, despite his continued efforts on behalf of the Progressive Bloc. But it also seems apparent that pressure from the Soviet pushed him in this direction.[13] In any event, the main consideration for Miliukov was the fact that the Duma was not democratically elected, but class-based, and never regarded by the left as a true national parliament. In the context of revolutionary democracy, with the broadest possible extension of political freedom and civil liberties, it was hardly likely that a cabinet responsible to its propertied (*tsenzovye*) delegates could long maintain popular support. The sources do not say so directly, but Miliukov most likely felt that *any* form of direct accountability was inappropriate for Russia in the context of revolution. With their own limited national constituency, the Kadets themselves could never claim the right to rule on the basis of representative principles; and politically inexperienced Russian workers and peasants were not accustomed to representational authority. No effective policies, moreover, were likely to be implemented if ministers were more interested in currying popular favor than in taking decisive, necessary action; the task of the new regime had to be national, not sectarian.

We do know, moreover, that Miliukov felt the Duma had lost its political initiative by obeying the prorogation decree on the 27th. "Legally," it now had no more claim to power than any other ad hoc group, such as the Petrograd Soviet. In retrospect, it is clear that Soviet leaders had no intention of taking state power, fearing this would provoke a ruthless counterrevolution, and reinforced by Marxist convictions which postulated a clearly defined bourgeois stage of development before Russia could move toward socialism. But in the hours of frenzied activity at the Tauride Palace, the left's possible

---

13 M. Paleologue, *An Ambassador's Memoirs*, 3 vols., London, 1923-25, III, 88.

political aspirations greatly concerned the tiring Miliukov. The only acceptable course, considering all factors, was a totally new regime, not based on the Duma, but independently vested with "the plenitude of power."[14]

The crucial element in Miliukov's vision, however, was the sanction of the tsar. Unless the monarchy continued to exist in some form to endorse a new government, preferably as a regency under Grand Duke Michael, Miliukov felt that neither the army command and conservative, upper-class Russia on one hand, nor the untutored mass of workers, peasants, and soldiers on the other, would recognize its authority. Soviet leaders negotiating with the Temporary Duma Committee felt Miliukov's concern was "utopian" in view of the "general hatred of the monarchy among the masses of the people," but were not prepared to make the question a major issue. The monarchy was simply not "an important factor"; in any event, a constituent assembly would certainly establish a republic in the not-too-distant future.[15] What was a factor, however, was the possibility of counterrevolution. Already by February 28 there were rumors of loyalist troops moving on the capital under General Ivanov. In dealing with this problem, a number of leftists thought the monarchy could prove useful.[16]

Thus the liberal plan for a responsible ministry collapsed as Miliukov, the country's leading Kadet and ostensible "boss" of right-wing Russia, negotiated a provisional government committed to political freedom and a constituent assembly, but sanctioned by a figurehead regent rather than the Duma. While obviously not the only member of the Temporary Duma Committee to take this position, Miliukov was clearly most influential. It is not too much to say that largely as a result of his efforts, the dejected Rodzianko was forced to wire General Ruzskii in the early hours of March 2 that the tsar's manifesto in favor of a responsible ministry was now too late.

Meanwhile, such was Miliukov's position of authority in the Tauride Palace that he himself wrote part of the Soviet's declaration supporting the new government on March 2 (in which, according to Sergei Melgunov, it was he who included the phrase that Russia was "not yet free from the dangers of military movement against the revolution").[17] And such was his self-assurance that, even before the delegates to Pskov brought back the tsar's sanction for an independent,

[14] Miliukov, *Istoriia*, pt. 1, pp. 46-48; S. I. Shidlovskii, *Vospominaniia*, 2 pts., Berlin, 1923, pt. 2, pp. 64-65. The attitudes of various Soviet leaders and the Soviet's negotiations with the Duma committee are most fully reported in Sukhanov, I, 271ff.

[15] Sukhanov, I, 218-19.

[16] *Ibid.*, p. 88; Zenzinov, "Fevral'skie dni," No. 35, p. 219.

[17] Mel'gunov, *Martovskie dni*, p. 43.

provisional regime, Miliukov stood in the Ekaterinskii Hall of the Tauride Palace, in one of the most famous incidents of the March period, and declared to an assembled throng that a new government "elected by the revolution" would govern under the regency of Grand Duke Michael.[18]

This particular speech would haunt the Kadet leader the rest of his life. While shrewd in calculating the monarchy's possible role in consolidating state authority in the face of right-wing opposition, Miliukov badly misjudged the temper of Petrograd. Instantly, on hearing the word "regency," the crowd at the Tauride roared its disapproval. ("Prolonged bursts of indignation," the transcript in *Izvestiia* reads; "Exclamation: 'Long Live the Republic!' 'Down with the Dynasty!'")[19] Moreover, Miliukov also overestimated the popularity of his scheme with the new members of the government, and even with Grand Duke Michael himself. On the morning of March 3, in a dramatic confrontation at the Grand Duke's apartment on Millionnaia Street, Miliukov found himself practically alone in arguing the necessity of monarchic symbolism. Michael refused to accept the crown without much hesitation. The monarchy dissolved, with the Kadet leader himself one of its last prominent defenders.

For the Kadet party as a whole, the political implications of Miliukov's actions were quickly apparent. From the left came charges of counterrevolution, of upholding the standards of reaction; on the right there was hostility over the collapse of Rodzianko's plan for a ministry responsible to the conservative Duma. Neither development could help the Kadets broaden their base of support, a necessary step if the party was to develop its strength in the forthcoming period of electoral democracy. Late on the afternoon of March 3, in fact, Miliukov determined to withdraw completely from government affairs, having earlier stated that the perpetuation of the monarchy was a condition for his accepting a ministerial position. Only a special delegation from the Kadet Central Committee, led by Vinaver and Nabokov, persuaded him to change his mind.[20]

Even within the Central Committee, there was much consternation over Miliukov's independent actions. Nekrasov was particularly bitter, having hoped the Kadets would help the abdication go smoothly; others felt divisions among Kadets were deepened when they should have been healed. Most important, there were fears that doubts would now develop among workers and soldiers about the orientation of the new provisional cabinet itself.

[18] *Izvestiia Revoliutsionnoi Nedeli*, Mar. 2, 1917.
[19] *Ibid.*
[20] Nabokov, p. 22; R. Vinavera, "Vospominaniia," MS, 1944, p. 93.

Though hardly a Kadet creation alone, the new regime was composed almost entirely of liberal figures. It sprang from the Progressive Bloc, which had been working on the composition of a possible liberal ministry since the summer of 1915, when it first proposed the famous "Cabinet of Defense."[21] Its head was Prince George Lvov, a nonparty zemstvo leader chosen more for his disassociation from politics than for political skills, and largely at the urging of Miliukov, who wanted to be sure the new cabinet had little direct connection with the Fourth Duma.[22] But the Kadet leader himself, who took the post of minister of foreign affairs, was clearly its dominant personality; and his closest associates from the Petrograd party group held important posts. Andrei Shingarev became minister of agriculture; Fedor Kokoshkin and Vladimir Nabokov became, respectively, chairman of the important Constituent Assembly Committee and state secretary; and Alexander Manuilov, former rector of Moscow University, was made minister of education. While the socialist Alexander Kerensky also joined the cabinet, and Nicholas Nekrasov, the new Kadet minister of transport, was generally considered a radical, the remaining ministers were all likely to support Kadet party views (particularly Alexander Konovalov, the progressive Moscow industrialist and future Kadet who became minister of trade and industry; and Michael Tereshchenko, a young Kievan sugar magnate who became minister of finance). Thus the regime was as much a Kadet government as party leaders could reasonably expect, though the party's Central Committee played no direct role in its formation, and some have even argued that masonry was a more important factor than politics in structuring its composition.[23]

What this would mean in terms of the government's programs and policies remained to be seen. Reflecting the Petrograd Kadet ethos, the new provisional regime was decidedly "nonpartisan" in all of its initial pronouncements, officially committing itself to national rather than sectarian interests. But it was hardly representative. Instead it reflected the emphasis on elite rather than mass politics which had characterized the approach of Petrograd Kadets generally (and which Miliukov himself may have felt was a necessary means of circumventing the political implications of the liberals' own narrow electoral base); it was concerned with political, not social democracy; and it reflected the intense desire to win the war and advance Russia's "national interests" which had largely impelled all of the Kadets' own policies in the preceding two and one-half years.

Meanwhile, however, elsewhere in Russia, new local authorities were

[21] *Utro Rossii*, Aug. 13, 1915.   [22] Nabokov, p. 40.
[23] E.g., Katkov, pp. 377ff.

also springing up, whose composition differed from that of the central regime. And as Petrograd Kadet leaders were shortly to learn to their surprise, an effort to orient these new local authorities toward social concerns and give them a very broad popular base was led in many places by Miliukov's own party colleagues.

THE PARTY'S RESPONSE IN THE PROVINCES

Most of Russia greeted the revolution calmly. So shallow was tsarist authority that almost no attempt was made to organize a restorationist *vendée*. On March 5, at the insistence of the Petrograd Kadets, the new government discharged all provincial governors and their assistants. Regional administration was entrusted to zemstvo board chairmen pending the appointment of Provisional Government commissars and the reorganization of local rule on democratic principles.[24] But the government's action, designed to quash any administrative counter-revolution, was not really needed. All over Russia, local public figures, led by the Kadets were already taking control.

The process started first in Moscow. As early as February 27, while Rodzianko in Petrograd was informing Nicholas of the government's inability to suppress disorders, Nicholas Kishkin, Nicholas Astrov, and other Moscow liberals met in a private conference. Fearing the Petrograd rioting might spread, the Moscow Kadets determined to take action on their own to preserve order. And reflecting their own political style of the last few years, in contrast to their colleagues in Petrograd, they called a meeting of representatives from all leading public organizations to ground new local authority in mass popular support.[25]

[24] The decree appears in both Browder and Kerensky, I, 243, and in *Izvestiia Petrogradskago Soveta Rabochikh i Soldatskikh Deputatov*, Mar. 4, 1917, but with a significant difference. The Kerensky and Browder version reads in part as follows: ". . . the Provisional Government has deemed it necessary to temporarily remove the governor and vice governor from the execution of their functions. The Chairmen of the Guberniya Zemstvo Boards are entrusted with the administration of the guberniya. . . ." *Izvestiia*, however, reports the decree with the word *temporarily* juxtaposed: "the Provisional Government has deemed it necessary to remove the governor and vice-governor . . . The Chairmen of the Guberniya Zemstvo Boards are temporarily entrusted. . . ." The significance of the change is that Kerensky and Browder's version releases the government from much of the blame for disrupting provincial administrations, something for which Lvov's regime was later very much criticized, since the governors appear to have been removed only temporarily. In fact, the governors and their staffs were permanently removed, and the decree of March 5 was understood at the time in the version appearing in *Izvestiia*. See e.g. *Rech'*, Mar. 7, 1917. Kadets themselves urged that the governors be removed in their Central Committee meeting of March 2. See *VPNS*, No. 1, May 11, 1917, p. 19, and *Rech'*, Mar. 5, 7, and 8, 1917.

[25] *Sbornik materialov komiteta moskovskikh obshchestvennykh organizatsii*, 2 pts., Moscow, 1917, pt. 1, pp. 2-3.

A preliminary meeting took place on the night of February 28-March 1, where it was decided the group's representative base was still not broad enough. New invitations were sent out to more than twenty groups to attend a second, larger meeting. In response, the Moscow Committee of Public Organizations held its "constituent conference" late on the afternoon of March 1. More than 170 "civic leaders" attended, including in addition to a prominent body of Kadets, a delegation of 20 from the newly formed Moscow Workers' Soviet.[26]

Here, moreover (again in contrast to Petrograd), Kadet party leaders joined enthusiastically in support of a series of radical resolutions: autocracy was declared "unsuitable" for Russia; the monarchy could not continue, and all members of the tsar's family were to surrender their official positions; a constituent assembly had to be elected as soon as possible on democratic principles to organize a permanent, representative government; and, since local government authorities were "incapable" of exercising power properly, authority in Moscow had to be vested temporarily in the Committee of Public Organizations itself, chaired by an Executive Board of fifteen persons.[27]

The Executive Board met for the first time at 9 p.m. on the same evening, March 1 (just as Miliukov was about to begin negotiations with the Petrograd Soviet). It was expressly a coalition. Its fifteen members were made up of five delegates from workers' organizations, five from democratic parties, and five from "upper-class" (*tsenzovye*) groups, including the Kadets. And on the grounds of this "representational base," it united "all authority for the city of Moscow" in its hands.[28]

A number of Moscow Kadet leaders enthusiastically supported this approach, which reflected their earlier efforts to join closer with workers' groups and left-wing parties in the War Industries Committees and the Zemstvo and City Unions. Nicholas Kishkin, the progressive Moscow Kadet physician who had served on the party's Central Committee since 1907, became the Executive Board's official chairman; Nicholas Astrov, one of the Moscow Kadets' most prominent figures, became its unofficial spokesman. Three other Kadets also joined the Executive Board, while a number of their party colleagues assumed other specific duties and responsibilities.[29] Kishkin, meanwhile, met

[26] *Ibid.*, which lists the groups sending representatives and their respective number of delegates.

[27] *Ibid.*

[28] *Ibid.*, p. 11. See also *Russkiia Vedomosti*, Mar. 2, 1917; *Russkoe Slovo*, Mar. 2, 1917.

[29] According to the *Sbornik Materialov*, pt. 2, p. 24, for example, a well-known Kadet educator, A. D. Alferov, was made "Commissar for Secondary Schools."

with the Moscow Military District Commander, General Vankov, on measures to prevent disorder; Astrov took steps to publicize the Committee's activities through *Russkiia Vedomosti*, where he was a member of the staff; and the Moscow Kadets as a group sent a telegram to Petrograd, stressing the absolute impossibility of retaining the monarchy.[30]

By March 4, consequently, although a local workers' soviet was also active in Moscow, the Committee of Public Organizations held effective power. Under Kishkin's leadership, its Executive Board appointed twenty-three different commissars and committee chairmen to deal with all aspects of city government, from military affairs to the administration of archives.[31] Supporting a democratic government, the end of the monarchy, but also the liberals' traditional national goals, Kadets regarded the Committee as a perfect vehicle through which their party could exercise its administrative talent, and "lift" Russia toward a constitutional order. By March 5 they had persuaded the Moscow Trade-Industrialists to assign 100,000 rubles for its emergency use; and on March 6 they convinced the new Provisional Government to rescind its appointment for the post of Moscow District Commissar, and designate Kishkin, the Committee's choice, instead.[32]

It was the Kadet group in Moscow, moreover, rather than Miliukov or the party's leadership in Petrograd, which set the pattern for Kadet committees elsewhere in Russia. Whether this was planned or not is unclear. As early as December 1916, Kishkin was telling his party colleagues that Kadets should form groups like the Moscow Committee of Public Organizations to take power into their hands "when the day comes."[33] In many places, like Kharkov, Kiev, and Odessa, where local Kadet committees were still active, he struck a responsive chord. Particularly in Kharkov, a radically oriented local committee resolved on February 5 to support "any revolutionary effort whatsoever to overthrow the old regime," making efforts at the same time to solidify contacts with local left-wing groups.[34] In any event, the first days of March saw Kadets all over Russia joining workers' representatives and leaders of other local groups to form governing committees like the

---

[30] *Ibid.*, pp. 17-24; E. N. Burdzhalov, *Vtoraia russkaia revoliutsiia. Moskva, front, periferiia*, Moscow, 1971, p. 66.

[31] *Sbornik materialov*, pt. 1, p. 17; pt. 2, p. 24.

[32] This was apparently done so that the Provisional Government would recognize the Committee's power, since the original appointment was made to M. V. Chelnokov, the liberal mayor of Moscow during the war, and a prominent Kadet. See *Utro Rossii*, Mar. 5, 1917.

[33] Rodichev MS, p. 1.

[34] *Izvestiia Khar'kovskago Komiteta Partii Narodnoi Svobody*, No. 1, Apr. 30, 1917.

one in Moscow, designed to maintain local control and assure the success of the revolution.

In Kiev, Kadet Mayor F. R. Burchak gathered "leading civic figures" to his office on March 1 to announce his intention of forming a new representative organization. By 9:30 p.m., a Council of United Public Organizations was holding its first meeting. Like its counterpart in Moscow, it assumed responsibility for maintaining law and order, and also elected an Executive Committee, which immediately established liaison with both the Kievan Soviet of Workers' Deputies and the city Duma. Agreeing to cooperate closely with the new Council, the Soviet and the Duma sent their own delegates to the Executive Committee. By March 5 a broad Kadet-led coalition was in provisional control of Kiev.[35]

Shortly afterward, Odessa's liberals followed suit. A Committee of Public Organizations formed here on March 3 "in light of the extreme seriousness of the present moment," according to one newspaper announcement.[36] The Odessa Committee included workers' representatives, representatives from the Zemstvo Union, the Union of Cities, the university, and professional organizations like the Odessa Technical Society; but Kadets were predominant. On March 4, the Odessa Committee elected twelve city "commissars" and a "permanent presidium." M. V. Braikevich, a long-time member of the Odessa Kadet Committee, was named the "City Manager."[37] In Odessa, he announced, citizens of all political persuasions would work together to meet the needs of the army and to consolidate the revolution.[38]

Thus it was throughout most of Russia. Kadets and other political figures in Saratov, Simferopol, Tashkent, Samara, Tiflis, Kharkov, and scores of other cities and towns followed the pattern of their Moscow, Kievan, and Odessa colleagues. In Voronezh, liberals organized a public committee on March 1; in Ekaterinoslav, they grouped together four days later. In Baku, a group formed from representatives of the local soviet, the city, and the Trade-Industrialist organization; in Tashkent, a public committee was created out of five "workers" and ten "liberals."[39]

The list could go on. In Simferopol, initiative for a Committee of Public Organizations came from Kadet representatives in the city duma after news arrived about the arrest of former tsarist ministers. In Saratov, an "Executive Committee" of public organizations an-

[35] *Kievskaia Mysl'*, Mar. 2, 1917; V. Manilov, ed., *1917 god na kievshchine*, Kiev, 1928, pp. 3-7, which gives Executive Committee membership and party affiliation.
[36] *Odesskii Listok*, Mar. 4, 1917.   [37] *Ibid.*, Mar. 8, 1917.
[38] *Ibid.*, Mar. 4, 5, and 6, 1917.
[39] Ia. A. Ratgauzer, *Revoliutsiia i grazhdanskaia voina v Baku*, Baku, 1917, pt. 1, p. 34; *Odesskii Listok*, Mar. 6, 1917; *Russkiia Vedomosti*, Mar. 7, 1917.

nounced its intention through Kadet spokesmen to "preserve order and . . . unflinchingly work with the army for final victory over the enemy." Nine of the seventeen members on the Saratov committee were Kadet party representatives; and on March 2 or 3, the military garrison placed itself at their disposal. Elsewhere the pattern was the same. In Rostov, a public committee held its first meeting on March 3 at the instigation of V. F. Zeeler and N. E. Paramonov, the city's two most prominent Kadets. The garrison declared its support on March 5.[40]

Thus most Kadet leaders in provincial cities and towns were anxious and willing to work closely with a broad spectrum of political leaders, including, perhaps even emphasizing, representatives of left-wing groups. Far more enthusiastic about the revolution than their party colleagues in Petrograd, provincial Kadets also showed relatively little concern for preserving the monarchy. In one or two places like Odessa, Kadet newspapers published statements supporting a regency, but these were the exceptions; despite the Kadet party program, most local groups followed their Moscow colleagues, rather than Miliukov, and endorsed a democratic republic even before Michael's final rejection of the crown.[41]

Kadet opinion in the provinces, as in Moscow and Petrograd, was not uniform. In Odessa, Kiev, Poltava, and a number of provincial towns, for example, there was a tendency among some Kadets to welcome the revolution as a means of "liberating" non-Russian nationalities; and despite the party program's adherence to a nonfederal, centralized system of government, some Kadets expressed themselves locally in favor of a new republican federation. In Poltava this issue even led at the beginning of March to an open division of the local party committee.[42] There were also differences of opinion about the potential radicalism of the peasantry, whether monarchism had deep or shallow roots in the countryside, and whether in Russia's new conditions of electoral democracy Kadets ought to avoid close ties with the gentry.[43]

[40] The Simferopol committee is described in detail in P. Nikol'skii, "Simferopol'skii gorodskoi obshchestvennyi komitet," *Revoliutsiia v Krymu* (Simferopol), No. 7, 1927, pp. 67-100; the Saratov committee is detailed in *1917 god v Saratove*, Saratov, 1927, pp. 6-7, and in V. P. Antonov-Saratovskii, *Pod stiagom proletarskoi bor'by*, Moscow-Leningrad, 1925, pp. 99-104. The best Petrograd newspaper on these committees is *Birzhevyia Vedomosti*. See also my article, "Les Libéraux russes et le changement de pouvoir en mars 1917," *Cahiers du Monde Russe et Soviétique*, IX, Jan.-Mar., 1968, pp. 46-57.
[41] *Odesskii Listok*, Mar. 2, 1917. [42] *Poltavskii Den'*, Mar. 17, 1917.
[43] "Iz protokolov plenarnago zasedaniia tsentral'nago komiteta i parlamentskoi fraktsii partii narodnoi svobody, 10-13 mart. 1917," *VPNS*, No. 1, May 11, 1917, pp. 15-20; *Rech'*, Mar. 26, 27, and 28, 1917 (protocols of the seventh party congress).

Yet despite these differences, it also became clear as local Kadets began to reconvene their committees and clubs, that in two important ways, both of which would prove to have a profound effect on the party's role in the revolution, provincial Kadets were not only united among themselves, but also wholly supportive of the Petrograd party leadership. One was an acceptance of the revolution primarily as an opportunity to win the war, and a hope that immediate social and political changes would serve to unite the country as a whole, strengthening the ability to win a military victory. By the end of the first week in March, organizational sessions of local Kadet committees had been held in over twenty cities, including Novgorod, Minsk, Simbirsk, Orel, Vologda, Nizhni-Novgorod, Revel, Tver, Simferopol, Poltava, Kharkov, Tiflis, Kazan, and Baku. And everywhere, Kadets were concerned that the "fresh air of freedom" be welcomed and celebrated in the first instance as a great opportunity for military victory, that "no patriotic Russian forget that a savage enemy stands in the west, ready to take advantage of any weakening of our effort."[44]

The second, closely related element of Kadet unity was that virtually all party members, even those tacitly oriented toward the left, were momentarily convinced that the appropriate political posture for all Russians was one of nonpartisanship and cooperation between all political parties and social groups who supported the revolution, despite past conflicts and differences. In Odessa, Kadets announced that they were not organizing "in order to struggle with other parties, a struggle which, by introducing dissension, would be a serious disservice to the country," but "to work in a friendly way, cooperatively and with enthusiasm, to inculcate the broad masses with principles of a new democratic order. . . ."[45] In Simbirsk, the popular lawyer S. P. Rudnev became chairman of the local Kadet committee despite "a deep aversion to politics" because it was known he could work cooperatively with other political groups.[46] In Kiev, Kadets urged *all* political groups to withhold partisan demands until democracy was firmly established and the war won.[47] And in the Petrograd Central Committee itself, as that group reconvened on March 1 in Vinaver's apartment, initial decisions endorsed "nonpartisan" Kadet participation in the various committees being set up by the Temporary Duma Committee, and instituted procedures through *Rech'* and other newspapers to disseminate both the government's decrees and the decisions of the Petrograd Soviet. The Committee's only "political" resolution

[44] Editorial in *Odesskii Listok*, Mar. 2, 1917.
[45] *Ibid.*, Mar. 14, 1917.
[46] S. P. Rudnev, *Pri vechernikh ogniakh*, Kharbin, 1928, pp. 49-50.
[47] *Poltavskii Den'*, Mar. 4 and Mar. 17, 1917.

was a demand for amnesty for political and religious prisoners, hardly something Kadets alone desired.[48] On March 2, in fact, nonpartisanship became explicit when the question was raised about the Central Committee supplying new Kadet ministers with lists of persons deemed capable of assuming responsible administrative posts. After discussing the question at some length, the Committee decided that such lists should *not* be submitted "in order to protect the ministers from any partisan (*partiinyi*) interference."[49]

To some extent, this nonpartisanship—or *nadpartiinost'*, as the Kadets themselves again pointedly called it—reflected the long decline in sectarian politics generally in Russia following the failure of the first two Dumas. In the provinces, this decline had reinforced a bias among Kadet intellectuals against activist partisan politics without at the same time erasing a fundamental radicalism. In Petrograd, it had prompted Miliukov and his colleagues to concern themselves almost entirely with "nonpartisan" legislative activity in the Duma, which in practice largely reflected the interests of Russia's professional middle class. In part, however, it was also a deliberate political style, developed in the prerevolutionary period, as we have seen, to compensate for the party's rather narrow constituency outside the capitals, and reinforced now by the fact that political authority in most places clearly depended on cooperating with the left. Nonpartisanship in this sense reflected Kadet concern about instituting social change too rapidly or at the expense of particular social groups, and thus represented the basic liberal value system underlying the party's official program. But in most cases, finally, Kadet *nadpartiinost'* in essence simply reflected a deeply felt belief in February 1917 that the revolution was a great *national* event, crucial to Russia's general interest and development, rather than an opportunity to secure sectarian class or party goals.

For many Kadets, as we shall see, this attitude would soon appear utopian and impractical; and discussions about "partisan" tactics and programs would soon rekindle long-standing differences of opinion. But for the time being, at least, the Central Committee spoke for virtually all party members when it declared in the party's first official post-revolutionary statement:

Let all differences of parties, classes, social estates, and nationalities be forgotten. Let a single Russian nation rise up in a peak of greatness, and create conditions for the peaceful existence of all citizens. Let order be strengthened so that each class, each estate, and each nationality can freely express its views and achieve the realization

[48] *VPNS*, No. 1, May 11, 1917, pp. 13-14.   [49] *Ibid.*, p. 13.

of its desires. Our main slogan now is "Organization and Unity." Organization and unity for victory over the foreign enemy; organization and unity for domestic reconstruction. Let every heart have hope that once and for all we have succeeded in eliminating all that would perniciously divide us.[50]

[50] *Ibid.*, p. 19.

Ministers, Party, and Country

THE EVENTS OF February 1917 were signs of the enormous pressures straining in Russia: rapid and uneven industrialization; disparate wealth; mass agrarian discontent; administrative incompetence; the brutality of workers' existence in wretched slums. There was also the savage war, whose objectives were incomprehensible to millions of peasant-soldiers, and whose cruelties by the late winter of 1917 had touched virtually every Russian household.

A few weeks before the revolution began, Russian conditions were graphically described by Duma President Rodzianko in a long memorandum to the tsar:

> Your Imperial Highness! At a moment of grave danger, the very worst policy is to close ones eyes to the profound seriousness of conditions which have developed. . . . Russia's situation at the present time is catastrophic, and also deeply tragic. Her army has not been beaten. It is better supplied with articles of war than at any time in the past. But behind the army, in the rear, disorganization is so great that it threatens to make meaningless all the sacrifices, all the blood that has flowed, all the unexcelled heroism, and—what is more—decisively tilt the military balance in favor of our enemies. . . .[1]

In detail, Rodzianko then described the situation in Moscow and Petrograd. Supplies of food to Moscow were less than half the required daily norms. Only 430,000 puds[2] of firewood were available when the daily need was 475,000; only 60,000 puds of coal and 75,000 puds of oil, when the daily needs were 100,000 puds of each. The average daily supply of essential raw materials was also running less than half of established norms; and scores of factories, even those essential to defense, were being forced to curtail their outputs. In Moscow, the city gasworks had reduced its production almost 75 percent. Tramways had ceased running in the evenings, and there was a possibility that service would be curtailed altogether. The temperature in homes

---

[1] *Ekonomicheskoe polozhenie Rossii nakanune velikoi oktiabr'skoi sotsialisticheskoi revoliutsii*, 3 pts., Moscow-Leningrad, 1957-67, pt. 2, p. 18.

[2] 1 pud = 36 lbs.

and apartments hovered around 10 degrees centigrade. Disease was rampant; unemployment was reaching epidemic proportions. In Petrograd, out of 73 major enterprises operating in December 1916, 39 had been forced to cease production for various lengths of time as a result of lack of fuel, 11 as a result of electricity shortages. Supplies of oil were at 50 percent of demand; and on January 31, the municipal transit system had only one day's reserve of fuel.

The situation elsewhere in Russia was the same. Serious shortages of iron ore were forcing metallurgical factories throughout the country to curtail their work, especially in the Urals. The Perm industrial region, with only a month's supply of grain on hand, was threatened with open famine; within three months, the country as a whole could expect similar conditions. In urban areas, food shortages were exacerbated by workers who could no longer find employment, and who were increasingly venting their frustration in rioting and strikes. The value of wages for those still employed, meanwhile, was dropping rapidly as a result of inflation. Administrators and other salaried employees were particularly hard hit.

The reasons for these catastrophic conditions, according to Rodzianko, were not hard to find. It was not a question of poor harvests, or even of reduced extractions of coal or other raw materials. Preliminary totals of the all-Russian agrarian census for 1916 showed that land under cultivation was 20-25 percent greater than necessary to meet population demands with an average harvest, while harvests for 1913, 1914, and 1915 had generally been favorable. The coal extraction capabilities of the Don basin alone for 1917 were estimated to be over 2,000 million puds compared to 1,544 million in 1913; and a similar situation existed with respect to other raw materials.

Rather, the problem lay first in the disorganization of transport, which lacked the capacity to move even existing stores of grain and raw materials, and which in some areas, such as on the trans-Siberian network, had resulted in the spoiling of millions of pounds of meat and other foods. Second, it was due to an irrational mobilization of skilled workers for the army, whose places had been taken by less able, and consequently less productive, substitutes. More than 50 percent of all capable workers between the ages of 16 and 50 had been drafted, according to Rodzianko, leaving industries in extremely tenuous circumstances. Third and fourth were the government's refusal to make effective use of local public organizations, like the War Industries Committees, and its financial policies, which had contributed to inflation, encouraged speculation, and developed an "absolute lack of confidence in the future" on the part of Russia's industrial and commercial classes. Finally, all of these factors, which were closely interrelated and which acted on each other to increase the seriousness of Russia's general condition, were exacerbated by a lack of government initiative and planning. "It is quite apparent," Rodzianko wrote, "that the interests of private individuals must be put aside, and that measures ought to be undertaken to assure maximum economic productivity." This meant comprehensive state planning, since it was "impossible to have confidence in the willingness of private individuals to refrain voluntarily from pursuing narrow personal gains, and to start acting only in accordance with their patriotic and moral duties." "The eleventh hour is upon us," the Duma president concluded: "The time is very near when any resort to the intelligence of the people will be too late and useless."[3]

Recent research has shown that Rodzianko's analysis was substantially correct. Grain supplies in particular, according to the Soviet historian A. M. Anfimov, were sufficient in the beginning of 1917 for both civilian and military needs, even without counting reserves in Siberia.[4] P. V. Volobuev has shown that this situation even improved somewhat in the early months of 1917, especially in the Caucasus region and Siberia, and that substantial stores of grain existed even in several European Russian provinces.[5] Natural resources and raw materials were also available, providing they could be moved. But the critical problem, as the Duma president pointed out, was transport.[6]

Rodzianko failed only to stress the negative effects that Russia's concentration of workers had on the economic situation. Almost half of the country's approximately 20 million[7] proletarians were located in the comparatively small district of central and northwestern European Russia, centered on Moscow and Petrograd, which constituted little more than one-fortieth of all Russian territory. The remainder was concentrated in a handful of other major cities and industrial areas: Saratov, Nizhni-Novgorod, and Ivanovo-Voznesensk in the central industrial region; Ekaterinburg in the Urals; the Don region; Kharkov, Odessa, and Kiev in the Ukraine; and the Caucasus area, particularly Baku.[8] Shortages of raw materials or foodstuffs in any one of these

[3] *Ekon. polozhenie*, pt. 2, p. 32.

[4] A. M. Anfimov, "Zernovoe khoziaistvo Rossii v gody pervoi mirovoi voiny," *Materialy po istorii sel'skogo khoziaistva i krest'ianstva SSSR*, Moscow, 1959, sbor. III, 493; see also his *Rossiiskaia derevnia v gody pervoi mirovoi voiny*, Moscow, 1962, esp. pp. 276-323.

[5] P. V. Volobuev, *Ekonomicheskaia politika vremennogo pravitel'stva*, Moscow, 1962, pp. 383-87.

[6] *Ekon. polozhenie*, pt. 2, pp. 211-33.

[7] L. S. Gaponenko, "Rabochii klass Rossii nakanune velikogo oktiabria," *IZ*, No. 73, 1963, p. 51.

[8] *Ibid.*, p. 65; P. V. Volobuev, *Proletariat i burzhuaziia Rossii v 1917 g.*, Moscow, 1964, pp. 36-37.

areas was thus likely to have a widespread effect on the productivity of the country as a whole, while continued unemployment or unrest in a handful of factories was likely to spread quickly into a serious regional depression. The effect of worker concentration was therefore to amplify enormously the consequences of existing difficulties, not only on Russia's economy, but in terms of politics and social relations as well.

If excited crowds all over Russia enthusiastically welcomed the events in Petrograd, if the threat of counterrevolution began to subside and even uneasy Kadet conservatives like Vasili Maklakov and Paul Dolgorukov began to think their colleagues might successfully assume the reins of power, the tasks facing the new government were still enormous.

Problems of Legitimacy, Accountability, and Authority

The problem most concerning Miliukov and his fellow ministers in the first days of March, however, was not Russia's economic condition, but the new government's authority. In effect, the regime had unilaterally declared itself in power. Though supported by the Petrograd Soviet, itself an ad hoc body, its legitimacy was tenuous; and unless the liberal ministers had effective power, it was unlikely that Russia's other problems could be solved.

The most obvious means of securing the nation's confidence, once Miliukov's plan of obtaining monarchic sanction had failed, was to stress a commitment to the rapid convocation of a democratically elected constituent (or constitutional) assembly. This became the government's "primary duty" according to its general declaration of March 6, equaled in importance only by national defense.[9] Yet for several reasons, Miliukov and his liberal colleagues had reservations about convening the assembly. One was the difficulty of holding fully democratic elections in the midst of a war, with millions in the fluid status of military service, and millions more completely ignorant of even the most basic democratic political processes. As we have seen, Miliukov and other Kadet party leaders, particularly in Petrograd, had come to assume a long period of political evolution before Russia was fully ready for representative democracy, despite the commitments of the Kadet party program; Miliukov's own goal in 1916 had been a liberal dictatorship on the model of Lloyd George's cabinet in England or Clemenceau's in France, at least until the end of the war.[10] Also, Russia's pressing economic and social problems could simply not

[9] *Vestnik Vremennago Pravitel'stva*, Mar. 7, 1917.
[10] Editorial in *Rech'*, Nov. 27, 1916.

wait until the country was organized for national elections. However unpopular they might be to different groups of the population, measures had to be taken by the provisional regime at once, particularly to support the army. Finally, there was the probability that any national election campaign would intensify partisanship in Russia, increasing social polarization perhaps even to the point of civil war, as class-oriented parties fought for support of their programs; at the very least, a campaign might undermine what Kadets saw as Russia's "national concensus," whose development and maintenance was necessary for military victory.

In effect, therefore, while proclaiming their democratic commitments, Russia's new liberal ministers had no intention of foregoing the "right" to address themselves to pressing national problems even before any elections were held; and implicitly, this meant the necessity of defining "acceptable limits" to revolutionary change, at least for the time being. Indeed, leaving aside any question of the Kadets' own class interests (which one might well argue would benefit from the postponement of many of the reforms being advocated by socialist radicals), it is difficult to see how they could have done otherwise, given the nation's needs and the lack of any established mechanism for effective democratic representation. Yet the revolution had been carried to fruition by a flood of mass frustration and hostility, which the new ministers could easily find turned against themselves. Also, unless new policies reflected mass aspirations, the new regime would have to enforce its decisions with the same coercive measures used by the tsarist autocracy, which again might easily lead to civil war.

The existence of the Petrograd Soviet posed special problems in this regard. Ostensibly a representative body itself, whose policies were to reflect the interests of Russia's workers, peasants, and soldiers, the Soviet clearly rivaled the government as an institution of authority. Moreover, other local soviets, modeling themselves on the Petrograd example, were springing up in virtually every significant city and town. By the end of March, they existed in more than 70 localities in the central region alone; and in the Ural industrial region, there were more than 100.[11] Peasant soviets were also organizing in the countryside, although in some places news of the revolution itself did not arrive for several weeks.[12] These groups raised obvious questions about the comprehensiveness of the government's own power—the specter of *dvoevlastie*, or dual authority, as Miliukov and others described it.

[11] A. M. Andreev, *Sovety rabochikh i soldatskikh deputatov nakanune oktiabria*, Moscow, 1967, pp. 59-74, esp. p. 63.

[12] O. N. Moiseeva, *Sovety krest'ianskikh deputatov v 1917 godu*, Moscow, 1967, p. 22.

The Petrograd Kadet leadership worried about "dual authority" from the first days of the revolution, arguing that whatever the new form of political control in Russia, authority could not be held effectively by more than one institution. What bothered Miliukov and his colleagues most was the soviets' obvious partisanship, at odds with their own hope of maintaining a sentiment of national unity. They also worried that "blinded radicals" might use the new organizations to launch a coup d'état in the future.[13]

Yet it was also clear that for the time being, at least, the new regime *needed* the power exercised by the soviets. When Demidov, Stepanov, Rodichev, Gronskii, and other Kadets went out to enlist the support of army garrisons in the first days of March, for example, they leaned heavily on Petrograd Soviet spokesmen who accompanied them for support and protection. Also, Soviet and Duma Committee proclamations were co-authored on several occasions; their military commissions were joined; and at one point Miliukov himself even insisted that published statements from both groups be printed together "to underscore their mutual relationship."[14] It was also Miliukov who insisted, along with other Kadets in Petrograd, that the Soviet leadership use its influence to prevent further demonstrations by workers. He also regarded it as the Soviet's obligation to restore and maintain civil order, assuring at the same time—since the socialists controlled the printers' union—that all parties, including those on the right, enjoyed freedom of the press and other civil liberties.[15]

The local soviets were also important to the government in terms of the army and the front. More than 7 million front-echelon soldiers, stretched along a 3,000 kilometer line from the Baltic to the Black Sea, hoped at the very least that the revolution would bring some relief from the hardships of discipline and short supplies. Any effective military posture required that the troops remain orderly. But in some places, soldiers were reacting to the news from Petrograd with an enthusiasm bordering on anarchy; and elsewhere, officers hostile to the revolution (or in some cases, those with German names), were wantonly shot.[16] On March 2, moreover, a group of radical leftists pub-

[13] *Rech'*, Mar. 7, 1917. See also Vladimir Nabokov, "Vremennoe pravitel'stvo," *ARR*, I, 1922, pp. 18-20; Baron B. E. Nol'de, "V. D. Nabokov v 1917 g.," *ARR*, VII, 1922, p. 7.

[14] P. N. Miliukov, *Istoriia vtoroi russkoi revoliutsii*, 3 pts., Sofia, 1921-23, pt. 1, p. 48.

[15] See, e.g., the resolutions of the Central Committee, Mar. 4, 1917, in *VPNS*, No. 1, May 11, 1917, pp. 13-14.

[16] E. N. Burdzhalov, *Vtoraia russkaia revoliutsiia. Moskva, front, periferiia*, Moscow, 1971, p. 139. The most recent statistics on the army are in L. M. Gavrilov, "Chislennost' russkoi deistvuiushchei armii v period fevral'skoi revoliutsii," *Ist. SSSR*, No. 3, 1972, pp. 198-202.

lished the famous Order Number 1, which not only freed soldiers from the humiliating rigors of tsarist military discipline, but also ordered the creation of soldiers' committees to direct and oversee each unit. At once scores of units both in Petrograd and at the front began to look to the Petrograd Soviet as their source of authority, rather than to the government.[17]

Kadets in Petrograd vigorously protested Order Number 1, but even before its publication, implicitly recognized Soviet power in the question of military discipline. On March 1 and 2, when Miliukov and other liberals were concerned that the Petrograd garrison could not defend the revolution if loyalist troops counterattacked, they relied on the Soviet to bring officers and men together and restore the garrison's fighting capabilities.[18] Similarly, when it appeared that scores of army units were stretching Order Number 1 (which supposedly applied only to the Petrograd garrison), and were electing their officers in total disregard for the traditional chain of command, it was the Soviet which was expected to bring them to their senses.[19]

Several left Kadets, particularly Nicholas Nekrasov, argued in the beginning of March that the network of soviets offered a temporary solution to the problem of government accountability. The authority exercised by these "unofficial" organs did not so much overlap the government's as run in parallel lines, with the composition of the provisional ministry reflecting Russia's professional classes, public organizations, bourgeoisie, and army officers; and that of the soviets representing millions of workers, peasants, and soldiers, particularly those in Moscow and Petrograd, and at the front. Until the convening of the Constituent Assembly, liberal ministers could "legitimize" their power by tailoring decisions to the soviets' wishes.[20]

But just as Miliukov and his supporters worried about a revolutionary cabinet responsible to the old Fourth Duma, they were equally adamant about the government's independence from the soviets. Accountability to one partisan group raised the problem of support from others; and if mass popularity became the basis for political power before the Constituent Assembly, the position of the Kadets themselves, judging by past Duma elections, was likely to become even more tenuous than it already was. In a context of revolutionary change,

[17] Though intended for the Petrograd garrison, Order Number 1 was soon regarded by most soldiers as applying to all units, much to the consternation of Kadets and moderate socialists alike. See the discussion by J. R. Boyd, "The Origins of Order No. 1," *Sov. Stud.*, XIX, Jan. 1968, pp. 359-72; and V. I. Miller, "Nachalo demokratizatsii staroi armii v dni fevral'skoi revoliutsii," *Ist. SSSR*, No. 6, 1966, pp. 26-43.

[18] P. Miliukov, *Vospominaniia*, 2 vols., New York, 1955, II, 305-06.

[19] Central Committee resolutions, Mar. 4; *Rech'*, Mar. 12, 1917.

[20] *VPNS*, No. 1, May 11, 1917, pp. 21-22.

moreover, an independent government of "national," "nonpartisan" liberals was far better able, in Miliukov's view, to determine what was truly in Russia's national interest than organizations which themselves were formed on an ad hoc basis. Consequently, Miliukov and his liberal colleagues insisted that the power of the new regime could not in any way be circumscribed. They took their posts instead as if they were a "ministry of confidence" under the old regime, warning the soviets not to encroach on their "legitimate authority."

In these circumstances, if the liberal ministers used their self-proclaimed legitimacy to introduce policies at variance with the desires of workers, peasants, and soldiers, as expressed through the soviets, it would only be a matter of time before Russia faced a new political crisis. And given the dual nature of power which existed in fact, as well as Russia's enormous practical needs, even minor disagreements were bound to have a serious effect on the political and social stability most Kadets so much desired.

MILIUKOV'S IMPERIALISM AND THE QUESTION OF RUSSIA'S WAR AIMS

One ready point of conflict between the government and the soviets was, of course, the war and foreign policy, where Miliukov himself took over the Ministry of Foreign Affairs. Even before the Provisional Government's first official declaration, the Kadet leader dispatched what amounted to a personal statement of principles to Russia's Allies through her diplomatic representatives abroad. In it he stressed the liberal foundations of the new regime, and insisted in typically Kadet language that Russia would now fight "shoulder to shoulder" with her democratic Allies to the hour of final triumph, "unswervingly and indefatigably," "faithful to the treaties which bind her by indissoluble ties."[21] These were precisely the themes of *Rech'*, and almost the same words Miliukov had used in May 1916, when he visited London. They were also sentiments echoed innumerable times since 1914 by Kadet spokesmen in the Duma. Russia's honor and duty was to uphold her foreign obligations, regardless of domestic strife, and the fact that they were incurred by the tsarist regime.[22]

Miliukov's thinking on this question was expressed many times, but never more clearly than in a pamphlet entitled *Pochemu i Zachem My Voiuem?* (Why and For What are We Fighting?), published shortly

---

[21] E. A. Adamov, ed., *Constantinople et les détroits*, trans. S. Volsky et al., 2 vols., Paris, 1930-32, I, 462-64.

[22] Thomas Riha, *A Russian European. Paul Miliukov in Russian Politics*, Notre Dame, Ind., 1969, pp. 249-59.

after the revolution.[23] In it Miliukov laid the blame for the war squarely at the feet of German "imperialists," arguing that Russia fought
simply to combat Germany's economic, political, and demographic
pretensions. But as we have seen in Chapter One, and as socialist
readers were undoubtedly quick to perceive in 1917, the Kadet leader
also displayed imperialist tones of his own, arguing that Germany's
guilt lay not in the striving for power and dominance, but only in
her effort to impose hegemony by force. Victory would protect for
Russia the right to free economic and political competition.[24]

Thus Russia was decidedly not fighting for "the most rapid securing
of peace," as many socialists desired. An early peace would not be
lasting. Rather, Russia was fighting for a "firm and enduring" peace,
one in which borders would appear "final" in the eyes of all peoples,
especially in the Balkans and the Dardanelles region.[25] Nations in this
area should certainly be allowed self-determination; but their interests
should not be prejudicial to the big powers. The Alsace-Lorraine
region, whose mineral deposits were vital to France, was a case in
point. So, too, were Constantinople and the Dardanelles Straits.[26]

The question of Russian control over the Dardanelles had preoccupied Russian foreign policy strategists for decades, since the Straits
provided the only Mediterranean outlet for military and commercial
transport from the Black Sea. For most of the nineteenth century,
Russian rights were ostensibly predominant, "guaranteed" by several
treaties. But tsarist statesmen never had much confidence in diplomatic
agreements on this question, and preferred physical control. Their
fears were confirmed most recently in 1912, when the temporary
closing of the Bosphorus and Dardanelles caused considerable losses
for Russian Black Sea shippers.

Before the outbreak of the First World War, all efforts to gain
French and British approval for anything resembling Russian control
proved unsuccessful. When the Germans began to expand their own
influence in this region, a top-level government meeting in February
1914 determined that Russian domination had to be a principal goal
of tsarist foreign policy. Physical control of the Straits, however, also
implied domination over the city of Constantinople, since security
otherwise was untenable.

When the war began, these views were coordinated in a memorandum on the question by an official of the Foreign Ministry, N. B. Bazili.
Bazili pointed out that virtually all proposals for control of the Straits
short of outright occupation had been tried in one instance or another,
and proved deficient. Neutralization had to be rejected since Germany

23 P. Miliukov, *Pochemu i zachem my voiuem?*, Petrograd, 1917.
24 *Ibid.*, pp. 30, 35.   25 *Ibid.*, pp. 39-42.   26 *Ibid.*, pp. 44-46.

had shown with Belgium that "scraps of paper" made little difference when national interests were at stake; an international patrol would also not be effective since each patrolling power could use its own ships for its own purposes; while a tripartite administration under Britain, France, and Russia would last only so long as the alliance. If old treaty agreements were renewed, there was no guarantee that Turkey would be held to its terms in the future; while a Russian naval patrol alone, without territorial occupation, would be subject to shore-based artillery. The only viable alternative was outright annexation.[27] After a brief exchange of diplomatic notes and opinions in the winter of 1914-1915, Russia finally got the agreement of France and England to this in the famous "Secret Treaties" of 1915.[28]

Miliukov fully supported tsarist policy on this issue. No one was the least confused when he began to speak of "strictly observing international obligations" after becoming foreign minister. Just before the revolution, in January 1917, he had published the first in a series of essays on precisely the problem of "Constantinople and the Straits" in the liberal monthly, *Vestnik Evropy*. Arguing here to forestall criticism from socialist "idealists," he distinguished Russia's need for the Straits from "traditional imperialism." Possession of the Straits for Russia was "completely necessary" for elementary reasons of defense and economic development.[29]

At the same time, Miliukov showed that his brand of "necessary" imperialism also involved ideas of racial and cultural superiority, precisely the components of "traditional" imperialism that "idealistic" Russian socialists found most repugnant. The acquisition of Constantinople by Russia, he maintained, could not be objected to on "moral" grounds as if it were simply the forcible seizure of another people's territory. Constantinople was not really a Turkish city. It was instead an "international trading center" belonging to a host of diverse nationalities. Dominated by the Turks, it was deprived of its historic status as a great center of Western civilization and culture; and like the Balkan lands whose growth and culture had been stunted by a "heavy and bloody tyranny," it could by right be "liberated" from the Ottomans in the name of Western values.[30]

This was also how other Kadet leaders saw the question both of Constantinople and the Straits, and Russia's foreign policy generally after the revolution; Miliukov was not lacking party support for his

27 Adamov, I, 43-80.

28 *Ibid.*, pp. 204, 232. See also W. A. Renzi, "Great Britain, Russia, and the Straits," *JMH*, XLII, Mar. 1970, pp. 1-20.

29 P. Miliukov, "Konstantinopol' i prolivy," *VE*, No. 1, 1917, pp. 355-65.

30 *Ibid.*, No. 2, 1917, pp. 225-32; Nos. 4-6, 1917, pp. 526, 535-42.

views. Kadet literature published in March 1917 repeatedly stressed Russia's war aims. So did the speeches of various party leaders at public meetings, and editorials in the press.[31]

There was no question, however, that these views would draw the sharpest opposition from Petrograd Soviet leaders, particularly internationalists like Nicholas Chkheidze, Iurii Steklov, and Nicholas Sukhanov. While the Soviet leadership had no clear view on the war in the first weeks of March, the range of opinion ran only from "defensism" to total withdrawal, with the dominant center clearly leaning toward internationalism. The principal Soviet slogan was "Peace without Annexations or Indemnities"; and by March 10, the Bolsheviks were loudly pushing their demand that the war be converted into a civil struggle of people against imperialist oppressors, a position which Lenin had steadfastly maintained since 1914. All Soviet parties recoiled at the thought of Russia's occupying part of Turkey. Even the moderate Menshevik newspaper *Den'* declared in an editorial on March 5 that "we shall fight against all chauvinistic, nationalistic, and imperialistic words, thoughts, or deeds, whatever their source. . . ."[32]

On March 7 or 8, Alexander Kerensky—the Petrograd Soviet's self-appointed spokesman in the Provisional Government—told Harold Williams of the English *Daily Chronicle* that Russia did not need Constantinople or the Straits, but simply desired free access. This infuriated the already touchy Miliukov, who rebutted Kerensky on March 8 by insisting that "now more than ever" possession of the Straits and Constantinople were necessary to Russian "freedom."[33] Thereupon a full-scale polemic on war aims broke out between *Izvestiia* and *Rech'*. The Soviet organ advanced the idea that it was time to explain "without undue passion" how the war arose, why it was continuing with such horrible intensity, and how it might be ended in the interests of all peoples. *Rech'* complained that utopianism and idealism might cost Russia the "fruits" of her revolutionary victory,

---

[31] For example, a party pamphlet by Arkady Borman (*Chto takoe anneksiia i kontributsiia*, Petrograd, 1917, pp. 7-8) maintained that it was difficult to argue against the "right of the loser" to pay for the war, and that the annexation of both the Dardanelles and Armenia was "just" on the grounds both of military and commercial necessity, and because the Turks were "undeserving." Similar views appeared in pamphlets by E. Korovin, *Vneshniaia politika obnovlennoi Rossii*, Moscow, 1917; A. A. Kornilov. *Partiia narodnoi svobody*, Petrograd, 1917; B. S. Serafimov, *Nemtsy v Konstantinopole*, Petrograd, 1917; and S. A. Kotliarevskii, *Voina i demokratiia*, Moscow, 1917. Leading newspaper articles by Kadets also appeared in March on the subject in *Russkiia Vedomosti*, Mar. 11, 1917; *Odesskii Listok*, Mar. 3, 1917; and a number of issues of *Rech'*. If Nekrasov, Manuilov, or others opposed Miliukov's perspectives in the first weeks of 1917 on this issue, as some later claimed, they kept their views to themselves.

[32] *Den'*, Mar. 5, 1917.   [33] *Rech'*, Mar. 9, 1917.

and suggested obliquely that the slogan "Peace without Annexations and Indemnities" was German in origin.[34]

In the meantime, Chkheidze, Sukhanov, and other Soviet leaders were working out their famous Manifesto to the Peoples of All the World, in which they opposed "the policy of conquest of [Russia's] ruling classes," and appealed to "all people destroyed and ruined by the monstrous war . . . to begin a decisive struggle against the acquisitive ambitions of governments of all countries." On March 14, the manifesto was accepted by the Petrograd Soviet as a whole, and published as a new basis for the foreign policy of democratic Russia.[35]

It therefore became apparent a scant two weeks after the liberal ministers took office that they and the Soviet leadership had different views of Russian "national interests." "Official" policy in foreign affairs was clearly that of the Kadet party and groups to its right; and clearly Miliukov and his party colleagues could not long pursue their own objectives in foreign affairs without calling into question among other things, the regime's ostensible nonpartisanship.

THE QUESTION OF LEGAL REFORMS: KADET POLICIES IN AGRICULTURE, INDUSTRY, AND EDUCATION

Similar difficulties soon emerged over other issues. One of the most important was agrarian reform. The Kadet minister of agriculture was Andrei Shingarev, son of a poor Voronezh bourgeois who had entered Kadet party ranks as a zemstvo physician. (It was said Kadet success in Voronezh during the early years of the party's history was due entirely to his energy. He was well known as a social worker and public speaker, and also helped edit the *Voronezhskoe Slovo*, an early Kadet newspaper in the region.)[36] While Shingarev's special competency was in the realm of finances, that post went to Nicholas Tereshchenko for reasons possibly related to the Masonic movement, but in any event unclear.[37] Instead, Shingarev was given the almost insurmountable problems of "legally" regulating rural production, providing for

[34] See esp. *Izvestiia*, Mar. 11, 1917, and *Rech'*, Mar. 11, 1917; also *Rabochaia Gazeta*, Mar. 7 and 8, 1917; *Pravda*, Mar. 10, 1917; and Iraklii G. Tsereteli, *Vospominaniia o fevral'skoi revoliutsii*, 2 vols., Paris, 1963, I, 33.

[35] *Izvestiia*, Mar. 15, 1917. The drafting of the manifesto is discussed fully in Nicholas Sukhanov, *Zapiski o revoliutsii*, 7 vols., Berlin, 1922-23, II, 197-203.

[36] A. Khrushchov, *Andrei Ivanovich Shingarev*, Moscow, 1918, p. 32.

[37] The post most likely went to Tereshchenko because he was considered more capable of maintaining close relations with industrial circles and the War Industries Committees, of which he was a member, though George Katkov claims Tereshchenko's Masonic affiliations were determinant, and asserts somewhat unfairly that he had "no qualifications whatever" for the post. See George Katkov, *Russia 1917: The February Revolution*, London, 1967, p. 380.

adequate distribution of food products, and containing peasant discontent.[38]

In the beginning of March, the new Kadet minister took a number of emergency measures. He directed the railroad administration to give top priority to all shipments of foodstuffs, gathered statistics on the location of grain supplies, sent directives to military commanders curtailing their practice of unrestricted requisitioning, and worked on plans in conjunction with local committees of public organizations to introduce rationing in several major cities. Working closely as well with the food commission of the Petrograd Soviet, and particularly its principal figure, Vladimir Groman, he also announced on March 10 that the government would introduce a national grain monopoly, requiring the compulsory transfer of all marketable grain to the state at fixed 1916 rates.[39]

At first Soviet spokesmen and supporters regarded the planned grain monopoly as a major concession of the new government. They also supported two further measures Shingarev took in March (again in accordance with the desires of Groman and the Soviet food commission) which promised far-reaching social consequences: the establishment of local food supply committees (charged with "administering the food supply and the organization of agricultural production within the framework of orders from Petrograd"); and the creation of a network of "land committees" (designed to accumulate factual data and deal with specific local problems). Both groups of committees were to be composed of appointed and elected representatives. The statute creating the land committees specifically allowed for local soviet delegates.[40]

These measures drew accusations from some quarters that Shingarev's aim was nothing less than the "illegal" destruction of private property.[41] An All-Russian Congress of Trade-Industrialists meeting in Moscow on March 19-22 also called his grain monopoly "a dangerous plan," and argued that the country was not "technically prepared."[42] But it soon became clear that the Kadet minister was

[38] Khrushchov, pp. 89-92. See also S. I. Shidlovskii, *Vospominaniia*, 2 pts., Berlin, 1923, pt. 2, p. 62, who denies Shingarev's competency in fiscal affairs.

[39] *Vestnik Vremennago Pravitel'stva*, Mar. 11, 1917.

[40] The decision to take these steps was made as early as March 10, and the statutes themselves were distributed several weeks later. See *Vestnik Vremennago Pravitel'stva*, Mar. 11, 1917, and R. P. Browder and A. F. Kerensky, eds., *The Russian Provisional Government 1917*, 3 vols., Stanford, 1961, II, 528-32, 618-21. An article by Manuilov reviewing early developments in agriculture under Shingarev is in *Russkiia Vedomosti*, Mar. 6/19, 1918.

[41] Shidlovskii, pt. 2, pp. 114-15; P. A. Buryshkin, *Moskva kupecheskaia*, New York, 1954, p. 324.

[42] Volobuev, *Ekonomicheskaia politika*, p. 393.

actually placing the problem of agrarian reform very much in the background. Despite appearances, his concern was not for measures which would satisfy the peasants' demand for land but for improving the food supply. This meant a *minimum* of disruption of existing agrarian relations, as Shingarev began to explain publicly later in the month, since even if the transfer of land might ultimately increase productivity, it would certainly not do so in 1917. Moreover, the problem of compensating landlords for expropriated land was now complicated by the treasury's acute shortage of funds; while the fact that millions of peasants were still in uniform meant that any fair redistribution of land would have to await their demobilization—i.e., be postponed until after the war. Despite his initial working relationship with the Petrograd Soviet, consequently, Shingarev soon came to be considered quite conservative, even by a number of his own provincial party colleagues. Very rapidly, opposition shifted from right to left. For the time being, it remained largely muted on the assumption that "the most important question for our country," as the government's own official journal described land reform,[43] would shortly be resolved in the Constituent Assembly. But by the third week in March, left-wing protests were already being heard.[44]

The situation regarding trade and industry was somewhat different, but equally troublesome to Kadets. In the aftermath of the February revolution, Russia witnessed the formation of countless different worker and factory committees. In some areas they were created in response to pressures from local soviets, and were concerned almost entirely with issues relating to the improvement of working conditions. Elsewhere they not only formed on the initiative of workers themselves, but attempted to take virtually all elements of factory administration under their control.[45] In any event, by the end of the first week in March, factory committees were meeting in manufacturing plants in almost all major industrial areas, including Moscow and Petrograd, where they had begun.[46]

At the same time, similar efforts at organization were also under way on the part of Russia's industrial and commercial bourgeoisie, who greeted the February revolution in part as signaling the end to past restrictions on War Industries Committees and other trade-industrial groups. At a special meeting of commercial and industrial representatives in Moscow on March 4, for example, it was decided that all trade-industrial organizations, bourse committees, commercial so-

43 *Vestnik Vremennago Pravitel'stva*, Apr. 23, 1917.
44 *Ibid.*
45 L. S. Gaponenko, *Rabochii klass Rossii v 1917 godu*, Moscow, 1970, pp. 90-91.
46 *Ibid.*

cieties, and other management groups were themselves to form new local committees, and to send representatives to a national congress on March 19 where a new All Russian Union of Trade and Industry would be formed. In the meantime, local management committees were also to address themselves to problems of production and supply.[47]

The new liberal minister of trade and industry, Alexander Konovalov, was a somewhat weak-willed progressive Moscow industrialist, who had served before the revolution as a principal link in that city between the local Kadet committee and the War Industries groups (and who himself would shortly join the Kadets' inner leadership circle in Petrograd as an official party member). Konovalov's initial approach to Russia's pressing economic problems was to rely on the initiative of the new local factory and management committees, using his office to help bring the groups together, and hoping mutual confidence and good will could alleviate at once some of the most troublesome difficulties with production.[48] When pressed by the Soviet for a strong policy of state regulation, his response instead was to invoke sentiments of national patriotism and self-sacrifice, precisely the attitudes that Duma President Rodzianko had earlier dismissed in his long memorandum to the tsar.[49] On March 10, Konovalov was greatly encouraged by an agreement between the Petrograd Association of Manufacturers and the Soviet, introducing an eight-hour working day in factories and mills (a long-sought goal of the labor movement), and promising to increase production. The agreement also formally recognized the operations of factory committees elected by workers on the basis of equal suffrage; and established mediation councils in all enterprises "for the purpose of settling all misunderstandings arising from labor-management relations."[50] It thus seemed exactly the way to handle local problems and avoid serious antagonism.

But like Shingarev, the minister of trade and industry was also placing questions of fundamental reform in the background. Once factory committees were sanctioned by the regime, they began demanding further control over management concerns, provoking the sharp antagonism of Trade-Industrialists; but when Konovalov urged self-restraint and sacrifice, he incurred the emnity of the left, who

[47] *Utro Rossii*, Mar. 7, 1917; V. Ia. Laverychev, "Vserossiiskii soiuz torgovli i promyshlennosti," *IZ*, No. 70, 1961, p. 37.

[48] *Utro Rossii*, Mar. 9, 1917; *Promyshlennost' i Torgovlia*, No. 8-9, Mar. 18, 1917, p. 214. Volobuev and other Soviet historians have portrayed Konovalov's policy as an effort to consolidate the bourgeoisie for the task of struggling politically and economically with the workers. See, e.g., Volobuev, *Proletariat*, pp. 68ff.

[49] *Vestnik Vremennago Pravitel'stva*, Mar. 7, 1917.

[50] *Ekon. polozhenie*, pt. 1, p. 511.

accused him of being a "bourgeois tool."[51] By the end of March, each side waited for more forceful policies; but both prepared to muster their opposition if new measures encroached on their interests.

In educational affairs, meanwhile, which were also under Kadet control in the beginning of March, a similarly cautious attitude toward reform was emerging, and also provoking the antagonism of the left. Alexander Manuilov, the new minister, was thought at first to be a popular appointment. As the rector of Moscow University, he had led the fight against the government's restrictive measures during the Stolypin period, and had lost his job as a consequence. From 1911 onward, he had also continued the struggle as an editor of the liberal *Russkiia Vedomosti*. It was assumed after the revolution that he would move quickly to revamp the entire educational network: restructuring primary and secondary systems to allow free access and upward movement for workers and peasants; ending the traditional system of centralized curriculum control; improving finances and construction programs; and allowing greater public involvement in local school affairs. Above all, the new minister was expected both to purge tsarist supervisory personnel (many of whom were odious figures to teachers and students alike), and to displace those on university faculties who had taken chairs made vacant by political persecutions.[52]

But the turmoil of revolution made Manuilov rather cautious. Scores of primary and secondary schools had closed with the end of the old regime; and universities had almost entirely ceased formal instruction. As soon as he took office he urged that all institutions be reopened.[53] But since this would be hampered by simultaneously removing the very people who were in charge of the schools, or by drastically reshaping their structure, the Kadet minister preferred at first to make only superficial changes.

On March 4, consequently, he proposed only that the government eliminate the *numerus-clausus* for Jews, and allow the return of those expelled for political reasons.[54] On March 11, he dismissed university professors who occupied the chairs of Kasso's victims.[55] But in almost all other matters, he simply established investigatory commissions, and postponed basic reforms. And like his Kadet colleagues, Manuilov also left most tsarist administrators at their posts. Thus his policies also seemed to be serving tradition, rather than the revolution, at odds with the aims of those who felt the February events would

---

[51] *Ibid.*, pp. 511-13.

[52] P. N. Ignatiev, ed., *Russian Schools and Universities in the World War*, New Haven, 1929, pp. 125ff.

[53] *Rech'*, Mar. 5, 1917.

[54] *Zhurnaly Zasedanii Vremennago Pravitel'stva*, No. 4, Mar. 4, 1917.

[55] *Ibid.*, No. 15, Mar. 11, 1917.

totally reform the educational network. Here, too, consequently, left-wing opposition began rapidly to emerge.[56]

The only liberal minister whose initial policies and appointments were greeted with unreserved enthusiasm by the left, in fact, was Nicholas Nekrasov, the minister of transport and the best-known left Kadet. In part this reflected a difference in affect and style. Unlike many of his Petrograd and Moscow Kadet colleagues, the Tomsk party radical was comfortable in factory shops and committees, and spent much of his time in early March meeting with workers, rather than with industrialists or administrators. Also in contrast to his colleagues' rather passive approach, Nekrasov began working soon after his appointment on a comprehensive plan to turn virtually all rights of supervision and control over to the railroad workers themselves. He began on March 5 by forming a special committee of workers and supervisors to deal with labor disputes; shortly afterward, he instructed local workers' groups on the railroads to use all possible initiative to speed the shipment of goods.[57] In his view, "democratizing the entire railroad structure" was the "primary means for renewing Russian transport," an attitude which obviously appealed to the workers and the left, but was not greeted with any noticeable enthusiasm by either his ministerial colleagues or the Petrograd Kadet party leadership.[58]

"UNIFYING" THE PARTY: THE SEVENTH CONGRESS

The contrast between Nekrasov's orientation and that of the other Kadet ministers reflected more general problems facing the Kadet party by the middle of March. With Russia's new commitments to the principles of representative democracy, and with the proliferation of democratic organizations, Kadets found themselves under increasing pressure to determine whether their traditional formal detachment from partisan class interests was still an effective basis on which to secure political power. In view of the promised Constituent Assembly elections, the formation of workers' soviets, local land committees, and other popular worker and peasant groups were tempting organizations through which to forge new alliances with the left, reinforcing strong past tendencies in this direction. By the middle of the month,

56 See the measures and discussions in *Russkiia Vedomosti*, Mar. 9 and 16, 1917; *Vestnik Vremennago Pravitel'stva*, Apr. 1 and 15, 1917; Ignatiev, p. 232; and M. M. Novikov, *Ot Moskvy do N'iu-Iorka*, New York, 1952, pp. 268ff. Manuilov was very severely attacked for his approach in *Izvestiia*, Apr. 1, 1917; see also, A. S. Izgoev, *Sotsialisty vo vtoroi russkoi revoliutsii*, Petrograd, 1917, pp. 38-39.

57 *Zhurnaly*, No. 5, Mar. 5, 1917; *Vestnik Vremennago Pravitel'stva*, Mar. 7, 1917; Nabokov, pp. 49-50.

58 *Rech'*, Mar. 29, 1917.

the tactic of a left alliance was already being pressed as a possible formal party course by Nekrasov, Frenkel, and particularly D. I. Shakhovskoi, who began laying plans in Moscow for "unifying all democratic elements," including the Socialist Revolutionaries and the Menshevik Social Democrats, in conjunction with the publication of the daily newspaper *Vlast' Naroda*.[59] At the same time, bourgeois groups like Riabushinskii's Trade-Industrialists were also pressing for closer ties with Kadets, hoping to build a new, strong liberal bloc. In contrast to Shakhovskoi, the prominent Moscow party figure S. A. Smirnov and others were taking an active role in organizing the new Trade-Industrial Union;[60] and on March 9, *Utro Rossii* announced plans to organize a new "Republican Democratic" party in Petrograd to unite "leading social and statesmanlike figures," which was alluring to more moderate and conservative Kadets as a basis for possible electoral alliances with the right.[61] Meanwhile, there were also questions of where the party as a whole should now stand on the nationalities issue, on agrarian reform, and even on the appropriate form of Russia's permanent state administration, all questions on which the events of February had outdated the party's official program.

A number of Kadets, particularly Shakhovskoi in Moscow, Nekrasov in Petrograd, and several provincial representatives, welcomed the need to resolve these issues as an opportunity to end long-standing party conflicts. They were confident the revolution would pull the Kadets as a whole in the direction of Russia's mass movements. But for Miliukov and his close associates in Petrograd, these issues again raised the question of a party split, just as they had in the past. And if unity for the Petrograd leadership seemed critical before 1917, as a means of compensating for a fairly narrow constituency, Miliukov regarded it as even more important now, when Russia was in danger of polarizing, perhaps into civil war, and when national, statesmanlike leadership was necessary to carry the country through the struggle against the Germans.

Exercising its prerogative as the Kadets' official leadership organ, the Central Committee in Petrograd began discussing these issues soon after the Provisional Government took power. At first, the fifteen to twenty Committee members available for the meetings generally reflected the party's right flank.[62] Energies were spent trying to con-

---

[59] Central Committee protocols, Mar. 17, 1917, in *VPNS*, No. 3, May 25, 1917, pp. 8-9.

[60] On March 17 Smirnov was elected president of the Regional Congress of Military Industrial Committees for the Moscow district. See *Russkiia Vedomosti*, Mar. 19, 1917.

[61] *Utro Rossii*, Mar. 9, 1917.

[62] The core of the group consisted of V. A. Maklakov, A. V. Tyrkova, I. S. Izgoev,

solidate the authority of the new regime: broadsides and press releases were prepared which criticized the Soviet's interference in questions of foreign policy and the army; and directives were sent to local party committees calling for a renewal of activities as a means of strengthening government power. Throughout, the Kadets' official *nadklassnost'* and "nonpartisan" political orientation were repeatedly stressed.

From March 10 to 13, however, a plenary session of the Central Committee was held in Petrograd, attended by some forty-three Moscow and provincial party figures as well as the Petrograd group. And here the differences in Kadet outlooks became apparent, indicating the revolution had not ended long-standing divisions among Kadets despite strong unifying elements in the response of the party as a whole to the transfer of power.

According to the somewhat fragmentary reports of the meetings, the dominant tone remained that of the Petrograd leadership. Reflecting Miliukov's special concern for party unity, as well as for solidarity and nonpartisanship in the country at large, the Committee decided that a final resolution of the agrarian question should await the end of the war, thus supporting (and implicitly directing) Minister Shingarev, and also implicitly protecting the existing interests of landowners. The possibility otherwise, according to the Petrograd leadership, was at best for serious tensions, and perhaps even forceful resistance to the new government from whatever group thought its rights were infringed. The Committee also censured the Petrograd Soviet for interfering in several instances with the publication of non-socialist newspapers; and it established a number of commissions to oversee the development of party propaganda activities.

But questions were also raised at the meetings about the desirability of forming electoral or other tactical party blocs with republican and soviet groups, and abandoning the posture of *nadklassnost'*. Also, several delegates urged that Kadets renew their past efforts to win peasant support by adopting a more radical agrarian platform; and a special subcommittee of provincial delegates brought in a resolution calling the government's attention to the fact that in Vitebsk, Kostroma, Tambov, and other provinces, persons "known for their reactionary activities" were still exercising power as a result of the government's decision of March 5 to transfer local authority to provincial zemstvo boards. These and other issues were left open at the plenary conference, but it was decided as the top order of party business to

A. A. Kornilov, V. A. Stepanov, M. N. Rostovtsev, V. I. Vernadskii, and M. M. Vinaver, though daily liaison was kept with party members in the government, and Miliukov, Shingarev, Nabokov, Kokoshkin, Nekrasov, and Gronskii found time to participate in a number of sessions.

convene a national congress on March 25. The ostensible task of the congress was to establish a new official viewpoint on the question of Russia's future government, to be organized by the Constituent Assembly. More important was the need to define future tactics.[63]

Two weeks later, more than 300 delegates gathered for the congress, the seventh since Kadets had organized in 1905. They came from more than fifty-two provinces and regions of European and Asiatic Russia, though Petrograd and Moscow party members predominated, and at the Mikhailovskii Theater, where the sessions were held, Miliukov and his closest colleagues sat on the stage. As the setting suggested, the Kadet leader hoped to use the congress to generate new party unity, reaffirming both the authority and popularity of the Provisional Government among Russia's liberal elements, and constructing as well a bulwark against any spreading soviet influence.

Unity was best assured by dealing first with issues of little controversy, and by hearing speeches from prominent right and left Kadets who were anxious to bury old disagreements. An introductory address by Paul Dolgorukov stressed the importance of "continuing the war until the enemy is completely driven from our borders," and called for the development of a "strong and durable" party organization. The venerable party leftist, Michael Mandelshtam, then told his colleagues that past divisions would have to be forgotten so that traditional liberal values could "endure"; and a prominent conservative, Prince Eugene Trubetskoi, announced that he was rejoining the party after ten years of protesting its "radical politics."[64] Thereafter, Fedor Kokoshkin presented a long report on whether or not the Kadets should abandon their support for constitutional monarchy, one issue the revolution itself had already determined; and Alexander Kornilov and Fedor Rodichev spoke on foreign policy. Neither report was expected to provoke debate.[65]

On the monarchy issue, where the only problem seemed to be one of injured sensibilities, Kokoshkin spoke so as not to recall Miliukov's speech of March 3, or otherwise alienate remaining monarchists. Kadets, he argued, had always distinguished support for constitutional monarchy from support for the monarchy itself; the Kadet program on this question was thus the result of political expediency rather than principle, since constitutional monarchy had simply been the form most likely to gain general acceptance between 1905 and 1917. In terms of their general beliefs, even monarchist Kadets had a right to "consider themselves socialists," not to mention democrats. Their basic

[63] *VPNS*, No. 1, May 11, 1917, pp. 15-21.   [64] *Rech'*, Mar. 30, 1917.
[65] *Rech'*, Mar. 26, 1917.

political commitment had always been to "full sovereignty for the will of the people," "civil freedom and equality," and the "realization of the principle of social justice." Consequently, Kadets might endorse without qualm the Central Committee's proposal to support a republic, presided over by a ministry responsible to a democratic parliament.[66]

On the question of the war, Kornilov and Rodichev both presented ringing endorsements of the policies being followed by Miliukov, and exhorted their colleagues from the provinces to carry a renewed enthusiasm and commitment for the struggle back to their home committees. Rodichev in particular offered a fiery denunciation of the Petrograd Soviet's slogan "Peace without Annexations and Indemnities," strongly defending Miliukov's policies toward Constantinople and the Straits:

> Where is annexation proposed? Constantinople? From whom do we intend to annex it? From the Turks? Citizens, you know that Constantinople is certainly not a completely Turkish city. You know that there are only 140,000 Turks living there if my memory does not fail me, with the remainder made up of Christians, Greeks, and Jews. From whom are we annexing the city? Constantinople is under the authority of a band of robbers! And in any event, it is not Constantinople that we need, but the Straits. They tell us: Organize free passage in the Straits. What does that mean? It means freedom for the German navy to enter the Black Sea unhindered, that is what it means! . . . Citizens, they say that these are the strivings of Russian imperialism and seizure. No! This is not seizure. It is the preservation of Russian independence.[67]

As Miliukov and the Petrograd party leadership undoubtedly expected, this and Kokoshkin's speech evoked great enthusiasm from the congress. But probably to their surprise, both reports also evoked criticism, which Dolgorukov, Vinaver, and Kokoshkin, acting as Congress chairmen, tried to stifle. In response to Kokoshkin, M. A. Kukharenko from Kostroma insisted the question was not really one of monarchy or republic, but of a federated vs. a nonfederated system. "Up until now," he argued, "the Ukrainians and other peoples have not been attracted to the Party of People's Freedom because . . . only a democratic *federated* republic can satisfy their interests." His suggestion that the congress add "just this one little word 'federated' " to its resolution drew laughter, but also a ruling from the chair that dis-

66 *Ibid.* Kokoshkin's speech was republished as a party pamphlet under the title *Respublika* (Petrograd, 1917).
67 *Rech'*, Mar. 28, 1917.

cussion should end. Although another provincial delegate, M. M. Mogilianskii, protested strongly, the troublesome nationalities issue was deferred to a subsequent congress.[68]

Opposition to Rodichev was dealt with even more harshly. When N. A. Gredeskul, a long time Central Committee member and First Duma delegate from Kharkov, voiced strong opposition to annexing Constantinople, and proposed that his colleagues exclude from their resolution the words "not infringing on the freedom of other peoples," N. K. Volkov from Chita wondered in rebuttal whether Gredeskul was really a Kadet. And when the Muslim delegate S. N. Maksudov protested that Miliukov's policies were destroying the Kadets' appeal among millions of Russian Turks, Kokoshkin answered that it was not Russia which had attacked Turkey but the other way around; and as Constantinople and the Straits remained in Turkish hands, "the question could not help but agitate Russia, since Turkish hands were really German ones."[69] According to Miliukov's *Rech'*, this response was also greeted with "stormy applause"; and whether accurately reflecting delegate sentiment or simply a device to present a unified front to a broader public, the congress passed Central Committee resolutions on both these issues with virtual unanimity.[70]

Conflict over the questions of convening the Constituent Assembly and instituting reforms in agriculture were also covered over by "unanimous" votes in favor of official resolutions. The Central Committee report on the Constituent Assembly stressed the need for its rapid convocation, but it left open the question of exactly when that should be. To some delegates, confident that a free peasantry would eventually support Kadet candidates, electoral fairness was more important than time. The Volynskaia province representative, for example, argued that fairness dictated delay. "Even if the elections are held in July or even September, neither the army nor the peasantry will be ready. . . . The Assembly ought to be convened only after the war, when each soldier has returned home. . . ."[71] But others, such as conservative Prince Trubetskoi and D. N. Grigorovich-Barskii from Kiev, argued that postponing elections would only amplify the difficulties of dual authority, "and in some areas, the existence of many authorities (*desiativlastie*)." Though the rights of the troops were important, they should not force the Assembly's postponement.[72] Implicit here was the notion that the Kadets' own electoral possibilities would not improve by extending the franchise immediately to soldiers and peasants, a concern which was now prompting conservative party mem-

[68] *Ibid.*, Mar. 26, 1917.
[70] *Ibid.*
[72] *Ibid.*

[69] *Ibid.*, Mar. 27, 1917.
[71] *Ibid.*

bers to urge that the Assembly be convened at once, in contrast to the attitude they would adopt later in the spring. But rather than confront this issue more fully, and possibly intensify divisions, Miliukov and the Central Committee leadership urged only that the "Assembly be convened in the shortest possible time, but with the protection of all guarantees necessary to assure that the voting correctly expresses the will of the people," in effect, leaving the issue up to the government's Kadet-dominated Constituent Assembly Commission. A resolution to this effect was unanimously endorsed.[73]

The agrarian issue also raised questions about the Kadets' constituency. Though considering it one of the major problems of the revolution, the Central Committee had not been able to draft any formal proposals in its few weeks of meetings, and proposed instead that an eighth Kadet congress be called in six or eight weeks to discuss the question fully. This infuriated provincial delegates like Tatishchev from Tula, Bukeikhanov from Semipalatinsk, and Kudriatsev from Kazan, who insisted that this "cardinal question" simply had to be solved as soon as possible "for political as well as social reasons," and in such a way as to take into account "the deeply socialist point of view which has emerged in the countryside." According to Desiatov (Kharkov) and Minaev (Kursk), the Kadets were still "extremely popular" in the countryside; but the party's "deep roots" among the peasantry could only be preserved if its leaders endorsed radical reforms. To Elachich and Radetskii from the Volga region, and to the Kostroma delegate Cheshikhin, this meant that Kadets should support the nationalization of agriculture; to Miakov from Tambov, it implied that the party at the very least should insist on an immediate end of sales in land, which many peasants feared as a means of preventing land transfers to them.[74] But for Miliukov and the Central Committee leadership, these arguments—so reminiscent of those heard at the third Kadet congress in 1906—not only emphasized the dangers of civil war in the countryside, but also the possibility of the Kadets own further fragmentation. Precisely *because* these issues were so crucial, they deserved much further study; and their resolution, like that of the difficult nationalities question, had to be postponed.

Most delegates eventually fell in line on the issue of postponement, but not before the question of party tactics raised by the agrarian debate had itself been fully examined. And here, finally, it was impossible for Miliukov or anyone else to prevent or camouflage disagreements. The crucial practical issue was whether Kadets should end

[73] *Ibid.*   [74] *Ibid.*

their formal commitment to *nadpartiinost'* and *nadklassnost'*—their posture of standing above partisan class interests—in many ways the most important question of the Congress. In a few short weeks, the revolution had transformed the party from one of splintered autocratic opposition to that of the most powerful and influential of all nonsocialist groups. Right-wing parties like the Nationalists and Octobrists had fallen away, and the Kadets were the only important nonsocialist party whose leaders held government posts. The party was also increasingly regarded by left and right alike as the political core of bourgeois Russia; and in a context where electoral partisanship would soon become the political norm, where particularistic interests were finding new expressions every day, and where *all* social groups would soon struggle bitterly in defense of their personal welfare, Kadets had to decide whether to restructure their own organizational base, and officially formulate a new political outlook.

The Central Committee keynote on this issue was sounded by Maxim Vinaver, who reflected the prevailing attitude of the party's group in Petrograd. In effect, he argued, Kadet *nadklassnost'* was a necessary party counterpart to the national orientation of the Provisional Government as a whole. On one hand, sectarian, representative politics would destroy the authority of liberal ministers; on the other, a non-class and nonpartisan orientation was crucial to the nation as a whole, avoiding "ruinous party struggles and social divisions." The Kadets, he argued, had to take the lead in the quest for national unity, just as they had when the Provisional Government was being formed; and the resolution on tactics he presented not only stressed these themes, but officially renewed the party's own "above class" designation.[75]

One can well understand why Miliukov, Vinaver, and others, continued to fear partisanship in Russia's revolutionary context, and wanted to preserve the attitudes Kadets in general had shown in the beginning of March. Kadet *nadklassnost'* stemmed in 1917, as it had throughout the party's history, from a fear of Russia's "uncultured" masses. It represented the Russian intelligentsia's historic paternalism, which assumed for Kadets the competence to make political and social decisions best serving the needs of the country as a whole. It also allowed Kadets to ignore—at least intellectually—any opposition on the part of workers and peasants to continuing at war, since these groups "lacked familiarity" with Russia's national interests; and just as before the revolution, it remained a convenient, although illusory, screen for the more subtle problem of the party's own narrow electoral base

[75] *Ibid.*, Mar. 29, 1917.

(as well as, perhaps, its actual posture of representing Russia's professional middle classes), since as national, nonpartisan liberals, rather than defenders of sectarian interests, party leaders could argue they "deserved" power even if they lacked massive popular support.

Yet if such an approach was perhaps tactically viable before 1917, when Kadets were largely concerned with demonstrating their respectability to an authoritarian monarchy, it now increasingly contradicted the premises of participatory democracy underlying Russia's new order. Moreover, in practical terms, it also implicitly placed the party in opposition to major new social reforms, at least for the time being, since changes in this area would invariably serve special interests. Thus whether Kadets admitted it or not, by now advancing *nadklassnost'* or *nadpartiinost'* in defense of "stable" social and political relations, they were attempting to hold back new revolutionary energies, rather than mount a positive social program of their own, and indirectly defending the interests of privileged Russia, just as in many ways they had done after their initial failure as a "non-class" party in the period of the first two State Dumas.

It was the political difficulties of this posture in Russia's revolutionary context which was pressed so strongly to the delegates by Dmitri Shakhovskoi, who presented a "supplementary" report on tactics reflecting the minority left on the Central Committee. According to Shakhovskoi, Kadet tactics had to be reformulated on the basis of the party's new acceptance of a republic, rather than a constitutional monarchy. "Accepting a republic, we recognize the Russian people as the most important factor in state life. . . . Thus it is necessary for us immediately to clarify our relations with the popular masses, and also to our friends on the left. . . . Having raised the republican banner, we have removed one of the barriers to a closer association . . . and while it is impossible to dream of one huge democratic or even socialist party . . . the field has been opened for extremely broad activities, and also for electoral blocs, with parties of the left. . . ."[76]

Shakhovskoi's views received strong endorsements from Mandelshtam and Z. G. Frenkel, both Central Committee members, and also from Prince Viazemskii from Tambov, who announced that Kadets in his area had already formed an alliance with Mensheviks and Trudoviks, much as Shakhovskoi himself had been trying to do in Moscow. But their strongest support came from Nicholas Nekrasov, the minister of transport, who by now was regarded by many as the party's leading democratic advocate. In a fiery speech, Nekrasov argued not for consolidating with Russia's bourgeoisie, as many in Moscow were in

[76] *Ibid.*

favor of doing, but for officially aligning Kadets with workers and peasants. The essence of his argument had been heard many times in the past: Russia's masses had to be brought into the political mainstream; their demands and aspirations had to be considered "legitimate"; and the Kadet party as a whole had to defend mass interests by adopting and implementing a program of popular social reforms. It was the workers and soldiers of Petrograd who had made the revolution, Nekrasov maintained, not the liberals; Kadets could not survive without their support; and this support required that social reforms not be shunted to the background or screened behind so-called national interests. "The basic question" of the moment was "whether the idea of revolution, of democratic creativity, of implementing the popular will, could be realized rapidly in all of its forms." If Kadets persisted in their paternalism, continuing to support "government from above" on the basis of *nadklassnye* tactics and principles, Russia was heading for either a left- or right-wing dictatorship.[77]

But most delegates—from the provinces and Moscow, as well as from Petrogard—rejected Nekrasov's views and were far more cautious. Critical to them, as with the Central Committee majority under Miliukov, was order, unity, and support for the war, not partisanship, or class-oriented sectarianism. If dictatorship emerged, it would come through partisan tactics or policies, which were likely to provoke resistance, and hence civil war. As Vinaver expressed it in concluding the debate, the Kadets would be foolhardy to move in any tactical direction likely to increase the possibility of polarization. Counterrevolution and civil war were very real dangers:

> Any decisive forays beyond the bounds of the agreement establishing the Provisional Government, or decisions on basic state questions or social reforms will very much increase the danger not only for the government, but for the whole revolution. There is no easier or more likely method of creating in the country a strong counterrevolutionary mood than the adoption . . . of a [partisan] line. . . ."[78]

The Kadets' role in these circumstances, both for national reasons and in the cause of their own political survival, was to remain a *nadklassnaia* party of the center, uniting right and left and assuring national unity.

In the end, two resolutions on tactics were adopted as a means of containing the "left opposition" and lessening the possibility of a split within the party. One stressed the Kadets' non-class and non-estate orientation, and was presented by Vinaver as reflecting most forcefully

[77] *Ibid.*   [78] *Ibid.*

the views of the Petrograd leadership. While no specific votes were tallied—again most likely as a means of masking internal party differences—it seems apparent from reports in the press that most delegates supported this view. The other resolution, presented by Shakhovskoi, called for closer cooperation with the left, and reflected the views of a number of provincial and Moscow delegates (though also Z. G. Frenkel and others from Petrograd). Kadets in sum would "defend general democratic principles," but the Central Committee would avoid issuing more specific directives, and urge only that Kadets "agitate among those sectors of the population which are not yet capable of readily grasping party slogans."[79]

On this somewhat paternalistic note, "with joyful consciousness of unity and courageous spirit," according to Vinaver, the delegates adjourned.[80]

[79] *Ibid.*   [80] *Ibid.*

CHAPTER FOUR

Dual Authority and Partisanship:
The April Crisis and Its Aftermath

In EVALUATING the seventh congress, the right-wing Petrograd daily *Novoe Vremia* congratulated the Kadets for maintaining their "high nonpartisan ideals."[1] Miliukov and his supporters accepted the accolade with appreciation. Strong criticism from Nekrasov, Shakhovskoi, and others had not shaken the party's overall orientation; in retrospect, the position of the Kadet left was far less damaging to party unity than at other times in the past. Strong differences of opinion obviously still existed, but the revolution had brought the party closer together; and most delegates at the seventh congress, from the provinces and Moscow as well as Petrograd, had united behind Vinaver, Miliukov, and the Central Committee leadership. Nonpartisanship was still accepted as the best possible means of protecting the state and preserving Russian unity, "the only patriotic ground" for Russia's "new democratic consciousness."[2] It also continued to legitimize Kadet authority in the Provisional Government.

The dominant Kadet outlook, however, assumed a vision of revolutionary Russia vastly different from that of millions of workers, peasants, and soldiers. Miliukov, Kokoshkin, Vinaver, and most of their colleagues still looked at their country through Spenserian lenses, as an evolving political organism moving toward a liberal democratic order in the style of England or France, and forced to defend its national interests in a competitive world. In their view, a massive political upheaval had occurred, and long-sought civil liberties were now being used by some radicals in a manner potentially damaging to Russia's "national welfare." Civil war was also a very real threat, and revolutionary contexts always posed dangers for liberals like themselves. But most still reasoned that if the country pulled together, if front lines held against the "German menace," if critical problems of food supply and transport were resolved, and especially if the authority of the new regime was strengthened, it was possible the revolution might even accelerate Russia's natural liberal evolution.

Notions of Russia's "liberal evolution" had very little meaning, how-

[1] *Novoe Vremia*, Mar. 28, 1917.　　[2] *Rech'*, Mar. 29, 1917.

ever, to millions of workers and peasants—the "uncultured masses" in the view of some right-wing Kadets. Their thoughts were turned not to politics or political systems, but to ending long-standing social grievances. Workers wanted new labor and living conditions; peasants and peasant-soldiers wanted land; troops in the field wanted an end to their pain and suffering. Civil liberties and a rule of law were far less important than social change; and the vital question was not whether "national" interests were protected or Russia secured the trappings of liberal democracy, but what the revolution would mean in the way of new social and economic conditions.

Kadet intellectuals and historians like Miliukov recognized Russia's deep social cleavages, and even their political implications. Yet as late as the beginning of April 1917, there was still very little clear evidence of any profound difference in the way they and others were interpreting the revolution, other than what came from the "intellectual left," as some Kadets called it, in the Petrograd Soviet. Here and there one heard alarming rumors of peasant attacks on the gentry; workers were obviously militant and showed frightening power; and conditions in the army were at best unstable. But if anything, the situation seemed much improved in comparison with the last weeks of the old regime. In scores of provincial towns and cities, Kadet groups were still working closely with other parties in the various Committees of Public Organizations; in Moscow, new contacts had been made with workers through groups like the War Industries Committee and the Trade-Industrial Union, actions which Shakhovskoi's resolution had sanctioned at the seventh congress. Even in Petrograd the dominant Kadet mood was still one of great relief: a lingering satisfaction that the revolution, while hardly without grave danger, had at least been accomplished without great bloodshed or civil war. This mood would begin to change very shortly, as we shall see; but as late as April 11, a full week after Lenin's return from exile, an editorial in *Rech'* noted with satisfaction that the country was "returning to its normal course of life."[3]

THE GROWING PROBLEM OF DUAL AUTHORITY

At the very moment "nonpartisan" Kadets were accepting congratulations from *Novoe Vremia*, their countrymen everywhere were organizing in pursuit of special interests. "Organize! Organize!" the Soviet organ *Izvestiia* urged: "Construct political and economic unions. Enter into parties, enroll in political organizations."[4] What Miliukov,

[3] *Rech'*, Apr. 11, 1917.   [4] *Izvestiia*, Mar. 9, 1917.

Vinaver, and their "centrist" Kadet supporters feared as leading to greater political instability, Soviet groups and even the Kadets' own left regarded as rightful privileges to be exercised at once as gains of the revolution.

At the end of March and in the beginning of April, this process led to a rapid intensification of conflict between the government and the Petrograd Soviet. On March 29, the First All-Russian Conference of Soviets opened in the capital, drawing delegates from scores of provincial organizations. The concern here, in contrast to that of Miliukov and his fellow Kadet ministers, was for less ministerial independence, rather than more, and for the immediate implementation of socialist reforms.

The person responsible for formulating the Conference view on Russia's general political situation was Iurii Steklov, editor of *Izvestiia*, radical internationalist, and future Bolshevik. Steklov's approach was to emphasize the degree to which the new regime depended on the authority of the Petrograd Soviet to keep order and prevent counter-revolution, and to contrast the "legalistic" (and therefore artificial) legitimacy of the provisional regime with the "healthy, broad masses of hundreds of thousands of people" who gave power to the Soviet:

> We are responsible to the Russian people to see that their labors have not been in vain, and that the maximum political gains are taken. And this we can achieve only if the center of revolutionary democratic forces preserves its complete independence, preserves its close, living ties with the masses, and continually acts upon the Provisional Government to force it to fight more determinedly with counterrevolution as well as to secure as much as possible the maximum gains of the revolution. . . . This is our direct responsibility; and our constant existence as an independent center is for the solidification of all revolutionary democratic forces.[5]

Following Steklov, the Conference adopted a strong resolution declaring the "necessity of gradually gaining control and influence over the Provisional Government to assure that it follows Soviet policies." It also tendered support for the government's foreign policy "only in so far as [*poskol'ku postol'ku*] it was based on a rejection of expansionist ambitions."[6]

As if to prove its commitment to maintaining dual power, moreover, the Conference also seemed to give license to any form of "advancing revolutionary goals." Speakers attacked the Lvov regime as if the liberals, rather than the autocracy, were responsible for Russia's

[5] *Ibid.*, Apr. 4, 1917.   [6] *Ibid.*, Apr. 6, 1917.

oppressive conditions. "Bourgeois" ministers were charged with following only "bourgeois" interests; the "national" objectives of the Kadets were denounced as a means of preserving old forms of class oppression. Liberals were also bitterly criticized for attempting to "drive a wedge between workers and soldiers," a reference to the implication in some nonsocialist newspapers that boycotts over wage and labor demands were keeping supplies from the front. In many cases where workers were idle, Conference spokesmen maintained with some justification that the situation was due to lockouts caused by lack of fuel or raw materials.[7]

Kadet ministers were also attacked individually. Manuilov's preference for established structures and curricula, for example, was seen as contrary to the "revolutionary" view of education as a means of social development and change. On April 1 *Izvestiia* charged the Kadet minister of education with retaining administrators who were "organically alien to the new demands. . . ." It indicated the Soviet would take steps to "establish a school-life atmosphere corresponding to the nature of the new order."[8] Shortly afterward, the Soviet journal called for a thorough overhaul of Russia's whole educational structure, so that its graduates "would not be frightened by the red phantom of social revolution which society will create, and in which there will be no place for parasitic gentlemen of leisure."[9]

Konovalov and Shingarev were also castigated, as much for what they were not doing as for what they were. The Soviet wanted a sharp limitation on profits in trade and industry, and the creation of a strong state regulatory apparatus. Vladimir Groman's plans, which were presented and endorsed at the March Conference of Soviets, included the expansion of regulation into virtually all areas of Russian economic life. They also called for the creation of a new centralized regulatory apparatus, and movement toward the development of a planned economy.[10] But Konovalov's program rested primarily on patterns established before the revolution, involving groups like the War Industries Committees. According to a comprehensive statement to the press on March 29, regulation was to be extended in industry, but almost entirely in those sectors dealing with defense; freedom and order were to be Russia's guidelines, rather than comprehensive control and change; and while "certain state interference in private Trade-

---

[7] *Ibid.*, Apr. 1, 5, 7, and 11, 1917. See also *Edinstvo*, Mar. 31, 1917; *Novoe Vremia*, Apr. 7 and 9, 1917; and *Rech'*, Apr. 1, 5, and 7, 1917. *Petrogradskaia Gazeta*, *Petrogradskii Listok*, and *Russkaia Volia* were also in the forefront of the campaign against the workers, even more so than *Novoe Vremia* and *Rech'*.

[8] *Izvestiia*, Apr. 1 and 18, 1917.   [9] *Ibid.*, Apr. 18, 1917.

[10] P. V. Volobuev, "Ekonomicheskaia programma burzhuazii i vremennogo pravitel'stva," *IZ*, No. 67, 1960, p. 55.

Industrial relations and interests" was "inevitable," its extent was to be "determined cooperatively by the government and industry committees."[11] In agrarian affairs, meanwhile, Minister Shingarev was accused of weakness on the specific question of lowering land rents, while *Izvestiia* insisted that *"Pomeshchik* ownership of the land" was the "flesh and blood of tsarism. . . . Not only the interests of the peasantry, but the interests also of the entire Russian democracy demand that the gentry's estates be confiscated and transferred to the democratic state. . . ."[12]

There was also the growing problem of military discipline. Revolutionary attitudes were beginning to take hold among even front-line troops in the first days of April, stimulated (though certainly not precipitated) by Order Number 1. Increasingly, army units were refusing to obey their officers. Unit committees were taking full command. Fraternization was also becoming common, while increasing numbers of soldiers expected a rapid conclusion of peace. In the view of Miliukov and his colleagues, attacks on "bourgeois ministers" and Soviet efforts to "control" the government only encouraged army units to regard socialist leaders, rather than the War Ministry, as the source of command. Front-line units were even beginning to pass resolutions in support of the Petrograd Soviet alone, rather than the government. That many of these were similarly worded added to the Kadets' anxiety, as did the taunt from Sukhanov to Miliukov early in April (which quickly went the rounds of Kadet circles) that the army was "not going over to you." ("But what are you saying?" was Miliukov's response. "How can you put the question that way? The army is not coming over to us! *The army must fight at the front.* That is the only way the question can be put, and the only thing we stand for. That is our entire policy in relation to the army.")[13]

To a certain extent the Soviet's growing radicalism and its rapidly developing hostility toward the provisional regime may have been stimulated by the Bolsheviks, and the publication on April 7 of Lenin's celebrated April Theses. These denounced the government unequivocally, demanding a policy of "no support," and the "exposure of the utter falsity of all its promises. . . ."[14] But Lenin did not so much pre-

11 *Ekonomicheskoe polozhenie Rossii nakanune velikoi oktiabr'skoi sotsialisticheskoi revoliutsii,* 3 pts., Moscow-Leningrad, 1957-67, pt. 1, p. 216.

12 *Izvestiia,* Mar. 26, 1917.

13 N. Sukhanov, *Zapiski o revoliutsii,* 7 vols., Berlin, 1922-23, III, 124. The italics are Sukhanov's. Resolutions in support of the Soviet rather than the government appear in *Izvestiia,* Apr. 9, 1917, *Rech',* Apr. 8, 1917, and esp. in G. N. Golikov and Iu. S. Tokarev, "Aprel'skii krizis," *IZ,* No. 57, 1956, pp. 43-44.

14 R. P. Browder and A. F. Kerensky, eds., *The Russian Provisional Government 1917,* 3 vols., Stanford, 1961, III, 1205-07.

cipitate a shift in rank-and-file sentiment as capitalize on a growing popular radicalism. Feelings against the social and economic inequities of tsarist society, which found only general expression in the February days, were now being articulated more and more clearly.

The most dramatic shift in popular outlook pertained to the war. With hindsight it is possible to argue that the acquisition of Constantinople and the Dardanelles Straits had not been popular goals even before the revolution.[15] But for liberals like Miliukov, who accepted the revolution primarily for the sake of military victory, developing agitation against Russia's war aims appeared as a crass attempt by the left to extend its power.

Several factors reinforced the Kadet leader's perspective. One was the pressure of Allied ambassadors, particularly Maurice Paleologue, whose arguments that Russia had a "moral" obligation to pursue the war to full victory found special resonance in Kadet commitments to the ethical content of law.[16] The integrity of the new political order seemed closely related to the government's fulfillment of treaty obligations, not to mention the treaties' specific advantages for Russia. Another was the apparent enthusiasm for the war shown by troops pledging loyalty to the new regime. In early March, delegates from scores of units came in an endless parade to the Tauride Palace, shouting themselves hoarse with patriotic slogans. On March 12 the entire Volynskii regiment appeared—the first major unit to go over to the revolution. With a full band playing the *Marseillaise,* the troops showed banners proclaiming "We are Ready!" "Do Not Forget Our Brothers at the Front!" and "War to Complete Victory!"[17] Other units paraded similar slogans.[18]

A third factor was the way in which soldiers seemed to be concerned with military production. When the March 10 agreement was reached for an eight-hour working day in Petrograd, front-line troops received

[15] In the fall of 1916, for instance, the tsarist regime considered publishing the secret treaties as a means of rekindling popular enthusiasm for the war. But when Trepov read the text of one convention to the Duma on November 16 (rightly assuming its terms would soon thereafter be general knowledge), there was little reaction, and certainly not the enthusiasm the government expected. Newspapers and journals, moreover, were full of internationalist sentiment in March, and at the time of the February disorders, some troops even raised banners denouncing the war, though they were quickly taken down.

[16] F. A. Golder to H. H. Fisher, Nov. 25, 1925, quoting Miliukov, in the Hoover Institution.

[17] *Izvestiia,* Mar. 14, 1917; *Rech',* Mar. 14, 1917.

[18] *Izvestiia,* Mar. 17, 1917. See also Sukhanov, *Zapiski,* II, 214-16; I. G. Tsereteli, *Vospominaniia o fevral'skoi revoliutsii,* 2 vols., Paris, 1963, I, 30-32; and S. I. Shidlovskii, *Vospominaniia,* 2 vols., Berlin, 1923, II, 70-71. The apparent attitudes of the soldiers were such that *Izvestiia* wondered rhetorically in an editorial on March 17 whether they actually understood what "War to Complete Victory" meant.

the impression through *Novoe Vremia* and other conservative newspapers that Petrograders were cutting back on the production of desperately needed war supplies. In effect, what had been formalized was the payment of overtime, rather than a reduction in the hours of work. But front-line units began sending delegations into the city to investigate whether workers were really at their benches.[19]

None of this meant that workers or soldiers were the slightest bit interested in Russia's obtaining Constantinople or the Dardanelles. In fact, anti-war sentiment among the troops was growing rapidly.[20] But for Miliukov, who was quite convinced the *narod* had no understanding of foreign policy matters anyway, it seemed endorsement for his programs. And as the Petrograd Soviet began to define its own foreign policy goals, Miliukov was sure its leaders were usurping the prerogatives of popular sovereignty which were "properly" reflected in the government.

As we have seen, the Soviet issued a dramatic Declaration to all Peoples of the World on March 14; several days later, *Izvestiia* also published an editorial which suggested "War for Freedom" as a substitute slogan for "War to Victory." But it was not until the "Siberian Zimmerwaldist" Iraklii Tsereteli returned to Petrograd on March 20 that the Soviet actually began a detailed reexamination of the foreign policy issue. Debate commenced in the Soviet Executive Committee on March 21, with Nicholas Sukhanov, the radical Social Democratic journalist, proposing a strong peace policy and the "mobilization" of workers and soldiers against Miliukov's "tsarist war program." In an effort to create an "open démarche with the Allies," Sukhanov also emphasized the formula which Miliukov had earlier called German in origin, "Peace without Annexations or Indemnities."[21]

Opposing Sukhanov were defensists like the Mensheviks Bogdanov and Gvozdev, who believed in minimizing internal agitation on the foreign policy question for fear it might weaken the army, and who advocated the strongest possible measures to assure that the revolution was adequately defended at the front. But between these two positions,

[19] *Izvestiia*, Mar. 30 and Apr. 7, 1917; *Novoe Vremia*, Mar. 18 and 31, 1917; *Rech'*, Mar. 12, 1917.

[20] See, e.g., O. N. Chaadaeva, ed., *Soldatskie pis'ma 1917 goda*, Moscow-Leningrad, pp. 18-53; N. E. Kakurin, ed., *Razlozhenie armii v 1917 godu*, Moscow-Leningrad, 1925, pp. 25ff; L. S. Gaponenko, ed., *Revoliutsionnoe dvizhenie v russkoi armii*, Moscow, 1968, pp. 24ff; M. Ferro, *La Révolution de 1917*, Paris, 1967, pp. 196-203. Ferro notes, however (p. 202), that the soldiers' desire for peace was expressed less forcefully than that of the workers or peasants. See also G. Wettig, "Die Rolle der russischen Armee in revolutionären Machtkampf 1917," *Forschungen zur osteuropäischen Geschichte*, vol. 12, 1967, pp. 260-79; and Gen. N. N. Golovin, *Rossiiskaia kontr-revoliutsiia v 1917-1918 gg.*, 5 vols., Tallin, 1937, bk. 1, pp. 74-91.

[21] Sukhanov, II, 334ff.

Tsereteli offered a compromise: a policy of "revolutionary defensism," which combined both an appeal for "peace without annexations and indemnities" with an insistence that the army's defensive capacities be fully supported. To the internationalists, this was a prostitution of Zimmerwald. But a majority in the Soviet saw "revolutionary defensism" as a perfect combination of idealism and practicality. A resolution supporting the notion was consequently adopted on March 22. Shortly afterward, the Soviet proposed that the Provisional Government also adopt it as an official statement of policy.[22]

Miliukov felt this was absurd. Not only was revolutionary defensism a utopian outlook, harmful to Russia's national interests; its very articulation by the Soviet could drastically affect the morale of Russian troops, making it appear that state power was divided. Miliukov was also convinced that Tsereteli and his colleagues represented little besides the views of some isolated left-wing intellectuals;[23] and he feared as well that Britain and France might themselves renege on the secret agreements if Russia failed to press them. With Britain's claims to hegemony in Persia and Egypt, and France's interests in Rumania, Russia would have a difficult time at a peace conference under any circumstances, secret treaties or not. The Soviet's very pretension to speak on this issue made matters worse in every direction.[24]

In a press interview on March 22, the Kadet foreign minister pulled rein on the left by again stressing Russia's "right" to Constantinople and the Dardanelles. He also belittled the Soviet's authority, again labeling "Peace without Annexations" a German formulation.[25] But this only further angered the left, setting the stage for full-scale discussions between the Soviet and the cabinet on the foreign policy question.

The discussions began on March 24, on the eve of the Kadets' seventh congress. To Miliukov's surprise, many in the government leaned toward compromise, perhaps hoping to isolate the Kadet foreign minister as a lightning rod for radical dissidence, and thus preserve their own credibility. Even Minister-President Lvov thought some agreement would have to be reached on this issue to preserve domestic harmony. And in the course of the argument, Andrei Shingarev accepted this position as well, largely because he felt a resolution

22 Tsereteli, I, 45-57. See also the excellent study by Rex A. Wade, *The Russian Search for Peace*, Stanford, 1969, chap. 2, and his "Irakli Tsereteli and Siberian Zimmerwaldism," *JMH*, xxxix, Dec. 1967, pp. 425-31.

23 Editorial by Miliukov in *Rech'*, Mar. 15, 1917.

24 See, e.g., his telegrams to the Russian ambassadors in Britain and France in "Perepiska Miliukova i Tereshchenko s poslami vremennago pravitel'stva," *Bor'ba Klassov*, No. 5, 1931, pp. 84-89.

25 *Rech'*, Mar. 22, 1917.

of the issue would increase the fighting spirit of the army. Miliukov himself, of course, vigorously objected. For him the question was not only foreign policy, but who held power, the government or the Soviet. Where was the "plenitude of authority" Russia's political leaders had agreed upon? And who, in any case, was better able to judge Russia's national interests in foreign affairs, the minister, or self-appointed representatives of an ad hoc peoples' council?

Nevertheless, the angry Kadet leader was overruled by the cabinet. Pressed by Nekrasov, Tereshchenko, Soviet leaders, and Prince Lvov himself, the ministers came out in favor of accommodation. On March 27, the government published a new "Declaration of War Aims," formally renouncing "domination over other nations," or "seizure of their national possessions."[26]

The document had some catches. It was specifically addressed only to the Russian people rather than to the Allies; it warned of a "powerful enemy" about to launch a determined assault; and it closed with the assertion that "the final solution to all problems" would be left to "the will of the people in close unison with our Allies," a neat twist which almost reduced its force to pious aspiration. But it also tacitly recognized the existence of Soviet influence, and hence dual power.

Resenting the new declaration bitterly, Miliukov only hoped it would finally prompt the full loyalty of Soviet leaders to the "legitimate" government.[27] He also continued to behave as if it had not been issued. Early in April he told the Manchester *Guardian* that Russia would still insist on the right to close the Dardanelles to foreign warships, "which would not be possible unless Russia possessed the Straits and fortified them."[28] He also reported to his colleagues that he considered the Declaration in no way abrogating his right to pursue policies in accord with his earlier viewpoints, "in agreement with the Allies and the national interests of Russia."[29] In public, he forcefully denied the existence, much less the utility, of dual authority, and rejected any notion of sharing power with the left; in private, he rejected as divisive and irresponsible the tacit recognition of Soviet power.[30]

But his was hardly the only Kadet view. As the days in April began to pass, even Vinaver and Nabokov were beginning to think socialists

[26] Sukhanov, II, 353-69; Tsereteli, I, 63-65, 68; V. Nabokov, "Vremennoe pravitel'stvo," *ARR*, I, 1922, pp. 58-60; Browder and Kerensky, II, 1045-46.

[27] Nabokov, pp. 58-60.

[28] *Manchester Guardian*, Apr. 13/26, 1917.

[29] P. Miliukov, *Istoriia vtoroi russkoi revoliutsii*, 3 pts., Sofia, 1921-23, pt. 1, p. 87; *Russkiia Vedomosti*, Apr. 9, 1917.

[30] E.g., Central Committee protocol, Apr. 7, 1917, in *VPNS*, No. 3, May 25, 1917, p. 8.

might have to be given greater political responsibilities, and perhaps even enlisted into government ranks. At the same time, there was new consideration of the idea that Kadets themselves should accept the growing partisanship of Russian society as an irreversible trend, relax their insistence on *nadpartiinost'* and direct their energies, as Shakhovskoi and others had argued, toward accommodating left-wing sentiment.

In the government, renewed efforts for accommodation were led by Nicholas Nekrasov. With close personal ties to Kerensky and the young left-liberal minister of finance, Michael Tereshchenko, Nekrasov was increasingly certain his Kadet colleagues failed to perceive the extent to which they themselves were opposing popular viewpoints. And while also warning against increasing "irresponsibility" and the threat of anarchy, he worked privately to force Kadet positions left-ward on a number of issues, again concentrating on foreign policy.[31]

In this he found at least partial support in the Kadet Central Committee from Adzhemov, Volkov, Gerasimov, Vinaver, Nabokov, and Nolde, all of whom recognized some validity in the accusation of "classical imperialism" being leveled against the party, and all of whom were also very anxious by now to establish closer controls over the actions of their own ministers, especially Miliukov.[32] At a Central Committee meeting on March 29, Dmitri Shakhovskoi raised the question directly as to whether the Soviet view of party "control" over ministers might not be an effective way of resolving the problem of "legitimacy," suggesting that each party send one "authoritative and competent" representative into the government. And in response, his colleagues now asked Maxim Vinaver (who had come to exercise the role of Kadet "liaison" with government) to begin lobbying specifically for Kadet positions. In the meantime, the issue also remained a continued topic of discussion.[33]

So, too, did the question of increased contact with the left. In early April, with the symbolic convocation of the Pirogov Physicians Congress in Moscow,[34] Z. G. Frenkel again raised the question in the

[31] For example, Nekrasov held a meeting of those he thought were "left" Kadets around the middle of April, and attacked strongly Miliukov's "uncompromising" position, which was "very much complicating" the government's relations with the Petrograd Soviet. Volkov, Gerasimov, Vinaver, Obolenskii, and four or five other Central Committee members attended. The incident is reported in V. A. Obolenskii, "Vospominaniia," MS, n.d., pp. 449-50.

[32] *Ibid.*; B. E. Nol'de, "Nabokov v 1917," *ARR*, VII, 1922, p. 10; *Novoe Vremia*, Apr. 11, 1917.

[33] Central Committee protocol, Mar. 29, 1917, in *VPNS*, No. 3, May 25, 1917, pp. 6-7.

[34] The Pirogov Society, founded in 1885, was an early professional nucleus of the Russian liberal movement.

Central Committee of creating a new Union of Liberation as a means of rapprochement (*sblizhenie*) with the left, just as he, Nekrasov, and others had done before the revolution, and as Shakhovskoi had urged at the seventh party congress. In a number of provincial committees there were similar suggestions being made; and in Moscow on April 9, S. A. Klivanskii continued the argument with Vinaver and Adzhemov, suggesting that Kadets would lose all possibility of developing mass electoral support unless they abandoned their *nadklassnost'* and supported legislation in the specific interests of workers and peasants.[35]

Rapprochement was again rejected, however, by Miliukov, Rodichev, and other members of the Petrograd leadership, who continued to condemn the left for its partisan outlook, and who still regarded the revolution as basically a constructive stage in winning the war. More emphatically than ever, Miliukov, Rodichev, and others denied that authority either could or should be shared with the left, or even that a condition of dual authority actually existed.[36] And once again, as in the first week of March on the monarchy question, Miliukov's self-assurance was destined to play a critical role both in structuring the sequence of revolution, and in ordering the future of his own party. The primary issue remained foreign policy, and the government's Declaration of March 27.

Miliukov's Note of April 18

The grounds for further discussion of foreign policy lay in the ambiguity of the March 27 statement, which coupled a denial of Russia's desire to "dominate other peoples" and "rob them of their territory" with a commitment to "fully honor" all treaties and obligations undertaken with the Allies, presumably including the Straits agreements. As we have seen, Miliukov had expressly accepted the Declaration as a political compromise. He suspected its ambiguity would be of little consequence if it was directed only for Russian consumption.

But when the Declaration was published abroad, it was accompanied by another statement from Kerensky, calling for the "internationalization" of the Straits, and implying a renunciation by Russia of her war goals. Since Kerensky held positions in both the government and the Petrograd Soviet, it was difficult to determine whether he was speaking officially or as a private person. Soon afterward, Miliukov began receiving pleas for clarification from his embassies. London and Paris were talking as if Russia had, in fact, renounced the secret treaties,

---

[35] *VPNS*, No. 1, May 11, 1917, p. 21.
[36] *Rech'*, Apr. 11, 1917; *VPNS*, No. 1, May 11, 1917, p. 22.

while American Secretary of State Lansing complained that "communications" by socialist "extremists" might jeopardize a war loan.[37] Joining the chorus were several prominent foreign socialists, particularly Albert Thomas, in Petrograd at this time to bolster Russia's military commitments. Thomas, the French minister of munitions as well as a leading socialist politician, was especially anxious to have the situation clarified. And it was he who now suggested to Miliukov that the Declaration of March 27 be officially conveyed to the Allied governments with a cover note of explanation.[38]

Pressure for clarifying Russian war aims also came from the Zimmerwaldian internationalists, but for different reasons. Having defined the meaning of revolution primarily in terms of the international peace movement, and having written the March 14 Declaration to All the Peoples of the World on this basis, Steklov, Sukhanov, Chkheidze, and others were also not assuaged by the compromise Declaration of March 27. The revolution to them was a powerful force for altering traditional attitudes about war and war aims; this meant spreading socialist peace doctrines abroad in an active fashion, just what Miliukov hoped the March 27 statement might prevent.

When the Socialist Revolutionary leader Victor Chernov returned from exile on April 8, the Zimmerwaldian viewpoint found a new and articulate spokesman. On April 11, Chernov, too, raised the question of sending the March 27 statement to the Allies as an official communiqué. The Russian revolution would then become as an international force for peace, combating ideas which had originally produced the war. At the same time, the troublesome question of the Allies' detention of radical emigrants could be laid out officially for Britain and France, with Britain in particular being placed on notice that free Russia would not tolerate interference with the rights of her citizens to travel, regardless of their political convictions.[39]

There was thus a fundamental difference between what Miliukov and the Soviet leadership hoped to gain from an "official clarification." When Miliukov accepted the proposal to send the Declaration of

[37] A. Popov, "Inostrannye diplomaty o revoliutsii 1917 g.," *KA*, No. 24, 1927, p. 132; E. A. Adamov, ed., *Constantinople et les détroits*, trans. S. Volsky, et al., 2 vols., Paris, 1930, I, 477-82; "Perepiska Miliukova," *Bor'ba Klassov*, No. 5, 1931, p. 86.

[38] Adamov, I, 486. See also Wade, *The Russian Search*, pp. 35-37.

[39] V. Chernov, *The Great Russian Revolution*, trans. P. Mosely, New Haven, 1936, pp. 193-202. See also Tsereteli, I, 84-85; Sukhanov, III, 203ff. There is some evidence that it was Kerensky who forced Miliukov to send the Declaration of March 27 abroad, by announcing to the press in an "official communiqué" that a special note to the Allies on war aims was being drafted. See M. Paleologue, *An Ambassador's Memoirs*, 3 vols., London, 1923-25, III, 313-14. Miliukov's own account appears in his *Istoriia*, pt. 1, pp. 91-95.

March 27 abroad, he did so convinced that the Straits were still obtainable, and with the expectation that his cover note would not only reinforce Russia's commitments to her Allies, but prevent them as well from reneging on war loans or the secret treaties. Chernov and his colleagues expected instead an extension of their own revolutionary attitudes into the arena of international diplomacy.

Small wonder, then, that on April 18, when Miliukov officially transmitted the government's March 27 statement to Russia's Allies under cover of a special note, his action evoked a storm of protest. It was not even so much a question of content. The Note itself simply expressed the "general aspiration of the whole Russian people to bring the war to a decisive victory." It also insisted that Russia would "fully observe" her treaty obligations. But Miliukov still indicated that the ideals in the Declaration of March 27 were the government's official basis for policy.[40]

Rather, the importance of Miliukov's Note was that it subverted the Soviet's effort to use the Declaration as a springboard for the ideas of Zimmerwaldian internationalism. Instead of suggesting a revision of treaty obligations, Miliukov endorsed them. And instead of emphasizing the need for a just peace, the Kadet foreign minister reinforced traditional militarism. Indirectly, Russia's Allies were put on notice that the new regime would continue to press her "national interests" in the Black Sea region. The Declaration of March 27 was thus made out to be little more than left-wing rhetoric.

It was this aspect of the Note—the government's subversion of the internationalists' goals—which even moderate left-wing newspapers like *Delo Naroda* responded to angrily on April 19 and 20; and it was this as well which brought demonstrators into the streets on April 20 and 21 against "Miliukov-Dardanelskii" and the "capitalist ministers."

THE APRIL DEMONSTRATIONS

On the day the demonstrations broke out, the Kadet foreign minister was driving in his automobile near the Tauride Palace when he suddenly encountered a large crowd of soldiers and workers, who blocked his way. The demonstrators slowed his car to a crawl and pounded it with their fists, making threatening gestures. Miliukov was forced to stop. But rather than becoming flustered, the Kadet leader stood up calmly in his seat, crossed his arms, and began giving a speech. His presumption and nerve impressed the crowd, which began to calm down, and soon allowed him to proceed.[41]

Because of incidents like this one, historians have often treated the

[40] Browder and Kerensky, II, 1098.   [41] Obolenskii MS, p. 450.

April demonstrations as an outburst of popular indignation against the war, and against the Kadets in particular.[42] And indeed, there is no question about the hostility many Russians felt toward Miliukov and his colleagues. A more accurate perception of the April days, however, must see the demonstrations as indicative of a broad crosscurrent of attitudes, the very complexity of which posed difficult problems for the Soviet and government alike.

The initial protests were anti-war and most likely induced by rank-and-file Bolsheviks.[43] But by April 21, as many demonstrators seemed to be coming out *in favor* of the government as against. In some cases, different groups clashed violently, indicating more a polarization of attitudes on the war than a consensus behind the socialists. Miliukov and his Kadet supporters could justifiably feel they had substantial backing, while Tsereteli and the Soviet leadership now had good cause themselves to fear the outbreak of civil war. The Petrograd garrison, moreover, was clearly more radical than the Soviet Executive Committee either suspected or desired. Many of the demonstrators were armed, and as much of the Executive Committee's effort was spent in trying to contain the dissidents as to identify the Soviet with their basic demands. But if Soviet leaders felt insecure enough to order military units in the surrounding districts *not* to march on the city, they also felt pressed toward radicalism by Lenin and the militant Bolsheviks, to whom workers and soldiers threatened to transfer allegiance.

Another complicating element was that Petrograd, as the capital, attracted many of Russia's most radical activists; attitudes here, consequently, often seemed more extreme than in other cities or the countryside. This was also reflected in the moods of different military units, with those closest to the "center" appearing more vocal than their comrades elsewhere in demanding change. For Miliukov and the Kadets, who read with great interest in April the resolutions of dozens of congresses and conferences supporting "War to Complete Victory," the Petrograd demonstrations thus raised the whole question of the capital's relation to the rest of Russia, and the liberals' "obligation" to defend "national interests" against the onslaught of a relatively small group of Petrograd rebels. Just one day before the Kadet foreign minister dispatched his Note of April 18, a large group of war-wounded in Petrograd had mounted the noisiest public attack yet on Lenin and the internationalists, calling the Bolsheviks "German agents," and de-

[42] E.g., W. H. Chamberlin, *The Russian Revolution*, 2 vols., New York, 1935, I, 144-47; V. S. Vasiukov, *Vneshniaia politika vremennogo pravitel'stva*, Moscow, 1966, pp. 123-32; Golikov and Tokarev, "Aprel'skii krisis," pp. 35ff.

[43] Alexander Rabinowitch, *Prelude to Revolution*, Bloomington, Ind., 1968, pp. 44-45.

manding war to complete victory. And such was the demonstration in support of the government on April 21 that the Kadet columnist for *Russkiia Vedomosti* could call the whole affair a "vote of confidence" for the regime.[44]

The basic issue, in other words, was not Miliukov's Note, but the problem of dual authority, social polarization, and the revolution's future goals and direction. And when left-wing demonstrators came out forcefully against Miliukov and the Kadet ministers on April 20, the first impulse of party leaders was to show the "Bolshevik rabble" that tens of thousands of their countrymen backed the regime. On April 21, after meeting for much of the night, the Kadet Central Committee issued one of its most militant declarations of the revolutionary epoch. It called "loyal" Russians into the streets, and demanded a massive anti-Bolshevik demonstration:

Citizens!
Russia is living through its most serious hour. The fate of the nation is being decided, the fate of future generations. The people unanimously overthrew the old regime. And the people, having entrusted authority to the Provisional Government, showed great wisdom. Now we must rally around that government. . . . We stand on the brink of an abyss. Citizens! Come out into the streets, show your will, participate in demonstrations and meetings, show your approval for the government. Save the country from anarchy! Long Live Free Russia! Long Live the Provisional Government![45]

Shortly afterward, thousands of Kadet supporters began a mass march through the city. Maxim Vinaver and Peter Gerasimov led the way in an open limousine. To many sullen workers and soldiers on the sidewalks, it must have seemed as if "privileged Russia" had finally taken to the streets.

Mixed with the green pennants of the party were a variety of liberal banners: "Victory for the Free Democracies!" "Down with German Militarism!" "Long Live Miliukov!" "Down with Anarchy!" "Long Live the Provisional Regime!" And as the demonstrators paraded down Liteinyi and Nevskii Prospekts, their ranks were swelled by scores of well-dressed supporters, undoubtedly drawn, in addition to the issues, by subtle class and social prejudices. Eventually the crowd found itself at the Mariinskii Palace, where Miliukov appeared with War Minister Guchkov as representatives of the government.[46]

[44] *Russkiia Vedomosti*, Apr. 25, 1917.
[45] Reprinted in *VPNS*, No. 1, May 11, 1917, p. 20.
[46] See the description in *Rech'*, Apr. 22, 1917.

Like many displays of this sort, the Kadet demonstration was little more than a cloudburst of emotional enthusiasm, let loose to muster courage for treating what all recognized was a governmental crisis of the first order. (Indeed, the Central Committee's resolution itself soon seemed anomalous; it appeared in the press and on broadsides only after an announcement by the Soviet urging that all demonstrations be halted, and ordering workers and soldiers off the streets. As a consequence, the episode brought down on Kadet heads the self-righteous scorn of left-wing editorialists, and also forced something of an official party apology.)[47] Russia and the Kadets in particular now had to decide whether order and stability required the reconstruction of the government, and whether the revolution's future goals had to be redefined. Moreover, party leaders had to resolve their own divisions on the role socialists might play in the regime before the Constituent Assembly, and what the political implications were of hostility toward Miliukov.

The Note itself was the easiest problem to resolve. By the night of April 20, Nekrasov and Tsereteli were already working on the text of a supplementary statement, which was approved the following afternoon not only by the government, but also by the Soviet and the Duma Committee. It was agreed that while Miliukov's statement had the unanimous approval of all ministers, the reference in his Note to "decisive victory" meant only what the government had set forth in the Declaration of March 27: that the aim of free Russia was not the domination of other nations or territories or the forcible occupation of foreign lands, but the creation of a stable peace on the basis of national self-determination.[48]

But the problem of state authority could not be so easily settled. On April 20 and 21, several delegates within the Petrograd Soviet had raised a cry for taking state power. And while only a small minority supported this view, a far greater number demanded Miliukov's ouster and the dismissal of Guchkov, the minister of war. The Kadet response was to demand instead that the Soviet cease acting as an independent authority. Central Committee members also intimated that if one party figure was forced to resign, the remaining Kadet ministers would also leave the regime. The problem of political stability was primarily the "fault" of the Soviet; and the demonstrations "proved" that socialists would have to commit themselves to maintaining law and order.[49]

[47] *Izvestiia*, Apr. 22, 1917; *Rech'*, Apr. 23, 1917.

[48] *Vestnik Vremennago Pravitel'stva*, Apr. 22, 1917.

[49] *Russkiia Vedomosti*, Apr. 21, 1917; *Birzhevyia Vedomosti*, Apr. 22, 1917; *Novoe Vremia*, Apr. 22, 1917. See also the discussion in Tsereteli, I, 86-96.

The problem was that the Kadets' position on this question was far less solid than it publicly appeared. Nekrasov in particular was making a strong plea for coalition within the Petrograd Kadet leadership; and at a massive party meeting of more than 1,000 persons on April 22, he repeated his viewpoints publicly. No governmental authority, he argued, ought to be without responsibility for its actions. The last few days had shown that the Petrograd Soviet, rather than the government, had the allegiance of large numbers of workers and soldiers; and in numerous instances, particularly that of bringing in government troops, it was the Soviet's orders which were obeyed, not the ministers'. The government consequently had to be reformed, either by means of a coalition, or through some institution that would make it more responsible to the popular will. In either case, Soviet power had to be recognized.[50]

Within the Kadet Central Committee, Nabokov, Vinaver, Adzhemov, Demidov, Gronskii, and one or two others were now sympathetic to these views, if not openly supportive. On April 23, with twelve members present, the Committee decided against supporting a coalition by only a single vote.[51] Astrov, Shakhovskoi, and Kishkin, meanwhile, were taking similar positions in Moscow, and suggesting that the "conciliationists" might find considerable party support in the provinces. Certainly a coalition regime in Petrograd would correspond to the types of administrations many local Kadet groups had already established in their own localities. In Rostov, in fact, Kadets were even coming to the conclusion that the Soviet should take all power since this seemed the best way to establish stability and order.[52]

But while conciliationist Kadets were especially impressed by the Soviet's ability to restore order and control the Petrograd garrison, it was precisely this point which induced Miliukov, Kokoshkin, and more conservative party leaders to demand that the government publicly condemn the Soviet for its "illegal, anti-government behavior."[53] In fact, the regime's official response was far different. On April 26, while asking all citizens to recognize its accomplishments,

[50] Report in *VPNS*, No. 1, May 11, 1917, pp. 23-24.

[51] Those present were Gerasimov, Makushin, Kornilov, Vinaver, Grigorovich-Barskii, Ruttsen, Stepanov, Glebov, Gronskii, Aleksandrov, Vernadskii, and Adzhemov, but there is no record of their individual votes. See *VPNS*, No. 11-13, Aug. 10, 1917, p. 21.

[52] *Rostovskaia Rech'*, Apr. 26, 1917; *Rech'*, Apr. 25, 1917; *Russkiia Vedomosti*, Apr. 25, 1917.

[53] The idea that the government should publicly condemn the Soviet was probably Kokoshkin's. See P. Miliukov, "Ne novyi svidetel'," *Posledniia Novosti*, No. 1439, Jan. 3, 1925.

Prince Lvov announced his intention to draw "new elements" into the cabinet.[54]

FORMATION OF THE FIRST COALITION

The extent to which Kadet and Soviet views on state authority had polarized during April was shown dramatically in two editorials which appeared in *Izvestiia* and *Rech'* at the end of the month. The *Izvestiia* article condemned a "juridical analysis" of governmental power, arguing that both the Soviet and the ministers exercised authority, since both had constituencies under their control. "Responsible" policies, in *Izvestiia*'s view, had to take this into account. If the government was to bring Russia to a Constituent Assembly, and successfully preserve the fruits of revolution, it had no choice but to work closely with the Soviet, and under its "supervision" (*kontrol'*).[55]

Rech', on the other hand, revealed Kadets as precisely the jurists *Izvestiia* complained about. Any talk of a "coalition," *Rech'* argued, indicated a misunderstanding of governmental processes. A coalition could only exist where individual ministers acted as party representatives, and pressed partisan party programs. Coalitions were also the result of specific party alliances; their members held their portfolios only as long as their parties held parliamentary majorities. It was "irrational" to discuss a coalition for Russia since the Provisional Government was not a cabinet regime in any parliamentary sense of the term, nor "responsible" to any legislature. Its goals, moreover, were national, not partisan. If socialists entered the government, it would not therefore be a question of "coalition" but of "reconstruction."[56]

The liberals and the left thus had very different concepts of what coalition meant. Miliukov, Kokoshkin, and their supporters saw the Provisional Government as a "national" regime, whose nonpartisan objectives would have to be served whether socialists or liberals held ministerial positions. Soviet leaders saw both coalition and *kontrol'* as a means of advancing definite popular programs. To a certain extent, the Kadet view derived from the statist orientation of Russian liberalism generally, and from the Kadets' particular conception of governmental legitimacy. It was also related to Miliukov's fear of civil war. But each view stemmed as well from a conception of why the revolution had been fought: the liberals, to pursue the war and provide the foundations for future economic and political maturation along the

---

[54] *Vestnik Vremennago Pravitel'stva,* Apr. 26, 1917.
[55] *Izvestiia,* Apr. 26, 1917.   [56] *Rech',* Apr. 29, 1917.

lines of Western liberal democracies; the socialists, to alter basic attitudes and institutions responsible for oppression both at home and abroad.

Kadet legalism, however, obscured several important political realities. The Provisional Government did *not* exercise "plenitude of power," as the April days had shown, not only because the Petrograd Soviet openly disagreed with some of its policies, but also because scores of workers, peasants, and soldiers were becoming increasingly disenchanted with government authority. The Soviet, moreover, could not support the government unequivocally without losing its own following. Workers demanding higher wages and an extension of the eight-hour day, peasants demanding land, and soldiers demanding release from the army were all pressing Soviet leaders into an anti-government position. Many on the left, like Kerensky, even hoped to bring socialist representatives into the regime not because they had any illusions about the "legalities" of parliamentary coalitions, but because they, too, were afraid of increasing ferment. To this end they also wanted the resignation of "Miliukov-Dardanelskii," whose reputation as a "reactionary monarchist" in the first days of March had now been amplified to the point where he seemed an arch-enemy of the whole revolution. It was imperative that the government become more popular to stem radicalism and prevent increasing polarization. And insofar as both Miliukov's ouster and the formation of a coalition was a means to social and political stability—a device by which the left could "contain" its own constituency while also keeping a close check on counterrevolutionary tendencies from the right—it was a conservative, not a radical, tactic.[57]

Largely because they feared the action would appear a compromise with right-wing elements, particularly in light of accusations from the Bolsheviks, a majority of Soviet Executive Committee members initially rejected the idea of coalition.[58] Kadet *verkhovniki* also remained opposed, staying closely allied with Miliukov. When a commemorative

[57] According to Tsereteli, the left's fear of a counterrevolution at this time was very pervasive. Miliukov, in his memoirs, castigates Nekrasov for contributing to the left's concern by spreading "rumors." Guchkov's later memoirs reveal, however, that Nekrasov's and the socialists' fears had some foundation. The minister of war set for himself the express aim at the end of April of "liquidating the Soviet, regardless of what happened," and he resigned his post to again become president of the War Industries Committee "in order to prepare cadres there for a march on Moscow and Petrograd." See Tsereteli, I, 87ff; Miliukov, *Istoriia*, pt. 1, p. 112; and A. I. Guchkov, "Iz vospominanii," *Posledniia Novosti*, Nos. 5661, 5665, and 5668, Sept. 23, 27, and 30, 1936, the quotations here being from Sept. 27.

[58] According to Tsereteli, I, 132, the vote was 24 against, 22 in favor, with 9 abstentions.

meeting gathered in honor of the First State Duma on April 27, with the Progressive Bloc leader Shulgin accusing the Soviet of "treachery," Rodichev demanding a struggle with "German slogans," and Tsereteli defending the concept of *kontrol'* but opposed to actual Soviet participation in the regime, there seemed little indication that coalition was a workable possibility.

What broke the impasse was the resignation of War Minister Guchkov on April 29. Shortly afterward, the Soviet received a frantic delegation of officers from the Petrograd staff, worried that Guchkov, General Kornilov, and possibly even the Kadets might be planning military action against the left. (Kornilov was the Petrograd District Commander. It was his orders which were countermanded by the Soviet on April 21 when he tried to bring troops from surrounding districts into the city to quell the demonstrations. Indignant, he had left the capital abruptly for the front. Miliukov and Shingarev had also just left Petrograd for army headquarters at Mogilev, for reasons which were not publicly explained, but which could be interpreted as an effort to lay the groundwork for a right-wight coup.) It was soon clear that fears of counterrevolution were exaggerated. (Miliukov and Shingarev's trip was actually planned well in advance of the crisis.) But there was now a much stronger argument in favor of coalition, since socialists in the government could more readily draw rein on the army's high command. Consequently, when Lvov sent the Soviet a new invitation to join the government on May 1, the Executive Committee reversed its earlier position.[59]

Lvov's second request for a coalition was a strong rebuff to Miliukov. On April 29, the Kadet leader had advised him to abandon the idea of coalition, and press instead for a program of "firm authority." Miliukov feared a new invitation would give the socialists special bargaining power, allowing them to pose conditions as their price for accepting government posts.[60]

This, in fact, is precisely what happened. On May 1 the Soviet Executive Committee worked out a set of eight demands as planks for a coalition regime, accepting Lvov's proposal on this basis. These included official support for "peace without annexation or indemnity"; "democratization" in the army; increased state control of industry; and the regulation of agriculture in the interests of the peasantry. Moreover, of fundamental importance to the legal-minded Kadets, the Executive Committee insisted that socialist ministers be "responsible"

[59] The vote was now 44 in favor, 19 against, with only 2 abstentions. See Tsereteli, I, 137.

[60] Protocol of the Kadet Group in Paris, Feb. 9, 1921, in the Archives of the Constitutional Democratic Party, Hoover Institution.

to the Soviet in a parliamentary sense, subject to recall if the Soviet desired.[61]

If the Soviet program was accepted, Miliukov could obviously not remain minister of foreign affairs. Now, however, a majority of Soviet leaders were no longer anxious that he leave the government entirely, for fear of hopelessly (and dangerously) alienating the army command. They proposed instead that he replace Manuilov as minister of education. In principle, the Kadet leader was not opposed to such a switch. Early in April he had raised the same possibility himself, when reservations about his effectiveness began to filter in through the Allied missions.[62] (Assuming that Russia stayed in the war, the Allies were naturally not unwilling to see their own territorial interests advanced by having a less forceful nationalist in the post of foreign minister, and may actually have leaked indications of their "discouragement" with Miliukov for this purpose.) But when the Kadet leader returned to Petrograd on May 2 to find negotiations already underway on the formation of a coalition, he exploded: nonpartisanship was being sacrificed to disruptive factionalism; a program was being forced on the regime which would weaken central authority; his advice to Lvov had been rejected. Adamantly refusing to change portfolios, he instead announced his resignation, and stalked out of the ministers' chambers.

This, in turn, brought the whole question of Kadet attitudes toward the government to a head. Miliukov intended his departure to signal the resignations of the remaining party ministers, the most effective leverage, in his view, for combating pressure from the left.[63] But once again he had acted independently, without consulting his colleagues; and for all his insistence, the Kadet Central Committee could not agree that he had been forced from the regime. ("Ousted involuntarily" was how he described it to a meeting of Duma members on May 4.) The Ministry of Education was open, and in any event, the resignation of *all* Kadet ministers would undoubtedly precipitate a prolonged government crisis. It was difficult to see in these circumstances how the liberal goals of order, social stability, and the effective pursuit of the war would be advanced.

For most of the night of May 2, a number of Central Committee

[61] *Izvestiia*, May 1 and 2, 1917.

[62] V. Nabokov, "Vremennoe pravitel'stvo," p. 62. British Ambassador Buchanan was convinced Miliukov was too weak to remain foreign minister. He notes in his memoirs that "Kerensky was the only man to whom we could look to keep Russia in the war." See Sir George Buchanan, *My Mission to Russia*, 2 vols., London, 1923, II, 109.

[63] Obolenskii MS, pp. 450-51.

members tried to persuade Miliukov to remain in the government as minister of education. The Kadet leader remained obstinate, however, and absolutely refused. The Committee then contacted Lvov, and tried to pressure his reinstatement as foreign minister, presumably by means of modifying the Soviet's demands. When this also failed, the party leadership finally had to decide whether to support Miliukov and his strategy of mass resignation, or join the coalition.

Opinion was divided, and in the discussions which followed, long-standing differences between Kadets on questions of tactics and even program again made themselves felt. Those in favor of joining the coalition were led by Nekrasov, once more the energetic leader of the party's left-wing. He had considerable support, moreover, from Demidov, Vinaver, and Nabokov, all generally regarded as "moderates"; and several members of the old Fourth Duma contingent, which in June and July 1915 had opposed the Progressive Bloc. Those in favor of total Kadet withdrawal, however, included Kokoshkin, Rodichev, Dolgorukov, Nolde, Manuilov, and Shingarev—the prominent *verkhovniki*, who in addition to raising questions about party ideology, called on their colleagues not to publicly "abandon" Miliukov.

The real question for all Kadets was what the coalition would mean in terms of the party's "national" objectives, and particularly Russian unity, which was almost impossible to answer. There was some feeling in the Central Committee that ministers *should*, in fact, be formal representatives of their party, and use their positions to press party programs. On the other hand, it was also thought that without Miliukov as foreign minister, a coalition would be deprived of any real substance. Shingarev, in particular, felt it would be "purposeless" to continue without Miliukov, and prepared to submit his own resignation. In his view, as well as Izgoev's, the best alternative was to have the Soviet itself assume full power, and let Russia realize the "poverty" of the left's position.

In the end, the Central Committee voted 18 to 10 to keep its members in the government. But the Kadet leadership left many major questions unresolved. Miliukov's plan for mass resignations failed largely because Nekrasov announced he would stay in the cabinet in any case, and resigned from the Central Committee; and because Nabokov, Manuilov, and others felt their responsibility to Russia was greater than their loyalty to Miliukov. Even Shingarev had second thoughts, questioning whether "conscience" could allow him to resign. But the Committee never clearly determined what its attitudes should be about coalition, about ministerial partisanship, or the degree to which the government should begin to meet popular demands. Nor did it determine whether Kadet ministers would consider themselves subject to party recall.[64]

After intensive negotiations, the Soviet's program for the new cabinet was modified somewhat to meet liberal objections. (In particular, it accepted the need to build up the army and launch offensive operations as the best way to defend Russian security.)[65] But the socialists formally announced on May 6 that their representatives "must consider themselves responsible to the Petrograd Soviet . . . and must commit themselves to render full account to it for their actions."[66] The Kadets prepared a similar statement, outlining their own tasks for the regime, and asserting that if the coalition did not meet them, they too retained for themselves the right to withdraw their members. In print, however, this statement was modified, speaking only of "representatives," and not threatening their withdrawal; and the "tasks" Kadets spoke of were national in scope, rather than particularistic or expressly class oriented.[67] In sum, the Petrograd party leadership decided awkwardly and with great hesitation to support what they roughly conceived of as a "national, nonpartisan coalition," unsure in actuality whether the left could be contained, whether the development of new counter-revolutionary forces on the right could be avoided, or where, in fact, the new arrangement would lead Russia as a whole.

PARTISANSHIP AND LOCAL PARTY ORGANIZATIONS

While the April crisis was essentially a conflict of political power and authority, limited to Petrograd, it shocked Kadets throughout Russia. Miliukov's ouster from the government a scant eight weeks after the end of the old regime clearly revealed the uncertainties for liberals of revolutionary politics. With mobs of unruly workers and soldiers in the streets, and veterans of the "Liberation" movement like Kokoshkin, Vinaver, and Shingarev objects of vituperation and scorn, the manner in which the crisis unfolded showed unmistakably for the first time the power of developing social forces. Even for those provincial and Moscow party members, whose concerns were more with local social issues than high politics, the incident could not fail to leave a sharp and painful impression, arousing deep feelings of fear and doubt.

[64] A. S. Izgoev, "Piat' let v sovetskoi Rossii," *ARR*, x, 1923, pp. 13-14; A. Khrushchov, *Andrei Ivanovich Shingarev*, Moscow, 1918, pp. 99-101; *Rech'*, May 5 and 6, 1917; *Russkiia Vedomosti*, May 2, 3, and 4, 1917; N. Gubskii, *Revoliutsiia i vneshniaia politika Rossii*, Moscow, 1917; Tsereteli, 1, 150-55. Tsereteli emphatically denies that Miliukov's resignation was a condition for coalition.
[65] Report by M. M. Vinaver to the eighth party congress, *VPNS*, No. 4-5, June 8, 1917, pp. 8-9.
[66] *Izvestiia*, May 6, 1917.
[67] Miliukov, *Istoriia*, pt. 1, pp. 113-14; Tsereteli, 1, 154; *Rech'*, May 6, 1917.

The April crisis was all the more unsettling for Kadets because it took place against a background of increasing economic difficulty and social unrest in the country at large. By the middle of April, this process was already undermining the mood of general optimism and satisfaction which had characterized the party after the seventh congress. In the cities, where the supply of food and fuel had improved somewhat in the first weeks of the Provisional Government (largely because local soviets and Committees of Public Organizations worked energetically to distribute the most readily available stores), new shortages had begun to appear. From April 10 to May 9, movement of foodstuffs was only about 60 percent of what it had been in March, and only about 28 percent of Russia's estimated need.[68] On April 15, Shingarev received an urgent wire from Moscow reporting that grain reserves there were once again "at critically low levels"; one day later, Minister of Transport Nekrasov informed Prince Lvov that the total available supply of fuel for the immediate future would be "absolutely insufficient to meet the needs even of defense industries alone."[69] The principal difficulty remained transport. In the second two weeks of April, the number of locomotives in repair shops increased from 4247 to 4658, almost 25 percent of the total; and some 7000 more freight cars were out of service in April, compared with the beginning of March.[70]

Shortages of goods meant increasing prices, both on articles of mass consumption and industrial materials. The price of cast iron increased from 155 kopecks a pud on February 21, for example, to 185 kopecks a pub on April 1; the price of steel rose from 370 kopecks to 480, almost 30 percent.[71] In many areas, inflation wiped out the wage increases that a number of factory owners had granted in the immediate postrevolutionary period; and as a result of higher costs for fuel and supplies, more factories closed, and thousands of additional workers became unemployed.[72] Meanwhile, workers themselves issued new demands for price and wage controls, both to prevent a further deterioration of their own situation, and "to curb the rapacious appetites of the capitalists," as those in the vast Putilov works in Petrograd expressed it on April 27.[73] Work stoppages became more frequent; and many of the tensions characterizing labor-management relations in the worst months of the old regime began to return. According to official statistics, 41 major strikes took place in April, including 13 at major indus-

[68] L. S. Gaponenko, *Rabochii klass Rossii v 1917 godu*, Moscow, 1970, pp. 227-28.
[69] *Ekon. polozhenie*, pt. 1, pp. 254-55; pt. 2, p. 293.
[70] *Ibid.*, pt. 2, pp. 228-31.
[71] P. V. Volobuev, *Ekonomicheskaia politika vremennogo pravitel'stva*, Moscow, 1962, p. 254.
[72] *Ekon. polozhenie*, pt. 2, pp. 38-43.   [73] *Izvestiia*, May 6, 1917.

trial enterprises (over 500 workers). In May this figure would almost double.[74]

The eight-hour working day was another source of increasing tension. Established in Petrograd by agreement between the Soviet and the Society of Manufacturers, as we have seen, it rapidly became a major (and symbolic) demand for workers throughout Russia. By the middle of April, sometimes as a result of unilateral action by the workers themselves, eight hours had become the norm in Omsk, Rostov, Ivanovo-Voznesensk, Orekhovo-Zuevo, Bogorodsk, Minsk, Podolsk, Serpukhov, and Kolomna, as well as in Moscow and Petrograd. Additional hours, which employers now tried hard to avoid, were compensated at higher rates.[75] According to one report to the Provisional Government on May 4, however, a shorter working day in some enterprises was resulting in production losses of up to 60 percent;[76] and whether or not this or other factors were actually the cause, the net result by the end of April was an even greater increase in the shortage of goods; more shutdowns (or lockouts, depending on one's viewpoint); increased hardships for workers; and the development of enormous hostility toward factory committees and soviets on the part of much of Russia's industrial bourgeoisie, many of whose members were losing complete control over their own private enterprises.

The situation in the countryside, meanwhile, was also deteriorating. In striving to preserve existing agrarian relations, Shingarev and other Provisional Government officials failed to consider the antagonism among peasants in many places over the Stolypin reforms, particularly against former members of the commune who had received especially favorable separate holdings. In the central black-earth region in particular, many villages regarded the end of the old regime as the end of the Stolypin system; and peasants in Kazan, Simbirsk, Perm, Penza, and other provinces began to move against the so-called *otrubniki*, or those who had separated from the commune.[77]

More important in terms of Russia's overall social stability, moreover, and also far more worrisome to the gentry and the Kadets, peasants in many places also began to "settle old scores" with landlords, moving under the pretext of "liberating the countryside from those who supported the tsarist regime, and who might be the basis for counterrevolution."[78] Seizures took place in Kursk province as early as March 11, coupled with the imprisonment of landlords; by April, they

[74] Gaponenko, *Rabochii klass*, pp. 377-78, 386.

[75] *Ibid.*, p. 349.

[76] *Ekon. polozhenie*, pt. 1, p. 514. See also Volobuev, *Proletariat*, pp. 283-84.

[77] P. N. Pershin, *Agrarnaia revoliutsiia v Rossii*, 2 vols., Moscow, 1966, I, 299; *Krest'ianskoe dvizhenie v 1917 godu*, Moscow-Leningrad, 1927, pp. 16, 19, 96.

[78] Pershin, I, 290.

had developed in the provinces of Riazan, Voronezh, Orlov, Tula, Kazan, Perm, Pskov, Novgorod, and Simbirsk, affecting scores of districts.[79] The government's response was to dispatch reliable troops to particularly troublesome areas, and to insist in a circular letter to provincial commissars on April 13 that it was "indispensable to suppress all manifestations of violence or plunder. . . ."[80] But to *Rech'*, *Russkiia Vedomosti*, and other liberal newspapers, the "various anarchistic forces" emerging in the middle of April were still "threatening to lead the country to new losses of sown areas, and . . . new national disasters."[81]

Culminating in the April crisis itself, all of this reaffirmed the worst fears of many Kadets, and could not help but affect their own party development. Russia was increasingly an arena of partisan social conflict, with sectarian goals and class interests more important to their advocates than unity or Russia's national welfare. Kadets had party committees in each of the provinces in which peasant violence erupted in April; and it was unnerving for liberals here and elsewhere to realize the gap that was rapidly opening between themselves and masses of their countrymen. Even left Kadets had to perceive that despite their own long years of struggle against the autocracy, their party was increasingly identified by workers and peasants with the gentry and privileged Russia, the "bourgeois enemy" to be flailed for long-standing social injustices. For conservative party members, the realization reinforced many deep-rooted prejudices about Russian backwardness. Where socialists saw peasant and worker "consciousness," many Kadets saw chaos. As Maklakov suggested to his former Duma colleagues on May 4, it was possible "Russia had received in the revolution more freedom than she could manage."[82]

The April crisis did have one salutory effect, however: it impressed even conservative Kadet leaders with the necessity of building up their national party organization. Partisanship meant Kadets would have to compete more intensely for popular support at all levels, propagandizing their programs and defending their policies even to unsympathetic workers and peasants. On May 3 a long editorial in *Rech'* recognized this clearly; and eight days later, the first issue appeared since 1908 of the party's official journal, *Vestnik Partii Narodnoi Svobody*, designed to coordinate local party activities.

[79] A. M. Andreev, *Sovety rabochikh i soldatskikh deputatov nakanune oktiabria*, Moscow, 1967, p. 122.

[80] Browder and Kerensky, II, 584-85; E. N. Burdzhalov, *Vtoraia russkaia revoliutsiia. Moskva, front, periferiia*, Moscow, 1971, p. 400.

[81] *Russkiia Vedomosti*, Apr. 18, 1917.

[82] *Rech'*, May 5, 1917. According to Obolenskii (MS, p. 452), Miliukov also told his colleagues on the Central Committee that he thought the revolution had "run off its rails."

Kadet organizational strength had actually been growing steadily since the middle of March. By April, Kadets in many places were already publishing their own local party newspapers; and in Tiflis, Moscow, Kiev, and Odessa, they had also organized special branch sections for military personnel, students, and women. On April 7, the Central Committee in Petrograd assigned some 25,000 rubles of party funds for local newspaper work; and 50,000 rubles for the publication of party literature.[83] By the end of the month, there were more than 180 local party committees functioning in 66 provinces and regions.[84]

The orientation of these local committees through most of April was quite varied. In some areas, particularly Kharkov in the Ukraine, the Volga region, the Ural industrial area, and western Siberia, the posture of cooperation which had characterized most party organizations in early March still held. Local committee chairmen made serious efforts toward transforming the party into the mass organization called for by Shakhovskoi at the seventh congress, and hoped to revive the energy, enthusiasm and perhaps even the popular support of the party in provincial cities and towns at the time of the first revolution in 1905. In Ekaterinburg, for example, local Kadets under Lev Krol moved into factories for agitation and discussion meetings, argued with Bolshevik speakers in passionate debates, and devoted all of their efforts to winning worker support (as well as preserving industrial peace).[85] Elsewhere, such as in Viatka province, Kadets spread through the countryside to enlist the support of the peasants.[86]

But with growing popular unrest in April, a far more pervasive tendency was developing among scores of provincial groups in favor of moving the party to the right. Kadets who had argued bitterly with one another over the best tactical means to overthrow the autocracy now began to close ranks against "broadening and deepening" the revolution. Also, many party figures still inclined to the left found themselves more and more frequently rejected by local soviet leaders; and results from committees like those in Ekaterinburg and Viatka were not encouraging. In the Urals, if workers were not yet pro-Bolshevik, they showed little inclination to ally with Kadets over Mensheviks or other moderate Social Democrats; and in the countryside, Kadet agitators often found open hostility, with peasants more interested in Socialist Revolutionaries or the Peasants' Union than the Kadets. In some places they even insisted they had "no need at all for Kadet party materials."[87] Some provincial party figures responded to worker and peasant hostility by urging their colleagues to take more, rather than

83 *VPNS*, No. 3, May 25, 1917, p. 8.   84 *Ibid.*, p. 17.
85 *Ibid.*, No. 17-18, Sept. 7, 1917, pp. 15-16.
86 *Ibid.*, No. 11-13, Aug. 10, 1917, p. 35.   87 *Ibid.*

less, radical positions; and there was a good deal of discussion in particular about curbing peasant violence with immediate land reform, a subject scheduled for resolution by the party as a whole at its forthcoming eighth party congress. But a much more common response was to abandon the quest for mass support, and seek new contacts instead with other forces of "law and order," particularly after the shock of the April crisis itself.

Kadet movement to the right was very much facilitated, moreover, by the fact that toward the end of March and in early April, large numbers of Octobrists, Nationalists, and members of other prerevolutionary parties began to filter into party ranks, altering the composition of a number of local committees quite dramatically. In Saratov province, for example, a new Kadet group composed almost entirely of gentry figures organized in April in the hope that Kadet political muscle could be used to protect their estates; and elsewhere party committees attracted conservatives and monarchists—"March Kadets" (*Martovskie Kadety*) the Central Committee labeled them—who apparently hoped the party's organizational looseness might enable them to pursue their own goals with a "safe" political label.[88] So great was the shift to the right in some areas that the party's official *Vestnik* urged local committees in early May "to think seriously about this right-wing danger" and take firm measures to combat it. One method suggested was a temporary slowdown on the admission of new party members, with the requirement that each new candidate present two recommendations from Kadets already in good standing. But in most places the suggestion went unheeded. In Mogilev, for example, the local Kadet committees admitted 55 new members in early May, and rejected only 4.[89]

In some places ties were also becoming stronger between Kadets and Trade-Industrial circles, particularly in Moscow, where relationships between the two groups were already well-developed before 1917, as we have seen. As the revolution plunged Petrograd Kadets ever more deeply into the affairs of high politics, so the Moscow Kadets became increasingly preoccupied with the vast problems of social and economic organization that concerned the Zemstvo and City Unions, and the War Industries Committees. Particularly with the formation of the All-Russian Union of Trade and Industry in late March, Moscow Kadets like S. A. Smirnov began working more closely than ever with progressive members of the Moscow bourgeoisie like Riabushinskii and Tretiakov.

Moreover, with the growing hostility of workers and their soviet

88 *Ibid.*, No. 6-7, Jun. 22, 1917, pp. 4-5, 11.
89 *Ibid.*, No. 14-16, Aug. 31, 1917, p. 32.

leaders in April, some Moscow party members began insisting that Kadets themselves take a more active "partisan" position in defense of bourgeois interests. The Moscow Kadet committee as a whole rejected this course, but when the Trade-Industrial Union opened a special "Political Section" to coordinate its party relationships, its membership included S. A. Kotliarevskii, a former Kadet Central Committee member, and P. A. Buryshkin and L. A. Katuar, both city duma delegates, as well as Smirnov.[90] And while the general spirit of the Union leadership itself was still one of cooperation with the left, its net effect on many Moscow Kadets was to draw them away from the party's official "above class" orientation.[91]

In Petrograd, however, *nadklassnost'* was still very much the dominant outlook, even in the face of mounting social tensions. And as a consequence of Central Committee influence over official party literature, it remained the dominant posture as well for the vast majority of local Kadet committees. When the Central Committee began coordinating agitation and propaganda activities, Kadet spokesmen were instructed to go out of their way to avoid identification with any particular social class. Thousands of placards were printed with such nonpartisan slogans as "Liberty, Equality, Fraternity"; "Remember the War"; and simply "Workers! Soldiers! Citizens!"[92] A pamphlet by Sergei Iablonovskii, *The Non-class Struggle and the Tasks of the Moment*, insisted that Kadets were "very much like moderate socialists" (but failed to inform the reader why he should therefore favor the Kadets); while an important and widely distributed piece by Alexander Kizevetter emphatically insisted that Kadets were not "a bourgeois group," but fighters for the "freedom, justice, and class interests of *all* groups from the standpoint of general social welfare."[93] Similarly, an official biography of Miliukov began with "Paul Nicholaevich Miliukov is not a capitalist and is not a landowner, contrary to what is now being frequently heard; he is a scholar, a politician, and a writer.

[90] Gaponenko, *Rabochii klass*, pp. 228-29; V. Ia. Laverychev, *Po tu storonu barrikad*, Moscow, 1967, pp. 40-41.

[91] According to Laverychev, "Vserossiiskii soiuz torgovli i promyshlennosti," *IZ*, No. 70, 1961, pp. 53-54, the Union granted funds to the Moscow Kadets for the publication of party literature, as well as sponsoring Kadet lecture tours, though some funds were also apparently granted to Plekhanov and other moderate socialists.

[92] To these inspiring broadsides were also added some of more specific content, though hardly designed to win converts among those to whom they were directed: "In Discipline is the Salvation of the Army!" "Soldiers Save our Army!" "Soldiers to the Front, Workers to their Benches!" Some of these were published in runs of more than 300,000 copies at considerable expense. See *VPNS*, No. 1, May 11, 1917, p. 18.

[93] S. Iablonovskii, *Nadklassovaia bor'ba i zadachi momenta*, Moscow, 1917; A. A. Kizevetter, *Partiia narodnoi svobody i eia ideologiia*, Moscow, 1917, pp. 4-7.

He has no factories, no property. He has only books."[94] And when the Central Committee published a pamphlet by V. I. Dobrovolskii, designed to attract new followers for Kadets and entitled *Why I Support the Party of People's Freedom*, its principal argument ran as follows:

> I support the Party of People's Freedom since this party desires to construct society in such a way as to ensure universal and equal freedom, and so that the national welfare will be shared by all, with no single sector of the population, no single nationality or class having rights that are detrimental to others.[95]

While one can hardly criticize the Kadets in Petrograd or elsewhere for their reluctance to assume the partisan posture to which liberal members of the intelligentsia had always objected (and which they now feared might accelerate a dangerous tendency toward civil war), it is still fair to observe that by the middle of April, there were increasing practical difficulties with this *nadklassnost'*, however sincere the Kadets' ideological commitment. One might argue that with a national bourgeoisie of little more than 6 million, and a gentry population probably less than one-tenth that size (compared with some 20 million proletarians and more than 100 million peasants), Kadets could hardly hope to maintain a dominant political position if they overtly became the party of the gentry and bourgeoisie; and thus from a practical viewpoint, a nonpartisan approach was worth maintaining even if most Kadets were actually moving to the right. Yet when many on the radical left accused Kadets of being "bourgeois," they referred in large measure not to personal involvement in commerce and industry, as the author of the pamphlet on Miliukov assumed, but to social values. And when the Novgorod Kadets stressed "respect for others" and "obedience to law and order" in the first edition of their local party newspaper on April 16; when Kadets in Rostov doubted whether elections of any sort could be held before all Russians committed themselves to "principles of order"; and when S. M. Gutnik wrote in *Odesskii Listok* on April 25 that, while Kadets would always carry the banners of "broad social reform," they opposed "social revolution," the widening gap between liberal and mass orientations was increasingly clear, even if not explicit.[96] Nonpartisanship or *nadklassnost'* in

[94] G. V. Vernadskii, *Pavel Nikolaevich Miliukov*, Petrograd, 1917, p. 1.

[95] V. I. Dobrovol'skii, *Pochemu ia stoiu za partiiu narodnoi svobody*, Petrograd, 1917, p. 9.

[96] *Novgorodskaia Zhizn'*, Apr. 16, 1917; *Rostovskaia Rech'*, Apr. 6, 1917; *Odesskii Listok*, Apr. 25, 1917. A similar attitude was displayed by Kadets in Nizhni-Novgorod when their paper, *Narodnaia Svoboda*, first appeared on Apr. 26; and even in

these circumstances was likely to appear as little more than a screen to hide the Kadets' actual orientation toward Russia's privileged elements. At the same time, however, from the standpoint of groups like the Trade-Industrialists or the Petrograd Society of Manufacturers, nonpartisanship was also likely to be regarded as a tactic of weakness and indecision, particularly considering the forthcoming national and local elections.

Most Kadets in April still felt deeply committed to the idea of national unity, just as they had at the time the Provisional Government was first organized; and they hoped with an increasing sense of urgency to stem Russia's growing social polarization. Yet in precisely these conditions, traditional *nadklassnye* values and a "nonpartisan" approach were also unlikely to win many converts to the liberal cause.

PARTY DEFINITION AT THE EIGHTH CONGRESS

Before Kadets could further define or reassess their strategy, however, several important programmatic matters still had to be resolved, particularly the question of agrarian reform and the nationalities issue, which had been postponed by the seventh congress in March. On May 8, consequently, more than 250 party representatives gathered again in Petrograd, including more than 150 from the provinces, 34 from Moscow, and more than 40 from the capital itself.[97]

The tenor of the eighth congress was set by the opening address of Miliukov, whose crusty rancor quickly disabused anyone who still thought he was equivocal about the current political situation. In his view, Russia was in great danger. Extremist elements had wormed their way into the army, and caused a collapse of spirit and discipline; desertion and fraternization were now common; and there was widespread expectation of immediate peace, which itself was weakening Russia's position among the Allies. In the countryside, reports of peasant disorders raised the spector of anarchy; while in the capital, the Soviet's pretensions had created an intolerable division of authority, leaving the government without control over its own instruments of power. Whether the new coalition would work depended on whether moderate socialists could control their extremist colleagues, and were willing to make practical concessions.[98]

What these concessions were, Miliukov spelled out indirectly by

Kharkov, when the *Izvestiia Khar'kovskago Komiteta Partii Narodnoi Svobody* published its first edition on Apr. 30.

[97] *VPNS*, No. 4-5, Jun. 8, 1917, p. 9.

[98] Protocols of the eighth party congress, *VPNS*, No. 4-5, Jun. 8, 1917, pp. 7-8. Major speeches also appear in *Rech'* and *Russkiia Vedomosti*, May 10, 1917 et seq.

defining what he considered the three principal political trends of the moment. The first was "counterrevolutionary," as yet unstructured and disorganized, and still no real threat. The second was "conservative," and stood for the preservation of what the revolution had already achieved. The third was "radical." It believed in the "deepening and broadening" of the revolution, and carried on its banner "Let the Revolution Continue." It was this tendency that was the source of danger, in Miliukov's view, since it encouraged "anarchism" and undermined the "creative" revolutionary energies of the Provisional Government. "What reason is there," the Kadet leader asked, "for continuing the revolution?"[99]

Miliukov thus asserted his leadership at the eighth congress to have Kadets resist further reforms. What was needed in terms of the party's political definition was a reemphasis of traditional Kadet guidelines on agrarian reform and the nationality question; organization, so that the party could bring a substantial number of delegates to the Constituent Assembly; and the concentration of unitary authority in the Provisional Government. These accomplishments alone would allow Russia to pursue the war effectively and remain a great power, the basic reasons why Kadets had agreed to participate in a coalition regime.[100]

But as Nicholas Nekrasov, A. V. Vasilev, and other delegates recognized, Miliukov's statist perspective was increasingly out of phase with practical reality. Soldiers were not fighting at the front precisely because they failed to revere the state and saw no purpose in the conflict. Workers were concerned with the quality of their daily existence. "Vital interests" expressed in terms of Constantinople and the Straits were becoming irrelevant. On the contrary, as Vasilev, a delegate from Samara pointed out, the Soviet was being obeyed not out of principle but because it supported popular goals. And the lesson from this, according to Nekrasov, was that Kadets had to spell out in clear detail exactly what they thought Russia's vital interests were, and define their goals in these terms.[101]

But Nekrasov's criticism only stiffened Miliukov's imperiousness. It also angered delegates like Trubetskoi, Izgoev, and Rodichev, who felt Nekrasov had "stabbed Miliukov in the back" in April by agitating in favor of a coalition. (The April crisis "was in the end of a victory of socialist intrigues," Izgoev insisted, "organized from inside the cabinet by N. V. Nekrasov himself.")[102] When Nekrasov charged Kadet spokesmen with concealing the party's imperialist designs, Miliukov readily admitted he thought Russia's "vital interests" required possession of Constantinople and the Straits. Those who disagreed simply did not

[99] Ibid., p. 8.   [100] Ibid., p. 9.   [101] Ibid., pp. 10, 12-13.
[102] A. S. Izgoev, Sotsialisty vo vtoroi russkoi revoliutsii, Petrograd, 1917, p. 43.

understand what served Russia's national welfare.[103] Miliukov's personal force, moreover, was sufficient to carry an overwhelming majority of delegates, and his views were officially endorsed.[104]

In turn, however, the argument on Russia's vital interests served to widen the already troublesome cracks in Kadet party unity. The real question at hand was whether Kadets should align themselves more closely with the masses, the same issue which had divided liberals in the early days of the liberation movement, created such ambivalence in Kadet politics before 1917, and preoccupied Nekrasov and Shakhovskoi at the seventh congress in March. When Fedor Kokoshkin presented the Central Committee's report on nationality problems and the structure of Russia's future government, therefore, and when Nicholas Chernenkov reported on agrarian affairs, questions of tactics reemerged. Debate became more bitter, and Petrograd party leaders once again faced considerable opposition to their views.

Kokoshkin followed a traditional line. Independent or even politically autonomous nationalities would "Balkanize" Russia, he maintained, and result in a loss of international power and prestige. The notion of a federal system based on nationalities also had to be rejected, both because disparities in the size of different nationality groups would result in disproportionate legislative representation, and because nationalities intermingled in the same geographical areas. Who would represent the rights of non-Ukrainians in the Ukraine, for example, or the interests of Russian Turks? A more appropriate state structure, one Kadets had always supported and should continue to support, was a unitary state administration with legislative competence exercised through a bicameral congress. Delegates in one house would represent geographically defined units like *uezdy,* while members of the other would be elected as representatives-at-large on a nationwide basis. Kokoshkin asked the delegates to endorse these views as the party's platform for the Constituent Assembly.[105]

The problem here was that Kokoshkin's approach bore little relation to the activities of nationality movements themselves. Federalists in the Ukraine were already demanding self-determination by means of an independent Ukrainian Constituent Assembly, and had organized their own "national Rada" (parliament). Similar rumblings could be heard from Belorussia, the Baltic States and Transcaucasia. In Helsinki, Finnish nationalists were demanding outright independence; and the Provisional Government itself had already given pledges of

---

[103] *VPNS,* No. 4-5, Jun. 8, 1917, p. 14.   [104] *Ibid.,* p. 15.

[105] Protocols continued in *VPNS,* No. 14-16, Aug. 31, 1917, pp. 10-20; *Rech',* May 11 and 13, 1917. This speech was also published as a separate pamphlet, *Avtonomiia i federatsiia,* Petrograd, 1917.

independence to Poland. As a number of regional delegates from Georgia and the Ukraine pointed out, the party's emphasis on "Great Russia, One and Indivisible" would sound dully familiar to national minorities accustomed to tsarist oppression. And according to P. E. Butenko, the president of the party's group in Kiev, Kokoshkin could not even read his report in the Ukraine without being hooted off the stage as a Great Russian chauvinist.[106]

Debate was all the more intense because Butenko, Mogilianskii, Imshenetskii, and others who spoke against the Central Committee were not themselves radicals or federalists, and certainly not partisans of Ukrainian, Georgian, or even Finnish independence. They simply recognized the practical need to attune party policy to regional conditions and popular sentiment, precisely the "sectarianism" which Miliukov, Kokoshkin, and their supporters insisted the party avoid. Some provincial delegates, Kokoshkin argued back, were making a mistake which he had warned about in his report. They were confusing the issue of local self-government, which the party supported, with the question of autonomy for nationalities, which it did not.[107] But how potential voters would react if party leaders themselves could not keep these matters clear, the Central Committee spokesman did not say.

On the agrarian question, Chernenkov insisted the crucial problem for Kadets was how to increase agricultural productivity while retaining conditions of relative social stability. Kadets well understood the peasants' demand for land. They had always supported the expropriation of property from large landowners (with just compensation), and opposed special privileges for the gentry. They even recognized that the issue of "private" property in Russian agriculture was less important than the question of land use, and endorsed the right of peasants or peasant communes to own or hold property in different tenure relationships. But they also understood the crisis of food productivity, Chernenkov argued, and its relation to the war. The politically expedient objective of satisfying peasant land hunger had to be balanced against the immediate national goal of increasing Russia's agricultural product. Since the process of implementing reforms would undoubtedly lead to a serious (though possibly only short-term) drop in productivity, and hence damage the war effort, fundamental changes had to be postponed.

Chernenkov suggested that the congress formally incorporate several basic principles into the party's program as a way of making their position clearer. Kadets ought to state that land should belong to those

---

[106] *VPNS*, No. 14-16, Aug. 31, 1917, pp. 12-13.
[107] *Ibid.*, pp. 18-20.

who worked it; and that local solutions should be applied for specific local problems. This was, in effect, the policy of Minister Shingarev. They might also endorse the preservation of communal tenure in regions where this was desired by peasants themselves; and while rejecting "nationalization," "socialization," or "municipalization" of land as "simplified slogans" for what had to be a complex pattern of reform, they could recognize the presence of "many partisans of nationalization" within their ranks, and make clear they were not advocates of "unlimited rights of property." One means of doing this was to support legislation guaranteeing the right of "perpetual use" in new lands granted to peasants by the state, thus satisfying land hunger without bestowing disposition rights on new holders. In any event, Chernenkov suggested, Kadets should reaffirm their support for forced expropriation of land from large landowners. In this way they themselves would "broaden" and "deepen" the revolution's commitment to the country's rural masses.[108]

This report, too, caused a furor, precipitating a discussion which went on for the better part of two days, and which sounded in the view of A. A. Spasskii very much like a meeting of the reactionary tsarist land commission on the eve of emancipation in 1860.[109] Now the sharpest criticism came from a group of conservative provincial delegates, and from Central Committee members like Vasili Maklakov and Fedor Rodichev, both of whom argued against even the general principle of transferring land to poor and landless peasantry on the unproved grounds that this would cripple production. For Maklakov, a reform of this sort was a political "luxury"; while Rodichev, focusing on the problem of rural stability (but avoiding the question of Stolypin's legislation or the further breakup of the commune), argued that the disruption he feared most was from the gentry, not the peasants, who would rise up in arms as an entire class against any large-scale effort to expropriate their lands.[110]

Here, clearly, the specter of counterrevolution was being used by Kadet leaders to defend privileged Russia and the liberal state against what seemed to be obvious popular demands. For some delegates, the speeches of Kadets like Rodichev and Maklakov constituted a full-fledged "scandal," revealing to the public an image of the party which conformed to the radicals' worst accusations. And again, D. I. Shakhovskoi spoke for a Central Committee minority, just as he had done at the seventh congress, rebutting Rodichev and Maklakov with arguments (also unproved) that small landholders were *more* productive in the aggregate than large estates. Others, like E. I. Kedrin, though himself

---

108 *Ibid.*
110 *Ibid.*, pp. 16-18.

109 *Ibid.*, No. 11-13, Aug. 10, 1917, p. 20.

a member of the hereditary nobility from Petrograd, went even further, demanding that land be given free to the peasants without any legalistic encumbrances.[111]

But when it came to voting, the conservative position carried on almost every point by more than 2 to 1. Delegates approved the idea of transferring land "in use" to the peasants with "special consideration" for the poor and landless, and introduced these concepts into Articles 36 and 37 of the party's program. But they rejected Gronskii's proposal that Article 36 read simply "Land ought to belong to the working agrarian population"; and voted 83 to 40 to add a number of "exceptions" to categories of land exempt from confiscation. There was also no change in the party's official position on compensating landlords whose property was taken; the majority beat back a proposal for the free transfer of land by 77 to 33.[112]

The agrarian debate and voting thus signified a very considerable division in the party's higher echelons on what was rapidly becoming a crucial issue of the revolution. More important for the future of Russian liberalism, it also showed the majority of Kadet party leaders defending vested agrarian interests. The party's new "official" platform was actually quite close to that of leading gentry groups, almost all of whom now recognized the inevitability of some changes in the countryside. Since Kadets reaffirmed the concept of forced expropriation, they were not, of course, presenting themselves as the mouthpiece of the gentry. But by failing to endorse more forceful reforms, as many delegates urged, the congress as a whole was defining a posture far removed from basic mass desires.

It was now quite clear, moreover, that this is what *nadpartiinost'* had come to mean generally at the eighth party congress. In Miliukov's demand that the revolution not be continued, in the Petrograd leadership's defense of Russia's "vital" international interests, in Kokoshkin's insistence on centralized state administration, in agrarian affairs, and finally, in the party's strong emphasis on law and order, Kadets at the eighth congress affirmed that liberal "nonpartisanship" was, in effect, a bulwark against change. Kadets thus openly reinforced a posture at their national congress, as they were increasingly doing on local levels, at odds with Russia's social context, where most Russians looked and hoped for immediate social and economic reforms, and where the strength of the new regime itself depended in large measure on massive popular support.

Many delegates to the eighth congress recognized this discrepancy, feeling, as one representative put it, a "tormenting anxiety" over the

111 *Ibid.*, No. 8-10, Jul. 20, 1917, pp. 13-20; and No. 11-13, Aug. 10, 1917, pp. 16-20.
112 *Ibid.*, No. 20, Sept. 28, 1917, pp. 8-15.

implicit conflict between "political responsibility" and mass pressure for reform.[113] And unquestionably, the Kadets faced a dilemma. An elemental mood of radicalism was affecting increasing numbers of Russians; and the critical question was whether basic liberal values had any relevance to the growing conditions of social, economic, and political disruption. If it were true that Russia's masses remained "politically unconscious" (as Nabokov maintained), that the "darkest Russian mass could not understand the present meaning of freedom" (as *Svobodnyi Narod*, the party's official paper in Petrograd, editorialized), that Russia was "drunk with revolution" (as Rodichev insisted), then "nonpartisanship" could be considered a responsible approach for Kadets even if it did mean the party's divorce from mass demands and further revolutionary development. On the other hand, if these fears were unfounded, if Russian workers did understand the principles of democracy and the need for social order, there was a better chance for liberal Russia to survive if party leaders made their own outlook compatible with mass desires, and in this way sought to broaden their constituency. But this clearly involved discarding many traditional values and established positions.

Just as in March, several Kadets at the eighth congress again urged their colleagues to take precisely this latter course, "merging" at least in principle with the left. E. N. Tatishchev from Tula insisted Kadets were divorcing themselves from both the revolution and the people, and warned that "a horrible responsibility" would lie on each party member unless the congress realized the left also represented principles of "statesmanship" and Russian "national interests."[114] Nekrasov, Shakhovskoi, Frenkel, and others supported the Petrograd Soviet's notion of "accountability," arguing it was an appropriate device for "organizing the real forces of the country," a means to allow the "peaceful evolution of Russia as a whole."[115] And D. N. Kvashnin-Samarin, from Tver, virtually pleaded with his colleagues to change their tactical orientation before it was too late:

Until now in Russia there has been no party based on genuinely broad support, only parties of the intelligentsia, or simple fictions and delusions. The Party of People's Freedom now has a great opportunity to become that broadly based group, perhaps even more so than the left parties, since we stand on fully democratic principles and recognize the absolute right of popular will without reference to class boundaries or other restrictions.[116]

[113] *Russkiia Vedomosti*, May 13, 1917.   [114] *Ibid.*
[115] *VPNS*, No. 4-5, Jun. 8, 1917, pp. 9-11.   [116] *Ibid.*, p. 13.

But Miliukov, Vinaver, and most Petrograd Central Committee members again held firm in defense of the Kadets' ostensible "non-partisanship," and argued in opposition to any tactics which might further "politicize" the authority of the Provisional Government. Now more than ever, law and order were the basis of effective government; and nonpartisanship, both at a local and national level, was the only "responsible" course to preserve the integrity of the Russian state. "Grave dangers" were threatening Russia "from the disruption of the army at the front and from internal anarchy." As a result of the April crisis, the threat to the regime from both right and left was intense; and so, implicitly, was the danger of civil war. National unity was the only means to avoid further chaos. Partisanship, and particularly a merger with the left, would lead to further polarization. The Kadets' proper place was still as a bridge of "statesmanship and responsibility" between right and left (though Miliukov himself defined it more precisely now as "left-center," since Kadet differences with the left were "not so much in goals as in the tactics to achieve them").[117]

Moreover, just as national unity was essential, so was that of the party itself. The existence of serious differences on programmatic issues could not lead, Miliukov insisted, to further divisions among Kadets without jeopardizing the stability of Russia as a whole. With a remarkable mixture of self-confidence and self-esteem, Miliukov thus continued to insist on the critical importance of liberalism for Russia's future, just as he had throughout long years of opposition to the tsar. Only now it was the country as a whole which had to appreciate the party's national purpose, rather than a faltering autocracy.

To a remarkable extent, most delegates agreed with these views, including those from the provinces like Podshibiakin from Baku, Mogilianskii from Chernigov, and Gurvich from Kiev province, who reflected the growing conservatism of provincial Kadet committees, and who attacked those in the party who would "emphasize the democratic aspect of the revolution over its national aspect."[118] Just before the congress ended, delegates elected a new Central Committee. With 223 persons voting, Miliukov and his closest associates—Vernadskii, Vinaver, Grimm, Kokoshkin, Gronskii, Adzhemov, Dolgorukov, Manuilov, Nabokov, Shingarev, and Kornilov—were all reelected to their posts with unanimous votes (or were only one vote shy, possibly their own). But concern for party unity was evidenced in the fact that each of the party's principal right- and left-wing spokesmen were also elected to the new Committee. Shakhovskoi, Nekrasov, Frenkel, Vinogradov, Svechin, Gerasimov, and Vasilev were returned from the "radicals"

117 *Ibid.*, pp. 7-8.   118 *Ibid.*, p. 10.

(with votes ranging from Shakhovskoi's 220 to Nekrasov's 173); and Rodichev, Maklakov, Tyrkova, and Izgoev were all reelected from among the party's prominent "rightists" (with votes here ranging from 221 for Rodichev to 174 for Izgoev). If one considers that 50 delegates refused to vote for Nekrasov, the most prominent left Kadet, and an almost equal number (49) refused to vote for Izgoev, who had contributed to the *Vekhi* critique of radicalism in 1909 and was one of the party's most outspoken conservatives, it is reasonable to assume that there were about the same number of "hard" right- and left-wing delegates, roughly 50 of each. (This would suggest, incidently, that the eighth congress included approximately the same proportion of party leftists as had the second and third party congresses in 1906, and the fifth gathering in 1907, a supposition supported in addition by the votes on the agrarian issues.) But in any event, a far more important fact is that almost all delegates voted for representatives of both viewpoints, like Shakhovskoi and Maklakov, thus following Miliukov's "unity" line to an impressive degree.[119]

There was also an almost even geographical distribution on the new Committee, although whether or not this was intentional is not clear. Twenty-two of the Committee's 66 members were from Petrograd, 17 from Moscow, and 27 were from more than fifteen different provinces (including Voronezh, Vladimir, Kursk, Tomsk, Kherson, Chernigov, Kazan, Astrakhan, Kharbin, the Don, and a contingent of 5 representatives from Kiev). In practice, however, Miliukov and the Petrograd group were bound to have the most influence on the party's national direction, just as in the past, since plenary sessions of the Committee were not frequently held.[120]

Thus reflecting their strong commitments to unity and balance, despite their often rancorous disagreements, the delegates to the eighth congress finally closed their sessions on a mixed note of hope and

[119] *VPNS*, No. 2, May 18, 1917, p. 11.
[120] The Committee elected at the eighth congress consisted of the following, listed in the order of most votes received: V. I. Vernadskii, M. M. Vinaver, D. D. Grimm, F. F. Kokoshkin, P. N. Miliukov, K. K. Chernosvitov, M. S. Adzhemov, S. V. Vostrotin, P. P. Gronskii, P. D. Dolgorukov, A. A. Manuilov, V. D. Nabokov, N. V. Teslenko, N. N. Chernenkov, A. I. Shingarev, N. I. Astrov, A. A. Kizevetter, A. A. Kornilov, F. I. Rodichev, F. A. Golovin, D. I. Shakhovskoi, P. V. Gerasimov, N. M. Kishkin, V. A. Maklakov, M. G. Komissarov, P. I. Novgorodtsev, D. N. Grigorovich-Barskii, N. N. Shchepkin, A. V. Vasilev, N. K. Volkov, V. A. Stepanov, V. A. Obolenskii, A. G. Khrushchov, A. V. Tyrkova, Z. G. Frenkel, N. P. Vasilenko, P. P. Iurenev, A. I. Makushin, D. D. Protopopov, I. P. Demidov, A. A. Dobrovolskii, E. M. Eshchin, Ia. K. Imshenetskii, N. N. Glebov, S. A. Levitskii, S. F. Oldenburg, F. R. Shteingel, A. N. Bukeikhanov, M. V. Sabashnikov, A. S. Izgoev, N. V. Nekrasov, D. S. Zernov, S. V. Panina, A. N. Ruttsen, V. A. Kharlamov, P. A. Sadyrin, V. A. Vinogradov, B. M. Ovchinnikov, G. B. Bykhovskii, A. K. Paramonov, M. D. Kalugin, A. A. Svechin, S. A. Ivanov, A. A. Shakhmatov, A. K. Dzhivelegov, G. M. Tumanov.

apprehension. While N. N. Kutler painted a gloomy picture of Russian industry, showing a drop in production in some areas of more than 40 percent (and blaming the "excessive demands" of workers for most of the trouble), Gronskii and Dolgorukov reported that much of what Petrograd was hearing about front-line troops was exaggerated. The soldiers were tired and wanted peace; but these feelings had existed for better than two years, and were not really impairing the country's ability to fight. Gronskii in particular was "completely convinced" that the new war minister, Kerensky, was making headway. And with normalcy returning to the army, Russia would win a military victory. After this, Miliukov concluded with a summation of the "intensive and productive" work of the sessions, exhorted the party to greater organizational efforts, and expressed the conviction that Kadets would now assume greater influence in practical affairs. He then declared the Congress adjourned.[121]

What emerged as the doors of the hall flung open was an assortment of well-dressed lawyers, professors, civil servants, and zemstvo administrators who considered themselves, despite their differences, the last best hope of Russian political moderation. As Miliukov himself said in evaluating the proceedings, the party's role remained essentially the same as it had been for eleven years: to preserve liberal values from adversaries on the right and left. And first among these values was now the integrity of the Russian state itself, whose territory was threatened with dismemberment by both foreign and domestic foes, whose hard won civil liberties were challenged by narrow-minded extremists, and whose future depended on the dispassionate willingness of the enlightened to elevate their culturally disadvantaged countrymen.[122] As the new order entered its eleventh week, the Kadets thus officially defined themselves anew as the "nonpartisan" defenders of Russia "as a whole."

121 *VPNS*, No. 20, Sept. 28, 1917, pp. 15-20.
122 P. Miliukov, "Itogi VIII s"ezda partii narodnoi svobody," *VPNS*, No. 2, May 18, 1917, pp. 1-4.

CHAPTER FIVE

The Politics of "State Consciousness"
In May and June

I N THE DAYS immediately following the eighth party congress, Petrograd Kadet leaders extracted an old weapon from their conceptual arsenal to explain their views to the country at large: the notion of *gosudarstvennost'*. The term is difficult to translate. Literally, it means "state system," "governmental organization," or even "statesmanship," but Russian liberals had traditionally used it to describe their *rechtsstaat* views: that law was the only effective basis of government; and that social stability required a general recognition of the ethical and moral bases of lawful behavior. Now, as Kadets continued their argument with Soviet leaders over the proper form of state authority and the meaning of coalition, *gosudarstvennost'* reappeared in the party press to characterize what Miliukov and others felt Russia most needed to avoid complete political disintegration and civil war: a new "state consciousness" among all classes and sectors of the population, a recognition that the country as a whole was in danger both internally and from abroad, and that the new coalition could preserve Russia's political integrity only if it acted "responsibly" and "lawfully." There could be no question of usurping the prerogatives of the Constituent Assembly by "illegally" reordering social and economic patterns, or nationality relationships. Nor could international commitments be violated. Socialist ministers in particular had to withstand the pressures of class and party demands, and recognize the importance of *gosudarstvennye* principles.

In effect, *gosudarstvennost'* corresponded on the level of state affairs to perspectives now underlying *nadpartiinost'* at the party level: a fear of the "mob," a desire to brake further social change and disruption, and an effort to combat increasing anarchy in government. It also bore a chauvinistic flavor, since established legal relationships generally supported Great Russian interests over those of minority groups like the Ukrainians; and it clearly implied continued strong support for the war. But most important, it represented a posture where popular needs and desires were subordinated to "state" interests, and where the new "democratic" coalition was pressured to reject popular demands.

Petrograd Kadet leaders supported their position in part by arguing that the principles of *gosudarstvennost'* were the only grounds on which the new coalition could prevent a counterrevolution from the right, something Rodichev warned about forcefully at the eighth party congress. In all likelihood, however, they exaggerated this danger in May. Miliukov himself admitted at the eighth congress that the right was "no real threat"; and events would reveal the meager powers of those hostile to the regime from this quarter. A much greater danger for Kadets lay in isolating moderate socialists from Russia's workers and peasants by forcing the coalition into unpopular policies, a process which Lenin and the Bolsheviks were only too anxious to encourage. Even if only to preserve national unity and civil peace, it was far more important for the regime to work cooperatively with the left than it was to mollify dissident gentry and bourgeois elements. If there was little chance for Kadets themselves to remain a dominant political force in the context of democratic politics without broadening their prerevolutionary constituencies, it was also unlikely that the coalition government itself could survive if it became too detached from Russia's popular mood.

In May and June, however, under the influence of Miliukov, Kokoshkin, Rodichev, and the party's *verkhovniki* in Petrograd, Kadets pursued the politics of state rather than popular consciousness, especially on the high level of cabinet affairs. In the coalition government, which now included the radical populist Victor Chernov as minister of agriculture, the Menshevik Skobelev as minister of labor, the Socialist Revolutionary Paul Pereverzev as minister of justice, and Iraklii Tsereteli, the spokesman of "revolutionary defensism," as minister of post and telegraph, Kadets pressed for policies of "stabilization" rather than reform, and insisted on the end to "arbitrary" acts by ad hoc groups like the soviets. According to the Central Committee, the order of the day was "to strengthen governmental authority," a task which required the "absolute refusal of all groups and organizations, without exception, to arrogate to themselves the right to issue directives which replace or alter acts of the Provisional Government, and which encroach on the area of legislation or administration."[1] Meanwhile, in Moscow, Petrograd, Kharkov, Kiev, Odessa, and scores of provincial cities and towns, party leaders began at a local level to prepare extensive campaigns in municipal duma elections on platforms designed to serve "the interests of Russia as a whole." Finally, in meetings of public organizations and local administrative bodies,

[1] *Rech'*, May 6, 1917.

Kadets mobilized all of their energies in support of a great military offensive, hoping with an increasing sense of desperation that "lasting freedom" would finally come with victory.

KADETS IN THE FIRST COALITION

On May 6, the Kadet Central Committee issued a formula for "statesmanlike" policies in a general resolution on the new coalition. Until the meeting of the Constituent Assembly, whose rapid convocation was the "surest means" of strengthening state authority, Russia needed "forceful measures" to assure order, and

> urgent measures having as their aim the establishment of a reasonable and expedient economic and financial policy, the preparation of land reform which transfers land to the working agricultural population, the protection of workers' interests, the development of local self-government, the proper organization of the judicial system, and the satisfaction of various other requirements of state administration.[2]

These tasks of government, in the Committee's view, imposed a "great responsibility on all citizens," particularly political leaders; their fulfillment would be impossible without a firm "state consciousness," that is, "an awareness of duty to the Motherland."[3]

The key words in this statement were "urgent," "reasonable," and "responsible"; and it soon became apparent that the key difference between Kadet expectations for the first coalition and those of many Soviet leaders lay in the distinction between "preparation" of reform, as opposed to implementation, and "protection" of popular interests, as opposed to the satisfaction of mass demands. Almost before the new ministers took their posts, these differences began to lead to problems. It also became clear that "urgent," "reasonable," and "responsible" had many meanings.

Difficulties emerged almost immediately in the area of industry and labor relations, an attenuation of problems the government had been facing for a number of weeks. Factory owners and labor leaders had been blaming each other for production difficulties since the beginning of March, as we have seen; and the task of the new coalition was not only to work out policies acceptable to both sides, minimizing class conflict, but just as urgently to find a way of meeting Russia's continued, drastic production and transport needs.

In the beginning of May, one major problem centered on the question of state regulation. In the various regulatory councils set up by the

2 *Ibid.*   3 *Ibid.*

tsarist regime during the war, labor representatives had been systematically excluded. They were granted only token voices in one or two groups like the War Industries Committees. The regulatory councils did manage to effect some coordination among Russian industries in the months before the revolution, but without much attention to labor needs.

Factory owners and manufacturers favored continuing the old regulatory system in the first weeks after the February revolution, partly because it guaranteed markets and profits with a minimum amount of risk. Minister of Trade and Industry Konovalov was also inclined to continue the prerevolutionary system, coming himself to the government as a prominent member of the War Industries Committee in Moscow. As we have seen, however, Menshevik economists like Groman and Cherevanin, working through the "Economic Section" of the Petrograd Soviet, pressed the first provisional cabinet in late March and early April toward a radical restructuring of state regulation, demanding in addition to a new centralized regulatory apparatus, the inclusion in administrative ranks of new and articulate labor representatives, and a drastic extension of industries under state control.

Konovalov's response was to disband the Special Council on Production, which was particularly onerous to the left, and shuffle personnel around somewhat in the remaining Special Councils on Fuel, Defense, and Transport. In most cases, however, new personnel came from the ranks of industry, usually through public organizations like the War Industries Committees, the Petrograd Society of Manufacturers, or the Trade-Industrial Union. The leadership of the Council on Fuel, for example, fell to Ia. D. Priadkin, a leading member of the South Russian Coal Producers Association; and P. I. Palchinskii, a talented administrator with close ties to leading Russian financial circles, became chairman of the Council on Defense. At the same time, as we have seen, Konovalov relied heavily on developing cooperative relations between management and labor through local factory and trade-industrial committees, and he pressed for voluntary cooperation on prices and wages. On March 29 he announced the government would "strengthen" regulatory work; and on April 23, largely as a result of his efforts, the provisional regime passed special legislation formally authorizing the extension of the workers' committee system.[4]

But Groman and other Soviet spokesmen continued to regard Konovalov as "protecting" industry interests. They noted the close relationship between government administrators and Russian com-

[4] P. V. Volobuev, *Proletariat i burzhuaziia Rossii v 1917 g.*, Moscow, 1964, p. 194; R. P. Browder and A. F. Kerensky, eds., *The Russian Provisional Government 1917*, 3 vols., Stanford, 1961, II, 718.

mercial circles; and they remained highly dissatisfied with the government's failure to take more stringent measures to regulate prices and profits. Toward the end of April, as Soviet leaders pressed for closer "control" over Provisional Government policies, they also began to insist more forcefully that regulation be used as a tool to improve workers' conditions, i.e., for social as well as economic purposes. And they argued that the government should forceably prevent factory closings which owners blamed on "increased expenses" and the shortage of materials, but which workers felt from past experience was a deliberate effort to keep their wages down.

The organization of the first coalition placed the whole question of "responsible" regulation in a new light. With their own "representatives" now in the government, socialist leaders saw regulation as a means to lay the foundations of a socialized economy, shifting the goal from efficiency in support of the war to domestic reconstruction. To offset the state councils, they encouraged new workers' "control" committees to involve themselves in regulatory questions, something Konovalov and his Kadet colleagues felt undermined government authority. In early May, consequently, liberals began a campaign to curtail workers' groups, and end forcefully the interference in production of "unauthorized" and "spontaneously formed" local organizations.[5]

The problem was made more difficult because the first coalition now included an independent Ministry of Labor under the energetic Menshevik internationalist Michael Skobelev. And unlike Konovalov and the Kadets, who equated "responsible" policies with those serving national interests, Skobelev specifically considered himself "labor's representative": he regarded his role as one of supporting the partisan demands of his labor "constituents," extending regulation so as to assure an equitable standard of living, and otherwise "guarding the interests" of Russian workers.[6] This left Konovalov even less able than before to restrain the growing anger of industrialists, greatly aggravating tensions.

In the meantime, productivity continued to decline. More than 125 new factories closed their doors permanently in May. Railroad shipments continued far below basic needs. And labor-management relations in a number of areas, particularly the Don basin and the Urals, reached critical proportions, with each side blaming the other for Russia's conditions. According to the Don worker Sandomirskii, for

[5] P. V. Volobuev, *Ekonomicheskaia politika vremennogo pravitel'stva*, Moscow, 1962, p. 147. See also the discussion in M. Ferro, *La Révolution de 1917*, Paris, 1967, pp. 385-98.

[6] *Izvestiia*, May 19, 1917.

example, who addressed the Executive Committee of the Petrograd Soviet in early May, employers were taking "no new steps towards reconditioning instruments and equipment so that production is becoming technically impossible. . . . Embezzlement of raw materials and products . . . is evident. Manufacturers refuse to provide food for workers and have permitted sanitation conditions to deteriorate to a dangerous point. The way has thus been paved for the cessation of production vital to the country."[7] But according to South Russian and Ural industrialists, high wages were already destroying capital reserves, the quality of production itself was at all-time low levels, supplies were short, and factories were closing because of a "situation absolutely bordering on industrial anarchy." The result, here and elsewhere in Russia, according to the industrialists, was "complete industrial disintegration."[8]

Pressed by even more radical left-wing elements to champion workers' control and the expropriation of private enterprises, Skobelev thought the "responsible" policy in these circumstances was to extend state involvement in production and to socialize enterprises. He wanted the government to regulate all profits and wages as a means of forcing pay increases without closing factories; and he wanted the government's promise to implement broad social reforms.[9] Konovalov and the Kadets argued to the contrary that owners would shut down rather than submit to increased regulation, using as evidence resolutions such as those from the Don and Ural executives. Also, the Kadet ministers felt the issue of socialization was specious, maintaining that workers themselves were not as interested in socialism as the leftist politicians, and desired simply the improvement of their material welfare.[10]

Recent research suggests the Kadets were not altogether wrong in their evaluation of worker concerns, but their response hardly dealt with the issue.[11] Without increased state regulation, much less socialization, it was hard to see how conditions would improve. If factory owners balked at new controls, Kadets should certainly have been willing to apply against them the "forceful measures" they spoke about

[7] Browder and Kerensky, II, 728.

[8] *Ekonomicheskoe polozhenie Rossii nakanune velikoi oktiabr'skoi sotsialisticheskoi revoliutsii*, 3 pts., Moscow-Leningrad, 1957-67, pt. 1, pp. 169-71, 174-80. *Promyshlennost' i Torgovlia*, No. 14-15, Apr. 29, 1917, pp. 265-69.

[9] Volobuev, *Proletariat*, p. 199.

[10] Volobuev, *Ekonomicheskaia politika*, pp. 172-82. Volobuev shows (p. 295) that the lack of fuel was causing many factory owners to close anyway, a problem which they could then blame for "ideological" reasons on government controls or worker demands. For some 568 factory closings between March and July, Volobuev attributes 375 (66%) to a lack of fuel.

[11] Ferro, pp. 399-409.

in early May in conjunction with illegal acts of workers. In fact, however, they called simply for "responsible" policies and a "sobering up of befogged minds," warning that the alternative was "death, destruction, misery, shattered credit, and a financial crisis provoking ruin for all" (a rhetorical ordering which might have suggested to some a curious hierarchy of values).[12]

Undaunted, the Petrograd Soviet demanded on May 16 the "immediate, total, and systematic" extension by the government of state control over the economy.[13] Two days later, throwing "consciousness of duty" aside, the besieged and frustrated Konovalov resigned. With Kadet archives still closed for 1917, the role other liberal leaders may have played in his resignation is unclear. It is possible that Miliukov, Izgoev, and other Petrograd Kadets urged the move as a means to pressure the left, as Miliukov had tried to do in April, and would do again in July. But directly involved or not, the Kadet leadership seized the occasion to issue a caustic blast against the left, insisting "the policies of a coalition government" could not "bear the character of the realization of demands from one class or other, or the implementation of party programs." Policies had to be "applied even-handedly in support of the most essential *gosudarstvennye* interests of the country."[14]

Shortly afterward, the task of imparting "responsibility," "legality," and "state consciousness" to the Trade-Industrial combatants fell on the shoulders of Kadet vice-minister Vasili Stepanov. Stepanov was an honest and intelligent liberal, with a good background in both legal and economic affairs. But in the words of a colleague, he was "a devoted slave" to Miliukov. Greatly sobered by events of the past weeks, like many of his comrades who had earlier felt some sympathy for radical programs, he took over the Ministry of Trade and Industry.

With typical liberal self-confidence, Stepanov also felt he knew what constituted "responsible" behavior. His test was the effect of any action on the war effort. If wage demands prompted the closing of factories with vital production, workers had to be repressed; if management stalled production, enterprises had to be more closely regulated by the state. Above all, what Stepanov considered the "anarchistic particularism" of various interest groups had to be controlled in favor of political stability and social order (though the new minister felt.

---

[12] *Vestnik Vremennago Pravitel'stva*, May 18, 1917.

[13] *Izvestiia*, May 17, 1917.

[14] *Rech'*, May 20, 1917. An editorial in *Promyshlennost' i Torgovlia*, No. 18-19, May 27, 1917, suggests Konovalov hoped in part to force the creation of an all socialist cabinet, thereby strengthening state authority and reducing the power of ad hoc workers' groups.

that it was labor, rather than management, which was guilty of causing disruption).[15]

Within a short period, Stepanov developed a specific program in conjunction with P. I. Palchinskii of the Council of Defense. In a memorandum presented to the government on June 8, he urged a series of measures designed both to end worker radicalism and reverse the disruption of industry. At their core was the demand that the government take a firm stand against socialism, a posture which had just been urged by a special conference of Trade-Industrial organizations in Moscow.[16] If this were done, and if the government was "especially sharp" in its denunciation of attempts to "socialize" individual enterprises, Stepanov felt the strength of socialist radicals would be weakened, while industrialists and manufacturers would be encouraged to put full effort into restoring their own plant operations. On the other hand, the regime also had to reject the demand of commercial capital for an immediate end to regulation and a return to a completely free economy. The main task in this regard was to determine the scope of necessary governmental intervention in each economic branch, and then determine the most appropriate control methods.[17]

Stepanov's concept of "responsibility" reflected a rapidly growing anti-labor sentiment in Kadet circles, signs of which were even finding expression in pamphlets challenging the patriotism and loyalty of workers as a whole.[18] By urging the regime expressly to reject socialism, he also hoped to encourage political support for the government on the part of bourgeois groups like the Petrograd Society of Manufacturers, some of whose members indicated they might acquiesce to increased regulation, providing workers' committees were curtailed and government actions had no anti-capitalist intent.[19] Socialist leaders were extremely critical of Stepanov, but his views were regarded as the

---

[15] See his speech to the Duma Committee on May 20, in A. Drezen, ed., *Burzhuaziia i pomeshchiki v 1917 godu*, Moscow-Leningrad, 1932, pp. 68-69.

[16] *Ekon. polozhenie*, p. 1, pp. 181-82.

[17] The memorandum appears in M. N. Pokrovskii, ed., "Ekonomicheskoe polozhenie Rossii pered revoliutsiei," *KA*, No. 10, 1925, pp. 86-94. An abridged translation is in Browder and Kerensky, II, 672-77. Stepanov also supported the formation of a special "Economic Council," which was discussed and endorsed by the Executive Committee of the Petrograd Soviet on May 16, and proposed to the government on May 27. An enabling statute was subsequently passed on June 21. The Council's specific task was "to prepare a general plan for the organization of the national economy, and of labor, as well as for the preparation of bills and general measures for the regulation of economic life." See Browder and Kerensky, II, 677.

[18] E.g., V. M. Shtein, *Nashi ekonomicheskiia i finansovyia zadachi*, Petrograd, 1917, esp. p. 12.

[19] *Zhurnal Zasedanii Sovet Petrogradskogo Obshchestva Zavodchikov i Fabrikantov*, June 6 and 15, 1917, as noted in Volobuev, *Ekonomicheskaia politika*, p. 39.

epitome of state consciousness by the two Kadet vice-ministers, Sophia Panina and Dmitri Shchepkin (who now attended cabinet sessions as representatives of the Ministries of Welfare and Internal Affairs) and by his fellow Kadet ministers, Alexander Manuilov and Andrei Shingarev.

Shingarev, in particular, valued the ideological thrust of Stepanov's program. The former Voronezh physician had moved over in the cabinet with the formation of the first coalition to the position of minister of finance; and in his new post he found Russia practically bankrupt. The only hope for relief were loans and credits pending from the Allies and the so-called Liberty Loan, a bond issue which the government had offered at the end of March. New taxes were imperative. And taking into consideration the impoverished state of the country's workers and peasants, Shingarev worked out legislation for new levies on individuals and enterprises with incomes or profits over 10,000 rubles. In the case of firms with very large profits, a new "extraordinary" tax was to be as much as 90 percent.[20]

As this legislation was enacted on June 12, Shingarev's main concern (and one that was well founded) was that resistance from the industrial bourgeoisie would further weaken the regime. This could be mitigated by adopting Stepanov's suggestions. If socialism was formally renounced, the regime would make clear that it was acting to preserve liberal values, that the "Motherland" as the bourgeoisie understood it was "on the brink of perishing," that *their* state system was in danger.[21]

Obviously, however, an official renunciation of socialism by the government was completely unacceptable to Chernov, Skobelev, and the socialist ministers. And indeed, it is difficult to see how Stepanov and Shingarev felt the government could possibly retain mass support if it appealed in this way to the bourgeoisie. After a brief but intense argument, the cabinet rejected Stepanov's plans. But the discussions themselves left new feelings of doubt and suspicion in the minds of all concerned.

These feelings were not assuaged, moreover, as Kadets in the government continued to pursue their "politics of state consciousness" in the critical areas of agriculture and nationality affairs. The nationalities issue emerged largely through the activities of the Ukrainian Rada and the National Ukrainian Congress, a representative body convened by the Rada to sanction its own authority and work out a

[20] *Zhurnaly Zasedanii Vremennogo Pravitel'stva*, No. 195, June 12, 1917. The actual rates were to be established by the chairmen of District Income Tax Offices. See also *Ekon. polozhenie*, pt. 2, pp. 400-401; Browder and Kerensky, II, 495-96.
[21] *Vestnik Vremennago Pravitel'stva*, May 25 and June 4, 1917.

draft statute for Ukrainian regional autonomy. Late in April, when delegates from the congress had visited Petrograd to discuss the project with government officials, they had received an extremely cool reception. Miliukov and Kokoshkin insisted in particular that federalism was not workable, that political autonomy based on a territorial unit was dangerous to Russian unity, and that the Ukrainians were not "prepared" for independence. As we have seen, these were also attitudes which the Kadets reaffirmed at their eighth party congress; and they were carried into the new coalition by Shingarev, Manuilov, and particularly Kokoshkin.

Kadet statism of this sort only reinforced Ukrainian nationalists in their separatist designs. "Unprepared" was an all-too-familiar denigration of Russia's popular masses, while Kadet opposition to federalism suggested to the Ukrainians only that Constitutional Democracy was at heart a chauvinist movement.[22] Late in May, consequently, the Rada formulated specific demands for Petrograd, convinced that further "preliminary discussions" were fruitless. These included a call for guarantees that the Ukraine would be represented at any international peace conference, permission to form separate Ukrainian army units, and the right to use Ukrainian tax funds at the Rada's own discretion.[23] On June 3, not surprisingly, the government rejected the Rada's demands, acting on the insistence of Shingarev, Kokoshkin, and the Kadets. The official argument was that the Rada was not a "legitimate" local government since it had not been popularly elected. Moreover, from the "formal as well as the tactical point of view" Ukrainian questions could be settled only by the Constituent Assembly.[24] At the same time, the Council of Ministers turned the question over to Baron Nolde's Juridical Commission for formal resolution. Two weeks later this Kadet-dominated body supported the government's decision with a statement corresponding exactly to the views of the party's own eighth congress.[25]

Here, too, consequently, Kadet policies in the government clashed with pressures for change. Suspecting the Ukrainians of collusion with the Germans, particularly on the question of forming separate army detachments, they equated federalism with disloyalty; and fearing the Rada's demands would be emulated by other minority groups, they insisted that the Juridical Council's decisions legally bound the Pro-

---

[22] A. Shul'gin (Choulguine), *L'Ukraine contre Moscou-1917*, Paris, 1935, pp. 111-13.

[23] S. M. Dimanshtein, ed., *Revoliutsiia i natsional'nyi vopros*, Moscow, 1930, pp. 143-49. See also Browder and Kerensky, I, 374-76.

[24] Browder and Kerensky, I, 376-77.

[25] P. Galuzo, ed., "Iz istorii natsional'noi politiki vremennogo pravitel'stva," *KA*, No. 30, 1926, pp. 51-55. The statement was signed by Kokoshkin, Maklakov, and Nabokov.

visional Government. Thus when the Rada issued its "First Universal" on June 10, declaring in effect its independent competency on all Ukrainian matters, Kadets felt the coalition's integrity "as a government" depended on the forcefulness of its response: unless the regime firmly contained the Ukrainians, every nationality group would feel free to act as it wanted; the war effort would be undermined; domestic strife would grow; and Russia's future as a great, unified state would be doubtful.[26]

In agrarian affairs, meanwhile, the perspectives and policies of Kadets in the first coalition ran directly counter to those of the new socialist minister, Victor Chernov, whose approach was to stress rather than obscure the new regime's socialist commitments. Chernov believed property in agriculture exploited Russia's peasants, pure and simple. He was also certain the only "responsible" agrarian policy was to transfer land to the peasants as rapidly as possible. As he told the All-Russian Congress of Peasants' deputies in May, "the only basis for right to land was labor."[27]

Most Petrograd Kadets profoundly distrusted Chernov. His internationalism in April had infuriated Miliukov, who despised him with a vengeance; and Shingarev had resisted leaving the agricultural ministry because Chernov would replace him. The SR leader, however, not only reciprocated the Kadets' dislike, but as a "socialist" minister, seemed to take every opportunity to contradict their views. He argued to the Peasants' Congress, for example, that the concerns of the state itself should actually play very *little* role in agrarian affairs. Instead, "the very working out of new legislation, its very preparation [had] to come from below, from the land, from the voice of the people themselves."[28] This horrified Kadets like Miliukov, Stepanov, and Kokoshkin: it totally disregarded the rights of the gentry and romanticized the peasants, who simply did not understand legal principles or concepts, and in no sense could be expected to work out an equitable solution to the land problem on their own.

Moreover, with an attitude reminiscent of their position in the First Duma, Miliukov and his colleagues were also convinced that for all the efforts expended by zemstvo statisticians, basic questions concerning agricultural productivity in the spring of 1917 were still unclear. How much extra land was available for redistribution, how readily peasant cultivators could absorb new acreage, and what effect agricultural

---

[26] *Rech'*, June 14, 1917; *Svobodnyi Narod*, June 25 and 27, 1917.
[27] V. Chernov, *Zemel'nyi vopros*, Petrograd, 1917, p. 7; see also his *The Great Russian Revolution*, trans. P. Mosely, New Haven, 1936, esp. chap. 8.
[28] Chernov, *Zemel'nyi vopros*, p. 34.

reforms would have on Russia's already drastic food shortages were all questions to be thoroughly investigated by the government's Main Land Commission, and presented to the Constituent Assembly. In any event basic reforms had to be postponed until the end of the war in fairness to peasant soldiers, and to avoid further disruptions at the front.[29]

In contrast, Chernov felt agricultural productivity could be increased if land and equipment were transferred rapidly from landlords to peasants. While responsible enough to realize the need to postpone formal reforms until the Constituent Assembly, he was also unwilling to intervene when peasant groups issued "revolutionary" statements supporting "in principle" the immediate expropriation of gentry estates. And in mid-May, he tried to place a moratorium on land transactions in general as a means of preventing landlords from adding new mortgages to their land, or otherwise encumbering their holdings to prevent expropriation.[30] The Kadets in the government vigorously opposed Chernov on these issues, despite the fact that precisely such a moratorium had been proposed by several left-wing provincial party members at the seventh and eighth Kadet congresses. Shingarev, Stepanov, Manuilov, and their colleagues in the cabinet argued that this not only violated an owner's inherent right to dispose of his property, as the Juridical Commission had ruled on a number of individual cases, but also that it threatened to wreck the financial underpinnings of most general production.[31] On May 17, however, apparently at Chernov's instigation, the socialist minister of justice P. N. Pereverzov ordered a halt to the notarization of land transactions, achieving Chernov's goal in an indirect way.[32]

In sum, Kadets felt Chernov (and other socialists) were using their positions in the government to "broaden" and "deepen" the revolution regardless of official state policy. When Chernov spoke to the Peasants' Congress (which Kadets rightly assumed was a political organization convened by the Socialist Revolutionary party to cultivate an alliance with local peasant leaders),[33] Kadets felt he was deliberately trying to break down social order in the countryside, undermining the very principles of *gosudarstvennost'* which they were trying to establish. In

[29] See the series of articles by V. A. Obolenskii in *Svobodnyi Narod*, beginning with June 8, 1917.

[30] I. G. Tsereteli, "Rossiiskoe krest'ianstvo i V. M. Chernov v 1917 g.," *NZ*, No. 29, 1952, pp. 231-37.

[31] *Ibid.*

[32] *Ibid.*, pp. 226-28. See also Oliver Radkey, *The Agrarian Foes of Bolshevism*, New York, 1958, pp. 255-57. The measure was later retracted.

[33] V. Gurevich, "Vserossiiskii krest'ianskii s"ezd i pervaia koalitsiia," *LR*, No. 1, 1923, pp. 177-78.

some ways, moreover, liberal fears were well founded. When the Peasants' Congress resolved that "all land, without exception, must be given to the land committees . . ." and that government policy should be based on the principle of transferring all land, without compensation, to the possession of the state "for equitable and free use by the peasants," many peasants did, in fact, assume that estates in their villages had been *legally* transferred to them, and forcibly seized them.[34]

All of this made Kadets in Petrograd and elsewhere exceedingly anxious about convening the Constituent Assembly. Since the beginning of March, Kadets had publicly insisted the Assembly was the only legitimate means of establishing permanent state authority, and urged its rapid convocation. These sentiments were repeated at the seventh and eighth party congresses, and officially reaffirmed by the Central Committee in its statement on the new coalition in early May. Yet with increasing suspicions concerning the goals of socialist politicians, and with popular radicalism reinforcing long-time doubts about the political maturity of the Russian people, Kokoshkin and other Kadets involved in the Special Commission on the Constituent Assembly found themselves in a growing quandary. On the one hand, they felt the Assembly was desperately needed as a stabilizing and legitimizing force; on the other, they worried whether it could be fairly elected, and whether it would support the interests of the state as a whole (never mind the Kadets' own program), given the conditions in which Russia found herself. These were extremely serious questions for Kadets, who thought of the Assembly not in terms of immediate social or political objectives, but "to determine Russian history for the next one hundred years."[35] Unless the Assembly was elected fairly, and regarded as "legitimate" by Russians of all classes, it would be worse than futile, a legislative "false Dmitri" whose decrees would provoke resistance and probably civil war.[36]

These fears were reflected in the great importance Kadets attached to the Special Council, which Fedor Kokoshkin, as its chairman, finally convened at the end of May. A number of factors caused this initial delay in the Council's work, including objections to the preponderance of Kadets in its membership.[37] But the Council proceeded very slowly

[34] *Ibid.*, p. 190. See also M. Martynov. ed., "Agrarnoe dvizhenie v 1917 g.," *KA*, No. 14, 1926, pp. 205-206; Tsereteli, "Chernov," pp. 224-31. The resolution of the Peasants' Congress appears in Browder and Kerensky, II, 597-98.

[35] *Stenograficheskii otchet osobago soveshchaniia dlia izgotovleniia proekta polozheniia o vyborakh v uchreditel'noe sobranie*, Sess. 1, May 25, 1917, col. 7.

[36] I. A. Il'in, *O sroke sozyva uchreditel'nago sobraniia*, Moscow, 1917, passim; K. N. Sokolov, *Uchreditel'noe sobranie*, Petrograd, 1917, passim, both publications of the Kadet Central Committee.

[37] *Den'*, May 11, 1917.

even after it convened because Kokoshkin and other liberal officers felt every issue deserved full discussion. Minor substantive questions such as whether the Imperial Family should have a vote became tests of the Assembly's commitment to major principles like universal suffrage; and the desirability of a proportional electoral system had to be analyzed in terms of the sociology of Russia's electorate. Debates on such issues were often rancorous, sometimes so much so that delegates walked out. Also, delegates concerned with other "urgent" matters often met only briefly, and then dismissed. Chairman Kokoshkin pleaded with the Council's members to attend sessions regularly, and to work with "extreme speed." But his primary concern was that all issues be thoroughly analyzed, and that the group avoid hasty decisions.[38]

Historians have sometimes victimized Kadets on the issue of convening the Constituent Assembly. The argument usually is that Kadets knew they would fail to gain much popular support for their candidates, and therefore wanted the elections postponed.[39] In fact, the issue is more subtle. Commitments to Russia's "national interests" and the principles of *gosudarstvennost'* prompted Kadets to proceed carefully. The Assembly had to be legitimate and authoritative, as Kadets understood these concepts, or it would fail in its purpose, regardless of composition. Above all a situation had to be avoided in which the Assembly took a radical position on the war, ignoring what Kadets like Miliukov regarded as crucial foreign concerns, and abrogating firm moral commitments to the Allies. What was disingenuous about the liberal approach in May and June was the party's constant public recognition of the need to convene the Assembly rapidly, while its own representatives worked with such exactitude as to force a delay. Most Kadets in fact hoped "rapidly" meant "at the end of the war."

PROBLEMS OF INCREASING SOCIAL POLARIZATION

While Kadets debated Russia's future "for the next one hundred years," a wave of social violence was sweeping the country, adding enormously to their concerns. As we have seen, serious incidents had occurred as early as late March and the beginning of April; but in May, in the aftermath of the April crisis, Russia seemed plagued by an epidemic of lawlessness. Many occurrences were quite dramatic. On

[38] *Steno. otchet*, Sess. 3, May 30, 1917, cols. 154-55; Sess. 6, June 2, 1917, and passim.

[39] E.g., Lionel Kochan, "Kadet Policy in 1917 and the Constituent Assembly," *SEER*, XLV, Jan. 1967, pp. 183-92, who also notes other literature on this question. Kokoshkin's call to the members to speed up their work appears, e.g., in Sess. 10, June 14, 1917, col. 631.

May 16, dissident sailors took over the fortress of Kronstadt, forcing the resignation of Victor Pepeliaev, the Kadet commissar, and refusing for a time to recognize the authority of the national regime. Anarchists sacked the newspaper *Russkaia Volia*, and set up an armed stronghold in the old Durnovo mansion in Petrograd. And on the Black Sea, sailors mutinied against Admiral Kolchak.

But it was the rapidly increasing number of "common" incidents that worried Kadets most: desertions at the front, assaults and the destruction of machinery in industrial areas, and attacks on landlords. In March, peasant "uprisings" were reported in only 34 districts (*uezdy*); by the end of April this number had increased almost fivefold, to 174; in May it grew to 236; and in June, to 280.[40] Meanwhile, according to the Petrograd Society of Manufacturers, acts of violence in industry were creating an "industrial catastrophe with headspinning rapidity."[41] Whether or not this description was accurate, a column listing acts of "anarchy" moved from the back pages of *Novoe Vremia* to the front in early June, and even the Soviet organ *Izvestiia* began sounding notes of alarm. When the Bolsheviks announced major demonstrations against the "bourgeois ministers" for June 10, Petrograd Kadets expected a full-scale riot. According to one sympathetic commentator, anxieties reached a "feverish" level.[42]

The importance of this disruption can hardly be underestimated; indeed, it gives unique tones to the whole course of revolution in 1917, and also to the civil war. In May and June, however, it served as well as a sounding board for the success of Kadet policies in the government. Obviously party leaders did not precipitate the breakdown of "law and order," and it would be absurd to thrust on them the burden of responsibility for Russia's condition. But their policies in both the first and second provisional cabinets were designed expressly to restore social stability, increase economic efficiency and production, and reinforce state authority. Clearly they were not succeeding.

Strong differences of opinion were growing within the party as to why this was so. Many in the Petrograd Kadet leadership continued to blame the government's failure on the partisanship of Soviet leaders, the "underdevelopment" and "low cultural level" of the Russian people, and particularly, the ubiquitous "committee": the ad hoc soviet, peasant group, or factory organization which attempted to deal on a local level with specific local problems. Miliukov, Kokoshkin, Shingarev, Stepanov, Maklakov, Tyrkova, and others despised these latter

---

[40] *Krest'ianskoe dvizhenie v 1917 godu*, Moscow, 1927, pp. iv-vi.

[41] *Ekon. polozhenie*, pt. 1, pp. 165-66.

[42] Boris Gurevich, "Krasnyi sfinks (vospominaniia)," MS in the Columbia Russian Archive, n.d., bx. 1, p. 366.

organizations not only because socialists were using them to their own partisan advantage, but also because they often acted in complete disregard of government directives, undermining national authority.

Ironically, one group of committees which many Kadets regarded as particularly troublesome, and which illustrate the problem of social disruption in May and June—the local land committees—were established when Shingarev himself was minister of agriculture. They were originally intended to gather new data for reform proposals, while at the same time acting to settle minor local disputes.[43] But under pressure from the peasants themselves (and encouraged by soviet leaders like Chernov), the committees in a number of places were now developing in a far more radical way than Shingarev and Kadets had intended. They were setting new regulations for rents, mortgages, the use of forests, the sharing of implements and livestock, and even the management of land "not being fully exploited" by its owners.[44]

Often, decisions reached by the local committees in specific cases were appealed to the Main Land or Juridical Commissions in Petrograd and overturned, only to be implemented afterward in complete disregard of the formal decision. A typical case was that decided by the Iablonovskii *volost'* land committee, which heard a report on June 11 from peasants in the village of Svistovskii that the landlord Otreshkov was not plowing his fields or spreading manure. The committee, "in the interests of using the land in the best possible way," decided the peasants should themselves work Otreshkov's fields, which they did. Thereupon the landlord appealed to the Main Land Commission, which decreed that the local decision was illegal. But the Iablonovskii committee, on hearing the new order, determined itself that "all acts of Svistovskii peasants were correct, and not in violation of any laws."[45]

Hundreds of similar cases developed in May and June. Although the Kadet-dominated Juridical Commission repeatedly insisted that landlords had the right to use their property as they saw fit, its rulings were generally ignored.[46] In Kursk province peasants decided "not to consider valid any lease concluded without the participation of land committees"; in Tambov, the provincial land committee reduced all rents by 50 percent; and elsewhere, in Riazan, Voronezh, Kharkov,

---

[43] The creation of land committees was not a new idea in 1917. They were proposed by Popular Socialists and Trudoviki in the State Duma as early as 1906 as a means both of preparing reforms and working out economic relations in the transition period. Kadets simply adopted the prevailing approach to the problem. See the tendentious but still useful essay by N. K. Figurovskaia, "Bankrotstvo 'agrarnoi reformy' burzhuaznogo vremennogo pravitel'stva," *IZ*, No. 81, 1968, pp. 23-67, esp. p. 29.

[44] P. N. Pershin, *Agrarnaia revoliutsiia v Rossii*, 2 vols., Moscow, 1966, I, p. 301.

[45] *Ibid.*, pp. 262-63.   [46] *Ibid.*, pp. 301-02.

Poltava, and Vitebsk, the committees themselves collected rent to hold in escrow until the land reform question was determined.[47] Meanwhile in Vologda province, local committees were already ordering the transfer of land and forests to the peasants;[48] in Kursk, the provincial committee on June 16 ordered all land to the control of local district committees;[49] and in Penza, local officials reported to Petrograd that peasants were treating small landholders and those who had been granted separate holdings through the Stolypin reforms (*otrubniki*) in exactly the same way they were treating the very largest landlords, demanding a share of their fields and the right to use their implements.[50] Following Chernov's speeches to the Peasant Congress, moreover, when a number of local land committees tried to prevent peasants from seizing estates they now thought "belonged" to them, the committees themselves were reorganized and became more radical.[51]

Yet while Stepanov, Rodichev, Tyrkova, and others both in Petrograd and the provinces regarded this process as clear indication that Russia's revolution had been "premature," other Kadets still felt local organizations like the land committees were a possible means of bringing political control into areas where authority was weak. At the same time, they could act like the old zemstvos to cultivate an understanding of democratic processes. The various "Committees of Public Organizations" had been a start of sorts in this direction in March and April; and it was precisely this "zemstvo mentality" which underlay the decision of Shingarev and others to establish land committees in the first place. In the view of men like Nekrasov and Shakhovskoi, the task now was for the government to *learn* from the local organizations, and for the Petrograd Kadets to break out of the cocoon of "high state politics" in which Miliukov and others invested so much of their concern.

Having himself authorized workers' committees on the railroads to assume supervisory control of their lines in his official capacity as minister of transport, Nekrasov in particular continued to argue that authority could only be strengthened in Russia through popular allegiance, a condition which required mass participation in committee activities, and the development of a close correspondence between committee and government goals.[52] Early in June, he and several other long-time left Kadets even attempted to form a new liberal organization on the basis of these ideas, "deeply patriotic and supportive of an evolutionary path towards moral, national, non-class

[47] *Ibid.*, pp. 364-66.
[49] *Ibid.*, p. 281.
[51] Pershin, I, 353-56.
[48] *Ekon. polozhenie*, pt. 3, p. 283.
[50] *Ibid.*, pp. 284-89.
[52] *Vestnik Putei Soobshcheniia*, No. 25, 1917, p. 270; *Izvestiia*, May 30, 1917; *Rech'*, June 8, 1917.

socialism."[53] Calling themselves the "Union of Evolutionary Socialism," their goal was again to create a close union of left-liberals and moderate socialists oriented toward the masses, without, however, breaking their ties to the Kadet party.[54]

Shingarev, Miliukov, Stepanov, and other Central Committee members could hardly have disagreed more with this "populist-liberal orientation" in May and June. Ordinary Russians were "completely unprepared" for the role of government and administration, and any attempt to thrust it on them was simply "utopian."[55] One major effect of the politics (and ethos) of state consciousness, consequently, was the further division of the Kadet party itself. Again, the precise lines of division are unclear. Unquestionably, most party members still supported Miliukov and the majority leadership in Petrograd; if anything, the wave of urban and rural violence moved provincial committees even more to the right in May and June than they were in April, as gentry figures like the landlord Otreshkov joined the party in increasing numbers. But Kadets of both viewpoints could still be found in Moscow and Petrograd, as well as in the provinces. And the greater Russia's problems in this regard, the more men like Astrov and Kishkin in Moscow, Shakhovskoi and Frenkel in Petrograd, Krol in Ekaterinburg, and Braikevich in Odessa questioned the wisdom of continued intransigent opposition to Soviet programs.

This "conciliationist" tendency among some Kadets was reinforced in May and June by the fact that incidents of anarchy and violence reflected the growing polarization of Russian society at large; far from producing national unity, Kadet policies seemed only to be galvanizing elements of Russia's traditional right, giving hope to conservatives and reactionaries who might otherwise have more readily acquiesced to the necessity of fundamental change, and pressing moderate socialist leaders to the left, forcing them to defend their official posture of cooperation with the Kadets against radical assaults. Socialist Revolutionaries like Nicholas Avksentiev and Abram Gots, for example, and even Mensheviks like Tsereteli and Skobelev were finding themselves in increasingly tenuous positions. While as concerned as the liberals about anarchism and social disintegration, they had to remain sufficiently radical to keep their leadership positions in the Soviet. But when Konovalov resigned, and when Kadets like Shingarev, Miliukov, and

[53] Gurevich MS, bx. 1, p. 344.

[54] *Ibid.* See also V. V. Komin, *Bankrotstvo burzhuaznykh i melkoburzhuaznykh partii Rossii v period podgotovki i pobedy velikoi oktiabr'skoi sotsialisticheskoi revoliutsii*, Moscow, 1965, pp. 210-11; Iraklii Tsereteli, *Vospominaniia*, 2 vols., Paris, 1963, II, 155.

[55] See, e.g., Miliukov's June 3 speech to the Duma deputies in Drezen, pp. 91-109; Gurevich MS, bx. 1, p. 364.

Kokoshkin pressed the government to oppose Soviet views, not only were they accused of "collusion" with the bourgeoisie—"cooptation" is the term in current fashion—but the tasks of the coalition as a whole were made more difficult, and thus more vulnerable to radical attack.[56]

These problems were dramatically illustrated at the First All-Russian Congress of Soviets in June, where socialist ministers were called to account for their actions. From the opening session, when Abramovich and Martov roasted the ministers for the expulsion from Russia of Robert Grimm (a Swiss pacifist accused of peddling German peace offers), the moderates were on the defensive. The 105 Bolshevik delegates constituted little more than 12 percent of the Congress, but coupled with left SR and radical SD factions, they were more than enough to raise the question of whether the socialist ministers were, in fact, supporting revolutionary interests. They also set the background against which Lenin could assert the Bolsheviks were ready to take state power.[57]

Responding to the left's assault, Tsereteli, Skobelev, and other moderates sounded almost like Kadets. According to the Menshevik minister of post and telegraph, it was impossible for responsible workers to press for an eight-hour working day under present conditions. "Everyone understands that this is an anxious time, a dangerous time. It is necessary to save the country. Workers must be ready to work more than eight hours a day."[58] Similarly, Skobelev's speech on Russia's economic condition might have been given by Shingarev or even Konovalov, whom he had so angered with his circulars when minister of labor. In his view, "the situation [was] such that the entire country, its entire economic life, was heading toward derangement."[59] Only Chernov, playing on widespread anti-war feeling among the delegates, bitterly attacked liberals for "their" war, and picked up the radicals' applause by "jokingly" declaring he stood on the side of those who wanted to solve economic problems by arresting factory owners.[60]

Yet political necessity forced Tsereteli, Skobelev, and other moderates to encase their views in radical frameworks. When Lenin posed the question "Do we go backward or forward?" in a fiery speech on June 4, Tsereteli and the moderates insisted they *were* going forward: "From the moment we entered the government," Tsereteli countered,

[56] I. Shteinberg, *Ot fevralia po oktiabr' 1917 g.*, Berlin, 1919, p. 36; *Izvestiia*, May 21, 1917. See also the interesting introduction by Ia. A. Iakovlev, *Pervyi vserossiiskii s"ezd sovetov rabochikh i soldatskikh deputatov*, 2 vols., Moscow-Leningrad, 1930-31, I, esp. p. v.

[57] *Pervyi vserossiiskii s"ezd*, I, 65.

[58] *Ibid.*, p. 221.

[59] *Ibid.*, p. 228.

[60] *Ibid.*, p. 97.

"we have prepared the ground through constant agreement with democratic organizations so that economic measures can be worked out and implemented in forms most favorable to all democratic strata. . . ."[61] This, of course, was insufficiently radical for the Bolsheviks; but it seemed the height of irresponsibility to many Kadets. Tsereteli was making the development of firm state authority dependent on the satisfaction of mass demands, and openly admitting he regarded the congress as a "revolutionary parliament" with the right to formulate state policy. Thus while Nicholas Sukhanov insisted the Soviet Congress was coming apart at the seams, torn by radical-moderate fissures, Miliukov and his supporters in the Kadet Central Committee were convinced it was usurping all-Russian authority.[62]

Meanwhile, the Kadets' opposition even to moderate socialists served as a lightening rod for more traditional right-wing groups. Toward the end of April, the former president of the Duma, Rodzianko, organized a rump group of conservative delegates from all four State Dumas into a "private conference" to discuss the political situation, and generally offer a right-wing critique. For a time, Kadet leaders had little to do with this group, and vice versa. But Miliukov's ouster, Konovalov's resignation, and the general growth of social disorder in May produced a kindred gloom. It was at a Duma conference on May 4 that Maklakov suggested that Russia had received more freedom than she could absorb; and on May 27 and June 3, Miliukov and Victor Pepeliaev took the lead at a Duma meeting in denouncing the "hideous" situation at Kronstadt and the "counterrevolutionary danger from the left."[63]

Just as during the tsarist regime, moreover, the old Duma leadership was again thinking of itself as a vehicle for political "opposition," this time, however, as the rallying point for right-wing forces. On June 16, the arch-reactionary Vladimir Purishkevich suggested that the Duma alone was the sole organ of Russian state authority, urging it move to the cossack capital of Novocherkassk "where there is sufficient strength to guarantee its existence."[64] And insofar as Miliukov shared the Duma platform with reactionaries like Purishkevich, who desper-

[61] *Ibid.*, pp. 62, 76.

[62] Sukhanov, *Zapiski*, IV, 305; *Izvestiia*, June 3, 1917; *Svobodnyi Narod*, June 4, 1917; *Rech'*, June 9, 1917.

[63] P. Miliukov, *Rossiia v plenu u tsimmerval'da*, Petrograd, 1917, pp. 38-39; Drezen, pp. 73, 91.

[64] Drezen, p. 127. Also, in a speech to the Duma group on May 4 (Drezen, pp. 14-15), Shulgin left the clear impression that only if the socialists fought to save Russia could they avoid a "stab in the back." See also A. I. Guchkov, "Iz vospominanii," *Posledniia Novosti*, Nos. 5665 and 5668, Sept. 27 and 30, 1936; V. V. Komin, "Kontr-revoliutsionnaia deiatel'nost' gosudarstvennoi dumy posle sverzheniia samoderzhaviia, mart-oktiabr' 1917 goda," *Uchenye Zapiski Kalininskogo Gosudarstvennogo Pedagogicheskogo Instituta*, No. 34, 1963, pp. 205-306.

ately wanted to preserve the old estate system of government, Kadets themselves could not help but become increasingly a political magnet for the right.

Anti-soviet sentiment was also linked increasingly to the Kadets through other groups. In some fourteen or fifteen provinces, an organization calling itself the "Union of Landowners" was organizing "in defense of private property and the estate system."[65] V. V. Meller-Zakomelskii, N. A. Melnikov, and others involved with this group were well-known monarchists, with close links to the Duma. But they secured the support of Grigorovich-Barskii, chairman of the Kadets' Kievan District organization and a Central Committee member, and thus had ties to Kadets. While Chernov was engineering to suspend land transactions, organizers of the Landowners Union were planning nationwide opposition, and scheduling their own All-Russian Congress for the first of July.[66]

Long-standing Kadet contacts with trade-industrial groups were also growing increasingly strong, particularly in Moscow among those associated with Riabushinskii's Trade-Industrial Union. According to the Soviet historian V. Ia. Laverychev, local committees of this Union came to work so closely with Kadets in May and June that it became impossible to tell them apart.[67] This view is exaggerated, since industrialists like Tretiakov, Buryshkin, Riabushinskii and others still kept their political independence, and in many cases, Trade-Industrial committees were planning to run their own candidates in the forthcoming local duma elections, in competition with the Kadets. But as Stepanov and other Kadet leaders took up the industrialists' cause, opposing regulation and wage demands, and insisting on a restriction of factory committees, ties between the two groups grew increasingly close not only in Moscow, but also in many other cities and towns. Each looked increasingly to the other for support against the left.[68]

Here, again, there were unforeseen effects on the politics of state

[65] O. N. Chaadaeva, "Soiuz zemel'nykh sobstvennikov v 1917 g.," *KA*, No. 21, 1927, p. 97.

[66] *Ibid.*, pp. 97-101. See also O. N. Chaadaeva, *Pomeshchiki i ikh organizatsii v 1917 godu*, Moscow-Leningrad, 1928, pp. 81-85; and A. V. Shchestakov, ed., *Sovety krest'ianskikh deputatov i drugie krest'ianskie organizatsii*, Moscow, 1929, pp. 136-75. The Union had also had a brief existence in 1906-07.

[67] V. Ia. Laverychev, "Vserossiiskii soiuz torgovli i promyshlennosti," *IZ*, No. 70, 1961, pp. 35-60.

[68] *Rech'*, June 3, 1917. In the first week of June, for example, the First All-Russian Congress of Representatives of Industry and Trade demanded—just as Stepanov was about to do—that the government recognize that "no economic organization other than capitalism is possible in Russia," and that "all attempts to create a partially socialistic regime in isolated firms are both harmful and doomed to fail." See *Ekon. polozhenie*, pt. 1, p. 181; *Promyshlennost' i Torgovlia*, Nos. 20-21, June 10, 1917, pp. 365-68.

consciousness. If we examine the social composition of the Central Committee elected at the eighth Kadet congress, it is clear that the party's leadership had changed very little in background or social affiliation since before the revolution. At least 58 of the Committee's 66 members had professional, rather than commercial or other occupations, a percentage just as high as at any other time in the party's history; 16 were attorneys or jurists, 19 were professors (many of law), 4 were doctors, and at least 10 were professionally associated with zemstvo activities as statisticians, agronomists, or economists. And while some were individuals of great wealth (N. N. Shchepkin, for example, owned property in Moscow valued at 30,000 rubles, and some 10,000 desiatins of land), most were of relatively modest means.[69]

But increasingly in May and June, the relationship between the Kadets' strong support for law and order and the defense of established class interests and privileges seemed clear. Property owners calling for a "rule of law" to protect their holdings and manufacturers declaring the "absolute inadmissibility of yielding to workers' demands" were echoing Kadet themes.[70] In Bakhmut, Vladikavkaz, Kiev, and other places, printers' unions refused to print Kadet newspapers and pamphlets with statements of this sort because they "offended" the revolution; elsewhere, local soviets regarded gentry and industrial groups as if they themselves were Kadet organizations.[71]

Moreover, the growing association between Kadets and groups like the Union of Property Owners and the Duma Conference was not only one of program and political philosophy. As the revolution inexorably drove a deeper and deeper wedge between Russia's old privileged elements and her masses of workers and peasants, the Kadets' position was also increasingly defined by such matters of "affect" as style, social bearing, and even appearance. Evidence on such matters is hard to come by, but early in May, one clear indication emerged when the Central Committee in Petrograd allotted the enormous sum of 20,000 rubles to support a private club, the rules of which left no question but that the party's leadership wanted a meeting center far removed from any "revolutionary" atmosphere. Membership was limited to 200-250 persons, and was almost entirely male (there were only two women among the 66 members of the party's new Central Committee). Constituent members were either recognized officials of the party, Central Committee members, former Kadet Duma delegates or members of the district committees. Other persons could be-

[69] Shchepkin's estate was probably the largest of Kadet Central Committee members. His was a distinguished old Moscow family; his mother was a Stankevich.
[70] *Utro Rossii*, May 9, 11, 1917; *Ekon. polozhenie*, pt. 1, p. 523.
[71] *VPNS*, Nos. 6-7, June 22, 1917, pp. 12-13.

come members only on the recommendation of at least 15 persons. Annual dues were set at 25 rubles.

While one should not exaggerate the political significance of restrictions such as these, it is obvious that few workers or ordinary peasants could possibly feel comfortable in such surroundings; and when one considers that similar places were also established in Moscow, Kiev, Odessa, and scores of other cities and towns, as well as on a district level in Petrograd itself,[72] it seems clear that Kadets were barricading themselves from popular currents not only in terms of policies and values, but also by means of their own party structure. As focal points of local Kadet activity, these clubs contrasted sharply to Bolshevik meeting spots or those of other socialist groups; and in effect, they allowed the "bourgeois" label to fit with increasing appropriateness on a party that still insistently defended its *nadklassnost'*. Even a special article in the party's *Vestnik* "officially" denying that the Kadets represented any particular class could not contradict a growing "bourgeois" image.[73]

There were two ironies in this. One was that many genuinely conservative groups felt little real comradeship toward the Kadets. For monarchists and prerevolutionary nationalists, liberals were an old nemesis, as demonic to the autocracy and traditional Russian institutions as the Bolsheviks now were to the revolution. Also, Rodzianko and others still resented Miliukov's opposition to preserving the Duma in February and March; and were particularly annoyed in May and June by the pretentious moralizing of Kadets like Rodichev, who reproached them for holding "obvious" class interests, and for outright attacks on the Duma conference by party leaders like Nicholas Astrov.[74] Many industrialists, moreover, resented the Kadets' tax policies and opposed even the tentative efforts made by liberal ministers in the direction of state regulation.[75] They also strongly objected to statements from Kadets like Shingarev, who told a press conference on May 30 that "propertied classes ought to understand that in the present situation, for the good of the state, it is necessary to sacrifice some of one's holdings."[76] The Union of Landowners, meanwhile, although appearing to left-wing observers to work hand in glove with the Kadets, was actually mounting a concerted effort in opposition to the

[72] *Ibid.*, No. 3, May 25, 1917, p. 8.

[73] A. S., "O burzhuaznosti," *VPNS*, No. 1, May 11, 1917, pp. 8-9.

[74] Drezen, p. 129; Gurevich MS, bx. 1, p. 344.

[75] *Ekon. polozhenie*, pt. 1, pp. 243-75; *Promyshlennost' i Torgovlia*, No. 14-15, Apr. 29, 1917, p. 265.

[76] *Vestnik Vremennago Pravitel'stva*, May 31, 1917. See also Volobuev, *Ekonomicheskaia politika*, p. 316.

party's program for agrarian reform.[77] As we shall see, bonds with privileged Russia were strong enough to discredit the Kadets among workers and peasants; but they would also prove too weak for the party to coordinate any effective conservative action.

The second irony was that just as Kadets appeared to be shedding their "non-class" image on a national level, many local party leaders were beginning election campaigns for city and town dumas with a firm restatement of the party's basic principles, which the eighth congress had reaffirmed. By the third week of June, there were more than 230 local Kadet committees; and in conditions of increasingly open partisanship, the party's task politically was to consolidate as much strength as possible throughout the country. Yet despite fears and reservations, and their own increasingly conservative bias and image, most Kadet groups still officially entered the local election process as the party of Russia's "state interests" and the "welfare of the people as a whole."[78]

The May and June Election Campaigns in Petrograd and Moscow

Serious work on the local duma election campaigns began after the eighth congress in early May, when Vinaver, Nekrasov, Nabokov, Shingarev, Miliukov and other Central Committee members began systematically to visit local party committees and stir campaign efforts. The first important elections were scheduled for Petrograd (May 27-29) and Moscow (June 25); but campaign activities were also getting underway in scores of other cities and towns.

In a typical locality, the Central Committee members found local Kadets grouped around their clubs, with little organization and a lack of adequate means for political agitation. In some places, such as Rostov, local party leaders thought this might actually be used to advantage, since Kadets would appear as a "fresh" force, while better organized leftists were already wearing out the public's patience.[79] There was also a tendency for local party groups to exaggerate their popular following. Reports of peasants urging the postponement of agrarian reforms or of workers favoring increased productivity were taken as indications of liberal support. So were demands for a vigorous military offensive. Liberal newspapers in the provinces repeatedly pointed to "facts" such as these, and spoke enthusiastically of "tides

[77] Chaadaeva, *Pomeshchiki*, pp. 96-97, 120-27; *Rech'*, June 1, 1917; *Novoe Vremia*, June 21, 1917.
[78] *VPNS*, No. 6-7, June 22, 1917, p. 14.   [79] *Rostovskaia Rech'*, May 20, 1917.

turning" in the Kadets' favor. The only areas in which the party felt it was having serious difficulty were Siberia and the Ukraine, where questions of regional autonomy were assuming paramount importance.[80]

Party committees were loosely organized even in Moscow and Petrograd. (One district committee in Petrograd, for instance, felt it could not work effectively until it secured space for its own local "club"; it delayed electing a permanent district bureau until July!) But there was still considerable local enthusiasm, and in actually campaigning, Kadets used all of the standard Western procedures—*po-amerikanskii*, as one commentator described it. They rang doorbells, distributed placards and posters, and held street-corner rallies. In one Petrograd district a "Kadet Day" was proclaimed, with parades and demonstrations. Moscow Kadets also issued their own special election newspaper, *Moskvich Izbiratel'*. So extensively, in fact, did Kadets cover buildings and tramways with their green banners and posters that the Socialist Revolutionary journal *Zemlia i Volia* suggested they were running scared.[81]

This was close to the truth, but for different reasons that *Zemlia i Volia* implied. Particularly in Petrograd, party leaders were nervous primarily because the political need to rouse popular feelings and win votes contradicted the national need for order, stability, and an end to particularism. There was no doubt that questions like the war, land reform, and the "deepening" revolution would determine the vote. But when Kadets tried to win support with moderate, disciplined appeals on these issues, they had either to rely on platitudes, which most other parties also accepted, or argue in a negative way against particular class or group demands.

Throughout Russia, for example, the party's municipal programs supported goals that would "serve all Russians equally, without regard to class." In Kharkov, the program began with a declaration of support for local self-government (something the elections themselves were going to provide), and went on in favor of "reconstruction" of run-down areas, increased medical assistance, better schools, a more extensive local court system, and new marketplaces. There were also suggestions for "protecting" labor which involved better vocational

[80] Particularly good reports on local party activities appear in *Narodnaia Svoboda* (Nizhni-Novgorod), May 20, 1917; *Odesskii Listok*, June 4, 1917; *Sibirskaia Rech'*, May 24, 1917; *Rech'*, May 16, 1917; *Russkiia Vedomosti*, June 15, 1917, and *VPNS*, No. 8-10, July 20, 1917, pp. 20-21.

[81] *Zemlia i Volia*, June 11, 1917. *Moskvich Izbiratel'* also worried the Social Democrats, who noted in *Proletarii*, June 10, 1917, that its appearance would force them to work harder.

training and the organization of a municipal employment bureau.[82] In Nizhni-Novgorod, the Kadets announced they were supporting a "more just" distribution of taxes, improvements in cultural well-being, better educational facilities, and a number of "measures for the protection of labor interests," none of which was clearly specified.[83] And in Petrograd itself, Kadets emerged in favor of improving city welfare ("struggle with smoke and dust"); education ("the most rapid introduction of universal, free, and obligatory education"); city services ("further development of the tramway network"); and more equitable tax legislation. Above all, local Kadets insisted they were concerned "with the legitimate interests of all citizens," an approach which represented the best traditions of Russia's liberal intelligentsia, but hardly held much promise in terms of winning vast numbers of new party supporters.

Compounding the problem, Kadet speakers frequently approached their audiences in a condescending way, lecturing *po-intelligentskii*, and irritating educated and uneducated listeners alike.[84] Difficulties were hardly lessened, moreover, when Miliukov published a new article in *Vestnik Evropy* which again justified Russia's need for Constantinople and the Straits, arguing that "even a significant part" of cultured society was not "sufficiently prepared" to understand Russian national interests.[85] Problems of rapport with the public also increased as tensions grew between the party's leadership and the Petrograd Soviet; and they came to a head in the Moscow campaign in mid-June, when Kadet fears prompted a panicky opposition to city-wide "solidarity" demonstrations scheduled by the Soviet for June 18, the last Sunday before the elections. At scores of gatherings on that date, absent Kadets lost an important campaign opportunity.

Here, in a capsule, was the whole dilemma of practical liberal politics, caught in the swirl of revolutionary change. Committed to civil freedom and the interests of Russia as a whole, yet fearful of social distintegration and the power of an unleashed mob, Kadets could only reach out hesitantly for support, urging the virtues of what they saw as unselfish national commitment. As in 1906, the election campaigns themselves were further polarizing Russian society, with left and right extremists becoming more and more virulent in their criticism and attacks. For Kadets to adjust their tactics for the

---

[82] *Izvestiia Khar'kovskogo Komiteta Partii Narodnoi Svobody*, No. 3, May 21-27, 1917.

[83] *Narodnaia Svoboda* (Nizhni-Novgorod), June 3, 1917.

[84] E.g., *Novoe Vremia*, May 25, 1917; *Sibirskaia Rech'*, May 23 and 24, 1917; *Proletarii*, June 20, 1917; *Vlast' Naroda*, June 17, 19, 21, 1917.

[85] P. Miliukov, "Konstantinopol' i prolivy," *VE*, Nos. 4-6, 1917, p. 525.

sake of mass appeal would again be, in the eyes of party leaders like Miliukov, Nabokov, Kokoshkin, and Vinaver, to encourage the very disintegration they desperately hoped to control. Yet the more moderate and principled their approach, the easier targets they became for partisan opponents. In Petrograd by the end of May, radical groups were already translating the implicit conceptions of April into public charges of Kadets as the "enemy of the people."[86] Shortly afterward, in Moscow, the journal *Proletarii* began insisting that the Kadets wanted city duma seats to "stop the revolution and liquidate the organs of revolutionary self-government."[87] Even moderates like the Popular Socialists found it expedient to attack Kadets; a writer in *Vlast' Naroda*, for example, declared his "shame" that so many of his party's followers had joined Kadet ranks in the past.[88]

Yet, rather than forcing a consolidation of the anti-Soviet camp, these attacks also prompted bourgeois groups and Kadets to stress their separate identities: the former, to avoid unnecessary hostility from workers; and the party, to reaffirm its *nadklassnost'*. For example, Kadets in the Vyborgskii district of Petrograd insisted their primary goal was to "disprove" accusations about their "bourgeois orientation," while groups like the "Union of Homeowners," "The League of Freedom and Order," and the "United Apartment Dwellers" found it expedient to organize separate slates.[89] As Ia. B. Dimanshtein wrote in support of the Trade-Industrialists, the bourgeoisie knew that "the Russian population could only be effectively organized at this moment on the grounds of defending their own social interests and only in this fashion could they enter political life," a tactic which at least in Petrograd precluded joining slates with Kadets.[90]

Party leaders were also extremely nervous that elections proceed without illegal acts of coercion and intimidation. This may even have mattered as much to some Kadets as the number of votes the party received, since the Constituent Assembly—and thus Russia's future—depended on electoral legitimacy. As a referendum on national issues, as a means of ascertaining party strength, and as a test of the country's political sophistication, the elections thus represented a heavy investment. And on almost all of these grounds, neither the Petrograd nor

[86] E.g., *Vpered*, June 23, 1917; *Trud*, June 7, 11, 1917; *Proletarii*, June 24, 1917; *Pravda*, May 25, 27, 1917.

[87] *Proletarii*, May 20, 1917.

[88] *Vlast' Naroda*, June 17, 1917. In the issue of June 21, E. D. Kuskova also leveled a heavy broadside against the Kadets, accusing the party of joining with Nationalists and Octobrists, and betraying the liberal movement.

[89] *VPNS*, No. 2, May 18, 1917, pp. 14, 20; No. 4-5, June 8, 1917, pp. 4-6.

[90] Ia. B. Dimanshtein, *Torgovo-promyshlennyi klass i uchreditel'noe sobranie*, Kharkov, 1917, p. 5.

Moscow voting was destined to give Miliukov and his supporters much cause for satisfaction.

In Petrograd, balloting was originally scheduled to last three days, starting on May 27. Procedures were so complicated, however, that two districts postponed their votes for a week. As a consequence, many Kadets were naturally suspicious of results in districts that did vote. And when the returns began coming in, doubts were increased when they showed substantially fewer votes for Kadet candidates than party leaders had hoped and expected.[91]

Standing in all twelve Petrograd districts, the Kadets received only 171,745 votes, or 21.9 percent of the total 784,910 votes. This compared to 61 percent of the total for Petrograd in the First Duma elections, the most open of Russia's prerevolutionary campaigns, and 58 percent in the Fourth Duma elections, when the Social Democrats also ran a strong campaign but received only 20 percent of second curia votes. In contrast, the united bloc of moderate socialist parties, standing in only ten of Petrograd's twelve districts, now gained 347,053 of the total ballots cast, or 44.2 percent. And the Bolsheviks themselves secured 159,936 votes, or 20.4 percent. Moreover, Kadets failed to gain a majority in any one of what they thought were their four strongest districts, the Petrogradskii (where they won only 21.8 percent of the total), the Spasskii (28.9 percent), the Rozhdestvenskii (30.5 percent), and the Kazanskii (where they received 42.5 percent, and made their best showing). And in the Vasilevskii district, where the university was to have given Kadets support, they actually lost to the Bolsheviks by 2 to 1. The only real satisfaction Kadets could gain from the balloting, in fact, was that minor socialist parties and competitive nonsocialist groups did most poorly. Complete returns by district are given in Table 1.

Without information on such factors as voter awareness, absenteeism, age participation, and the like, it is very difficult to analyze the Petrograd returns with any degree of precision. But we can say what the returns *seemed* to indicate, particularly to observers in 1917. Moderate socialist spokesmen were delighted with what they took as a vote of confidence. According to the Socialist Revolutionaries, the election meant an end to Kadet influence in Russia; according to the Mensheviks and Plekhanovites, voters had decisively rejected Bolshevik defeatism (despite that party's impressive showing in some districts), and Lenin taught "an excellent lesson."[92] But most important, the Petrograd vote suggested general support for the policies of the Soviet,

[91] See my article "The Russian Municipal Duma Elections of 1917," *Sov. Stud.*, XXI, Oct. 1969, pp. 131-63.

[92] *Zemlia i Volia*, June 2, 1917; *Edinstvo*, June 2, 1917.

TABLE 1. PETROGRAD DISTRICT DUMA ELECTION RETURNS
(Popular Vote by District)

	Socialist Bloc	SR	Trudovik-Popular Socialist	Bol-shevik	Men-shevik	Radical Democrat	Kadet	Minor Non-Socialist[a]
Admiralteiskii	11,105			2,983			4,503	340
Aleksandro-Nevskii		41,363	1,282	8,737	7,246		9,116	574
Kazanskii	9,253			2,219			9,382	1,223
Kolomenskii	22,726		998	6,035		237	10,241	389
Liteinyi	30,583			5,085		617	22,507	631
Moskovskii[b]	41,517[c]			6,758			21,667	
Narvskii	73,293			18,202			12,625	2,272
Petrogradskii	72,750			30,348		754	29,323	1,170
Rozhdestvenskii		16,729	1,897	2,944	19,045		18,126	617
Spasskii	16,832		3,378	4,945		569	10,885	972
Vasilevskii	49,293			37,377		631	19,299	2,375
Vyborgskii	19,701		867	34,303			4,071	
TOTALS[d]	347,053	58,092	8,422	159,936	26,291	2,808	171,745	10,563

SOURCES: *Rech'*, June 3, 8 and 9, 1917; *Novoe Vremia*, June 2 and 9, 1917. Returns in other newspapers vary slightly. See, e.g. *Delo Naroda*, June 1, 2, 8, 9, and 16, 1917.

a Includes Trade-Industrial Group, Nonparty groups, and *Domovladel'tsy.*
b Known to be incomplete.
c Includes totals for Trudoviks and Popular Socialists though these parties were not in the bloc.
d Total votes cast: 784,910.

and the socialist ministers in the first coalition. Voters were repudiating the Kadets, and rejecting the party's politics of state consciousness.

For Petrograd Kadet leaders themselves, however, the numerical results only reinforced suspicions about procedure, and the whole question of the suitability of partisan politics. With circular logic, Petrograd Kadets also explained their failure in terms of the low cultural level of Russia's people, and thus emerged from electoral combat even more elitist than before. In every district, Kadets believed "irregularities" had occurred. In some areas, voters simply did not understand what to do, and in addition to their own ballots, cast large numbers of proxies; elsewhere, there were not enough candidate lists (which became ballots when dropped by voters into the urns), and hence restrictions on freedom of choice.[93] Most important, there were widespread reports of excesses against Kadets: candidates being manhandled, party bureaus being ransacked, electors being harassed.[94]

93 *Novoe Vremia*, May 28, 1917.
94 E.g., *Russkiia Vedomosti*, May 30, 1917; *Novoe Vremia*, May 30, 1917; *Rech'*, May 30, 1917.

How much of this actually occurred is less important than the fact that many Kadets believed the elections were unfair. In particular, Miliukov's supporters were alarmed by the degree to which the Bolsheviks had apparently mobilized the garrison vote. If the soldiers could be so easily manipulated, the whole question of holding elections to the Constituent Assembly during the war was even more troublesome than Kadets had suspected.[95] Paradoxically, however, the very irregularities of the voting in Petrograd gave liberals an excuse for minimizing their losses. New elections would soon occur in Moscow, according to the stricter procedures of the Provisional Government's April 15 statute. (The Petrograd vote was on the basis of a special decree enacted in March.) Under better conditions of "law and order," Kadet policies would "undoubtedly" be supported more strongly. In the final analysis, *Rech'* therefore told its readers, the Petrograd elections did not give "any real basis for pessimism."[96]

This relieved the party of any necessity to change campaign techniques. As a consequence, despite real differences in the past between Moscow and Petrograd Kadets on questions of political involvement and tactics, party members plunged into campaign activities in Moscow almost exactly as they had in Petrograd, despite the outcome of earlier balloting. Again, national issues became the center of attention, and again familiar rhetoric was heard: radical socialists were for "deepening and broadening the revolution"; Kadets were for "controlling anarchy" and "strengthening government authority"; moderate socialists were for "organizing revolutionary democracy" and "strengthening class and civil consciousness."[97] When Kadets began publication of *Svobodnyi Narod*, their new "official daily," on June 1, its lead article by Miliukov, "How to Conclude the War Most Rapidly," offered only the Kadets' established imperatives: hard work, postponement of sectarian demands, increased military activity, ultimate victory.[98]

The one significant difference between Moscow and Petrograd Kadets in their approach to the elections had to do with allying with Trade-Industrial groups. In Petrograd, where Shakhovskoi and Nekrasov still prodded for closer alliances with the socialists, most local Kadets groups had campaigned entirely on their own, without overt

---

[95] *Svobodnyi Narod*, June 1, 1917.   [96] *Rech'*, June 2, 1917.

[97] See, e.g., the Kadet pamphlet *Ocherednyia zadachi moskovskoi gorodskoi dumy*, Moscow, 1917, pp. 1-3; the Menshevik Internationalist pamphlet by M. Kakhiani, *Kogo izbirat' v gorodskiia i raionnyia dumy?*, Moscow, 1917, pp. 1-5; *Proletarii*, May 20, June 4 and 6, 1917; *Zemlia i Volia*, June 11, 1917; *Vpered*, June 13, 1917; *Trud*, May 30, 1917; and *Vlast' Naroda*, June 14, 1917.

[98] *Svobodnyi Narod*, June 1, 1917.

assistance from recognized bourgeois groups like the Petrograd Society of Manufacturers. But in Moscow, building on close associations of long standing, Kadets moved toward an open alliance with Riabushinskii's Union of Trade Industrialists. P. A. Buryshkin and S. N. Tretiakov, for example, both became official Kadet candidates, despite some protests from local party members; and so did the former minister of trade and industry, A. I. Konovalov, who was now considered one of Russia's most prominent bourgeois spokesmen, particularly by groups on the left. Partly as a result of the Kadet–Trade-Industrialist alliance, preelection debates became more focused in Moscow as the campaign progressed. Moderate socialists seemed to scramble to avoid appearing too liberal; and Bolsheviks launched into impassioned attacks against all of their opponents, particularly after the start of the military offensive on June 18, which, as we shall see, increased for moderate socialists the uncomfortable appearance of collusion with Kadets. Toward the end of the campaign, Bolshevik printing shops even censored the Kadets' *Moskvich Izbiratel'*, turning it out with large blank spaces; and again, Kadet leaders worried about the "fitness" of Russian workers and peasants for democratic procedures.[99]

When the balloting here was completed on June 25, moreover, it was again the Kadets who suffered the greatest disappointment. Gaining only 108,781 of Moscow's 646,560 votes (16.8 percent), the liberals found themselves running behind the Bolsheviks in 17 of the city's 53 election districts, behind the Mensheviks in 16, and behind both in 13. In 32 districts, moreover, the Kadets gained less than the combined Menshevik and Bolshevik totals. The Socialist Revolutionaries, with 374,885 votes (58.0 percent) were clearly most successful. Then, after the Kadets, came the Mensheviks (76,407, or 11.8 percent), the Bolsheviks (75,409, or 11.7 percent), the Popular Socialists (8132 or 1.3 percent), Plekhanov's Edinstvo (1506 or 0.2 percent), and the Liberal Democratic Union (1440, or 0.2 percent). This compared with First and Second Duma election results for Kadets in Moscow of 63 percent and 54 percent, and Third and Fourth Duma returns in the second curia of 61 percent and 65 percent, though now, of course, more than 20 times the number of voters were participating in the elections in both Moscow and Petrograd. Detailed returns for the Moscow elections are presented in Table 2, although for the sake of convenience, results from some smaller adjoining electoral districts have been consolidated. The returns here and for Petrograd can be compared with those for some districts in the State Duma elections by referring to Chapter 1, above.

[99] *Russkiia Vedomosti*, June 23, 1917.

TABLE 2. Moscow Municipal Duma Election Returns, June 1917
(Popular Vote by Major District)

	Kadet	Popular Socialist	SR	Menshevik	Bolshevik	Edinstvo	Liberal Democratic Union
Alekseevskii	704	38	5,311	934	918	4	9
Arbatskii	7,354	566	8,897	1,720	500	155	52
Basmannyi	4,069	289	10,890	2,245	2,393	46	66
Blagushinskii	845	30	8,068	2,354	2,605	7	15
Bogorodskii	560	54	2,401	2,090	720	6	12
Butyrskii	1,431	72	5,922	1,377	1,603	24	25
Cherkizovskii	1,356	33	8,544	1,204	1,516	8	24
Dorogomilovskii	1,090	49	9,045	1,174	539	12	24
Gorodskoi	1,146	81	3,392	340	259	13	17
Iakimanskii	5,177	304	14,349	2,883	2,302	65	114
Iauzskii	4,622	480	7,726	1,437	1,151	80	44
Khamovnicheskii	4,805	408	16,128	3,896	3,078	66	57
Lefortovskii	4,765	253	22,418	6,054	9,934	27	78
Marino-Roshchinskii	706	47	10,040	2,643	2,208	10	74
Meshchanskii	10,584	784	37,597	8,668	5,808	149	77
Miasnitskii	4,673	500	9,796	1,441	529	69	44
Novo-Androvskii	861	29	11,515	3,107	1,788	14	46
Petr-Presnenskii	2,442	202	16,209	2,009	7,271	64	22
Petr-Razumovskii	635	109	4,108	432	347	15	7
Piatnitskii	5,546	426	20,207	3,568	3,244	51	60
Prechistenskii	7,564	555	8,628	2,608	731	106	59
Presnenskii	6,336	415	29,830	4,935	2,878	97	116
Rogozhskii	5,737	436	22,713	3,479	3,025	49	64
Serpukhovski	3,052	246	17,396	3,966	10,589	18	41
Simonovskii	697	49	9,892	1,074	1,941	5	41
Sretenskii	4,826	382	12,340	1,801	1,344	71	38
Sushchevskii	10,078	721	30,417	7,310	5,295	168	147
Tverskoi	7,120	574	11,108	1,658	893	107	67
TOTALS	108,781	8,132	374,885	76,407	75,409	1,506	1,440

SOURCES: Adapted from A. Ul'ianov, *Pervye demokraticheskie vybory v moskovskuiu gorodskuiu dumu*, Moscow, 1917, pp. 40-42; *Russkoe Slovo*, July 2, 1917; *Russkiia Vedomosti*, June 28, 1917.

NOTE: Total votes cast: 646,560. Totals differ somewhat in different newspapers and various other sources. Elsewhere the Kadets are given 115,051, the SRs 359,875, the Mensheviks 80,896, and the Bolsheviks 73,386, but the above totals now appear to be most nearly accurate. I am grateful to Diane Koenker for pointing out some discrepancies in the district totals and for helping me sort out the figures in general.

In sum, Russia's first elections of the revolutionary period showed Kadets with a staggering loss of city influence and prestige in their two strongest centers of past support. Hope that the party could build on its earlier urban constituencies in Moscow and Petrograd and retain its virtual monopoly over the official affairs of both cities had obviously proved futile; and what this might mean in the all-Russian Constituent Assembly vote, with all of Russia's peasants and workers participating, was frightening for Kadets to contemplate.

It was not, moreover, simply the extent of the socialist triumph, but the degree to which the moderate socialist vote represented defections from the traditional liberal camp. In district after district in Moscow and Petrograd, elements who were earlier considered firmly liberal voted for SRs as the *force majeure* behind the coalition regime, the party which in May and June appeared to be Russia's most significant political entity. In Moscow, SRs may also have ridden a short-lived wave of enthusiasm for the government which developed, as we shall see, after the start of the June offensive, and also benefited strongly, as Professor Radkey has pointed out, from close ties which still existed between Moscow and Petrograd workers and soldiers (particularly garrison troops) and Russia's peasants in the countryside. As Radkey reports, the SRs promise to give "Land and Liberty" to the peasants proved enormously popular even in Russia's two largest urban centers.[100] What is most apparent, however, in an examination of the returns district by district, is that socialists overwhelmed Kadets even in parts of the city that were heavily bourgeois.[101] While district boundaries had been changed in 1917, and the social composition of particular areas was too fluid for electoral analysis by class, the Kadets themselves recognized their losses in "bourgeois" areas, and reacted despondently.

Again they tried to explain defeat in terms of the "underdeveloped state of Russia's political consciousness," and again they saw the passion for the immediate satisfaction of grievances as overwhelming any tendency toward cool-headed problem solving. "The larger part of the dark masses of people simply are not able to understand the present meaning of freedom," *Svobodnyi Narod* editorialized. "Freedom has been understood to mean the conquest of life for the use of the individual, and is not considered related either to a rule of law or the interests of the state as a whole."[102] In fact, the opposite was

[100] Radkey, *Agrarian Foes*, p. 241.

[101] For example, the Kadets expected to do well in the Arbat, where the SRs gained 8897 votes to their 7354, and in the fashionable Prechistenskii area, where the SRs gained 8626 to the Kadets' 7564. See Table 2.

[102] *Svobodnyi Narod*, June 21, 28, 1917. See also, *Narodnaia Svoboda* (Nizhni-Novgorod), July 1, 1917; *Rech'*, June 30, 1917; *Russkiia Vedomosti*, June 28, 1917.

probably the case. Kadets most likely lost even in "bourgeois" districts because moderate socialism appeared politically germane, and willing to satisfy popular demands.

"To Freedom Through Victory"

The only bright note for many Kadets in May and June came with the start of Russia's long-planned military offensive on the Galician front, just before the Moscow Duma elections. As the news broke, liberals all over the country momentarily forgot their deepening anxiety over the course of the revolution, and again felt some sense of exhilaration and hope. While Soviet leaders also welcomed the news, seeing the renewal of action at the front as an effective way to "defend the revolution" and bring the war to a close, the offensive served for many Kadets as a psychological crutch, an unreasoned hope that Russia's national interests would be saved, political wounds healed, and solutions found to social and economic problems. However great the country's domestic turmoil, and however weak the party's own popular support, Miliukov and his followers could at least feel that the "politics of state consciousness" had helped Russia toward what many regarded as the one great goal of the February revolution: military victory. To them the offensive represented a "noble fight for freedom."[103]

The agreement with Britain, France, and Italy to launch simultaneous operations in the spring of 1917 had actually been worked out at an inter-Allied conference at Chantilly in November 1916, and confirmed at a second conference in Petrograd shortly before the Provisional Government took power. According to the general understanding, Russian troops would strike not later than three weeks after the Allies had launched their attack in the West. Despite some reservations within the high command, Miliukov, Shingarev, and other Kadet leaders had enthusiastically taken up the idea from the first days of the revolution. Miliukov in particular carried on an energetic propaganda barrage in its behalf, partly because the idea of a general offensive fit in with his plans for Constantinople and the Straits, and partly, as we have seen, because Buchanan, Paleologue, and the other Allied ministers suggested Russia might lose her place at the peace conference unless she met her military obligations.

The offensive also had political value. The commitment of troops to battle was a way of generating patriotism, consolidating support for the authority of the Provisional Government, smothering social con-

---

103 E.g., V. Ia. Ulanov, *Vsem kto protiv voiny*, Moscow, 1917, pp. 2-4, and passim, a publication of the Kadet Central Committee.

flict, and triggering a new willingness for sacrifice. It also justified Kadet desires to postpone social reforms, and even to delay the Constituent Assembly. Nekrasov, Shakhovskoi, and possibly even Nolde on the Kadet Central Committee may have doubted the political advantages of the offensive in April and May, but their reservations were not mentioned publicly. And there were no objections whatsoever to the pro-war, pro-offensive resolutions passed by the eighth party congress. As *Svobodnyi Narod* editorialized in its lead issue of June 1, Kadets everywhere were convinced that military victory was the most rapid means to peace and freedom, and that rapid peace was crucial to Russia's economic and political future.[104]

With the exception of militant internationalists like Lenin, who opposed the offensive entirely, Soviet leaders were also motivated as much by domestic concerns as by considerations of military strategy. For War Minister Kerensky, the offensive was "dictated absolutely by the inner development of events in Russia." For the "sake of the nation's life, it was necessary to restore the army's will to die." ("Forward to the Battle for Freedom!" he rallied the troops. "Forward . . . to death!"[105]) Tsereteli and Skobelev were less hyperbolic, but neither acted in May to change what had become full-scale military planning. *Izvestiia*'s insistence on May 17 that it was the *possibility* of an offensive that was being planned rather than an offensive itself was apparently simply a device for quieting anti-war radicals.[106]

Moreover, a close review of the liberal press in May and June suggests a reason why Kadets and moderate socialists may have expected the offensive to succeed, despite all that was known about problems of discipline, morale, and supply. For every piece of evidence that front-line troops opposed the war, there was another declaring the soldiers were ready "to die in defense of freedom." *Novoe Vremia, Rech'*, and other papers filled their columns in May and early June with resolutions from units ready for the offensive; while even the Conference of

---

[104] *Svobodnyi Narod*, June 1, 1917. Similar editorial views were expressed in *Promyshlennost' i Torgovlia*, No. 20-21, June 10, 1917, pp. 363-68.

[105] Alexander F. Kerensky, *The Catastrophe*, New York, 1927, pp. 195, 207.

[106] *Izvestiia*, May 17, 1917. The Soviet was, of course, actively attempting at this time to organize an international socialist conference at Stockholm to discuss peace conditions; and as Rex A. Wade points out in his *The Russian Search for Peace*, Stanford, 1969, Russia was actually presenting to the outside world two separate policies and two separate agencies of implementation, the government and the Petrograd Soviet (p. 50). At the same time, however, no one within the government was seriously considering a separate peace. According to Tsereteli, "no government could lead the country on the path of a separate peace without suppressing by armed force the opposition of a majority of the population. The idea of a separate peace was rejected by all social opinion of the country, without regard to political tendencies" (*Vospominaniia*, I, 380). For a different perspective, see V. S. Vasiukov, *Vneshniaia politika vremennogo pravitel'stva*, Moscow, 1966, chap. 2.

Delegates from the Front, which met in Petrograd in the middle of May, expressed its support for a "mighty army" and its willingness to fight.[107]

Most of this was sheer bravado. In some cases, the very speeches and resolutions seized upon by liberals as evidence of the army's desire to fight were only verbal retorts to the Kadets' own charges of cowardice and malingering.[108] In others, it was a case of Kerensky's indiscriminate enthusiasm blurring reality in a whirl of frenzied speeches and reports.[109] Newspaper accounts were often selective, reflecting a desire to "balance" reports of anarchy and desertion with more hopeful news; and many Kadets were simply ready by early June to seek some form of "miracle" cure for Russia's profound social and political problems. Smokescreens of zeal raised hopes and expectations of success.

In any event, when news of the offensive broke on June 19, just before the elections in Moscow, Kadet excitement knew no bounds. "Again the sun rises," the party's official newspaper, *Svobodnyi Narod* enthused. "Again one wants to live and believe. Our brothers have gone on the offensive; they are moving forward; everything is saved: freedom, our dignity, our national honor."[110] For Miliukov, the day ranked with February 27 as the most important of the revolution. Kadet policies were finally proving justified. Russia had reached a "great turning point."[111]

Indeed it had, but not in the way Miliukov hoped.

[107] *Novoe Vremia*, May 17, 1917.   [108] *Izvestiia*, June 25, 1917.

[109] See, e.g., Kerensky's interview with *Novoe Vremia*, May 31, 1917, on his return from a tour of the front. The war minister found the army "completely healthy." Morale, allegedly, was high, there was complete readiness to fight, and reorganization on the basis of democratic principles had already "borne fruit."

[110] *Svobodnyi Narod*, June 20, 1917.   [111] *Novoe Vremia*, June 20, 1917.

CHAPTER SIX

The July "Interregnum"

KADET EXCITEMENT over the start of the June offensive was one more measure of divorce from practical reality. In equipment and supplies, as well as morale, Russian soldiers were ill-prepared for such a drive; and the moment it began, resistance was bound to develop against the Provisional Government as it had against the old regime. Moreover, few Kadets recognized the degree to which the offensive would further exacerbate the Petrograd Soviet's relationship with its own anti-war left, or the effect this would have on the development of Bolshevism. Much popular support for moderate socialist leaders turned on antipathy to Kadet imperialism. Now, as Kerensky and the coalition ministers seemed to be effecting liberal goals, the offensive identified Soviet moderates with Kadets, and indirectly substantiated Bolshevik charges of "collusion." If many Soviet leaders greeted the news from the front almost as enthusiastically as Miliukov, moderates like Tsereteli, Avksentiev, and even Kerensky were also bound to reemphasize their differences with Kadets, pressing their own domestic policies even more forcefully than before. Political tensions were thus bound to flow as naturally from the offensive itself as they had from conditions the offensive was expected to resolve.

THE COLLAPSE OF THE FIRST COALITION

For their part, Kadet *verkhovniki* in Petrograd moved immediately to use the new military action as grounds for tightening civil order. Meeting shortly after the offensive began, Central Committee members demanded the government deal as firmly as possible with "anarchists, Bolsheviks, dissident workers and separatists." An editorial to this effect also appeared in *Rech'*, bearing the unmistakable stamp of Miliukov. In the Kadet view seizures of property, wage demands, and the like now bordered on sedition.[1]

Moreover, when *Novoe Vremia* published an article entitled "Anxious News from the Country" on June 21, describing hordes of Bolshevik agitators moving into the provinces to encourage "anarchy" and the seizure of estates, Kadets demanded unequivocally that the

[1] *Rech'*, June 24, 1917.

Soviet leadership try to stop them. They also wanted tougher requisition policies from the socialist minister of food, Peshekhonov, and launched a new assault at Chernov, who reported to the cabinet on June 23 that change, rather than firmness, was the key to rural social stability.[2] Also disturbing were rumors that the Petrograd Soviet was about to press anew for the nationalization of industry, using the offensive as justification. Petrograd Kadets again decried any move in this direction, echoing sentiments of the June Trade-Industrial Conference, and supporting a circular drafted by representatives of the metallurgical industry, which insisted management would not be bound to any promises made under duress.[3]

But it was in nationality policies that Kadets thought the coalition might show its greatest weakness toward the end of June. And here, too, with the start of the offensive, Kadets insisted that firmness was absolutely essential to the war effort. Difficulties centered on both the actions of the Finnish Sejm, which was now moving to proclaim full independence for Finland, and on the continuing efforts of the Ukrainian Rada to take full charge of all Ukrainian affairs, not excluding the disposition of Ukrainian troops or representation of Ukrainian interests abroad. In addition to striking at the very heart of the liberal conception of *gosudarstvennost'*, these separatist tendencies posed conflicting demands on soldiers' loyalties, increased the possibilities of German interference in Russian domestic affairs, and diverted attention from efforts at the front. Any immediate resolution of nationality problems along separatist lines would also usurp the prerogatives of the Constituent Assembly, as Kokoshkin had pointed out to the eighth party congress, not to mention its effect on the interests of the state as a whole.

On June 20, a scant two days after the offensive began, the Finnish Social Democrat Khuttunen informed the Congress of Soviets that Finland would soon declare her independence.[4] Russians were not sure what form this declaration would take (the Sejm was drafting the bill secretly), but it was certain to be "illegal" in terms of the Constituent Assembly's prerogatives. Within a few days, Kadets learned that the question would come before the Sejm in July. Angrily, Nolde, Maklakov, Nabokov, and Kokoshkin spoke out against this "unilateral" procedure in their official capacities as members of the State Juridical Commission; and while unable to blame the Soviet directly for the Finnish problem, which they recognized as having deep historic roots,

[2] *Novoe Vremia*, June 21 and 25, 1917; *Rech'*, June 24, 1917.
[3] *Novoe Vremia*, June 28, 1917; *Rech'*, July 2, 1917.
[4] *Izvestiia*, June 23, 1917.

they complained bitterly that the coalition government had not acted forcefully enough to head off the crisis.[5]

The Ukrainian problem was also exacerbated by the offensive. As we have seen, the Rada on June 10 had declared its exclusive competence in Ukrainian affairs, including authority over some 900,000 Ukrainian troops, which it wanted to form into separate detachments. Concerned that these soldiers might disobey his orders, General Brusilov, the army's Supreme Commander, urged the government and the Rada to resolve their differences as soon as possible. On June 22 or 23, Nekrasov suggested in the Council of Ministers that a special negotiating committee go to Kiev for this purpose. The Petrograd Soviet was in favor, but the Kadet Central Committee, fearing a Canossa and distrustful of Nekrasov, strongly disapproved.[6] Over Kadet objections, however, a delegation composed of the socialist ministers Tsereteli, Peshekhonov, and Kerensky left for Kiev on June 27, accompanied by Nekrasov. The departing ministers felt the Rada enjoyed almost universal Ukrainian support, and expected the government would have to come to terms.[7]

In the meantime, other developments also worried the Kadets. For several unrelated reasons, the left began at this time to mount a particularly sharp attack on the Kadet minister of education, Alexander Manuilov, accusing him of ignoring the resolutions of the Soviet dominated State Committee on Education. The State Committee wanted immediate implementation of reforms supported by the first All-Russian Congress of Soviets, especially a change in enrollment policies. Manuilov insisted on postponement. The basic question was not so much education as the right of the Soviet vs. the government to decide policy; and on July 1, *Izvestiia* called for Manuilov's resignation.[8]

Then, too, new warnings came from the Trade-Industrialists on June 27 and 28 that unless worker committees were sharply curbed and wage demands moderated, a number of additional enterprises would close. But few Soviet leaders either in or out of the government seemed concerned. And on July 1, *Izvestiia* noted in connection with the Finnish problem that the position of the Sejm "generally corresponded" to the views of the All-Russian Congress of Soviets.[9] It thus appeared that the expected unilateral declaration of Finnish independence in the first week of July would meet no Soviet resistance,

---

[5] *Russkiia Vedomosti*, July 1, 1917; *Svobodnyi Narod*, June 24, 1917.

[6] *Svobodnyi Narod*, June 25, 1917.

[7] Iraklii Tsereteli, *Vospominaniia o fevral'skoi revoliutsii*, 2 vols., Paris, 1963, II, 133.

[8] *Izvestiia*, July 1, 1917; *Novaia Zhizn'*, July 2, 1917; "V zashchitu A. A. Manuilova," *Narodnaia Svoboda* (Kharkov), No. 23, Aug. 11-12, 1917.

[9] *Rech'*, June 28, July 1, 1917; *Izvestiia*, July 1, 1917.

while labor-management relations and problems of production seemed about to get much worse.

Finally, and most important, Kadets all over Russia were abruptly confronted at the end of June with the realization that two of their greatest hopes for the survival of liberal values and institutions in the revolution were probably unfounded. On June 27 and 28, the full import of the Moscow Duma results became clear, showing the socialists' enormous popularity. In combining the Moscow and Petrograd election results, there was no escaping the eclipse of liberal strength: Kadets would not remain a dominant political power even in their past urban strongholds. At the same time, first indications arrived that the offensive was in serious trouble. Troops in many units had refused to leave their trenches. Elsewhere army committees were preventing their men from following up initial successes. Near Galich, disciplined troops under General Kornilov had caught the enemy unawares, and had taken thousands of Austrian prisoners. But fresh German soldiers were moving into the breach, supplies were running short, and even here some soldiers refused to continue fighting. The situation was unclear, but on June 30 Soviet leaders Lebedev and Skobelev hurriedly left for the Fifth Army to rally the troops. Disaster seemed imminent.[10]

All of this left Kadet leaders profoundly troubled. From their great investment in the success of the offensive now came a deep anxiety, a sense of utter frustration, much of which was readily channeled into anger and hostility toward the Soviet and the left. More than ever, Miliukov, Kokoshkin, Vinaver, and their colleagues in the Petrograd Kadet leadership were convinced that the root of all Russia's immediate problems lay in the failure of socialist ministers to commit themselves to firm state authority and national goals: "Russian people now thirst for authority and a *gosudarstvennaia* organization of life," *Svobodnyi Narod* editorialized; "They instinctively feel that only a statesmanlike government [*gosudarstvennaia vlast'*] and a strong army can save the country from ignominious historical death."[11] Earlier fears that socialists did not "understand" the meaning of coalition were also proving justified. Tsereteli, Skobelev, and particularly Chernov were acting as socialist "partisans," not as the official caretakers of Russia's national interests. "The fundamental idea of a true coalition, an all-national agreement," was not being realized "in its true form."[12] The fate of Russia's very state existence was in doubt.[13]

[10] *Rech'*, July 2, 1917; *Novoe Vremia*, July 1, 1917; *Narodnoe Slovo*, July 1, 1917.
[11] *Svobodnyi Narod*, June 10, 1917.   [12] *Rech'*, July 5, 1917.
[13] *Ibid*. See also Miliukov's report to the Duma Conference on July 2 in A. Drezen, ed., *Burzhuaziia i pomeshchiki v 1917 godu*, Moscow, 1932, pp. 158-59.

So much turned on a strong national government, in fact, that Miliukov again began to consider having the Kadet ministers leave the cabinet. The tactic of mass resignations had failed in April, but the Kadet leader was convinced events had proved him right. If socialists were still unwilling to take full power (as would probably be the case, given the likely opposition of the army command, the support for Kadets from Russia's liberal bourgeoisie, and the socialists' own ideological biases), a Kadet withdrawal might at least shock the left into an awareness of their political shortcomings, bringing "firm authority" and "forceful measures."[14] The tactic was risky. It involved the danger of greater social polarization and perhaps new popular demonstrations. But military defeat was unthinkable; the offensive had to be saved. A victory at the front made virtually any risk worth taking.

Consequently, when the government's delegation returned from the Ukraine on July 2 with an agreement accepting most of the Rada's major demands, Miliukov resolved to put his strategy into action. The agreement was the last straw. The only alternative to resignation was for Kadets to defeat the accord from within the cabinet, but they lacked the necessary votes. As D. D. Grimm, a Central Committee member and assistant minister of education expressed it, the agreement reached in Kiev was "a criminal document"; members of the government "were obligated by oath to preserve the sanctity and indivisibility of the Russian state." It was time for Kadets to draw the line.[15]

Not surprisingly, there was strong opposition to this view in the Central Committee, even among several of Miliukov's close friends, just as there had been in April. Vinaver, Nabokov, and particularly Moisei Adzhemov (the Armenian doctor and long-time member of the Kadet Duma faction), were convinced that the end of the coalition would weaken rather than strengthen state authority. They also worried about "deserting" the government at the height of the offensive. Astrov and Kishkin in Moscow strongly agreed with these views, and hurriedly conveyed their feelings. So did Shakhovskoi, who argued that conciliation, not intransigence, was the best way to preserve government strength and national unity.[16]

The Central Committee members in Petrograd met on the question during the evening of July 1, when news first arrived from Kiev. (Only 27 of the Committee's 66 members were present, most of the others having left Petrograd after the eighth party congress.) Debate went on

[14] Report of the Central Committee meeting of July 1-2 by Ariadna Tyrkova in the newspaper of the Nizhni-Novgorod Kadet committee, *Narodnaia Svoboda*, July 22, 1917.
[15] *Ibid.*   [16] *Ibid.*

through most of the night. Kokoshkin, Dolgorukov, Maklakov, Stepanov, Tyrkova, Grimm, Oldenburg, Vernadskii, and Rodichev resolutely
followed Miliukov in favoring Kadet withdrawal, and under pressure,
Shingarev, and Manuilov were also inclined to agree. The sources are
not explicit, but Nolde and Iurenev apparently leaned toward Nabokov, Vinaver, and Adzhemov in opposition, although probably without
great conviction. The others were undecided.[17] Discussion finally
ended with Kokoshkin, Shingarev, and the Kadet ministers going off
to meet the whole of Prince Lvov's cabinet. There they demanded the
agreement be canceled, insisting that only the Constituent Assembly
could accept the Rada's proposals.[18] When the cabinet refused, the
Kadets resigned. The final vote in the Central Committee supporting
the resignations was 16 to 11.

As the first coalition crashed to a halt, the Committee's majority felt
a sense of satisfaction that Kadets were finally taking strong action to
disassociate themselves from "responsibility" for the country's condition, falling back on what Paul Novgorodtsev, the party's resident religious philosopher, rather prosaically described as "the depths of our
ideals."[19] Deeply believing in the sanctity of the Russian nation, considering their actions a sign of true loyalty to the army, Miliukov and
his supporters desperately hoped they would "shock" the socialists to
their senses, turning the government around so that the country at
large—and particularly troops at the front—might finally receive the
backing of firm state authority. They also hoped that a new cabinet
could be "easily and peacefully reconstructed."[20]

What the Central Committee majority failed to realize, however,
and what the closeness of the Committee's own vote alone should have
signaled, was that Russians of all political views would prove profoundly out of sympathy with their action. Patriotism, a fear of the
left, and a deep historical sense of the Russian state blurred perceptions
of current national realities. Even within the Kadet party, the decision
to withdraw marked the exacerbation of significant divisions.

THE "JULY DAYS" AND THEIR AFTERMATH:
CONTINUING CONFLICT OVER STATE AUTHORITY

Miliukov and his followers also failed to reckon with the Bolsheviks.
On the morning of July 3, a little more than twelve hours after the
Kadets submitted their resignations, Lenin's supporters attempted to
seize power in Petrograd. As Alexander Rabinowitch has shown, the

[17] *Ibid.*   [18] *Ibid.*
[19] *Ibid.*
[20] A. G. Khrushchov, *Andrei Ivanovich Shingarev*, Moscow, 1918, p. 117.

Bolshevik move had little to do with the Kadets. Encouraged by the rapid growth of his party apparatus, and the increasing popularity of his positions on workers' control, the transfer of land to peasants, and especially the war, Lenin had talked about seizing power for weeks; and a group of his followers in the Petrograd garrison, led by the First Machine Gun Regiment, took his words more literally than he had intended.[21] In any event, the armed uprising sent Petrograd into chaos. For two days, the rump cabinet struggled to retain order and control, assisted by the Executive Committee of the All-Russian Congress of Soviets.

For their part, the Petrograd Kadets were only vaguely aware the Bolsheviks were preparing a coup; they had no idea as to organization, scheduling, or timing, and used the rumors which had circulated for weeks simply as grist for the editorial mills of *Rech'*. And perhaps because no one in the Central Committee felt Lenin was very strong, the matter was not considered seriously in the debate over whether Kadets should resign their ministerial positions.[22] When the uprising came, Miliukov and his colleagues even feared at first that it was directed against them, rather than against the government as a whole. Seeing Bolshevik soldiers approaching the party club, a number of party leaders had a particularly bad moment, thinking they were about to be seized. Even after the soldiers passed, Miliukov was urged to go into hiding.[23]

In fact, the Bolsheviks had little intention of seizing the Kadets; and after two difficult days of sporadic shooting and general disorder, they were suppressed. But the effect of the uprising was to harden political attitudes on all sides. For Miliukov and his supporters, Bolshevik guns simply underscored the government's incompetence. The question was: "Who is guilty?" And the answer was: "Those who tolerated the Bolsheviks," at least as much as the actual mutineers.[24] According to *Rech'*, the coalition had collapsed and the Bolsheviks had launched their attempted coup not because the Kadets resigned, but because Soviet spokesmen had attempted to "command" the country, had "converted national [*obshchenatsional'nye*] tasks into the systematic implementation of partisan [*partiinye*] viewpoints by means of an accidental coalition majority."[25]

[21] Alexander Rabinowitch, *Prelude to Revolution*, Bloomington, Ind., 1968, chaps. 5 and 6.

[22] *Narodnaia Svoboda* (Nizhni-Novgorod), July 22, 1917. By the same token, the course of the Bolshevik mutiny was little affected by the Kadet withdrawal. As Alexander Rabinowitch indicates (p. 148), there was nothing about the Kadet resignations in the Bolshevik appeals, and at most, the ministerial crisis simply further weakened the government's prestige among already disaffected soldiers.

[23] Obolenskii MS, p. 454.   [24] *Svobodnyi Narod*, July 6, 1917.

[25] *Rech'*, July 5, 1917.

But for Miliukov's opponents in the Kadet Central Committee, as well as for a number of Moscow and provincial party leaders, the Bolshevik uprising only scored the impropriety of the Kadet resignations. Like the April crisis, the "July days" were an important moment in the internal development of the party in 1917, but one which caused many Kadets to rethink the party's basic "above class" approach to revolutionary politics, and which sharpened rather than reduced party divisions. For those like Shakhovskoi and Nekrasov in Petrograd, who were still convinced that Russian state authority depended on a consolidation of the liberal and moderate socialist movements, Miliukov and the *verkhovniki* were again acting with elitist independence, not considering the country's real needs or conditions. Vinaver, Adzhemov, Frenkel, Gerasimov, and others in Petrograd also spoke out sharply against the decision to withdraw the ministers, and indicated their fears in district committee meetings that the party was placing itself in a position of hopeless isolation. And in Moscow on July 6, a full-scale debate took place between Novgorodtsev and Astrov, revealing the two distinct groups into which Kadets in the "second capital" were now divided. According to Novgorodtsev, the party's strength lay precisely in its refusal "to depend on the mood of the masses in making decisions, in contrast to other political parties." Astrov on the contrary argued that the withdrawal was neither desirable nor necessary, that coalition required a partisan give and take, and that it was Miliukov and the Petrograd *verkhovniki*, rather than the Soviet leaders, who were now attempting to "command" the country in a destructive way.[26]

Moreover, in Kiev on July 5, the party's district committee voted in a special session to support the Rada, rather than the central regime or their own Petrograd leadership. The withdrawal of Kadet ministers was "incomprehensible," and "not without dangers for the interests of the state as a whole."[27] In Tiflis, the local Kadet newspaper stressed the party's basic commitment to the principles of "national self-determination," affirming its desire for "territorial autonomy" in the Caucasus.[28] And in Chernigov, the Ukrainian Rada was also given support, its decisions declared "correct."[29] Opinion again in the provinces was hardly uniform. In Rostov, attacks on the Petrograd leadership were considered so strong as to warrant "serious reflection" about whether Kadets of this viewpoint should be kept in the party.[30] And the dominant posture of provincial committees was still strongly nationalistic and conservative, even more so after the Bolshevik up-

[26] *Russkiia Vedomosti*, July 9, 1917; *VPNS*, Nos. 11-13, Aug. 10, 1917, p. 32.
[27] *Kievskaia Mysl'*, July 6, 1917.
[28] *Narodnaia Svoboda* (Tiflis), July 5, 1917.
[29] *Svobodnyi Narod*, July 9, 1917.   [30] *Rostovskaia Rech'*, July 13, 1917.

rising, in fact, than before. But all over Russia Kadets were also convinced that the Petrograd leadership had made a serious tactical error; and as right and left alike accused the party of deserting both the nation and the army at a moment of high crisis, unwittingly helping the Bolsheviks, provincial Kadets also found their own local situations much more difficult.

For their part, meanwhile, the Soviet leadership not only bridled at the Kadets' attempted power play, but bitterly resented the liberals blaming them for the Bolsheviks' assault. Some even suspected the Kadets had resigned for Machiavellian reasons, hoping on the basis of advance knowledge either to discredit the left by forcing the Soviet itself to suppress Lenin, or else to set up sufficient grounds for a military counterattack, assuming the Bolsheviks temporarily succeeded.[31] Potresov, Panin, and other Mensheviks were as concerned as many Kadets about Russia's political "underdevelopment," and equally as frightened about the fate and the revolution and the possibility of civil war. But in terms of the Kadets' whole anti-Soviet critique, and particularly the argument that firmness rather than popular support was needed for political stability, they rightly felt the July days proved just the opposite: it was the *insufficiency* of reforms that had led to conditions where the uprising was possible.[32]

At the same time, Martov and other more militant left-wing leaders also felt the Petrograd Soviet's success in ending the revolt was proof that Kadets were no longer needed for Russia to have an effective government. (The party's only "contribution" to dispersing the Bolsheviks came in the form of outsize headlines in *Svobodnyi Narod*, "breaking" the news that Lenin had used German funds; shortly afterward, Miliukov and Tyrkova drafted a scorching statement demanding that the cabinet they had just abandoned take steps to arrest the Bolshevik leadership.)[33] Opinion within the Soviet Executive Committee was divided on this as on other issues, but a number of Menshevik and SR leaders felt the rump ministry should now begin to govern exclusively on the basis of resolutions passed earlier by the various Soviet conferences. This meant the further development of Chernov's agrarian program, and an active government peace policy. To some on the left, it also meant the formal dissolution of the old State Duma, and the proclamation of a Russian republic.[34]

It was the head of the government, Prince Lvov, who prompted a crystallization of these views into a specific "Declaration of Principles."

[31] E.g., *Izvestiia*, July 13, 1917.
[32] *Novoe Vremia*, July 8, 1917; *Rabochaia Gazeta*, July 7, 1917.
[33] *Svobodnyi Narod*, July 6, 1917; *Rech'*, July 7, 1917.
[34] Tsereteli, *Vospominaniia*, II, 375-81; *Izvestiia*, July 6 and 7, 1917.

As soon as the Kadets resigned, Lvov announced he, too, would leave his post unless a new coalition could be organized on the basis of a definite social and economic program. The program was to include a decisive fight against anarchists and Bolsheviks, and the end of anarchic tendencies in the country at large. It was also to repudiate all types of "seizures" of land and goods, and the reversal of Chernov's agrarian policies (about which Lvov and the minister of agriculture had been disputing for some time).[35]

But most socialists had other ideas. At a plenary session of the joint Soviet Executive Committee on July 4, there was considerable pressure not only to restructure the government's program in conformity with the left's demands, but to have the Congress of Soviets itself assume all state power. Land would be transferred immediately to the peasants, and local soviets would establish control over industry. And while the Soviet leadership in Petrograd ultimately decided to continue pressing for a coalition, it was on these terms, rather than those spelled out by Prince Lvov, that the remaining ministers drafted a new declaration.[36] Thereupon Lvov resigned, convinced, as he put it, that the left "was sacrificing national and moral values to the masses in the name of demagogy. . . ."[37] Responsibility for forming a new cabinet was given to Kerensky, ostensibly the most neutral of the remaining ministers.

Somewhat concerned about the effect this new resignation might have on the army command and the right, Kerensky and his colleagues reworked their declaration. They deleted demands for the proclamation of a republic and for the formal dissolution of the old State Duma and State Council. On July 8, the statement was then published in the government's own journal as an official "Declaration of the Provisional Government." With German armies breaking the Russian offensive, with "anarchism" in the cities and countryside, with the "national organism" infected with a "contagious sickness," the remaining ministers heralded the arrival of a "fateful hour," declaring their confidence that Russia would recover as a new cabinet brought into practice the principles of soviet democracy.[38]

It is difficult to underestimate the importance of the July 8 Declaration for Miliukov, Kokoshkin, and their liberal supporters. The

---

[35] *Novoe Vremia*, July 8, 1917.

[36] Tsereteli, *Vospominaniia*, II, 375-81; *Izvestiia*, July 6 and 7, 1917.

[37] *Russkiia Vedomosti*, July 9, 1917.

[38] *Vestnik Vremennago Pravitel'stva*, July 8, 1917 (translated in R. P. Browder and A. F. Kerensky, *The Russian Provisional Government 1917*, 3 vols., Stanford, 1961, III, 1386-87). See also the discussion in Oliver H. Radkey, *The Agrarian Foes of Bolshevism*, New York, 1959, pp. 285-93.

Declaration indicated the new government would unilaterally abolish social estates [*soslovie*], liquidate civil ranks and orders, work out and introduce measures to regulate economic life and control industry, implement laws on labor unions, workers' conditions, insurance and arbitration, and finally, take measures which would "completely do away with the old agrarian policy . . . [while] expanding and consolidating the network of land committees. . . ."[39] Thus the socialists were officially setting goals for the provisional regime whose implementation would fly in the face of the Kadets' own conception of legal procedures, preempting the Constituent Assembly, undermining any sense of "law," "responsibility," or "respect for individual rights," and pandering to the "hysteria" of individuals "absolutely incapable of determining what constituted Russia's national interests." Russia "was not a socialist society," in the view of Miliukov and Kokoshkin, nor was there "any soil for socialism at the present moment," considering the extent of popular anarchy and the unwillingness of Russians to work together for their own greater good. Thus the subordination of government power to a Soviet program was not only "irrational," but "treacherous."[40] Moreover, as Izgoev insisted, the question was not simply one of domestic policies, but whether Russia was to be "a great world power, democratic, liberal, and free, or a tiny Muscovite principality, subordinate to foreign interests." A strong regime required the nonpartisan statesmanship Kadets had tried to create. It was for this reason alone that party leaders had taken the drastic step of submitting their resignations.[41]

It was now quite clear to the Soviet Executive Committee, however, that Miliukov and his Petrograd supporters did not speak for all Kadets. Nekrasov had kept Kerensky and Tsereteli well informed of party disputes; and in any event, Kadet divisions over the ministers' resignations were public knowledge in a matter of days. Most members of the Soviet Committee still wanted liberals in the cabinet. Some convinced Marxists were simply unable to accept a "bourgeois" revolutionary phase without liberals in power; others worried about worsening relations with Russian industrialists, who controlled vitally needed supplies, and the danger of armed counter-revolution. (With the start of the offensive, this latter fear was well founded. Already by July 8 General Brusilov had told his five major field commanders that civil war was "inevitable," and indicated the need for "energetic action" in order to lead Russia to a Constituent Assembly; on July 14, a noisy meeting of officers from the Petrograd garrison condemned

[39] Browder and Kerensky, III, 1386-87.   [40] *Novoe Vremia*, July 13, 1917.
[41] *Svobodnyi Narod*, July 11, 1917. See also *Novoe Vremia*, July 13, 1917; *Rech'*, July 18, 1917.

the "irresponsible organs of democracy," and demanded a strong disciplined government; and two days later at headquarters, Generals Alekseev, Ruzskii, Gurko, Dragomirov, and especially Anton Denikin insisted to Kerensky in the strongest possible terms that the army would not stand idly by while anarchistic groups and ad hoc commissars destroyed Russia.)[42]

Consequently, the approach of the socialist ministers to forming a new cabinet was to try to take advantage of Kadet divisions, relying in particular on the close relationship between Kadets and Trade-Industrialists in Moscow, and building a new coalition out of those who both before the revolution and after, had advocated a "coming together" [sblizhenie] of socialists and liberals. Sympathetic Kadets from Moscow like Nicholas Astrov and Nicholas Kishkin would be brought into a "government to save the revolution" under Kerensky, displacing their Petrograd colleagues. And with them would come left-wing liberals from the Radical Democratic party like I. N. Efremov, and progressive Trade-Industrialists like S. N. Tretiakov. While the sources are again unclear, Shakhovskoi and particularly Nekrasov apparently played a considerable role in convincing their socialist friends that a new coalition of this sort was possible, though whether Nekrasov was again trying to discredit Miliukov in the process, as some argued he had done in April, will not be known until Soviet archives are opened for careful scrutiny.

In any event, Kerensky on July 12 bypassed the Kadet Central Committee group in Petrograd, and rang up Astrov, Kishkin, and Tretiakov in Moscow, asking them to come immediately to the capital. Before leaving, Astrov and Kishkin met with their Moscow party colleagues and received "party sanction" to enter the government—an indication of how deep feelings were running at this time between the Moscow and Petrograd Kadet committees. The dominant feeling here was that the July 8 Declaration was less important than a new commitment from socialist ministers to break from direct Soviet control, and accept measures to reestablish army discipline. Meanwhile Tretiakov caucused in a special conference of the Moscow Trade-Industrial Committee, which likewise sanctioned his entry into the government, providing that "a defined framework of social legislation" was agreed upon in Petrograd which would not usurp the prerogatives of the Constituent Assembly. The Trade-Industrialists also apparently stipulated

---

[42] Browder and Kerensky, II, 980-82; Izvestiia, July 9 and 15, 1917; Rech', July 15, 1917. One speaker at the Petrograd garrison meeting, a Captain Zhuravlev, went so far as to suggest the Soviet itself might be reorganized to include not only democratic elements, but also non-socialist bourgeois groups! The Stavka conference protocols appear in N. Bukhbinder, "Na fronte v predoktiabr'skie dni," KL, No. 6, 1923, pp. 18-52, and partially in Browder and Kerensky, II, 989-1009.

that Chernov would not continue as minister of agriculture, something Kishkin and Astrov agreed to as well when they and Tretiakov met together before leaving for the capital. War and navy posts were also to be in the hands of military specialists, preferably General Alekseev and Admiral Kolchak. The main objective of the Muscovites was to avoid further civil disruption, and recreate a firm central authority as rapidly as possible.[43]

Once in Petrograd, however, Astrov and Kishkin found Miliukov and his followers adamant against allowing any Kadets in the government unless the socialists disavowed their Declaration of July 8. Kerensky also had to "guarantee" that committees and soviets at all levels would be replaced by "real authorities." Otherwise, the Kadet resignations would produce precisely the opposite effect to that the Petrograd Kadets had intended. Astrov and Kishkin objected, arguing that some reforms were necessary to guarantee the new cabinet's popularity. But Miliukov, Kokoshkin, Rodichev, and others virtually made retreat from reform a question of Russia's "national honor." Not only did changes of the type proposed in the July 8 statement have to await the Constituent Assembly; but discipline and order had to be established before a lawful assembly could sit.[44]

The one strong point of agreement between the Moscow and Petrograd Kadets was on Victor Chernov. Of all the Soviet leaders, Chernov seemed most responsible for the "illegitimate" socialization of Russian society—the implementation of "illegal" social and economic reforms through ad hoc groups like Shingarev's disinherited land committees. At a meeting of party leaders in Petrograd on July 14, just after the Muscovites arrived, no firm conclusions were reached on the question of accommodation with the left; but all agreed that the removal of Chernov was to be a precondition to the Kadets joining any new cabinet. Later in the evening, the two Moscow Kadets met Kerensky in the Winter Palace (where the frenetic "acting prime minister" was already ensconcing himself in the tsar's former apartments). Chernov's ouster headed their list of demands.[45]

According to contemporary accounts, the palace meeting took place amicably. The papers that afternoon had quoted Tsereteli to the effect that the time was not right for partisan activities; and Kerensky had also indicated his desire for an agreement in discussions with Maklakov and Nabokov. The Soviet leadership had left negotiating responsibility almost entirely in Kerensky's hands, and he was extremely nervous

[43] Newspaper interview given by Astrov to *Russkiia Vedomosti*, July 18, 1917. See also *Novoe Vremia*, July 15, 1917; *Utro Rossii*, July 18 and 19, 1917; V. Ia. Laveryshev, *Po tu storonu barrikad*, Moscow, 1967, pp. 196-98.
[44] *Russkiia Vedomosti*, July 18, 1917.   [45] *Ibid*.

at the possibility of a prolonged Kadet boycott.[46] Without discussing a formal renunciation of the July 8 Declaration, there seemed to be general agreement on all points but one—the removal of Chernov. Kerensky himself was on very poor terms with the populist radical, but insisted that for the time being, at least, the left would simply not accept his removal. Indicating that they understood Kerensky's problem, Kishkin and Astrov then returned to the party club, prepared to thrash out the issue with their colleagues the rest of the night.[47]

The sources don't reveal the actual scope of subsequent Kadet discussions, but it is clear that many Central Committee members were somewhat uncertain about how to proceed after hearing Astrov and Kishkin's report. While Miliukov himself remained adamant, others were much more willing to accept Kishkin and Astrov's arguments about the government's need to implement reforms. Miliukov, however, proved quite insistent, acting almost as if the matter was a test of his own personal judgment in prompting the Kadet resignations. And with characteristic persuasiveness, he rallied his coterie of close supporters, especially Kokoshkin. For their part, meanwhile, Astrov and Kishkin now felt they could not enter a cabinet themselves without Kokoshkin or other prominent Petrograd leaders, and without the full support of the Petrograd Central Committee. Whatever their tactical differences, Kadets had to continue struggling together for the eventual realization of liberal values.[48]

By morning, a rough compromise had been worked out. On one hand, it was decided not to include the question of Chernov's ouster (and thus of "individual personalities") among the party's formal demands, but to press his removal instead through private channels. Each prospective Kadet minister, moreover, would ultimately be allowed to decide the question for himself; there would be no blanket Central Committee control over sending party representatives to the cabinet.[49] On the other hand, the Kadets now established their own preconditions for entering the government, which followed almost exclusively the views of Miliukov. They were summarized in a "personal" letter to Kerensky, dated July 15, from Kishkin, Astrov and Nabokov (whom the acting prime minister had also invited into the cabinet):

[46] *Svobodnyi Narod*, July 13, 1917; *Novoe Vremia*, July 15, 1917; Alexander Kerensky, *The Catastrophe*, New York, 1927, p. 250.
[47] *Svobodnyi Narod*, July 16, 18, 1917; *Izvestiia*, July 16, 1917; *Rech'*, July 15 and 16, 1917; *Russkiia Vedomosti*, July 15, 16, and 18, 1917.
[48] *Rech'*, July 16, 1917; *Russkiia Vedomosti*, July 16, 1917.
[49] *Russkiia Vedomosti*, July 16 and 18, 1917; *Rech'*, July 16, 1917; *Svobodnyi Narod*, July 16, 1917.

1) All members of the Government are to be responsible only to their conscience, regardless of their party affiliations, and their actions and presence in the cabinet are no reason for interference in the direction of state affairs by any kind of committee or organization.

2) In matters of internal policy, the Government is to limit itself to guarding the conquests of the revolution, and not undertake measures that might lead to civil strife. All basic social reforms and all questions relating to the form of government are to be left absolutely to the Constituent Assembly.

3) In matters of war and peace, the Government is to be guided by the principle of complete union with the Allies.

4) Steps are to be taken to develop a strong army by restoring strict military discipline, and putting a definite stop to interference by soldier committees in questions of tactics and strategy.

5) As a fundamental of internal administration, an end is to be made to the pluralism of government authority; order re-established in the country; a vigorous fight waged against anarchistic, anti-governmental and counter-revolutionary elements; and a stable local administration organized as soon as possible so that the new, legitimate local organs of government can begin to function.

6) State courts are to be brought back to a position from which they might carry on their functions properly. Prosecuting attorneys and judges are not to be interfered with by politicians and other outsiders.

7) Elections to the Constitutent Assembly are to be conducted so that the people might express the true national will. Elections are to be under the supervision of legally selected organs of local government or institutions formed by them. They are to guarantee the freedom of electoral campaigns.[50]

This, in effect, was the official Kadet response to the Declaration of July 8. The basic difference between the two documents was that the socialists' statement pledged to meet Russia's crisis conditions with new social legislation, and set the transfer of land to the peasants as a definite principle for Constituent Assembly land reform, while the Kadet letter demanded a halt to any additional measures over which there were significant public disagreements. Suppressing their own internal differences, the Kadets were also insisting on an end to the authority of soviets and committees, while the July 8 declaration, reflecting the majority viewpoint of the Petrograd Soviet, assigned an important, continued role to these organizations. The Kadet leadership

[50] *Rech'*, July 18, 1917, translated in Browder and Kerensky, III, 1401-02.

in Petrograd was thus picking up the challenge hurled by the socialist rump ministry on July 8 and throwing back their own positions on the basis of traditional liberal views. In effect, Miliukov and his supporters were returning to their platform of March and April, refusing to admit of any changes which required an alteration of basic liberal perspectives.

"THE REAL DEMANDS OF RUSSIAN LIFE"

Miliukov insisted that the position of Petrograd Kadets "corresponded absolutely to the real demands of Russian life." Above all, Russia needed firm state authority, not to suppress the "legitimate" achievements of the revolution, but to consolidate its gains, preserve the army, and protect the country from the chaos of future radical uprisings. Further social reforms would lead to new bloodshed. Now more than any other time since February, the government had to be "independent," a "nonpartisan" body whose members were "responsible only to their conscience." Partisanship, and even electoral competition between political parties was only further weakening Russia's ability as a nation to endure what had become her greatest national crisis.[51]

At the very moment he and his supporters were defending this position in Petrograd, however, Kadets and other nonsocialists elsewhere were developing quite a different view of the "real demands of Russian life." The results of the Moscow and Petrograd Duma elections could not be ignored; and in cities with large non-Russian populations like Kiev and Odessa, in provincial industrial centers like Ekaterinburg and Rostov, and in areas of serious peasant unrest like Vitebsk, Riazan, Penza, and Kursk, the demand for new and comprehensive social reforms was only too apparent. Peasants and workers were unwilling to wait for a Constituent Assembly even if it was only several months off; and appeals to "support the offensive" and to "remember our brothers at the front" seemed echoes from a day that many thought had passed.

On July 14 and 15, at the height of the "interregnum," Kadets held a regional conference in Moscow to discuss the Constituent Assembly campaign, with delegates coming from a score of important provincial cities. Uniformly, reports told of growing support for parties responding to demands for "real" reforms, and of a corresponding decline in the popularity of Kadets. In Kazan, party members were having no success whatsoever with traditional slogans like "War to Complete Victory"; and from a position of great strength immediately

---

[51] Drezen, 217-18; also, P. N. Miliukov, *Istoriia vtoroi russkoi revoliutsiia*, 3 pts., Sofia, 1921-23, pt. 2, pp. 29-35.

after February, the Kazan organization was now reduced to secondary importance. In Tambov, there were too few party speakers, and those available had difficulty gathering an audience. Elsewhere Kadets were having trouble recruiting new party cadres, even from among non-socialists. No one seemed interested in supporting the "interests of Russia as a whole." In Smolensk, only half the provincial districts were organized, and the party lacked workers. In Voronezh, "all authority" was now in the hands of workers and soldiers.[52] Even Central Committee representatives like Paul Gronskii and Alexander Kornilov had to admit that Petrograd Kadets seemed "temporarily divorced" from the party's rank and file, who were urging not concessions to workers and peasants, but the adoption of specific programs which potential supporters in their districts would recognize as meeting immediate needs. The party now had more than 300 local committees, the most in its history; and its national organization included seven "regional" committees in Petrograd, Moscow, Kiev, Tiflis, Odessa, Rostov, and Kharkov, each of which was officially charged with coordinating party activities in its area. Just as the Petrograd Soviet had instructed workers and peasants in March to "Organize! Organize!" it was now time for the liberals to build these committees into partisan, activist groups.[53]

The need for activism was affirmed by new results from municipal duma elections, which began to come in just as negotiations in Petrograd were reaching a stalemate. In Tsaritsyn in early July, Kadets elected only 1 member out of 102 to the new city legislature.[54] In Rostov, where Kadet leaders had insisted that the party committee was still "very strong" (and where Kadets had won 70 percent of the electoral seats in the First Duma balloting), party candidates received little more than 10,000 votes in balloting on July 11, while the socialist total was more than 50,000.[55] Similar results occurred in Kostroma (where the Kadets gained only 13.7 percent of the vote), in Ufa (12.0 percent) and Batum (where the total was only 3.3 percent); and in Kursk and Saratov, where Kadets had been elected to every seat in the First Duma electoral assemblies in 1906, party candidates now won only 17 percent and 9 percent, respectively.[56]

Nonpartisanship and a platform of "strong state authority" seemed to have little appeal even after the full details were known of the Bolsheviks' attempted coup. In Nizhni-Novgorod, where balloting took

[52] *Svobodnyi Narod*, July 18, 19, and 21, 1917.
[53] *Rech'*, July 18, 1917; *VPNS*, Nos. 14-16, Aug. 31, 1917, pp. 42-48.
[54] *Svobodnyi Narod*, July 14, 1917.   [55] *Rostovskaia Rech'*, July 12, 1917.
[56] *Povolzhskii Vestnik* (Kostroma), June 28, 1917; *Russkiia Vedomosti*, July 12, 1917; *Trud*, Aug. 8, 1917; *Utro Rossii*, July 20, 1917; *Sibirskaia Rech'* (Omsk), July 17, 1917.

place on July 15 and where Kadets campaigned heavily on a program of "law and order," they won less than a quarter of the available duma seats. The SRs gained almost half, and various SD blocs, including two favorable to Lenin, gained almost a third.[57] In Omsk, where Kadets would set up their Eastern Central Committee during the civil war, they received only 1,733 ballots out of a total of more than 17,000. The SRs won 9,069, the SDs 3,291, and even a group of nonsocialist "Home-Owners" (landlords), campaigning on an openly partisan program, out-polled them with 2,580.[58] Everywhere, in fact, returns from local duma elections in the first weeks of July read very much like First Duma results in terms of their lopsided results, but with socialists replacing Kadets as the dominant party, and to such an extent in many places that Kadet candidates were obviously being denied even the support they had won in the past.

Returns also showed that the activities of Kadet leaders in Petrograd were more important in forming popular attitudes in the provinces than the specific tactical orientation of local party groups. In Ekaterinburg, for example, where Lev Krol had led a strong effort toward closer association with workers' groups, only 2,788 out of 24,687 voters supported Kadet candidates in the local duma elections, or 11.7 percent. The Bolsheviks, despite the July days, received almost 22 percent of the vote; and the SRs, 51.5 percent. In Kharkov, where local Kadets had formed one of the party's most radical groups before the revolution, SRs captured 46.5 percent of the vote compared to the Kadets' 13.8 percent.[59]

Similar results emerged even from those regions which had the greatest amount of peasant or worker violence in June and July, like Mogilev, Minsk, Vitebsk, Tula, Tambov, Penza, Podolsk, and Kursk. The level of fear and anxiety in these places was very high, as local party officials reported, but even those desperately anxious for civil peace and firm state authority shied away from associating with the Kadets, apparently believing that other groups would be better able to meet their needs. In each of these areas, it was the SRs who emerged as the primary political force in new town dumas; and in some places, especially where SRs formed electoral blocs with anti-Bolshevik SDs, their victory was overwhelming. In Tambov on July 21, for example, the SRs alone received 59 percent of the vote; in Kursk the same week, a socialist bloc received 62.7 percent; and in Penza, 74 percent. The Kadets' only real reported victory in these weeks came from

[57] *Narodnaia Svoboda* (Nizhni-Novgorod), July 22, 1917.

[58] *Russkiia Vedomosti*, July 7, 1917.

[59] *Russkiia Vedomosti*, July 12, 1917; *Narodnoe Slovo*, July 18, 1917; *Sibirskaia Rech'*, July 21, 1917.

Riazan, where party representatives won 29 of the city duma's 60 seats, as opposed to 22 for the socialist bloc. Elsewhere, local party figures reported that even private landholders were refusing to support them, not so much because of their agrarian program (though this was undoubtedly a factor), but also because it was simply unclear how effective Kadets could be in meeting the "real demands" of their areas.[60]

Results were virtually the same, moreover, in small towns as well as large. While returns from outlying areas were still very scattered in July, elections in some 28 towns with populations of less than 50,000 showed Kadets in only 8 winning more than 15 percent of the seats. In some places, such as the small town of Belev in Tula province, and Cherepovets in the Novgorod region, this represented fewer than 1,000 voters. Moreover, in five towns of Voronezh province, where Kadets had a relatively extensive provincial organization, they elected only 22 out of a possible 188 representatives, and 17 of these were in the city of Voronezh itself.[61] Meanwhile, the returns for 21 elections in other provincial capitals of European Russia during the period between June 26 and July 30, were much the same. The results appear in Table 3 below.

In sum, the low level of Kadet popularity in July was dramatic, so much so that the liberal Moscow daily *Russkiia Vedomosti* noted in an editorial that "the Kadet organization has little influence in the present revolutionary moment of our history."[62] Even the Duma Conference leadership began attacking Miliukov for his "independence" in leaving the cabinet "on his own."[63] And when the Trade-Industrialists issued their own seven-point declaration to back Sergei Tretiakov in his negotiations with Kerensky, this most bourgeois of all Russian public organizations resolved that there should be *no* place in the government for individuals who stood "above party," precisely the opposite of the Petrograd Kadet view. According to the Trade-Industrialists, "The cabinet must be composed of persons who are the *actual* representatives of *authoritative* social and political organizations."[64]

Yet the impression all of this made of Miliukov and his Petrograd supporters was not of a sort to weaken their position in the negotia-

[60] *VPNS*, Nos. 11-13, Aug. 10, 1917, p. 25.

[61] B. M. Lavygin, *1917 god v voronezhskoi gubernii*, Voronezh, 1928, p. 74.

[62] *Russkiia Vedomosti*, July 7, 1917.

[63] Drezen, pp. 18off., and esp. pp. 199, 209, and 217. One representative, A. M. Maslennikov, went so far as to recommend that the Duma be called back into session to take control over the formation and program of any new provisional government. See also *Russkiia Vedomosti*, July 16, 1917.

[64] *Russkiia Vedomosti*, July 16, 1917 (my italics). See also, V. Ia. Laverychev, *Po tu storonu barrikad*, Moscow, 1967, pp. 208ff.

TABLE 3. Municipal Duma Election Returns for Provincial Capitals, European Russia, June 26 - July 30

(Seats Obtained Displayed as a Percentage of Total Seats Available)

	June 26 - July 16	July 17 - July 30
	(9 elections)	(12 elections)
Socialist Parties (Excluding Bolsheviks running independently)a	62.2	57.9
Bolsheviks	6.6	4.5
Kadets	15.1	17.7
Other Nonsocialists	3.7	5.4
Nationality & Religious Groups	12.4	14.5
	100.0	100.0

SOURCES: Election returns were gathered from a number of different provincial newspapers, particularly *Odesskii Listok, Kievskaia Mysl', Rostovskaia Rech',* and *Sibirskaia Rech',* as well as from *Rech', Russkiia Vedomosti, Novoe Vremia, Izvestiia, Utro Rossii,* and other Moscow and Petrograd papers of various political viewpoints.

NOTE: Excludes Smolensk, Kamenets-Podolsk, Petrozavodsk, and the capitals of Baltic provinces.

a Includes some seats won by Socialist Blocs which included Bolsheviks.

tions for a new coalition, and may actually have strengthened their resolve. "The real demands of Russian life" still required an "independent, nonpartisan government" whose members were "responsible only to their conscience," and whose goal, in effect, would be to save liberal Russia. If Kadets were destined to be the party of only a small minority, as Miliukov and the Petrograd leadership undoubtedly realized in mid-July they were, there was all the *more* reason to seek their goals through negotiation and hard bargaining, rather than by capitulating (as the Trade-Industrialists seemed to be doing) or by seeking broad popular support through the ballot box.

In retrospect, however, it seems clear that there were serious, harmful consequences to this posture (which seemed to many observers at the time as abject intransigence). While Miliukov tried to argue the Soviet leadership into retreat, Russia, in effect, had no legal government; and what the Kadets themselves deplored as the corrosive power of ad hoc local soviets and committees was rapidly increasing as the "interregnum" continued. So was the frequency of "anarchistic" acts in factories and the countryside. And at the front, the offensive was collapsing. (In fact, appeals from units for help and reinforcements began appearing in the liberal press just as the Kadets were awaiting Kerensky's reply to their letter of July 15; and within a day or so, rumors that the Germans were moving toward Petrograd on the Riga front became front-page news.)[65] The task of creating a strong national authority would certainly have been assisted in these circumstances had Kadets rallied quickly behind the moderate Soviet leadership, helped defeat the Bolsheviks, and agreed on at least a minimum program of clearly defined social reforms, as those within the party's own left wing had urged. This, perhaps, would have been a public admission that the resignations had been a mistake; and it would undoubtedly have infuriated those on the party's far right, like Izgoev and Novgorodtsev. But the immediate political crisis would have ended; and the result over a longer period of time might even have been a lessening of social and political antagonism.

As it was, however, Miliukov, Rodichev, Kokoshkin, and their supporters stood fast. On July 18 and 19, Kerensky held discussions with the combined Executive Committees of the Workers' and Peasants' Soviet Congresses. Ironically, the peripatetic Simbirsk lawyer was himself confused about the strength of the Kadets, believing they had now "organized all the political and social forces of the country representing the interests of the propertied classes, the high command, the remnants of the old bureaucracy, and even fragments of the aristocracy."[66] He therefore insisted that Kadets come into the cabinet and, not unwilling to use another's weakness to his own advantage, was now more than ready to sacrifice Chernov. (For a number of reasons, not the least of which had to do with Chernov's role in denying Kerensky a seat on the SR Central Committee at the party's third congress, Kerensky actually despised his party colleague; he was delighted to see pressure directed against him, and even sent out signals to this effect as negotiations for a new ministry were getting underway.)[67]

The Soviet leadership also was finally willing to drop Chernov, but now refused to yield on the July 8 Declaration. This still had to be the basis for any new coalition. Consequently, while Kerensky could announce with some glee on July 20 that Chernov would resign, insisting as well on the "independence" of the new regime from any "public" organizations, he was also forced to indicate that the government would "invariably" be guided by the principles of the July 8 Declaration. And this, once again, Miliukov and the Petrograd Cen-

[65] E.g. *Novoe Vremia*, July 18, 20, and 23, 1917.
[66] Kerensky, *Catastrophe*, p. 250.   [67] Radkey, *Agrarian Foes*, pp. 304-05.

tral Committee refused to accept.[68] Shortly afterward, consequently, the acting minister-president was forced to announce that discussions had completely broken down.[69]

FORMATION OF THE SECOND COALITION

Three and a half years later, when Miliukov, Rodichev, Maklakov, Dolgorukov, Grimm, and other Kadets were regrouping in Paris and assessing their misfortunes through émigré lenses, they came to recognize the effect their position had on the protracted July crisis. The three-week interregnum had actually marked the effective end of state power in democratic Russia. Though a new coalition was formed, Russia's political leaders failed to find a firm basis for national authority, one capable of treating the increasing problems of social and economic instability while also satisfying Russia's various interest groups and parties. Instead, Russians everywhere came increasingly to expect that if problems were to be treated at all, they would be done so in an ad hoc fashion by local committees and commissars, or else by independent-minded military commanders. And by the time the second coalition was officially constituted, no one really expected very much in the way of effective national leadership.

The manner in which the July crisis finally ended did no credit to any of Russia's major political figures. On July 21, Kerensky himself resigned, flying off in a dusty cloud of false pride to escape the pressures breaking from all sides. This suddenly frightened Kadets and the left alike, for without Kerensky in the middle, neither side felt any new cabinet could be organized. Consequently, when Nekrasov (as Kerensky's deputy) called representatives from each of the major factions to an emergency all-night conference in the Malachite Room of the Winter Palace, each party finally accepted a new government with candidates selected on an "individual" rather than party basis. The subterfuges were all too obvious; but they allowed each side to feel the other had made major concessions. Socialist ministers would not be Soviet "representatives" in the government, or be "responsible" to any Soviet organization; they would merely "inform" their colleagues regularly of their actions; the government *as a whole* did not stand *officially* behind the July 8 Declaration, but individual ministers were free to join the regime on these grounds. And the Kadets, accepting the regime as officially "national" and "nonpartisan," would take their places alongside Victor Chernov.[70]

[68] *Rech'*, July 21, 1917.   [69] *Ibid.*; *Novoe Vremia*, July 21, 1917.
[70] *Rech'*, July 22 and 23, 1917; *Izvestiia*, July 22 and 23, 1917; *Novoe Vremia*, July 25, 1917.

The new Kadet ministers were Kokoshkin (who rejoined the government as state controller at the special insistence of Miliukov), Peter Iurenev (transport), Sergei Oldenburg (education), and Anton Kartashev (ober-procurator of the Holy Synod). They assumed their posts under Kerensky's presidency, and alongside the "renegade" Nekrasov, who was now deputy minister-president and minister of finance. In addition to Kerensky, the socialists were represented by Chernov, Skobelev, Peshekhonov, Zarudnyi, Prokopovich, Nikitin, and Avksentiev, and thus had a majority. And while all four Kadets were past or present members of the Central Committee, none represented the progressive views of men like Kishkin and Astrov. (In Sergei Oldenburg's first speech as minister of education, in fact, the former secretary of the Imperial Academy of Sciences declared that the events of July 3-5 only showed how "ignorant" the masses were, and how urgent the tasks of national education!)[71] Only Kokoshkin and Iurenev, moreover, had any real stature within the party. Kartashev and Oldenburg were precisely the type of "accidental" (*sluchainye*) officials propelled to power "by chance" that *Svobodnyi Narod* itself criticized in an editorial on the new regime.[72]

More important, the way in which the second coalition was organized failed to resolve the questions of political authority initially precipitating the Kadet resignations. Perhaps the most prominent spokesman for the Petrograd Soviet in May and June, Iraklii Tsereteli, was gone from the cabinet; but the hated Chernov remained; and as *Svobodnyi Narod* and *Rech'* both bitterly complained, he and other Soviet Executive Committee members were privately insisting that their "parent" bodies still had the right to "withdraw" them, despite the "independence" of the regime. Thus the Soviet's former leverage was tacitly preserved.[73]

The committee problem was also still open, precisely what had agitated Kadets through most of May and June. On July 16, in fact, just as Kadet pressures against him were reaching a peak, Chernov had actually strengthened the powers of local land committees by issuing a special circular granting them almost unlimited power to exploit estates which, in their own judgment, were not being fully utilized; and in special cases, where the estate owner was "completely" unable to cope with production problems—again in the judgment of local committees—seizures of estates were specifically authorized. "Land committees," Chernov wrote, "must look upon themselves as organs of state authority"—the very fragmentation of power statist Kadets like Kokoshkin desperately wanted to avoid—and "must go

---

[71] *Rech'*, July 28, 1917.   [72] *Svobodnyi Narod*, July 26, 1917.
[73] *Ibid.*; *Rech'*, July 26, 1917.

quite far in satisfying the just demands of the toiling peasantry . . ."—
precisely the preemption of Constituent Assembly powers that drove
Kadets from the first coalition.[74] Chernov's "instructions" were soon
countermanded by Tsereteli, who dispatched a circular to all provincial commissars on July 18, categorically ordering the cessation of
further land seizures on the part of local committees; and in a number
of places, particularly in the vicinity of the Southwestern Front, army
units were ordered to prevent the resolution of agrarian disputes
through "independent acts."[75] But there was little question that the
impact of the SR leader's "instructions" would still be felt.

There were also the persistent problems of production and supply.
These, too, had grown more serious since the beginning of July. According to material in the *Torgovo-Promyshlennaia Gazeta* (Trade-Industrial Gazette), 206 more factories closed their doors between the
time of the Kadet resignations and the formation of the new coalition,
throwing additional thousands of workers out of their jobs.[76] The
situation was most acute in Petrograd itself, where again, in spite of
many accusations from factory owners about new interference from
workers, the principal cause was lack of raw materials and fuel. Almost 10 percent less coal was mined in July 1917, for example, compared with February and March; and only two-thirds of that was carried on the railroads.[77] Production in general in some areas (like the
Donets basin) was now down 50 percent from the start of the year;
"delivered" goods were off by two-thirds; and transport almost everywhere remained "in crisis."[78] What was significant about these dreary
statistics in terms of the second coalition, however, was not so much the
magnitude of the problem, but the fact that the new ministers had
no clear set of policies with which to deal with the crisis other than
the July 8 Declaration, whose implementation the Kadet ministers
were pledged to prevent. As a consequence, the critical question of
state control (and thus of the relationship between governmental
authority, popular support, and the war) remained obscured; and the
result was bound to be an increase in the conflict between labor and

[74] Browder and Kerensky, II, 558-62. See also V. Chernov, *The Great Russian
Revolution*, trans. P. Mosely, New Haven, 1936, pp. 243-45. The editors of *Russkiia
Vedomosti* were particularly incensed by the secrecy of Chernov's circular, and
published a bitter editorial on the subject on August 4. See also the comments in
Chernov, pp. 243-48.

[75] *Ekonomicheskoe polozhenie Rossii nakanune velikoi oktiabr'skoi sotsialisticheskoi revoliutsii*, 3 pts., Moscow-Leningrad, 1957-67, pt. 3, pp. 249-50; P. N. Pershin,
Agrarnaia revoliutsiia v Rossii, 2 vols. Moscow, 1966, I, 379-85.

[76] *Torgovo-Promyshlennaia Gazeta*, Oct. 1/14, 1917.

[77] *Ekon. polozhenie*, pt. 1, pp. 74-77.

[78] *Stenograficheskii otchet zasedaniia ekonomicheskago soveta pri vremennom
pravitel'stve*, No. 1, July 21, 1917, and No. 2, July 22, 1917.

management that Kadets regarded as one root cause of political instability.

In only three areas—nationality affairs, the Constituent Assembly, and the army—did Kadets see the possibility of improvement. On July 18, the Finnish impasse was temporarily resolved by a government manifesto dissolving the Sejm for "predetermining of its own accord the will of the forthcoming Russian Constituent Assembly." The Finns accepted the decree, though reluctantly and with symbolic protests.[79] The more complicated Ukrainian problem was largely dealt with by a comprehensive statute on local administration, worked out by Rada leaders in accordance both with own demands and the fateful Ukrainian-Russian agreement of early July. Largely as a result of Nekrasov's efforts, the Ukrainian's work was also turned over to Baron Nolde's Juridical Commission for review.[80]

With respect to the Constituent Assembly, there was finally some indication that the elections scheduled for mid-September would be postponed. This promised to solve certain legal problems the Kadets considered crucial, such as the statutory requirement that electoral lists be published forty days before the elections. It also helped mitigate the danger pointed out with increasing stridency by local Kadet organs like *Rostovskaia Rech'*, that the current disorganization of local government would effectively disfranchise whole geographic areas[81] (though with results arriving in Petrograd of municipal duma elections, it is doubtful many Kadets felt that postponing the Assembly would actually improve their own party's chances).

Finally, the Kadets were pleased with Kerensky's efforts to repress the Bolsheviks and tighten discipline in the army. On July 15, in his

[79] *Vestnik Vremennago Pravitel'stva*, July 21, 1917; S. M. Dimanshtein, ed., *Revoliutsiia i natsional'nyi vopros*, Moscow, 1930, pp. 68-69; *Rech'*, July 22, 1917. Some Kadets continued to equate national self-determination with German subversion in Finland, but were satisfied after Finnish SDs failed in their attempt to reconvene the Sejm that Kerensky had the situation fairly well in control. See *Rech'*, Aug. 4 and 10, 1917.

[80] P. Khristiuk, *Zamitky i materialy do istorii ukrainskoi revoliutsii, 1917-20*, 4 vols., Vienna, 1921-22, II, 93-115; J. S. Reshetar, Jr., *The Ukrainian Revolution, 1917-1920*, Princeton, 1952, pp. 67-72. The statute further limited the territorial jurisdiction of the Ukrainian government, and lopped off from the Rada's own statute the ministerial posts of justice, war, post and telegraph, and communications. This affirmed in institutional terms the Ukraine's attachment to Petrograd. Other provisions retained for the Provisional Government the right "in pressing and urgent matters" to bypass normal administrative channels (which were Ukrainian organs) and contact local authorities directly. This kept police under Russian control. At the same time, the government reserved the right to veto legislation enacted by the General Secretariat.

[81] For example, *Rostovskaia Rech'* argued on Aug. 8 that if the elections were actually held on September 17, the whole Don region would simply not be represented, as local government organs, which were to supervise the elections, had not yet been organized. See also *Svobodnyi Narod*, July 28, 1917.

capacity as acting minister-president, Kerensky closed *Pravda, Okop-naia Pravda*, and other "seditious" publications, adopting at almost the same time a series of special measures for investigating the events of July 3-5. Particularly gratifying for the liberals was Tsereteli's special telegram to local soviets and committees, insisting that the government would not tolerate any further "anarchic" outbursts or "allow appeals to civil war, acts of violence or arbitrary actions which threaten the very existence of the country."[82]

Similarly, with respect to the army, Kadets welcomed Kerensky's seeming acceptance of Generals Brusilov and Kornilov's views on military discipline, presented at the headquarters conference of July 16; and they also applauded Kerensky's appointment of Kornilov as commander-in-chief on July 18.[83] Kornilov had presented a set of strict conditions—the Kornilov "Program"—before accepting the post: (1) that the Supreme Commander be responsible only to his "own conscience"; (2) that there be no interference with his orders or appointments; (3) that capital punishment be applied to army reserve units, like the Petrograd garrison; and (4) that specific proposals for army reform presented at the July 16 conference be formally accepted.[84] It was not clear how the new cabinet would respond to these conditions, and Kerensky himself seemed to hedge. Kornilov was assured, however, through Tereshchenko and Kerensky's assistant, Boris Savinkov, that his demands would be met.[85]

All sides, consequently, affected satisfaction with the reorganization of state authority. But in fact, the new coalition was essentially a repetition of the old; on one hand, it lacked even the veneer of authority needed to implement Soviet reforms in the face of forceful right-wing resistance; and on the other, it had little power or perhaps even desire to halt the "deepening" of the revolution. The right-wing editors of *Novoe Vremia* rightly feared that the government's future was doomed like its predecessor's; and many liberals must have joined them in their laconic hope that when the cabinet fell again, it would not carry all of Russia with it![86]

[82] *Vestnik Vremennago Pravitel'stva*, July 18, 1917. See also the discussion in Vera Vladimirova, *Kontr-revoliutsiia v 1917*, Moscow, 1924, pp. 19-21.

[83] The Kadets themselves had much to do with Kornilov's appointment, pressuring Kerensky, and while not making it a contingency for participation in the government, at least making it very clear that it would greatly increase Kerensky's support. See the discussion in J. D. White, "The Kornilov Affair," *Sov. Stud.*, xx, Oct. 1968, pp. 192-97.

[84] Kerensky, *Catastrophe*, pp. 306-07.

[85] B. Savinkov, *K delu Kornilova*, Paris, 1919, pp. 19-20; *Rech'*, July 28, 1917; Boris Gurevich, "Krasnyi sfinks," MS in the Columbia Russian Archive, 3 boxes, n.d., bx. 1, p. 416.

[86] *Novoe Vremia*, July 25, 1917.

CHAPTER SEVEN

Kadets and Kornilov

O<small>NE OF THE</small> most *simpatichnyi* members of the Kadet Central Committee was the hard-working former zemstvo physician from Voronezh,
Andrei Shingarev—the minister of agriculture and finance in the first
two cabinets. Devoted to his family, a conscientious and gentle hu-
manist, Shingarev felt one of the heaviest burdens of revolution was
the need to be away from home. Whenever he could, he traveled to
his small country estate and visited his wife. Other times, he wrote her
long and revealing letters.

In a letter he wrote at the end of July, Shingarev indicated he had
little confidence in the second coalition. Kerensky he regarded as
hysterical and incompetent; Nekrasov he distrusted. Kadets joined
the new cabinet because they felt "duty bound" to Russia. They also
felt no personal obligations had been placed on them in terms of the
July 8 Declaration, and that their own program was a basis for firm
authority.[1]

Kadets were certain, however, as Shingarev expressed it, that they
could no longer "sit on two stools," supporting one set of policies,
and watching the government implement another. They had to move
quickly and forcefully in some clear way to give the government power.
"Judging by my own observations," Shingarev wrote "the government
enjoys neither authority nor the hope of support from among the
so-called bourgeoisie; and left elements in the soviets are directly hostile." The crucial question was: "which way are the Kadets to move,"
which was very hard to answer.[2]

As Shingarev noted, a number of his colleagues still wanted the
party to move toward conciliation with the left, and finally to begin
working closely and cooperatively with moderate socialists. Until Kadet
archives for 1917 are opened for Western scholars in the Soviet Union,
we cannot know for certain how extensive this "left" faction had become after the July crisis, or who now supported this view in the
Central Committee. It is clear that Astrov, Kishkin, and Nicholas
Shchepkin still felt this way in Moscow, and so did Butenko in Kiev,
Krol in Ekaterinburg, Braikevich in Odessa, Vasilev in Samara, and

---

[1] A. G. Khrushchov, *Andrei Ivanovich Shingarev*, Moscow, 1918, pp. 123-25.
[2] *Ibid.*, p. 125.

Kedrin, Volkov, Gerasimov, Spasskii, Shakhovskoi, Adzhemov, Frenkel, and perhaps even Nabokov and Vinaver in Petrograd. In effect, these Kadets were ready to accept a subordinate role in terms of the party's relationship with the socialists, and for the sake of national unity, use their influence to calm the right, mobilizing "bourgeois" sentiment in favor of reforms and mutual understanding. Kadets might also work to smooth relations with the army command. A military coup now seemed a constant danger, and party leaders could certainly try to preserve the generals' support.

The validity of this viewpoint rested on the fact that liberals could no longer hope to govern by themselves, or even to establish an authoritative, liberal, provisional regime. These possibilities had disappeared with the prolonged crisis in July, and perhaps even before. Social disruption in the countryside, unease and dissension among workers, growing anarchy, and above all, the constant deterioration of Russia's military forces all pressed in the direction of social reforms, particularly in the countryside. They also impelled a rapid end to the war, as well as the election of a popular democratic government through the Constituent Assembly. At the level of high politics, consequently, the best hope—and perhaps the *last* best hope—for civil liberties, a permanent rule of law, and other traditional liberal goals, was to preserve and protect the Provisional regime, just as Kadets had tried to preserve and protect the Second Duma in 1907. This meant cooperation and close relations with Soviet leaders.

Social and political stability at a local level also required cooperation with the left. Kadets all over Russia complained bitterly of "anarchy" and "chaos," but what they were describing in effect was the extent to which political and social administration in the country was coming increasingly under the control of committees, soviets, and other ad hoc local organizations. By the end of July 1917, the influence of these groups could be felt in every city, town, and village, every factory and workshop, every railroad junction, school, and garrison. In one ironic sense, in fact, Russia in the summer of 1917 may have been better organized than at any other time in her history, in that virtually all institutional life was at least to some extent in committee or soviet hands. These groups lacked coordination or even clear policies. They were simply attempting in a chaotic fashion to remedy pressing, deep-rooted social problems on a particularistic and piecemeal basis, with scant regard for questions of political order. Nevertheless, these groups were now clearly managing most Russian affairs at a local level, just as zemstvos had done in many parts of Russia before the revolution; and for Kadets and other liberals to have any positive effect on the country's local affairs, it was necessary to begin working closely and cooperatively with them, and attempt to influence their activities from within.

The problem was, of course, that on a local level most Kadets strongly disagreed with the direction in which the committees and soviets were moving. There was also an enormous amount of mutual distrust, as Kadets appeared increasingly to represent "bourgeois" and gentry interests, while committees and soviets seemed increasingly the tools of radicals like the Bolsheviks. The conflict was, in a word, whether Russia's revolution had meaning primarily in terms of social or political democracy, whether national interests superseded popular ones. In seizing estates and taking control of factories and even army units, the "dark people" and their leaders were corrupting the very values and institutions on which liberals felt their country's future rested.

At the level of high politics, meanwhile, the problem was that liberals who favored conciliation lacked power within the government, or even authority within the party. Nekrasov was now completely discredited among most Petrograd and Moscow party members; and while nominally still a Kadet, was soon to be ceremoniously "disowned" at the ninth party congress. The other Kadet ministers were all virtually handpicked by Miliukov; and despite the divisions in the Central Committee over both the July resignations and the terms for further Kadet participation in the government (as well as a good deal of hostility toward the Kadet leader personally, whose somewhat arrogant personality had become even more abrasive through fatigue and anxiety), Miliukov and his supporters still held sway.

For them, in fact, the July crisis had resulted in a shift away from what earlier could be described as a "centrist" posture, and the assumption of a position much closer to that of the party's clear conservatives like Maklakov, Rodichev, and Izgoev. Having finally been forced into what he regarded as an unacceptable solution to the July crisis, and finally accepting Russian polarization as a present fact rather than future threat, Miliukov was assuming what Leopold Haimson has called a "civil war mentality," one which saw the future of liberal Russia absolutely dependent on the strict—and perhaps forcible—containment of the soviets and committees, rather than cooperation or conciliation. Even the Kadet party's own internal unity was becoming much less important, as would shortly be clear at the ninth congress. As Maklakov argued, there could be no freedom *bez Rodiny*, without, that is, the Great Russian State of the liberal's nationalist conception. If Kadets moved in any direction, it had to be to consolidate and strengthen Russia's "healthy elements."[3]

[3] *Svobodnyi Narod*, Aug. 17, 1917.

By the end of July, this had also become the firm view of a majority of provincial party leaders. Pressed by the anxiety and fear of increasing local violence, discouraged by the results of municipal duma campaigns, increasingly harassed by Bolsheviks and other radicals in public meetings, and unable to recruit new cadres, most provincial committee members now felt more strongly than ever that the party had to end its ostensible "nonpartisanship," and ally firmly with right-wing groups. This required the adoption of a much more partisan program, a clearer statement of the Kadets' own national and class biases. And while again, as in the past, the views of Kadets were hardly uniform in provincial areas (any more than they were in Moscow or Petrograd), Kadet newspapers increasingly carried statements like that in Omsk by Victor Zhardetskii, a future leader of the Eastern Section of the Kadet Central Committee, who wrote that the leaders of the Petrograd Soviet were worse than Sukhomlinov, Miasoedov, and other wretched tsarist officials: they had betrayed the army, covered the offensive with shame, and even "provoked" the Bolshevik insurrection.[4] Elsewhere, opinions were similar. In Kharkov, former Kadet "radicals" now publicly lauded Manuilov for trying to keep control of the schools from soviet reformers; and in Rostov, despite earlier criticism of the Kadet resignations, the outspoken Rodichev was welcomed by his colleagues after the July crisis as a conquering hero.[5]

The obvious advantage of moving openly to the right would be a consolidation of anti-socialist political strength, and the development of new abilities to coordinate political and economic pressures against the left. But there was also the obvious danger of further polarizing Russian society as a whole, and the much greater likelihood of civil war. And what then about Russia's role as a great power? Even Kadets like Novgorodtsev, Dolgorukov, Rodichev, and Izgoev shied away from considering open civil combat. Just as most Kadets could never become militant revolutionaries against the tsar, most could not see themselves now as militant counterrevolutionaries against the mass of Russian people.

What seemed to be the logical course for most Kadets in these circumstances was to shift openly from the position of "left-center" (as Miliukov had described it at the eighth congress) to "right center," playing on new hostility toward the Bolsheviks which had developed even in moderate socialist quarters after the July days, identifying the party programmatically with more openly conservative groups, and in particular, giving full support to the army and its forceful new com-

---

[4] *Sibirskaia Rech'*, Aug. 20, 1917.

[5] V. Zeeler, "Rodichev na iuge (iz vospominanii)," *Posledniia Novosti*, No. 2892, Feb. 21, 1929.

mander, General Kornilov. At best, this might lead party cadres in the provinces to closer associations with groups like the Union of Landowners (completing, in effect, the swing in this direction which had begun as early as April, and perhaps bringing some new sense of personal security); and there was even some possibility that discipline throughout society as a whole could be restored through the use of "loyalist" troops like the cossacks, sanctioned by the government as a result of pressures from the Kadet ministers. Perhaps in these circumstances Kadets could even return a reasonable delegation to the Constituent Assembly (though it would obviously be a minority), whenever that body convened.

As time would tell, however, the optimism underlying such a course for Kadets was bred of despair, rather than a clear perception of viable politics. More important, it meant firing up General Kornilov's own ambitions, which for many liberals would create the greatest dilemma of all.

THE NINTH KADET CONGRESS

The ninth Kadet congress, which opened on July 23, just as negotiations over a new government were ending, was convened specifically to prepare the party for the Constituent Assembly campaign; and most delegates arriving for the sessions were prepared to convince Miliukov and the Petrograd leadership that the only effective way to enter the electoral struggle was in alliance with clearly anti-soviet groups. Each came from an area with its own particular tale of trouble: in Barnaul, the local soviet had ordered a search of the Kadet print shop, and confiscated party literature; in Kursk, printers had refused to publish the Kadet paper before the city elections; in Perm province, the Kadet club was invaded by soldiers, and party members threatened with bayonets; and in Sriazi, a prominent Kadet landowner well known for his radical views (and who earlier had worked for a local alliance between the Kadets and the left), was seized by a crowd of peasants, taken to the railroad station to "join the army," and lynched.[6]

It turned out, however, that Miliukov and most of his colleagues now needed very little convincing. As the congress opened, just before the new government organized itself, Paul Novgorodtsev told the delegates that Kadets would never join a cabinet that would implement the socialists' program. The word "coalition" was "falling on all ears" and "unthinking, would-be patriots" from all sides were calling on the party to yield to the left; but Kadet firmness was "absolutely right";

6 *VPNS*, No. 19, Sept. 21, 1917, pp. 24-25.

Russia's future depended on containing the socialists and creating instead a government based on a "truly national program."[7]

Moreover, when Miliukov himself addressed the delegates after the cabinet had been formed, he took little time to align himself clearly with the party's right. Gone was his past role of "unifier." A coalition had indeed been organized with Kadet participation, he argued, contrary to what many Kadets had hoped or been led to expect. (Novgorodtsev's speech had made a "tremendous impression" on the delegates, according to *Rech'*, and many were quite surprised to learn of what seemed at first to be an abrupt turnaround.)[8] But Kadets had entered the cabinet only because Russia had been plunged into a situation where the alternative would have been no government at all. The Petrograd leadership fully recognized Russia's condition, and appreciated the needs and desires of provincial delegates. The country was in chaos: ". . . chaos in the army, chaos in foreign policy, chaos in industry, and chaos in nationality questions, which had resulted in the recognition of the Ukrainian Rada and the departure of the Kadet ministers." In particular, Miliukov went on angrily, there was chaos in communications and transport—the preserve of Nicholas Nekrasov; and abandoning the "balanced" viewpoint he had taken at other congresses to keep the party together, Miliukov now laid blame for these conditions squarely at the feet of his ertswhile party colleague and his left-Kadet supporters, even applauding the fact that Nekrasov had "finally been driven" from his former government position. In sum, Miliukov declared, the Kadet ministers remained determined now as before to defend the country's best interests; they would pull the regime away from soviet domination and strengthen state authority "from within."[9]

Many were displeased with Miliukov's presentation, but not because he attacked Nekrasov or otherwise appeared uncompromising. On the contrary, while leftist delegates like Frenkel and Shakhovskoi looked on with dismay, their right-wing colleagues responded by insisting that the Petrograd leadership had been *too* conciliatory, and greeted Miliukov's condemnation of Nekrasov with "strong applause." Davydov from Moscow was incensed that "the traitor" Chernov remained in the cabinet, and that the Program of July 8 had essentially been accepted, despite public Kadet denials; and A. M. Evlakhov from the Kuban bitterly assailed the entire Soviet, blaming Kerensky himself for Order Number One in March (a charge some delegates

---

[7] *Russkiia Vedomosti*, July 25, 1917.
[8] *Rech'*, July 26 and 27, 1917; *Russkiia Vedomosti*, July 26 and 27, 1917.
[9] *Rech'*, July 26, 1917.

loudly refuted). "The sole guilty party responsible for the present dreadful situation in Russia is the Soviet of Workers' and Peasants' Deputies," he argued, with whom any accommodation whatsoever was "completely unacceptable." What the country needed at once was a "national regime" concerned with "national interests," and staffed by prominent "national figures."[10]

But in concern for Russia's national interests, no one in the party had better credentials than Miliukov. The Kadet leader quickly mollified his critics by insisting that the party was ready to "fight." When the Central Committee introduced a resolution in support of the party's Petrograd leadership, there was no "minority report" in favor of *sblizhenie* with the Left, as Shakhovskoi had introduced at the seventh congress in March; and despite the fact that a number of the approximately 200 ninth congress delegates were still partisans of conciliation (including now some prominent new adherents in the Central Committee like Astrov, Kishkin, and perhaps even Vinaver and Nabokov), the course charted by Miliukov was enthusiastically endorsed. (According to *Rech'*, support was "unanimous," though only a voice vote was taken.) Kadets would undertake a new struggle against sectarian left-wing elements, and in the face of "a most critical danger threatening the very existence" of the country, "dedicate all forces to saving the Motherland."[11]

What these forces were the leadership soon made clear. First among them was the army, particularly its officer corps. Traditionally, liberals had insisted that the military be kept out of politics. But now Kadets were clearly anxious to show support for General Kornilov, and argued they had to "agitate" to win soldiers from the radicals. These were extraordinary times, Miliukov declared, and extraordinary times demanded special measures.[12] The official report of the Central Committee's military commission obscured the question somewhat, stating only that "mutual relations between military personnel must be founded on principles of legality and firm military discipline, and correspond to the basic principles of democratic government." But a suggestion that a statement be added to the effect that the army was "nonpolitical" was specifically rejected; and despite a certain ambiguity in the report (which some delegates, in fact, protested), its general meaning was clear. The validity of Nicholas Sukhanov's challenge to Miliukov in April, which assumed the army would become *the* crucial political battleground of revolutionary Russia, was now being formally recognized.

10 *Ibid.*, July 26 and 27, 1917; *Russkiia Vedomosti*, July 26 and 27, 1917.
11 Resolutions of the ninth party congress, *VPNS*, Nos. 11-13, Aug. 10, 1917, p. 10.
12 *Rech'*, July 18, 1917.

Also clear were the implicit purposes underlying the party's statements on agriculture and industry. Ariadna Tyrkova and V. A. Kosinskii attributed rural unrest directly to Chernov's "socializing adventures." Socialism ran "counter to innate peasant attachment to property." The lack of peasant productivity, the weakening of labor intensity, the decline of peasant willingness to work—all these developments were the result of "socialist experimentation." Tyrkova and Kosinskii even insisted that Kadets take up Stepanov's earlier call and urge the regime to renounce socialism officially: if peasants understood that socialism threatened property in land, they would "follow no other political party but our own. This will lead us out of the horror and chaos which threatens our agrarian life."[13]

Here there was a good deal of resistance from left-leaning Kadet "conciliationists," who recognized the effect any statement of this sort would have on their relations with the soviets. Even Shingarev spoke about the need for state control of industry, and perhaps even some degree of socialization in agriculture, stressing that this might be the only way out of a "gloomy" situation in which every local committee wanted to decide production questions by itself. Others, like Manuilov, while "deeply pessimistic," straddled both camps; and as a consequence, no single statement on either issue was formally adopted. But the congress majority clearly indicated that it thought Russia's economic life had to be based on "free initiative," and that Kadets would move "forward" with those who supported this view.[14]

This, clearly, was an abject ploy for new support from gentry groups like the Union of Landowners, as well as from others who generally felt Kadet economic policies in the past had been too radical. For the first time at an official party congress, the question of economic "initiative" was being advanced as a way of setting Kadets off clearly from even moderate socialist groups like the Trudoviks, and identifying the party with the basic principles of capitalism and the bourgeoisie. Ironically, the party's career in the civil war would show how few friends the Kadets had among other organized nonsocialist groups; and that rather than the "bourgeoisie," moderate socialists were the party's strongest allies in the pursuit of liberal democracy. But at the ninth party congress, in the anxious aftermath of what scores of Kadets felt was clear display of the "socialist danger" for Russia, party members from Petrograd, Moscow, and the provinces alike were insistent on drawing clear lines between them and the left.

The most dramatic indications of the party's move to the right, however, came not on economic matters, but on the nationality issue,

[13] *Rech'*, July 28, 1917.   [14] *Ibid.*

and the question of the church. According to Baron Nolde, a member of the government's Juridical Commission and a distinguished professor of law, the Central Committee had resolved "in a final way" to reject the territorial basis as the framework for resolving the nationality question. Kadets would press instead for nationality "unions," to be recognized as quasi-official organizations, and enjoying the prerogatives of administering all *cultural* affairs pertaining to their particular ethnic group.[15]

As Grigorovich-Barskii pointed out—and he was certainly no radical—Nolde's theses meant that Kadets absolutely rejected autonomy for the Ukraine in geographic terms. This not only contradicted what party committees in the Ukraine believed themselves, but made absurd the Kadets' past positions on "other nationality groups," as Barskii described them, like Poland and Finland.[16] But the congress as a whole accepted Nolde's theses as amendments to the party's program. Grigorovich-Barskii was rebutted when Miliukov announced that the Central Committee considered the Ukraine a "special case," and would set up a special commission to work out legislation for Ukrainian autonomy to present the Constituent Assembly.[17]

The question of the church was even more scandalous, at least to left Kadets. Here delegates were not only asked to change the party program so that orthodoxy was designated an "institution of public-legal (*publichno-pravovyi*) character," but also to sanction state aid so that Kadets did not appear "to recommend separation of church and state as the socialist parties do."[18] Such a position corresponded to the programs of prerevolutionary rightist parties, and would obviously appeal to Russia's remaining conservative elements. But it also clearly violated the Kadets' own program (paragraph 2 of which clearly committed Kadets to the separation of church and state); and it implicitly threw into question the whole liberal attitude toward religious discrimination, as several of the delegates pointed out. Not surprisingly, the Central Committee's position on this question drew heated opposition, some of the delegates even accusing its leaders, particularly Novgorodtsev, of wanting "to turn the clock back 11 years or more." But the amendments to the program were approved nevertheless. Despite their own Western intellectual heritage (and perhaps as an indication of the depths of their own anxiety and fear), Kadets after five months of revolutionary tumult officially became champions of the orthodox church.[19]

As the delegates dispersed, Astrov, Frenkel, Gerasimov, and other

15 *Ibid.*, July 26, 1917.   16 *Ibid.*

17 *VPNS*, Nos. 11-13, Aug. 10, 1917, p. 13.   18 *Rech'*, July 27, 1917.

19 *Ibid.*; *VPNS*, Nos. 11-13, Aug. 10, 1917, pp. 13-14.

left Kadets felt the congress had only added to Russia's confusion, not to mention their own. As at earlier sessions, the party's official resolution on tactics left the matter of alliances and electoral blocs up to local committees. But most Kadets were no longer insisting on their own "nonpartisanship"; and the traditional role of the party as the unifying center for Russia was implicitly discarded. It was quite uncertain in these circumstances how (if at all) Kadets were to approach masses of workers and peasants in the campaign for the Constituent Assembly, something left Kadets still regarded as essential for the future of Russian liberalism; and it was even doubtful whether local party committees were expected to support the second coalition.

For their rightward drifting colleagues, however, the future was clear. Kadets had only to translate the angry, conservative mood of the congress into political force.

Allies on the Right

Immediately after the ninth congress, Rodichev, Kharlamov, and M. S. Voronkov left for Novocherkassk to develop closer ties between Kadets and the Don cossacks, the traditional defenders of state authority. Kharlamov and Voronkov were prominent members of the Kadet committee in Rostov, while Rodichev had now become one of the party's foremost right-wing spokesmen. Kharlamov was also president of the Don Voisko, the cossacks' military administration, in addition to being a member of the party's Central Committee. The task of the three Kadets was to form a Kadet-cossack "united front," and to consolidate efforts for the Constituent Assembly elections.[20]

Local party organizations in the Don had actually developed excellent relations with the cossacks in May and June, largely because both groups were resisting the efforts of non-cossack *inogorodnye* to organize into soviets and local committees, and secure greater privileges. The *inogorodnye* were non-cossack peasants, who had traditionally labored for the cossacks very much like serfs. Among other deprivations, they were denied the right to own land in cossack territories. They constituted a sympathetic base for radical agitation, and the containment of their efforts at local government and organization seemed an important means of preserving "order" in the region.[21]

At the height of the July crisis, moreover, the Kadets had also publicly demonstrated their support for the cossacks by sending a special delegation to the funeral of several cossack officers killed in the

20 Zeeler, "Rodichev."
21 See the discussion in Peter Kenez, *Civil War in South Russia*, Berkeley, 1971, pp. 38-39.

Bolshevik uprising. This had caused a furor within the Petrograd Soviet (whose spokesmen wondered why Kadets had not similarly honored *all* Russians killed in the episode), but it was very much appreciated by cossacks on the Don, particularly the officers.[22]

When the three Kadets arrived in early August, they received a tumultuous welcome. The weather was scorching hot, but more than 1,000 persons jammed an assembly hall to hear them speak. On August 2, Rodichev and Voronkov were also specially presented as "honored guests" to the Don military council. Shortly afterward, assisted by local Kadets like V. F. Zeeler, they succeeded in forging exactly the type of alliance they felt the party needed to consolidate its national positions: Don cossacks and Kadets would run on a single slate for the Constituent Assembly, and would stand in support of the party's platform in all areas under the military council's jurisdiction.[23]

Meanwhile, Kadets also worked at building their ties with the regular army, or more precisely, the regular army's officer corps. Here, too, contacts had been made in May and June. In early May, when a newly formed Union of Army and Navy Officers held its organizational conference, Rodichev, Shingarev, and Miliukov had all addressed the group as keynote speakers. (Rodichev in particular knew how to strike a responsive chord. "There is a banner," he orated, "under which each citizen must stand in readiness to sacrifice all, even his life—the Holy Banner of Defense of the Motherland!")[24] Prodded by Miliukov, the delegates had passed resolutions condemning "collective decision-making" and the "elective principle," and asserting that the "sole guarantee of national economic welfare" was "access, if not military control, over the Dardanelles Straits."[25]

But before the July interregnum, Kadets had generally followed the party's traditional rule of keeping the army out of politics. An official Kadet pamphlet, "The Army in Free Russia," declared, for example, that armies "in all democratic countries are apolitical . . . independent of parties and governments, and defending the civil liberties of all citizens equally."[26] The Officers Union also made efforts to show its impartiality. Its administrative head was a colonel named Novosiltsev, who openly declared his allegiance to the Kadets, but it also established contacts with the Petrograd Soviet in May and June, and listened attentively to the radical Steklov at its opening conference, along with the Kadets.[27]

[22] *Birzhevye Vedomosti*, July 11, 1917; *Izvestiia*, July 13, 1917.
[23] Zeeler, "Rodichev"; *Svobodnyi Narod*, Aug. 5, 1917; *Novoe Vremia*, Aug. 4, 1917.
[24] *Novoe Vremia*, May 13, 1917.   [25] *Ibid.*, May 24, 1917.
[26] Gen. Maj. P. D. Burskii, *Armiia svobodnoi Rossii*, Moscow, 1917, pp. 9-10.
[27] *Novoe Vremia*, May 10 and 11, 1917; *Rech'*, May 14, 1917.

All of this changed in July. Shortly after the Kadet ministers resigned, the party's Central Committee organized a special "Military Commission" under Vasili Stepanov. It was divided into four sections: agitation, organization, legislation, and literature; and its official goals were to "establish links between the party and soldiers, sailors, officers, and other members of the army and navy, and to familiarize army personnel with the party's views on the meaning of the military in state affairs."[28] As with the cossacks, these efforts were accelerated immediately after the ninth party congress, having now been officially endorsed. The commission drafted a comprehensive set of rules, "Instructions for the Organization of Party Groups in Military Units of the Army and Navy," and published them in the party's official *Vestnik* on August 10. Local Kadet committees in districts where army units were stationed were to move at once to form a comprehensive network of Kadet "military factions," admitting anyone who declared their support for the party's program. Their purpose was to distribute party literature, agitate in favor of party goals, and organize meetings where Kadet Central Committee members could speak.[29]

Meanwhile, Miliukov and other party leaders in Petrograd also developed their contacts with the army's high command. Shortly after Kerensky appointed Lavr Kornilov Supreme Military Commander on July 18, Miliukov was visited by Boris Savinkov, the assistant minister of war and General Kornilov's political commissar. Savinkov's task was to present Kadets with Kornilov's "Program" to extend capital punishment, and implement new disciplinary measures. With Russia still in the midst of the government crisis, he also sounded Kadet opinion on the desirability of creating a three-man military dictatorship, to be composed of Kerensky, Kornilov, and a leading Kadet. Its base of operations would be at army headquarters at Mogilev, rather than Petrograd; and its attention would be focused primarily on problems of military and civil discipline. (Other governmental affairs were to be left to the competence of the vice-ministers and their assistants, who would remain in the capital.)[30]

Miliukov categorically rejected the dictatorship scheme as unworkable and undesirable (though some evidence suggests his attitude was "for the time being").[31] But he and the Kadet leadership enthusiasti-

<hr>

[28] *Rech'*, July 13, 1917.

[29] *VPNS*, Nos. 11-13, Aug. 10, 1917, p. 24.

[30] Boris Gurevich, "Krasnyi sfinks," unpubl. MS, 3 boxes, n.d., bx. 1, pp. 416-17, 467.

[31] V. Obolenskii, "Vospominaniia," MS, n.d., p. 460. According to N. G. Dumova, "Maloizvestnye materialy po istorii kornilovshchiny," *VI*, No. 11, 1968, p. 72, Miliukov may have "entered into personal conversations on the establishment of a military dictatorship with Admiral Kolchak in the beginning of June." Dumova's

cally supported Kornilov's demands. To mobilize public pressure, they began to develop their contacts with several civilian organizations which were also strongly endorsing Kornilov, particularly the so-called Republican Center, a group which had formed in May to press for strong government, victory over the Germans, and stricter military controls. The Center was not a secret organization, nor did its members generally consider themselves conservatives. In its public statements and declarations, which occasionally appeared in the press, it urged tight control over monarchist groups as well as the satisfaction of "just demands" from the workers. It also urged the rapid convocation of a Constituent Assembly.[32]

The Center maintained close contacts with the army, however, through a special Military Section under L. P. Desimeter, a colonel on the General Staff, and with Petrograd and Moscow commercial circles. In July, it also established close ties for the first time with overtly right-wing organizations like the so-called Society for the Economic Rehabilitation of Russia, a funding group led by the Octobrist and former war minister Guchkov, and Aleksei Putilov, one of Russia's leading industrialists. In addition to moral support for General Kornilov, these people were willing to contribute substantial amounts of money for a campaign in his behalf. They were also more interested than Miliukov in the possibility of a military dictatorship.[33]

The details of this organizational maze are hard to sort out and not very important. The significant point is that the Kadets were the only major political party involved in these groups and discussions, and the only nonsocialist party with officials in the cabinet of ministers. Central Committee figures like Miliukov and Rodichev thus

---

source is apparently a document of Novosiltsev's, though this is not clear; and she has Novosiltsev learning of this from Kolchak himself, rather than from Miliukov, although the two Kadets were in frequent contact.

[32] Memoirs of P. N. Finisov, vice president of the Republican Center, in *Posledniia Novosti*, No. 5818, Feb. 27, 1937; see also O. N. Chaadaeva, *Pomeshchiki i ikh organizatsii v 1917 godu*, Moscow-Leningrad, 1928, p. 141; A. I. Denikin, *Ocherki russkoi smuty*, 5 vols., Paris-Berlin, 1921-25, II, 27-29; V. Vladimirova, *Kontrrevoliutsiia v 1917*, Moscow, 1924, pp. 41-42. A declaration of the Center signed by Finisov, K. Nikolaevskii, and A. Bogdanovskii, and stating its program, appeared, for example, in the Kadet paper in Baku, *Narodnaia Svoboda*, July 23, 1917.

[33] The Society for the Economic Rehabilitation of Russia was formed by Guchkov, A. I. Vyshnegradskii, A. I. Putilov, N. A. Belotsvetov, N. N. Kutler, V. A. Kamenka, and A. P. Meshcherskii shortly after Guchkov's resignation as minister of war. Its function was to propagandize, and to fund right-wing agitators, but it was generally inactive in May and June, and had no contact with the Republican Center. According to the Finisov memoirs, in fact, Guchkov was quite unpopular with many army officers, and could not have worked closely with the Center had he wanted to. See also, "Kornilov i fevral'skaia revoliutsiia. Lektsiia V. A. Gurevicha," *Poslednia Novosti*, No. 4118, July 1, 1932, and Vladimirova, p. 42.

became the political focal point for support of the army generally, a posture they cultivated and welcomed.

As Kartashev, Iurenev, Oldenburg, and particularly the pessimistic Kokoshkin took their posts in the new coalition, they began immediately to champion Kornilov's cause. They pressured Kerensky to accept the general's "program," urged tighter control over committees, and even spoke out forcefully in favor of extending capital punishment, a measure the party still officially opposed.[34] When Kerensky appeared to stall on the question (he was, in fact, quite distrustful of Kornilov, fearing him as a "usurper" and worried about civil war),[35] Kadets also helped arrange a special meeting between the two. And when this failed to produce an agreement, Kokoshkin began attacking Kerensky both for personally trying to assume all governmental power and selfishly protecting his own personal relations with the soviets.[36] On August 11, Kokoshkin went so far as to threaten that the Kadets would again resign if the cabinet did not immediately accept the general's demands.[37]

It was also in their roles both as government officials and local party leaders that many Kadets began extending their contacts with bourgeois organizations like the Trade-Industrialists in the days immediately following the ninth congress, in some places completely discarding even a theoretical commitment to the notion of *nadklassnost'* and openly defending sectarian class interests. On August 3, when a Trade-Industrialist conference met in Moscow, prominent Kadets from all over Russia were in attendance as speaker after speaker described the chaotic and critical conditions of Russian industry, and attacked the socialist leadership in the government. ("A pack of charlatans," was how the conference president, Riabushinskii, described them: "We ought to say . . . that the present revolution is a bourgeois revolution, that the bourgeois order which exists at the present time is inevitable, and since it is inevitable, one must draw the completely logical conclusion and insist that those who rule the state think in a bourgeois manner and act in a bourgeois manner. . . .")[38] Kadets responded sympathetically, despite the fact that Riabushinskii also criticized party leaders like Shingarev for their constant call "to sacrifice." The con-

[34] *Rech'*, July 28, 1917; B. Savinkov, *K delu Kornilova*, Paris, 1919, pp. 19-20.

[35] A. F. Kerensky, *Prelude to Bolshevism*, London, 1919, pp. 51-64.

[36] Report of F. F. Kokoshkin to the Kadet city committee in Moscow, Aug. 31, 1917, in the Panina Archive, bx. 2, fold. 3, pp. 2-3, 5.

[37] *Ibid.* See also Vladimirova, p. 62. Kokoshkin's threat came on the heels of a second meeting between Kerensky and Kornilov on August 10, at which time Kornilov presented his program in person.

[38] *Russkiia Vedomosti*, Aug. 4, 1917; *Ekonomicheskoe polozhenie Rossii nakanune velikoi oktiabr'skoi sotsialisticheskoi revoliutsii*, 3 pts., Moscow-Leningrad, 1957-67, pt. 1, pp. 196-99.

ference was "an occasion where the bourgeoisie finally strikes back at the unjustified attacks from the left," according to *Rech'*; while in the cabinet, Kokoshkin and Iurenev took up the Trade-Industrialist call for tight controls on workers' committees.[39] The conference leadership also met with Shingarev, Manuilov, and other Kadets to develop further coordination.[40]

Similar ties were also developed with N. N. Lvov's "Union of Landowners." A plenary session of this group's Central Council was held on July 29-31, where socialists (and particularly Victor Chernov) were denounced in scathing terms. Lvov himself had been a Kadet deputy in the State Duma before the revolution, and a charter member of the party's first Central Committee in 1905. And as we have seen he and the Union had earlier begun to explore the possibility of closer contacts through Grigorovich-Barskii and other landowning Kadets, particularly through the use by the Union of the Kadet provincial press.[41] On July 31, Lvov told his colleagues that he was beginning the work of "organizing groups of industrialists, bankers, Kadets, and others" in order to "boldly defend our interests, because by defending property, we defend statehood. . . ."[42]

All these efforts at liberal consolidation were finally brought into clear focus at a huge Conference of Public Figures, which convened in Moscow on August 8. According to the conservative Kadet E. N. Trubetskoi, who played a prominent role in convening the sessions, the conference was "to gather and strengthen the statesmanlike [*gosudarstvennye*] and nationalist [*natsional'nye*] elements of the country, and to give them an opportunity to express their views on the general state of affairs . . . ," particularly in view of the fact that Minister-President Kerensky had called for a conference of *all* Russian political elements to meet in Moscow on August 12.[43] The meetings were closed to the general public to prevent disruptions. But more than 400 individuals attended, bringing together for the first time since the February revolution representatives from all segments of non-socialist Russian society. Generals Alekseev, Brusilov, and the cossack general Kaledin were there from the army; Rodzianko and Shulgin from the old Fourth Duma leadership; Riabushinskii and a host of

[39] *Rech'*, Aug. 5, 1917. See also *Promyshlennost' i Torgovlia*, No. 28-29, Aug. 5, 1917, pp. 71ff.

[40] V. A. Laverychev, "Vserossiiskii soiuz torgovli i promyshlennosti," *IZ*, No. 70, 1961, pp. 48-49; and his *Po tu storonu barrikad*, Moscow, 1967, pp. 173-88.

[41] O. N. Chaadaeva, "Soiuz zemel'nykh sobstvennikov v 1917 g.," *KA*, No. 21, 1927, p. 106; A. V. Shchestakov, ed., *Sovety krest'ianskikh deputatov i drugie krest'-ianskie organizatsii*, Moscow, 1929, pp. 152-77.

[42] Chaadaeva, "Soiuz," pp. 120-21.

[43] *Otchet o moskovskom soveshchanii obshchestvennykh deiatelei 8-10 avgust 1917*, Moscow, 1917, p. 3.

Trade-Industrialists; and Miliukov, Shingarev, Maklakov, Konovalov, and others from the Kadets. Miliukov himself also played a prominent role in the main working committee of the conference, introducing the reports of the Resolutions Committee. To outside observers, and particularly workers, peasants, and soldiers who read the left-wing press, no gathering could have better illustrated the deep social cleavage that now rent Russian society.

The tone of the sessions, moreover, corresponded very closely to the dominant mood of the Kadets' own ninth party congress: "nonpartisan" in the statist and conservative sense this term had come to mean, nationalistic, deeply patriotic in the traditions of old Russia, and passionately supportive of General Kornilov and his efforts to restore strict discipline in the army. "The causes and root of Russia's present evils are evident," one resolution introduced by Miliukov declared:

> Its sources are the subordination of the great national [obshche-natsional'nye] tasks of the revolution to the visionary aspirations of socialist parties. . . . Time will not wait; it is impossible to delay. In the name of Russia's salvation and the rebirth of freedom, the government must immediately and decisively break with all servants of utopia.[44]

With battle lines thus clearly drawn, scores of reports were then given from all corners of privileged Russia describing with passionate detail the disruption and agony revolutionary change had wrought on a dying way of life.

It is hard to say whether the conference accomplished anything specific. In one sense, its greatest achievement was psychological, bringing together scores of persons who could take some small comfort in knowing many others shared their anxieties and fears. As the sessions closed, Rodzianko, Guchkov, Miliukov, Maklakov, Shingarev, Shulgin, Tretiakov, Riabushinskii, and a number of other "leading public figures" met at a special private session with Generals Alekseev, Brusilov, Iudenich, and Kaledin. They discussed the need for "the most severe measures" for establishing military discipline, and also examined the need for yet another change of government, this time one "which would finally give the possibility of setting up a firm, unlimited [neogranichennaia] state authority." This, "in the opinion of the participants" was something "absolutely necessary for the present time."[45] Whether steps were also taken to set such strong ideas in motion is unclear, though not unlikely. According to the Soviet

---

[44] Ibid., p. 3, 132-36. Vladimirova, p. 128, gives the number of delegates as 300; the official Otchet reports 400.

[45] Svobodnyi Narod, Aug. 10, 1917.

historian N. F. Slavin, who has used archival materials still unavailable to Western scholars, a number of Kadet Central Committee members "categorically" insisted at a meeting on August 11 that "an end must be put to the 'Bolshevik' revolution," while Miliukov emphasized to his colleagues that "the path toward creating a dictatorship was already being followed," and that it was "impossible to change in the middle."[46] Whether or not Slavin is accurate, Miliukov and his supporters at the very least had succeeded in bringing together what their Central Committee leadership now considered the only "healthy elements" in Russia to discuss future tactics, consolidating *tsenzovoe* society as a whole. Openly admitting, in effect, that the country was now thoroughly polarized, they publicly shed at a national level any remaining pretense about their own social and political orientation.

THE MOSCOW STATE CONFERENCE

We know in retrospect that there were very serious weaknesses in the Kadet effort to consolidate Russia's anti-socialist forces. Progressive Kadets like Shakhovskoi, Astrov, and Frenkel themselves disagreed with this posture, and it further weakened the remaining bonds of party unity. More important in practical terms, a number of the Kadet's right-wing contacts were still quite tenuous. The Union of Landowners, for example, continued to blame Kadets (particularly Shingarev) for the Provisional Government's weakness, and castigated party leaders for "capitulating" to a cabinet which still included Victor Chernov; while many Trade-Industrialists also felt Kadets had acquiesced to a new cabinet which had only the appearance of authority, and sharply criticized those who wanted an expansion of state monopolies and control, precisely what was being suggested by Manuilov and Shingarev.[47] Moreover, when army leaders prompted Kerensky to revive the government's power of "administrative arrest and deportation," one of the old regime's most hated instruments, and thus gave the ministers of war and interior authorization to arrest and deport "anyone whose activity constitutes a particular threat to the defense and internal security of the state . . . ," even *Russkiia Vedomosti* worried in an editorial whether these weapons might not be "misused" for "partisan purposes" if the regime fell completely under socialist dominance.[48]

[46] N. F. Slavin, "Krisis vlasti v sentiabre 1917 g. i obrazovanie vremennogo soveta respubliki (predparlament)," *IZ*, No. 61, 1967, p. 35.

[47] Chaadaeva, *Pomeshchiki*, pp. 94-97, 125-27; *Russkiia Vedomosti*, Aug. 4, 1917; *Novoe Vremia*, July 26, Aug. 5, 1917.

[48] *Russkiia Vedomosti*, Aug. 4, 1917.

In terms of their own practical political activities, moreover, organizations like the Union of Landowners were still keeping some distance from many local Kadet committees, still afraid, apparently, of becoming more open targets themselves for the wrath of local radicals. In most places, they refused to consolidate electoral slates for municipal duma elections in August, or even back mutual candidates, much more so than in July. In Iaroslavl on August 1, Orel on August 2, Tula on August 3, Stavropol and Serpukhov on August 6, and Chernigov on August 8, for example, Landowners, Trade-Industrialists, and a surprising number of other bourgeois groups all elected their own "partisan" representatives to new local city dumas. In Kremenchug and Dmitrov, the Union of Homeowners surpassed the Kadets in numbers of candidates elected. In Iaroslavl they came close. In the process, moreover, the popular strength of Kadets themselves continued to drop, even in the old second curia districts. While Kadets received some 17.7 percent of the available local duma seats in elections between July 17 and 30, they received only 12.8 percent from July 31 to August 9. (At the same time, despite the July uprising, there was no real change in the percentage of seats obtained by the Bolsheviks. In twelve elections held in the capital cities of European Russia between July 17 and 30, they received 4.5 percent of all available seats; in the 9 elections between July 31 and August 13, they received 4.8 percent.)[49] According to reports in the Kadet *Vestnik*, Kadet meetings were now increasingly attended by officers, local industrialists, and other clearly "bourgeois" elements, in addition to the party's traditional following among the intelligentsia.[50] But while attendance of this sort very much strengthened the popular conception of local Kadet committees as organs of counterrevolution, it did nothing to increase the party's real political strength. New local dumas were still entirely dominated by the socialists, particularly the SRs.

In addition, Kadet ties with the army command were also seriously flawed, so much so, in fact, that it was very unlikely that even a successful military coup would propel Kadets into power. The full consequences of the party's poor relations with the army would become apparent in the civil war, as we shall see. But even in August 1917, General Alekseev resented the party's "desertion" from the government in July, at the height of the offensive; and Kornilov felt almost all political leaders, Kadets included, were not to be trusted.[51] According

[49] See my article, "The Russian Municipal Duma Elections of 1917," *Sov. Stud.*, XXI, Oct. 1969, pp. 148-50.

[50] E.g., *VPNS*, Nos. 11-13, Aug. 10, 1917, p. 25; Nos. 17-18, Sept. 7, 1917, pp. 13-22.

[51] Gen. M. V. Alekseev, "Iz dnevnika generala M. V. Alekseeva," *Sbornik russkii istoricheskii arkhiv*, I, Prague, 1929, pp. 19-20.

to General Brusilov, the majority of officers had sympathy for the Kadets. But some groups, like the Petrograd Officers Council, were clearly hostile, and there was suspicion at all levels about the general competence of civilian administrators.[52] When the local garrison in Rostov participated in a city duma election in July, for example, only 10 of the army's 1,997 votes—officers and enlisted men included—went to Kadets. The overwhelming majority here and elsewhere went to socialist bloc candidates, and a good proportion (331 in Rostov) went to the Bolsheviks.[53]

Even the party's vaunted union with the Don cossacks had problems. Not only did the *inogorodnye* react with bitterness to the merger of Kadet and cossack electoral slates; many rank-and-file cossacks themselves were developing great antipathy toward their own officer leadership, emulating their non-cossack comrades throughout the army. A division was thus opening which would prove to have fateful consequences in the Don region during the early months of the civil war, and Kadet activities at "unification" were actually contributing to its development.

But by far the most serious consequence of Kadet efforts to consolidate the right was that they virtually precluded cooperation with moderate socialist leaders, particularly in the Petrograd Soviet and the Executive Committee of the All-Russian Congress of Soviets. While the time had surely passed in mid-August when such cooperation would have significantly increased the authority of the provisional regime, it might have been sufficient to keep counter-revolutionary tendencies under control, and thus preserve such state power as existed until the convocation of the Constituent Assembly. In addition, left-wing radicals were now insisting that Kadets and the right were plotting against the revolution. Demonstrable support for the second coalition would have undermined their arguments, and perhaps even their popular appeal. More important, the moderate socialists themselves were now anxious for liberal cooperation and support. They also felt national unity behind even a weak provisional government would protect the revolution, and lead the way to an authoritative national regime elected by the people themselves.

This became clear at the famous State Conference in Moscow, which was originally conceived after the Kadet resignations in July as a forum for discussing new programs and developing national unity, and which convened on August 12. Initially the Kadets were supportive, even enthusiastic. But as the party moved rapidly to the right, attitudes began to change, particularly among the Petrograd *verkhov-*

---

[52] Gen. A. Brusilov, *Moi vospominaniia*, Moscow, 1929, p. 210.
[53] *Rostovskaia Rech'*, July 11, 12, and 13, 1917.

niki. By early August, Kokoshkin, Shingarev, and especially Miliukov felt such a clear difference existed between liberals and socialists that the government would do far better simply to "choose" between one or the other.[54]

As the moderate socialist *Narodnoe Slovo* pointed out, however, this was hardly the road to compromise or national unity.[55] On one hand, Petrograd Kadets were still insisting that the second coalition be "above politics"; on the other, they wanted the regime to commit itself to partisan Kadet positions. And while calling publicly for national "solidification," the Kadet leadership failed to recognize that unity could be achieved only if the party itself established some workable relationship with the Executive Committee of the Soviets. Unity was somehow to be reached only through the implementation of liberal programs.

As the Moscow Conference got underway, debate began to mirror these contradictions. Kadets like Maklakov, Rodichev, and now Miliukov spoke with unbridled hostility against the left and refused to pledge support for Kerensky's regime. So far had Miliukov's own views shifted about the "dangers" of provoking further social polarization, in fact, that the Kadet leader himself wanted to end his own address with an open declaration of *non*-support and failed to do so only by "taking into consideration the mood of some provincial sectors of the party, and the fact that party comrades were still members of the government. . . ."[56] By contrast, Tsereteli, Chkheidze, and other Soviet spokesmen extended the hand of compromise. Tsereteli even embraced the Trade-Industrialist Bublikov in a much noted symbolic gesture; while Chkheidze, who spoke as the official representative of the Soviet Executive Committee, promised he and his colleagues would place "the interest of the whole country, of the revolution, above the interests of classes or specific groups of the population."[57] "The interests of Russia," he also insisted—sounding remarkably like the Kadets themselves—could not be "sacrificed to the importunities of irresponsible or self-interested groups."[58]

The left, moreover, accepted the need for firm state authority, insisting only in the correlation between strength and popularity. But Kadet speakers like Maklakov and Rodichev were still unwilling to

---

[54] *Rech'*, Aug. 2 and 12, 1917; Khrushchov, p. 125; Miliukov, *Istoriia*, pt. 2, pp. 111-12; P. P. Iurenev, "F. F. Kokoshkin vo vremennom pravitel'stve," *Posledniia Novosti*, No. 1452, Jan. 18, 1925.

[55] *Narodnoe Slovo*, Aug. 15, 1917.

[56] P. Miliukov, "Denikin—istorik i memuarist," *Posledniia Novosti*, No. 839, Jan. 14, 1923.

[57] *Gosudarstvennoe soveshchanie*, Moscow, 1930, p. 78.

[58] *Ibid.*, p. 85.

associate a strong government with the satisfaction of mass demands. It was true, Maklakov admitted with a typical elitist aside, that the "deep dark masses" were now "quietly casting their votes for party lists." But they were doing this "without understanding" the democratic process; and the regime was mistaken if it believed it "would lose its real strength" if it "parted ways with political parties." On the contrary, if the regime stopped appealing to Russians in political terms, "the masses . . . would instinctively understand who is destroying them . . . and surround those who are leading them to salvation with love, sympathy and loyalty, against which the malignity of political parties would be powerless."[59] The contradiction here, as Tsereteli was quick to point out, was that if the Kadets were right, events themselves would render politics superfluous; masses would "instinctively" reject those who did appeal in "political terms," and follow the liberals.[60]

Similar problems emerged in the discussion about a national program. Here Chkheidze and the Soviet representatives were not only more accommodating than Kadets on specific matters of policy; but the non-socialists as a whole disagreed among themselves, and had very little to offer in the way of counterproposals. On the question of strengthening the army, both sides agreed that the "salvation of the country and the revolution" depended on the "restoration of the army's military might." (Chkheidze's words.) The left insisted this could be done, however, only by retaining the army's committee structure for all nonmilitary questions, and using it to infuse spirit and morale among the troops. Complete independence of command would have to be enforced in all matters of strategy and tactics; but any return to prerevolutionary methods of discipline would lead to precisely the defeatism and low spirit which so weakened the army in 1915 and 1916.[61] In opposition, Miliukov and the nonsocialists argued that a return to prerevolutionary methods of discipline was the only way the army could be saved, and showed by their rousing reception of General Kornilov that the man whom the Soviet had driven from Petrograd in April was now their national hero. But while Rodzianko wanted an end to *all* political agitation among the troops, which the Kadets could not accept since it would eliminate their efforts as well as the socialists', the Kadets wanted an end to all military committees, which even Kornilov and the high command still recognized as having some role to play in social and economic questions.[62]

Similarly, all speakers agreed that the powers of committees in factories and villages should be clearly defined. But while bourgeois

59 *Ibid.*, pp. 116-17.
61 *Ibid.*, pp. 77-86.
60 *Ibid.*, pp. 118-19.
62 *Ibid.*, esp. pp. 64-65, 106-07, 130.

spokesmen like Riabushinskii, Sokolovskii, and even Gruzinov saw real value in some aspects of worker and peasant organizations (Riabushinskii even recalling the role he himself played in setting up labor groups in Moscow), the Duma group called for their total elimination.[63] And here, too, there was paradox. The Duma committee wanted functions exercised by committees and soviets turned over to "legitimate organs of local government."[64] But as Kadet leaders themselves were aware, local elections all over Russia were returning large socialist majorities to these bodies. There was thus as much division and confusion within the nonsocialist camp as a whole on this question as there was antagonism between the liberals and the left.

The left was also more willing to make concessions on questions of finance, taxation, production, and food supply. Despite the sacrifice it implied for the peasants, for example, the Soviet's resolution pledged the left to support the continuation of the grain monopoly and fixed prices. It also called for strict regulation of industrial prices, and for state control over wages. Even more dramatic, the resolution officially pledged Soviet support for private commerce in support of food supply groups, accepted labor conscription as a means to meet industrial shortages "if the need arises," and declared the necessity of repudiating all arbitrary seizures of land in the countryside.[65] But again, the nonsocialists refused to show support for the Soviet's positions, while offering little in the way of alternatives. Kornilov demanded "urgent" measures to meet production needs, but failed to describe specifically what he had in mind. General Kaledin joined the Soviet in calling for labor conscription; but by demanding restrictions on profits as well, he antagonized von Ditmar and other Trade-Industrialists.[66] And while Chkheidze advanced the suggestion both of a mass capital levy and an increase of taxes on articles of mass consumption, Gruzinov and other nonsocialists could only respond with references to their past contributions to the liberty loans. They, too, had no new proposals.[67]

There was, finally, no clear liberal position on the most crucial question of all: whether or not to support Kerensky and the coalition. F. A. Golovin, the former president of the Second Duma, felt support was imperative.[68] Bublikov, Kapatsinskii, Riabushinskii, Sokolovskii and other "bourgeois" speakers agreed, and Nicholas Astrov, speaking for Volkov, Gerasimov, Shchepkin, and other Kadets (who now defined themselves as "progressives" and "conciliationists") went so far as to suggest that his "political ear" heard "notes sounding very much like the reconciliation of previously irreconcilable tendencies."[69]

63 *Ibid.*, pp. 161-65, 253-55, 269-71.   64 *Ibid.*, pp. 165-66.
65 *Ibid.*, pp. 80-86.   66 *Ibid.*, pp. 64-65, 76, 259-67.
67 *Ibid.*, pp. 82-83, 161-64, 253, 269-71.   68 *Ibid.*, p. 54.
69 *Ibid.*, p. 141.

Astrov's ear was certainly not cocked in the direction of Maklakov, however, or Rodichev, Kokoshkin, Shulgin, Guchkov, or even Miliukov, whose sympathies lay with right-wing authoritarianism.

In summarizing the results of the Moscow Conference, *Rech'* told its readers the meetings showed Russia divided into two vast "irreconcilable camps." At first glance, these seemed to be "the bourgeoisie and the democracy," though "more attentive analysis" showed that the line ran between "the utopianism of partisanship and the statesmanship of nonpartisans."[70] This was hardly an adequate description, however, or even the only Kadet view. It suggested simply that after months and even years of stressing the need for Russian national unity, of great fear of mass unrest and a deep concern for civil law and order, Miliukov and his supporters among the Petrograd Kadets were girding for civil war. More appropriate would have been the observation that efforts toward accommodation and compromise had been made at the sessions by the moderate socialists and their left-wing liberal supporters, but that right-wing elements offered no positive response. Whether this indicated a "full victory" for the idea of coalition, as Nekrasov told reporters,[71] is very dubious; but equally doubtful is the notion that those who in the past had been the loudest champions of national unity and authority took any constructive steps at the conference to achieve their goals.

"PETROGRAD IS IN DANGER!"

Immediately after the Moscow Conference, the situation in Russia began to deteriorate sharply, particularly in Petrograd. Symptomatic of the times, even the newsstand price of *Izvestiia* rose on August 16 from 12 to 15 kopecks, while bourgeois newspapers like *Birzhevye Vedomosti* began to carry long columns of newly vacated apartments, deserted by owners fearful of new disorders. Reports from the front also sounded more ominous. The Germans were now advancing. In several areas, especially along the Baltic, defenses were collapsing entirely. On the night of August 19, Russian troops evacuated Riga. Many now became thoroughly alarmed that the enemy would march on Petrograd itself.

In the midst of these developments, the inhabitants of Russia's capital city held what were destined to be their last free municipal elections under a democratic government. The balloting was scheduled for August 20, to elect a new city duma. And here, too, the results were hardly encouraging for Kadets. Parties approached the campaign

[70] *Rech'*, Aug. 17 and 18, 1917. *Den'* took a similar view, Aug. 18, 1917.
[71] *Izvestiia*, Aug. 18, 1917.

with a noticeable lack of enthusiasm. Mensheviks stressed the value of the ballot box in combating the liberals' growing truculence; the Kadets spoke for order and national unity; and radical newspapers like *Proletarii* aimed their editorial guns at "the growing strength of bourgeois-landowner counterrevolutionary dictators," warning workers and soldiers that the Constitutional Democrats were threatening their freedom.[72] But the Mensheviks were disorganized as a result of an attempt by their internationalist faction to exclude Tsereteli and other defensists from a new city committee; the Bolsheviks had to campaign covertly as a result of the July fiasco; and the SR leadership appeared too busy with state affairs to pay much attention to city business. *Delo Naroda* ran a campaign banner on August 12 and 13, but then virtually ignored the election until just before the balloting on August 20. And on election day, even the SRs admitted the vote could not count for much "while the revolution itself was in danger."[73] The Popular Socialists were even more indifferent. *Narodnoe Slovo* announced the "opening" of their campaign only two days before the election itself.[74]

The elections were also marked by a high degree of absenteeism, especially in the well-to-do Kazanskii and Liteinyi districts. This had characterized other towns in late July and August, particularly Vologda, Voronezh, Viatka, and Ekaterinburg. But nowhere was the voters' indifference more evident than in the revolution's capital. According to *Rech'*, one could walk past a polling station on August 20 and not notice that an election was taking place.[75] And indeed, the total number of ballots cast was some 235,000 less than in district duma elections in May, despite the inclusion of six additional election districts from the city's immediate suburbs.

This hardly encouraged even left Kadets about the feasibility of democratic processes. Predictions of party figures like Vasili Maklakov about Russia not being sufficiently "mature" to utilize the freedoms of liberation seemed to be coming true. According even to the mild-mannered Shingarev, "socialistic instincts" were conquering "*gosudarstvennyi* reason"; what was necessary was "ceaseless cultural work" of the kind Kadets had begun twelve years before.[76]

But the results of the elections revealed that even "ceaseless cultural work" was hardly likely to reverse the course of events, as Table 4 indicates. Out of 549,350 ballots (including the suburban vote), socialist candidates (including the Bolsheviks) secured 427,087 or almost

---

[72] See, e.g., *Delo Naroda*, Aug. 8, 1917; *Rabochaia Gazeta*, Aug. 8, 1917; *Rech'*, Aug. 12, 1917; *Proletarii*, Aug. 18 and 20, 1917.

[73] *Delo Naroda*, Aug. 20, 1917.   [74] *Narodnoe Slovo*, Aug. 18, 1917.

[75] *Rech'*, Aug. 22, 1917.   [76] Khrushchov, p. 129.

TABLE 4. PETROGRAD MUNICIPAL DUMA RETURNS, AUGUST 1917
(Popular Vote and % Change from May District Duma Elections Relative to Total Votes Cast in Each Election)

	Socialist Bloc[a]		SR		Bolshevik		Kadets		Menshevik		Trudovik Pop. Socialist Edinstvo		Other[d]	
	vote[a]	%	vote	%	vote	%	vote	%	vote	%	vote	%	vote	%
Admiralteiskii	(4,763)	−18.5	4,252	......	4,233	+19.9	2,531	−2.6	257	......	254	......	338	−1.3
Aleksandr Nevskii		......	22,820	−6.2	12,180	+15.5	5,993	+0.8	1,463	−7.0	611	−0.4	485	−0.4
Kazanskii	(4,864)	−5.6	3,993	......	2,284	+7.0	5,478	−1.6	471	......	395	......	754	−4.6
Kolomenskii	(10,138)	−15.2	9,042	......	7,015	+14.9	6,179	+1.1	543		553	−0.1	277	−0.5
Liteinyi	(13,169)	−13.0	10,999	......	5,293	+8.4	12,038	+0.6	1,259	......	911		736	−0.5
Moskovskii	(17,233)	−16.0	13,917	......	8,508	+12.0	13,190	+3.3	1,784	......	1,532		1,036	
Narvskii	(27,747)	−22.2	24,969	......	23,177	+21.5	7,892	+0.5	2,218	......	833		884	−1.7
Petrogradskii	(24,166)	−19.9	18,232	......	26,781	+15.3	18,582	+4.5	3,785	......	2,149		986	−0.5
Rozhdestvenskii		......	13,477	+11.1	5,321	+12.0	11,530	+3.1	1,688	−27.2	1,113	0.0	1,158	−0.4
Spasskii	(8,356)	−1.5	7,141	......	3,026	+2.0	5,927	+4.1	650	......	565	−5.9	661	−0.2
Vasilevskii	(28,055)	−2.9	21,290	......	24,691	+3.8	11,463	0.0	5,281	......	1,484		517	−2.0
Vyborgskii	(10,205)	−6.1	8,519	......	22,487	+4.8	2,703	+0.6	1,264	......	422	0.0	316	
TOTALS[b]			205,659b		183,624b		114,483b		23,552b		12,744b		9,288bc	

SOURCES: Adapted from *VPNS*, No. 17-18, Sept. 7, 1917; *Rech'*, June 3, 8, 9, 1917; *Novoe Vremia*, June 2, 9, 1917.

NOTES: Total Votes cast: 549,350.
Ellipsis (......) indicates no % comparison possible because party did not run independently in May election.

a There were no Socialist Bloc slates in the August election. Bloc figures for May are compared with combined August tallies of former Bloc parties (in parentheses).
b Totals include returns for 6 additional suburban districts not voting in May.
c Includes votes for several minor socialist parties and groups, though largely nonsocialist.
d Trade-Industrialist, Homeowners (Landlords), Republican Democratic Party, and others, including several minor socialist groups.

78 percent. The Kadets won only 114,483 or 20.9 percent, a relative decrease of little more than 1 percent from May, but an absolute decrease of 57,262 votes in what was supposed to be the city of their strongest popularity. Most shocking and significant of all was the great increase in Bolshevik support, both in absolute and relative terms. Lenin's followers secured a full 33 percent of the total vote, only 4 percent behind the front running Socialist Revolutionaries. Not only was this a gain of almost 13 percent over what the Bolsheviks had won in May (relative to the total vote in each election); it represented an absolute increase of 23,688 despite the drastic reduction in the total number of voters. A comparison of Tables 1 (above, p. 162) and 4 (above, p. 220) shows that most of this new strength undoubtedly came from those who had earlier supported socialist moderates. It came primarily in the Alexander Nevskii, Narvskii, Petrogradskii, and Admiralteiskii sections of the cities, where SRs and Mensheviks had been strongest in May; and in the Rozhdestvenskii, where Mensheviks won 19,045 votes (32.1 percent) in the district duma elections, and now returned only 1,688 (4.9 percent). This indicated that workers had become even better organized and politically radical since the July uprising, despite the arrest of Trotsky and other Bolshevik leaders and Lenin's retreat to Finland; while any new liberal and SR supporters either failed for some reason to go to the polls, or had already fled the city. It meant as well, though few Kadets chose to interpret the returns this way, that Kadets and moderate socialists were both being strongly challenged from the same source, reinforcing the desirability of a *sblizhenie* between liberals and the left which Astrov, Frenkel, and others still advocated. Finally, the elections meant that the new administration of Russia's capital, long dominated by Kadets and a liberal stronghold, would finally be under strong radical influence.

Petrograd was thus "in great danger" according to the Kadet Central Committee. The crucial question was whether any firm authority could possibly be found to save the city, and indeed, the country as a whole.[77]

PLOTS AGAINST THE GOVERNMENT

One obvious possibility for reestablishing firm authority, of course, and one now being talked about freely in liberal circles, was a military dictatorship under General Kornilov. The tumultuous reception the army commander received at the Moscow Conference testified to the

[77] D. A. Chugaev et al., eds., *Revoliutsionnoe dvizhenie v Rossii v avguste 1917 g.*, Moscow, 1959, pp. 371-77.

popularity of this idea in right-wing circles; while the base for organizing such an effort existed in army groups like the Military League, and civilian societies like the Republican Center. From August 20 onward, even *Novoe Vremia* carried articles warning of anti-government plots (though insinuating the greatest danger in this regard was still from the radical left); while on August 23, the Grand Duke Michael Alexandrovich was placed under house arrest in Gatchina as a precautionary move.

As we have seen, right-wing groups had been considering the possibility of a military dictatorship for quite some time. The Military League and the Union of Officers discussed it as early as May and June, and even talked about it with members of the high command, including Generals Kornilov and Alekseev, and Admiral Kolchak.[78] In July, Boris Savinkov had sounded out Miliukov on the notion; and at the Conference of Public Figures in early August, the subject was mentioned frequently. Kadets themselves discussed the possibility of using troops against the soviets at Central Committee meetings on August 11 or 12, and again on August 20; and they repeatedly explored the question of dictatorship in private conversations.[79]

Within the Central Committee, however, there were several views on the issue, ranging from sympathetic to hostile. The grounds for sympathy were simply that Russia was in imminent danger of collapse, and however much dictatorial methods compromised liberal principles, Russia's survival as a strong, united power was the primary consideration. This meant the application of strict authority and discipline to the country at large by forceful measures. It also meant the elimination of committees and soviets, nationalization of railroads and key military industries, and the exercise of whatever force was necessary to control radicals.

This was Rodichev's view, and it found expression in his exhortation to Kornilov when the General arrived for the Moscow Conference: "Save Russia, and a grateful people will revere you."[80] It was also the view of Tyrkova, Novgorodtsev, Dolgorukov, and others, who argued to the Kadet Central Committee that an imminent (and "inevitable") Bolshevik uprising could be put down only with dictatorial force.[81]

[78] B. A. Gurevich, "Kornilov," *Posledniia Novosti*, No. 4118, July 1, 1932; Denikin, II, 28; Vladimirova, pp. 43-46.

[79] Obolenskii MS, pp. 460-61; P. Miliukov, "Po povodu soobshcheniia P. N. Finisov," *Posledniia Novosti*, No. 5825, Mar. 6, 1937; Slavin, p. 35; Chugaev, pp. 373-77.

[80] Vladimirova, p. 84; Denikin, II, 31.

[81] These arguments emerged with particular force at Central Committee meetings on August 11, right after the second meeting between Kornilov and Kerensky, and on August 20. Protocols for the August 11 meeting, first used in his doctoral dissertation by the Soviet historian A. M. Mal'tov, are quoted extensively by N. F.

Yet other Kadets were more circumspect—even those who considered the Moscow Conference a dismal failure, and who abhored Nekrasov and Kerensky. The problem was not whether military authoritarianism was desirable, but whether it could be extended into a civilian dictatorship—even temporarily, until the convocation of the Constituent Assembly—without hopelessly dividing the nation and precipitating a disastrous civil war.

This was the dilemma Kornilov posed for the liberal moderates: there was little question about endorsing a Kornilov dictatorship *once it had been established*; but most party members in Moscow and Petrograd felt dictatorial efforts could not succeed unless both the cabinet and the Soviet acquiesced voluntarily. This ruled out participation in a conspiratorial coup d'état. As Maklakov himself acknowledged, a unilateral move on Kornilov's part would be "disastrous," serving only to strengthen the Bolsheviks and unite the "very revolutionary democracy that was eroding and defeating the revolution."[82] And when Miliukov himself talked to General Kornilov on August 13, it was this perspective which underlay his insistence that Kadets could not involve themselves directly in any action against Kerensky which "took the form that many in Moscow are discussing."[83] Rather, the party's task was to apply maximum pressure against the second coalition's "triumvirs"—Kerensky, Nekrasov, and Tereshchenko —if not to remove them, at least to assure the adoption of forceful programs like General Kornilov's.

Meanwhile, both the Republican Center and the Union of Officers were stepping up their conspiratorial activities. These groups were now more convinced than ever that Kerensky's regime had to be replaced by one under General Kornilov. Whether their plans involved eliminating Kerensky from power entirely, or simply reorganizing his cabinet under Kornilov's direction, is not clear. Nor is the nature of Kornilov's own personal involvement (though the general almost certainly had a firm hand in discussions at Mogilev, the army's headquarters). What is clear is that while Kadets worked for authoritarian measures within the cabinet, Kornilov's supporters elsewhere

---

Slavin in his article "Krisis vlasti." According to the document in the Chugaev volume, Tyrkova told her colleagues on August 20 that Kadets "must support a dictator even more than Kerensky; there is no other way—only through blood" (p. 374).

[82] Letter to Miliukov, dated Jan. 24, 1923, in the Miliukov Archive, bx. 1662.

[83] Miliukov, "Denikin"; In his memoirs in *NCS*, No. 5, 1924, p. 6, V. Obolenskii notes that he and others were convinced Miliukov supported Kornilov wholeheartedly; Soviet historians have frequently taken this as evidence of Miliukov's direct involvement in the conspiracy. Support of Kornilov was not incompatible, however, with reservations about a unilateral coup.

contemplated more drastic actions, none of which boded well for the future of the second coalition.

The crux of the anti-government plots involved marching on Petrograd to put down a Bolshevik "uprising," and under this pretext, replacing Kerensky's cabinet with a "Council of National Defense." (There is abundant evidence as well that many hoped to arrest leaders of the Petrograd Soviet.)[84] The plotters were naturally worried about left-wing resistance, however, fearing the outbreak of civil war and the effect this would have on the front. Consequently, in an apparent effort to persuade Kerensky to yield voluntarily, several of those involved contacted V. N. Lvov, the procurator of the Holy Synod in the first two provisional cabinets, and a centrist with close ties to the regime. While details here are especially vague, it was probably hoped that Lvov could work out some means whereby Kerensky and Kornilov could cooperate, allowing a change of government without forceful opposition. Perhaps Kerensky might even be given a place in Kornilov's Council, at least temporarily.[85]

Meanwhile, Boris Savinkov, Kerensky's assistant minister of war who was still acting as a go-between for the cabinet and Kornilov, had finally worked out a draft of Kornilov's program acceptable to the government. On August 23 he took it to Mogilev, more than a full month after Kornilov himself had first proposed it.[86] The principal stumbling block during this time had been the role of commissars and committees, both in the army and in the country at large. Kornilov was initially willing to have committees retained, recognizing they served some useful functions in keeping the army together. But he wanted their activities sharply circumscribed, something socialists like Victor Chernov objected to on principle, and which other ministers

[84] The following account is distilled from a number of sources, the most important of which are the memoirs of Finisov, Lukomskii, Savinkov, Putilov, Shidlovskii, Vinberg, Miliukov, and Kerensky. There is a great deal of secondary literature on the mutiny, both Soviet and Western, the most recent being by J. D. White, "The Kornilov Affair," *Sov. Stud.*, xx, Oct. 1968, pp. 187-205; N. G. Dumova, "Maloizvestnye materialy po istorii kornilovshchiny," vi, No. 11, 1968, pp. 69-93; and Harvey Asher, "The Kornilov Affair: A Reinterpretation," *Rus. Rev.*, Vol. 29, July 1970, pp. 286-300. These studies footnote the important reference material, and the reader is referred to them for additional citations. The question of the composition of the new government as well as the arrest of Soviet leaders apparently caused considerable antagonism between the different conspiratorial groups. See the Lvov memoirs in Browder and Kerensky, III, esp. 1565-67. White goes so far as to suggest that it was this antagonism which "finally disrupted the Kornilovist movement" (p. 204).

[85] On this see in particular Lvov's testimony to the Special Investigating Commission on Sept. 14, 1917, in Chugaev, pp. 425-28.

[86] There is also evidence that Savinkov was to investigate counter-revolutionary activities at Stavka, and to disperse the Republican Center. See Miliukov, *Istoriia*, pt. 2, p. 175; and the Lukomskii memoirs in Browder and Kerensky, III, 1550.

(though not apparently Kerensky himself) feared might unleash new civil disorders.

In accordance with Kornilov's earlier views, Savinkov's "final" version of his program provided for the retention of commissars and committees, but limited their functions entirely to nonmilitary affairs. The sources suggest, however, that Kornilov and his aides—particularly General Lukomskii—were less sanguine on this question than even two weeks earlier, and now felt commissars and committees should be eliminated. (This question probably provoked Kornilov's harsh judgments of Kerensky, reported in the latter's *Prelude to Bolshevism*.)[87] In discussions between Savinkov and Kornilov on the question on August 24, Savinkov won out. But even with the committee provisions retained, he and Kornilov both agreed the publication of the program would outrage the left, possibly triggering another mass "Bolshevik" demonstration. This also worried Kerensky. It was therefore apparently decided on all sides that troops should be sent to the capital to deal as necessary with whatever resistance developed, a "precautionary move" which corresponded exactly with the tactical schemes of those hoping to oust the coalition, whether or not Kornilov, Savinkov, or Kerensky himself actually intended it that way.

The somewhat devious V. N. Lvov, meanwhile, having earlier met with Kerensky as an emissary of unnamed right-wing political figures, was himself hurrying out to army headquarters to discover exactly what kind of government Kornilov wanted in place of the coalition. Arriving on August 24, while Kornilov was busy with Savinkov, Lvov cooled his heels until later in the evening, possibly talking in the meantime with members of the Union of Officers or Military League. Then, with Savinkov heading back to Petrograd with Kornilov's agreement on a program preserving the army committees, Lvov confronted the army commander with what he said were Kerensky's own plans for a new cabinet. What these were (or whether they were Kerensky's) is unclear. But Lvov apparently brought word that Kerensky was ready to yield to a directorate or even a dictatorship under Kornilov.[88]

What Kornilov himself made of Lvov and this new information, having just met with Savinkov, is hard to determine. Perhaps he was

[87] Kerensky, *Prelude*, pp. 212ff.

[88] According to Lvov's testimony in Chugaev, and his memoirs in *Posledniia Novosti*, No. 186, Nov. 30, 1920, et seq., he met with Kerensky on August 22 on the prompting of I. A. Dobrynskii, a member of the St. George Cavaliers with close ties to the Republican Center, the Officers Union, and the Moscow industrialists. Lvov says Kerensky authorized him to enter into "negotiations" with Kornilov for a new regime, implying his acceptance of a dictatorship. He also reports that his discussion with Kornilov touched only on a dictatorship, rather than a directorate. Kerensky denies Lvov's account categorically. See *Prelude*, p. 160.

simply pleased to think that the various conspirators had finally convinced Kerensky to come around. Perhaps he thought Kerensky had suddenly gotten new evidence about a possible Bolshevik uprising. In any event, Kornilov certainly preferred the idea of dictatorship to continued coalition; and he undoubtedly said so to Lvov.

Lvov for his part, meanwhile, now had either a general agreement between Kerensky and Kornilov to establish a new cabinet (as he later testified), or simply an open statement of Kornilov's personal desires and intentions (as Kerensky's memoirs would have us believe); and he hurried back to Petrograd to meet again with the minister-president, no doubt convinced he held in his hands the keys to resolving Russia's crisis of authority. If Kerensky himself could now be convinced to accept a change of regime, bloodshed would be avoided. Troops moving toward Petrograd to prevent the disorders which were expected when Kornilov's program was published could be used instead to prevent resistance to the coup. They could also root out radical groups like the Bolsheviks, acting on the pretext of preventing civil war. (At precisely this time, in fact, representatives from the Republican Center were contacting Putilov and other industrialists for funds, planning to stage a Bolshevik "uprising" as a pretext for repressive action if one did not develop on its own.) But when Lvov told Kerensky that Kornilov was actually moving to replace the coalition, Kerensky panicked. Confirming Lvov's account on the wireless with Kornilov (in a conversation during which the hapless general neglected to ascertain exactly what it was in Lvov's message Kerensky was asking him to confirm!), the frenetic minister clapped Lvov in jail, convened his cabinet in emergency session, and declared Kornilov a traitor to the revolution.[89]

What, in all this, was the role of the Kadets? While the details presented here may not be fully accurate, given the contradictions in available source material, they do suffice to indicate that few if any leading party members took personal roles in actively planning or executing the conspiracy, and that official Kadet organizations, such as the Central Committee or the Petrograd or Moscow city groups, stood entirely aloof. Conspiracy was the work of the Republican Center, in conjuction with army groups like the Union of Officers and individual members of the General Staff. Here, military figures like Colonel Novosiltsev, the Kadet leader of the Officers Union, undoubtedly took active roles. And as the competent Bolshevik historian Vera Vladimirova indicates, Kadets were also doubtlessly involved through conversations and discussions with Republican Center leaders, perhaps even being approached by people like Putilov for funds.[90] Discussions

[89] Browder and Kerensky, III, 1568-73.   [90] Vladimirova, pp. 41ff.

along the way must also have touched on realigning the cabinet, a subject constantly preoccupying the Kadets from virtually the first days of the revolution, and something they now very much desired.

But even in terms of their support for such a venture, much less their participation, Miliukov, Kokoshkin, and most of the party's *verkhovniki* were ambiguous at best, refusing to encourage a unilateral move on Kornilov's part while supporting his goals in the government; and the evidence shows that Kadet supporters close to leading financial circles, like S. N. Tretiakov, president of the Moscow Stock Exchange, unceremoniously rejected requests for funds from Putilov, and kept the Moscow and Petrograd Kadet committees clear of the "conspiracy bankers." Neither Tretiakov nor Miliukov also had a clear idea of exactly what was being planned.[91]

Nor, the evidence suggests, did any other of the party's principal leaders. The only specific charge to the contrary is the accusation leveled by P. N. Finisov in 1937 that sometime in August, Rodichev, Dolgorukov, and Struve closeted with Republican Center representatives over their plans, and that on August 23, these three liberals came to Miliukov with the request that he himself enter into Republican Center discussions.[92] Miliukov categorically denies this, and while we know Kadets met frequently with Center members in a variety of contexts, there seems to be no other evidence to support the contention that they were directly involved as conspirators.[93] On the contrary, when the Kadet Central Committee met on August 20, not one of the group mentioned the mutiny, which was now in its final stages of preparation, or suggested they were party to special information. Also, no Kadets were included in the cabinet proposed by the conspirators to replace the second coalition;[94] and on August 22, when V. N. Lvov recalls he told Nabokov that General Lukomskii felt it "would not be a bad idea" for Kadets to resign from the government on August 27, the Kadet's response was a surprised "What is going to happen on August 27?"[95] This was not the voice of conspiracy; and if Kadets themselves were about to participate in overthrowing Kerensky by force, it would hardly have been necessary to urge them to resign.

From all this one must finally emerge with two conclusions. On one hand, Vasili Maklakov was undoubtedly right when he complained in a letter to Miliukov in 1923—and it *was* a complaint—that the "affair" went "right past the party."[96] In the near panic seizing Petro-

[91] Miliukov, "Denikin . . ."
[92] Miliukov, "Po povodu . . ." On this see also Dumova, "Maloizvestnye materialy," pp. 84-85.
[93] *Ibid.*   [94] Denikin, II, 42.
[95] V. N. Lvov, "Kerenskii-Kornilov," *Posledniia Novosti*, No. 186, Nov. 30, 1920.
[96] Letter to Miliukov, Jan. 24, 1923, in the Miliukov Archive, bx. 1662.

grad after the fall of Riga, with government offices frantically preparing to move east, the Bolsheviks about to take an important role in city administration, and newspapers of all persuasions falling over themselves with charges of mutiny, treason, and counterrevolution, Kadets undoubtedly expected—perhaps even nervously awaited—an attempted military coup. And for their part, Kornilov and the conspirators in Mogilev were undoubtedly—and justifiably—confident that once their effort was successfully launched, most Kadets would give them wholehearted support. This, after all, was certainly the direction in which Kadet efforts to consolidate Russia's right-wing forces were headed. But despite their counterrevolutionary attitudes, Kadets as individuals and the party's organization as a whole were not the leaders of the plot, allegations of Soviet historians to the contrary.[97]

On the other hand, one must also ask whether this made them significantly less culpable than the actual conspirators. As we shall see, Kadets later separated themselves from the mutineers by insisting they remained firmly committed to legal methods. Yet commitment to "legality" and "legal methods" is certainly transparent when those who uphold these principles are fully aware that their own goals are being advanced by others who do not. Kadets may not have actively plotted with Kornilov; but their speeches and attitudes clearly encouraged those who did. And more important, they took no steps whatsoever to prevent a mutiny from developing, despite their knowledge that plots were underway, and their political position as Russia's leading nonsocialist party. With little effort, Kadet leaders might have easily contained the mutineers. They could have prevented the "affair" from developing by persuasion, by official pressure, or even by exposure. They thus might have helped Russia avoid what would prove to be a fatal blow to civil liberty and political democracy. Instead they stood silent; and like fellow liberals in other times and places, they bore their own particular responsibility for the sequence of events which followed.

[97] The Soviet historians Slavin, Dumova, and N. Ia. Ivanov (*Kornilovshchina i ee razgrom*, Leningrad, 1965), argue that Kadets themselves were actually conspirators. But V. V. Komin, writing about the problem in his *Bankrotstvo burzhuaznykh i melkoburzhuaznykh partii Rossii v period podgotovki i pobedy velikoi oktiabr'skoi sotsialisticheskoi revoliutsii*, Moscow, 1965, notes that, until the completion of the Mal'tov dissertation, "we did not have direct documentary proof on the direct leadership of the Kadet party and the State Duma in the mutiny of General Kornilov, and based our discussion about that only on indirect materials and a logical reconstruction of events" (p. 359). But if Mal'tov's material is the same as that used recently by Slavin, as it appears to be, it again shows only that the Kadets would have welcomed a dictatorship if it could have been established successfully, not that Kadets themselves were organizing its leadership.

THE KORNILOV REBELLION

Without taxing the reader's patience too much further with detail, we can quickly sketch the Kadet role in high Russian politics after Kornilov began moving toward Petrograd on August 26. Three of the factors operating before the march continued to structure events after it began: a compelling desire among both Moscow and Petrograd Kadet leaders to replace Kerensky, Nekrasov, Tereshchenko, and Chernov with more competent and authoritarian officials; an intense fear of civil war; and a lack of any clear idea for much of the time what either Kerensky or Kornilov was doing.

Kadet desire for a new cabinet helps explain one of the early "mysteries" of the Kornilov episode, the resignation of Kadet ministers on the night of August 26-27. Historians have sometimes offered this as evidence of the party's complicity with the mutineers, particularly in light of Lukomskii's warning.[98] In fact we know from special reports given the Moscow Kadets by Kishkin and Kokoshkin on August 31 that the situation was somewhat different. From the fall of Riga, the Kadet *verkhovniki* in Petrograd felt the leadership of the coalition had to resign; Kadets simply had no confidence in the ability of Kerensky or his principal colleagues to meet the crisis. *Rech'* said as much publicly on August 24; and on August 25, after a particularly stormy cabinet session, Minister of Food Aleksei Peshekhonov indicated to his colleagues that he felt the same way.[99] On the evening of August 26, the cabinet assembled to pursue the question. But before it could be worked out, Kerensky burst in with news of Kornilov's "ultimatum," brought moments earlier by Lvov. This changed matters drastically: suddenly it was no longer a question of resigning in favor of a stronger group of ministers, but of giving Kerensky himself "extraordinary powers" to deal with an army revolt.[100]

The problem this posed for Kokoshkin and the Kadets was that regardless of whether Kornilov was actually moving against Petrograd —and on the night of August 26-27 this was by no means clear— dictatorial powers in Kerensky's hands were a dangerous weapon against both the liberals' and Kornilov's objectives. Whether or not Kerensky used full powers to destroy the alleged conspiracy, there was certainly the danger he would use them to enact the socialists' program

[98] E.g., Ivanov, pp. 110-11; Dumova, pp. 87-89, and esp. V. Chernov, *The Great Russian Revolution*, trans. P. Mosely, New Haven, 1936, p. 350.

[99] Reports of F. F. Kokoshkin and N. M. Kishkin to the Kadet City Committee in Moscow, Aug. 31, 1917, in the Panina Archive, bx. 2, fold. 8; *Rech'*, Aug. 24, 1917; *Svobodnyi Narod*, Aug. 25, 1917.

[100] Kokoshkin report, pp. 5-7.

of July 8, rallying workers and soldiers against both Kadets and the high command. Kornilov, in other words, would be the excuse for Russia's socialization, as well as the means by which Kerensky would satisfy his own Napoleonic fancies.

Kokoshkin in particular was determined to resist giving Kerensky full powers. When it appeared that the socialist majority in the cabinet would grant the minister-president's demands, he and his colleagues tried to employ their party's basic weapon: resignation. Meanwhile, precisely because Kerensky reported that Kornilov was marching against the government, Kokoshkin indicated he and his Kadet colleagues intended to stay temporarily in their posts as "private individuals"; their design was not so much to make things easier for the mutineers, but to assure that the conflict was satisfactorily resolved, and to prevent full power from falling to the left.[101]

Kokoshkin's tactic failed, however, because while Iurenev supported him, the other two Kadet ministers, Kartashev and Oldenburg, did not. The cabinet thus had little fear of a wholesale Kadet boycott, and felt it could vote Kerensky full powers without precipitating another July crisis. But even as it did this, Kerensky made it clear that he also wanted the ministers to remain at their posts "unofficially"; and the following afternoon, when a second full-scale cabinet meeting was held on Kornilov, even Kokoshkin attended.[102]

In the meantime, the Petrograd Kadets were frantically trying to ascertain Kornilov's real intentions. Kerensky's first use of his full powers was to replace the Supreme Commander with General Klembovskii, announcing publicly as he did so that his action was based on Lvov's report.[103] Kornilov responded with a furious denial of Kerensky's premises: in his version, it was not he who sent Lvov to Kerensky, but Kerensky who sent Lvov to him. Refusing to resign, he insisted instead by open radio-telegram that a "great provocation" was taking place, and that the government, under pressure from the Bolsheviks and in harmony with the Germans, was preparing the way for new enemy advances. For himself, Kornilov wanted nothing "except the preservation of Great Russia"; and he vowed to bring the country to a Constituent Assembly where Russians themselves—instead of Bolshe-

101 *Ibid.*, pp. 8-9.
102 The meeting, in fact, turned out to be fruitless, since Kerensky, Nekrasov and Tereshchenko did not attend. Kokoshkin later recalled how the socialist and nonsocialist ministers alike fell into a friendly discussion about their strange position, sitting in the Winter Palace, with the absent Kerensky enjoying full powers. The meeting lasted well into the evening, and eventually concerned itself with matters of production. *Ibid.*, p. 10.
103 *Vestnik Vremennago Pravitel'stva*, Aug. 29, 1917. The telegram was sent on the morning of August 27.

viks or Germans—would "decide their fate and choose their form of government."[104]

This made the Kadets very suspicious of Kerensky. Maklakov and others consequently spent most of the afternoon of August 27 on the wire with Mogilev, trying to determine the basis of Kornilov's action. Their hope was that Kornilov was *not* in open rebellion, and that they could use factual information to persuade Kerensky to repeal his dismissal order.[105] Meanwhile, however, the frantic Kerensky had already responded to Kornilov's insurbordination with a new declaration, branding the general a traitor.[106] With this, the die was cast. Now Kornilov could not retreat unless Kerensky repudiated his accusation, while Kerensky could not repudiate his accusation without appearing totally ridiculous. And if a "mutiny" had not previously been intended, it was now certainly underway. Kadets gathering for a Central Committee meeting on August 28 realized this, and saw their task now as preventing the outbreak of civil war at all costs.[107]

Meanwhile, the situation looked bleak for the government. First reports from army headquarters indicated the command stood behind Kornilov. Troops were allegedly approaching Petrograd, bypassing all resistance. According to Kerensky himself, Kornilov would soon arrive in the city: the outlook was "hopeless."[108] This very much worried the Kadets. The Petrograd Soviet was mustering workers and soldiers in the city, and Kadets had become sure that Kornilov's advance into Petrograd would precipitate full-fledged civil war, fatal for Russia. Miliukov himself was sufficiently concerned on the evening of August 27—when Kerensky was lamenting that all was lost—to try personally to intercede between the minister-president and Kornilov.[109]

At the same time, however, the Central Committee also recognized that the situation lent itself to replacing Kerensky's cabinet with one more competent and authoritarian, precisely the objective Kadets had been struggling toward for several weeks. If Kerensky surrendered his power to someone Kornilov respected before his troops reached the city, such as General Alekseev, and the government was reconstructed to include moderate socialists, military figures, and Kadets, Kornilov would undoubtedly yield. Civil war could then be avoided; the

[104] Browder and Kerensky, III, 1573.

[105] Kokoshkin report, pp. 11-12; Miliukov, *Istoriia*, pt. 2, pp. 227-28; Chugaev, pp. 448-52.

[106] The second telegram was apparently written by Nekrasov, which infuriated the Kadets. See Pav. V . . . skii, "Vremennoe pravitel'stvo v avguste 1917 g. (Vospominaniia P. P. Iurenev)," *Posledniia Novosti*, No. 1211, Apr. 3, 1924.

[107] Kokoshkin report, pp. 11-12.   [108] *Ibid.*

[109] Miliukov, *Istoriia*, pt. 2, pp. 251-52.

Bolsheviks could be suppressed; and both Kornilov and Kerensky could retreat gracefully.[110]

This, consequently, was the goal set by Petrograd Kadets on August 28. At first there were high hopes of its success. For one thing, Nicholas Kishkin, the moderate Kadet leader whom Kerensky had specially invited from Moscow to assist him in the crisis, supported his colleagues' plan. For another, Kokoshkin himself had been invited back to the Winter Palace for another private conference, and felt he could obtain the support of the cabinet. There also seemed to be little doubt about Alekseev, with whom Miliukov was in contact, and intended to meet again shortly.

Indeed, the plan almost worked. According to Kokoshkin's account, verified by Kishkin, a majority of Kerensky's "suspended" ministers supported it, including the socialists. Miliukov, moreover, managed to secure Alekseev's support at precisely the moment Kishkin was meeting with Kerensky, and passed the information by phone—along with a repeated offer to go personally as mediator to Kornilov—just as Kishkin was leaving Kerensky's office.[111] But there were two problems. First, despite pressure from Avksentiev and Nekrasov, both of whom apparently supported the Kadet plan in some degree (and felt Alekseev should definitely be brought into the cabinet, though not necessarily as head of state), Kerensky himself felt honor bound to continue holding supreme power. Whether this was megalomania, as the Kadets later charged, a fear of the left, as Kishkin implied, or simply an honest belief that Alekseev and the Kadets would "betray" the revolution, is certainly unclear. But the fact is that Kerensky stood firm, agreeing only on the following afternoon that Alekseev should become his chief-of-staff.

Second, it quickly developed that reports about Kornilov's strength on August 28 were wrong: the army was not, in fact, behind the general. Troops on the way to Petrograd had been stopped by railroad workers, and in massive confusion about their goals, readily laid down their arms. Moreover, as these new reports reached Kerensky, his confidence began to return. By August 30, early anxieties were being covered up; in Kerensky's mind at least, there was now no question about his continuing to lead the government.

This galled the Kadets (particularly Kishkin, who was repulsed by Kerensky's new aloofness toward those he had nervously leaned on

110 Kokoshkin report, pp. 11-12.

111 *Ibid.*, pp. 11-12, 15. See also the discussion in Miliukov, *Istoriia*, II, 250, and the comments by Maklakov on the relationship between Kornilov and the constitutional base of the provisional regime in *La Chute du régime tsariste: interrogatoires*, Paris, 1927.

two days earlier).[112] It was obvious that Kornilov now had to submit to Russia's "legally constituted" government, but it was not at all obvious that the government had to be headed by Kerensky. On August 29, therefore, the Kadet Central Committee set out a last-ditch plan to stiffen national authority as much as possible. If Alekseev could not be head of state, he could at least be commander-in-chief. And assuming the left would again require liberals in the cabinet, as in July, the Kadet Central Committee decided to hold out for Alekseev's appointment as the basic condition for its own continued participation. In addition, it set three further conditions: that other members of the military be given ministerial posts; that all government members be equal; and that the Kornilov affair be liquidated in such a way "as not to aggravate or deepen the differences which had initially made the episode possible," i.e., without excessive penalties imposed on the mutineers.[113]

But now the Kadets were again weakened by their own lack of party discipline. On August 30, under reproach from the left for not supporting Kerensky more forcefully in his moment of crisis—and thus acting indirectly as Kornilov's ally behind the lines—Kishkin agreed to join Kerensky regardless of what his colleagues on the Central Committee decided. The Moscow Kadet was also worried about the impetus Kornilov's defeat might give the Bolsheviks; and to abandon Kerensky now, he explained, would further open the right-left gap he and others were trying to close. Kishkin felt justified, moreover, since Kerensky indicated he would invite three military figures—Verkhovskii, Verderevskii and Alekseev—into his cabinet, discharge Nekrasov, and "go soft" on Kornilov.[114]

Kadet pressure consequently collapsed, though the party's demands were partially met; and the uprising dissolved in a welter of confusion. Kornilov was arrested, his troops dispersed, and to the relief of everyone, not least of all the "conciliationist" Kadets, civil war was temporarily avoided. But this was the only positive note liberals could sound.

[112] Kishkin report, p. 17.   [113] Kokoshkin report, p. 13.
[114] Kishkin report, pp. 17-18. General Verkhovskii was commander of the Moscow military district in 1917, and somewhat sympathetic to the left. He later emigrated and then returned to join the Red Army. Admiral Verderevskii was commander of the Baltic Fleet.

CHAPTER EIGHT

Concessions and Conflicts in the Last
Weeks of the Provisional Regime

In the first week of September, peasants sacked the country home of Andrei Shingarev, the former Kadet minister of agriculture, killing his domestic animals, and terrorizing his wife. Shortly afterward she died of nervousness and anxiety.

Nothing more tragically symbolized the hopeless and desperate condition of Kadets in the aftermath of the Kornilov mutiny. Had leftists set out deliberately, they could not have better destroyed the power and influence of Russia's partisans of authority, or set the stage more neatly for Bolsheviks coming to power. Nor could anything have more increased the liberals' sense of insecurity, the terrifying anxiety that new acts of violence would now be directed against them broadside by "uncultured" workers and peasants, the "dark" masses Kadets had worried about for so long. One reads the liberal press for early September, with its endless lists of "incidents" and long columns of apartments for rent, and cannot help feeling the Kadets' sense of despair.

The irony of Andrei Shingarev's personal tragedy was that he himself had had the opportunity as minister of agriculture to improve Russia's agrarian conditions. In a similar way, the party's encouragement to General Kornilov did much to foment the new conditions of terror. While the Petrograd *verkhovniki* still explained events in elitist terms, falling back on arguments about Russia's "underdeveloped state consciousness" and the "tragedy of excessive freedom" in an "embryonic democracy," they themselves had failed to produce effective programs or policies. They had also withheld full support from the first and second coalitions. They demanded "plenitude of power" for the government, but when this was exercised in behalf of socialist goals, they either resigned or encouraged right-wing subversion; and they demanded the legitimation of all basic reforms by a democratically elected Constituent Assembly, but were fearful of democratic processes, and insisted balloting be postponed. If Kornilov *had* succeeded in taking Petrograd, Kadets would have readily accommodated themselves to his authority. In all likelihood, however, Russia's protracted, devastating civil war would have started then and there.

The question of liberal rectitude turned on whether commitment to "legality," "order," and "legitimate authority" justified postponing basic social reforms; whether Russian "national interests" justified the war and Kornilov. Miliukov, Shingarev, and their followers championed the international welfare of the state—the Kadets' cherished abstraction—over the domestic welfare of her people, arguing that the two were closely related, that strength in the competitive world arena was necessary for Russia's liberal evolution. But in fact, Kadet nationalism in 1917 hindered social change, and served to protect privileged interests. And while Kornilov's effort to topple the government may well have represented the "anarcho-syndicalist" psychology infecting all sectors of Russia's "broad social milieu," as Shingarev maintained, the reason "hundreds of laws" were not being obeyed was not because Russia's "self-formed mass psychology" was "irresponsible," as he also argued, but because little correlation could be made in the popular mind between obedience to the government's laws and social betterment.[1]

THE AFTERMATH OF KORNILOV: NEW
PROBLEMS OF KADET CREDIBILITY

In the weeks following the Kornilov debacle, a number of leading Kadets came to realize the relationship between political stability and social welfare. Some, like Astrov and Adzhemov, needed little prompting. Others, like Nabokov and Vinaver, were increasingly persuaded by pressure from moderate socialists.

This pressure began to intensify almost from the moment Kornilov was arrested. At first Kadets attempted to absolve themselves from complicity in the affair by contrasting their commitment to "legitimate struggle" with the "criminal methods" of the mutineers; then they admitted support for Kornilov's goals while still condemning his methods.[2] But even to the party's "friends" on the left, this seemed sophistic. Many even discounted the government's own version of events, feeling Kerensky himself must have been directly involved; others thought it unlikely that Kornilov would have moved without Kadet support. More probable was the *Izvestiia* account of August 28, which quoted "unnamed sources" to indicate the Kadet ministers had attempted to cripple the government behind the scenes, and then tried

---

[1] Shingarev to his wife, Aug. 30, 1917, quoted in A. G. Khrushchov, *Andrei Ivanovich Shingarev*, Moscow, 1918, p. 134. See also A. Shingarev, "Krisis vlasti," *VPNS*, No. 20, Sept. 28, 1917, pp. 1-2; *Rech'*, Sept. 7, 1917.

[2] *Rech'*, Aug. 31, 1917; *Novoe Vremia*, Sept. 6 and 7, 1917.

to free their own hands.[3] Even if Kadets were only passively involved, many felt their encouragement of the mutiny should be punished.[4]

These arguments were made most forcefully by Bolsheviks like Riazanov and Kamenev, for whom the Kornilov episode served to vindicate earlier suspicions about counterrevolution, but they were also made by moderate SDs, and by the so-called near Kadets among the moderate SRs like Avksentiev. Even the moderate journal *Delo Naroda* scathingly attacked Kadets on September 1, arguing that "no public leader loyal to the revolution or socialism could participate with Kadets in the exercise of government power."[5] And while much SR hostility was directed with equal force against Kerensky (whom Chernov accused in a celebrated attack of selling out the revolution), the Kadets faced what Miliukov later called a "declaration of war"; in Moscow and Petrograd, party members were even threatened with expulsion from city councils.[6]

The behavior of Miliukov and the Petrograd *verkhovniki* reinforced radical suspicions. Miliukov and Kokoshkin left immediately for the Crimea, as if fleeing arrest. Maklakov took up an ambassadorial appointment to France. Tyrkova and others withdrew to their country homes. Moreover, on August 30, *Rech'* appeared with yawning white spaces on its first page, suggesting the deletion of material tying the party directly to the mutiny (although what had actually been dropped was an editorial lauding Kornilov's goals but again criticizing his methods).[7] And even after Kornilov's arrest, Petrograd party leaders not only continued to praise the general, but while arguing in favor of extending capital punishment, as he had urged, now insisted it should not be applied against the mutineers. Again, they seemed bent on a course to shield their own complicity.

The Kadet argument in favor of extending the death penalty was based on "new appreciation" of the dangers of social disintegration. Nabokov's rationalization was that for all its evils, there were times when any government had to "murder" in the interest of national self-preservation; according to Shingarev, there were moments when theoretical and moral considerations had to yield to demands for a "higher order," when all other methods were incapable of "fighting

[3] *Izvestiia*, Aug. 28, 1917.

[4] *Ibid.*, and esp. Sept. 2, 1917. Bogdanov, for example, argued to the Petrograd Soviet on September 1 that the Kadets "provided the ideological inspiration" for the revolt, and should be punished on these grounds alone.

[5] *Delo Naroda*, Sept. 1, 1917.

[6] P. N. Miliukov, *Rossiia na perelome*, 2 vols., Paris, 1927, I, 105-06. *Rabochii*, Sept. 1, 1917; *Vpered*, Sept. 2, 1917; *Russkiia Vedomosti*, Sept. 2, 1917; *Zhurnal Petrogradskoi Gorodskoi Dumy*, No. 74, Sept. 1, 1917.

[7] *Rech'*, Aug. 30, 1917. See the discussion of the incident in *Rech'*, Sept. 19, 1917, and the report by Nabokov in *VPNS*, No. 20, Sept. 28, 1917, p. 24.

the horrors of life."[8] But when opponents of the death penalty argued that by this reasoning, Kornilov and his accomplices should be executed, Kadets in Petrograd insisted Kornilovites were different offenders altogether. Like prerevolutionary terrorists, whom the party had also refused to condemn in the Second Duma, they were "honest democrats" and "sincere republicans"; only their tactics were misguided.[9] How much these arguments were divorced from public opinion was clear when the Petrograd City Duma voted against the death penalty on September 4 by 137 to 16.

All of this resulted in a profound loss of Kadet credibility. The party's position on capital punishment alone stood in dramatic contrast to earlier liberal views, suggesting a total disaffection from the basic goals of revolution. ("Death Penalty Abolished Forever!" *Rech'* had exulted in March. "Only four words, but what a thundering echo they call forth from the whole Russian land . . . forever and ever this act shall remain solemn evidence of the greatness of the popular soul, a manifestation of nobleness. . . .")[10] Among the consequences of distrust, moreover, was the collapse of Kerensky's efforts to reconstruct the coalition. As we have seen, the minister-president had succeeded on August 30 in getting Kishkin's acceptance for the post of interior minister; and on August 31, he could announce the formation of a cabinet which included 4 Kadets, 4 Social Democrats, 3 SRs, and several others. But at precisely this moment, the Petrograd Soviet was voting 279 to 115 in favor of excluding Kadets from government ranks entirely; and later in the evening, the SR Central Committee did the same.[11] Faced with a socialist boycott, Kerensky at first tried to form a coalition out of other bourgeois elements, particularly Trade-Industrialists. (Avksentiev ironically justified this effort in terms of the latter being less committed to *partiinost'* than Kadets.)[12] But this also failed when the Trade-Industrialists refused to be in a cabinet without Kadets. The best Kerensky could do was temporarily entrust state affairs to a special five-man directorate.[13]

A further consequence was that Kadets found themselves excluded from the All-Russian Democratic Conference, a new national gathering called in the aftermath of the Kornilov affair to bolster socialist unity and generate new support for the government. The purpose of the

[8] *Zhurnal Petrogradskoi Gorodskoi Dumy*, No. 75, Sept. 4, 1917.

[9] *Ibid.*; *Izvestiia*, Aug. 31, 1917; *Rech'*, Sept. 6, 1917; *Svobodnyi Narod*, Sept. 1 and 23, 1917; and esp. *VPNS*, No. 21-22, Oct. 12, 1917, p. 34.

[10] *Rech'*, Mar. 10, 1917.

[11] N. Avdeev et al., eds., *Revoliutsiia 1917 goda. Khronika sobytii*, 6 vols., Moscow-Leningrad, 1923-30, IV, 138-39, 143.

[12] *Rech'*, Sept. 1, 1917.

[13] The five were Kerensky, Tereshchenko, Nikitin, Verderevskii, and Verkhovskii.

Conference was to assemble "all forces of the country," according to *Izvestiia*, "to organize for national defense, assist in internal organization, and pronounce the final word on conditions which would guarantee the existence of a strong revolutionary authority, capable of uniting all Revolutionary Russia for the purpose of repelling the foreign enemy and crushing challenges to our newly won domestic freedoms."[14] Many Kadets shuddered at the implications this might have for liberal programs, or even the Constituent Assembly; and they found their worst fears confirmed on September 5, when Kerensky unilaterally declared Russia a republic, arrogating to himself a right which was to have belonged to the people's representatives. But there was little Kadets could do by way of response; it appeared they were no longer needed by the left, and would have little hand in Russia's future.

In the provinces a number of Kadet committees were far more ready than their colleagues in the capital to condemn the mutiny, but nothing stopped the wholesale onslaught from the left. *Rostovskaia Rech'* published a sharp attack on Kornilov, for example, at the very moment he appeared to be entering Petrograd, despite Kadet ties to the cossacks. Russia, the journal argued, was being thrown back to the early seventeenth century, to the Time of Troubles.[15] In Tiflis, *Narodnaia Svoboda* predicted civil war if Kornilov won; while the party's organ in Nizhni-Novgorod insisted the mutiny violated all basic liberal principles.[16] Provincial Kadet committees also offered similar statements in various public meetings, and submitted anti-Kornilov resolutions to local dumas and zemstvos. Yet all over Russia, Kadets found their clubs attacked, their papers shut, their leaders censored. In Kiev, the soviet declared Kadets "publicly discredited"; in Tiflis, the party's journal was forced by typographers to run a front-page notice titled "Down with Kadets." As *Russkiia Vedomosti* noted on September 5, it was as if the left was coordinating an all-out national attack.[17]

All of this naturally contributed, finally, to the further disintegration of government authority itself (if, indeed, the regime had any authority left to lose). For many workers and soldiers the moderate socialists were as tainted by Kadets as Kadets were tainted by Kornilov. One direct result of this was the formation throughout the country at the height of the Kornilov uprising of ad hoc "Committees to Save the Revolution," largely dominated by the Bolsheviks. Whether local

14 *Izvestiia*, Sept. 3, 1917.   15 *Rostovskaia Rech'*, Aug. 31, 1917.
16 *Narodnaia Svoboda* (Tiflis), Sept. 1, 1917; *Narodnaia Svoboda* (Nizhni-Novgorod), Sept. 2, 1917.
17 *Russkiia Vedomosti*, Sept. 5, 1917; see also *Odesskii Listok*, Sept. 2 and 3, 1917; *Narodnaia Svoboda* (Baku), Sept. 16, 1917; *Rostovskaia Rech'*, Sept. 3, 1917; *Russkiia Vedomosti*, Sept. 3, 1917; *Odesskii Listok*, Sept. 2 and 3, 1917; and *Narodnaia Svoboda* (Tiflis), Sept. 17, 1917.

radicals followed the lead of Petrograd, where a Committee to Struggle against Counterrevolution armed workers on August 27, or organized on their own in conjunction with Bolshevik directives, is not clear. What is clear is that groups of this sort took effective control in scores of localities in early September, and that specific government directives ordering their dissolution were largely ignored.[18]

KADET CONCILIATION

Thus Kadet politics virtually ground to a halt. Such few Central Committee meetings as took place were apathetic and lifeless. Bolsheviks spied openly on the party club. Conservative *verkhovniki* stayed away. The ground was disappearing from beneath the feet of "legitimate power," most Kadets felt, and what was left of Kerensky's government was "flopping around like a wounded bird, shaming itself with new pronouncements and slanders, as if under hypnosis, understanding nothing. . . ."[19]

In these circumstances, Miliukov's "opposition" in the Petrograd Central Committee finally secured a position of temporary dominance over the party's high politics, if "opposition" is not too strong a word for those who had tried to resist the party's steady drift to the right throughout the spring and summer of 1917. To Vinaver, Grimm, Kishkin, Adzhemov, Gerasimov, Shakhovskoi, Frenkel and others who had urged a more conciliatory policy toward the Soviet and the left, the Kornilov affair was a tragic but logical end to the "politics of state consciousness," a clear indication in particular that the Committee had erred in bringing down the first coalition in July. And with Miliukov, Maklakov, Tyrkova, and others temporarily gone from Petrograd, they were ready, finally, to consider new ways of building state authority "from below." While deeply pessimistic over Russia's future and the fate of the revolution (as well as aware of their own grave personal danger), they retained some hope that a *modus vivendi* could still be worked out with the moderate left.

Growing concern among the socialists about the dangers of Bolshevism, and new fears of the Germans also provided some encouragement. The Germans had occupied Riga even before the Kornilov affair, as we have seen; and there were now reports that "disorganized masses of soldiers" were "pouring in an uncontrollable stream down

[18] Ministerstvo vnutrennago dela vremennago pravitel'stva, *Izvestiia Otdela po Delam Mestnago Upravleniia*, No. 4, Sept. 23, 1917. A description of the activities of one such local group appears in *Odesskii Listok*, Sept. 1, 1917. See also *Vestnik Vremennago Pravitel'stva*, Sept. 5, 1917.

[19] Fedor Rodichev, "Vospominaniia o 1917," unpubl. MS in the Hoover Institution, 1924, p. 24.

the Pskov highway." Once again, government offices prepared to evacuate.[20] Meanwhile, on the afternoon of August 31, as the Petrograd militia was mopping up the remnants of Kornilov's forces, Lenin's followers passed a sharply worded resolution through the Petrograd Soviet, indicating their own new self-assurance. The government was to proclaim a democratic republic, end private property in land, publish all secret treaties, authorize full workers' control in industry, and send immediate peace proposals to all warring countries. Bolsheviks also noisily demanded the election of new commissars by local soviets, dissolution of the State Duma, elimination of all class privileges, and the immediate convening of a Constituent Assembly.[21]

On September 1, the Central Executive Committee of the All-Russian Congress of Soviets (TsIK) rejected the Bolsheviks' demands and called for the Democratic Conference.[22] But the new strength of Lenin's supporters was not ephemeral. Reports from the front lines indicated Kornilov's arrest had effectively nullified past orders, meaning the virtual end of discipline. Bolshevik journals reappeared in the trenches, and army committees on all three major fronts passed Bolshevik-sponsored resolutions.[23] Violence also flared up against command personnel suspected of pro-Kornilov sympathies. On September 2, *Izvestiia*, *Rech'*, and other Petrograd papers reported particularly grim atrocities at Vyborg. On September 4, pressure from the left also forced the government to accept bail for Trotsky, arrested after the July disorders. And the following afternoon, the Moscow Soviet adopted an even sharper Bolshevik resolution than the one passed in Petrograd, expressing no confidence in the Central Executive Committee. It also demanded the right to arm workers and organize a Red Guard.[24] When the Petrograd Soviet reaffirmed its earlier condemnation of the Kadets on September 8 and 9, and elected a Bolshevik majority to the board of its workers' section (simultaneously forcing the resignation of socialist moderates from the ruling presidium), the most prominent local organ of revolutionary democracy fell largely into Bolshevik hands.[25]

All of this had a dramatic impact on Kadets and moderate socialists alike. As the war continued, and as new factory closings turned out thousands of additional unemployed workers, Bolshevik strength was rapidly growing. New shortages of food and rising prices also contributed to Lenin's support, as did fears of new hardships in the

[20] *Rech'*, Sept. 6 and 7, 1917; *Novoe Vremia*, Sept. 12, 1917.
[21] *Revoliutsiia 1917 goda*, IV, 139.   [22] *Ibid.*, p. 351.
[23] Notes on the condition of the Russian army in September and October, 1917, in the Bylevskii Papers, pack. 7.
[24] *Revoliutsiia 1917 goda*, IV, 155-72.   [25] *Izvestiia*, Sept. 8 and 10, 1917.

coming winter, and the growing realization that Kerensky was unlikely to organize anything but a poor excuse for national authority, absolutely incapable of stemming the pain and suffering of everyday Russian existence. Many even suspected the Bolsheviks themselves would make a new coup attempt in a matter of days; and rumors to this effect spread freely from the Nevskii Prospekt to trenches in Galicia.

When the SRs and Mensheviks refused to back Kerensky's coalition cabinet on August 31, they assumed the Democratic Conference would unite moderate soviet leadership with democratic elements in zemstvos and cooperatives, many of whose leaders had supported the socialists' "Program of August 14" (read by Chkheidze to the Moscow Conference). On these grounds they hoped finally to force a broadly based socialist regime with sufficient power to restore a strong defensive posture at the front, and carry the country to a Constituent Assembly.[26] But German advances and the Bolshevik capture of the Moscow and Petrograd Soviets shattered what little chance there might have been of unity on the question of an all-socialist regime. Tsereteli, Gots, and other Menshevik and SR leaders again argued forcefully that the government had to include Kadets, or at least "propertied" elements, to build its strength against both left and right extremists, and to preserve as much unity as possible in the army. Plekhanov's *Edinstvo* even published a "Long Live Coalition" banner in its editions of September 7 through 10, despite articles continuing to link the Kadets with Kornilov. And moderates in both the SR and Menshevik camps hoped the Democratic Conference would settle the issue in favor of a continued sharing of power.[27]

The Kadet Central Committee was initially hostile to the Democratic Conference. Instructions were sent out to party leaders urging them to dissuade local public organizations from sending delegates; and in Petrograd, Shingarev and Kedrin spoke bitterly when the city duma voted 5,000 rubles for the project.[28] But when the anti-Bolshevik and "patriotic" posture of moderate socialist leaders was reaffirmed, "conciliationist" Kadets felt new grounds for accommodation could well develop; and soon, with the approval of the Central Committee, Smirnov, Kishkin, and Konovalov joined several others in asking Kerensky to organize a new coalition under six very general conditions:

[26] F. Dan, "K istorii poslednikh dnei vremennogo pravitel'stva," *LR*, No. 1, 1923, pp. 164-65.

[27] *Edinstvo*, Sept. 7, 8, and 10, 1917. See also *Izvestiia*, Sept. 7, and the discussion in N. Sukhanov, *Zapiski o revoliutsii*, 7 vols., Berlin, 1922-23, VI, pp. 86ff.

[28] *Zhurnal Petrogradskoi Gorodskoi Dumy*, No. 77, Sept. 11, 1917; and *Svobodnyi Narod*, Sept. 12, 1917.

a decisive war on "anarchy"; guarantees of free Constituent Assembly elections; equal rights for all ministers; measures to "strengthen" the army; the independence of the government from "irresponsible" parties or class organizations; and general acceptance of the Kadet role in the cabinet, something the Democratic Conference itself might now provide. Strikingly absent were statements about local committee or soviet authority, agrarian or economic reforms, or the "representative" status of ministers—stumbling blocks to previous ministerial negotiations.[29]

Meanwhile, an even more conciliatory line was emerging on the difficult question of war and peace. Kadet moderates were by no means becoming Zimmerwaldian internationalists; but there was an increasing feeling on the part of Nolde, Adzhemov, Vinaver, Nabokov, and several others that Russia would have to begin "very carefully" to explore peace possibilities. The obvious danger otherwise was that Russia would fall either to the Bolsheviks or to the Germans. In the middle of September (and in Miliukov's continued absence), the Kadet Central Committee heard Nolde present a long report in favor of asking the Allies to start peace discussions.[30]

Nolde's report may well have represented a fear that peace would soon be negotiated anyway, and at Russia's expense. This was the implication of a circular letter issued to the various belligerents by Pope Benedict in August, and was also the gist of a report on the question by Henrik Erlich, a well-known Bundist, who spoke to the Soviet Central Executive Committee on September 12.[31] Defense of Russia's interests in this case would best be served if her political factions could approach discussions as a united front, a condition which suggests the Kadets' new found "pacifism" did not, in fact, represent any significant lessening of nationalistic ardor. Still, Nolde's report was a great step toward the moderate socialists' viewpoint, and one which made a new coalition all the more desirable.

The problem was to overcome the resistance not only of Bolsheviks and left SRs, but of scores of "moderate" socialists as well, who now very much doubted whether a "united front" with Kadets made much sense. A swing away from the notion of coalition had been growing steadily even before the Kornilov uprising, as Miliukov and his colleagues became increasingly identified with "forces of counterrevolution" on the right, and as the party's tactics in the government seemed

---

[29] *Rech'*, Sept. 15, 1917.

[30] V. Nabokov, "Vremennoe pravitel'stvo," *ARR*, I, 1922, pp. 81-82; Baron B. B. Nol'de, "V. D. Nabokov v 1917 g.," *ARR*, VII, 1922, p. 11.

[31] *Revoliutsiia 1917 goda*, IV, 203-04; Fritz Fischer, *Germany's Aims in the First World War*, New York, 1967, pp. 416-20.

increasingly obstructionist. At a "unity" congress of Mensheviks just after the Moscow State Conference in August, Tsereteli, Potresov, and others in favor of coalition had barely maintained a majority; and among the SRs, the aftermath of Kornilov saw the eruption of violent disputes on the question, with Chernov leading a strong "left-center" faction in favor of coalition but without the Kadets, and the SR Central Committee as a whole instructing Kerensky on August 31 not to include Kadets in any new ministry, as we have seen.

When the Democratic Conference finally convened on September 14, it was thus a far cry from the unifying organ its sponsors had anticipated. Tsereteli, Gots, and other Soviet leaders were again sharply attacked by the Bolsheviks, just as they had been at the first All-Russian Congress of Soviets in June. But now large numbers of more moderate SRs also hurled accusations of weakness. Kerensky was openly ridiculed. Avksentiev was virtually driven off the stage. Some assaulted Tsereteli, and then whipped around to attack Martov, Lenin, and "left-wing extremists" with equal passion. As a canvas of unity, one observer noted, the gathering resembled nothing so much as a "hastily constructed lean-to, full of gaps and crevices, into which people have crowded for warmth and shelter from the cold and bitter winds of a revolutionary autumn." There was little comfort to be found.[32]

On the central issue of whether a new regime should be a coalition, there was no unity whatsoever. While Gots and Tsereteli fought for accommodation, scores of their SR and Menshevik colleagues stoutly resisted, and were joined by a number of representatives from even such "nonpartisan" organizations as the cooperatives and food-supply organs.[33] It was also obvious that many delegates were simply uncertain about which course Russia should follow. When the issue came to a vote, delegates passed a motion in favor of coalition by a margin of 766 to 688; but they then adopted an amendment to exclude the Kadets by 595 to 493; and finally, by an overwhelming margin of 813 to 183, rejected the original motion as amended, leaving the issue more confused than before. The best the Conference could do was to entrust a specially elected presidium—dominated by moderates like Gots and Tsereteli—to negotiate a new government with Kerensky.[34]

[32] Telegram from George Williams, husband of Ariadna Tyrkova, to the London *Daily Chronicle*, dated Oct. 2, 1917 (n.s.), in the A. V. Tyrkova Archive, sec. 3, cart. 12, gp. 3.

[33] For example, a group of representatives from local dumas favored coalition only by 114 to 101 (with 15 abstaining); the economic and food supply organizations voted 34 to 16 in favor of coalition; and the nationality representatives (representatives from "nationality organizations") 15 in favor, 40 opposed. See *Izvestiia*, Sept. 20, 1917, and Browder and Kerensky, III, 1685.

[34] *Revoliutsiia 1917 goda*, IV, 204. See also *Rech'*, Sept. 20, 1917; *Izvestiia*, Sept. 20 and 21, 1917, and the discussion in Sukhanov, VI, 86-92.

The minister-president himself, meanwhile, had already taken new steps to reconstruct his cabinet. After negotiating individually with a number of persons as the Democratic Conference was getting underway, he convened a meeting of all leading political representatives on September 22. For Kadets, it was now a question of whether or not the view of their own party moderates was to prevail, whether a government was to be organized with Kadet participation on the basis of significant programmatic concessions. The question had come up before: at the seventh party congress, when Miliukov had insisted concessions would weaken national unity; and at the eighth and ninth party congresses in May and July, when the dominant theme turned out to be the unification of "healthy statesmanlike elements," which in practice had meant a recognition of Russia's growing national polarization, and an effort to consolidate the right. But events had shown the futility of this course, even driving those who represented a "civil war mentality" out of the capital. And with Smirnov, Adzhemov, Nabokov, Kishkin, and Konovalov now leading the Central Committee, that group as a whole was finally willing to compromise. It remained only for two major issues to be resolved: whether Chkheidze's statement to the Moscow Conference on August 14 could stand as a program for the new government; and whether the new regime would in any way be responsible to a new, all-Russian "Provisional Council" or "preparliament," which the socialists wanted to convene before the Constituent Assembly to draft legislation and set state policy.

For all their desire to reach an accommodation with the socialist moderates, Kadets strongly objected to the preparliament. Again it was a question of "legal power," and "legitimate" authority, just as throughout 1917. Tsereteli and the representatives of the Democratic Conference wanted the new coalition to be "factually" responsible to the new institution, formally reflecting its policies. Kadets felt this would create a surrogate legislature, even less representative than the Dumas, and certainly less likely to reflect the liberals' views. When it became clear, however, that Kadets were drawing the line of compromise here, the left backed down. A "Council of the Republic" would be convened, but only as a consultative body, and without the capability of issuing formal directives. Hopefully, the moral weight of the Council would both strengthen the coalition, and establish a mutual interdependence bordering on parliamentary responsibility. But authority for creating a new government structure still rested with the Constituent Assembly.[35]

Chkheidze's so-called Program of August 14 caused other problems. For one, it seemed to undercut a main premise of liberal politics in

[35] *Russkiia Vedomosti*, Sept. 23, 24, and 26, 1917.

1917 by sanctioning the authority of local "democratic" committees, and charging them with the implementation of major social and economic reforms. For another, it seemed to recognize the legitimacy of secessionist tendencies, especially in Finland and the Ukraine. But here liberals were more ready to yield. Adzhemov, Kishkin, Smirnov, and others had actually been conciliatory toward the program in August; and they were now even further convinced that only a moderate bloc could save Russia from extremists. Chkheidze's statement, moreover, had the advantage of being acceptable not only to soviet groups, but to cooperatives, zemstvos, and liberal professional organizations; while any attempt to work out a new program would require going back to the Democratic Conference. Kadets consequently felt they were left with the alternatives of accepting the statement, and joining the cabinet on this basis; or turning over the reins of government entirely to the socialists. In the latter case, with the cabinet forced to rely for support on the Moscow and Petrograd Soviets, it seemed only a matter of time before the Bolsheviks controlled the government itself.

Thus it developed that the Kadets made perhaps the greatest concession of their entire political history, and decided to join a cabinet formally committed to the implication of a forthright socialist program. In making this decision, the Central Committee consented in effect to the "immediate improvement of land relations" through existing land committees, thus reversing one of the positions they had held most tenaciously for the previous six months; and they accepted "the right of all nationalities to self-determination" on principles to be laid out by the Constituent Assembly, a stance which, had it been adopted earlier, might conceivably have precluded the whole July crisis. The new regime also declared its intention to "guarantee" the introduction of special legislation relative to state control over industry "with the participation of laboring and industrial classes, and *active interference* in the management of enterprises with the goal of increasing productivity" (my italics). And perhaps most symbolically, the Kadet Central Committee officially buried Miliukov's foreign policy, accepting the socialists' belief in the importance of an immediate, universal peace, obtained through the pursuit of an active foreign policy "in the spirit of the democratic principles proclaimed by the Russian Revolution."[36]

But if this alone was not enough to stagger party conservatives, the government's new program had other statements of significance for Kadets. To strengthen the army, it accepted the principle of selecting commanding officers on the basis of their loyalty to republican govern-

---

[36] *Vestnik Vremennago Pravitel'stva*, Sept. 28, 1917. A translation appears in Browder and Kerensky, III, 1714-17.

ment, as well as their willingness to cooperate with army committees and commissars. And it pledged to introduce new taxation on profits, luxuries, and property. In sum, the four Kadets accepting posts in the coalition—Kishkin, Kartashev, Konovalov and Smirnov—recognized that the government "in all its struggles and activities" would consider itself the "spokesman of the will of the revolutionary people," and would "collaborate closely with the organizations of the people."[37]

"Conciliationists" vs. the Right

With the advantage of hindsight, one is tempted to assign very little practical significance to these concessions. The story was over by now in terms of establishing a firm provisional authority, and however crucial their own acts seemed to Kadets in Petrograd, the only important political question was whether Lenin and his supporters would make their move before or after the Constituent Assembly convened, and whether they would have the strength to succeed when they acted.

But the events of mid-September are quite important in terms of understanding the liberals' whole revolutionary experience. They show that the Central Committee could, in fact, make the kind of concessions which might earlier have led to much greater popular support, had they been offered during the first provisional cabinets. The Committee had finally accepted in September that Russia was a sea of red flags; had they been more willing in the spring to respond positively to the social demands these flags paraded, moderation and liberal democracy might well have had a chance to survive.

Now, however, even conciliatory Kadets remained properly skeptical that the new cabinet could effectively meet Russia's problems. The very fact that Kerensky remained head of state boded ill for government authority. He was an accident of history, the wrong man in the right place, who held his position only because circumstances left Russia's divided political leadership with no other mutually acceptable candidate. (Miliukov even felt the minister-president needed a full-time psychiatrist, caustically suggesting his own party colleague Nicholas Kishkin might fill the bill.)[38] In order to provide as much liberal backbone as possible for the new cabinet, Kadet ministers finally began meeting on a daily basis with the Petrograd Central Committee, the first time Kadets had attempted such coordination since the revolution began. But with increasing violence in the countryside, transport virtually at a standstill, productivity at an all-

[37] *Ibid.*   [38] Miliukov, *Istoriia*, pt. 3, p. 78.

time low, the growing strength of the Bolsheviks, and finally, the constant menace of the Germans, the best Kadets could hope was that the new regime might somehow limp to the Constituent Assembly on the crutch of a radical program.

Their very anxiety, however, not only prompted Central Committee support for the government's new positions, but pressed Kadets on two other courses they had resisted throughout the year: support for an ad hoc, socialist-dominated national assembly, the "preparliament"; and active campaign work for the Constituent Assembly elections. The preparliament still raised questions of government "legitimacy," even though it had been reduced to purely consultative status in the negotiations over the new coalition: by what right, Kadet legalists still inquired, could such a body structure national policy, even indirectly, and prepare programs for the Constituent Assembly? But once Adzhemov and the other party negotiators agreed to its convocation, the Central Committee as a whole accepted its validity, and hoped simply to prevent its becoming a socialist rubber stamp. Adzhemov began to work full time on the body's governing statutes; and he, Vinaver, and Nabokov met with various Soviet representatives to plan its program. Thus "cooperation" between the Kadets and the moderate left was also finally institutionalized, though too late, of course, to significantly affect the course of the revolution. In an editorial on the preparliament on October 3, even *Rech'* reversed its earlier hostile line.[39]

Kadets also began to work hard on the Constituent Assembly elections, though their deep concern about Russia's readiness to vote was hardly mollified by either Russian conditions or the experience of local duma elections in September and October. On September 10 and 24, Pskov and Moscow went to the polls; and Samara and Tomsk followed on October 1. While balloting in each case was characterized by listlessness and apathy, Lenin's followers scored dramatic victories, especially in Moscow, Samara, and Tomsk, roundly defeating all competition, including the SRs; and in Moscow, they secured a staggering 193,489 votes, fully 51 percent of the total. In contrast, the SRs gained only 54,479 votes, while all other socialist parties together won barely 20,000. Such was the "revolutionary temper of the masses" that some Bolsheviks even felt a "Council of District Dumas" in Moscow might

---

[39] *Rech'*, Oct. 3, 1917; Nabokov, "Vremennoe pravitel'stvo," p. 79; N. F. Slavin, "Krisis vlasti v sentiabre 1917 g. i obrazovanie vremennogo soveta respubliki (predparlament)," *IZ*, No. 61, 1957, pp. 57-59. Right-SR support for Kadet conciliationists, meanwhile was suggested by a *Volia Naroda* article on October 7, entitled "Oboroncheskii blok"; while a regional Kadet gathering in Rostov reversed an earlier decision of the Rostov committee on October 3, and determined the tactic was now worth trying. See *Rostovskaia Rech'*, Sept. 23 and Oct. 5, 1917.

possibly become a "legitimate" steppingstone for seizing control of the revolution.[40]

Curiously, however, the Kadets also saw hope in the Moscow election results. Without much effort, the liberals themselves had finally "defeated" their moderate socialist competitors, winning 101,100 votes or 27 percent. Moreover, they now interpreted their earlier defeat in Petrograd to garrison votes and the high rate of absenteeism. In August, *Rech'* had claimed that Kadets actually "won" 40 percent of the "basic" popular vote, reasoning that most who stayed away from the polls were liberal supporters. By the same logic, the Moscow returns now indicated a "significant victory."[41]

Consequently, as the Moscow results became known, party leaders began to devote themselves in earnest to the Constituent Assembly campaign. After three long months of work in the Assembly's Election Commission, Kokoshkin and his colleagues had finally produced what they considered to be an acceptable electoral statute: Russia would have "one of the most satisfactory and most democratic electoral laws in the world."[42] And with a desperate hope that perhaps the Assembly *could* provide Russia with a moderate, authoritative government, they began once again to gather their forces, scheduling new special sessions on "agitation." In Moscow a special course was to begin on October 2: Paul Novgorodtsev would speak on "The Ideology of the Party of People's Freedom and Socialism"; P. A. Velikhov on "City and Zemstvo Self-Government"; and Michael Mandelshtam on "The Main Questions of Our Times." Similar sessions were set for other cities.[43]

Once again, however, these efforts raised tactical problems for Kadets, the same ones they had struggled with since the first days of the party's organization: how to seek new popular support for the party, and how to translate this support into votes. The basic question was: should Kadets continue appealing to right-wing interests, as they had in July and August (and particularly at the ninth party congress)? Should they enter the elections instead with gestures of support for

[40] M. Vladimirskii, "Moskovskie raionnye dumy i sovet raionnykh dum v 1917-1918 gg.," *PR*, No. 8 (20), 1923, pp. 79-80. See also A. Shlikhter, "Pamiatnye dni v Moskve," *PR*, No. 10, 1922, pp. 173-74; and my article, "The Russian Municipal Duma Elections of 1917," *Sov. Stud.*, XXI, Oct. 1969, pp. 158-62, which gives sources for actual returns. In Samara, out of a total of 54,537 votes, the Bolsheviks secured 20,318, the SRs, 18,956, as reported in V. V. Trotskii, *Samarskaia organizatsiia VKP v gody voiny i okt'iabriskaia revoliutsiia*, Samara, 1927, pp. 134-35; in Tomsk, Lenin's supporters won 7605 out of 23,463 total votes, compared to the SRs' 5422, as reported in *Znamia Revoliutsii* (Tomsk) Oct. 3, 1917.

[41] *Rech'*, Aug. 23, 1917; *Russkiia Vedomosti*, Sept. 28, 1917.

[42] A. Iu. Blok, "Vybory v uchreditel'noe sobranie," *VPNS*, No. 19, Sept. 21, 1917, p. 4.

[43] *Russkiia Vedomosti*, Sept. 26, 1917; *Odesskii Listok*, Sept. 26, 1917; *Svobodnyi Narod*, Sept. 21, 1917.

the interests of workers and peasants? Or should local party organizations remain officially committed to traditional positions, advancing the virtues of *nadklassnost'* and *nadpartiinost'* as they had in most city duma elections?

Not surprisingly, there was considerable confusion on these issues. But with conciliationists in control of the Central Committee, that body finally took the significant step in mid-September of trying to reverse the party's general rightward drift, and swing the tactics of local organizations back toward the left. On September 11 or 12, the Committee voted to form a special "Peasant Committee" for the party, and actively solicit peasant representatives for local party slates. Also, just as Kadets had done in their "radical" years of 1905-1906, it authorized local party groups to include peasants as official Kadet candidates even if they were not party members, provided only that they "accepted" the basic premises of the Kadets' agrarian program.[44] At the same time, cooperation was urged with socialist moderates, even to the extent of forming electoral blocs; and there was genuine disappointment in early October when a congress of the moderate Popular Socialist party rejected such alliances, despite a recognition that they and the Kadets shared a similar understanding of social needs and tasks.[45]

Thus the Central Committee adopted an electoral strategy in September which corresponded to its new spirit of conciliation and cooperation at the level of high politics. There was, however, something ironic and even curious about this course. In June, July, and August, when all indications showed the party's prerevolutionary electoral base had collapsed, party leaders both in Petrograd and elsewhere were still almost rigidly intransigent on the question of concessions to popular demands in local election campaigns. Despite its obvious lack of mass appeal, the party's standard had continued to be *nadpartiinost'*, which was increasingly a shield for associations with bourgeois groups and the right, and a defense of Russia's propertied interests. But now, with Russia fully polarized and the party's base reasonably firm with right-wing groups (as the most recent Moscow and Petrograd elections indicated), Petrograd Kadets backed off, proposing tactics instead which they hoped would appeal to the left.

Perhaps the best explanation of this shift lies in the psychology of

[44] *Svobodnyi Narod*, Sept. 13, 1917.

[45] *VPNS*, No. 21-22, Oct. 12, 1917, p. 33. At a regional party conference in Moscow on Sept. 23-24, delegates were read a specific directive from the Central Committee forbidding their local groups from taking financial contributions from groups like the Union of Factory Owners or the Trade-Industrialists (although donations from individuals without group affiliation were still welcome, regardless of their personal group affiliation). See *VPNS*, No. 28, Nov. 30, 1917, p. 12, and the discussion in *Utro Rossii*, Oct. 4, 1917.

the Petrograd party leadership itself. From the first days of the revolution in February, the greatest fear of Kadets in the capital was the outbreak of civil war. *Nadpartiinost'* as a tactical orientation in local politics was specifically designed to mitigate interclass conflict and social polarization, while also preserving national unity in support of the war. As partisanship was increasingly pressed on Kadets, both through the actual social polarization of cities and the countryside and the practical needs of local elections, the party followed a natural course to the right in defending its own interests and values; but developing associations with "healthy, statesmanlike elements" were still thought of as an effort to resist, rather than encourage polarization, and again, to prevent civil conflict. For many Kadets (and especially for those in Petrograd and Moscow who had argued all along in favor of a more conciliatory approach to the left) the tragedy for Kadets in the Kornilov affair was that civil war, in effect, had almost become a logical end of the party's own tactics. And now, in the tense aftermath of that episode, the Central Committee was ready to lead the party away from the right in a new quest for civil peace.

The problem with the conciliationists' approach, however, was that it underestimated the degree to which right-wing party members in Petrograd and Moscow, and particularly the party's provincial leadership, had now come to assume a full-fledged civil war mentality. In the provinces, a willingness to fight seemed increasingly the sole route to survival. And for Miliukov, Kokoshkin, Novgorodtsev, Dolgorukov, and others in both Moscow and Petrograd, the Kornilov episode and the Democratic Conference together only reinforced a desire to consolidate conservative forces, girding for future conflict. At the very moment Kishkin and Adzhemov were negotiating the governments' new radical program, for example, *Svobodnyi Narod* questioned whether any "sensible" person "could seriously think about basic social reforms":

> When the Germans are threatening Petrograd, and our army is disintegrating; when the city is hungry and the peasants refuse to provide bread; when factories are closing for lack of fuel; when senseless pogroms and riots are breaking out everywhere and no one knows what tomorrow will bring—in these times it is absolutely impossible to think of the basic reconstruction of Russia.[46]

One could think only of winning the war and maintaining order: "The country does not await reforms from the government, but order—order without which even the best democratic reforms will only be scraps of paper."[47]

[46] *Svobodnyi Narod*, Sept. 17, 1917.   [47] *Ibid.*

In the provinces, moreover, Miliukov and his supporters were encouraging local party groups in September to adopt precisely the opposite strategy from the one recommended by the Central Committee, and form electoral alliances with right-wing groups, rather than those on the left. And whether or not as a result of their efforts, this was the course most groups began to follow. In Vitebsk, for example, Kadets attempted a bloc with the openly right-wing Union of Landowners; in Penza they wanted to group with tradesmen, industrialists, landlords, and the Landowners Council; and in Orenburg and Orlov provinces, they offered to unite with the Trade-Industrialists.[48] While the Kievan Kadets openly declared their support for "democratic ideas in the face of rising opposition," and their colleagues in Odessa actively recruited peasants in conformity with the directives of the Central Committee, these local groups were the exceptions, not the rule.[49]

Again, however, while many local bourgeois groups accepted Kadet overtures, others still preferred very much to maintain their independence: the tenuous nature of the party's bonds to the right, caused basically by past refusals to take a partisan "bourgeois" orientation but now attenuated by the Kornilov debacle, was becoming more and more clear; and Kadets seemed thwarted in any direction they wanted to move. In the municipal duma elections in Tomsk and Samara on October 1, for example, local bourgeois groups insisted on running independent slates. And significantly, they did almost as well as the Kadets. In Tomsk, where Kadets won 3,871 out of 23,463 votes, the Landlords' group (Domovladel'tsy) itself won 2,328. Apartment Owners, Civil Servants, and other nonsocialist groups gained an additional 1,221. In Samara, meanwhile, Landlords won 3,478 votes, as compared to the Kadets 7,560.[50]

Nevertheless, Kadet conservatives still worked hard at consolidating right-wing strength. Returning north in late September, Miliukov in particular pursued these efforts in conjunction with yet another bourgeois conference, this time the Second All-Russia Congress of Public Figures which met in Moscow on September 28. And here party conservatives had more success. The "Public Figures" not only determined to unify their own slates with those of the Kadets for the Constituent Assembly elections, but to thwart any Kadet-socialist alliance in either the elections or the preparliament. Russia's strongest nonsocialist party was to stand as the political core of the right, not as a bridge between dissident factions of leftists and moderates. And

[48] Ibid., Oct. 12, 1917.
[49] Odesskii Listok, Sept. 26 and Oct. 4, 1917.
[50] Trotskii, Samarskaia organizatsiia, pp. 134-35; Znamia Revoliutsii (Tomsk), Oct. 3, 1917.

despite the lack of any apparent alternative to Kerensky's third coalition (though some delegates actually discussed the possibility of setting up their own rival cabinet),[51] the Public Figures openly disavowed the premises on which the new regime had been organized. Instead, they formed a special coordinating group to consolidate all right-wing organizations, including the Kadets, and presented themselves as a firm counterweight to any efforts—by socialists or "conciliationists"—to undermine "liberty, social justice, or Russian national unity."[52]

THE TENTH PARTY CONGRESS

Thus in early October the Kadet party leadership was clearly and openly divided. And just as antagonism between individual Kadet leaders was reaching the point of explosion, party delegates from all over Russia arrived in Moscow for their last major gathering of the revolutionary period, the tenth party congress. Ironically, the basic tactical questions of Russian liberalism thus emerged to be highlighted and debated at the moment the Bolsheviks began their final drive for power.

Understandably, feelings on all sides were intense, since even at this late stage no one dared assume the inevitability of Bolshevik success, and adherents of each viewpoint looked at their adversaries as purveyors of catastrophe. In the Central Committee, most agreed with Adzhemov, Nabokov, and the recently returned Vinaver that conciliation was the Kadets only choice. Despite Miliukov's arguments to the contrary, his colleagues considered necessary "the further development of the same tactical agreements which had led to the third coalition and the acceptance of the preparliament," that is, concessions to the left. The goal here was to create "a healthy [national] majority, supporting the government's point of view," and carry it into both the preparliament and the Constituent Assembly elections.[53]

But at the tenth congress itself, a majority lined up squarely behind the forceful Miliukov, convinced as he was that only a consolidation of right-wing forces could save their interests, and Russia's. Delegates from Moscow, Petrograd, and especially the provinces overwhelmingly indicated their approval of the conservative leadership, enthusiastically endorsing positions like those of the Congress of Public Figures, pre-

---

[51] S. P. Mel'gunov, *Kak bol'sheviki zakhvatili vlast'*, Paris, 1953, p. 45.

[52] *Russkiia Vedomosti*, Oct. 14, 1917; *Utro Rossii*, Oct. 14, 1917, Mel'gunov, *Kak bol'sheviki*, pp. 44-48; A. S. Dem'ianov, "Sluzhba pri vremennom pravitel'stve," *ARR*, IV, 1922, p. 72.

[53] B. Gurevich, "Krasnyi sfinks," MS in the Columbia Russian Archive, bx. 1, p. 474/20; Miliukov, *Istoriia*, pt. 3, p. 145.

sented them by Paul Novgorodtsev: the program agreed upon as the basis for the third coalition was "illegitimate"; it usurped the prerogatives of the Constituent Assembly in favor of specific social groups. Instead of the immediate implementation of reform, the Kadet task was to build a phalanx of groups standing for lawfulness and order, even if they were considered "reactionary" or "right wing." The party had to bring these people "into the liberal orbit," and consolidate legal-minded sentiment around Kadet ideals.[54]

In Miliukov's characterization, moreover, Russia was experiencing a period of "official dissimulation"; the socialists, not understanding the meaning of statesmanship, were hypocritically avoiding the best methods of obtaining national authority for fear of being challenged as Kornilovites. Kadets had to introduce some backbone into the third coalition; it was the moderate socialists who were split and confused, and who needed the Kadets to retain power. Thus the party had an advantage; and the best tactic was to press it hard. In particular, Kadets were to use the preparliament to insist their programs be adopted. If the socialists refused, if a majority in the preparliament could not be pressured behind the liberal outlook, Kadets should "seek allies elsewhere," from the ranks of the Public Figures and the cossacks—"the country's healthy elements."[55]

The implications of this were clear. In effect, as the Rostov delegate Leontev pointed out, Miliukov was arguing that Kadets should now play exclusively the role of an opposition party, avoiding all cooperation with moderate socialists which might alienate potential electoral allies on the right. The delegate Velikhov put the matter more directly. "I think," he told his colleagues, "that we must support the government *only in so far as—poskol'ku postol'ku*—it moves without hesitation on the path toward reestablishing lawful conditions in the country."[56]

This was indeed an ironic manner of expression for Kadets. Velikhov and his supporters had come full circle from the first days of March, when *poskol'ku postol'ku* was considered the root of government weakness. In a moment of grave crisis for the revolution, when qualification and opposition seemed to serve *their* interests, these Kadets themselves took a position which their own party had consistently and vociferously opposed as destructively partisan and nonstatesmanlike.

It was this that so outraged Adzhemov and the other so-called conciliationists. Adzhemov in particular turned on his colleagues after

[54] *Russkiia Vedomosti*, Oct. 15 and 17, 1917.
[55] *Ibid.*
[56] *Ibid.*, Oct. 17, 1917, my italics. Only an abbreviated account of Velikhov's speech appears in *Rech'*, Oct. 17, 1917.

Leontev and Velikhov, had spoken, castigating them for their "partisanship." Miliukov wanted the preparliament as an arena for winning right-wing votes. If the Kadets followed this advice, if they avoided "in a spirit of conciliation to find common roads with the huge Russian masses" for the sake of "pure principles," they would ignore both practical politics and the pressing immediate needs of Russia. "We, as a strong party," he continued, "should not be afraid to hear the truth. . . . In an extraordinary way, our comrades, the former ministers, have taken the most uncompromising position with regard to the government; here they represent the wing most to the right. . . . They are busy trying to destroy the coalition. But there can be no other."[57]

In the end, however, Miliukov again prevailed. The party's task for the immediate future was to form "a leading center for statesmanlike thinking which unites all healthy political elements. . . ." The meaning of this was clear: no one *wanted* civil war, but it was now the left which would have to realize the danger, while the right prepared; *nadklassnost'* and *nadpartiinost'*—with the hopes they bore in the spring of avoiding civil conflict—were policies of the past. For the time being, at least, conciliationist efforts had been effectively forestalled.[58]

Persistent Liberal Illusions on the Eve of the October Revolution

Kadets adjourned their tenth congress only ten days before Lenin came to power. Little had been accomplished. *Rech'* insisted a party split was "impossible," but divisions were clear. It was just possible that the Council of the Republic, the so-called preparliament, might preserve the government until the Constituent Assembly, or that Miliukov's "healthy elements" might coordinate their activities to stave off the radicals. But with those pressing most for accommodation officially defeated within the party, the preparliament hardly seemed promising. In the countryside, meanwhile, the popular mood was so overwhelmingly against the party that many local government organs did not even try to prevent Bolshevik harassment. The reality of October was agrarian and urban chaos, government impotence, unemployment, shortages of food and supplies, Kadet retrenchment, and the Bolshevik plans to take control.

At a series of meetings to celebrate the party's twelfth anniversary on October 18, however, Miliukov, Shingarev, and others still argued that the party's basic commitments were "unquestionably correct," that its

---

[57] *Ibid.*
[58] Resolutions of the tenth congress, *VPNS*, Nos. 28 and 30, 1917, pp. 8-12.

role was still to educate the masses politically, rather than in any sense respond to them, that Kadets represented the "statesmanlike" forces of the country, committed to lawful and orderly resolution of grievances. "In its difficult twelve years of experience," Shingarev told his colleagues with an appropriate professorial allusion, "the party has passed its examinations. All principles established by it at its foundation have proved justified."[59] Thus Kadets with Shingarev's outlook either failed to see how divorced the party had become from the process of revolutionary change, or found themselves unwilling and perhaps unable to break traditional liberal habits and forms.

The preparliament itself was rapidly becoming one such traditional form, and is worth examining briefly simply to show how unmovable right-wing Kadets still remained. Organized by the Democratic Conference in September as a permanent council to support the new coalition, its membership was divided among all major parties and public organizations, though numerically weighted in favor of the "democracy." But under pressure from Miliukov and his supporters, it was quickly converted into something very much like the old State Duma: a council of elders was elected, commissions were formed, and parliamentary practices were adopted. If Kadets and others on the right were to participate, there would be no repeat of the Democratic Conference in September. At the first session, the Bolsheviks walked out.

Many recognized that time-consuming legislative procedures were hardly suited to Russia's crisis situation, but on virtually all issues, Miliukov, Shingarev, Chernosvitov, and even Adzhemov continued until the very eve of the Bolshevik seizure to insist "legitimate" procedures be followed. As late as October 18, when a group of Mensheviks proposed that the Council deal with the urgent question of anarchy and counterrevolution, Kadets insisted the matter be sent first to a "special commission" for "analysis."[60] At the moment they were doing so, moreover, party "whips" were moving around the floor, reminding Kadets "in even voices" that fees for their club were due, and telling them what commission meetings were scheduled.[61] The preparliament was an attractive obfuscation.

Nor were most Kadets ready to change their perspectives on the state, on the meaning of the revolution, or on Russia's posture toward her Allies. These questions all came up early in the preparliament, as matters of defense and foreign policy became the principal issues of debate. At hand in particular was the question of instructing a special delegation to the Allied war conference in November, which the Pro-

[59] *VPNS*, Nos. 24-25, Nov. 9, 1917, p. 28.   [60] *Russkiia Vedomosti*, Oct. 19, 1917.
[61] I. V. Gessen, *V dvukh vekakh*, Berlin, 1937, p. 375.

visional Government mistakenly thought would deal with general matters of policy, as well as specific war plans. In early October, the Soviet Executive Committee delegated its own representative, Skobelev, to present certain peace proposals. This infuriated Miliukov's group of Kadets, who still insisted on "unitary" state authority; and even the Kadet "peace faction"—Adzhemov, Dobrovolskii, Vinaver, Nolde, Nabokov—feared Skobolev would seek a settlement unfavorable to Russia's national interests. For both groups of Kadets, the meaning of the revolution was still seen largely in terms of Russia's international position.[62]

What the government itself thought Russian national interests were on the eve of the Bolshevik coup was spelled out at the preparliament by the young liberal industrialist Michael Tereshchenko, Kerensky's foreign minister. Russia had to secure access to the Baltic, had to obtain guarantees of free passage through the Dardanelles, and had to "preserve her economic independence." A "real threat" to the first of these goals existed in the independence of Poland, Latvia, Estonia, Finland, and Ukraine; and Tereshchenko was reluctant to accept neutrality for the Dardanelles. Russia could not return to the "so-called imperialist plan," he argued, but neither could she allow a situation to exist whereby any military force whatsoever could close the straits to Russian ships. And as far as Russia's economic independence was concerned, defeat would be tantamount to becoming Germany's client; however great the difficulty, Russia had to continue fighting.[63]

This pleased most Kadets immensely. Tereshchenko's statement reflected precisely the goals Miliukov and his supporters had set for the revolution in March, with the same implications for military discipline and preparedness. The question for Kadets of this viewpoint was still how to build up the army. Tereshchenko himself spoke with some optimism on this point. There was no doubt, he argued, that Russia was in *better* economic circumstances than her enemies, despite grave problems. The main cause for her military difficulties "was not material conditions at all, but that reversal (*perelom*) in national psychology, to which we all are witness."[64]

But here was the source of a different set of persistent liberal illusions. Kadets still failed to recognize that the problem of army morale had to be treated at its source: the inability of workers and

---

[62] See in particular Adzhemov's speech to the pre-parliament on October 12, in *Russkiia Vedomosti*, Oct. 13, 1917.

[63] "Nakanune oktiabr'skago perevorota," *Byloe*, No. 12 (6), 1918, pp. 14-17 (accounts of the secret sessions of the pre-parliament).

[64] *Ibid.*, p. 14.

peasant-soldiers to see any relationship between liberal war aims and Russia's domestic welfare—the needs of the "state" vs. land, peace, and bread. This was pointed out by several Soviet spokesmen in the pre-parliament, and its implication in practical terms was that any government policy on continuing the war had to be explained in terms of meeting popular demands.

But on October 18, when several resolutions embodying this explanation were submitted, all were successfully countered by a statement from the liberal "bloc" (which on this question also included a number of right-wing socialists like N. V. Chaikovskii). The liberal's formula rested simply on the need to establish order, and the relationship between an effective military defense and "lawlessness, lynch-law, and anarchy." Matters such as land reform and ideological statements about "democratic peace" were superfluous.[65]

The liberal resolution did not gain a majority, but enough delegates supported it to split the preparliament virtually in two. On one side were those who felt they saw clearly the dangers (and even likelihood) of further conflict, both civil and foreign, and who insisted on firmness and military strength as a last defense. Like Miliukov, they represented a conviction that support for "worker and peasant interests" was tantamount to encouraging even further social disintegration, and thus, indirectly, the Germans and the Bolsheviks. On the other were those who saw Miliukov's group (and its "near Kadet" supporters among the SRs and the moderate Mensheviks) as the force of counterrevolution from the right, and who represented a hope that truly popular government could both throttle dangers from the left and protect Russia from future German domination. Popularity (and hence authority and strength) meant support and commitment to basic socialist ideals, especially on the war and reform.

For many, moreover, the division of the preparliament into two clear camps was an even more critical development than the formulation of the defense question per se. It implied that the preparliament would not form a solid phalanx behind the third coalition, with its Program of September 25, and that the government's weakness would continue.[66] It also suggested that Kadet concern for "state" interests in international terms still obscured domestic realities, even at this late moment.

This was also the problem of liberal attitudes toward General Verkhovskii, the left-leaning minister of war who painted a dismal picture of Russian conditions at a special meeting of the preparliament's defense and foreign affairs commissions on October 20. Ver-

[65] *Russkiia Vedomosti*, Oct. 19, 1917.   [66] *Ibid.*

khovskii's effort was to untie the Gordian knot of Russian defense by simply posing the question, "Can we continue fighting?" His answer, after a careful survey of material needs and conditions, was a forthright "No!" The minister could not, therefore, endorse with confidence any plans to improve the fighting capacity of the army; and he concluded that only immediate peace could avoid a Bolshevik coup.[67]

But for Miliukov and his supporters this was scandalous. And partly in response to their pressure, Kerensky asked for Verkhovskii's resignation the next morning. What angered liberals most, however, was not so much the content of Verkhovskii's report as Russia being served in such an important post by a man avowedly blind to Russian "honor" and what Kadets considered the interests of the state. Kadets advanced as their arguments against Verkhovskii his naiivité, defeatism, and sheer incompetence; but the thrust of their critique was his sense of priorities. These pressed a resolution of domestic problems regardless of their consequences in terms of the war on Russia's Allies.[68]

Finally, the continued intensity of Kadet statist concerns was also evident in the discussions of the Juridical Commission on Finland. After the Provisional Government had dissolved the Sejm in August, ostensibly to prevent a unilateral declaration of Finnish independence, the Finns had elected a new, more militant body, due to convene on October 21. Among other things, it was to hear various new proposals for regulating Russian-Finnish relations. In order to avoid open hostilities between Helsinki and Petrograd, Nicholas Nekrasov (now governor-general) recommended that the Russian government transfer all power over Finnish internal affairs to a person elected by the Sejm; as before, however, military and international matters were to be left in Russian hands.[69]

But not only did the Kadets on the commission respond harshly to Nekrasov; their objections to his proposal were based entirely on a consideration of Russian, rather than Finnish interests. Baron Nolde, for example, characterizing Finnish socialists as "utterly unreliable . . . ignorant people," argued that the Finns would respond to Nekrasov's proposals by staking out an independent foreign policy. And even for conciliationists like Grimm and Adzhemov, "vital Russian interests" would become the items of a Russian-Finnish bargain, with the outcome depending on Finnish, rather than Russian good will. For his

[67] "Nakanune," pp. 28-41.

[68] A. I. Verkhovskii, *Rossiia na golgofe*, Petrograd, 1918, pp. 113-34. See also Miliukov, *Istoriia*, pt. 3, p. 173; and Nabokov, "Vremennoe pravitel'stvo," pp. 79-81.

[69] Browder and Kerensky, I, 364-70. Nekrasov's plan was actually quite complicated, and involved applying maximum pressure on the Finns to accept what amounted to a Russian ultimatum. Moreover, it was clear that the grant of power over domestic affairs was to run only until the Constituent Assembly.

part, Grimm preferred to postpone all questions of this sort until the Constituent Assembly; in this way, if the Finns "seized" power *de facto* (and hence "illegally"), their actions could "be liquidated" by superior Russian force. According to the Kadets, Russia could not "give way to compromise on the grounds of expediency," for in effect, any such action "would also predetermine the question of the extent of autonomy for all other Russian borderlands . . . who would demand for themselves the rights granted Finland."[70]

With fifty years' hindsight, and with the knowledge of what lay just ahead for Kadets, one cannot help but be extremely impatient with these arguments. With Bolsheviks organizing in the wings, this time with such noise and commotion that all Russia knew what they were about, Kadets in the preparliament still evaluated policies through the glass of Russian state interests. National-liberalism, statism, *gosudarstvennaia mysl'*—whatever one wants to call it, it was the persistent ideological counterpart in October to the party's retreat behind the parliamentary façade of the Council of the Republic, a nationalism which was all the greater now, in October, in fact, than perhaps at any other time in the party's history, as the Russian state seemed about to disintegrate and liberal hopes were collapsing. This was the prevailing Kadet viewpoint, moreover, despite the fact that it reflected an attitude which had constantly led to failure, despite the concessions made over the third coalition, despite continued divisions within the party, and despite the "terrible, heavy anxiety" which virtually all Kadets felt hanging over Russia.[71]

And tragically for the liberals, their perspectives in the context of revolutionary democracy still meant a deep suspicion of the *narod*, an inability to relate to masses of workers and peasants. It may well be, as the scholars among Kadets continually argued, that Russia's conditions were simply a function of political and social backwardness, that the party cannot be faulted for what was essentially the consequence of general historical developments. One can still recognize, however, that with attitudes about "uplifting" the masses, with visions of ordinary citizens as "utterly unreliable, ignorant people," as Nolde characterized the Finns, Kadets stood little chance of carrying the masses with them; and without a sanctified, authoritative state apparatus, Russian society was open for whoever could muster effective force in support of their beliefs.

Thus the liberals waited dourly for Russia's second revolution. No one doubted that the Bolsheviks would attempt to take power; the

---

[70] *Ibid.*, pp. 369-70; and P. Galuzo, ed., "Iz istorii natsional'noi politiki vremennogo pravitel'stva," *KA*, No. 30, 1923, pp. 65-70.

[71] V. Nabokov, "Shest' mesiatsev revoliutsii," *VPNS*, No. 19, Sept. 21, 1917, p. 3.

only question was whether Kerensky could suppress them. Some party leaders—even those like Konovalov, who had felt in September that progress might be made—now lost all hope whatsoever. Every evening around 6:00 p.m. in the week or so before October 25, he, Shingarev, and Miliukov, Kishkin, Kartashev, and other leading Kadets met in Alexander Khrushchov's apartment to discuss the day's events. But for all their understanding of the government's lack of power, they themselves did nothing. On October 19, *Svobodnyi Narod* began a full-size daily column entitled "Bolshevik Preparations." Shortly afterward, Miliukov's apartment was placed under armed guard. The best the party could hope was that the Bolsheviks might again be crushed, as in July; and that Russia's wounds were less than mortal.

PART THREE

THE CIVIL WAR

CHAPTER NINE

The Agony of Political Irrelevance: Kadets
in Moscow and Petrograd after October

W<small>HEN THE</small> Bolsheviks finally struck on the night of October 25-26, the issues of popular radicalism, social polarization, and revolutionary change in Russia were finally joined. In a broad sense, the revolt represented the massive break in Russian society between its privileged and common social elements, the logical culmination of complex, long-term social forces. More narrowly, it reflected the Provisional Government's own inability to mobilize popular energies behind liberal, great-power objectives, and the unwillingness of workers and peasants to postpone basic social reforms. In towns and villages all over Russia "revolution" promised an end to social injustice and inequity, not simply the liberals' civil liberties; and if Lenin and the new Soviet power was "our" government for only a small fraction of the country's total population in October 1917, Miliukov, Kokoshkin, Nabokov, and their liberal colleagues clearly represented "them" for countless millions of others. Here, in brief, was the social symbolism of Russian liberal weakness.

The division between leaders and led not only helped explain the past in October 1917, but also largely defined the limits of effective future action for Kadets. Restoring "legitimate" government obviously required military force in Petrograd, but "privileged" Russia could hardly regain a dominant or stable political role without new support from ordinary citizens. Thus the outcome of any civil conflict, whether localized in Petrograd and Moscow or spread massively throughout the country as a whole, hinged from the outset on the ability of those opposing the Bolsheviks to popularize their goals and coordinate their energies and forces.

"LEGITIMACY" AND "STRUGGLE"

The initial response of Kadets in both Moscow and Petrograd to Lenin's action was a mixture of confusion, self-justification, hesitant militance, and misplaced hope in the power of existing "legitimate" institutions. Many liberals actually felt a sense of relief. The coup itself was in some ways easier to confront than the fears and anxieties which preceded it, particularly since few if any Kadets thought Lenin could hold state power permanently. Conciliationist party leaders and their more conservative colleagues alike both saw what was happening as one more episode in the unraveling of Provisional Government authority. Many even expected that the Bolsheviks might do for liberals what Kornilov had done for Lenin in August, restoring party credibility and unleashing a flood tide of new support.

The Central Committee's first reaction to the coup, consequently, was to stress the validity of the Kadets' own ideals and past perspectives. Ignoring their own earlier differences over coalition government and the policy of conciliation, the Committee reminded Russia in what were undoubtedly Miliukov's words that "from the time power was transferred to the first coalition regime, the Party of People's Freedom has not ceased to warn loudly of the threatening danger . . . and of the government's ruinous course in voluntarily sharing its power with soviets and partisan organizations of the so-called 'revolutionary democracy.'" Lenin was "proving" the weakness of socialist moderates, demonstrating anew the need for "firm, statesmanlike authority." With confiscated copies of *Rech'* burning in the streets, Miliukov and his colleagues urged Russians not to "recognize" Bolshevik power, but to work for "unity and social peace" by rallying at institutions still representing "legal" authority. In Petrograd and Moscow, this meant the remnants of the Provisional Government and the local city dumas.[1]

For a brief period, on October 26 and 27, the on-going apparatus of the Provisional Government seemed the best instrument for preserving legal power. The Bolsheviks' Military Revolutionary Committee had seized major government buildings and offices, but in the confusion, Kerensky left for Gatchina to rally loyalist troops, and granted "extraordinary powers for restoring order in Petrograd" to Nicholas Kishkin. He also appointed Alexander Konovalov as acting prime minister. Together, the two Kadets tried frantically to muster the Petrograd garrison in the name of legality. Discharging Colonel Polkovnikov as "irresolute" from command of the city's "Military District," they replaced him with General Major Bagratuni, called the army to action, and publicly insisted on the legitimacy of their authority alone. At the same time, they ordered lower-level government personnel to secure funds and records to prevent their falling into Bolshevik hands.[2]

[1] Statement of the Central Committee on "Current Events," October 27, 1917, republished in *VPNS*, Nos. 24-25, Nov. 9, 1917, p. 24; *Russkiia Vedomosti*, Nov. 10, 1917.
[2] *Volia Naroda*, Oct. 26, 1917. See also A. Kerensky, "Gatchina," *SZ*, No. 10, 1922,

But the task was hopeless. ("What kind of party is it," Kishkin telephoned A. G. Khrushchov on October 26, "that cannot even send us a mere three hundred armed men?")[3] When Bolsheviks began arresting government ministers, Kishkin and Konovalov's order to lower administrators proved their only act of consequence. On October 28 or 29, a group of assistant ministers, largely Kadets, gathered secretly in the apartment of Sophia Panina, herself a Central Committee member and an assistant minister of education. In accordance with Kishkin and Konovalov's order, arrangements were made to transfer government funds to foreign banks, payable only to Russia's "legal" regime, and to dispatch "official" emissaries to other Russian cities in an effort to retain government control. With Lenin's Council of People's Commissars (Sovnarkom) organizing its own administrative apparatus, this Underground Provisional Government began to meet regularly in Panina's apartment to coordinate the "legal" ministries.[4]

Thus a rudimentary groundwork was laid for a coordinated anti-Bolshevik struggle by Kadets, although the political situation in general remained unclear, and the party's leadership as a whole had no clear strategy. On October 29 the Central Committee publicly sent its "greetings" to "all institutions and organizations uniting against the Bolshevik seizure" in a statement printed by the SR newspaper *Volia Naroda*; but Miliukov and others were leaving the capital for Moscow; Kishkin, Konovalov, Smirnov, and Kartashev were imprisoned in the Peter Paul fortress; Vladimir Nabokov had been detained at Smolnyi with the Constituent Assembly Commission; and most remaining Central Committee members were prudently avoiding the party's clubs. Within the Underground Provisional Government, meanwhile, discussion was stymied over the form which the struggle against the Bolsheviks should take, a problem which became more difficult as party leaders learned of Kerensky's failure to rally troops at Gatchina. A call for massive armed resistance might create conditions in which Russia would lose any remaining ability to protect herself against the Germans, much less pursue her own vital national interests; while to resist

---

pp. 147-81; "Iz zapisnoi knizhniki arkhivista: poslednie chasy vremennogo pravitel'stva v 1917 g.," *KA*, No. 56(1), 1933, p. 137; P. N. Maliantovich, *Revoliutsiia i pravosudie*, Moscow, 1918, pp. 184-237.

[3] P. N. Miliukov, *Istoriia vtoroi russkoi revoliutsii*, 3 pts., Sofia, 1921-23, pt. 3, p. 232.

[4] Panina Archive, pack. 6, fold. 37. A manuscript in the A. V. Tyrkova Archive, cart. 3, gp. 2, attributes the initative for the strike of the Provisional Government office workers to Panina. The Underground Provisional Government met additionally on Nov. 6, 7, 10, 11, 13, 14, 15, and 16, before dispersing. The principal published source on this group, A. Dem'ianov, "Zapiski o podpol'nom vremennom pravitel'stve," *ARR*, VII, 1922, pp. 34-53, must be used cautiously. See also M. Fleer, ed., "Vremennoe pravitel'stvo posle oktiabria," *KA*, No. 6, 1924, pp. 195-221.

passively might be to acquiesce to radical dictatorship, internationalism, and the enactment of drastic social reforms.

As Panina and others discussed these issues, Kadets also clustered around two other "legal" institutions still capable of representing "legitimate authority," the Petrograd and Moscow City Dumas. Concentrating on the central government, the Bolsheviks made no immediate move against either, and both continued to meet after October 25. The Duma in Petrograd presented an especially curious spectacle. On the night of the coup, some ninety delegates remained at their benches until 3:00 a.m., led in part by V. A. Obolenskii and Andrei Shingarev. As messengers raced in with news of unfolding events, "special delegations" were dispatched to try to prevent bloodshed, one to the Winter Palace, one to the Bolshevik-controlled Soviet, and one to the cruiser *Aurora*, maneuvering into position on the Neva. Each was blocked by Red Guards. In frustration, the delegates then determined to march *en masse* to Palace Square. After justifying such an "extraordinary" action with a resolution on the "special dangers" of the moment, they set off around 1:30 a.m. in ranks of eight, but went only three blocks before being ignominiously turned back by an armed patrol.[5]

The Duma convened again in Petrograd on October 26, and continued to gather on succeeding days. At each session, Kadet representatives spoke with increasing forcefulness in defense of "legality" and "constitutional principles," but still gave little indication they appreciated the significance of Lenin's move. With the Duma still sitting, and orders still emanating from the Kadet-run remnants of the Provisional Government, the façade of "legitimate authority" obscured both political and social realities. On October 26, Shingarev insisted the Military Revolutionary Committee and "others acting illegally" would soon be arrested and brought to trial.[6]

In two longer speeches on October 30 and November 1, moreover, Shingarev also indicated how deeply he and his Kadet colleagues in Petrograd felt justified for their own past judgments, how convinced they were that the present crisis was solely the result of socialist ineptitude, rather than deeper social causes or their own political weakness: "The horrifying position of the nation," he declared, "is not only that a mutiny has occurred, but that mutiny has been allowed to fester so long in the country"; it was not so much the Bolsheviks who were

---

[5] *Zhurnal Petrogradskoi Gorodskoi Dumy*, No. 93, Sess. of Oct. 25, 1917 (p.m.).

[6] *Ibid.*, No. 94, Sess. of Oct. 26, 1917 (p.m.). One of the more anomalous appeals of the Petrograd Duma appeared on October 29, calling on all owners of automobiles "having passes from the Military Revolutionary Committee" to place them at the disposal of the Duma's "Committee to Save the Revolution"! It appeared in the *Vestnik Gorodskogo Samupravleniia*, Oct. 29, 1917.

responsible for the present catastrophe, as the socialist moderates, whose lack of concern for Russia's "real" needs and constant pandering to popular demands had led to a massive corruption of legality.[7] This theme was also echoed by Kadets outside the Duma in Petrograd. According to Vladimir Nabokov, for example, whom the Bolsheviks had just released, the cause of "all misfortunes" was the "demagogy which has been preached by all socialist parties without exception from the first moment of the revolution"; while even the more moderate Vinaver argued that "Trotsky and Lenin are simply continuing what Tsereteli, Chernov, and others began. . . ."[8]

Kadets in the Moscow City Duma were similarly preoccupied with the problems of "legal authority," although here they were less caustic toward the moderate socialists, a legacy, perhaps, of past conciliationist sentiment. The Moscow Duma met only three times after the Bolshevik coup, but at each session Kadet spokesmen continued to stress the importance of political legitimacy and legality. According to Astrov, the Provisional Government continued "legally" to exist despite the Bolsheviks; there was no "new authority" in the country, and the Provisional Government's "weakness" (!) did not destroy its legal foundation. "There is no need to create any new authority at the present time," he declared as late as November 15. "The Provisional Government must continue its work to the Constitutional [Constituent] Assembly." N. V. Teslenko also asserted these views, arguing that whatever force was used against it, the Duma should not disperse, but continue meeting as a "legitimate power"; the "usurpers were to be ignored"![9]

This was not isolated irrationality on the part of individual Kadets, nor was it simply naive. By the second week of November General Krasnov's cossacks had been beaten back from Petrograd near the Pulkovo heights, and resistance had collapsed in Moscow. It seemed unlikely that new forces could be brought to bear quickly and successfully against Lenin, or that the anti-Bolshevik struggle could in any case be confined to Petrograd and Moscow; and many Kadets remained deeply concerned about civil conflict spreading in a massive way throughout the country. Miliukov, Rodichev, and several others were clearly thinking in terms of an extended armed struggle, and Miliukov himself soon left Moscow to meet with cossack leaders in the

[7] *Zhurnal Petrogradskoi Gorodskoi Dumy*, No. 102, Sess. of Oct. 30, 1917 (p.m.) Shingarev's speeches were also reported in *Volia Naroda*, Oct. 31 and Nov. 1, 1917.

[8] *VPNS*, Nos. 26-27, Nov. 23, 1917, p. 9.

[9] *Russkiia Vedomosti*, Nov. 16, 1917; *Utro Rossii*, Nov. 16, 1917. See also M. Vladimirskii, ed., "Moskovskaia gorodskaia duma posle oktiabria," *KA*, No. 27. 1928, pp. 58-109, and No. 28, 1929, pp. 59-106; and V. Pobel'skii, "V gorodskoi dume," in N. Ovsiannikov, ed., *Moskva v oktiabre 1917 g.*, Moscow, 1919, pp. 56-58.

Don. But for the time being at least, most of his colleagues were far more cautious, and now inclined to think the restoration of "legal" rule might better come through nonviolent popular resistance to Lenin than through armed force.

Moreover as Vladimir Nabokov indicated to a meeting of city and provincial leaders in Petrograd in early November, some Kadets even found it possible to maintain that Lenin and his followers had not in fact "seized power" at all in any important sense, but merely accomplished the "simple" task of taking over political offices. Despite his own recent detention, Nabokov insisted that what really mattered was "psychological authority," the ability to command voluntary obedience, something Lenin could never develop on a national scale. When the Constituent Assembly convened on November 28, its task would be to remove political power from the Bolsheviks by winning psychological control of the people, and securing mass national support for an alternative cabinet. What the nation required in the meantime, and what Kadets were to do until the Russian people "rejected" the Bolsheviks, was to occupy themselves with the urgent everyday problems of economic and social administration—*delovye voprosy*—doing "everything possible to stop the decay of the government apparatus, and with it, the economic life of the country."[10]

The problem with this approach—in one sense a reflection of the same concern for legitimacy and legality which had structured liberal politics generally for the past twelve years, but also an indication that many Kadets seriously underestimated Bolshevik capabilities and the extent of popular radicalism—was that it made new efforts to cooperate with moderate socialists extremely difficult, thus hindering the formation of any broad anti-Bolshevik coalition. On the morning of October 26 a group of right-wing SRs, Popular Socialists, and moderate SDs formed an ad hoc anti-Bolshevik organization called the Committee to Save the Fatherland and Revolution (*Komitet Spaseniia Rodiny i Revoliutsii*—KSRR). The KSRR intended to fight the Bolsheviks with "all available means," forming local units in other parts of Russia, and uniting "all responsible democratic forces." It had the endorsement of the Petrograd City Duma.[11]

[10] *Novaia Zhizn'*, Nov. 11, 1917. Nabokov was speaking to the Zemsko-Gorodskoi Sobor, a gathering of provincial and city civic leaders which opened in Petrograd on November 9 with approximately sixty delegates attending.

[11] *Volia Naroda*, Oct. 27 and Nov. 4, 1917; *Zhurnal Petrogradskoi Gorodskoi Dumy*, No. 93, Sess. of Oct. 25, 1917. The KSRR was formed after the unsuccessful march by the Petrograd City Duma delegates to the Winter Palace at the urging of Petrograd mayor G. I. Shreider. Its first members were all Duma representatives, but according to the *Zhurnal*, no Kadets were included despite the organization's being formed in the Duma chambers. V. Vladimirova, *God sluzhby 'sotsialistov' kapitalistam*, Moscow-Petrograd, 1917, p. 20, lists almost a dozen organizations as

But while some left-wing Kadets applauded the KSRR, and urged the party's Central Committee to participate, Shingarev and other leaders in Petrograd looked askance at the committee as another effort to "usurp" the authority of the Provisional regime. Moreover, the manner in which liberals attacked the moderate socialists in the Petrograd and Moscow Dumas infuriated KSRR leaders. Consequently, when Obolenskii, Panina, and Nabokov tried to sit in on KSRR discussions, they were treated coolly.[12] And shortly afterward, when Bramson, Demianov, and other KSRR figures urged the transfer of government funds to the committee at a stormy session in Panina's apartment, hoping to raise troops and flood Russia with anti-Bolshevik proclamations, Panina and the Kadets became especially indignant. What right had they, they asked, to give the nation's money for partisan political struggle? When the socialists responded by accusing the Kadets of absurd attachment to "bourgeois legalism," relations broke down completely.[13]

Similarly, when Vinaver engaged Tsereteli in a lively debate in early November (at the same Petrograd conference to which Nabokov insisted the Bolsheviks had not really seized power), he also argued against any anti-Bolshevik "democratic center" on the ground that it would be a "direct usurpation of the rights of the Constituent Assembly."[14] The same weary argument affecting so much of Kadet policy in the earlier months of 1917 seemed to take new lease on life. Even when Tsereteli indicated that the "democratic center" would expressly preserve the power of the Assembly, Vinaver insisted Kadets could not participate.[15]

For the time being, consequently, Kadet-socialist conciliation was as much a victim of the Bolshevik coup as the third coalition it had constructed. Freed from the hapless duty of professing support for a

---

belonging to the committee, including the All-Russian Central Executive Committee of the Congress of Soviets (first convocation), and the Central Committees of the Menshevik, SR, Edinstvo, Bund, and Popular Socialist parties. Oliver Radkey gives extensive treatment to SR-KSRR relations in his *Sickle Under the Hammer*, New York, 1963, pp. 19ff. See also V. I. Ignat'ev, *Nekotorye fakty i itogi chetyrekh let grazhdanskoi voiny (1917-1921)*, Moscow, 1922, pp. 4-5.

12 V. Nabokov, "Vremennoe pravitel'stvo," *ARR*, I, 1922, 88-89; S. P. Mel'gunov, *N. V. Chaikovskii v gody grazhdanskoi voiny*, Paris, 1929, pp. 34-35. There was substance to Kadet suspicions about the KSRR wanting to supplant the Provisional Government. See the discussion in Radkey, pp. 73-91, and Ignat'ev, pp. 6-7.

13 Dem'ianov, "Zapiski," pp. 47-48. Shortly afterward, while most of the remaining figures in the Provisional Government fled the capital, the Bolsheviks moved against the KSRR. While it is not clear exactly when the Committee stopped functioning, *Utro Rossii* carried a notice of its dissolution on Nov. 10, 1917. See also Vladimirova, pp. 85-86.

14 *Novaia Zhizn'*, Nov. 12, 1917.   15 *Ibid.*

cabinet in which they actually had no faith, most Kadet spokesmen were momentarily fixed on the notion that fighting Bolshevism with Bolshevik methods would be to abandon constitutional legality on the eve of its promised institutionalization by Russia's first legitimate Constituent Assembly. The only practical militancy of party leaders came on the same day *Utro Rossii* noted the collapse of efforts to organize the KSRR, and was itself a very circumscribed call to "struggle." In a broadsheet called *Bor'ba*, Ariadna Tyrkova, A. S. Izgoev, and several other right-wing Kadets compared Lenin and Trotsky to Stürmer and Rasputin, and called Russians to an active struggle (*bor'ba*) "to reconstruct representative government on a correct and intelligent basis."[16] But while the very name *Bor'ba* suggested action, and the paper called Russia "to arms" with rhetorical flourish, the envisioned "struggle" was still to be fought essentially with the traditional weapons of the liberals' arsenal:

> To Arms, Citizens, to Arms!
> Freedom has been bayoneted.
> In the place of Russian leaders, forced aside by bayonets, false persons, dark personalities have appeared. . . .
> A bayonet has been thrust in the breast of the people.
> Freedom of the Press has been eliminated.
> Machine guns and bestial mob law threaten anyone who dares raise his voice in defense of the will. and honor of the Russian State.
> Citizens! Bayonets, machine guns and bombs are the weapons of brigands.
> We have—only our bare hands.
> We have no lethal bayonets
> We have no Red Guards
> We have only the greatest weapon of any in the land. That is Faith. The faith of law, justice, freedom and the honor of men. . . .
> Our Revolution has had everything with one exception: Reason.
> The nation must acquire Reason immediately if it does not want to perish.
> Of all the Russian parties, only one can truly bring Reason to Russia:
> *The Party of People's Freedom!*
> . . . Let the Party stand as a shield for our state, our freedom, our civil order and peace.

16 *Bor'ba*, Nov. 10, 1917. *Bor'ba* was intended to be a daily newspaper, but only two issues appeared, the third being confiscated by the Bolsheviks after a press run of 50,000 copies.

Long live Reason!
It is our only salvation.
The Struggle is beginning.
To Arms, Citizens, to Arms![17]

Thus even for Kadets with a "civil war outlook," it was faith in reason and a sense of justice, legality, and freedom which were to lead to Russia's "salvation," presumably through their expression in the Constituent Assembly, and despite the strength of Bolshevik troops. Red Guards now patrolled the capitals; the offices of *Rech'* had been smashed; Miliukov had fled for his life; and the editor of *Bor'ba* was herself afraid to spend the night in her apartment. In Moscow, the Bolshevik Military Revkom had closed Kadet offices, burned the party's papers, and threatened its leaders with arrest or worse. But despite all this, most Kadets in the capitals still felt they had good grounds for not abandoning past ideals or methods. Far from being a momentous turning point for Kadets, the establishment of a Bolshevik regime simply pressed most party members closer to their basic system of values.

ELECTING A CONSTITUENT ASSEMBLY

It consequently developed that those most suspicious of participatory democracy in 1917 came in the beginning of November to invest quite heavily in the Constituent Assembly, not owing to any burst of liberal democratism, but because most party leaders saw no immediate "legitimate" alternatives. Elections were scheduled for November 12-14. While Lenin himself wanted them postponed, the Bolsheviks had persistently criticized the Provisional Government on this issue, and the campaign was already underway. After debating the question, the Sovnarkom determined to confirm elections on these dates, feeding in the process liberal fantasies about recouping authority through democratic methods. And once it was clear that balloting would take place, local Kadet committees began to regroup. Public meetings were renewed in Petrograd on November 7.

For the most part the dominant themes of these sessions were those set down by Miliukov at the tenth party congress: commitment to the "legitimate principles" of the February revolution; alliance with "healthy elements"; and continued bitterness toward the socialist moderates. At the same time, however, Kadet spokesmen also affirmed the party's basic programmatic positions, despite the increased disdain of right-wing party figures like Tyrkova for "democratic" as opposed

[17] *Ibid.*

to "national" concerns: the Constituent Assembly was to declare
Russia a democratic republic with leadership vested in an elected
executive; legislative authority was to be held by a national assembly;
and local self-government (but not *soviet* self-government) was to be
developed and guaranteed. Almost every Kadet speaker also dwelt on
basic civil liberties the party would support in the Assembly: equality
of all citizens before the law; freedom of conscience and speech; right
to assembly (even for Bolsheviks); inviolability of personality and
domicile; a guaranteed right of workers to strike. If Lenin brought
out the nationalist passions of Kadets, he also evoked their deep
liberal commitment to basic civil liberties.

In Petrograd, some party spokesmen still clearly showed a desire to
reach out for broader popular support, an indication that despite the
mollification of differences among Kadets in the capital, conciliationist
sentiment had not disappeared entirely. Some, like Z. G. Frenkel, reaffirmed the party's "ideal" commitment to an eight-hour working day,
and stressed the Kadets' desire to divide land among the working
peasantry through forced expropriation of landed estates. Others
called for cooperation and unity among all "democrats," regardless of
party affiliation. Much stronger, however, was Kadet bitterness on
questions of national unity, civil order, and the war, where at almost
every preelection meeting speakers angrily condemned socialist "uto-
pians," and called for the repression of "internal disorders" and their
instigators. There were also poignant pleas for continuing the struggle
against Germany.[18]

In Moscow and the provinces, meanwhile, most Kadet spokesmen
also reflected the "Miliukov line" of the ninth and tenth party congresses, although here, as in the past, the pattern was somewhat more
diverse. In places like Samara and Novgorod, where gatherings in early
November drew large audiences and where Kadets were clearly regarded by local bourgeois and gentry elements as the only significant
political force of nonsocialist Russia, party leaders made new efforts to
consolidate with the right. In Vitebsk, Kadets forced a strong anti-
Bolshevik resolution through the city duma, which here as elsewhere
became the focal point of "legitimate" authority. And in Batum,
Vologda, Ustiug, Irkutsk, Ekaterinodar, Novgorod, Kursk, Ekaterino-

---

[18] Kadet speakers at these meetings included Nabokov, Vinaver, Kutler, Nolde,
Tyrkova, Ryss, Gerasimov, Pepeliaev, and Stepanov, all leading party figures.
A. V. Tyrkova, herself quite skeptical, noted in her diary that some Kadets ex-
pected to win as many as 150 seats in the Assembly. See A. Borman, *A. V. Tyrkova-
Vil'iams*, Louvain-Washington, 1964, pp. 140-41, and the editorial in *Nash Vek*,
Nov. 30, 1917. Kadet party meetings were reported in *Utro Rossii*, Nov. 14-16, 1917;
Russkiia Vedomosti, Nov. 17-19, 1917; *Volia Naroda*, Nov. 24, 1917; *Bor'ba*, Nov.
10, 1917, and the official *VPNS*, Nos. 26-27, Nov. 23, 1917, pp. 9-12.

slav, and Vladivostok, they pursued the electoral campaign with new vigor, sharply disassociating themselves from even the moderate left: "While the socialists march hand in hand with the Bolsheviks," V. F. Zeeler told party members in Rostov, for example, "we will resist! We will struggle for freedom, even if it turns out that we are cut off from Moscow and Petrograd. . . . We will stand unequivocally for the legitimate rights of the nation!"[19]

At the same time, however, in some provincial towns like Iaroslavl and Kharkov, and also in Moscow, a number of Kadets continued to press for the "conciliationist" tactic of September and early October, albeit with somewhat subdued voices. In Moscow, for example, while Paul Novgorodtsev and others denounced the socialists bitterly, Kishkin, Astrov, and particularly Nicholas Shchepkin worried instead about the very real dangers of massive, full-scale civil war, and sought ways to reduce rather than aggravate social polarization. In the early part of November, the Trade-Industrialists formally asked the Moscow Kadet committee to organize their candidates for the Constituent Assembly into a bloc in order to offer voters a single slate. According to reports in *Utro Rossii*, "leading representatives" of the national Kadet organization in Moscow were in "full agreement" with the plan, but the local committee, to whom the request formally had to be made, "answered with a categorical refusal." Moscow Kadets had no opposition to any individuals on the Trade-Industrialists list, but "for tactical reasons" preferred to remain independent from "clearly bourgeois organizations."[20] Meanwhile in Iaroslavl, N. A. Morozov, a longtime radical and one of the founders of the revolutionary organization Narodnaia Volia (The People's Will) joined the local Kadet slate because he felt the Party of People's Freedom was the "natural" heir of the radical populist movement. It was important, he declared, for peasants and other "true" Russians to see the Kadets as representing the best interests of the country "as a whole," and not simply the welfare of one particular social group.[21]

Despite their energies spent in campaigning, however, Kadets returned only a handful of delegates when the Assembly elections finally took place, as Oliver Radkey and others have shown.[22] And whatever one might want to say about electoral irregularities (and for their part, the Kadets generally regarded the vote as having taken place

[19] *Novgorodskaia Zhizn'*, No. 2, 1917; *VPNS*, No. 31, Dec. 28, 1917, pp. 31-32.
[20] *Utro Rossii*, No. 19, 1917.   [21] *Russkiia Vedomosti*, Nov. 16, 1917.
[22] O. H. Radkey, *The Election to the Russian Constituent Assembly of 1917*, Cambridge, Mass., 1950; L. M. Spirin, *Klassy i partii v grazhdanskoi voine v Rossii*, Moscow, 1968.

"properly" [*pravil'no*], "despite pessimistic predictions"),[23] the over-whelmingly radical orientation of Russian voters was the clearest testi-mony yet of the liberals' divorce from popular aspiration and mood. Interestingly enough, however, this was not immediately apparent. With communications erratic at best, and many provincial localities cut off from Moscow and Petrograd, it actually seemed at first that a Kadet triumph was in the making. In Moscow, as Table 5 indicates,

TABLE 5. SUMMARY OF MOSCOW ELECTION RETURNS, 1917

	City Duma June 25		District Dumas Sept. 24		Const. Assembly Nov. 24	
	%	(vote)	%	(vote)	%	(vote)
SR	58.0	374,885	14.4	54,479	8.2	62,260
Minor Socialist	1.5	9,638	1.2	4,449	4.9	37,813
Bolshevik	11.7	75,409	50.9	193,489	47.9	366,148
Menshevik	11.8	76,407	4.1	15,618	2.8	21,597
Kadet	16.8	108,781	26.6	101,100	34.5	263,859
Minor Nonsocialist	0.2	1,440	2.8	10,504	1.7	13,086
TOTALS	100.0	646,560	100.0	379,639	100.0	764,763

SOURCES: For Duma returns, see Table 2, and *Russkiia Vedomosti*, Sept. 27-29, 1917; Constituent Assembly returns from O. H. Radkey, *The Election to the Russian Constituent Assembly of 1917*, Cambridge, Mass., 1950, appendix.

the party more than doubled the number of votes it had gained in the city duma elections of June, trailing only the front-running Bolshe-viks. In Petrograd (shown in Table 6) Kadets increased their support from approximately 115,000 votes in August to more than 245,000. As the liberal editors of *Utro Rossii* observed with some jubilation, "If one remembers how weak a contingent of electors the Kadet party had in the Moscow City Duma elections, the present results must be considered a great victory for Constitutional Democracy."[24]

In fact, however, the Kadets' "great victory" was evidence of the profound social polarization which had developed in Russia during 1917, and which had led by the end of November to the Kadets' almost total identification in the mind of workers and peasants with the interests of privileged society. Precise analysis of the returns by class is impossible on the basis of available data, but the implication of the Moscow and Petrograd returns is that intellectual and petty bourgeois elements who identified with the moderate socialists under

[23] *VPNS*, Nos. 26-27, Nov. 23, 1917, p. 3.   [24] *Utro Rossii*, Nov. 24, 1917.

TABLE 6. SUMMARY OF PETROGRAD ELECTION RETURNS, 1917

	District Dumas May 27-29		City Duma Aug. 20		Const. Assembly Nov. 12-14	
	%	(vote)	%	(vote)	%	(vote)
Socialist Bloc	44.2	347,053a				
SR	7.4	58,092b	37.4	205,659	16.2	152,230
Minor Socialist	1.4	11,230c	2.6	14,252	3.7	34,947
Bolshevik	20.4	159,936	33.4	183,624	45.0	424,027
Menshevik	3.4	26,291b	4.3	23,552	3.1	29,167
Kadet	21.9	171,745	20.9	114,483	26.2	246,506
Minor Nonsocialist	1.3	10,563d	1.4	7,780	5.8	55,456
TOTALS	100.0	784,910	100.0	549,350	100.0	942,333

SOURCES: For the Duma returns, see Tables 1 and 4; Constituent Assembly returns from O. H. Radkey, *The Election to the Russian Constituent Assembly of 1917*, Cambridge, Mass., 1950, appendix; and *VPNS*, Nos. 26-27, Nov. 23, 1917, p. 4.

a Vote for 10 out of 12 districts only.
b May figure for 2 districts compared to August figure for 18.
c May figure for 5 districts compared to August figure for 18.
d May figure for 10 districts compared to August figure for 18.

the Provisional Government now voted for Kadets to indicate their anti-Bolshevik partisanship, while workers and soldiers left the moderates for Lenin. Hence, the liberals' "victory" was, in effect, the firming up of social boundaries for civil war.

A similar pattern emerged in provincial towns and villages in the meantime, while in the countryside peasants threw their support overwhelmingly behind the SRs. A synopsis of the returns for a number of representative provinces and provincial cities and towns appears in Table 7, taken from the recent compilations of the Soviet historian L. M. Spirin. Above all they indicate the dramatic crystallization of nonsocialist "bourgeois" sentiment in cities and towns behind the Kadets, and the almost total isolation of the Party of People's Freedom from other social elements.

It was the Bolsheviks themselves, however, who in a violent manner paid the greatest compliment to Kadet electoral "success" in the capitals. As soon as it became clear how many Russians in Moscow and Petrograd still stood behind Constitutional Democracy, repressions against the party began in earnest. On November 17, armed sailors appeared at the apartments of Miliukov and Shingarev, seeking their arrest.[25] Vinaver's home was ransacked on the eighteenth, and shortly

[25] *Izvestiia*, Nov. 29, 1917.

TABLE 7. Selected Constituent Assembly Election Returns

(Percentage Vote in Provincial Capital or Major City and in
Provincial Election Districts, including Towns)

	Bolshevik city prov.		Kadet city prov.		SR city prov.		Menshevik city prov.		Natl. & Bourg. city prov.		Other city prov.	
Archangel	29.7	21.6	28.9	7.2	26.9	63.2	14.2	4.3	......	......	0.3	3.7
Astrakhan	27.5	18.6	25.8	6.7	12.4	51.8	4.3	1.1	18.3	10.5	11.7	11.3
Chernigov[a]	6.0	27.9	21.0	3.0	3.0	10.9	6.0	1.1	50.0	52.9	14.0	4.2
Ekaterinoslav	26.3	17.9	11.7	2.3	8.4	19.4	5.8	2.3	40.5	53.8	7.3	4.3
Iaroslavl	47.3	29.8	23.6	13.5	11.1	49.3	9.6	4.1	......	......	8.4	3.3
Irkutsk	30.6	14.3	21.7	4.0	33.9	54.4	6.3	2.9	0.1	16.7	7.4	7.7
Kaluga	24.7	60.2	49.2	6.8	5.5	29.3	16.7	1.9	2.3	0.3	1.6	1.5
Kazan	26.0	5.8	24.8	3.7	21.0	31.5	3.2	0.5	19.4	52.5	5.6	6.0
Kharkov	27.7	10.5	25.3	5.3	16.7	3.9	7.4	1.7	8.3	74.0	14.6	4.6
Kiev	16.7	4.0	10.3	1.4	4.2	1.3	3.7	0.8	43.8	88.9	21.3	3.6
Kostroma	43.6	40.8	22.4	7.5	10.3	45.0	11.3	3.5	......	......	12.4	3.2
Kursk	26.0	11.3	45.1	4.5	17.4	82.0	3.1	0.6	......	......	8.4	1.6
Minsk	26.6	63.2	5.8	1.2	2.7	19.8	8.0	1.8	52.7	12.6	4.2	1.4
Moscow[b]	47.9	55.8	34.5	6.7	8.2	26.2	2.8	4.2	1.7	......	4.9	7.1
Nizhni-Novgorod	22.8	23.1	31.6	6.0	14.4	54.1	5.0	1.3	0.7	3.5	25.5	12.0
Novgorod	20.3	41.9	37.6	6.5	20.0	45.4	6.4	1.9	......	......	15.7	4.3
Odessa[c]	28.6	10.2	16.2	6.3	5.5	52.9	4.6	1.1	37.9	27.9	7.2	1.6
Omsk[d]	27.5	6.4	21.8	1.7	10.8	87.0	24.9	0.5	9.0	1.1	6.0	3.3
Orel	27.6	29.7	28.6	2.3	16.5	62.8	12.9	2.0	......	......	14.3	3.2
Orenburg	34.0	23.6	17.7	3.5	7.8	15.9	4.9	1.4	14.5	22.5	21.1	33.1
Penza	15.6	8.6	24.8	4.0	47.9	81.3	6.4	0.7	2.8	4.7	2.5	0.7
Perm	27.0	21.4	25.9	8.9	22.7	53.1	4.7	2.2	5.4	6.2	14.3	8.2
Petrograd[b]	45.0	48.7	26.2	13.7	16.2	25.4	3.1	1.3	5.8	6.6	3.7	4.3
Pskov	38.7	33.7	29.6	5.0	16.4	57.3	3.0	0.9	3.9	0.8	8.3	2.3
Riazan	25.7	36.2	43.2	4.1	15.3	56.8	3.9	0.7	......	......	11.9	2.2
Rostov	37.5	14.6	20.0	3.1	11.1	34.1	6.8	1.2	......	......	24.6	47.0
Samara	42.0	16.1	13.8	3.7	26.5	57.1	3.7	0.5	6.0	20.2	8.0	2.4
Saratov	37.7	24.0	19.9	2.5	14.5	56.3	6.8	1.4	4.1	10.1	17.0	5.7
Simbirsk	19.5	13.0	21.2	3.1	36.0	72.2	4.9	0.7	5.9	10.5	12.5	0.5
Smolensk	40.8	54.9	28.6	4.4	16.1	38.0	7.4	1.2	......	0.3	7.1	1.2
Tambov	28.2	20.5	26.8	4.1	16.6	71.2	17.4	1.9	0.3	0.5	10.7	1.8
Tauride[e]	7.5	6.7	19.6	7.4	39.2	52.1	8.4	2.5	21.9	29.1	3.4	2.2
Tomsk	40.2	8.1	19.6	2.9	23.0	85.2	3.3	0.9	......	......	13.9	2.9
Tula	34.0	44.2	23.4	4.2	20.9	47.5	14.6	2.0	......	......	7.1	2.1
Tver	47.2	53.1	19.8	5.0	16.9	37.5	12.3	2.2	......	......	3.8	2.2
Ufa	19.2	5.0	12.0	1.6	26.5	33.7	2.5	0.3	25.5	55.4	14.0	4.0
Vitebsk	34.9	51.2	6.9	1.5	8.9	26.8	11.2	2.2	33.6	14.7	4.5	3.6
Voronezh	11.9	13.8	58.1	3.3	12.2	79.7	7.2	0.8	1.7	1.1	8.9	1.3

* sources: L. M. Spirin, *Klassy i partii v grazhdanskoi voine v Rossii*, Moscow 1968, pp. 416-25; O. H. Radkey, *The Election to the Russian Constituent Assembly*, Cambridge, Mass., 1950, appendix.

a Figures do not include garrison vote.

b Figures for Moscow and Petrograd are from Radkey. There are slight discrepancies between his and Spirin's figures, particularly for Moscow.

c Provincial figures are for Kherson province.

d Provincial figures are for the Altai election district.

e City figures are the combined totals for Simferopol and Sevastopol.

afterward, the party's Petrograd club was virtually destroyed. With Astrov, Shingarev, Kokoshkin, Dolgorukov, and other party leaders due to gather for the opening of the Assembly, Kadets began to sense the future's terrible dangers. On November 28, the very day the Assembly was to convene, the Sovnarkom declared Kadets outside the law. Russia's leading liberals officially became "enemies of the people."[26]

What, then, was the future of Russian constitutional democracy? This was the question Astrov and Shingarev grimly contemplated as they made their way by train toward Petrograd on November 26, two days before the scheduled opening of the Constituent Assembly. It seemed incredible that there was no national authority in the villages and towns which sped by their window, or that Russia as a whole stood practically defenseless against the Germans. With the shipment of goods and foodstuffs virtually at a standstill, staggering shortages loomed in the months ahead; and without a firm national government, it seemed almost absurd to discuss the restoration of normal industrial productivity. The opening of the Assembly itself was now a cause for apprehension as well. It was finally clear that Kadets would secure only seventeen seats in a body of more than 700 delegates, while the Bolsheviks themselves would have almost ten times that number, and the Assembly as a whole would clearly be dominated by SRs. Continued adherence to "legitimate" tactics thus not only meant great personal danger, but participation in an overwhelmingly anti-liberal body. Moreover, not enough delegates were yet in Petrograd to enable the Assembly to begin its work. Even if the Bolsheviks allowed it to meet (and there was every indication they would not), weeks might pass before anything useful could be done.

On November 27, the Kadet Central Committee gathered in Petrograd in Sophia Panina's apartment. The discussion was lively, as Astrov later recalled, with some Committee members ready to abandon legitimate tactics altogether. Kishkin and Konovalov were already in prison (along with other government ministers), and there was some indication that the remnants of Russia's officer corps were grouping in the south. Though Kadets had no definite information on the anti-Bolshevik military forces, Miliukov himself had already gone to Rostov. Civil war seemed to some the only possible course.[27]

[26] Ibid.; Nash Vek, Nov. 30, 1917. See the discussion by the Bolshevik Central Committee in Protokoly tsentral'nogo komiteta RSDRP (b), Moscow, 1958, Sess. of Nov. 29, 1917, pp. 148-59.

[27] Communication from "D. K." to Miliukov, June 2, 1918, Miliukov Archive, bx. 1661, fold. 1. Miliukov was one of the few leading Kadets still at large who failed to attend this session. As he noted in an autobiographical fragment (Miliukov Archive, bx. 8141, sec. 19a), he feared being arrested. Astrov describes the meeting in Posledniia Novosti, No. 1452, Jan. 18, 1925.

But in the best liberal tradition, Shingarev and Astrov insisted Kadets were "duty bound" to bear their electoral mandates, and attend the Constituent Assembly regardless of the consequences. Petrograd was a shambles. Rubble littered the street in front of the Kadet party club, and rag-tag bands of soldiers aimlessly "patrolled" the boulevards, stopping well-dressed passers-by in the hope of finding "counter-revolutionary" valuables. Kadets in particular, with their vests and warm overcoats, walked alone at their peril. But "duty" stood high in the liberal spectrum of values. And as the hours passed in Panina's apartment, the views of Astrov and Shingarev prevailed. Kadets would participate in the Assembly's first session. They would propose that a temporary president be elected to preside at each session until a quorum could be formed and the business of drafting a new Russian constitution could begin in earnest.[28]

The Kadet Central Committee did not disperse until early on the morning of November 28. Because the hour was late, Shingarev, Kokoshkin, and Dolgorukov stayed with Panina, intending to go directly from her apartment to the Assembly's convocation at the Tauride Palace. But at 7:30 a.m., Red Guards suddenly appeared. The four Kadet leaders were searched and arrested. Shortly afterward, soldiers also seized Kutler and Rodichev.[29]

THE TRIAL OF SOPHIA PANINA

So difficult was it, however, for Kadets to conceptualize the possibility of permanent Bolshevik authority that even the imprisonment of figures like Shingarev, Kokoshkin, Dolgorukov, Rodichev, and Panina was not enough to shock many party leaders into a recognition of their weakness. Bolshevik power still seemed pretty well confined to the capitals—so much so, in fact, that some Kadets even continued to worry about the effect civil war might have on defense against the Germans. Also, the problems of provisioning and supply loomed so large in November 1917 that many were sure the Bolsheviks would sooner or later have to recognize the country's dependence on non-proletarian social and political groups, and come to terms.

[28] Communication from "D. K." to Miliukov. See also N. Astrov, "Proobraz russkoi tragedii," *Posledniia Novosti*, No. 1452, Jan. 18, 1925; and A. Shingarev, *Kak eto bylo (dnevnik)*, Moscow, 1918, p. 1.

[29] *Nash Vek*, Nov. 30 and Dec. 1, 1917; Astrov, "Proobrazh." Despite the arrest of their colleagues, Astrov, Kutler, Rodichev, and Novgorodtsev attended the preliminary session of the Assembly on November 28. Kutler, who was arrested soon afterward, was wounded in a skirmish for his custody between Latvian soldiers and a group of Red Guards, but was only slightly hurt. Rodichev was seized on November 29 as he was going again to the Tauride Palace.

The arrest and trial of Sophia Panina also dulled liberal perceptivities. Panina was renowned in Petrograd as a Russian Jane Addams, having dedicated most of her life to improving the lot of St. Petersburg poor. Her Narodnyi Dom—People's House—resembled Hull House in Chicago. At the height of its activities before the war, hundreds of people came each day to participate in trade and industrial courses, use the recreation room, and experience the refinements of higher Russian culture. When Prince Lvov formed the first Provisional Government he appointed Panina assistant minister of social welfare; and Kerensky himself later made her assistant minister of education, a post he regarded as essentially nonpolitical.

The outcry against Panina's arrest was immediate, and surprisingly strong. Workers rallied to her support at meetings in the Narodnyi Dom. Twenty-eight different social and educational organizations, including such groups as the All-Russian League of Female Equality and the Petrograd Society for the Promotion of Literacy, sent a long letter of protest to Petrograd newspapers. Letters defending Panina also flooded the women's prison where she was being held. Among them was even a note from the sister of the Bolshevik commissar of welfare, N. A. Semashko. On December 9, the faculty council of Petrograd University held a special meeting to express its indignation, issuing a public declaration honoring Panina for her educational and social work.[30]

The Bolsheviks specifically charged Panina with sequestering 93,000 rubles from the Ministry of Education and refusing to turn the money over to the new administration.[31] Far from refuting the accusation, Panina readily admitted taking the money and transferring it to foreign banks. It was payable only to a "legal regime" she told Krasikov, president of the Investigating Commission, "protected" from the "usurpers" in accordance with the instructions of the Kadet Provisional Government ministers. She could not withdraw the funds even if she wanted to.[32]

Sophia Panina was a symbol of intransigent liberal opposition to the Bolsheviks. She typified the enlightened Kadet intellectual, certain of the need for social change and dedicated to the basics of political democracy, but convinced as well that social and political development should take place gradually in Russia, through the cultural

30 *Nash Vek*, Dec. 3 and 7, 1917; *VPNS*, Nos. 29 and 30, Dec. 14, 1917, p. 10. The letters defending Panina are in the Panina Archive, pack. 6, fold. 37, and pack. 6, fold. 9.
31 Panina later wrote that the sum was 97,000 rubles (Panina Archive, pack. 6, fold. 37), but contemporary accounts say 93,000, or more precisely, 92,802.
32 Unpubl. recollections of S. V. Panina, Panina Archive, pack. 6, fold. 37. See also Shingarev, *Kak eto bylo*, pp. 5-6.

advancement of the nation as a whole. Panina was precisely the type of individual the Kadet party attracted in Russia's towns and cities: idealistic, essentially nonpolitical and nonpartisan, anxious to preserve economic and cultural amenities but without gross social disparities, and unable to develop any clear notion of effective ways to achieve desired goals. And apparently because her arrest had provoked such a hue and cry, the Bolsheviks felt impelled to "expose" her publicly as a "class enemy." In any event, her case was chosen to be one of the first tried by the new Revolutionary Tribunal, a body specifically charged with exposing counterrevolution.

The Revolutionary Tribunal convened "triumphantly" on December 10.[33] According to contemporary accounts, the palace of Grand Duke Nicholas Nicholaevich, where the court held session, was overflowing with spectators. P. I. Stuchka, the People's Commissar of Justice, led the Bolshevik dignitaries, while a handpicked panel of four workers and two soldiers constituted judge and jury. In opening the session, the presiding officer, I. P. Zhukov, stressed its great historical significance. Like their French predecessors, he declared, the present courts would prove themselves "strong and rigorous defenders of the people's rights."[34]

But Zhukov was not alone in assessing the trial's propaganda value. Petrograd Kadets themselves realized the Bolsheviks were placing liberalism on the stand with Panina, and saw the court—in the best prerevolutionary tradition—as a forum from which to expose the baselessness of the "enemy of the people" charge.[35] In leading Panina's defense, Ia. Gurevich made no attempt to answer specific accusations. Instead he hammered on Panina's long record of social welfare achievements, stressed her contact with the Petrograd poor, and emphasized the great esteem in which both she and the Narodnyi Dom were held by rank-and-file workers. Of what was Panina guilty, Gurevich asked the court rhetorically? Only of trying to prevent funds which belonged to the people from entering political coffers. No doubt she would be punished; but the workers knew her as a friend, and the whole world would see the absurdity of repaying good with evil in the people's name.[36]

Gurevich caught the tribunal unprepared. When the presiding officer Zhukov asked for public accusations (one of the many "revolutionary innovations" of the trial), no one spoke! But when the defense

---

[33] The most complete account of the trial appeared in *Nash Vek*, Dec. 10-17, from which most of my account is taken. There is also an article on the trial by the defense attorney, Ia. Ia. Gurevich, in *Russkoe Bogatstvo*, Nos. 11-12, 1917, pp. 283-98.

[34] *Nash Vek*, Dec. 10, 1917.   [35] *Ibid.*, Dec. 1, 1917.

[36] *Ibid.*, Dec. 12, 1917; Panina, *Recollections*, pp. 2-4.

was granted a similar privilege, one N. I. Ivanov took the stand, a barely literate worker from a Petrograd munitions plant. Ivanov was not a Kadet, nor personally acquainted with Panina. But he had often visited the Narodnyi Dom, and in his crude ungrammatical fashion, recalled for the court the "great benefits" Panina had brought him and his fellow workers. "Such a one could not be a counterrevolutionary . . . ," he insisted. "It is impossible to allow the people to repay her work with black ingratitude!"[37]

After Ivanov, the rest was anticlimax. Panina was guilty, and sentenced to prison until the 93,000 rubles were repaid to the government. But even the socialist *Volia Naroda* could not help noticing that the Kadets had won a "stunning triumph." Crowds left the palace talking of how foolish the Bolsheviks had appeared, and how absurd their attempt had been to promote the trial as "the people's defense against counterrevolution."[38] It was an easy matter for different social organizations to raise the required ransom. Shortly after the trial, Panina was freed.[39]

Liberals in Petrograd could scarcely suppress their sense of satisfaction. Panina's conviction aside, the trial's outcome seemed to vindicate the party's hope that Lenin and the Bolsheviks could not long survive on their own. While the Kadet *Vestnik* congratulated Panina for having shown all Russia the absurdity of declaring liberals "enemies of the people," *Severnoe Ekho* insisted the Bolsheviks' "fear" of the party could no longer be concealed.[40]

Thus it still seemed possible as late as December 1917 to continue the anti-Bolshevik struggle with legal methods. The Constituent Assembly had functioned only briefly on November 28, but its official opening was rescheduled for January 5. *Nash Vek—Rech'* under a new masthead—was appearing daily in Petrograd; the *Vestnik Partii Narodnoi Svobody* could still be published; local Kadet organizations could continue holding open meetings. When a party speaker asked a large Petrograd gathering on December 6 whether it wanted to hear "an enemy of the people," he was greeted with laughter and prolonged applause.[41] And with Panina's "victory," Kadet city and district organizations in Petrograd began to insist that no threat of force could deter the party from struggling for "law," "freedom," and the "nation's welfare." P. V. Gerasimov wrote in the official party journal that it was

[37] *Ibid.*   [38] *Volia Naroda*, Dec. 12, 1917.

[39] Panina was released on Dec. 19. According to her own account, the ransom was paid by the Woman's University in Petrograd on condition that it be returned when a public subscription had secured sufficient funds.

[40] *VPNS*, No. 31, Dec. 28, 1917; *Severnoe Ekho*, Dec. 17, 1917.

[41] *Nash Vek*, Dec. 7, 1917.

the Kadets' very adherence to legality and statesmanship which made them anathema to the Bolsheviks.[42] Meanwhile in Moscow, the city committee announced its "unswerving support" for the Constituent Assembly. Declaring its belief that the "ideals of democracy" would "triumph," it scheduled a regional party conference for December 17.[43]

When the regional conference convened, moreover, Kadets continued to show themselves unable to perceive political realities clearly. In response to a call for "practical measures" designed to "organize social forces," speakers presented plans to open a new party library, publish more propaganda, and form a national committee to supervise the *Vestnik*'s distribution. A new "agitational course" for party workers was also set up, scheduled to open in Moscow on January 2. Its highlights were to be speeches by Novgorodtsev on "The Constituent Assembly and the Faith of the Kadet Party," Iurenev on "Stages in the Russian Revolution," and A. K. Shneider on "Methods of Holding Party Meetings."[44]

With many of their leaders arrested and others forced to move from apartment to apartment to avoid being seized; with Bolshevik guards disrupting meetings and confiscating literature; with the party officially outlawed, one cannot but wonder what "methods" Citizen Shneider had in mind for his liberal colleagues. To be sure, cloudy vision was not universal. When a prominent SR deputy to the Constituent Assembly was arrested on December 18, *Nash Vek* uttered new sounds of alarm. And in Moscow, a worried Novgorodtsev urged his comrades to consider new forms of action.[45] But as the new year dawned, the Central Committee as a whole still clung to the shredded cloth of political legitimacy. A shock greater than those already experienced was needed to jar the party from its paralyzing fix on past ideals and tactics.

THE SHOCK OF AWARENESS

The shock came in two waves. On January 5, Bolshevik troops dispersed the first and only official session of the Constituent Assembly, despite Lenin's assurance that it would function; two days later, Fedor Kokoshkin and Andrei Shingarev, still Bolshevik prisoners, were mur-

[42] P. V. Gerasimov, "Voprosy partiinoi zhizni," *VPNS*, Nos. 29-30, Dec. 14, 1917, p. 4.

[43] *VPNS*, No. 31, Dec. 28, 1917, p. 15. See also *Nash Vek*, Dec. 10 and 12, 1917; *VPNS*, Nos. 29-30, Dec. 14, 1917, pp. 12-14. On December 12, *Nash Vek* optimistically opened a campaign for subscriptions for 1918.

[44] *Russkiia Vedomosti*, Dec. 24-29, 1917; *VPNS*, No. 1, Jan. 4, 1918, cols. 24-25, and No. 4, Mar. 21, 1918.

[45] *Nash Vek*, Dec. 19, 1917; L. Krol', *Za tri goda*, Vladivostok, 1922, pp. 12-14.

dered in the Mariinskii Hospital. Their deaths were not part of any
terrorist plot or even officially engineered, but simply two more incidents of the wanton bitterness and hatred that was now infecting all of
Russia.

Both events numbed Kadets. From his cell in the Peter Paul
Fortress, Paul Dolgorukov wrote Panina of the deep shame and
disillusion felt by those in the prison. Kadets had "relied too long on
reason"; now Kokoshkin and Shingarev had "paid the price for the
party's myopic idealism."[46] In a similar vein, Ariadna Tyrkova wrote
ruefully in her diary that January 7 was a "watershed" in the history
of Russian liberalism.[47]

In Moscow, where most Kadet leaders were still free, the Central
Committee once again convened to discuss its future course. Its mood
was sharply changed. Vinaver had begun sleeping in a different place
each night; Rodichev, whom the Bolsheviks had released shortly after
the Panina trial, had begun to grow a beard. A warning system had
also been devised to protect Committee members from arrest. While
most still believed Lenin's power would be short lived, almost all
were ready to admit that "legitimate" tactics were no longer appropriate.[48]

The question was, however, what to do. Information had been received that an anti-Bolshevik military force was forming in South
Russia under Generals Alekseev and Kornilov; but many thought it
would be a magnet for reactionaries, unable to gain broad support. Yet
various former Duma members and other conservatives were already
discussing the possibility of organizing an uprising inside the capitals
to coincide with the army's attack. From a strategic point of view, a
plan of this sort was appealing. On the other hand, a group of moderate socialists was considering the possibility of reconvening the
Constituent Assembly in another part of Russia, thinking such a move
might rally sufficient popular backing to force a Bolshevik collapse,
especially if the Assembly leadership could secure recognition and aid
from the Allies.[49]

The choice for Kadets thus seemed to divide again between cooperation with the moderate left and alliance with the right, the same
cleavage which had torn the party through the latter months of the
Provisional Government. And just as before, Paul Novgorodtsev—now

[46] Dolgorukov to Panina, Jan. 9, 1918, in the Panina Archive, pack. 2, fold. 12.
[47] Borman, *Tyrkova*, p. 147. See also *Nash Vek*, Jan. 9, 1918; *Russkiia Vedomosti*,
Jan. 10, 1918.
[48] R. Vinavera, "Vospominaniia," MS in the Hoover Institution, 1944, p. 100;
Krol', *Za tri goda*, pp. 9-15.
[49] Krol', *Za tri goda*, pp. 12-15; N. Oganovskii, "Dnevnik chlena uchreditel'nago
sobraniia," *GM*, Nos. 4-6, 1918, pp. 143-72.

acting chairman of the Kadet Central Committee—argued for further consolidation with the right. Was their party committed more to liberalism or democracy, he asked his colleagues? In his view, Kadets had no choice but to postpone concerns about their programmatic goals, and work for reestablishing order in Russia by supporting Kornilov. This, in fact, is what they should have done in August.

But Vinaver, Astrov, Lev Krol, and other Central Committee members were reluctant to follow Novgorodtsev's lead. With the necessity of practical action, divisions again began to reemerge among Kadets. Vinaver and Astrov worried about mass support. Even if the party backed Kornilov completely, right-wing authoritarianism would not succeed any better now than in August 1917 if it lacked massive popular support, or even the confidence of "loyalist" moderate socialists. A better possibility perhaps was to rally both the generals and Russia at large behind the Constituent Assembly. Governmental authority would then be backed with the legitimacy of a nationally elected body.

For hours the Central Committee discussed the matter, trying to assess the national mood pragmatically, and whether Russians could better be united against the Bolsheviks behind the standards of Kornilov or those of the disorganized Constituent Assembly. Opinion was split, and the agony of decision was compounded by the fear that Kadets might actually have little relevance to either course. The Constituent Assembly had fallen under the domination of SRs, with the hated Chernov emerging as its spokesman; while few believed Kadets could greatly influence the anti-Bolshevik armies, particularly in view of the residue of hostility left by the Kornilov affair. At the same time, however, the murders of Shingarev and Kokoshkin were as great a blow for many moderate socialists as they were for the Kadets. Several "near Kadet" SRs even hoped to minimize differences between socialists and liberals on this basis, joining forces in a new national, anti-Bolshevik coalition. This was particularly attractive to conciliationist Kadets like Astrov. On the other hand, it seemed that Alekseev, Kornilov, and the Volunteer Army would obviously be in need of Kadet administrative talent. Liberals might thus have a practical role to play in the south, even if limited initially in terms of defining the movement's character and goals.[50]

One compromise solution was suggested by Alexander Kornilov. "We are a party of realistic politics," he said with revealing exaggeration, "which knows the necessity of participating in the organic work of governmental administration." Kadets could support right-wing

[50] *Ibid.*

groups, providing they divorced themselves from autocratic principles, by assisting in the work of administration. In doing so, Kadets could remain "republicans," even if the groups themselves were monarchistic. At the same time, party leaders could also maintain contacts with the left. The Central Committee would not commit Kadets *as a party* to the tactics of either the conservatives or the socialists, but it would be perfectly compatible with liberal ideals for Kadets *as individuals* to assist any organization fighting the Bolsheviks. Party members had never been bound by rigid party ties, and in any event, the Kadets' own organization was beginning to crumble under increasing Bolshevik pressure.[51]

Kornilov's projected *modus vivendi* provided a bridge between the party's right and left flanks, but it implied the end of Kadet political leadership, and most Central Committee members now wanted more than just a supporting role in the anti-Bolshevik struggle. The deaths of Kokoshkin and Shingarev had to be avenged; Russia had to be saved. Moreover, events had strongly reinforced the "partisan" views of party leaders like Miliukov and Novgorodtsev, who had argued since midsummer for firm alliances with the right. If the extent of Russia's social polarization was clear in the Constituent Assembly returns, dictatorship and force now seemed a better way to bridge the cleavage than coalitions or new popular programs, which might even collapse what social support the party did enjoy. In any event, few at the secret Moscow conclave were willing in January to endorse anything like a turn to the left; and although Kornilov's formula was deemed acceptable as the basis for individual action, Novgorodtsev's views found formal expression in a lengthy resolution adopted to express the "official" party position.[52]

In the struggle with "Bolshevik anarchist elements" the resolution declared, the only way to succeed was to "unite all available forces around the authority of a single person, and establish a temporary military dictatorship." The future form of Russia's state administration could be decided after victory was won. For the present, Russia needed only "authority" and "order." Creating a military dictatorship and unifying all social forces in a "united national front" were the party's immediate tasks.

At the same time, the "legal authority" of the dispersed Constituent Assembly had to be repudiated. The Assembly had lost its ability to establish civil order and had no practical significance. The Kadets would support the convocation of a new national body, but considered

---

[51] Krol', *Za tri goda*, p. 15. The sources actually refer to Kornilov only as Professor "K." Conceivably, they could mean Alexander Kizevetter.

[52] Panina Archive, pack. 3, fold. 3.

this feasible only in conditions of domestic peace, and only if the Assembly could work with sufficient freedom to translate its decisions into reality.

Thus, as Novgorodtsev himself later described the Kadets' new stance, traditional principles of democratic self-determination and full civic freedoms were being temporarily abandoned. These goals could not be obtained while a state of civil war existed; victory over the Bolsheviks came first. Traditional tactics also had to be dropped. Without firm military leadership, the struggle would be lost. Central Committee members realized their resolution violated the party's basic program and its historic commitment to concepts of legality and political legitimacy. But Novgorodtsev could easily rationalize this in the familiar terms of *nadpartiinost'* and "national" interests, as well as the Bolsheviks' own usurpation. The question now was one of political relevance, and of the future of the Russian state. If left-leaning Kadets disliked the resolution as a party document, they could consider it a "national" declaration.[53]

"From the Depths"

Thus national unity and state welfare remained the Kadet leadership's foremost goals in January 1918; Bolshevik "anarchism" was synonymous with Russia's underdeveloped political consciousness, an infection to be lanced with surgical determination. For some on the party's right, the Moscow resolution was the final step in a long flirtation with authoritarianism, representing a clear break with "false hopes" about revolutionary democracy. For others, social and political democracy were now simply irrelevant to the cause of Russia's "survival," and theirs.

Yet even a resolution as forceful as this one could not lift most Kadets from the depths of their despondency in the early months of 1918. The murder of Kokoshkin and Shingarev symbolized the assassination of the liberals' whole way of life. In both capitals, bands of hooligans roamed the streets almost at will. Bolsheviks seemed less able to cope with the desperate problems of anarchism and food supply than their Provisional Government predecessors. Bread was virtually nonexistent. Flour was obtained largely from bagmen, who bought cheaply in the countryside and resold in the cities at exorbitant prices. Fuel was also incredibly scarce. Apartments were plundered and smashed for wood, while scores of factories closed their doors, sending workers into the streets. Hundreds of refugees, meanwhile, streamed

[53] Report by Novgorodtsev to the Kadet Central Committee in Ekaterinodar, July 19, 1919, in the Panina Archive, pack. 3, fold. 3.

south and east out of Moscow and Petrograd, joined on the road by
ruined landowners escaping from plundered estates, and by "miscel-
laneous throngs of men and women who were finding the results of
the slow labor of years crumbling away in their hands, who had lost
occupations, who had no use for their talents, their painfully acquired
knowledge."[54] If the Bolsheviks themselves worried enormously about
these conditions in the winter and spring of 1918, they verified the
liberals' most awful predictions. But self-righteousness was scant compensation.

Late in February 1918 (early March by the new calendar), Lenin
finally brought Russia out of the war by signing the treaty of Brest-
Litovsk. In one stroke, the tsarist empire was formally abandoned,
with Poland, the Ukraine, Transcaucasia, Finland, Lithuania, and
the Baltic states surrendered to independence and German domination. The Bolsheviks acted only with great reservations and after
much bitter infighting, forced by the overwhelming pressure of a new
German advance. They feared not only severe consequences from the
loss of Ukrainian and West Russian grain supplies, but the Kaiser's
ability to transfer troops for use against German revolutionaries. The
overthrow of German and West European capitalism was still the
crucial determinant of communist success in Russia. Lenin, Trotsky,
and the Bolshevik leadership peered anxiously through the gloom of
Russian winter for the sparks of world conflagration.

But for Novgorodtsev, Rodichev, and other liberals, anxiety was
felt in terms of the corruption and disintegration of the Russian
state, and the apparent lack of effective means to reverse it. It also
sprang from a remorseful sense of the Kadets' own failure, and from
that of the whole Russian intelligentsia. For weeks after the murder
of Kokoshkin and Shingarev, Kadets met and discussed these questions in relative freedom. Bolshevik authority was still superficial, particularly outside Petrograd. Organizations like the Cheka—the future
instrument of red terror—were largely preoccupied with ordinary
problems of hooliganism and social control.[55] Many Kadet leaders arrested earlier in the fall had also been released, while well-known
anti-Bolsheviks like Struve and Savinkov, who had spent much of
December and January in the Don region, found they could return to
Moscow with relative impunity. In these circumstances, liberals spoke
out with increasing sharpness. Despite the risk of censorship and heavy
fines, they still found sounding boards in liberal newspapers like

[54] Dispatch from Harold Williams (husband of Ariadna Tyrkova) to the London
Daily Chronicle, Feb. 1/13, 1918, in the Tyrkova Archive, sec. 3, cart. 9, gp. 4.

[55] The Bolsheviks themselves condemned the murders of Kokoshkin and Shingarev, for example, and launched an investigation into the incident. See Spirin,
Klassy i partii, p. 80.

Russkiia Vedomosti and *Nash Vek*. Both appeared daily in Moscow and Petrograd. Even the liberals' official *Vestnik* was still published on a more or less regular basis.[56]

The most scorching liberal criticism still turned not so much against the Bolsheviks, however, as against moderate socialists and the whole radical intelligentsia—a bitter, contemptuous revulsion against impractical cosmopolitanism, and divorce from what many saw as the essential components of Russian national development and existence. For men like Struve, Novgorodtsev, Kotliarevskii, and Izgoev, these components were essentially subjective and spiritual, aspects of an orthodox Christian reverence for the collectivity of Russia and the nation as a whole. In their view, moreover, expressed not only in journals like Struve's *Russkaia Mysl'* and *Russkiia Vedomosti*, but also in the Kadet party's own *Vestnik* and in a special compendium called *From the Depths [Iz Glubiny]*, commitment to authority derived from an awareness of how true Russian leaders and genuine legality served community welfare. The basic cause of the present extraordinary destruction of Russian state life lay in the failure of Russia's radical intelligentsia to understand either the nature of Russia's people, or the interrelationship between Russian society and the state. Thus radicals failed to comprehend the conditions necessary for national strength and growth. Falling slavishly at the feet of Western economic materialism, infatuated with material rather than spiritual well-being, they used "false" teachings to arouse the bestial and destructive passions of individualism and class hatred. The basic values of a socialist outlook, ironically, were coincident with Russian collectivism. But they were accepted by uncultured Russians as reinforcement for individual betterment, rather than societal welfare. As Struve wrote in August 1918, the idea of socialism and class struggle had force in Russia only as a destructive tendency, not as a collective or creative one. Russia's collective spirit was to be found instead in a profound sense of nation, a national (*narodnyi*) spirit; and it would have to be resurrected in these terms.[57]

In part, this view reflected the liberal commitment to *nadpartiinost'* and *gosudarstvennost'* which had supported much of Kadet policy in 1917 and which in practice defended the interests of privileged Russia,

[56] In Petrograd, copies of newspapers had to be presented to the press commissariat at Smolnyi before 8 o'clock in the morning. Lateness resulted in heavy fines. Often, the Bolshevik couriers in Smolnyi held up final delivery to the censors. A similar procedure was followed in Moscow. An editorial on this appeared in *Nash Vek*, No. 66 (90), Apr. 5, 1918. The first serious censorship of *Russkiia Vedomosti* occurred with No. 31, Mar. 8, 1918.

[57] Peter Struve, "Istoricheskii smysl russkoi revoliutsii i natsional'nye zadachi," in the compendium *Iz glubiny*, 2nd ed., Paris, 1967, pp. 301, 304.

although it was now heavily layered with tones of crisis and doubt similar to those which had followed the revolution of 1905; in part, it stemmed as well from the same religio-philosophic idealism structuring the *Vekhi* essays. In large measure, it argued for what was essentially a spiritual retreat toward authoritarianism. As Tkhorzhevskii wrote in the Kadets' *Vestnik*, there were no interests higher than those of the state; the Bolsheviks' "destructive success," itself the logical derivative of efforts to "broaden and deepen" the revolution, was simple proof of the Russian masses' inability to participate creatively in the processes of state development. The responsibility of Kadets, consequently—and there was "nothing to hide" in this—was to "unite persons of all political hues who had one slogan: the restoration of Russia . . . its national resurrection."[58]

Yet the liberals' task now, as in 1917, was to give these values practical relevance. And despite party resolutions in support of military dictatorship, the deep psychological agony of Kadets in February and March 1918 was the gnawing fear that perhaps there was little they could do. Their main goal now was the unification of right-wing elements in support of anti-Bolshevik forces on the Don. Shortly after the Bolshevik coup, efforts toward this end were centered around the Union of Public Figures, carrying through the resolutions of that group's second congress in October. A special committee of three representatives each from the Union, the Trade-Industrial Congress, and the Kadets began meeting together as "The Nine" (*Deviatka*) sometime in November 1917; and after tentatively establishing ties to the South, directed its attention to securing funds. Liaison was also made with officers' groups in the capitals, using contacts made at the time of the Kornilov mutiny.[59]

The collapse of the Constituent Assembly and the crystallization of Kadet positions in the Moscow Central Committee led to a rapid expansion of The Nine's activities in January and February 1918, so much so that the group now generally came to be known as the "Right" or "Moscow" Center. Novgorodtsev, Stepanov, Kotliarevskii, and

[58] S. Tkhorzhevskii, "O partiia na zapade i v Rossii," *VPNS*, Nos. 11-12, Aug. 8, 1918, pp. 342-44. See also A. Izgoev, "Pis'ma o bol'shevizmom," *VPNS*, No. 4, Mar. 21, 1918, pp. 76-81; No. 5, Mar. 28, 1918, pp. 137-52; No. 6, Apr. 18, 1918, pp. 177-83; and No. 7, Apr. 30, 1918, pp. 209-14; and B. Maliutin, "K sporu o tvorcheskikh silakh naroda," *VPNS*, No. 8, May 23, 1918, pp. 246-49.

[59] N. Astrov, "Moskovskiia organizatsii, 1917-1918," unpubl. MS in the Panina Archive, pack. 5, suppl. 2, fold. 2. Astrov lists the original members of "The Nine" as Belorussov, Leontev, and D. M. Shchepkin from the Union of Public Men; Fedorov, Chelnokov, and Cherven-Vodali from the Trade-Industrialists; and himself, Sabashnikov, and N. N. Shchepkin from the Kadet party. He also caustically relates the unwillingness of Moscow financial circles to provide funds for the embryonic Volunteer Army, pp. 6-7.

others joined Astrov, Sabashnikov, and N. N. Shchepkin in representing the Kadets; while other participants included the well-known
conservative nationalists Krivoshein, Berdiaev, Ilin, Urosov, Gurko,
Meller-Zakomelskii, and Struve. Since one main thrust of the group
was to secure Allied military assistance, E. N. Trubetskoi, Struve,
Krivoshein, and Astrov also began tentative negotiations with the
French Consul in Moscow, M. Grenard.[60]

Simultaneously, however, the more extreme right-wing elements of
the Moscow Center began to think in different terms. In their view,
the possibility of an Allied landing was not only remote, but also
raised again the specter of Russia's simultaneous involvement in both
a European and civil war. On the other hand, if one considered Bolsheviks the real cancer of European and Russian social disintegration,
it was logical—though perhaps difficult in terms of Russian national
feelings—to contemplate assistance from the Germans. As Gurko,
Trepov, and Prince Trubetskoi himself expressed it, the danger of
Bolshevism to European and Russian civilization was so serious that
there could be no place for narrow "patriotic" feelings. Russians had
to cultivate whatever anti-Bolshevik alliances they could.[61]

By the end of the first five months of Bolshevik rule these were not
unpopular ideas even for a number of Kadets. It is a revealing characteristic of liberal statism that Bolshevik radicalism was now considered
by many a more terrible danger to Russia than the country's foreign
military enemy itself, under whose guns so many had died. Despite almost four years of bloody war, many liberals could still conceive of
the Germans as competitors, with whom one could reach a businesslike
agreement; while Lenin cut at the very heart of liberal values. So great,
in fact, was the sense of isolation and despair within the Right Center
that Grenard himself thought "it should surprise no one" that Germanophilism "has made considerable progress . . . particularly among
those who tremble for their lives and their bank-accounts."[62] The
problem was, however, that while Kadets like Trubetskoi fit neatly
into Grenard's categories, others clearly did not. For those like Astrov
and Nicholas Shchepkin, whose sense of sacrifice and duty throughout
most of 1917 had so frequently been expressed in terms of Russia's

[60] Astrov, "Moskovskiia organizatsii," pp. 12-13; V. Gurko, "Iz Petrograda cherez
Moskvu, Parizh i London v Odessu," *ARR*, xv, 1924, p. 13. On the "Nine" and the
"Right Center" see also Vladimirova, *God sluzhby*, p. 233; "Natsional'nyi tsentr' v
Moskve v 1918," *NCS*, No. 9, 1925, pp. 132ff; "Sovet obshchestvennykh deiatelei v
Moskve, 1917-19 gg.," *NCS*, No. 9, 1925, pp. 93ff.
[61] P. Stepanov, "Nemtsy v Moskve v 1918," *GMNCS*, No. 1 (14), 1926, p. 180; V.
Kazanovich, "Poezdka iz dobrovol'cheskoi armii v krasnuiu Moskvu," *ARR*, vii,
1922, pp. 192-93. See also "Sovet obshchestvennykh deiatelei v Moskve 1917-19 gg.,"
p. 96; and "Natsional'nyi tsentr' v Moskve v 1918," p. 129.
[62] Letter from Grenard to P. Boyer, Maklakov Archive, ser. B, pack. 6, fold. 2.

"integrity" and "loyalty" to her Allies, the Right Center's German orientation proved increasingly disturbing.[63]

Germanophilism also undercut new Kadet efforts to establish a workable association with the moderate left, a second possible practical course for active anti-Bolshevism. When the Central Committee of the Popular Socialist party transferred to Moscow in the middle of March, several of its members renewed the idea of creating a broadly based "conciliationist" front. Led by Titov, Miakotin, Chaikovskii, and Peshekhonov, the Popular Socialists entered into discussions with moderate SRs. Late in March, Astrov, Volkov, and N. N. Shchepkin were invited to join them on behalf of the Kadets.[64]

Initial discussions were held in the apartment of Dr. I. Kovarskii. Both the Popular Socialists and the moderate SRs (Avksentiev, Argunov, and B. N. Moiseenko) were anxious to reach an agreement with the Kadets. For their part, Astrov and Shchepkin reciprocated favorably, much in the terms they had used the previous September in what now seemed the distant past. There were, however, two serious stumbling blocks. First, the SRs insisted that the new union recognize the competency of the Constituent Assembly; and second, they demanded that military organizations be subordinated to the Assembly's control. Since Kadets still feared the dominance of radicals like Chernov in the Assembly, and worried about its acceptability in military circles, they found both these conditions unacceptable. Consequently, discussions were suspended until the beginning of April, when Popular Socialists borrowed one of the Kadets' own pet conceptions, and suggested that a "left center" be formed on the basis of "nonparty," rather than party ties. Moderate socialists and liberals could then work together in pursuit of common general goals, to which each subscribed as individuals, rather than parties. Astrov, Kishkin, Shchepkin and other left Kadets were now more receptive. If the SRs could set aside their commitment to the disbanded Constituent Assembly, they saw no further barrier to a practical association.[65]

[63] On March 12, 1918, for example, Kadets repudiated any contact or association with the Germans in *Russkiia Vedomosti*, and expressed the party's fidelity to the "political, ideological, and military goals" of the Allies (*Russkiia Vedomosti*, No. 34, Mar. 12, 1918).

[64] Astrov, "Moskovskiia organizatsii," pp. 8-9, 12; and his "Grazhdanskaia voina," unpubl. MS subtitled "Vospominaniia Astrova," in the Panina Archive, pack. 3, suppl. 3, esp. pp. 83ff. See also Mel'gunov, *Chaikovskii*, pp. 47ff; Vladimirova, *God sluzhby*, pp. 200ff; V. Miakotin, "Iz nedalekago proshlago," *NCS*, No. 9, 1925, pp. 205-36. A lengthy article describing the preliminary discussions of the group appeared surprisingly in *Nash Vek*, No. 70 (94), Apr. 11, 1918.

[65] Letter from Astrov to Denikin, Aug. 17, 1923, in the Panina Archive, pack. 5, suppl. 6, fold. 10; Miakotin, "Iz nedalekago," p. 180.

Thus divisions in the anti-Bolshevik movement began to reflect the differences which had existed among Kadets themselves through much of 1917, and even before. As Dolgorukov, Novgorodtsev, and the party's right concentrated on creating a "firm military dictatorship" without regard for the problems of social reform or popular sentiment, Astrov, Kishkin, Shchepkin, and the Kadets' former "conciliationists" continued to recognize the need for broad political unity, and hoped to give their moment mass support. In the middle of April 1918, a new "left center"—the Union of Regeneration (*Soiuz Vozrozhdeniia*)—was formally established with Kadet participation, an association of "various social figures . . . grouped together on the basis of personal agreements, as either nonparty figures or as members of various parties standing for the principles of statesmanship (*gosudarstvennost'*)."[66] Its platform read as follows:

> The Union for the Regeneration of Russia establishes as its task the resurrection of Russian state authority, the reunion with Russia of the regions forcefully cut off from her, and the defense of these regions from foreign enemies.
>
> The task of reunifying and defending Russia should be accomplished, in the Union's opinion, in close agreement with Russia's Allies, while they together carry on the struggle against Germany and the powers allied with her, who have seized parts of Russia's territory. The Union will strive to achieve the task of resurrecting the now corrupted Russian state in accordance with the will of the people, expressed by means of universal and equal elections.
>
> In conjunction with this the Union considers it necessary that the new power, which will arise in the struggle for freedom and the unity of Russia, and to which [the Union] will give its support, must be based as it is created on organs of local self government; and when the territory of Russia is liberated from its enemies, it will convoke a Constituent Assembly which will [finally] establish the forms of Russia's government.[67]

The Union thus skirted the ticklish questions of whether the Constituent Assembly (which would ultimately define the nature of the new Russian state) would be elected anew, and what the nature of the relationship would be between the anti-Bolshevik military forces and civilian political authorities. For the time being, it simply formed a base for new tactical associations.

---

[66] Soiuz Vozrozhdeniia Rossii, *Informatsionnyi Listok*, Aug. 16, 1918, in the Melgunov Archive, file B, fold. 9.

[67] *Ibid.*

Thus, Kadets became the center of conspiratorial activities in Moscow, with ties to both right- and left-wing groups. Taking advantage of their own capital resources and the Bolsheviks' still relatively lenient attitude toward the press, they began an effort to rally Moscow and Petrograd sentiment. To some extent, eulogies in honor of Shingarev and Kokoshkin provided a convenient (and relatively safe) vehicle for this, particularly when those accused of the murder were brought to trial in May.[68] But Kadet editors were also more direct. *Nash Vek* readers were told in March, for example, that the Moscow Kadet Committee was calling on every possible person to participate in a "general-national defense" of Russian interests, and that only through such a mass "defense" could Russia escape "its present catastrophic circumstances."[69] The address of the Kadet party club in Petrograd (Nevskii 72) was also frequently given, as were reports of various local party meetings. As late as May 11 *Nash Vek* reported in detail on a twelfth anniversary celebration by Kadets of the first State Duma. Readers were told how A. V. Vasilev had compared the present circumstances with the difficult days of the First Duma, drawing a parallel between the odious characteristics of tsarist autocracy and the Bolshevik regime; how Peter Ryss had stressed the necessity for organization, and declared the need for a "united, reorganized Russia"; and how Victor Pepeliaev had pointed out that Kadets had always striven for the good of the nation as a whole, and would continue to do so now: "Now we have no state, no territory, no authority, and no unification of our people," Pepeliaev declared. "The only escape is to strive with all our might to create a new Russia. The Ukraine must be united with Great Russia; Russia must again become whole. . . . A Great National Power must again be built. The Soviet regime can never save the nation."[70] Meanwhile, the Kadet Central Committee continued to meet in Moscow, sometimes in the Kadet party club on Briusovskii Lane, sometimes in private apartments. For the most part, its members spent their time dealing more or less "routinely" with problems of securing financial aid and recruits for Alekseev and Kornilov.

As the weeks went by, however, the Committee also found itself increasingly preoccupied with the problem of German "orientation," as it was termed. By late spring, the idea of a liberal-German alliance was even more attractive to members of the Right Center than it had been in February and March. Not only was there growing evidence that the German high command was itself considering a move in this

---

[68] *Nash Vek*, No. 29 (54), Feb. 20, 1918; *Svoboda Rossii*, No. 36, May 28, 1918.
[69] *Nash Vek*, No. 37 (61), Mar. 1, 1918.   [70] *Ibid.*, No. 93 (117), May 11, 1918.

direction, but Panina, Rodichev, and several other leading Petrograd
Kadets now believed the Germans would seize the capital anyway;
Kadets would thus stand a better chance of eventual success by cooperating with the "deliverers," rather than opposing them—an attitude showing just how flexible Kadet nationalism could be when
faced with the threat of Bolshevik radicalism.[71] In Moscow, however,
the party's mood remained unalterably opposed to cooperating with
the Germans. Some even believed that *any* foreign assistance would
harm the Kadet cause: Russia's peasants and workers would think the
party had sold out to foreign domination. Here Kadet nationalism
still meant the defense of Russian territorial integrity. The party's
only tactical course was vigorous assistance to the "national leadership" of Alekseev, Kornilov, and their fledgling anti-Bolshevik army,
the course decided upon in January.[72]

Late in April, the Kadet Central Committee learned the Allies had
decided to make a full-scale landing, ostensibly to reopen a strong
second front, and eliminate the Bolsheviks.[73] On April 13/26, the
Committee began discussing this new development, reaching several
conclusions within a few days which revealed how tortured many
party members had now become over the competing demands of anti-
Bolshevism and the advancement of Russian state interests. The
Allied landings would be officially welcomed by the Kadet party provided they were accompanied by a specific declaration supporting the
territorial integrity and sovereignty of Russia. (This was directed
specifically toward Japan, whom many liberals rightly suspected of
harboring territorial designs in the Russian Far East.) The Russian
people were also to be told that the Allies had landed not for the
purposes of occupation, but to wage war against a "common enemy";
the Russian descent was to be compared to English and American
landings in France; and finally, the Allied plan would be acceptable
to Kadets only if all powers participated (again, a reflection of concern
about Japan).[74] Simultaneously, the Moscow Kadets officially condemned any further attempts to solicit aid from Germany. "It is unanimously resolved," the Committee recorded, "that the Central Committee considers any motions—direct or indirect—which appeal to the

[71] R. Vinavera, "Vospominaniia," p. 101; Letter from Tyrkova to Maklakov,
Apr. 26, 1918, in the Maklakov Archive, ser. B, pack. 6, fold. 2. See also P. Dolgorukov, *Natsional'naia politika i partiia narodnoi svobody*, Rostov, 1919, pp. 6-9.

[72] "Memorandum" on the Russian situation, Apr. 8, 1918, unsigned, in the
Maklakov Archive, ser. B, pack. 1, fold. 2.

[73] Report on the Central Committee session in Moscow, Apr. 26, 1918, in the
Miliukov Archive, bx. 1661, fold. 1. The report states simply that "The Central
Committee was informed . . ." without divulging the source of information.

[74] Reports of the Central Committee meetings of May 8 and 12, Miliukov
Archive, bx. 1661, fold. 1.

Germans to invade Russia for the purpose of forming a new government absolutely unacceptable, and finds no possible basis for supporting such plans."[75]

What gave this statement particular urgency, however, was not so
much the inclinations of Kadets like Nolde and Rodichev, but rumors
from Kiev that Miliukov himself was actively seeking German support.[76] It was thus decided to resolve the "orientation" question more
definitively, by calling a general party conference, and setting a firm
line for local Kadet organizations throughout Russia. The Moscow
group was not yet confident that Kadets as a party had a significant
anti-Bolshevik role to play; but if they did, party unity on this basic
question of Russia's "national honor" was essential.[77]

THE TACTICS OF NATIONAL UNITY

The Kadet conference opened in Moscow on May 14/27. Most
delegates arriving from the provinces were shocked at the city's condition, but had also seen awful sights elsewhere. All over Russia,
authority seemed to have broken down completely. Commerce was at
a standstill; industrial plants lay idle. Where workers had driven out
burzhui managers, they often found themselves unable to cope with
everyday administrative problems; and with rampant inflation, and
nothing in the way of goods to receive in return for their grain,
peasants were refusing to part with their crops. *Izvestiia* itself estimated
on May 10, 1918, that 70-80 percent of Russia's industrial force was
unemployed. And as many workers returned disillusioned to their
villages, agitation against the Communists began to grow. Reports of
violence appeared uncensored in Moscow papers, while Lenin himself
began seriously considering the methods of war communism.

In these circumstances, few Kadets were ready to believe that the
Bolsheviks could possibly remain in power. Despite Lenin's obvious
charisma and authority for Moscow and Petrograd workers and soldiers, most Kadets in the capitals still regarded him and his comrades
as totally alien to what was basically and fundamentally Russian.
Yet there was also very little recognition that Kadets themselves might
seriously address social or economic questions, or attempt to broaden
their own base of support by drafting and articulating new proposals
for reform. For many it was almost a question of the country itself
being out of step with Constitutional Democracy, rather than the
other way around; and despite the fact that Bolshevik rule seemed

[75] *Ibid.*, Report of May 12.
[76] Astrov, "Moskovskiia organizatsii," p. 15.
[77] N. Astrov, "1918 god," MS in the Panina Archive, n.p., n.d., pack. 2, fold. 15.

tenuous, and that new social commitments from the liberals might have been precisely the way to undermine Lenin's own popular support, most Kadets gathering in Moscow felt these were the least of their problems. First, Russia's statehood had to be preserved; then order reestablished and the war won; finally, social reconstruction. Despite the views of Astrov, Shchepkin, and other persistent "conciliationists," most Kadets never felt more deeply than in the spring of 1918 that social goals were subordinate to "national purpose."

These, in any case, were the themes of the Kadets' May conference, forcefully expressed by spokesmen like Novgorodtsev and accepted with little discussion or dissent. The German question was also dispatched in these terms, as well as the task of constructing a future party line. While right-wing Kadets like Trubetskoi still remained doubtful, Vinaver insisted an anti-Bolshevik alliance with the Kaiser and Ludendorff would more firmly crush Russian state existence than even Bolshevik rule. Financially, politically, economically, Russia would become a German satellite. The essential fact of the current situation was its instability. There was every indication now that the Allies would win the war, and that Bolshevik-German agreements would be nullified. If Kadets themselves abandoned Russia's moral and legal commitments, Russia would become a social outcast in the postwar world. In Vinaver's view, and in the view of the conference as a whole (as expressed in five major "theses" on the problem), an agreement with the Austro-German coalition was morally and politically untenable. Instead, Russia's resurrection would "be the result of: (a) the struggle of the Allied powers (including Russia) to eliminate the German hegemony; (b) the inevitable tendency of different parts of Russia to unite; and (c)—most important—the internal union of popular forces, which, though they have not yet manifested themselves as a result of fatigue with the war and revolution, cannot nevertheless remain long in a condition of apathy and servility."[78]

It was Novgorodtsev's task at the conference to reformulate these views into a specific set of tactical guidelines. As the Central Committee had determined in January, Kadets were to support all "general-national" (obshchenatsional'nye) efforts to reconstruct a "free Russian state," whether they originated from the right or the left. Questions of program were less important than national commitment. Kadets had to realize that current conditions precluded the resolution of basic questions concerning Russia's political future; but they had to insist as well that any force with which they associated support the concepts of national unification, regional autonomy (rather than in-

---

[78] Untitled MS summary of the proceedings, Miliukov Archive, bx. 1661, fold. 1.

dependence), equality of nationalities, freedom of the church, and "basic political reform." In the meantime, Kadets would stand behind their traditional program on specific social and political issues.[79] Like Vinaver's theses, Novgorodtsev's were also adopted unanimously.

Finally, there was the tricky problem of defining an appropriate tactical course for party groups under German occupation. The task here was left largely to Astrov, a convinced Germanophobe. The essence of his report (and of its supporting resolution, adopted by the conference) was that Kadets in occupied areas "must remain and carry on their work in accordance with general directives from the party's central organs." Specifically, Kadets were "not to enter into any agreement with the Germans, and under no circumstances invite them to construct a government, establish order, or organize local affairs." The only exception to this might be in case where pressing local needs (such as food supply) could be met only by occupying powers. Where there was no effective government, local party groups were directed to cooperate in the formation of "local committees," just as they had in February 1917. These could take on executive functions themselves.[80]

In adopting Astrov's report, the Moscow conference was thinking specifically of Kadet activities in the Ukraine. There was no definite information yet, but a coalition of Kadets with the German puppet Skoropadskii was widely rumored. Consequently, as the conference closed, it was decided to send Vinaver personally to Kiev to convey the party's decisions. The Central Committee would postpone any further action on the matter until it received a formal report.[81]

As the May conference adjourned, Kadets withdrew from the now pro-German Right Center. In its place they organized a new "National" Center, dedicated to traditional liberal values. Officially non-party, the new group was almost entirely Kadet; its principal figures—Astrov, Fedorov, Shchepkin, Stepanov, Novgorodtsev, Volkov—were all members of the party's Central Committee. Tactically, the task of the National Center was to implement party resolutions, creating a broadly based anti-German alliance in support of Alekseev and Denikin; it would funnel men and funds to the south, and provide needed help in administration and logistics. It was also to continue efforts at organizing an anti-Bolshevik uprising in the capitals, timed perhaps to coincide with an attack by other anti-Bolshevik forces.[82]

[79] *Ibid.*   [80] *Ibid.*

[81] Communication from the Moscow Central Committee Branch to Miliukov in Kiev, June 4, 1918, in the Miliukov Archive, bx. 1661, fold 1.

[82] Astrov, "1918 god," pp. 6, 17-18.

Whether or not by design, the Center also began to stand as a surrogate for the Kadets' own party apparatus. When Vinaver spoke to his colleagues at the May conference about the "internal union of popular forces," he had in mind not the emergence of new support for the Kadet party specifically, but a general, nationalist coalition, which transcended party lines. For such a force, a "center" was more appropriate than a "party," especially when the Kadets themselves had become generally identified with privileged society, and when there was actually no practical need for party groupings.

A Center was also more suitable to the growing peril of Bolshevik police. Kadet groups and meeting places were well known, and in the late spring of 1918, Red Guards were becoming more vigilant. On May 17/30 Guards invaded the Andreevskii Dom, where the Kadet conference had been held; and soon thereafter a crackdown against all "enemies of the people" began in earnest. Cheka members arrested several Central Committee members and seized a number of important party documents, among which was a list of all Kadets still active in the Moscow city committees. Most local party meetings were consequently suspended.[83]

Mirroring its Kadet base, the National Center also stood firmly in support of military dictatorship, now the best weapon in the view of most liberals for fighting Bolshevism effectively. It was generally thought that Alekseev would be the most suitable "national leader," not only because he headed the Volunteer Army, but also because his moderation at the time of the Kornilov affair might enable him to gather socialist support. He was also thought to be staunchly anti-German. The problem here, however, was working out an understanding with the Union of Regeneration, whose socialist goals definitely did not include military dictatorship. The Union's SRs argued in particular that dictatorship would alienate the masses, destroying any chance of anti-Bolshevik success.[84]

In late May and June, Kadets once again discussed these questions in the National Center and the Central Committee, which now met furtively, and always with lookouts posted at the windows. Reports had begun arriving from the south on the growth of the anti-Bolshevik armies, while new indications were also being received of assistance

[83] *Ibid.*, pp. 4-5. The arrested Kadets were paraded through Moscow on their way to prison, and were seen by many. Astrov asserts that the Germans themselves were primarily responsible for the arrests, retaliating for the anti-Germanophile position adopted by the party at its May conference (p. 5) but this is not confirmed by German sources.

[84] M. Slonim, "Nashi raznoglasiia," *Volia Rossii*, No. 2 (18), 1923, p. 36. Chernov was even urging the SRs to withdraw from the Union of Regeneration over this issue.

from the Allies. Despite the precariousness of their own day-to-day existence, therefore, Kadets in Moscow and Petrograd again began to envision a significant role for themselves in Russia's political future.

Within the Central Committee new hopes brought new passion to the debate over the degree to which liberals should coordinate their activities with moderate socialists, with Stepanov, Dolgorukov, and Novgorodtsev again arguing emphatically for an authoritative, anti-socialist dictatorship, while Astrov and Shchepkin worried that commitment to one-man rule would reopen the struggle between moderate socialists and liberals, and assure ultimate Bolshevik victory.[85] Late in June, party leaders unofficially hammered out a compromise formula. Liberals would continue to support *in principle* a strong, unitary authority; but they would relax their insistence on a dictatorship if a directorate could be organized with left-wing support, headed by a military figure.[86] Largely through the insistence of Avksentiev, this soon proved acceptable to the Union of Regeneration, whose members met and discussed the question with Astrov and Shchepkin. One of the Directorate's members would be General Alekseev; his two associates would be prominent civilians, representing both socialist and non-socialist opinion. The Union also bowed to liberal pressure, however, by unofficially rejecting the competency of the first Constituent Assembly, and deciding a new convention of parties and social groups would have to be held in non-Bolshevik Russia sometime in the future. All agreed that the new assembly would have the ultimate responsibility for determining the Directorate's membership. In the meantime, the Union settled on Boldyrev, Avksentiev, Chaikovskii, and Astrov as acceptable candidates. Miliukov's name was also mentioned.[87]

Neither the National Center nor the Kadet Central Committee specifically committed itself to supporting this plan, but both agreed that it was feasible. The Center also accepted the idea that Astrov and Shchepkin should continue as contacts between the liberals and the left by participating in both organizations.[88] It was hoped that with

[85] Astrov, "1918 god," pp. 14-16.   [86] *Ibid.*

[87] *Ibid.*; Astrov, "Moskovskiia organizatsii," p. 20. See also V. Ignat'ev, *Nekotorye fakty*, pp. 11-13; Miakotin, "Iz nedalekago proshlago," *NCS*, No. 3, 1923, pp. 191-92; V. Gurevich, "Real'naia politika v revoliutsii (Kadetskaia taktika)," *Volia Rossii*, No. 12, 1923, p. 28. Details of the discussions in the National Center and the Union of Regeneration on this issue were received by Maklakov in Paris, apparently from Grenard. It is likely that the French government was therefore fully informed. These communications are in the Maklakov Archive, ser. A, fold. 2. In an unsigned letter to Miliukov, dated June 2/18, 1918, the Kadet leader was told that the Union of Regeneration had "unanimously designated" him as one of the members of the directorate. The letter is in the Miliukov Archive, bx. 1661, fold. 1.

[88] Astrov, "1918 god," pp. 14-16.

Kadet influence on anti-Boshevik military leaders, and moderate socialist popularity among Russia's peasant masses, national unity could again be created and the revolution brought to a positive conclusion. What remained now was for Kadets and the Centers to dispatch representatives to non-Bolshevik regions, and coordinate activities.

The exodus began in July. Kadets continued to meet two or three times a week, but the danger of arrest was growing daily, and it was becoming extremely difficult to find safe lodgings. *Nash Vek* shut down on May 11. Though it reappeared on June 16, it obviously lived on borrowed time. *Nashe Slovo* reported, meanwhile, that the Cheka's "offensive" against the Kadets was moving into high gear, and on July 17, the Bolsheviks even closed Gorky's left-wing *Novaia Zhizn'*. Under these conditions, there was little point in Kadets remaining in Moscow.

On June 18 Vinaver left for Kiev dressed as a laborer, with peaked cap, false passport, and a small supply of cash. His was the task of personally meeting with Miliukov and the Ukrainian Kadets over the German question. Astrov left a few weeks later, first to inform General Alekseev of the Moscow decisions, and then to proceed to the Volga region and the Constituent Assembly conference being organized by the Union of Regeneration. In the meantime, the National Center dispatched Pepeliaev directly to Siberia. Astrov expected to see him in a month or so, linking up southern and eastern military efforts.[89] Others followed suit, with hope and apprehension. "The first categorical imperative . . . for all national-minded parties is Unity!" *Nash Vek* told its readers in one of its last editorials.[90] And while planning an all-Russian government in the apartment of an obscure member of the Union of Regeneration seemed somehow strange and not altogether serious, Astrov later recalled, Kadets were now convinced their tasks were real.[91] By the beginning of September, only a skeleton group remained in the capitals.

[89] Astrov, "Grazhdanskaia voina," pp. 2-3; letter from Pepeliaev to the National Center, undated, in the Wrangel Military Archives, file 153.
[90] *Nash Vek*, No. 128 (152), July 27, 1918.
[91] Astrov, "Grazhdanskaia voina," pp. 1-3.

CHAPTER TEN

Conflicting Liberal Tactics: Kadets in the Ukraine and South Russia, 1918

W HILE Kadets in Moscow and Petrograd struggled over the "tactics of national unity," the flames of civil conflict spread throughout Russia. The few restraining bonds of national authority lying tenuously over the country in the last months of 1917 were now completely severed; in the Ukraine, in South Russia, along the Volga, into Siberia, vital questions of life and death for millions of Russians, of food, of land, of shelter, of personal safety, were now entirely in local hands. Those who held arms, held power. Those who did not, lived fearfully and in real peril, whether workers or merchants struggling to feed their children, angry peasants hoarding precious grain in the countryside, demobilized soldiers or "counterrevolutionaries" making their way from junction to junction in steamy, overcrowded railroad cars.

For uncountable numbers of Ukrainians, the collapse of national authority heralded the end of Great Russian domination. Even before the Bolshevik coup, the Kievan Rada had decided a special Ukrainian Constituent Assembly would determine the region's future, rather than an all-Russian one; and after Lenin seized power, a "Third Universal" proclaimed the Ukraine an autonomous "People's Republic," though insisting on continued membership in a Russian "federation." What was important to Rada leaders was not whether Bolsheviks or liberals ruled in Petrograd, but whether Ukrainians ruled in Kiev. When the Bolsheviks themselves attempted to gain control of the region, worrying much like their predecessors about grain supplies, the Rada declared the Ukraine's independence. Its representatives also signed a separate peace treaty with the Germans. Just as the treaty was concluded, however, the Bolsheviks reached Kiev, and drove the Rada to Zhitomir.

In the Don and Kuban regions of South Russia, meanwhile, the question was not so much one of Great Russian domination but of class rivalry, and the extension of rights from traditional cossack oligarchies to the so-called *inogorodnye*: non-cossack workers and peasants who had largely come south after the emancipation of 1861, and found themselves either in the unhappy condition of most Russian workers at the time of the revolution, or as landless fieldhands, virtually indentured to cossack overloads. Throughout 1917, the *inogorodnye* proved ready supporters for more radical soviet elements They also secured extensive representation in local organs of government like the Kuban Rada. While cossack congresses in Moscow and Petrograd insisted on the "inviolability" of private property, the *inogorodnye* refused to pay rent, and demanded that land be nationalized.[1]

The situation in the Don region was further complicated toward the end of 1917 by the return from the front lines of large numbers of radicalized younger cossacks—*frontoviki*—whose sympathies, while not particularly with Don or Kuban workers and peasants, were also not with their officer-elders like Ataman Kaledin, whom they considered reactionaries. If *inogorodnye* staffed the few scattered Military Revolutionary Committees that formed in support of Lenin in October, it was the attitudes of the *frontoviki* that allowed the Reds to gain ground.[2] For each group, however, the settling of local grievances mattered more than national politics. All assumed the autonomy of the cossack territories would be preserved. The crucial question was: under whose control?

By early spring of 1918, the cherished abstractions of constitutional democracy—above all, concern for state welfare, social order, and the interests of the nation "as a whole"—bore little direct relation to the vital concerns of any local group in either the Ukraine or South Russia. This did not mean, however, that there was not a potentially important role for Kadets. The Bolsheviks were still quite weak. Having assumed power, they now faced the same popular pressures as the Provisional Government they replaced. Given Russia's general condition, dissidence was bound to develop against their policies, just as it had against the liberals'; and the more forcefully Lenin attempted to deal with specific problems, the stronger resistance was likely to become. In these conditions, a well-armed, coordinated White movement could possibly retake the capitals.

Coordination could only be developed among the Whites, however, if political leaders in each anti-Bolshevik camp shared similar outlooks, and were able to orient the struggle so as to maximize popular

[1] G. Ladokh, *Ocherki grazhdanskoi bor'by na Kubani*, Krasnodar, 1923, pp. 44-45; *Oktiabr' na Kubani i Chernomor'i*, Krasnodar, 1924, pp. 107-09; Ia. N. Raenko, comp., *Khronika istoricheskikh sobytii na Donu, Kubani, i Chernomor'e, 1917-1920*, Rostov, 1941, pp. 26-37; A. N. Grekov, "Soiuz kazach'ikh voisk v Petrograde v 1917 goda," *Donskaia Letopis'*, No. 2, 1923, pp. 229-39.

[2] Ladokh, pp. 10-17; A. P. Filimonov, "Kubantsy, 1917-18 gg.," *Beloe Delo*, II, 1927, 68-69; V. V. Dobrynin, "Vooruzhennaia bor'ba Dona s bol'shevikami," *Donskaia Letopis'*, No. 1, 1923, pp. 95-98.

support, particularly in their base areas. If a root social cause for the outbreak of civil war in Moscow and Petrograd involved the rebellion of "dark" proletarian elements against privileged Russia, the White movement, for its part, could succeed only if its leaders developed their own broad popular following. Guns alone in the south or east would be worthless without the willingness of men to shoot them.

With many of their own regional committees still functioning, and with their own local leaders generally prominent community figures, the Kadets were in a particularly good position to assist in the task of political coordination among the anti-Bolsheviks in South Russia and the Ukraine; but it remained to be seen whether after a year of revolutionary tumult, Kadet leaders themselves could develop a unified political outlook; and more important, whether those who had stoutly resisted efforts to "popularize" their party in 1917 and before had now either the ability or the desire to help develop for the Whites a firm, broad, base of support.

KADETS IN THE UKRAINE: THE GERMAN OCCUPATION

While never very great to begin with, the influence of Russian liberals in the Ukraine temporarily ended in the beginning of October 1917 when the nationalist Rada moved toward its own Constituent Assembly and the institution of a number of radical social and economic reforms. As we have seen, Ukrainian Kadets had been at odds with their Moscow and Petrograd colleagues over the autonomy issue for most of the year. But even they could not countenance what seemed to be full-blown separatism. On October 6, 1917, they withdrew their Rada delegation, though still insisting on the sincerity of their commitment to "the national-cultural resurrection of the Ukrainian people," and the "legality and justice of Ukrainian aspirations for autonomy."[3]

After Lenin seized power in Petrograd, however, the crucial question for Kadets was whether separatists were better than Bolsheviks. For most of December and January, they worked at creating a new "third force" around the Kievan city duma, meeting with moderate socialists like the Russian SRs, and conservative groups like the Union of Landowners.[4] But the "United Counterrevolutionary Front," as both separatists and Bolsheviks called it, had no appeal. Its offices were sacked by both sides, and its Kadet leaders—men like Grigorovich-

---

[3] *Kievlianin*, Oct. 6, 1917.

[4] P. Khristiuk, *Zamitky i materialy do istorii ukrainskoi revoliutsii, 1917-1920*, 4 vols., Vienna, 1921-22, II, 43-44, 156-59; A. A. Gol'denveizer, "Iz kievskikh vospominanii," *ARR*, VI, 1922, pp. 195-96.

Barskii, Butenko, Nicholas Vasilenko—found themselves in a political no-man's-land. When Red troops under Antonov-Ovseenko moved toward Kiev in January 1918, some liberals moved slightly in the direction of support for the Rada, but without real conviction. The truth of the matter was that they found themselves paralyzed, unable— except in terms of helping refugee officers reach the Don—to take any positive steps in support of their own ideals. They sat "singing their songs, but doing nothing."[5]

Bolsheviks entered Kiev the first week of February. Ukrainian resistance had left the city a shambles, without water or electricity. Armed bands of all sorts roamed the streets. For three weeks, Kadets lived a terrorized existence, afraid to venture from their apartments, isolated, fearful there would be no escape.

They soon learned, however, of the Rada's agreement with the Germans at Brest-Litovsk. And shortly afterward, rumors spread that German troops, at the Rada's invitation, would march on the city. Despite all the dispositions of their Russian statist bias, Kievan Kadets by now so hated the Bolsheviks that they found themselves looking anxiously for the arrival of the foreigners.[6] Ironically, the "enemy" now meant order; and when Germans finally marched into the city, in neat, well-disciplined files, Kadets welcomed them, despite all their party had sacrificed in the name of the war. For the first time in months they felt secure.[7]

The Germans, meanwhile, soon had problems of their own. It was important for purposes of stabilizing the Eastern front to regard the Ukraine as a sovereign power and avoid excessive interference in local affairs. Yet both the Rada's weakness and its commitment to radical land and labor reforms jeopardized grain supplies. Its leaders had proclaimed the right of Ukrainian peasants to confiscate church and crown lands, and to seize private holdings not being worked by proprietors. But here as elsewhere in Russia, there were many conflicts when local land committees attempted to implement these measures. One consequence of this was the reluctance of many peasants to sow the spring crop, particularly in view of the uncertainty as to whom the harvest would belong. Another was forceful opposition

---

[5] P. Skoropadski, "Uryvok iz 'Spomyniv' Hetmana Pavla Skoropads'koho," *Khliborobs'ka Ukraina*, bk. 5, 1924, p. 55.

[6] S. Sumskii, "Odinnadtsat' perevorotov," in S. Alekseev, ed., *Revoliutsiia na Ukraine po memuaram belykh*, Moscow-Leningrad, 1930, pp. 99-114; N. M. Mogilianskii, "Tragediia Ukrainy," in *ibid.*, 115-35; Gol'denveizer, "Iz kievskikh," pp. 204-08; N. M. Golovin, *Rossiiskaia kontr-revoliutsiia*, 5 vols., Tallin, 1937, II, bk. 4, pp. 7-14.

[7] Sumskii, "Odinnadtsat'," pp. 106-07; Mogilianskii, "Tragediia," p. 116.

to the Germans, whose army units came to secure grain.[8] With much pressure but little guidance from Berlin, German authorities soon found themselves pursuing contradictory policies, trying to strengthen the Rada's authority in the hopes of preventing disorders, while undermining its programs in the field. In early April 1918, Ambassador Mumm and the German Foreign Office resisted efforts to attach military advisers to Rada agencies, but General Eichhorn ordered land to be sown "by the initiative of military authorities themselves," if necessary. From this point onward, the Rada's authority was generally disregarded.[9]

German attitudes toward the Rada thus came to resemble those of liberal and landowner groups, and both sides soon began exploring the possibility of changing regimes. The Germans wanted a forceful civilian authority capable of maintaining civil order (with German help), and willing to implement "official" policies in support of German needs; Ukrainian and Russian liberals wanted a bulwark against radical reform and the possibility of "legally" crushing the left. By the end of April, both sides felt they had an answer in General Paul Skoropadskii, a former tsarist officer of Ukrainian descent and commander of Ukrainian military detachments in 1917. With encouragement from the Germans, Ukrainian liberals, and Kadets, Skoropadskii himself finally agreed that the Rada should be replaced by a directorate under his (and the Germans') control. On April 16/29, after German troops themselves disbanded the Rada, Skoropadskii appeared at a congress of agriculturalists, and by prearrangement, was acclaimed Ukrainian Hetman.[10]

While the evidence is unclear, Ukrainian Kadets do not seem to have participated directly in Skoropadskii's coup; but as with General Kornilov ten months before, they encouraged those who did, and made it clear they would cooperate willingly with the new regime.[11] No one could have been surprised, therefore, when the Hetman asked N. P. Vasilenko to organize his cabinet. Vasilenko was a longtime Kievan Kadet, a member of the party's national Central Committee, a specialist in Ukrainian history, and one of the leading figures in the Ukrainian Scientific Society. While not considered a Ukrainian nationalist,

---

[8] Khristiuk, *Zamitky*, II, 156ff; D. Doroshenko, *Istoriia Ukrainy, 1917-1923 rr.*, 2 vols., Uzhgorod, 1930-32, II, 14-21, 29-35.

[9] W. Baumgart, *Deutsche Ostpolitik, 1918*, Vienna, 1966, pp. 119-26; W. Groener, *Lebenserinnerungen*, Göttingen, 1957, pp. 385-97. See also the recent study by D. S. Fedyshyn, *Germany's Drive to the East and the Ukrainian Revolution*, New Brunswick, N.J., 1971, pp. 158-83.

[10] Baumgart, pp. 127-28; Doroshenko, *Istoriia*, II, 29-42; John Reshetar, *The Ukrainian Revolution, 1917-1920*, Princeton, 1952, pp. 124-30; Fedyshyn, pp. 133-57.

[11] Doroshenko, *Istoriia*, II, 18-29.

he was known as a defender of Ukrainian culture, and opponent of Russified schools. More important, he and his Kadet colleagues were now convinced not only that the Germans would win the war, but that they would also march against Lenin in Moscow.[12] They could thus join Skoropadskii, convinced they were helping create a "stable regional authority," not altogether alien to basic liberal principles. Moreover, Skoropadskii's first proclamation on April 16/29 largely corresponded to the Kadets' own program. It stressed the need for order and legality, and promised land reform on the basis of fair compensation to landlords.[13] And it was the Hetman's "liberalism" which Vasilenko stressed when he announced a cabinet including no fewer than seven Kadet party members.[14]

The anomalous character of Skoropadskii's Kadet cabinet derived from the self-proclaimed independence of the Ukrainian state: Kadets in effect were participating in an enterprise more "separatist" than any of those condemned by their party leaders in 1917. (Later Kadets and others argued that Skoropadskii was really concerned primarily with Russian, rather than Ukrainian interests; but his own foreign minister Doroshenko suggests that even Vasilenko was ready to accommodate himself "without apology" in April 1918 to Ukrainian independence.)[15] In any event, Kievan Kadets felt sufficiently awkward about their new positions to seek "legitimation" for their actions in a regional Kadet party congress, which they convened on April 26/May 8.

More than 100 party members arrived for the meeting, testimony both to liberal resourcefulness—some came from as far away as Odessa, Kherson, and Chernigov—and to the importance with which Kadets all over the Ukraine regarded the question of collaborating with the Germans. What is interesting about the sessions, however, is not so much the *crise de conscience* that one might expect from knowing the Moscow experience, but the ease with which Russian liberal-nationalism could adapt to German occupation, particularly in com-

---

[12] Mogilianskii, "Tragediia," p. 126; Gol'denveizer, "Iz kievskikh," pp. 206-07.

[13] Doroshenko, *Istoriia*, II, 49-50, partially translated in J. Bunyan, *Intervention, Civil War and Communism in Russia*, Baltimore, 1936, pp. 16-17.

[14] *Svoboda Rossii*, No. 21, May 10, 1918. The most prominent were A. K. Rzhepetskii, a banker and landowner, as minister of finance; B. I. Butenko, an engineer from Kherson, minister of transport; S. M. Gutnik, the Odessan minister of industry and trade; and I. O. Kistiakovskii, a prominent Kievan and Moscow jurist, as state secretary (later minister of the interior). Apparently at his own request, Vasilenko became minister of education, yielding the post of prime minister to F. A. Lizogub, a prominent Kievan Octobrist.

[15] E.g., S. Dolenga, *Skoropadshchyna*, Warsaw, 1934, pp. 32-33, 44-58, 79-82; Gol'denveizer, "Iz kievskikh," p. 217; Mogilianskii, "Tragediia," p. 126; and esp. D. Doroshenko, *Moi spomyny pro nedavne mynule (1914-1920)*, 2nd ed., Munich, 1969, pp. 318-20.

parison with Bolshevik rule. No matter that millions of Russian lives had been lost for the better part of three years in fighting "a cursed foe," "a fiendish enemy"; or that Kadet politics throughout 1917 had been set concrete-like in support of the war. No matter as well that a strong Hetmanate might be the first step toward Russia's "Balkanization," a policy against which Kadets like Kokoshkin and Dolgorukov had warned for months. In the spring of 1918, Germans represented order. Skoropadskii's puppetry meant an end to the chaos of revolutionary change, and at least some protection against radical social reform. In these terms, as another national Central Committee member, Grigorovich-Barskii, declared to his colleagues, Kadet collaboration was "in the best interests of the country—I repeat, in the best interests of the country." The partisan interests of the party had to be "subordinate to the needs of the nation at large."[16]

Most delegates agreed. Rzhepetskii and Vasilenko, two of the Hetman's new Kadet ministers, went so far as to describe the Germans as "a true friend and ally of democratic Russia," and stressed the benefits of collaboration on the Russian economy. "Our history shows," Vasilenko insisted, "that Russia's interests have always been tied more closely to Germany than to England."[17] This drew considerable opposition from a number of non-Kievan delegates, as well as demands that the ministers pledge their support to a single, indivisible Russian state, rather than Ukrainian independence. But when the issue came to a vote, the overwhelming majority—71 to 13 (with 5 abstentions)— approved Kadet participation in the new regime. They also considered it "imperative" that liberals everywhere assume responsibility for state administration, insisting at the same time, however, on continued "loyalty" to Kadet "ideals and programs."[18]

What this "loyalty" meant in the Ukraine was soon apparent in resolutions on labor and land. Workers were to be allowed any measures which did not lead to a decrease in "normal" productivity, which in effect meant the abrogation of workers' control in factories. Peasants were promised assistance in increasing their holdings and removing "existing abnormalities in the use of land" (because "an adequate solution to the land problem . . . is the most pressing task of the day"), but were also informed that "unrestricted freedom to sell land without state regulation" was bound to lead to "chaotic liquidation of land ownership, speculative buying, and the transfer of land to foreigners."[19] Though vague and confusing, the thrust of these strictures was to place a "hold" on the Rada's earlier plans for reform.

[16] *Zaria Rossii*, No. 19, May 14, 1918.   [17] *Kievskaia Mysl'*, No. 72, May 11, 1918.
[18] *Nashe Slovo*, No. 23, May 15, 1918.
[19] *Svoboda Rossii*, No. 30, May 21, 1918, partially translated in Bunyan, *Intervention*, p. 19.

Kadets were pressing instead for a "stabilization" of labor and agrarian relations which would promise both adequate production and a minimum of antagonism with the Germans.

Kadets in Kiev thus opted for "responsible" and "forceful" government administration, echoing the principal themes of their Petrograd colleagues in 1917 despite the fact that many Ukrainian Kadets in the past had been active party leftists. And although Skoropadskii's social base rested almost entirely with large landowners (who had pushed his candidacy for the Hetmanate), delegates to the Kievan conference made no effort to address themselves to the problems of this limited support, nor did they contemplate its future implications if the Germans were forced to withdraw. As Grigorovich-Barskii expressed the party's position, circumstances simply required the "tactics of accommodation."[20]

KADETS IN THE DON REGION; THE VOLUNTEER ARMY

An entirely different liberal posture, meanwhile, was developing in the Don, where General Alekseev was struggling to build his so-called Volunteer Army. The former Supreme Commander had come to Novocherkassk in early November 1917, hoping to organize a strong anti-Bolshevik force with cossack support. His goals were not only to defeat Lenin militarily, but to drive out the Germans and establish a new national government. Within a matter of weeks, he was joined by several prominent civilians, including Miliukov, Stepanov, and Shingarev (who shortly afterward made the fateful decision to return north); and by a number of well-known officers, including the famous "Bykhov Generals"—Denikin, Romanovskii, Lukomskii, Markov, and later Kornilov—who were arrested and imprisoned at Bykhov at the time of the August mutiny.

What few of these figures initially recognized, however, was the indifference with which they would be regarded by local populations, and the manner in which their presence would complicate relations between cossacks and *inogorodnye*, drawing the resentment even of cossack leaders in the Don and Kuban military Krugs. On one hand, local political leaders were much more concerned with protecting their regional autonomy than they were with displacing the Bolsheviks in Moscow; they thought in terms of defending their own interests, and at first refused even to consider enlisting in the Volunteer brigade.[21] On the other, they resented the pretensions of Kadets in Rostov, Ta-

[20] Quoted in Khristiuk, *Zamitky*, II, 26.
[21] K. P. Kakliugin, "Voiskovoi Ataman A. M. Kaledin i ego vremia," *Donskaia Letopis'*, No. 2, 1923, pp. 108-70; K. N. Sokolov, *Pravlenie generala Denikina*, Sofia, 1921, pp. 4, 8-9.

ganrog, and Novocherkassk—men like N. E. Paramonov, publisher of *Rostovskaia Rech'*—to speak for the region on national issues. While Petrograd *verkhovniki* had been welcomed enthusiastically to Rostov in August 1917, and had worked out joint slates with the cossacks for the Constituent Assembly elections, subsequent events had very much changed the region's mood. Even Ataman Kaledin regretted the electoral association, feeling Kadets were not an integral part of the cossack community and therefore not capable of acting as its representatives; and even before the Constituent Assembly elections in November 1917, the Kadet-cossack bloc had been dissolved.[22]

The tenuous nature of the party's earlier alliances with right-wing groups thus made itself felt in the Don region even before the end of 1917. So did the resistance of Miliukov and his supporters during the Provisional Government to social reforms. By December, workers and *inogorodnye* peasants indiscriminately considered Volunteers and cossacks "Kadets," and showed their hostility to both. Trying to organize a national anti-Bolshevik organization, Alekseev and his Kadet colleagues found themselves isolated and attacked from all sides. Cossacks stressed their independence, workers and peasants their allegiance to the socialists. At one point Kaledin even asked Alekseev and the Kadets to leave Novocherkassk.[23]

The reason the Volunteers eventually won "the right to legal existence in the Don," to use Denikin's phrase,[24] was that in mid-November 1917, local Bolsheviks attempted to seize Rostov. Unable to rally his own men, Ataman Kaledin asked Alekseev for assistance. Though few in numbers, the Volunteers were eager to fight, since recapturing Rostov would presumably give them a bigger base for their operations than Novocherkassk, and also smooth relations with the cossacks. Thus there was much jubilation when Alekseev's forces drove the Bolsheviks out. For their part, Miliukov, Stepanov, Fedorov, Trubetskoi, and other liberal politicians with Alekseev felt the time had finally come for a "national crusade."[25]

These developments raised again for Kadets, however, what must be considered two of the most crucial problems of the whole revolutionary period: the relationship between military goals, popular demands, and social reforms; and the connection between political stability and a broad popular social base. It also raised the question of whether civilians or officers would dominate the anti-Bolshevik leadership.

[22] Unpublished memoir of F. I. Rodichev, n.d., in the Columbia Russian Archive, section dealing with October 1917.

[23] V. Vladimirova, *God sluzhby 'sotsialistov' kapitalistam*, Moscow-Leningrad, 1927, pp. 127-30; A. I. Denikin, *Ocherki russkoi smuty*, 5 vols., Paris-Berlin, 1921-25, II, 160.

[24] *Ibid.*, p. 173.   [25] Sokolov, *Pravlenie*, pp. 3-4.

With incurable arrogance, Miliukov and his Kadet supporters in the south felt the Volunteer movement now had to have "national" civilian character; and when they met with Alekseev after his victory in Rostov, they persuaded him to form a "Political Council," thus providing themselves not only with a formal voice in White affairs, but also an opportunity to give political definition in the south to the anti-Bolshevik movement as a whole. The first act of the Council, in fact, was a declaration of purpose, drawn up by Miliukov.

Both the tone and substance of the declaration clearly revealed, however, that insofar as the Kadets in Rostov were concerned about popular support for the Whites, their design was to play on nationalistic and patriotic sentiments, rather than endorse popular programs or social reforms. Whether or not this was a conscious effort to win new adherents to the White cause is unclear. Perhaps, given the extent of social polarization in Russia in the late fall of 1917, Miliukov and his colleagues simply felt their best course was to consolidate and extend their strength among conservative sectors of society; perhaps they thought a nationalistic appeal was precisely the way to attract new recruits more broadly. In any event, what is clear is that the declaration carefully avoided touching local political issues, such as regional autonomy, and gave no hint of any intention to satisfy popular social grievances or otherwise bring reforms. Instead, it stated simply that the Volunteer movement would be "universal," and that "just as 300 years ago," it would "defend Russia's holy relics." Its goal was a "united Russia" under a "free government"; and its watchwords were "law," "order," and "national honor," sentiments which, not surprisingly, drew no special outburst of local enthusiasm.[26] The Petrograd politicians' vision was still fixed on distant abstractions; and the political content of their declaration had clear implications in terms of the defense of social privilege. Workers, *inogorodnye* peasants, rank-and-file cossacks, and even members of the cossack leadership regarded issues such as land reform and regional self-government as vital questions of the moment. To the Kadets, they were matters for the future.

Within the Volunteer ranks themselves, meanwhile, the question of civilian vs. military roles was even more troublesome. General Alekseev himself was willing to work with the Kadets, and welcomed the considerable economic support they could provide. (Paramonov and Zeeler from the Rostov Kadet committee had already organized an "Economic Conference of the Don," and were channeling aid both from local sources and the capitals.)[27] But General Kornilov had little use for politicians, particularly the Kadets. He bitterly resented their weakness at the time of the August uprising, and he now wanted to

[26] Panina Archive, pack. 8, fold. 1.   [27] Sokolov, *Pravlenie*, p. 3.

control affairs himself. He also disliked Alekseev, who had replaced him briefly after his arrest as Kerensky's chief military aide; and his feelings were shared by an influential group of his supporters, particularly Generals Lukomskii and Markov. Miliukov, meanwhile, with his typical hautiness, was willing to "allow" military involvement in civil affairs, but wanted political administration exercised by the Political Council. Kornilov, on the contrary, wanted the movement entirely under army control. At one point, he even threatened to leave the Don entirely, and set up his own anti-Bolshevik army in Siberia.[28]

Such were the shaky foundations of the White armies of South Russia, confused and conflict-ridden in part by the Kadets' own failure to generate solid support even from among their natural allies. On December 18, 1917, issues were joined at a bitter meeting in Novocherkassk. No minutes have survived, but after intense discussion, the Kadets and the generals finally reached a mutually acceptable solution (possibly because all were dependent on the same limited material resources). Miliukov and the Kadets insisted that General Kornilov stay with the Volunteers, on the assumption that his name would attract large numbers of recruits; they also demanded that Alekseev control political affairs. Kornilov was worried about his relations with Moscow circles if he went to Siberia, and respected the liberals' purse strings. Alekseev was willing to yield his military command, provided the movement remained nominally under his control. In the resulting compromise, Kornilov was given military command, Alekseev (and the politicians) made responsible for civil affairs, and Ataman Kaledin brought in to lead the cossacks, with the triumvirate as a whole collectively responsible for major decisions.[29]

But the arrangement satisfied no one. Alekseev's "political kitchen," as Denikin disparagingly called the Political Council, formally became the army's "cabinet," with Miliukov, Trubetskoi, Struve, and Fedorov appointed to official positions along with Generals Denikin, Lukomskii, and Romanovskii.[30] But while Kornilov felt the Council could only "meddle" in army affairs, and resented being "forced" to remain in South Russia "involuntarily," the Council resented Kornilov's lack of trust, and the way he appeared to usurp the anti-Bolshevik movement as his own. Ataman Kaledin, meanwhile, pressed for more local representation. He also agreed with Kerensky's former aide Boris Savinkov, who had also arrived in Novocherkassk to work against the

[28] Denikin, *Ocherki*, II, 187-88; A. S. Lukomskii, *Vospominaniia*, 2 vols., Berlin, 1922, I, 280-84.

[29] *Ibid.*

[30] Denikin, *Ocherki*, II, 189-90. The Council was charged with organizing economic support, ordering relations with foreign and local governments, and preparing the apparatus of political administration as the Army occupied new territory.

Bolsheviks, that moderate socialists should be added to the Council to give it a more representative appearance.[31]

This, however, only made matters worse. Early in January 1918, three relatively unknown local socialists were, in fact, admitted to the Council, along with Boris Savinkov.[32] But this so incensed Kornilov that he considered a "coup d'état"! The matter was resolved only after more angry meetings, and new threats of resignations. And it resulted in the reduction of the Council's status to that of a "purely consultative organ" under the three military leaders.[33]

Even so, Kornilov was soon drafting a new "Political Program" for the Volunteers, without the knowledge of Miliukov or other civilians. Essentially, it corresponded to liberal principles, pledging full civil rights for all citizens without distinction, the end of ad hoc committees and commissars, restrictions against land seizures and other "anarchistic acts," "broad" regional autonomy, and firm adherence to Russia's treaty obligations with the Allies. It also indicated that the Volunteers' authority would pass to a Constituent Assembly when new elections could be freely held.[34] But when Kornilov presented the program to Alekseev, he noted that "sad experience" showed the "complete insolvency of governments created from representatives of the various contemporary political parties";[35] while for their part, Kadets were incensed that the program's publication would be entirely a one-sided act, belieing liberal pretensions that the Volunteers had created an "all-Russian" organization.[36]

About the only issue on which there was still agreement in the Don was that of orienting toward the Germans. Miliukov and his liberal colleagues might still be unable to address themselves to vital questions of social reform, or to construct a popular government, but what they could do—and with the army's wholehearted endorsement—was insist on Russia's "national honor," and the "patriotic" struggle against Germany.[37]

Thus by the early spring of 1918, Kadets and the Volunteer Army

[31] B. Suvorin, *Za rodinoi*, Paris, 1922, pp. 22-23; B. Savinkov, *Bor'ba s bol'shevikami*, Warsaw, 1920, pp. 16-23.

[32] Savinkov, *Bor'ba*, p. 21. The three others were Ageev, Mazurenko, and Vendziagolskii.

[33] Denikin, *Ocherki*, II, 193-94.

[34] Miliukov Archive, bx. 8161, fold. 13. See also Ia. M. Lisovoi ed., *Belyi Arkhiv*, II, 1926-28, pp. 180-82.

[35] *Belyi Arkhiv*, II, 174.

[36] Undated letter (but Feb. 1918) from Miliukov to Alekseev, Miliukov Archive, bx. 8161, fold. 13.

[37] According to the unpublished memoirs of I. A. Poliakov, "General Kornilov," n.d., in the Columbia Russian Archive, it was officially announced that the Bolsheviks were marching toward the Don under German leadership. Thus the German-Bolshevik fight was meshed together.

were identified with each other in the popular mind, despite their serious differences and the markedly different tactics of Kadet leaders here and in the Ukraine: Kiev, cooperation with the Germans and support for an independent Ukrainian government; in the Don, support (but shaky relations) with a staunchly anti-German force, not only opposed to regional regimes, but prone to repeating the mistakes of 1917, and convinced it possessed "all-Russian" competence. The identification could be made because everywhere in South Russia liberal anti-Bolshevism had come to have clear social meaning in terms of countering revolutionary change; and in large measure, the party's tactical diversity was not due to fundamental ideological conflict, as Miliukov's own course was about to show, but because liberals everywhere were desperately grasping for order and an end to popular radicalism.

MILIUKOV SHIFTS GROUND

This was the situation in South Russia in early 1918 when the civil war began to intensify. Local Bolshevik forces, organized with the help of the party's leadership in Moscow but staffed largely with local figures, began moving toward Rostov and closing a ring on the Don. Disaffected from their own leadership, the cossacks offered little armed resistance; and despite the Bolsheviks' brutality, civilians in many places were also indifferent. As Lenin's supporters approached Rostov, Ataman Kaledin found himself so powerless to rally his cossacks that, in desperation, he committed suicide.

Shortly afterward, Alekseev and Kornilov led the Volunteers out of the Don. The Whites were now a motley band with only eight guns and very few shells, short of food and supplies and numbering little more than 3,000 men (most of whom were officers). They presented a striking picture. The weather was bitter cold. The way south crossed several rivers and streams, and the icy waters caused terrible suffering. Toward the middle of April, after a number of bitter running battles, the hardened Volunteer survivors attempted to take Ekaterinodar, capital of the Kuban, but the Bolsheviks held firm. In the course of attack, a stray shell hit the group's headquarters, and Kornilov was instantly killed. Demoralized, the Volunteers beat a retreat back toward the Don, where they finally found relief from pursuit in the sparsely settled border region between the Don and Kuban territories.

Some political figures followed the army on its "Icy March," but Miliukov and the Rostov Kadets remained in the Don, even after the Bolsheviks arrived. As with Kiev, the Reds held on only until the arrival of the Germans in March. But here, too, Bolshevik control made Kadets want to welcome foreign occupation. With German patrols on the streets, order was reestablished. The Bolsheviks fled, and along with other liberals, Miliukov emerged from hiding, no longer fearing for his safety.[38]

Before the Germans arrived, the Kadet leader had planned to return to Moscow. Disillusioned with the leadership of the Volunteers, he felt cut off from constructive activity. Many of the new arrivals in South Russia seemed far more hostile to politicians like himself than even Lukomskii or Kornilov; and in Miliukov's view, they were hardly capable of national responsibility. The Kadet leader now thought new efforts against Lenin might have to be launched from the capital.[39]

But when the Germans entered Rostov and established a working relationship with the new cossack Ataman, General Krasnov, Miliukov had second thoughts. Just as in Kiev, the very fact that the Germans could restore civil order raised the question of using their troops against Lenin. For Miliukov, however, in contrast to his colleagues in the Ukraine, the possibility of "reorienting" toward the Germans raised serious personal problems. As the acknowledged leader of a party basing much of its revolutionary politics on upholding Russia's foreign commitments; as a former foreign minister whose obstinacy on the question of the war had splintered the first provisional cabinet; and as a Central Committee spokesman whose tenacity on this and other issues had virtually split the party in October, when many felt compromise was necessary, Miliukov felt painfully aware that he himself was responsible for much anti-German sentiment.[40]

Nevertheless, the arrival of the Germans changed his mind. Despite the past, Miliukov now saw something "positive," as he expressed it, in what was happening in Kiev and Rostov.[41] He realized that autonomous governments, set up in different regions liberated from the Bolsheviks and capable of maintaining order, might well become "steppingstones" for the liberation of the country as a whole. Anti-Bolsheviks in Moscow were still too weak to defeat Lenin on their own; and with its feuding leadership and lack of respect for political figures, the Volunteer Army also offered little promise.[42]

Miliukov now felt as well that the Central Powers would win the war. The Allies were unsure of themselves, and had also lost the opportunity for a crucial second front by not attacking the Bolsheviks.

[38] Miliukov to Alekseev, May 3/16, 1918. This and subsequent Miliukov-Alekseev correspondence is in the Miliukov Archive, bx. 8161, fold. 13.

[39] *Ibid.*

[40] Miliukov to the National Center, May 25/June 7, 1918, in the M. M. Vinaver Papers, Yivo Institute for Jewish Research, New York.

[41] *Ibid.*   [42] *Ibid.*

The Germans, obviously, were not sympathetic toward Russian "national interests." They wanted bread and supplies, and whatever else they could easily extract. But in Miliukov's view, the Germans also recognized the dangers posed by the Bolsheviks. Thus they might be persuaded to do for Russia as a whole what they had done for the Ukraine: establish and support on a "businesslike" basis a government of Kadets.[43]

Here as before, Miliukov's outlook was quintessentially statist. Having just emerged from three weeks' hiding in Rostov, his interest still focused on preserving the values and structure of the European nation-state system, of which old Russia was a part, and which the Bolsheviks now threatened. Russia's war aims were no less valid now than in 1917, but conflict between the Central Powers, Russia, and the Allies could be seen as a struggle between competitive equals. What the Bolsheviks represented was an entirely new order, corrosive not only to liberal values and social interests, but to the whole European system of national development. And as Miliukov expressed it in May 1918, the "law of national self-preservation" stood higher than any "moral commitments" to former allies.[44]

In the middle of May, therefore, Miliukov wrote confidentially to General Alekseev in the hope he might "transform the Volunteer Army to the service of this task." He himself would go to Kiev, and further "explore" the situation.[45] Before receiving a reply, he learned from N. Lvov that the general would shortly be in Novocherkassk; and after securing an expression of support from Paramonov and other Rostov Kadets, he set out to meet the Volunteer leader personally. Due to some confusion, however, the meeting never took place; and shortly afterward, after meeting himself with Ataman Krasnov and urging restraint in the question of Don "independence," Miliukov set out for Kiev.[46]

This last mix-up soon caused new trouble. Alekseev not only felt it hopeless to try to "reorient" the Volunteers, but now worried about bitterness developing toward Kadets as a consequence of Miliukov's new "desertion."[47] Undaunted, the Kadet leader asked him by letter to attack the army's mood in a "logical" fashion. Traditional concepts of "treason" and "desertion" were no longer applicable in Russia. The Volunteers would have to understand that there were no longer any axioms in politics or international relations. The only inviolable principle was the good of the nation. His and the Kadet task generally was nothing less than the "resurrection" of the Russian state.[48]

---

43 *Ibid.* Miliukov wrote in a similar vein to General Alekseev on May 3/16.
44 *Ibid.*   45 Letter of May 3/16, 1918.
46 Miliukov to Alekseev, May 10/23, 1918.
47 Alekseev to Miliukov, May 10/23 and May 12/25.
48 Miliukov to Alekseev, undated but May 20/June 2, 1918.

NEGOTIATING WITH THE GERMANS

With this pretentious baggage, Miliukov arrived in Kiev at the end of May 1918, and immediately began discussions with local Kadet party leaders. His first concern was that his colleagues were yielding too much to Ukrainian independence. If his own plans were to be effective, the Germans would have to believe that all responsible Ukrainian public figures supported the concept of a single Russian state. To press his position, he asked the Kadet ministers to meet with the Germans and, if possible, to prepare the ground for him to present his own viewpoints.[49]

On the German side there were differences of opinion about negotiating with Kadets, particularly Miliukov. Baron Riezler, the German legate in Moscow, was insisting to the Foreign Office that the Bolsheviks might collapse, and that Germany should "dip as deeply as possible into the ranks of the Kadets" in preparing the way for a new, friendly government.[50] This view was shared by a number of high-ranking military figures, and particularly by General Groener, Chief of Staff of Army Group Eichhorn in Kiev, and his assistant, Major Hasse, chief of German Military Intelligence in the Ukraine, who detested all that the Bolsheviks represented despite the obvious political benefits to Germany of the Brest-Litovsk treaty.[51] But the Foreign Office in Berlin was committed to the idea of Ukrainian separatism, "a kind of Bavaria," as the Ukraine's proposed relationship to Germany was described, and anxious to prevent the restoration of old Russian borders, even if Germany lost the war in the west. Thus while Ludendorff and other General Staff officers encouraged their subordinates in Kiev to maintain contact with various anti-Bolshevik groups, including the Kadets, the Foreign Office and its Ukrainian representative, Baron Mumm, discouraged such associations, devoting their energies instead toward building the authority of Hetman Skoropadskii.[52]

On June 3/16, General Eichhorn, General Groener, and Major Hasse met with Vasilenko, Rzhepetskii, Gutnik, and Kistiakovskii, the four most prominent Kadets in the Hetman's regime. Most of the session was given to a general analysis by the Germans of their own circumstances. Hasse told the Kadets that Berlin was disturbed by the idea of a permanent Bolshevik state on her eastern border, and was explor-

[49] P. Miliukov, "Dnevnik," unpubl. diary in the Columbia Russian Archive, pp. 1-7. Pagination follows the typed version of the MS. See also Miliukov's *Rossia na perelome*, 2 vols., Paris, 1927, II, 64-73.

[50] Riezler to Berlin, May 22/June 4, in Z.A.B. Zeman, ed., *Germany and the Revolution in Russia*, London, 1958, p. 131.

[51] Baumgart, pp. 138-39; Groener, pp. 100-103.

[52] E. von Ludendorff, *My War Memories, 1914-1918*, 2 vols., London, 1919, II, 624-26; Baumgart, pp. 138-39; Groener, pp. 101-03.

ing alternative possibilities. In his view the Foreign Ministry had not entirely ruled out the idea of a unified Russia, although "current thinking" had the Ukraine retaining a special status, and the rest of Russia joined economically to a greater German Empire. It was important, moreover, for the Germans to know whether Kadets would support the monarchy. "We can have business," Hasse reported, only with monarchist parties."[53]

While little in the German outlook bothered the liberal Ukrainians, Miliukov reacted in a sharply different vein. Interestingly enough, it was not the question of monarchism which disturbed him, but the idea of Ukrainian separatism. The idea of restoring tsarevich Aleksei, with Grand Duke Michael as Regent, seemed a definite possibility, perhaps even the best means to rouse support from the peasants. The Balkanization of Russia was not. And under no conditions, Miliukov told Vasilenko, could the Kadets agree to any form of "union" with Germany. The best they could offer was "benevolent neutrality."[54] To protests from his Ukrainian colleagues that the Kadets were hardly in a position to force their own terms, Miliukov insisted their position was not as unfavorable as it might appear. Assuming the Germans were as troubled as Kadets by the Bolshevik "menace," Kadets were "the last political party with whom they might negotiate."[55]

As so often in 1917, Miliukov was assuming more than was warranted about his and the Kadets' political prospects, with scant respect for broad, popular social feeling. There was no indication whatsoever that ordinary Russians would support the monarchy, or that some new "False Dmitri" was lurking in the wings who could rally the peasants. Nor was there much to support the contention that "the last political party with whom the Germans might negotiate" could themselves find massive popular backing, surely a requisite to political or social stabilization. Still, when Miliukov himself met Hasse a short time later, his tone was equally tough. "My first and foremost aim" he insisted, "is the unification of Russia. . . . We want nothing like your Bundesrat, with its legalistic unification of nationalities."[56]

Miliukov's attitude took Hasse by surprise. After establishing that the former foreign minister was not opposed to certain "priority" relationships between Germany and the Ukraine, providing these were "as few as possible," the German turned to the "Allied orientation" of

[53] Miliukov, "Dnevnik," pp. 9-11. For the German side of this and subsequent negotiations with Miliukov and the Kadets in Kiev, see Ambassador Mumm's reports in the German Foreign Office Archive (GFOA), microfilm reels 52, 144, and 147. In a message to Berlin on July 26, 1918, Mumm stressed the monarchic orientation of the Kadets. See telegram No. 1354, GFOA, reel 144.
[54] *Ibid.*, p. 11.   [55] *Ibid.*
[56] *Ibid.* pp. 16-17.

the Kadet Central Committee in Moscow. Miliukov again responded as if the cards he held were good ones. Of course, he intimated, the formation of a second front by means of Allied landings in Siberia was a definite possibility. The Kadets could not alter their former associations all at once. But the party was prepared to deal with accomplished facts. If Russia was unified and the Bolsheviks eliminated, it would not be difficult to profess "neutrality" and eliminate the possibility of a new second front. And how, Hasse inquired, did Miliukov propose to accomplish unification? Certainly not with foreign arms, was the reply. It was imperative that Moscow be liberated by Russians alone, for only in this way could national support be generated for a new regime. But German assistance was also needed. If the Central Powers guaranteed the western frontier of the Moscow *oblast'* while at the same time supplying the Volunteer Army with weapons and matériel, the Bolsheviks would be hemmed in and the Whites could finish the task themselves. When Hasse suggested the Volunteers were not only too weak for such an effort, but also bitterly anti-German, Miliukov demurred. It is true, he said, that there are strong feelings against the Central Powers. "But I have reason to think on the basis of my conversations with Alekseev that he is not averse to considering the necessity of dealing pragmatically with objective facts."[57]

Miliukov was again in his own private world. The best he could honestly say about the Volunteer Army was that some younger officers might possibly support his position. The leadership was stoutly opposed, as were almost all line officers. General Lukomskii himself reported this to Kadets during a visit to Kiev at this time; and Miliukov soon received personal confirmation in a letter from Alekseev.[58] But Hasse did not know this, and Miliukov pressed his advantage. Insisting the Brest pact be revised, the Kadet leader went so far as to suggest the Germans admit they had erred![59]

The meeting concluded on a friendly basis. Hasse noted that he considered their conversation "purely personal," but would transmit Miliukov's ideas to higher authorities. Asked if he would be willing to meet with others, the Kadet leader readily agreed. "It is my duty to Russia!" he responded.[60]

Miliukov's Germanophilism was now "official"—a calculated effort, Astrov later described it, "to seek a base of support and real power in

[57] *Ibid.*, pp. 17-20.
[58] Lukomskii, *Vospominaniia*, II, 64-67; Alekseev to Miliukov, Jun. 5/18, 1918.
[59] Miliukov, "Dnevnik," p. 20.
[60] *Ibid.*, p. 25; Mumm to the Foreign Office, telegram 1055, June 22, 1918, GFOA, reel 147.

the midst of chaos and disorder, to resurrect the fallen Russian state."[61] As a political tactic, however, it was based on several serious misconceptions: that the Germans were capable of winning the war; that the rag-tag forces of Bolshevik opposition were capable of overcoming their internal differences; that they knew how to translate military success into political and social stability if victory was achieved; and even that other Kadets would themselves fall into line. What impressed Miliukov most was the orderliness of everyday existence in areas under German control. That he could develop this into a full-blown political strategy only suggested his lack of attention, for the time being, at least, for the basic social forces of revolutionary change. Such had the chaos in Russia affected even the party's most experienced politician.

Miliukov's least tenable assumption was about the Kadets themselves. At precisely the moment he was orienting toward the Germans, the Central Committee in Moscow was emphatically declaring its allegiance to the Allies, and dispatching emissaries to coordinate party activities elsewhere in Russia. On the very day of his meeting with Hasse, in fact, Maxim Vinaver arrived in Kiev from the capital, bringing the conflict to him face to face.

Vinaver was shocked at Miliukov's position. His Moscow colleagues had sent him to deal with "renegade Ukrainians"; he hardly expected his close friend and colleague to be standing in their lead. On the night of June 9/22, the two Kadet leaders talked the problem through. Miliukov's arguments were the same as he had used to Alekseev: an obligation to Russia stood above all; the Allies had now proved completely indifferent to Russia's future; even if France and Britain did win in Europe, they would hardly be inclined to protect Russian interests, considering their own reconstruction difficulties.[62] The Germans, on the other hand, had a healthy respect for the dangers of radicalism. If they could be persuaded to recognize Russia's territorial integrity and vital interests, they could be useful. For his part, Miliukov further insisted (once again dusting off his favorite political weapon), he would rather resign from the Kadet party entirely than change his mind.[63]

Against this combination of self-pity, indignation, and *realpolitik*, Vinaver could do very little. The majority of Kievans agreed with

---

[61] N. I. Astrov, "Grazhdanskaia voina (vospominaniia)," unpubl. MS in the Panina Archive, n.d., pack. 3, suppl. 3, p. 23.

[62] "Zapiski M. M. Vinavera o svoei poezdke v Kiev letom 1918," n.d., in the M. M. Vinaver Papers, pp. 1-3.

[63] *Ibid.*, pp. 4-10. Miliukov later repeated his arguments in a long letter to the Moscow Central Committee, included in the "Dnevnik," pp. 262a-262z.

Miliukov, insisting their arguments were also based on a "realistic evaluation of the present circumstances."[64] A few days later Vinaver left Kiev, disappointed and deeply concerned about the Kadets' and Russia's future.

Meanwhile, having received what he felt was a vote of confidence from his Ukrainian colleagues, Miliukov proceeded with his German contacts. On June 14/27 he talked with Baron Mumm, the German Ambassador to Kiev; on June 28/July 11 he met again with Hasse. Now, however, he found the Germans considerably more distant. The Foreign Office in Berlin had been shocked to learn that Miliukov himself—the sworn enemy of Ukrainian separatists and bitter foe of the Triple Alliance—was under German protection in Kiev, and expressed grave fears to Mumm and Hasse that he would form a center of Great Russian agitation.[65] The Germans now were also much more concerned about the renewal of military action on the Eastern front, largely because a considerable force of Czech soldiers, moving across Siberia with the intention of being evacuated in Vladivostok and joining the Allies in France, had seized a number of critical junctions on the Trans-Siberian railroad. As a consequence, Berlin was more determined than ever to strengthen Ukrainian-German relations and keep the Bolsheviks as a buffer against the Allies.[66]

Thus, when Miliukov again raised the question of a unified Russia, Mumm's reply was a curt "That is difficult!"[67] Hasse went even further, stating that the Germans were no longer interested even in discussing a revision of the Brest treaty. Apparently, even chaos now seemed better than Russian unification.[68]

CONFLICTS CONTINUE: UKRAINIAN KADETS COOPERATE
WITH THE GERMANS; KADETS IN THE KUBAN REASSERT THEIR
ROLE IN THE VOLUNTEER ARMY

Thus Miliukov's "German policy" collapsed. Its results included the further isolation of Ukrainian Kadets and the aggravation of party relations with the Volunteers, but little more. Hearing the news in Moscow, Kadet leaders there were "shocked" and "stupefied."[69] *Nash Vek* went so far as to deny that Miliukov and Vinaver were even in Kiev, or that the party leaders had had any "official" contacts with the

[64] Miliukov, "Dnevnik," pp. 30-33.

[65] Baumgart, p. 139. See also Mumm's telegrams to the Foreign Office, No. 1091, June 27, 1918, and No. 1156, July 3, 1918, GFOA, reel 147.

[66] *Ibid.*, pp. 60-92.   [67] Miliukov, "Dnevnik," p. 38.

[68] *Ibid.*, pp. 39-41.

[69] Panina to Vinaver, June 28/July 11, 1918, in the Vinaver Papers.

Germans whatsoever.[70] When Dolgorukov subsequently arrived in Kiev, tensions were such that Miliukov resigned as Central Committee chairman.[71]

Throughout the summer of 1918, however, despite the increasing harshness of German occupation, Kadets continued to work for Skoropadskii. Outside the Ukraine, Russians were experiencing increasing shortages of food. In May, Lenin had organized a Central Food Commissariat with dictatorial powers over supply and distribution; in June, Committees of the Poor, *Kombedy*, began seizing grain. These drastic measures very much aggravated rural conditions, resulting not only in an increase in agrarian disorders, but a growing wave of hostility against the Bolsheviks. In turn this hostility was soon translated into acts of incredible barbarism, committed on all sides. But food shortages still increased, and as the situation deteriorated, fears grew about the possibility of massive famine. Bolshevik troops, meanwhile, concentrated most of their forces around Moscow and Petrograd. Some units still operated in the Don and Kuban regions, but fronts were irregular, and for the moment, all sides worried more about food than territory—the food which Ukrainian Kadets were diligently helping Germans ship off to Berlin.

By August, however, the problem of food shortages had also begun affecting the Ukraine; and as new directives on land cultivation issued from the German command, peasants here also began to take up arms. Soon a new system of military courts-martial was in effect, laying down the most severe penalties for even minor infractions. Little of this affected Kiev, which still remained something of a bourgeois oasis; but it turned the countryside into shambles, and generated the deepest animosities for Kadets and the Hetman alike. By September 1918, the liberals' regime was little more than a "ministry of public order."[72] The full-time task of its press department, by its director's own admission, was propagandizing to improve Skoropadskii's image.[73]

The civilian overseer of all this—at least indirectly—was the Kadet "state secretary" (and then minister of internal affairs), Igor Kistiakovskii. The 42-year-old liberal had formerly enjoyed wide popularity both in Kiev and Moscow, where he served on the law faculties of

[70] *Nash Vek*, No. 106 (130), July 2, 1918.

[71] P. Dolgorukov, *Velikaia razrukha*, Madrid, 1964, p. 119. On July 7/20, 1918, Astrov telegraphed to Maklakov in Paris that Miliukov's German orientation had engendered opposition "of the most energetic sort" from the Central Committee. The telegram is in the Archives of the Russian Embassy in Paris, Hoover Institution, fold. 2.

[72] Mogilianskii, "Tragediia," pp. 128-30.

[73] A. Maliarevskii, "Na pereekzamenovke—P. P. Skoropadskii i ego vremia." *Arkhiv Grazhdanskoi Voiny*, II, 192?, pp. 118-20.

both city's universities, and developed a broad civil practice. Now even some former associates thought him shockingly unprincipled. German arms and his energy—"evil genius," according to one observer—kept the Hetman in power.[74]

Kistiakovskii's principal Kadet assistants, Nicholas Vasilenko, S. M. Gutnik, and A. K. Rzhepetskii, also earned widespread scorn, but not from the Germans. Late in the summer, Berlin awarded Gutnik and Rzhepetskii the Kronenorden First Class for exceptional service.[75] What observers even to the right of Kadets could not understand was how these liberals could follow policies so obviously designed to further Ukrainian independence. Acquiescing in German rule was comprehensible in terms of law and order; working for Skoropadskii seemed a violation of all basic party traditions.[76]

Much of the answer lay in the same logic which would later help explain Kadet roles with Denikin and Admiral Kolchak: the belief that it was the Kadets' own "rightful" responsibility to try to "control" events; the conviction that events could only be controlled from *within* administrative circles, however harsh the regime; and the insistence that political stability had to precede "legitimate" social reform. But Kadet "control" of events in the Ukraine bore little direct relation to the overall anti-Bolshevik cause, and even less to the aspirations of most Ukrainians themselves. With the possible exception of Kistiakovskii and Vasilenko, Skoropadskii's Kadet ministers did not even fully support Ukrainian independence; they had joined the regime in part to "take the Ukrainian movement into their own hands."[77] Moreover, their desire to "control" events stemmed not from a realization of the need to develop a solid social base for the Whites or to coordinate the anti-Bolshevik movement as a whole, but to protect their own local interests and to remain in the forefront of events if Bolshevik rule collapsed. Many, in fact, still retained an irrepressible conviction that Russia would eventually evolve in a liberal direction, and that their party as a whole would again head a national government; whether Volunteers of Germans marched on Moscow, or Lenin's regime fell of its own weight, the Bolsheviks simply could not remain permanently in power. Some also felt with Miliukov that in all likelihood the peasants would again turn to the tsar. Postwar Russia would

74 Gol'denveizer, "Iz kievskikh," pp. 223-24.

75 *Die Deutsche Okkupation der Ukraine—Geheimdokumente*, Strassburg, 1937, pp. 118-19. See also Mumm's report to Berlin, No. 160, July 1, 1918, GFOA reel 52.

76 Doroshenko, *Istoriia*, II, 115-20; Dolenga, *Skoropadshchyna*, pp. 41-58; V. Vinnichenko, *Vidrodzhennia natsii*, 3 vols., Kiev-Vienna, 1920, III, 61-121. At their own party conference in May, the Socialist-Federalists prohibited their members from cooperating with the Kadets or joining the Hetman's regime. See C. Dubreuil, *Deux années en Ukraine, 1917-1919*, Paris, 1919, p. 36.

77 Miliukov, "Dnevnik," p. 133.

thus finally become the constitutional monarchy of the party's initial conception. With Nationalists and Octobrists discredited as a result of their attitudes toward the revolution, and socialists blamed for the failures of 1917, Kadets would emerge as the only remaining statesmen with both the ability and support to head an all-Russian government or federation.

It was this outlook, in any case, which moved Kadets in Kiev, and prompted Miliukov later in the summer to begin planning a new monarchic constitution.[78] It also pressed other members of the party in June and July to try to reestablish a role for themselves with the Volunteer Army. In the Don and Kuban regions, however, the distinguishing attitude of influential liberals was not allegiance with separatists, but the continued absence of any clear regard for popular local interests. The situation in the Kuban had begun to change in July. Just a few weeks earlier, Alekseev had written to Miliukov that the Volunteers would probably disband if large amounts of money and supplies were not received quickly.[79] Shortly afterward, however, a decision was made to turn again toward Ekaterinodar, the Kuban capital, where the army this time found considerable support. Bolshevik rule in the region had proved exceedingly harsh. Often Red commanders shot cossacks and other suspected Whites on the spot, even regarding tsarist army boots as "proof" of complicity with the Volunteers. The Whites benefited accordingly. Morale improved, recruitment increased, and Denikin's troops even got some assistance from local villages. By the middle of August, the Kuban capital was finally secure.

As the Whites entered the city, however, the reception they received indicated a complicated crosscurrent of local political feeling. From refugees and the local bourgeoisie (including the Kadet committee) there were flowers, and a feeling of profound relief. This group was "deeply grateful" for its liberation.[80] But like their counterparts in the Don, the Kuban cossacks and Ataman Filimonov were now themselves quite wary of the degree to which Alekseev and Denikin would usurp their own authority; and left-leaning *inogorodnye* went so far as to raise banners of protest.[81]

Earlier in March, an agreement had been reached between the

---

[78] Miliukov to the Right Center in Moscow, July 29/Aug. 11, 1918, in *Volia Rossii*, III, Nos. 18-19, 1924, pp. 206-10. See a discussion of the letter by E. Stalinskii, "Patriotizm i liberalizm v belom dvizhenii," *Volia Rossii*, III, Nos. 8-9, 1924, pp. 140-58.

[79] Alekseev to Miliukov, May 10/23, 1918.

[80] M. P. Vatasi, "The White Movement, 1917-1920: Memoirs," MS in the Hoover Institution, n.d., p. 53.

[81] *Ibid.*, p. 54.

Volunteers, Ataman Filimonov, and L. L. Bych, the president (premier) of the Kuban Regional Government, which provided for cossack troops to submit to Volunteer military command while retaining their separate organizational status and a large degree of administrative autonomy. But the Kuban Rada (parliament), which generally reflected the views of the non-cossack population and which was separate from both the military leadership of the cossacks and Bych's civilian cabinet, indicated its own intention to continue meeting independently.[82] The direction its leadership would follow remained unclear, as did the question of how the various Kuban leadership groups and even the cossack and Volunteer military commands would work together. Ataman Filimonov, for example, considered all revolutionary attitudes to be treasonous, was bitterly anti-*inogorodnye*, and suspected the loyalties of the Rada. But he also resented General Denikin, who by now had become the actual head of the Volunteers.[83] Both Bych and the Rada leadership, meanwhile, leaned to the left, indicating their support for the basic social and political gains of the revolution and their intention to press for further reforms. To them, both cossack and Russian military leaders raised the threat of reaction.[84] The Volunteers, finally, hardened veterans of the Icy March, regarded almost any local interests with disdain. There was even some resentment at having to reach for shelter in an out-of-the-way provincial town like Ekaterinodar.[85]

In August 1918 the task of straightening all this out was assigned by the Volunteer command to V. A. Stepanov and K. N. Sokolov, the two most prominent Kadets still with the army. Both men had close ties with the anti-Bolshevik organizations in Moscow, and as Kadet Central Committee members, both were also thought capable of imparting additional national stature to Denikin's forces. Moreover, the Kadets themselves had an active party committee in Ekaterinodar, led by I. S. Khlebnikov, N. M. Kaplin, and the former Provisional Government commissar, K. L. Bardizh, an old-line cossack. The Volunteer command consequently hoped that Stepanov and Sokolov could use their party authority to help create local political stability.[86]

Thus the Kadets found themselves with a good opportunity to demonstrate their value to the White movement as Russia's leading anti-Bolshevik party. Their task was to create a local political base so that the Volunteers could begin moving north, while also assuring a suf-

---

[82] Filimonov, "Kubantsy," p. 99. [83] *Ibid.*, pp. 65-75.

[84] Raenko, *Khronika*, pp. 26-37; A. P. Filimonov, "Razgrom kubanskoi rady," *ARR*, v, 1922, p. 324; Denikin, *Ocherki*, III, 205ff.

[85] Lukomskii, II, 178-80.

[86] Denikin, *Ocherki*, III, 266; Sokolov, *Pravlenie*, p. 29.

ficient degree of regional popularity so that the movement as a whole could sustain its national pretensions. In the stifling heat of the Kuban summer, however, the consequences of past political diversity within the Kadet movement soon became apparent. The two Central Committee members, Stepanov and Sokolov, were both men of strong conservative biases, who had firmly resisted the efforts of Kishkin, Astrov, and others to lead the party in a conciliationist direction of 1917. (Stepanov in particular had urged the Provisional Government to "renounce" socialism during his tenure as acting minister of trade and industry, as we have seen, in order to consolidate its position among industrial and manufacturing groups; and Sokolov had been an outspoken supporter throughout 1917 of firm social discipline and the extension of state authority.) Both also reflected the past orientation of Petrograd Kadets in general toward "high politics," and were anxious to reinforce the Volunteers' claim to national competence, which implied Denikin's "legitimate right" to control Kuban affairs. They differed only on whether a mixed military-civilian triumvirate (Stepanov's choice) would be preferable to a one-man military dictatorship (Sokolov's preference).

The party's Kuban committee, on the other hand, was deeply interested in local conditions and the possibility of further social reforms, more so, in fact, than in abstract questions of national competence. In meeting with the Central Committee members, Khlebnikov, Kaplin, and their colleagues stressed for their part the correlation between popular support and political stability, arguing the need for Whites to build a firm, popular, social base. And while Stepanov and Sokolov wanted regional politics subordinated absolutely to the army, the Ekaterinodar Kadets insisted that the Volunteers help create a viable parliamentary democracy in the Kuban region as an indication that they represented progressive liberal tendencies. In fact, the Kuban Kadets were already at work on a provisional constitution for an autonomous Kuban government.[87]

Eventually, and with great reluctance, the local Kadets accepted a compromise with Sokolov and Stepanov, and helped draft a "Statute for the Administration of Territories Occupied by the Volunteer Army." This provided that all "occupied" local areas be subordinated to direct military control, but established a special set of provisions for the Kuban and Northern Caucasus which left the Rada free to set its own social policies and write its own constitution. This hardly solved local problems, however. Filimonov and the Rada both balked at accepting the statute, as indeed the Kuban Kadets had warned

[87] Sokolov, *Pravlenie*, pp. 28-30.

they would; and the Volunteers had to establish themselves as Russia's national government as if they were occupying enemy territory. Unwittingly, Kadets thus extended rather than mollified basic political difficulties.

In the beginning of September, meanwhile, the Petrograd Kadets also helped lay down the rudiments of a new Special Council for the Volunteers, based on an earlier draft proposal by the well-known conservative nationalist V. V. Shulgin. The new arrangement "officially" gave the army command dictatorial authority. While the Council was to be responsible for guidance in all civil affairs, and staffed largely by civilians, it would only prepare and discuss legislation, not enact laws.[88] There was little doubt, therefore, that the army leadership would retain supremacy even in nonmilitary matters, and that the Special Council, in part, was a means of institutionalizing a bias against independent politics. For Stepanov, Sokolov, and the army's Kadet supporters, however, the importance of the new structure was not that it implied the eclipse of political figures like themselves, but that it clearly staked out a national competence. It was this, moreover, that also impressed Moscow and Petrograd Kadets as they began arriving in South Russia at the beginning of September.[89]

KADET PRETENSIONS AND THE NEED FOR PARTY UNITY

From the perspective of more than fifty years of Soviet development, one might find it hard to comprehend the new assurance of liberals in the summer of 1918 that Bolshevik power would be short-lived. Yet as Astrov, Dolgorukov, and others set out from Moscow to implement National Center policies, it was this conviction that gave them a sense of urgency. For them, there was nothing irrelevant about the questions of liberal policy, or the need for party unity. Constitutional Democracy was to become the "fabric of statesmanship" from which a new Russia would be tailored.[90]

This very assurance also made the Moscow Kadets more and more concerned about the problems of postwar politics, and again raised the question of whether they could best preserve their national role by staying relatively free from the army leadership (and thus the inevitable abuses of civil war), or operating within the chain of command, as the Ukrainian Kadets were doing in Kiev. The Kornilov episode still left moderate Kadet leaders like Astrov and Vinaver wary

[88] Ibid., pp. 40-41; Denikin, Ocherki, III, 264. Shulgin discusses his own role in the organization of the Special Council in Kievlianin, No. 2, Aug. 22, 1919.
[89] Denikin, Ocherki, III, 261; Astrov, "Grazhdanskaia voina," pp. 16-17.
[90] Astrov, "Grazhdanskaia voina," p. 16.

about over-identifying their party with the generals, despite the Central Committee's support for military dictatorship. Lukomskii, Pokrovskii, and other White leaders were clearly not liberals. On the other hand, Denikin and Romanovskii considered themselves supporters of the February revolution, while Kadets still felt themselves most competent as state administrators, despite their experiences in 1917. Remaining aloof from the Volunteer command might thus deny the army badly needed talent.

There were also the continuing problems of how to respond to pressures for reform, and what relations were to be with socialist groups. There was little question that military needs were paramount for the moment, but the Moscow Kadets seemed to recognize more than their South Russia colleagues that other matters would both affect the outcome of the war and determine its aftermath. Kadets in the north had dwelt on these questions abstractly for a number of months—and "resolved" them at their conferences. They were, in fact, the problems which had always defined the dilemmas of Russian liberal politics. Now they took on new importance as Vinaver, Krol, and others set out from Moscow to deal with new practical situations.

A lion's share of responsibility fell on the 49-year-old Moscow attorney, Nicholas Astrov, one of the few liberals who still kept good relations with moderate socialists. Astrov's task was not only to terminate the German orientation of Kadets in Kiev, but to persuade Volunteer leaders to join an anti-Bolshevik "national" government supposedly forming east of the Volga. He was also to secure support for a series of policy proposals that the National Center had worked out as a basis for a new, all-Russian provisional regime.[91]

He had his work cut out. When he went first to Kiev in the middle of September 1918, the city was already sliding into the uncertain panic and confusion which inevitably forecasts the changing fortunes of war. It was now quite clear that Germany was being defeated in the west; and what would happen when the neatly uniformed troops left Kiev was anyone's guess. Already sidewalks were filled with émigrés and speculators, people bent on saving themselves and their fortunes, with little thought for tomorrow and even less for anything liberals' might call "Russia." These, at least, were Astrov's impressions when he arrived in the early fall of 1917, and they underlay his amazement when he found Miliukov and the Kievan Kadets still hoping for German assistance.[92]

Like Vinaver and Dolgorukov before him, moreover, Astrov soon found his arguments to no avail. The best he could get from the

[91] *Ibid.*, pp. 7, 14.   [92] *Ibid.*, p. 25.

328—Part III. The Civil War

Kievan Kadets was a pledge to remain "neutral" in the event German military fortunes further turned for the worse.[93] Miliukov also continued to press his monarchism, arguing against the National Center-Union of Regeneration idea of a directorate.[94] And much to Astrov's regret, these views were now supported by a new organization of former Duma members, calling themselves the State Council for National Unification (later the Council for the State Unification of Russia—SGOR). The leaders of this group, including Miliukov, were even more pro-German than the Kievan Kadet committee. They presumed a resurrected monarchy would grant them governing powers, much as they had expected to become a "ministry of confidence" in the days of the Progressive Bloc.[95]

When he moved on to the Crimea, however, Astrov found the views of other leading Kadets very close to those of the party in Moscow. The Kadet center here was the villa of the aging party venerable Ivan Petrunkevich, a place of lush quietude and splendid scenery, well isolated from most Russian turmoils. There were some reservations from Vinaver, Teslenko, and Nabokov about overidentifying the Kadets with Denikin, but general enthusiasm about the idea of merging the Volunteers with the anti-Bolsheviks in Siberia. This was not far from Astrov's own perspective; the Kadet task, he now believed, was to "organize Russian social forces, crystallize our ideas, provide specific formulas, and translate them into definite organs of government capable of speaking in Russia's name."[96] Together, Astrov and his Crimean colleagues determined to reserve a leading role for the party by convening a regional conference in Ekaterinodar, and officially uniting all Kadets behind these goals.[97]

When Astrov finally arrived in the Kuban capital, he found it a bustling counterrevolutionary military center. The Volunteers were now in full control. Officers wore epaulettes, enlisted men saluted smartly. Newspapers published in the old orthography, carrying dates of the old calendar. "Look! Look!" Stepanov greeted Astrov as he stepped off the train. "There are our gendarmes, yes, indeed, our old, prerevolutionary gendarmes!"[98]

In these surroundings, Astrov's first task was to sound out Denikin on moving toward the Volga. The White leader may well have been unwilling to move east in any case, having just established his base in the Kuban and his own authority in the anti-Bolshevik movement.

[93] Miliukov, "Dnevnik," pp. 150-51.   [94] *Ibid.*, pp. 157-59.
[95] Reports of the Volunteer Army's "Azbuka" agent in Kiev, Sept. 20, 22, and 25, 1918 (o.s.), in the Wrangel Military Archive, file 141.
[96] Astrov, "Grazhdanskaia voina," p. 29.   [97] *Ibid.*, p. 35.
[98] *Ibid.*, p. 36.

But he now also had recent information which made the deployment a virtual impossibility. Astrov assumed a coalition government was being organized in Siberia as both the National Center and Union of Regeneration had determined: a three-man directorate (one of whose members would be the head of the Volunteer Army) which supported the principle of firm military authority and rejected the first Constituent Assembly as a competent governing organ. But Denikin produced a stenographic account of a conference just held at Ufa. It showed the organization of a government of five men rather than three (thus greatly weakening the principle of firm military government); and subordination to the old Constituent Assembly. The SRs were clearly in control. For Denikin and his fellow officers, this meant a replay of all they detested in 1917. Astrov's arguments thus collapsed, and with them, for the time being, at least, the scheme of the Moscow centers for unifying the anti-Bolshevik movement.[99]

The question remained, however, what exactly the Kadets' own posture would be as a party toward the anti-Bolsheviks in South Russia. The issue still seemed of enormous importance. Those most likely to lead a postwar Russia could now set out their own explicit program, asking the army to pledge its adherence and using whatever leverage they still possessed to direct its politics; or they could subordinate themselves to military control, as the Central Committee had suggested in Moscow, sharing onus and responsibility alike for whatever the generals decreed. It was also possible, finally, for Kadets to abstain from involving themselves altogether, staying out of harm's way until the war was over. On October 15/28, consequently, when the Kadets convened their conference in Ekaterinodar to resolve these issues, there was great interest and excitement on all sides. Everyone waited to see what the party would do.[100]

About one tactic there was now no longer any question: Germany was about to lose the war, and would be of no use to the anti-Bolshevik cause. But this in itself did little to bring Kadets together. For one thing, Skoropadskii still ruled in Kiev, and Kievan Kadets continued to support him. "Accommodation" sentiment thus persisted, though the tactic itself did not, and it left a strong residue of resentment. For another, Germanophilism basically represented a tendency toward expediency rather than principle, which remained in some Kadets despite the change in factual circumstances. The most significant aspect of the whole Ekaterinodar conference, in fact, was the breadth of tactical range displayed by Kadets. Sokolov supported one-man military dictatorship without reservation, but opposed the monarchy;

[99] Astrov, "Grazhdanskaia voina," pp. 43-44.
[100] *Ibid.*, p. 37.

Stepanov and Astrov insisted on a directorate, but one in which the army's command would play a dominant role; Miliukov wanted a monarchy; Vinaver, Nabokov, and their Crimean colleagues wanted some indication from Denikin that the Volunteers would adopt the Kadet program: in their view, broad popular support was still crucial to the White's success, and the party could not afford further taints of reaction.[101] Kadets thus stood with no clear tactical concensus on the brink of what was possibly their last concentrated opportunity to influence Russia's future.

In the end, it was Astrov who prevailed. Speaking as an emissary from the Central Committee in Moscow and a delegate from both the Union of Regeneration and the National Center, he proposed a long resolution to his colleagues which reflected the views of these groups: Kadets were to aid any anti-Bolshevik movement that was not bent on regional separatism, as was Skoropadskii's Hetmanate. "Russia One and Indivisible" had to be the party's slogan as well as Denikin's; and Kadets would assist the White commander in administrative capacities. Hopefully, the army would soon cooperate in forming a new Provisional Government with all political groups supporting a statesmanlike (*gosudarstvennoe*) point of view. Kadets would then be in a position to exercise primary political responsibility. In the meantime, they could cooperate with the socialists, but through the army, and from a position of strength; and they could leave the monarchy question aside.[102]

Interestingly enough, Astrov's rationale thus closely resembled that used by Kadets in Kiev to justify working with Skoropadskii, although now it was White Guard militarism with which liberals were formally ready to compromise, rather than the Germans. Kadets would work *within* the movement to channel anti-Bolshevik energies most constructively, as they perceived it, despite the obvious contempt with which many army leaders viewed liberal politics and programs, and despite the way in which Kadets would thus be linked closely to political reaction. As in the Ukraine, compromise was justified because both groups shared a basic, pressing objective: suppressing the radicals, unifying Russia, and "resurrecting" the Russian state; and because many Kadets still remained hopeful about the movement's ultimate chance of success. Whether the Bolsheviks could be defeated without liberals themselves becoming advocates of worker and peasant social interests, however, was something most Kadets at the Ekaterinodar conference could not bring themselves to consider seriously. If anything, "partisanship" in defense of the masses seemed far more

101 Miliukov, "Dnevnik," pp. 204-13.
102 Astrov, "Grazhdanskaia voina," p. 39-40.

inappropriate now than in the past; and in fact, would clearly have threatened (and probably collapsed) the party's association with the main anti-Bolshevik military forces, not to mention the liberals' own social and political interests. For most delegates, there consequently seemed no logical or even desirable alternative to the party's course. The Central Committee had already endorsed the concept of military dictatorship in Moscow; the task of Kadets in the south was to make dictatorship work.

Ironically, the strongest opposition to this position at Ekaterinodar now came from Miliukov, and largely on the grounds Astrov himself had earlier used in Kiev. The generals, he argued, would certainly retain close control of their forces, and thus would undoubtedly mismanage political affairs. Too close an association on the part of the Kadets would hopelessly compromise the party, further reinforcing its image as a rightist group, and minimizing its role in postwar politics. Kadets had to be their own people, not agents of the army.[103]

But despite the fact that Miliukov's approach was now much more sound politically than it had been earlier in the year, and represented, in fact, considerable movement for one who cultivated the party's "civil war mentality" in the latter months of 1917, the Kadet leader failed to carry his colleagues with him. When the issue came to a vote, a majority supported Astrov, 43 to 14.[104] Kadets in Ekaterinodar thus officially endorsed Denikin's dictatorship. They also adopted a resolution committing themselves to continued cooperation with the Allies and condemning their party colleagues in Kiev.[105]

What they failed to do, however, was address themselves seriously to problems of local vs. national authority, Russia's general social polarization, or the need for a popular anti-Bolshevik program and a broad base of social support. Nor did they issue the type of statement Vinaver and the Kadets in the Crimea had proposed, stating their own goals and principles clearly, and demanding Volunteer adherence as a general condition for joining ranks. Five years later, in emigration, Miliukov would argue that there was "no question" as to the cause of the White movement's failure, that its "obvious anti-democratic tendencies" were clear "from the very beginning," that it was "ruined in the eyes of the masses because it was a *class* army."[106] What he neglected to say was that the Kadets at the Ekaterinodar conference reinforced the White movement in this regard, rather than demanding a change in orientation or direction. Whatever the moment might have brought in terms of broadening the movement's political or social

[103] Miliukov, "Dnevnik," pp. 211-12.   [104] *Ibid.*, p. 213.
[105] Archives of the Russian Embassy in Paris, fold. 2.
[106] *Posledniia Novosti*, No. 878, Mar. 1, 1923 (italics are Miliukov's).

base—and to some, at least, it seemed to promise a lot—the opportunity passed.

The conference closed on a note of harmony. In a rare display of
abjuration, Miliukov told his colleagues he was glad it was he who
was mistaken about working with the Germans, rather than the
party.[107] The delegates then dispersed, fully expecting they would
soon return to Moscow, where social and political questions could
again be carefully examined. Few realized they had just helped doom
the anti-Bolshevik cause to defeat.

[107] Miliukov, "Dnevnik," p. 211.

CHAPTER ELEVEN

First Months with Denikin:
The Struggle for Balance

The importance of Kadets' adopting a more forceful line on political and social questions was soon apparent. By October 1918 the officer clique at Volunteer headquarters was profoundly disinterested in these matters, far less so than even during the army's early days at Rostov. Now numbering almost 40,000 men, Denikin's forces concentrated instead on clearing the North Caucasus of Bolsheviks, attempting to develop a large base area from which to launch a northern offensive. The Kuban was already reasonably secure, with Bolshevik units disorganized and short of supplies; and the capture of Novorossisk had provided an opening to the Black Sea. With new victories coloring their perspectives, most officers looked back on 1917 as a national catastrophe, instigated and encouraged by traitors. Their worlds were now strictly defined by the values of a patriotic militarism, in which social issues and politics had no part.

Denikin himself was something of an exception. Coming from a peasant background, and having climbed the army's ranks through a labyrinth of social prejudice, he well understood the revolution's social and psychological underpinnings. But most of his lieutenants detested anyone even suspected of sympathizing with the left. General Pokrovskii, for example, developed a special fondness for killing "radicals." (Group hangings became his speciality; he became one of the most feared men in South Russia.) General Dragomirov closely associated the revolution with the Jews, whom he despised. Almost all Volunteer officers also deeply resented the way in which politics had corrupted "their" army in 1917; and even Denikin was soon telling the Kuban Rada that defeating the Bolsheviks was the army's only important goal, that the tricolored Russian flag was vastly more important than any political program.[1] Within days of the Kadet conference, General Lukomskii insisted to Miliukov that the anti-Bolshevik movement was essentially none of the liberals' business.

---

[1] S. Piontkovskii, ed., *Grazhdanskaia voina v Rossii (1918-1921 gg.)*, Moscow, 1925, pp. 503-04.

Kadets could debate all they wanted; the army would follow its own men and its own designs.[2]

These attitudes seriously undermined any chances for Volunteer success. The struggle simply could not be won by the army alone, even with adequate financial and material backing. By ignoring social and political questions, the generals were declaring their indifference to issues some 150 million of their countrymen considered vital, regarding Russia almost like enemy territory. While the remnants of Russia's gentry and aristocracy might give them support, along with some sectors of the urban bourgeoisie, the vast majority of Russians would have little reason to follow Denikin rather than Lenin, for sacrificing themselves in his cause rather than that of radical socialism. The Whites assumed a desire for order and a general spirit of patriotism would turn their effort into a national "crusade," but their army was being organized in the midst of regional separatists who still revered the goals of the 1917 revolution, and in a socially polarized country whose overwhelming majority considered themselves supporters of social reform, as the Constituent Assembly elections had shown. To defeat the Bolsheviks, their outlook had to change, their movement made more responsive to popular moods.

This was the Kadet party's vital task in the fall of 1918, as a number of leading Kadets themselves perceived. In the Crimea, Vinaver, Petrunkevich, Nabokov, and several others still wanted to set specific conditions for the party's participation in Volunteer ranks, and force a more liberal pattern of administration. Astrov also saw the problem, and hoped the Ekaterinodar conference itself might lead to new roles for moderate or "conciliationist" party figures, perhaps even the creation of a civilian anti-Bolshevik cabinet. But without even the tenuous unity binding them in 1917, Kadet leaders themselves could develop no clear approach to questions of this sort, and even the harmony of the party conference proved short lived. For Miliukov, the army's intransigence only reinforced the need to resurrect the monarchy, an idea which had caused so many problems at the beginning of the revolution; and with incurable self-possession, the former foreign minister again argued in the days following the conference that only a tsar could command mass loyalty or minimize political bickering, even after learning firsthand from Denikin how opposed the Volunteers were to "political questions" of this sort.[3] In turn, Miliukov's new monarchism made the situation much more difficult for Astrov, Vinaver, Adzhemov, and others to his left, threatening their

[2] P. N. Miliukov, "Dnevnik," unpubl. diary in the Columbia Russian Archive, pp. 210-12.
[3] *Ibid.*, pp. 208-23.

hope, as Astrov put it, that the Kadets themselves could "unite sufficiently to become the living fabric joining all newly formed anti-Bolshevik movements."[4]

Astrov himself soon had further doubts as to whether he could work effectively with the Volunteers. When the Moscow Kadet first learned that a leftist directorate had been formed in Siberia by a State Conference at Ufa, he agreed with Denikin's decision not to strike out for the Urals, since the situation in the east seemed too confused and unstable. In turn, Denikin offered him the responsibility for managing "internal affairs" in regions occupied by the Volunteers. Although tempted to accept, an incident occurred before he could make up his mind which suggested the post would not carry any significant authority. G. I. Shreider, the former mayor of Petrograd and a nationally known socialist, was arrested in Ekaterinodar, ostensibly for "criticizing" the army in *Rodnaia Zemlia*, a left-wing newspaper. Since Shreider was an active, moderate SR, prominent in the Union of Regeneration, his arrest aroused many local socialists; but more important, it jeopardized the possibility of even a passive attitude on the part of leftist parties toward the Volunteers, and reinforced the army's reactionary image. It also demonstrated how little the generals cared about developing mass support. When Astrov went to Dragomirov and Lukomskii to secure Shreider's release, they insisted that the former mayor leave the Kuban, and forcibly expelled him.[5]

Consequently, Astrov himself began to wonder whether he should stay in the south. Toward the end of October 1918 he received several messages from Kadets in Moscow, urging him to go on to Siberia and join what was hoped would become a more moderate anti-Bolshevik coalition there.[6] And after attending several sessions of Denikin's Special Council, he found its "general tone, its manner of discussing questions, and the . . . very questions themselves giving reasons to conclude it had neither the men nor the ideas necessary to accomplish its tasks."[7]

All of this, finally, reinforced Maxim Vinaver and the Crimean Kadets in views they had held even before the Ekaterinodar conference: that the best method of constructing a strong anti-Bolshevik

[4] N. I. Astrov, "Grazhdanskaia voina (vospominaniia)," unpubl. MS in the Panina Archive, n.d., pack. 3, suppl. 3, p. 102.

[5] *Ibid.*, pp. 47-48. Vinaver attributes Shreider's arrest to the publication over his signature of a resolution by the Petrograd city council against Kornilov in August 1917. See his *Nashe pravitel'stvo*, Paris, 1928, p. 49.

[6] One of these is a letter written on cloth from the Moscow Central Committee, and sewn into the jacket of a refugee officer, now in the private collection of Mme. A. I. Denikin.

[7] Astrov, "Grazhdanskaia voina," p. 50.

movement was by "building from below," using strong regional governments to maintain local authority until anti-Bolshevik armies took Moscow. Vinaver and his colleagues now became quite anxious to put their ideas into practice, to make operational, in effect, many of the ideas which had been behind their conciliationist sentiment toward the end of 1917. Plans for building precisely such a popular regional government were already underway in Yalta. And Vinaver and others saw the Kuban Rada as another logical regional power. "Building from below" would finally end the need of imposing "artificial" state authority from above, from forcing Russians to accept the primacy of national interests over their own immediate needs. Hopefully, it would also produce a series of governments enjoying local support and confidence. Denikin, meanwhile, could concentrate on the war; once he was in Moscow, the question of national politics and an all-Russian government could be reopened at a new Constituent Assembly.[8]

Thus Kadets were anything but a "living fabric" capable of "joining all anti-Bolshevik governments," as Astrov had hoped. Vasili Stepanov and Konstantin Sokolov fully supported Denikin, objecting only to the general's own reluctance to assume the full mantle of dictatorship.[9] But Miliukov insisted the decisions of the Kadets' Ekaterinodar conference had "various meanings" and were "subject to differing interpretations"; and he decided to leave the Kuban.[10] Having heard that the Allied command in Rumania was inviting a group of prominent Russians—himself included—to present their opinions on foreign military assistance, he again decided to seek support for his views abroad. With guns and supplies again at stake—this time from the French and British, rather than the Germans—Miliukov was convinced the anti-Bolsheviks would finally come around; and he was now fully prepared to have the Kadet party split in two if others rejected his views.[11] Vinaver and Nabokov, meanwhile, returned to the Crimea to "build from below"; Paramonov, Zeeler, and the Don Kadets set up a South-Eastern Regional Kadet Committee to channel new aid to the army; and Astrov, after much soul-searching, finally accepted a post on Denikin's Special Council as minister without portfolio. The former Moscow attorney still had little faith in Volunteer politics; but with noble patience, remained convinced that the best way to affect the movement was by working from within. His would be a twofold "struggle for balance": an effort to counter the army's militarism with liberal politics; and a continued attempt to coordinate diverse viewpoints within the Kadet party itself.[12]

[8] *Ibid.*, pp. 128-29.
[9] *Ibid.*, p. 36.
[10] Miliukov, "Dnevnik," p. 232.
[11] *Ibid.*, pp. 226, 232-33.
[12] Astrov, "Grazhdanskaia voina," pp. 40-41; Reports on the South-Eastern

DENIKIN'S "KADET ADMINISTRATION"
NOVEMBER 1918–MARCH 1919

Astrov's immediate concern was the relationship between the Volunteers and the government of the Kuban. The future of the anti-Bolshevik effort largely turned on this issue, for if Denikin and his generals could not even establish friendly relations with the loyalist regions of South Russia, there was little chance of gaining support from the heavily leftist territories in the north. To legal-minded Kadets, the problem seemed at first glance to center on the degree of authority the Volunteers had a right to exercise in regions under their control. If they indeed bore national power, and were successors, in effect, to the Provisional Government, their authority was unlimited. Questions of regional power and social reform had to await resolution by an All-Russian Constituent Assembly. But in fact, the question really centered on the Volunteers' overall approach to defeating the Bolsheviks: the choice was whether their effort would be a "national crusade," in which particularistic interests were subordinated to the single goal of resurrecting a unified Great Russian state; or whether they would build through firm, popular regional governments in whom local populations had confidence, moving gradually toward the confederation of these regimes until Russia as a whole was united in a single, federal, anti-Bolshevik republic.

The importance of Kadets working closely with Denikin in the formative weeks of the army's Special Council was that they firmly insisted on the first approach, resolutely opposing any thought of federalism, as they had throughout 1917. They thus gave political legitimacy to the nationalist instincts of the Volunteer command. It was soon apparent that the statute worked out by Kadets for the administration of territories "occupied" by the Volunteers in the beginning of September would not be acceptable to the Kuban regime. The army promised autonomy, but made it clear at the same time that supreme dictatorial power remained with Denikin. The Kubantsy responded to this with their own draft Declaration, worth quoting here in part because of the clarity with which it indicates a different approach to the whole problem of Russian unification and the anti-Bolshevik struggle:

1. The formation of independent governments on the territory

Regional Kadet Committee, in the Iu. F. Semenov Papers, Boris Nicolaevsky Archive, sec. 10, bx. 3, file 34. The South-Eastern Committee was divided into six sections, for organization, finances, publications, aide to the Volunteer Army, policy, and agitation. Its officers included Zeeler (president), Paramonov, V. M. Bukhshtab, and M. S. Voronkov (vice presidents), and Z. V. Zelenskii (secretary).

of the former Russian state and the assumption by them of supreme authority was an unavoidable act, and . . . one of self-preservation.

2. The basic task of all these governments is to fight Bolshevism.

3. To accelerate the struggle, it is necessary as soon as possible to form a united military front with a single command.

4. It is also necessary to organize a single representation from the South Russian governments for the current peace conference. . . .

5. To accomplish the goals stated in 3 and 4, it is necessary to form a South Russian Union on federal principles.

6. A resurrected Russia is [only] possible in the form of an all-Russian federated republic.

7. The Kuban region [will] enter the Russian federation as a member of the federation.

8. The Kuban Regional Rada, setting for itself the task of fighting Bolshevism, strives to put into practice principles of broad popular sovereignty.

9. The population of the Kuban region believes the . . . future form of Russian government . . . [must be determined by] a new All-Russian Constituent Assembly.[13]

These proposals were supported by a broad cross section of the Kuban population. They won near unanimous approval in the Kuban Rada, which, though four-fifths cossack, was socialist led and largely composed of men from the ranks; and they were seen by *inogorodnye*—or at least their representatives in the Rada—as a first step toward settling local problems. The Kuban military under Ataman Filimonov was also anxious to preserve local authority, though less committed to the federative idea than the Rada, and staunchly opposed to the type of social and economic reforms that the Rada seemed inclined to pursue. Ataman Krasnov from the Don region also supported the plan, as did a number of local socialist party groups, and local cells of the Union of Regeneration, who were now meeting regularly in a number of southern cities.[14]

But to Kadets and the Volunteer leadership, the Kuban position was completely untenable. Federalism was simply a cloak for regional independence, the fragmentation of what had to be a united Russian movement. It also challenged Kadet pretensions to national leadership (though no one said so openly) since virtually all Central Committee members had stood firmly on a platform of anti-federalism throughout

13 A. I. Denikin, *Ocherki russkoi smuty*, 5 vols., Paris-Berlin, 1921-25, IV, 49.
14 *Ibid.*, pp. 45-49; A. P. Filimonov, "Kubantsy, 1917-18 gg.," *Beloe Delo*, II, 1927, pp. 68-71; N. M. Melnikov, "Grazhdanskaia voina na iuge Rossii," MS in the Columbia Russian Archive, n.d., pp. 130-31; V. Miakotin, "Iz nedalekago proshlago," *NCS*, No. 3, 1923, pp. 191-93.

1917. And in the army's Special Council, it was the two leading Kadets, Vasili Stepanov and Konstantin Sokolov, who took the lead in denouncing the plan, insisting that a single authoritative dictatorship was absolutely essential to the anti-Bolsheviks' success.[15]

While one can never determine precisely just how much the Kadets' position affected the Volunteers, it clearly was not without some influence. In an effort to resolve the question, Denikin appointed a special commission, the civilian members of which were almost all Kadets. Presumably, if the liberals were not so opposed to federalism, or concerned themselves as much with local as with national interests, relations between the Rada and the Volunteers might not have reached an impasse. (It might also be true, however, that if Kadets *were* more sympathetic to local demands, Denikin would not have asked them for assistance.) As things turned out, the arguments of Rada leaders fell on deaf ears. When Rada President L. L. Bych stressed that his government was duly elected (and thus more legitimate than the Volunteers' Special Council), insisting as well on a rigid division between political matters within his competence and military matters within Denikin's, the Kadets condemned his plans as "too complicated," "time consuming," and "diversionary" in terms both of defeating Lenin and unifying Russia.[16] Nothing was settled; and the issue continued to disrupt the whole South Russian anti-Bolshevik movement. The Kubantsy, thinking and acting as if they were independent, repeatedly protested Volunteer interference in their affairs; Denikin, while maintaining command of Kuban troops, increasingly resented disloyal separatists, and blamed the Rada for difficulties of supply and support. The only major change in anti-Bolshevik administration was the formal reorganization of the Volunteer command into the Armed Forces of South Russia (AFSR), in which Kuban divisions were organized as essentially separate units. Otherwise, a new system of dual authority prevailed, reminiscent of 1917.

Astrov himself was not particularly sympathetic to Bych's demands, but the conduct of his liberal colleagues also filled him with foreboding.[17] Vasili Stepanov was suggesting that Denikin appease the Rada with a phony South Russian directorate, which he could transform later into one-man military dictatorship simply "by the nature of things."[18] Konstantin Sokolov—whom Vinaver later dubbed the "song-

[15] Melnikov, pp. 131-33.

[16] Protocol of the Lukomskii Commission on Mutual Relations between the Volunteer Army and the Kuban Regional Government, Oct. 26, 1918 (o.s.), in the N. M. Melnikov Collection, gp. 2, fold. 3.

[17] Astrov, "Grazhdanskaia voina," p. 73.

[18] *Zhurnal Osobago Soveshchaniia pri Glavnokomanduiushchem Dobrovol'cheskoi*

bird" of military dictatorship[19]—rejected the legitimacy of *any* local demands, insisting the army deal harshly with all those who resisted Volunteer goals, Bolshevik or not.[20] What worried Astrov most was the same concern that had preoccupied him and many of his moderate colleagues throughout 1917: that the army leadership, military *and* civilian, would alienate large numbers of ordinary Russians, and that any claim to national authority would be sterile without massive popular support. For most of November he discussed these problems almost daily with socialist friends in Ekaterinodar, and repeatedly toyed with the idea of continuing on to Siberia.[21]

Each passing week, however, made the debate over power arrangements more academic. The Volunteers were now a hardened, driving, military force, with scant regard for legalistic niceties. While Bych and the Kadets struggled over administrative formalities, General Wrangel was engaging a well-armed Red force near Stavropol, and implementing his own occupation policies. The Reds fought desperately, fearful of being cut off from Bolshevik troops to the north. The Volunteers were equally determined to secure their southern flank. In the course of the fighting, as towns and villages came increasingly under Volunteer control, Wrangel's troops began to regard the region as if it were captured enemy territory. Soldiers began to pillage freely, and there were a number of awful scenes where women were raped and killed, and children cut down with no conceivable reason. In one or two cases, local duma leaders were even executed in the streets.

Moreover, as the territory became "secure," Denikin sent General Uvarov to take charge of administration as "Governor-General," who soon proved worse than the field commanders. Arriving with a determination to implement his own narrow-minded conception of social order, he placed in force all laws governing the Russian empire *before* February 1917.[22]

Scenes like this were repeated in many other places in the fall of 1918, as Astrov himself later recalled:

Complete horror reigned in local areas. Lawlessness and all sorts of arbitrary acts—this is what the representatives of the Volunteer army brought with them. One situation more tormenting than the next, more pitiful than the next, this was what was brought to us by

Armiei, No. 6, Oct. 16, 1918, in the General Baron P. N. Wrangel Personal Archives, file 1.

[19] M. N. Vinaver, *Nedavnee*, 2nd ed., Paris, 1926, p. 43.
[20] Astrov, "Grazhdanskaia voina," p. 52.　[21] *Ibid.*, pp. 40ff.
[22] V. M. Krasnov, "Iz vospominanii o 1917-20 gg.," *ARR*, XI, 1923, pp. 114-25.

people coming from local areas. There was no malice in these reports, no anger. These people were strong partisans of the Volunteers. They understood that in the chaos of civil war, it was impossible to think of an orderly, peaceful life. But just the same, it was necessary to do something radical, something drastic, to force the agents of military authority into some new way of thinking, to prevent the continuation of methods whereby military authority ran roughshod over local populations and social organs.[23]

The question was, of course, what to do? Astrov's own policy was a mixture of administrative reorganization, liberal declarations, and despair. When the Stavropol problem first came before the Special Council in late October, he suggested that the army's whole structure of civil administration be overhauled. He also wanted the army to frame clear statements of policy on vital social questions, so its goals would be more popular. Denikin, however, was reluctant to politicize in this way, fearing disagreements over particular issues would fragment his ranks. He much preferred questions of this sort to await the Bolsheviks' defeat.[24] Astrov was rightly convinced these matters were as important to White success as military victory; but the best he could do was to persuade the Special Council to pursue them in various special commissions.

The most important of these was the commission to reorganize the army's administration, which began functioning at the end of November 1918. Since it was almost entirely a Kadet group, Astrov at first was reassured in his decision to stay with the Volunteers, thinking liberals like himself might still have a chance to affect the army's policies from within. His hope was that the Special Council could be broadened into a governing organ of independent competence. If staffed by a broad spectrum of representative civilians, including socialists, it could free the army from direct responsibility for political concerns, and at the same time represent a broader cross section of Russia's population than simply the soldiers themselves. There was even some thought about heading the group with the type of three-man directorate suggested by the Union of Regeneration.[25]

But party membership soon proved of little consequence. Stepanov and Sokolov, two other Kadet members on the commission, again proved themselves uncompromising adherents of strict military dictatorship. The furthest they would go toward broadening the Council's base was to accept the idea that the Council presidency, held by

23 Astrov, "Grazhdanskaia voina," p. 53.   24 Denikin, *Ocherki*, IV, 213-18.
25 Letter from Astrov to Denikin, Oct. 23-26, 1924, in the Panina Archive, pack. 5, suppl. 6, fold. 12.

General Dragomirov, be transformed into a post resembling that of the minister-president during the Provisional Government, and be occupied by a civilian. This person would still be subordinate to the army's command, but would symbolize the separation of military and civilian administration.[26]

But even this small token soon proved worthless. By the time the commission finished its work in January 1919, the Kadet contribution had been to "streamline" the Special Council into a consolidation of military government, rather than "weaken" it with civilian administrators or by otherwise taking local political sentiments into account. General Denikin was given ultimate competence in both legislative and executive matters; the role of the Special Council remained limited to discussion and consultation; there was no provision whatsoever for any form of popular representation on either an appointed or elected basis; and the responsibility for drafting various legislative programs was left entirely to individual council sections organized along the general lines of prerevolutionary ministries. The only fully civilian departments were the Bureau of Propaganda and the Department of Laws, the latter established to clarify legislative drafts, not to introduce them. And the minister-president idea, which was now quite inconsistent with the commission's other recommendations, was rejected. As Astrov himself unhappily recognized, all important administrative responsibilities were left in military hands.[27]

More important, membership of the Council remained entirely nonsocialist, with Astrov himself constituting the "extreme left wing." The incongruity of this in a nation which had recently voted more than 70 percent in favor of socialist candidates in the Constituent Assembly elections was hardly lost on the frustrated Moscow lawyer, or on Denikin either, for that matter. The Volunteer commander was constantly being bombarded with demands from outside the army that he strengthen his authority with socialist assistants but felt the army's "psychology" would not admit such liberalization. And Astrov alone could do nothing.[28]

A similar fate awaited Astrov's hopes to correct the abuses of Volunteer field commanders. Here, too, the question was studied by a commission made up largely of Kadets; but again, governing responsibility was left entirely in army hands. Areas conquered from the Bolsheviks were divided into special regions, each under a military governor. The governor was to be aided by appointed assistants whose posts corresponded to the divisions within the Special Council. Officially, the

[26] K. N. Sokolov, *Pravlenie generala Denikina*, Sofia, 1921, pp. 76-77.
[27] Astrov, "Grazhdanskaia voina," p. 89; Melnikov, pp. 5-6.
[28] Denikin, *Ocherki*, III, 270-71; Astrov, "Grazhdanskaia voina," p. 52.

governor-general's office was to work closely with local public organizations, such as zemstvo councils; and it was to fulfill responsibilities in accordance with local customs and traditions.[29] But as Astrov and others quickly recognized, most officers favored tsarist bureaucrats for their civilian assistants, rather than zemstvo or local duma leaders. And the new legislation itself was not fully implemented until late in March 1919, by which time harsh patterns of "occupation" were already well established.[30]

What all of this meant was that the Volunteers were further isolating themselves from any expression of popular desires or representative national voices; and they were doing so with the support and encouragement of most Kadets. The Whites' hope was to build a national movement, but with the exception of Astrov and one or two others, few recognized they were working without regard for public opinion or the country's general mood, thus making virtually impossible the development of broad popular support. In effect, the traditional elitism of Kadet intellectuals like Sokolov and Stepanov was merging with the army leadership's own myopic tendency to see everything in military terms.

Thus it developed that the two most important policy statements Nicholas Astrov had hoped to extract from the Volunteer leadership, on agrarian policy and on labor reform, were issued virtually without reference to all that had happened on these fronts in 1917. On the agrarian question, a majority of the Special Council (strongly supported by Sokolov and Stepanov) did not want to issue any statement whatsoever. Their official explanation now was the totally vacuous assertion that matters of this importance were properly left to an all-Russian Constituent Assembly. In actuality, of course, the Whites opposed reforms, fearing they would indirectly sanction the goals of the revolution, and alienate vested landed interests.[31] The labor issue, meanwhile, was simply not considered important. Workers were written off as Bolshevik supporters; and it was argued that problems of wages and hours could hardly be regulated in conditions of civil war.[32] The best Astrov could do was to persuade Denikin to draft two special memoranda, which were then sent to the Special Council as proposals for possible action. In each case, Denikin's position generally conformed to those of the Kadets' own party program, but as statements of principles, they had no binding authority, and the Council itself did not deem it fit to make official public pronouncements.[33]

[29] Melnikov, pp. 20-21. [30] *Ibid.*, p. 28.
[31] Denikin, *Ocherki*, IV, 211-14. [32] Melnikov, p. 40.
[33] Denikin, *Ocherki*, IV, 212-14. The letter on agriculture stated five principles: (1) the interests of the laboring peasantry had to be protected; (2) small and

Actual legislation on these questions was not seriously contemplated until later in the summer of 1919.

Perhaps most symptomatic was the Council's relation to its own department of public information—Osvag—set up specially to win popular support for the army. At first Osvag was headed by N. E. Paramonov, the wealthy Kadet publisher in Rostov. Though certainly not a leftist, Paramonov recognized with Astrov the dangerous nature of the Volunteers' reactionary image, and began steering his department on a relatively liberal course. Press dispatches presented different viewpoints; efforts were made to link the Volunteers' goals with those of more leftist anti-Bolshevik groups; and a number of socialist refugees from the north were put to work in a variety of positions.[34] While none of this particularly pleased Denikin, his lieutenants on the Special Council became infuriated. Paramonov was soon replaced by Sokolov, who by now had thoroughly reactionary credentials, and who pledged reform from top to bottom, beginning with a purge of Jews and socialists.[35] The former Kadet Central Committee member soon made Osvag the army's loudest trumpet. Its literature became crudely rightist, appearing as if specially designed to slander even moderate left-wing parties.[36]

The pattern of Denikin's "Kadet administration" in the winter of 1918-1919 suggests the Volunteer movement could not succeed, regardless of Red Army strength. Military success brought no end to popular dissension, and in some cases increased it considerably. To some extent, the cause of this lay as it had in 1917 in the insistence of liberal leaders like Stepanov and Sokolov that authority had to be imposed from above, that order had to precede social reform, and that the security and welfare of the Russian state as a whole take precedence over meeting popular desires. Of all the political figures in South Russia at this time, the Kadets themselves should have clearly

---

middle-sized farms had to be created and strengthened at the expense of public and private land; (3) property rights had to be preserved, but quantities of land above designated amounts in particular regions had to be forcibly expropriated, with just compensation paid to former owners; (4) cossack land and certain other categories of holdings were to be excluded; (5) technological improvements in agriculture had to be introduced and developed. On the question of labor legislation, Denikin asked for recognition in principle of the eight-hour day; liberal provisions on unions, workers' insurance, and the employment of women and children; and compensation of some sort for the unemployed.

[34] Melnikov, pp. 121-22.   [35] Sokolov, *Pravlenie*, pp. 93-115.

[36] See, e.g., the Osvag pamphlets, A. I. Bezrodnov, *Spasaite Rossiiu!*, which linked socialism and the Jews in a crudely anti-Semitic fashion; A. I. Ksiunin, *Obmanutyi narod*, which simply cataloged a list of "left-wing" atrocities; and I. V. Laptev, *Lezhachego ne b'iut*, which called on the populace to turn in the names of socialist "traitors" to Volunteer authorities.

seen the difficulties of this outlook. But with the exception of Astrov, M. M. Fedorov, and several local party figures like Paramonov and Zeeler, they did not. The crucial question of what the Whites *represented* for the vast majority of Russia's common masses was simply buried in a quest for "unity" and "order."

Ironically for the increasingly despondent Astrov, his own efforts only provoked growing resentment on all sides. After Denikin issued his memoranda on agrarian and labor affairs, the General himself was accused of being a "plaything" in Astrov's hands.[37] Field commanders also ridiculed the Special Council as "Kadetskii"; and early in January, General Dragomirov began organizing a restorationist group to oppose the liberal "left."[38] "From ear to ear," Sokolov wrote, "traveled the phrase said to have been uttered by General Denikin to Astrov: 'I deputize you to be the opposition leader in my government.' "[39] A number of officers even thought the "noxious" Kadet influence would have to be forcibly eliminated.[40]

At the same time, socialists attacked Kadets from the other direction. Few outside the Special Council clearly understood Astrov's position. The only obvious facts were that Denikin's troops were often as barbaric as the Bolsheviks; that the Special Council vigorously supported the concept of one-man military dictatorship; and that Kadets and generals alike were turning deaf ears to popular voices. When the prominent Progressist Vladimir Miakotin visited a number of Union of Regeneration branches in early 1919, he found them uniformly hostile to both Kadets and Denikin. Even when Astrov, Iurenev, and other party moderates offered him explanations in Ekaterinodar, he found them "less than convincing."[41]

In these circumstances, Astrov again considered resigning his post, and leaving Ekaterinodar altogether. His socialist friends urged him to do so, insisting that his presence only compromised his politics. The Kadet leader was still hopeful, however, that the situation might improve when the army enjoyed greater military success. His own experience, he recognized, epitomized the dilemma of all moderates in conditions of revolution and civil war. The situation was inherently difficult and cruel. He could only believe in Denikin and assist the White movement as effectively as he could.[42]

[37] M. S. Margulies, *God interventsii*, 3 vols., Berlin, 1923, III, 170.

[38] N. N. Bogdanov, "Krymskoe kraevoe pravitel'stvo," unpubl. MS in the Archive of the Crimean Regional Government, file 19, p. 26; Denikin, *Ocherki*, IV, 207-08.

[39] Sokolov, *Pravlenie*, p. 126.

[40] V. A. Obolenskii, *Krym pri Vrangele*, Moscow, 1927, p. 5.

[41] Miakotin, "Iz nedalekago," *NCS*, No. 9, 1925, p. 283.

[42] Astrov, "Grazhdanskaia voina," p. 55.

THE NATIONAL CENTER, KADETS, AND DENIKIN'S
MARCH INTO THE UKRAINE

Astrov also began to hope the political climate could be improved if liberals outside Ekaterinodar played a greater role in local affairs He had in mind not only local Kadet groups, but also the various cells of the National Center, which in some places had by now completely replaced party committees as focal points of liberal political activity. Late in December, after raising the question in the Special Council, Astrov secured a resolution asking local National Center groups to establish ties with other public organizations, and help smooth the way for Volunteer rule.[43] His hope was to build on the Kadets' traditional *nadpartiinost'*, gathering a variety of talent in support of the Volunteers without regard to party affiliation. He also wanted to counter the army's own biases, and create a pattern of anti-Bolshevik cooperation which could carry past military victory as the political foundation of postwar Russia.

It is somewhat confusing to follow the activities of Kadets and National Center groups outside Ekaterinodar in the Winter of 1918-1919, but well worth the effort both as a means of observing liberal sentiment, and as a way of showing how unable the Kadets themselves were to unite the anti-Bolshevik movement during the first months of Denikin's rule. Throughout most of this period the Center's base was still in Moscow, where conditions were now far more bleak than even during the difficult winter of 1918. Bolshevik security had become quite stringent. Foodstuffs were strictly rationed, and despite a flourishing black market, were distributed largely according to social class and occupation. Somehow, Nicholas Kishkin, Nicholas Shchepkin, Peter Gerasimov, and a number of other Moscow Kadets managed to survive. They now had little hope of organizing an armed uprising, since most of the former officers' groups had long since dissolved; but they continued to meet as a National Center group two or three times a week, and struggled to stay in touch with other parts of the country.[44]

One might expect these conditions to have hardened the attitudes of Moscow Kadets, making them even more forceful advocates of strict military dictatorship, but such was not the case. Kishkin, Shchepkin and other former conciliationists continued to support the decisions of the May 1918 conference, backing one-man military rule; but by now they were also convinced that a non-socialist dictatorship divorced from the people had no chance of success. White leaders like Denikin had to disassociate themselves from the image of counter-

---

[43] *Zhurnal Osobago Soveshchaniia*, No. 21, Dec. 18, 1918.
[44] "Natsional'nyi tsentr' v Moskve v 1918," *NCS*, No. 8, 1924, p. 140.

revolution, staffing their administrations with persons in whom workers and particularly peasants could have confidence. They also had to enact reforms, especially in agriculture, and offer special guarantees to workers. From their perspective behind Bolshevik lines, Moscow liberals could see an increasing alienation from communist rule. Peasants were fighting to protect their grain; and even hard-bitten workers were increasingly angered by the harshness and disruption of war communism. Kishkin, Gerasimov, and others were now convinced that if anti-Bolshevik leaders took advantage of this dissidence, Lenin would fall. "But it must be specially emphasized," they wrote their colleagues in the south and east, "that there can be no return to the past."[45]

Moscow Kadets were particularly bothered by Denikin's Special Council. They rightly perceived it as precisely the type of narrow and uncompromising body which would prevent anti-Bolshevik unification. They also wanted Denikin to adopt a political program acceptable to a broad spectrum of organizations and parties, including the socialists.[46] Late in February 1919, they moved to implement these views themselves, outlining a common tactical program with two other social groups, the left-wing Union of Regeneration, and the bourgeois Union of Public Figures (some of whose leaders had also struggled through the bleak winter in Moscow). The program called for an interim all-Russian authority to take direction of the anti-Bolshevik movement, capable of creating a rule of law, implementing reforms, and guaranteeing civil rights for all citizens. The groups agreed that private property should be preserved in principle, but were committed to agrarian reform, and called on a new democratic assembly to outline Russia's future more precisely. Most important for the time being was the unification of right and left political forces, and the recognition that anti-Bolshevik programs had to relate to mass desires.[47]

[45] Letter from the Moscow Kadets to N. Astrov and V. Pepeliaev, n.d., in the Panina Archive, pack. 3, fold. 16; also: unsigned communication from Moscow Kadets to V. Maklakov, Jan. 24/Feb. 6, 1919, in Wrangel Military Archives, file 151.

[46] Moscow Kadets to Astrov, n.d., Panina Archive, pack. 3, fold. 16.

[47] *Informatsionnyi Listok* (illegal publication of the Union of Regeneration in Moscow), typed copy, dated Mar. 4/17, 1919, in the Melgunov Collection on the Civil War. Apparently the three Moscow organizations also agreed to continue working closely together, and formed for this purpose a new joint council called the "Tactical Center." Their subsequent activities, however, are shrouded. S. P. Melgunov later denied that the Tactical Center even existed in an independent form, and maintained that the joint agreement simply associated the three groups in a loose manner. (S. P. Mel'gunov, "Sud istorii nad intelligentsiei," *NCS*, No. 3, 1923, p. 156.) But later in the summer, the Bolsheviks seized a number of their opponents who remained in Moscow, and at the time of their trial, *Izvestiia* claimed the Tactical Center had a definite structure and had made efforts to construct a clandestine military organization. Its purpose, according to *Izvestiia*, was

Quite a different attitude prevailed, however, in National Center branches in South Russia. While committees here were also staffed largely by Kadets, the rightist influence of men like Stepanov and Sokolov was far greater than in Moscow, and there was little interest in interparty cooperation. In Ekaterinodar, for example, the Center broke decisively with local socialists over the question of a collegiate command; and it wired a "Declaration of Greetings" when Admiral Kolchak overthrew the recently established Directorate in Siberia.[48] In effect, the Ekaterinodar Center was little more than an auxiliary to the Special Council. It worked on various administrative regulations, sent memoranda to the Allies demanding support, and was largely responsible for Denikin's letters on agriculture and labor. It also offered the generals lists of reliable personnel. What encouraged Astrov, however, was that here as in Moscow, a number of Center members were aware of the army's need for competent administrators and popular support. And as the Volunteers began advancing into the Don and Ukraine, treading the paths of retreating Germans, Center leaders were already in contact with other local committees.[49]

The most difficult problems of administration were expected to be in the Ukraine, particularly in Kiev, Kharkov, and Odessa. As the Germans began to pull back in November 1918, local figures in these places found themselves in strong political crosscurrents. On one side

to prepare an armed uprising behind Bolshevik lines, aiding the Whites as they advanced on Moscow. (*Izvestiia*, No. 183 [1030], Aug. 19, 1920.) There is no independent confirmation of the Center's activities in this regard, however.

[48] Journals of the National Center in Ekaterinodar, Dec. 1918-Mar. 1919, in the Semenov Papers, sec. 35; Azbuka report on National Center activities, Feb. 11/24, 1919, in the Wrangel Military Archives, file 136; letter from the Ekaterinodar National Center branch to Admiral Kolchak, Jan. 31, 1919, in *Sibirskaia Rech'*, No. 166, July 20/Aug. 2, 1919. The Kadet core of the Center in Ekaterinodar included Astrov, Dolgorukov, Fedorov, Panina, Sokolov, Novgorodtsev, and Stepanov. Other members in the winter of 1918-19 included G. A. Meingardt, A. A. Neratov, Pr. G. N. Trubetskoi, V. N. Chelishchev, E. P. Shuberskii, N. N. Lvov, S. D. Sazonov, A. V. Desiatov, N. N. Nikolaev, A. N. Ratkov-Rozhnov, N. N. Chebyshev, and others.

[49] At a Center meeting in December, for example, Dolgorukov warned his colleagues that any all-Russian popular assembly was likely to take a more leftist position on land and labor questions than the Center itself preferred, and urged moving towards a "compromise" position which did not explicitly or exclusively endorse the concept of private property. N. N. Nikolaev, N. N. Lvov, and other of his colleagues, however, insisted a firm stand be taken on the question in favor of private ownership, Lvov at one point describing the peasantry as an "inert mass." Eventually the Center did endorse private property, but not "large landownership," supporting the "broad development" of "medium" and "small" landholders which Denikin later urged in his "Letter." See esp. the Center's *Zhurnaly*, Nos. 5 and 6, 1918, in the Semenov Papers, sec. 35; Reports on National Center policy decisions, Semenov papers, sec. 36; and Astrov's "Grazhdanskaia voina," pp. 98-101.

were the Rada's old forces under Simon Petliura, an impetuous separatist who insisted on issuing his own "universals" despite nominal subordination to a new Directory, organized by the Ukrainian National Union. On another were several groups of Bolsheviks, one in Kiev cooperating with the Directorate; another in Kursk under Grigorii Piatakov, which expected to create a Ukrainian Soviet Republic with Lenin's backing. Still a third force was made up of groups of armed peasants, some of whom under Nestor Makhno were creating their own independent anarchist movement. (Makhno's "Greens" would soon swirl through the Ukraine virtually unimpeded, preserving their independence for the better part of the next two years.) Finally there were Skoropadskii's old supporters, now desperately anxious for occupation by the Whites. The withdrawal of the Germans thus ushered in a period of almost complete political chaos in the Ukraine, which lasted for most of 1919. Even when Denikin's troops occupied Ukrainian towns and cities there was little authority in the countryside.[50]

Kadets in the Ukraine had grown increasingly nervous about the situation even before the Germans withdrew. Skoropadskii's cabinet was reorganized in October 1918, and began making overtures to the Allies. The Hetman's policy now was federation with a non-Bolshevik Russia.[51] Meanwhile, a small group of Kadets who had persistently opposed accommodation with the Germans formed themselves into a Kievan section of the National Center, and worked diligently in support of Denikin. Their leaders were E. A. Efimovskii and V. M. Levitskii, both lawyers and publicists, with good contacts in Moscow. For most of the Fall of 1918, they provided funds and assistance for officers heading toward the Kuban, maintaining only the coolest of relations with the regular Kadet committee. At one point the Kadet minister of internal affairs, Igor Kistiakovskii, even prohibited the press from mentioning the Center's existence.[52] Efimovskii and Levitskii also sought to cooperate with the Union of Regeneration. They met frequently with its Kievan leader D. M. Odinets, who also refused, in turn, to have anything to do with the regular Kadet committee.[53]

As the Germans prepared to withdraw in November 1918, the Ukraine consequently became an important testing ground for Astrov's concept of the Kadet party's becoming "the living fabric" of Russian

---

[50] R. Pipes, *The Formation of the Soviet Union*, Cambridge, Mass., 1954, pp. 137-50; P. Miliukov, *Rossiia na perelome*, 2 vols., Paris, 1927, II, 79-81.

[51] J. Reshetar, *The Ukrainian Revolution, 1917-20*, Princeton, 1952, pp. 193-207.

[52] Report of Azbuka on the Center branch in Kiev, Nov. 6/29, 1918, in the Wrangel Military Archives, file 141.

[53] *Ibid.*, Nov. 1/13, 1918.

anti-Bolsheviks. But as party leaders gathered in Kiev to discuss their future course, the picture they presented was anything but hopeful. From Moscow, Paul Novgorodtsev arrived as the Central Committee's latest "official" emissary, determined to head off any new separatism on the part of his party colleagues. Linking up with Miliukov, who had again stopped in the Ukrainian capital on his way to meet the Allied representatives in Rumania, Novgorodtsev fought against the efforts of Efimovskii and Levitskii to take a more cooperative attitude toward left-wing groups like the Union of Regeneration.[54] Miliukov, meanwhile, attempted to get Kadets in Kiev to associate more directly with the irrepressible old State Duma committee under Nicholas Rodzianko, which was also regrouping in Kiev, and with other right-wing organizations like the Church Council, the Trade-Industrialists, and the All-Russian Union of Landowners. On October 27/November 9, 1918, seven of these groups had met together with Miliukov's encouragement and formed the new, consolidated right-wing Council for the National Unification of Russia (SGOR). Under the Russian nationalists Meller-Zakomelskii, A. V. Krivoshein, and the right Kadet S. N. Tretiakov (all of whom had strong monarchist leanings), this new group considered itself a potential all-Russian government, and voted to send its own representatives to negotiate with the Allies in Rumania. Its leaders also hoped that Denikin himself would recognize their own "legitimate" authority, and use them, rather than the Kadet party, to unite the anti-Bolshevik movement. Miliukov himself became the group's vice-president.[55]

Thus conciliationist Kadets in the Ukraine found themselves squeezed between conservatives like Novgorodtsev and Miliukov within the party, and right-wing party allies from without. And rather than coordinate their activities, Kadets instead began to fight among themselves. After a series of particularly stormy meetings, where questions concerning the Kadets' relations with left-wing groups were thrashed out with great bitterness, Levitskii, Efimovskii, and the moderates finally submitted to the formation of the new South Russian National Center, under the chairmanship of the reactionary V. V. Shulgin. Staunchly opposing any form of federalism, and unwilling to cooperate with left-wing groups, this new group sharply opposed the policies of broad, nonpartisan cooperation which the National Center was press-

[54] Ibid., Dec. 17/30, 1918, in the Wrangel Military Archives, file 136.
[55] Miliukov, "Dnevnik," pp. 239-40, and his Rossiia na perelome, ii, 80-81; Denikin, Ocherki, iv, 185-86; P. P. Mendeleev, "Vospominaniia," unpubl. MS in the Columbia Russian Archive, n.d., bk. 4, pp. 156-58. Mendeleev was the representative of the Ukrainian Church Council in the SGOR. Other prominent SGOR members included A. D. Golitsyn, P. P. Riabushinskii, I. G. Kogan, and E. N. Trubetskoi.

ing in Moscow, and which Astrov had hoped might remedy Volunteer administrative problems.[56]

The practical significance of these somewhat tiring details was soon apparent. In December 1918, Denikin's troops neared Kharkov. As they did so, socialists and moderate Kadets attempted to organize a coalition city board, hoping to secure cooperation between Denikin's forces and those of the socialist Ukrainian Directorate, whose republican troops were camped some 15 miles from the city. But right-wing Kadets and the South Russian National Center seized the occasion to announce the mobilization of all former officers—and only officers—to aid the Volunteers. And while the moderates frantically cabled Ekaterinodar for permission to publish democratic slogans in the army's name, the conservatives insisted that the army avoid any statement which might suggest sympathy with either socialism or the new Ukrainian Directorate. This effectively undermined any desire the Ukrainians themselves might have had to unite with Denikin; and as the Whites entered the city, the Directorate's forces retreated to the north, carrying with them attitudes of suspicion, resentment, and distrust.[57] Rather than unifying the Whites, the whole episode only furthered anti-Bolshevik divisions.

THE JASSY CONFERENCE

An even more explicit example of Kadet disunity was emerging, meanwhile, at the conference called by the Allies in Rumania, which got underway in late November 1918 in the small provincial town of Jassy. And here, too, the consequences were significant for the Whites, though this time in terms of possible foreign assistance. Three separate organizations attended the meetings on behalf of Russia: the South Russian National Center, the Union of Regeneration, and the Council for the National Unification of Russia. Significantly, Kadets had been instrumental in organizing all three groups; and each delegation included Kadets among its members. Under the party's influence, consequently, the delegations should have been able to work out a coordinated, forceful approach, leading possibly to substantial Allied aid.

But as Robert McNeal had shown in his detailed study of the Jassy conference,[58] the proceedings led instead to a "fiasco" for the White

[56] V. M. Levitskii, *Chto kazhdyi dolzhen znat' ob Ukraine*, 2 pts., Paris, 1939, pt. 1, p. 14.

[57] *Ibid.*, pp. 14-16; Letter from N. Karinskii to N. Astrov, Dec. 12/25, 1918, in the Astrov papers, Panina Archive, pack. 5, suppl. 4.

[58] R. H. McNeal, "The Conference of Jassy; An Early Fiasco of the Anti-Bolshevik Movement," in J. S. Curtiss, ed., *Essays in Russian and Soviet History*,

movement. Delegates from the Union of Regeneration, led by the Kadet mayor of Odessa, Michael Braikevich, pressed the Allies to support the creation of a national coalition directorate, and insisted on the necessity of building a future Russian democracy from below.[59] In opposition, the Council for the National Unification of Russia, led by Miliukov, not only insisted the Allies back a dictatorship, but also declare themselves in favor of a regency under Grand Duke Nicholas Nicholaevich.[60] Finally, the National Center delegation under the moderate Kadet leader M. M. Fedorov, one of Astrov's closest associates in Ekaterinodar, pressed the conference to back Denikin and his Special Council.[61] (Miliukov was now ready to accept Denikin as the Whites' principal military leader, but wanted the establishment of a broader civilian government, under a regent.)[62] When the delegates voted, Denikin got nowhere near unanimous support; and more important, those voting against him gave no indication they would abandon their separate goals. The Council for National Unification remained committed to monarchy; the Union of Regeneration continued to oppose any type of one-man military dictatorship.[63] Thus the delegates failed to present the Allies with a single coherent position; and the latter refused to take the delegation seriously as a "representative" Russian body. Hence, the primary purpose of the sessions—to coordinate the Allies' plans with those of the South Russian anti-Bolsheviks—was not accomplished.

THE VOLUNTEER OCCUPATION OF ODESSA

In December 1918, the Russian delegates to Jassy moved on to Odessa, where they finally adjourned their discussions without resolving their differences. At Miliukov's insistence, a "subsidiary" (*maloe*) delegation under his chairmanship was sent on to Paris to talk directly with the Allied heads of state, but it too had no clear mandate or program.[64] The other delegates remained in the city to again seek a unified course of action. They were soon joined by other members of their respective organizations from Kiev, as the Ukrainian capital fell to separatist troops under Petliura on December 1/14.

New York, 1963, pp. 221-36. The *Protokoly* from the Jassy conference are in the Wrangel Military Archives, file 143. See also N. Astrov, "Iasskoe soveshchanie," *GMNCS*, No. 3, 1926, pp. 36-76.

[59] Soveshchaniia delegatsii v Iassakh s soiuznymi poslannikami, *Protokol*, No. 9, evening Sess., Nov. 7/20, 1918 (henceforth *Protokol*).

[60] *Ibid.*, No. 8, morning Sess., No. 7/20.　[61] *Ibid.*

[62] *Ibid.*; Miliukov, "Dnevnik," pp. 364-65.

[63] *Protokol*, No. 11, evening Sess., Nov. 8/21, 1918.

[64] *Ibid.*, No. 21, Nov. 17/30, 1918; No. 22, Nov. 19/Dec. 2, 1918.

The political situation in Odessa at the time the Jassy delegates arrived was even more complicated than it had been elsewhere in the Ukraine. At the end of November 1918, authority was nominally in the hands of a regional Muslim leader, Mustafin, who had administered the city under Skoropadskii and the Germans. As the Jassy group arrived, however, they found the city in the grip of a general strike, led by radical socialists. Mustafin's control was rapidly deteriorating, and a short while later, workers and soldiers loyal to the Ukrainian nationalist Petliura toppled him completely.

Within days, however, French transports arrived, part of an ill-conceived and disorganized Paris plan to aid Denikin by occupying regions evacuated by the Germans. For the sake of appearances, the transports brought a small detachment of Volunteers under one of Denikin's more wild-eyed lieutenants, Grishin-Almazov. Clearing the city with his own men in order to avoid any question of foreign intervention, Almazov soon set himself up as military governor; meanwhile, French troops were deployed on Odessa's outskirts both to protect the city, and to maintain a beachhead in case the Allies decided on future large-scale intervention.[65]

Almost at once, however, Grishin-Almazov met strong opposition from the Odessa City Duma. Elected in the summer of 1917, the Duma, like so many other similar bodies in Russia, was largely composed of moderate socialists, though almost one-sixth of its members were Kadets, and its leader was the Kadet mayor, M. V. Braikevich (the same moderate liberal figure who had attended the Jassy conference as a member of the Union of Regeneration). What angered local leaders was that Almazov unilaterally assumed dictatorial powers, taking full control of city government. He seized city funds, replaced duly elected officials with his own men, and also arrested a number of local leaders whom he suspected of Bolshevik sympathies. In turn, Duma members boycotted the Volunteers, demanding their city "be returned." Almazov not only refused, but began to deal harshly with Duma figures themselves, arresting several, and forcing others out of the city.[66]

In these circumstances, Kadets once again found themselves in a unique position to mollify discord; indeed, this was precisely the type

[65] Miliukov, "Dnevnik," pp. 162-76, and his Rossiia na perelome, II, 91-92; Denikin, Ocherki, V, 8-10; V. Kantorovich, Frantsuzy v Odesse, Petrograd, 1922, pp. 4ff; F. Anulov, "Soiuznyi desant na Ukraine," in A. G. Shlikhter, ed., Chernaia kniga, Ekaterinoslav, 1925, pp. 164-66. The Allies' role in Odessa is discussed in detail by George Brinkley in his The Volunteer Army and Allied Intervention in South Russia, 1917-21, Notre Dame, 1966, pp. 113-45.

[66] M. Braikevich, "Iz revoliutsii nam chto-nibud'," NCS, No. 5, 1924, pp. 224-25; Margulies, God, I, 107ff; A. S. Sannikov, "Vospominaniia, 1918-1919," unpubl. MS in the Columbia Russian Archive, 1926, pp. 2-3.

of situation Astrov had envisioned in deciding to work with Denikin, and which he hoped could be remedied by a revitalization of party and National Center activities. Again, Kadets were prominent both in the major public organizations in Odessa and in the local city government; and this time they were in reasonably close communication as well with party leaders on the Special Council in Ekaterinodar.

But once again—with a repetition which might be tiresome if it did not portend such disaster for the anti-Bolshevik cause—the Kadets themselves proved bitterly divided; Astrov's "fabric of unity" was little more than shredded cloth. Moderates in the Union of Regeneration continued to insist that a coalition directorate be established for all of South Russia, and refused to recognize Almazov's authority. And while ready to grant a leading role to Denikin and the Volunteers—the directorate most talked about consisted of Astrov, Denikin, and a moderate socialist—the Union still insisted that the main requirement for firm authority was broad popular support. It also demanded that Almazov be recalled pending the specific investiture of local power by a broad conference of popular representatives.[67]

Kadets in the Council of National Reunification, meanwhile—now including Miliukov's staunch supporter Fedor Rodichev[68]—again demanded local power for themselves, specifically suggesting the creation of a temporary South Russian Regional Government. The responsibility of such an administration would be to govern those portions of the Ukraine previously ruled by Hetman Skoropadskii—the effort was, in effect, to establish a liberal regional regime rather than allow the formation of a separatist Ukrainian one—and its source of power would be Denikin himself, who would support it with troops and appoint its minister of war and foreign affairs. Council members hoped this would take care of generals like Grishin-Almazov, since local administration would be entirely under their control.[69]

Finally, while Braikevich and local Odessa Kadets fiercely resented the pretensions of "national" figures like Rodichev on the Council for National Reunification, Kadets in both the Odessa branch of the Moscow National Center and V. V. Shulgin's separate South Russian National Center continued to support Denikin. And while Braikevich and his colleagues remained close to the Union of Regeneration, insisting that full power be returned to the Duma,[70] the two independent National Center groups continued to back Volunteer rule

[67] Miakotin, "Iz nedalekago," *NCS*, No. 6, 1924, pp. 87-88; Astrov, "Grazhdanskaia voina," pp. 139-40.

[68] Astrov, "Grazhdanskaia voina," p. 139.   [69] Margulies, *God*, I, 138-40.

[70] Astrov, "Grazhdanskaia voina," pp. 135-39; *Odesskaia Pochta*, No. 3536, Jan. 30/Feb. 12, 1919.

(though they too felt Almazov was hopeless, and pressured Ekaterinodar to replace him).[71]

Thus Kadets once again found it impossible not only to agree among themselves, but to coordinate the policies of their respective organizations in any constructive way; military crisis and civil war did nothing to bring them together in Odessa, or even to prompt the development of any effective party cohesion. How weak the party actually was became apparent at the end of January 1919 when the Volunteers, convinced that the City Duma was "impeding" their efforts to maintain order, "prorogued" that body and set up a new, special Political Section to deal with the populace.[72] This caused an enormous commotion, the reverberations of which were soon felt back in Ekaterinodar.[73] Within days, the order came down to reopen the Duma; and Grishin-Almazov was finally replaced. But Kadets in each of the public organizations now found themselves in a withering crossfire. From the left they were blamed along with Astrov, Sokolov, Stepanov, and their party colleagues with Denikin for the stringencies of military rule; and from army circles and the right they were scored for discrediting Almazov.[74] It thus became impossible for Kadets to secure any form of general political settlement whatsoever in the city.[75] And here again, the legacy of the party's ineffectuality was a distrust and mutual animosity among the public organizations, which would last well into the emigration.[76]

In the end, none of this had any bearing on Odessa's future. By the beginning of March 1919, Bolshevik troops were already approaching the city from the north, and the Volunteers were not able to gather a sufficient number of men to defend it. The French, meanwhile, anxious not to get directly involved in the fighting, determined somewhat precipitiously to withdraw. By the middle of the month, White supporters were fleeing in large numbers, cramming every available boat. And as the exodus became a nightmare, the city fell into Bolshevik hands.

But the loss of the city aside, what all of this indicated was that Kadets simply could not be effectively mobilized in support of Denikin's army in regions under White control. This in turn confirmed the bitter judgments of military men like Lukomskii about civilian

---

[71] *Rossiia*, No. 3, Jan. 11/24, 1919; Document entitled "Informatsiia odesskago otdela natsional'nogo tsentra," dated Feb. 13/25, 1919, in the Wrangel Military Archives, file 132.

[72] *Odesskaia Pochta*, No. 3523, Jan. 15/28, 1919; No. 3529, Jan. 22/Feb. 4, 1919.

[73] *Rossiia*, No. 6, Jan. 15/28, 1919; No. 7, Jan. 16/29, 1919.

[74] Azbuka Report, Odessa, Jan. 29, 1919, in Wrangel Military Archives, file 132.

[75] Telegram from P. P. Iurenev to M. M. Fedorov, Jan. 31, 1919, in the Wrangel Military Archives, file 132.

[76] Miakotin, "Iz nedalekago," *NCS*, No. 6, 1924, p. 93.

politicians generally, and made the task of moderates like Astrov, Fedorov, and Iurenev infinitely more difficult. In Ekaterinodar, Astrov and his colleagues looked at the situation in despair. It seemed obvious what the Kadet experience implied not only for the army, but for Russia's political future as well, should Lenin still by some miracle be defeated, and Kadets try again to assume responsibility for defining the interests of the nation "as a whole."[77]

[77] Astrov, "Grazhdanskaia voina," pp. 139-40.

CHAPTER TWELVE

A "Model Solution" to the Problem of Power: The Kadet Government in the Crimea

Tнᴇ ᴄᴏʟʟᴀᴘѕᴇ of Odessa marked the end for the time being of Astrov's efforts to use Kadets as the "living fabric" of the anti-Bolshevik movement in South Russia. Divided among themselves, deeply disillusioned over White Army administrative practices, Kadets also faced the growing strength of the Bolsheviks, whose forces in the spring of 1919 were sweeping rapidly through the Ukraine. By April 1919 Kadets were fleeing toward Ekaterinodar or going abroad, taking stock of their own political movement and awaiting a more favorable military situation.

Meanwhile, quite a different party effort was also beginning to crumble in the south, revealing even further the Kadets' inability to work constructively in the anti-Bolshevik cause, or even cooperate among themselves. While Astrov and others were trying to forge administrative links in support of Denikin, Maxim Vinaver, Vladimir Nabokov, Solomon Krym, and other Kadets were creating a new liberal administration of their own in the Crimea, "building from below." The Crimean effort represented a culmination of conciliationist tendencies on the part of the party's moderate left—an attempt finally to build political authority on the basis of popular support and create a firm, lasting, political administration capable of realizing basic liberal principles:

> The Crimea was to serve for all Russia as an example of cultured, democratic government, satisfying all just demands of the population, avoiding all mistakes of socialist passion, and fighting with Bolshevik demagogy. In a word, a model laboratory experiment.[1]

In contrast to the policies of right-wing Kadets like Stepanov and Sokolov, whose actions often reinforced an indiscriminate military ruthlessness, the experiment of Kadets in the Crimea represented the best of liberal traditions. The fate of the Crimean regime is all the more revealing, consequently, in terms of the Kadets' general destiny in the revolution and civil war.

[1] D. S. Pasmanik, *Revoliutsionnye gody v Krymu*, Paris, 1926, p. 113.

THE CRIMEAN POLITICAL BACKGROUND

Like the liberal effort in the Ukraine, the Crimean experiment had shaky foundations. The Kadet party had no deep roots in the region, which had extensive Ukrainian and Tatar populations. While Kadet groups formed in Yalta, Simferopol, and Sevastapol as early as 1905, they were more concerned with national than local affairs. As one party member observed, Kadets showed a "manorial" (*gospodskii*) attitude toward other Crimean parties and groups, considering themselves almost too important to be closely involved in local political currents.[2]

Three such currents dominated Crimean affairs in 1917, each of which would later affect the "model laboratory experiment": Tatar nationalism; SR activism in the countryside; and a developing anarchism among soldiers, sailors, and workers in Crimean port cities. Led by militant young intellectuals, largely educated in Constantinople, the Tatars were organized in a nationalist party, the Millî Firka (Crimean Tatar National Party), which considered the region ethnically part of Turkey. Tatar spokesmen bitterly opposed the Kadets' policy toward Constantinople and the Straits, and demanded cultural autonomy, nationalization of land, and a Russian federation.[3] The SRs, meanwhile, cultivated a largely Russian peasantry in Taurida province. While somewhat less volatile than their brethren in other parts of the country in 1917, peasants here as elsewhere were still militantly in favor of agrarian reform, and gave overwhelming support to SR programs and leaders.[4] In the elections to the Constituent Assembly, SRs secured more than 300,000 of the region's 500,000-odd votes, their closest competition coming from the Ukrainians and Tatars, each of whom secured about 60,000.[5] SRs were also very strong in local zemstvo organizations, which, unlike the Kadet groups, stressed the importance of regional autonomy.[6]

The most radical elements in the Crimea in 1917 were the soldiers and sailors in Sevastopol, the principal port of the Black Sea fleet. They were not well organized politically, however, since few Bolsheviks were in the region, and other left-wing groups were tainted by their

[2] *Ibid.*, p. 47.

[3] D. Seidamet, *La Crimée*, Lausanne, 1921, pp. 66-71; R. Pipes, *The Formation of the Soviet Union*, Cambridge, Mass., 1954, pp. 79-81; A. Bennigsen and C. Lemercier-Quelquejay, *Islam in the Soviet Union*, New York, 1967, pp. 25-29, 70.

[4] Bennigsen and Lemercier, p. 50.

[5] O. H. Radkey, *The Elections to the Russian Constituent Assembly of 1917*, Cambridge, Mass., 1950, appendix. Radkey's figures for this region are slightly incomplete.

[6] M. Bunegin, *Revoliutsiia i grazhdanskaia voina v Krymu, 1917-20*, Simferopol, 1927, pp. 31-32.

identification with the war. The result was a strong current of anarchism and civil disorder.[7]

Kadets in this context remained well organized, but without an extensive popular base. In the Constituent Assembly elections, they won only some 7 percent of the vote, most of which came from professional elements in Simferopol and Sevastopol.[8] Kadets did maintain close contact with zemstvo groups, however; and one of their members, Nicholas Bogdanov, was both a member of the regional zemstvo board, and Provisional Government commissar for the entire Tauride area. Kadets thus maintained a considerable degree of influence among elements best able to handle the problems of civil administration, an important factor in 1918 in the formation of the Crimean regional government.[9]

After the Bolshevik coup, political control in the region was divided: Lenin's supporters established a tenuous hold on Sevastopol, while Tatar military detachments asserted authority in the region around Simferopol. In this situation, Kadets and the zemstvo elements moved together in opposition to both camps, though they offered no organized resistance, and soon suspended their activities as Bolsheviks and Tatars battled for control.[10] At the end of January 1918, Bolshevik sailors launched an assault on Simferopol and, defeating the Tatars, established the first Crimean Soviet administration.[11]

The new regime was exceedingly harsh. Since even the Bolsheviks found it difficult to control the sailors, whose excesses were appalling, the situation soon bordered on complete anarchy. By April 1918 it had sapped the Bolsheviks' strength to such a degree that they were unable to return a majority of delegates to the Sevastopol Soviet. Before they could regroup, however, the Germans arrived; and the Bolsheviks evacuated so hastily that they even neglected to leave instructions or directives for cadres remaining behind.[12]

Nowhere in Russia was the German occupation welcomed so enthusiastically as in the Crimea. To liberals, German arms brought order and the containment of rampaging sailors; to Ukrainians and Tatars, they promised greater regional independence. When members

[7] Iu. P. Gaven, "Vosniknovenie krymskoi organizatsii R.K.P. (bol'shevikov)," *Revoliutsiia v Krymu*, No. 2, 1923, pp. 6-10.

[8] Bunegin, p. 31; see also Table 7 above. [9] Pasmanik, pp. 48, 67.

[10] V. Obolenskii, "Krym v 1917-1920 gg.," *NCS*, No. 5, 1924, pp. 29ff.

[11] A. Vasil'ev, "Pervaia sovetskaia vlast' v Krymu i ee padenie," *PR*, No. 7, 1922, pp. 3-11.

[12] Iu. P. Gaven, "Bor'ba bol'shevistskogo podpol'ia za sovetskii Krym," *Revoliutsiia v Krymu*, No. 9, 1930, pp. 5-6; A. Vasil'ev, "Pervaia sovetskaia vlast'," p. 28.

of the occupation command arrived in Yalta, a festive city greeted them as liberators.[13]

The Crimean Kadets had ridden out the Bolshevik storm in complete isolation. "The most difficult aspect of our life," Vladimir Obolenskii wrote later in describing this period, "was the fact that we were completely cut off from the rest of the world. . . . We did not receive any newspapers, and when Bolshevik journals occasionally fell into our hands, we found in them only an endless series of 'decrees' and ungrammatical news articles, whose content we could not believe."[14] But if the Germans ended this isolation, restoring as well a modicum of order, they also presented Crimean liberals with the same "orientation" problems that had faced their colleagues elsewhere. And here, too, Kadets found no easy resolutions.

One obvious possibility, strongly urged by those convinced of the Germans' inevitable victory in the war, was to follow the lead of Kadets in Kiev and openly cooperate with Russia's formal enemy. Nabokov himself led the way in justifying a policy of accommodation, rationalizing a change in Kadet policy on historical grounds:

Insofar as we have become cultured Europeans it is only thanks to the Germans. Our science, our technology, our philosophy are fruits of the German cultural influence. Even economically we are tied to Germany, and not to England or France. . . . We must therefore make peace with the Germans, if that is still possible.[15]

The problem was to work out a regional government the Germans would accept. Kadets wanted an end to the fighting, but also a clear recognition of Russia's territorial sanctity. And, as in the Ukraine, the Germans pressed a regional independence that Kadets found unacceptable. Shortly after their arrival, the Tatar Kurultai (Assembly) convened in Simferopol, and with German approval, structured its own Provisional Crimean Government under Dzjafer Seidamet on an openly separatist platform. Seidamet and the German commander, General Kosch, both wanted broad liberal participation in the regime as a means of securing its authority with commercial elements, whose help Berlin wanted for the war effort. But in contrast to their colleagues in Kiev, the Crimean Kadets responded with a program of their own demands, designed both to limit the Tatars' influence and contain Crimean separatism. Seidamet's plans consequently collapsed. Thereupon the Germans gave regional authority to General Suleiman

[13] F. Wertheimer, *Durch Ukraine und Krim*, Stuttgart, 1918, p. 112; Pasmanik, p. 89.

[14] Obolenskii, "Krym," p. 23.   [15] Pasmanik, p. 94.

Sulkevich, a universally disliked Lithuanian Muslim who had earlier fought against the Allies in Rumania. Sulkevich's first acts were to close a regional zemstvo conference, prohibit further sessions of Crimean city dumas, and proscribe public political meetings.[16] In effect, he became the Crimea's Skoropadskii, though without Kadet assistance.

With these developments Kadets themselves again "retired," following a policy of passive non-cooperation. They thus avoided any identification or responsibility for the Germans' own harsh administration, and incidentally demonstrated to their party colleagues in Kiev an alternative to outright collaborationism. Sulkevich made several new attempts to lure them into his cabinet, but they consistently refused. Only one regional party meeting was held during the summer of 1918 at Yalta, where a small gathering voted to continue their policy of "detachment."[17]

KADETS CONSTRUCT A "MODEL GOVERNMENT"

Kadet activity revived only toward the end of the summer, when General Sulkevich recalled the zemstvo and city councils, and allowed a new regional zemstvo conference to convene. The German puppet was bidding for popular support, but Solomon Krym, Nicholas Bogdanov, Vladimir Obolenskii, and the other Kadets active in zemstvo affairs returned to the councils convinced that the days of the occupation were numbered. Their thoughts were on replacing Sulkevich with a popular administration of their own choosing.[18]

While the Germans ignored a zemstvo demand to dismiss Sulkevich, Crimean politics were now in a state of flux, with Kadets themselves once again in an excellent position to influence the sequence of events. In Bogdanov, Krym, and Obolenskii, they had three of the zemstvo movement's most respected figures; and the presence of Petrunkevich, Nabokov, Vinaver, Pasmanik, and other Central Committee members gave their local party organization national stature and prestige.

This was the situation when Nicholas Astrov reached Yalta in the beginning of October 1918, on his way to the Kuban. The Moscow Kadet was not concerned with local politics, however, but with coordinating different Kadet groups in support of a united anti-Bolshevik movement, as we have seen. He regarded the Crimea pri-

[16] Gaven, "Bor'ba," pp. 11-12; Pasmanik, pp. 98-99; E. Kirimal, *Der Nationale Kampf der Krimturken*, Emsdetten, W. Germ., 1952, pp. 179-83.

[17] N. N. Bogdanov, "Krymskoe kraevoe pravitel'stvo," unpubl. MS in the Archive of the Crimean Regional Government, file 19, pp. 6-7.

[18] M. Vinaver, undated "Memorandum" in the Crimean Government Archive, file 6.

marily as a base for future Allied support to the Volunteers, favoring a local administration directly subordinate to Ekaterinodar.[19]

But both the local Kadets and Central Committee members like Vinaver and Nabokov now had very different views about uniting anti-Bolshevik Russia. Solomon Krym, Nicholas Bogdanov, and the Crimeans insisted regional stability depended on a local government capable of meeting local needs, and wanted an administration closely related to the zemstvos. Liberal programs could then be implemented independently of outside directives. Vinaver and Nabokov, meanwhile, also favored the creation of a strong local regime. While still opposed to regional separatism, their isolation during the summer of 1918 had finally convinced them that state authority imposed from without was doomed to failure in the turbulent conditions of revolution. They were now convinced that Kadets should follow the policies a number of local party groups had begun back in March 1917 in the committees of public organizations, and create strong local (although not separatist) administrations.[20]

Thus in the midst of what was rapidly becoming the worst civil conflict in all Russian history, Kadets in the Crimea finally retreated from the party's traditional statist orientation, and began to think practically of organizing a government administration directly related to local needs and aspirations. Now as in 1917, however, their views were not shared by many of their colleagues. Astrov and Panina continued to insist on the region's subordination to Denikin, fearing the Whites would be left with little support if regions like the Crimea failed to think beyond their own immediate needs. And the views of other leading party figures in the Crimea fanned out with the same broad diversity which had characterized the Kadets from 1905 onward. Gregory Trubetskoi and Nicholas Teslenko supported strict military dictatorship; the time was not right for experiments, and even Astrov's arguments in favor of cooperation with the moderate left were viewed suspiciously. Dmitri Pasmanik thought the views of local and national Kadets should be compromised; while Vinaver and even Petrunkevich, now the grand old man of the liberal movement, pressed with Bogdanov and Krym for Kadets to develop as many regional "building blocks" as possible, enjoying the confidence of local populations and uniting Russia "from below."[21]

The Yalta discussions thus came to no clear resolution. Astrov soon departed for the Kuban with Vinaver, leaving Bogdanov, Krym, and

[19] N. Astrov, "Grazhdanskaia voina," unpubl. MS in the Panina Archive, pack. 3, suppl. 3, n.d., pp. 28-33.

[20] Pasmanik, p. 113; M. Vinaver, *Nashe pravitel'stvo*, Paris, 1928, pp. 7-8.

[21] Astrov, "Grazhdanskaia voina," pp. 34-35.

other Crimean Kadets to their own devices, at least for the time being. And while Kadets met at the Ekaterinodar conference to formulate a unified course of action, their party colleagues in the Crimea continued their discussions in local zemstvo councils with the SRs, determined to put their own regional plan into effect.

Two problems were now at hand for the Crimeans: preventing the German puppet Sulkevich from preserving his authority once the Germans withdrew (as it now became apparent they would); and securing some new military force to preserve order and defend the region against the Bolsheviks. At a zemstvo conference in Yalta during September, both SRs and Mensheviks responded favorably to the idea of Solomon Krym heading a new administration. The Kadet agronomist possessed all the needed attributes. A long-time Crimean social figure, sympathetic, compassionate, and well known throughout the province, he had never taken a militant anti-socialist stance in more than a dozen years of public service; and his mild-mannered disposition made him generally well liked. He had also served as president of the Tauride zemstvo council; and while conservatives respected him as a landowner and former member of the Russian Senate, he was admired by the left for his work in social welfare. Krym also spoke the Tatar language, and for a short period, represented a predominantly Tatar constituency in the State Duma. Both Kadets and SRs consequently hoped he could also blunt the antipathies of Muslim nationalism.[22]

So that relations with other local Russian administrations might be as smooth as possible, and also to imbue a Crimean regime with some aura of national competence, Krym was willing to assume political responsibility only if members of the Kadet Central Committee took posts in his administration. He specifically wanted Maxim Vinaver to handle foreign relations, and Vladimir Nabokov, the ministry or department of justice.[23] Nabokov readily agreed, so readily in fact, that his colleagues in Ekaterinodar later accused him of grabbing for power.[24] But Vinaver had deep reservations. He and Krym were both Jews, and Vinaver feared the prejudice of Denikin and the Volunteers. He was persuaded only when Ivan Petrunkevich, the doughty *starik* of the constitutional democratic movement, insisted with unconscious prophecy that Volunteer anti-Semitism would destroy any chance of saving Russia.[25] Krym's choices were then approved by the

22 Feuilleton on S. Krym in *Posledniia Novosti*, No. 5656, Sept. 18, 1936.
23 M. M. Vinaver, undated "Memorandum" in the M. M. Vinaver Papers, Yivo Institute for Jewish Research, New York.
24 Astrov, "Grazhdanskaia voina," p. 116.
25 R. Vinavera, "Vospominaniia," MS in the Hoover Institution, 1944, p. 108.

Provincial Zemstvo Board, which called a second regional conference in Simferopol to work out the government's new program in detail.

The most interesting aspect of the discussions which followed is that Kadets again found themselves with familiar liberal dilemmas, despite all the exigencies of revolution and civil war. While they believed the zemstvo conference should establish a temporary regional government, willing to surrender authority to an all-Russian Constituent Assembly, their socialist colleagues felt that the only viable political form for a future Russian state was a federal republic, and wanted the Crimean administration to establish itself as a permanent component of a future federation. The socialists also urged that a new Crimean regime declare itself in favor of democracy and a republic, but Kadets still feared this would "usurp the prerogatives of the Constituent Assembly." Thus, while accused of being separatists in Ekaterinodar, Krym and his colleagues were challenged in Simferopol for their Great Russian nationalism.[26]

The socialists also desired to convene a regional legislature (Sejm) to which the executive component of the Crimean regime would be responsible. But Kadets feared the voting strength of Tatar nationalists, arguing that a democratic Sejm might detach the Crimea from Russia, and form an association with Muslim Turkey.[27] Here, for liberals, were the old familiar problems of ministerial responsibility, separatism, and the anti-statist tendencies of an uncultured electorate. Affirming their support for political democracy in principle, the Crimean Kadets insisted that it could develop on a constructive basis only, insuring the unity of a future Russian state.[28]

In the end, these and other problems were worked out in a series of compromises. The liberals yielded by agreeing to the Sejm, but secured a postponement of elections for at least two months. Zemstvo leaders agreed instead that the Crimean administration would be temporarily accountable to periodic regional zemstvo conferences. On the question of Russia's future political organization, an SR resolution in favor of a federal republic was replaced by a milder affirmation of faith in the ability of a new, democratically elected Constituent Assembly to decide the issue. Also passed over was a specific condemnation of military dictatorship. Eventually, all parties agreed to the following six-point program:

> The Conference of Provincial Zemstvo members of the Crimean districts considers it necessary to take on itself the formation of a government in the Crimea, so long as this can be done in conditions

[26] Vinaver, *Nashe pravitel'stvo*, pp. 12-13; Pasmanik, p. 114.
[27] Bogdanov, "Krymskoe," pp. 9-10.   [28] *Ibid.*

of absolute political independence, and on the basis of the following principles:

1. The government is to be responsible for taking all measures to unify Russia, and with this goal, to seek a rapprochement with all governing organizations which have arisen in other parts of Russia, and which have established for themselves the basic task of resurrecting a united nation; the problem of constructing a united Russian government and the question of its form is to be finally decided by an all-Russian Constituent Assembly, for which elections must be held again.

2. In the areas of legislation and administration, the new government is to be responsible for establishing all civil rights abrogated by former regimes, and when issuing additional laws in the future, is to be guided by democratic principles. The organs of city and zemstvo self-government are to be reestablished. To this end, the government is to call immediately for new local elections on the basis of universal suffrage, with an age qualification of twenty-five years, and a one-year residence requirement.

3. Until the creation in the Crimea of a representative government, the new administration is to be granted all legislative and executive authorities; and with the aim of continual contact with the Zemstvo Conference, is to convene the provincial Zemstvo members on a periodic basis. The government will give a short account of its activities to the Conference, and allow it to review its affairs; in this way the government will become familiar with the conditions of the region. It will not, however, be politically responsible to the Zemstvo Conference; and if, after a short while, not to exceed two months, there has not been created a united all-Russian government . . . the Crimean administration will convoke a regional Sejm on the basis of a universal, direct, and equal election law. . . .

4. From the moment a Crimean representative assembly [Sejm] is elected, legislative functions will be its responsibility; the administration is to be politically responsible to the assembly for actions taken both before and after its convocation.

5. The present Conference is electing a head of government, who will form a cabinet through agreement with political parties, and who will take into consideration the national pecularities of the Crimean region.

6. S. S. Krym is elected head of government.[29]

The charter thus corresponded very extensively to basic liberal principles. The periodic convocation of a consultative zemstvo assem-

[29] Vinaver, *Nashe pravitel'stvo*, p. 225.

bly provided a form of popular representation which would not interfere with the government's daily operation, and allowed the ministers a breathing space in which to cultivate popular political consciousness. The Kadets could thus establish civil liberties, and control a disorganized populace with an unencumbered hand. For the time being, social issues and major reforms would be postponed, as not in the government's competence. The only awkward passage in the document referred to conditions of "absolute political independence." The phrase was inserted because the Crimea was still under German control, and zemstvo leaders wanted it clear they would brook no interference from German authorities.[30] But the wording was subject to misinterpretation, and would later become a source of trouble.

In the beginning of November 1918, as the Germans prepared to withdraw, Krym and the Kadets were ready. Cabinet appointments were completed, with Krym selecting carefully from Menshevik, SR, and Tatar ranks.[31] Professing they had no desire to act as an all-Russian regime, members of the new government were even reluctant to call themselves "ministers," doing so only on the insistence of the Moscow Kadets, who felt the title would enhance their authority. Their purpose was simply to administer a liberated Crimea on liberal principles, and demonstrate to the rest of Russia that a coalition government, formed in a spirit of interparty cooperation and attentive to the needs and views of the populace, could perform effectively.[32]

CRIMEAN POLITICS AND THE VOLUNTEER ARMY

As Krym and his cabinet took power, the other major problem facing the zemstvo conferences in September and October 1918, that of securing some military force to replace the Germans in defending the region against the Bolsheviks, became their primary concern. Since the

[30] Article on the Crimean government by N. Bogdanov in *Posledniia Novosti*, No. 2100, Dec. 22, 1926.

[31] In addition to Krym (prime minister), Vinaver (minister of foreign affairs), and Nabokov (minister of justice), the cabinet included two other Kadets: N. N. Bogdanov (minister of internal affairs) and A. P. Bart (minister of finance). From the SRs and Mensheviks, Krym appointed A. A. Steven (trade, industry, and communication), P. S. Bobrovskii (controller and secretary), and S. A. Nikonov (education). Admiral Kanin, a commandant of the Black Sea navy nominally subordinate to Denikin, and General Butchik, a Tatar officer, rounded out the appointments as ministers in charge of army and navy relations. According to a memorandum in the Vinaver Papers, Yivo Institute, Krym accepted the prime minister's position only on condition that a majority of the cabinet be composed of Kadets; and despite its coalition character, the government was generally considered a Kadet regime.

[32] Crimean Regional Government, "Declaration of Aims," in A. I. Gukovskii, ed., "Krymskoe kraevoe pravitel'stvo, 1918-1919," *KA*, No. 22, 1927, p. 128; M. Margulies, *God interventsii*, 3 vols., Berlin, 1923, III, 187.

logical source of troops was the Volunteer Army, Vinaver and Bogdanov took instructions with them to explore this possibility with Denikin when they went to Ekaterinodar to attend the Kadet conference in October. The problem was that while Vinaver and the Crimeans worried about Volunteer occupation policies, and insisted on the strict subordination of any White detachment to their own civilian administration, Denikin and his generals regarded the Crimea as they did the Kuban: a troublesome political fragmentation of the anti-Bolshevik movement. Denikin in particular felt the time was inappropriate for political experiments. What was needed was a union of all social forces behind the army and the help of political parties in extending military rule.[33]

As we have seen, this view was widely shared among the Ekaterinodar Kadets, who warned their colleagues that a coalition regime in the Crimea was likely to be subverted from within by radical socialists.[34] Astrov and others also began to suspect their colleagues' political ambitions, feeling they had staked out "ministerial" positions with an eye to their own future careers.[35] In response, Vinaver and Bogdanov could only reiterate the efficacy of building "from below," while arguing their own lack of personal ambition, and continuing to insist the region had to be protected from the Bolsheviks. But by stressing the Bolshevik danger as a means of securing Volunteer assistance, the Crimeans only reinforced the views of those who felt the region should be under strict military control.[36]

Events themselves settled the question temporarily. While Vinaver negotiated, Krym's regime came into power. Denikin consequently agreed with much reluctance to send a small force of 600 men into the region, accepting in principle a restriction against interfering in the Crimea's internal affairs. There was, however, one important catch: Denikin expected his small detachment to be augmented by a mobilization in the Crimea of officers and soldiers, and he placed his own lieutenant, Baron de-Bode, in charge of this operation.[37]

Mobilization and the principle of noninterference were potential contradictions, epitomizing the difficulties of meshing military and civilian rule. Initially, as the Volunteers began arriving and received an enthusiastic reception, voluntary enlistments exceeded the army's

[33] Vinaver, *Nashe pravitel'stvo*, pp. 37-38; A. I. Denikin, *Ocherki russkoi smuty*, 5 vols., Paris-Berlin, 1921-25, v, 55-56.

[34] Bogdanov, "Krymskoe," pp. 25-26.

[35] Astrov, "Grazhdanskaia voina," pp. 106, 113.

[36] *Ibid.*

[37] Telegram No. 495, Denikin to General de-Bode and minister of internal affairs M. M. Vinaver, Nov. 7, 1918, in the Crimean Government Archive, file 1. See also Vinaver, *Nashe pravitel'stvo*, p. 229.

processing capacities, making the question of mobilization irrelevant, or at least so it seemed to the Crimeans, who expected any specific decision in this regard would be left to them.[38] On November 14/27, 1918, when Vinaver had an amicable meeting with the Volunteer commander, General Korvin-Krukovskii, neither mentioned the need for a draft.[39]

Yet a scant two days afterward, the Volunteer command plastered the walls of Simferopol, Yalta, and Kerch with an "official" mobilization order, calling up all able-bodied officers who had previously served in the Russian Army. Completely unexpected, the order provoked a considerable outcry, even among those whose social interests the army most protected. It implied not only the imposition of martial law, but the subordination of the government itself to the army's command. Angrily, the ministers telegraphed Denikin to rescind it and to demand that the army act only in conjunction with the government.[40]

Now it was Denikin who was angry and surprised. At first assuming mobilization had been decided on earlier, and backing his commanders in the field, he yielded only after a barrage of telegrams from Vinaver recalled his own personal pledge of noninterference, and insisted de-Bode's procedures would create new disorder.[41] But while the order was rescinded, and placards removed, the incident badly damaged the Kadet ministers' credibility, creating serious tensions.[42]

These were not reduced by a growing conviction among the Volunteers that Crimean liberalism was strengthening the Bolsheviks; or by repeated complaints to Simferopol of abusive Volunteer practices. Especially in the three northern districts of the Tauride, de-Bode and Korvin-Krukovskii thought foodstuffs and matériel that should be going to support the Volunteers was finding its way into Bolshevik hands. To curtail this "uncontrollable theft," as the Volunteers described it, Denikin's officers introduced a more stringent control.[43] In practical terms, this meant arbitrary searches, arrests, military courts-martial, and the general panoply of abuses which accompanied Volunteer occupation in other parts of South Russia. Yet additional protests by the Crimean ministers were regarded in Ekaterinodar as "proofs" of a "dangerous separatism."[44]

---

[38] Vinaver, *Nashe pravitel'stvo*, p. 138.   [39] *Ibid.*, p. 139.

[40] *Ibid.*, pp. 139-41; copies of the ministers' telegrams are in the Crimean Government Archive, file 1.

[41] *Ibid.*

[42] Vinaver, *Nashe pravitel'stvo*, pp. 140-41; Pasmanik, pp. 131-32.

[43] *Zhurnal Osobago Soveshchaniia pri Glavnokomanduiushchem Dobrovol'cheskoi Armiei*, No. 21, Dec. 18, 1918, in the Wrangel Personal Archives, file 1.

[44] Report of direct wire conversation between N. Astrov and S. Krym, Dec. 17,

By the first week of December 1918, the situation was deteriorating badly. De-Bode was now demanding that the government itself institute a general mobilization and take forceful steps against "criminal elements" who were "slandering" the Volunteers. Public groups like the zemstvo committees, on the other hand, were showing increasing reticence to continue giving the government support. Yet the louder the public outcry, the more the Volunteers were convinced that the only acceptable solution was a military dictatorship. And the more they pressed the ministers to act.[45]

On November 29/December 12, Krym's cabinet finally decided to give ground and publish their own mobilization decree.[46] But the very next day, when they communicated via telegraph with Denikin and Stepanov, they were accused of excessive tardiness on the question, and a passive attitude. Their shock and indignation was hardly appeased by Stepanov's patronizing reminder that every day was valuable, and that all Kadets were essentially involved in a common cause.[47]

The Ekaterinodar leaders simply did not understand the Crimean context. While Denikin was attempting to control local policies from a distance, Stepanov was assuming the Kadets in the Kuban had a clearer perception of Russia's political circumstances than their Crimean party colleagues. But even as Stepanov was on the wire, the Tatar Kurultai was issuing a manifesto condemning the draft and directing Tatars not to cooperate; *Priboi,* the vigorous journal of Crimean SDs, was castigating the Volunteers as invaders and demanding their removal; and the Crimean Trade Union Council was calling for public meetings to protest de-Bode's excesses, asking members to resist the army's policies. There was even talk of a general strike.[48]

But predictably, this only stiffened the determination of the Volunteers. Reports to Denikin now called for even sterner measures.[49] In response, Denikin ordered General Shilling to advance against suspected Bolshevik detachments in the three northern Crimean districts. And as Shilling cleared the area, he declared it under martial law, establishing his own military government. Since the three districts were nominally part of the Crimean government's jurisdiction, this constituted a direct usurpation of its prerogatives; and when new reports of

---

1918, in the Crimean Government Archive, file 17. See also Pasmanik, pp. 126-27; Vinaver, *Nashe pravitel'stvo,* pp. 140-41.

[45] Vinaver, *Nashe pravitel'stvo,* pp. 147-48; Pasmanik, pp. 128-29.

[46] Crimean Government Archive, file 1.

[47] Vinaver, *Nashe pravitel'stvo,* pp. 153-54.

[48] Newspaper reports on Crimean affairs, Nov.-Dec. 1918, in the Crimean Government Archive, file 9.

[49] Wrangel Military Archives, file 164.

Volunteer atrocities began to circulate, tension built to the point of explosion.[50]

The Crimean Kadets now determined to try once again to use their party's influence in Ekaterinodar to settle differences. But the dispute was not only between military and civilian administrations; it was also between two different Kadet perspectives on how to defeat the Bolsheviks. Ekaterinodar Kadets, moreover, saw the Crimean regime as a manifestation of egoism and of disruptive political separatism, pointing to the government's Statement of Aims with its clause concerning absolute political independence.[51] But to Kadets in the Crimea, it was Denikin's Special Council which was harboring personal ambitions.[52] Animosities thus ran deep, products of both the Kadets' own lack of internal party cohesion and the desperate conditions of civil war, which left field commanders on both sides virtual autocrats in regions under their control.

Discussions between the Crimean and Volunteer leaders consequently led to very little. Vinaver and Bogdanov urged their Ekaterinodar party colleagues to disengage themselves from the Special Council as a means of forcing the generals into recognizing civilian control; but Astrov rejected their arguments out of hand, knowing full well how little influence he and the Ekaterinodar Kadets actually had. While the Volunteers' own unpopularity might be ruining the White cause, Astrov still insisted that the liberals' involvement was preventing an even sterner reaction.[53]

On an official level, one or two decisions were reached that did, in fact, smooth relations slightly. The Volunteers accepted the Crimeans' complaints concerning the administrative excesses of their troops in the field, and reluctantly agreed that the Crimean regime would have jurisdiction over all agitators. The government's full responsibility for requisitioning and supply was also acknowledged, as was its "exclusive right" to determine measures for preserving social order. The Volunteers thus reaffirmed the principle of noninterference; while for their part the Crimeans reiterated support for the Volunteers, and their own commitment to a unified Russia.[54] But it remained to be seen whether any of this would affect actual conditions. Suspicions continued, along with complaints against the army's tough behavior on one hand, and reports of the government's leftist sympathies on the other.[55]

[50] Bogdanov, "Krymskoe," pp. 13-15.   [51] Astrov, "Grazhdanskaia voina," p. 113.
[52] Bogdanov, "Krymskoe," p. 19.
[53] S. S. Krym, "Otchet po poezdke v shtab dobrovol'cheskoi armii chlenov krymskogo kraevago pravitel'stva," in the Crimean Government Archive, file 17.
[54] Memorandum on relations between the Volunteer Army and the Crimean Regional Government, n.d., but Jan. 1919, Crimean Government Archive, file 9.
[55] Reports in the Wrangel Military Archives, file 164.

In these circumstances, it was logical for Vinaver and his Crimean colleagues to look in another direction for assistance. Late in November 1918, an Allied squadron arrived in Sevastopol. Its mission was officially restricted to protecting Black Sea shipping, but like the detachment in Odessa, it also served to establish a beachhead in the event of more active Allied intervention. At first both Vinaver and the Volunteer commander, General Korvin-Krukovskii, wanted Allied troops to replace the departing Germans.[56] Vinaver moved his Office of Foreign Relations to Sevastopol, and on November 27/December 10, gave a long speech of welcome aboard the H.M.S. *Superb*, linking his government with the Volunteers in a "close and noble effort."[57]

But as relations deteriorated between the two White groups, Vinaver began to press for a greater Allied commitment behind his policy of reconstructing Russia from below. Toward the end of December, he called for *de facto* recognition for the Crimean regime. He also wanted an expeditionary force of almost 3,000 men to replace the Volunteers.[58] And he continued his efforts in January and February 1919, despite the new government-Volunteer accords.[59]

Vinaver's plans failed, however, because neither London nor Paris was inclined toward full-scale intervention in the south, and Allied commanders feared taking measures on their own which might overly commit their governments. As in Odessa, the French disembarked in Sevastopol, and set up a strict but limited control of the city. The Crimeans tried, but could not entice a further extension of their operations. The H.M.S. *Superb*, meanwhile, sailed for Batum, revealing a British disinterest Vinaver later described as having "fateful consequence" for the Russian liberal cause.[60]

Programs and Policies

Despite these troubles, Crimean liberals struggled valiantly after taking power to institute a rule of law and uphold civil rights, efforts regarded in Ekaterinodar as foolish experiments in the midst of civil war, but which the Crimean Kadets themselves saw as the keystone to any effective reconstruction. In effect, they placed into practice on a

[56] "Deklaratsiia podannaia krymskim pravitel'svom sovmestno s komandovaniem voiskami dobrovol'cheskoi armii v Krymu admiralu Kol'sorpu, 7 XII 1918 goda [n.s.] v Sevastopole," Crimean Government Archive, file 17.

[57] *Bulletin* [of the Crimean Ministry of Foreign Affairs], No. 10, March 4, 1919, in the Crimean Government Archive, file 3.

[58] Vinaver to Maklakov, Dec. 21, 1918, in the Maklakov Personal Archive, ser. B, pack. 2, doss. 10; Vinaver to French Commander in Sevastopol, n.d., Crimean Government Archive, file 9.

[59] The telegrams are in the Vinaver Papers, Yivo Institute.

[60] Pasmanik, p. 155; Vinaver, *Nashe pravitel'stvo*, pp. 115-16.

local level many of the basic policies of Kerensky's third coalition, to which they and other conciliationists in the Kadet Central Committee had agreed in the aftermath of Kornilov's mutiny.

One of the government's first acts, for example, was to abrogate all decrees of previous regions restricting the press, assembly, worship, or the inviolability of person, even though this meant giving encouragement to Crimean Tatar separatists. Indeed, civil freedoms of this sort soon led not only to new expressions of Tatar nationalism, but also to vituperative attacks on both the Volunteers and the government itself as "bourgeois" and "repressive." Nevertheless, the Kadet cabinet kept its composure, and continued trying to build popular confidence. Maxim Vinaver could later claim with substantial pride that during its entire five months of existence, the government never intentionally violated the rights of any group or citizen.[61]

One of the most impressive liberal efforts was Vladimir Nabokov's revitalization of the local judiciary. Just after becoming minister of justice, the former attorney and head of chancellery for the Provisional Government formed a special commission to reestablish judicial institutions; he himself personally drafted a comprehensive program for their reconstruction, setting up new courts on every level.[62] The ministry also dispatched a series of memoranda to administrative agencies, specifically warning them not to interfere with legal procedures. And it was at Nabokov's personal insistence that many persons seized by the Volunteers were returned to civilian tribunals.[63] Even critics were impressed.[64]

The government also implemented its program of civil rights by supporting local organs of self-government and by creating a network of local administrative bureaus to assist in the execution of official policy. Almost 18 million rubles were granted to zemstvo and city boards to restore essential services, some of which came from private sources. The Kadet ministers also abrogated prerevolutionary laws restricting libraries, reopened the provincial university, and granted complete freedom to private educational institutions.[65]

On larger questions such as land reform, the Crimean Kadets still considered themselves bound by the provisional nature of their regime, just as they had in 1917. And whether from self-interest or consistent

[61] M. Vinaver, "Spravka," in A. Gukovskii, ed., "Krym v 1918-1919 gg.," *KA*, No. 28, 1928, p. 130.

[62] Report of the Commission on the Construction of Juridical Institutions in the Crimea, Crimean Government Archive, file 18.

[63] V. Nabakov, "Memorandum" on the Judiciary in the Crimean Government Archive, file 18.

[64] Pasmanik, p. 180.

[65] Vinaver, "Spravka," p. 131; *Nashe pravitel'stvo*, p. 190.

legalism, they avoided programs which might have national ramifications. They did, however, pass a law which carefully regulated leases and mortgages in the Crimea, and forced land to be leased at a fixed price if it had been done so at the beginning of the war. Prices were set on the basis of "just evaluations," calculated on area yields.[66] The results of this program were impressive. The regional yield of barley increased twofold between 1918 and 1919, that of wheat almost doubled, and that of oats almost tripled, though the harvest came too late to help the Kadets.[67]

Similarly, while the Crimean government failed to introduce any comprehensive program of taxation, it did exact a levy on export profits, and imposed minor excise imposts. By design, these fell heavily on the region's more prosperous city dwellers.[68] Otherwise, the government deliberately spared its constituents from a heavy tax burden by borrowing extensively from the State Bank of the Don, securing almost 53 million rubles from this source, and meeting in this way almost all of its financial needs.[69]

This, in fact, was only one aspect of the government's broader concern for labor and nationality problems, a concern which derived from the obvious realization that if either Tatars or workers turned forcefully against the regime, it would collapse very quickly. Crimean Kadets remained opposed to regional separatism, but they permitted the Tatar Kurultai (Assembly) to meet freely; and at least for the first few months of their rule, they allowed the publication of *Krym* and *Millet*—two Tatar papers which often bitterly attacked both the regime and the army and adopted a nationalist tone. At one point, just as the Volunteers were demanding that the papers be closed, Maxim Vinaver even tried to get them newsprint from the French, a commodity in very short supply.[70] At the same time, the government insisted on the right of labor and peasant associations to meet freely, and condoned the assembly of local political groups, some of which were obviously Bolshevik fronts.[71] They also introduced a certain amount of social insurance legislation in a deliberate effort to demonstrate to workers the "privileges" of liberal democracy.[72]

In pursuing these programs, the Crimean regime remained loosely responsible to the Conference of Zemstvo Representatives, though there

[66] Pasmanik, p. 178-79; Vinaver, "Spravka," p. 130-31.

[67] S. Urov, *Istoriko-ekonomicheskie ocherki Kryma*, Simferopol, 1925, p. 257.

[68] Vinaver, "Spravka," pp. 130-31; Pasmanik, pp. 179-80.

[69] Pasmanik, p. 179.

[70] Vinaver to the French Commander in Sevastopol, Feb. 11, 1919, in the Vinaver Papers, Yivo Institute.

[71] *Sobranie uzakonenii i rasporiazhenii krymskago kraevago pravitel'stva*, in the Papers of V. D. Nabokov, Crimean Government Archive, file 18.

[72] *Ibid.*; see also "Spravka," pp. 130-31.

was no legal relationship between the two, and the cabinet had full legislative and executive powers pending the convocation of the Sejm. Since periodic reports were required, the ministers presented themselves for inspection several times during the government's five-month existence. Most of the sessions were given over to discussing relations with the Volunteers. But despite growing criticism of the latter's role in Crimean affairs, the cabinet continued to enjoy the zemstvos' official support.[73]

The Regional Sejm posed greater problems. Despite their fear of Tatar voting strength, Kadets were committed to its eventual convocation; and when Solomon Krym met Volunteer Army representatives at the end of January, he rejected their suggestion that elections be postponed to the end of the war.[74] Kadets were cautious, however, and procrastinated in working out a draft election statute, which was ready only in February. And while the new Legislation corresponded closely to Russia's own Constituent Assembly law (providing direct, secret, equal and universal election rights), the Tatars complained that their districts had been gerrymandered, and the government collapsed before elections could actually be held.[75]

Voting did take place, however, for new city dumas. And here, to everyone's surprise (including their own), the Kadets did quite well, securing almost a third of all votes cast.[76] The election in Simferopol resulted in a duma of 20 Kadets, 17 Tatars, 13 SDs, 11 SRs, 3 Zionists, 3 Industrialists, and 2 nonparty.[77]

THE GOVERNMENT LOSES CONTROL

But Kadet success was ephemeral. Even without the Bolshevik invasion, which swept through the Tauride at the end of March, the fatal flaw in the liberals' "model laboratory experiment" was its close identification with the excesses of the Volunteer Army. Military commanders simply could not accept the liberal premises on which Crimean rule was based. And supported ironically by Kadets like Rodichev, Sokolov, and Novgorodtsev in Ekaterinodar, who were sure their

---

[73] Pasmanik, pp. 144-45.

[74] Krym, "Otchet." The Ekaterinodar Kadets were so opposed to elections being held for the Sejm that Astrov at one point threatened Krym with expulsion from the Kadet party ("Grazhdanskaia voina," p. 125).

[75] Seidamet, *La Crimée*, p. 83; Plans for a Statute on Elections to the Crimean Regional Sejm, Crimean Government Archive, file 18. Kadets, Social Democrats, SRs, Edinstvo, and eight other parties prepared independent slates for the elections. Their lists are in file 14 of the Crimean Government Archive.

[76] Pasmanik, p. 175.

[77] A. Gukovskii, ed., "Krym v 1918-1919 gg.," *KA*, No. 29, 1928, p. 62.

Crimean colleagues had been duped by left-wing socialists,[78] Volunteer leaders persistently undercut the Crimea's liberal democracy with their own brand of military government.

The Volunteers also became increasingly alarmed over Bolshevik activity in the Crimea in early January 1919. They expected an uprising in Simferopol, and blamed the Reds for a series of minor shooting incidents in the Sevastopol region. New searches were conducted, weapons seized, dozens of persons arrested, and in the laconic words of the army's own report, "several were beaten."[79] In the northern districts, measures were even more harsh. When General Tillo ordered the arrest of zemstvo board members in Melitopol for "agitating against mobilization," among those taken into custody was the Mayor, Alekseev. And while the army was convoying its prisoners, a number were killed "attempting to escape."[80]

Thereafter, bitterness toward the army mounted quickly. The Volunteers almost surely exaggerated local Bolshevik strength, confusing a general undercurrent of hostility with an organized *apparat*. By the spring of 1919, unemployment in some Crimean industries was as high as 80 percent, and strikes were common. Volunteers interpreted this as evidence of Bolshevik subversion, particularly when striking ship workers, in a dispute over wages, refused to repair French and Volunteer vessels.[81] Yet the more repressive the army's own behavior, the more attractive the Bolsheviks actually became.

Under these conditions, Crimean leaders felt increasing pressure to take strong measures themselves. Imposing a curfew at the end of January, the cabinet also adopted administrative measures to restrict leftist agitation in the press. A special commission was appointed to impose fines against editors, and suspend newspapers in especially severe cases, though exceptional care was exercised to assure that these powers were not abused, and in fact, they were not widely applied.[82] At the same time, the Council of Ministers directed its own department of internal affairs to search for weapons, and to deport those convicted of threatening regional security.[83]

But even this failed to satisfy the Volunteers. General Korvin-

[78] Astrov, "Grazhdanskaia voina," pp. 116, 126.

[79] Gukovskii, "Krym," No. 28, p. 147.   [80] *Ibid.*, No. 29, pp. 61-62.

[81] Evidence on the Bolsheviks' actual weakness appears in Bunegin, *Revoliutsiia*, p. 126-27. Bunegin himself was an active party member. See also A. Lysenko, "Krym do vtorogo prikhoda sovetskoi vlasti," *Revoliutsiia v Krymu*, No. 2, 1923, pp. 21-23; A. Gukovskii, *Frantsuzskaia interventsiia na iuge Rossii, 1918-1919*, Moscow-Leningrad, 1928, p. 79.

[82] Materials on the press, Crimean Government Archive, file 18; Gukovskii, "Krym," No. 29, p. 62.

[83] Vinaver, *Nashe pravitel'stvo*, pp. 202-03; Bunegin, *Revoliutsiia*, p. 211.

Krukovskii demanded the army itself be given censorship control, and insisted his headquarters be moved to Sevastopol, where it could watch the government more closely.[84] Late in January, Krym, Bogdanov, and several others journeyed again to discuss the situation with Denikin. Arguing that the Crimea was "almost entirely free" from Bolsheviks, they stressed the Volunteers' own responsibility for increasing local tensions.[85]

This appalled Denikin. The Volunteers were having difficulty maintaining their supplies, railroads were not functioning properly, dock workers were striking, the press was bitterly hostile, the enemy's regular troops were regrouping near Melitopol—and all the Crimean experimenters could suggest was that the Whites themselves were to blame![86] Nothing better indicates the hopelessness of the Crimean effort than the contrast between the Volunteers' intractibility at this time, and their own determination not to allow the spread of military dictatorship. Returning to the Crimea convinced their relations with Denikin would not improve, the ministers again tried to secure military assistance from the Allies and relieve Denikin's troops for service at the front.[87] They made no new headway, however; and when Korvin-Krukovskii learned of their efforts, relations were even further exacerbated.[88]

By February 1919, Crimean liberals were steadily losing ground. Living conditions were becoming increasingly more difficult as food supplies began to dwindle and prices rose. Agitation persisted; speculation increased.

Bolshevik troops also began to drive the Volunteers from the three northern Crimean districts. An invasion of the isthmus itself was thus a strong possibility. In the city dumas, meanwhile, the government came under increasing attack; and several regional newspapers now began to turn their attention away from the Volunteers, and on to the Kadets themselves. Tatar agitation was also on the rise. On February 22 or 23, 1919 (New Style), the Volunteers searched the homes of leading Kurultai members, seizing a number of documents. Shortly afterward, the army itself began assessing fines against the "slanderers," and closing down offensive publications. March thus found the Council of Ministers searching desperately for support.[89]

---

[84] Memorandum on relations with the Volunteer Army, n.d., Crimean Government Archive, file 18.

[85] Krym, "Otchet."   [86] Denikin, *Ocherki*, v, 57.

[87] Vinaver to Maklakov, Feb. 21, 1919, in the Crimean Government Archives, file 9.

[88] General Korvin-Krukovskii to Vinaver, Feb. 24, 1919, Crimean Government Archive, file 9.

[89] Bogdanov, "Krymskoe," pp. 16ff.

In these conditions, the Crimean Zemstvo Conference met for the final time in Simferopol to hear an account of the government's activities. General Borovskii, representing the Volunteers, reported on the military danger; Nabokov and his colleagues explained the necessity for "exceptional" measures. But this time the Conference responded harshly. Nabokov was condemned for sanctioning the illegalities of the Volunteers, and for choosing a "false means" for combating the Bolsheviks. The SRs threatened to withdraw Nikonov, their representative in the cabinet, if improvements failed to come at once.[90]

In Sevastopol, meanwhile, other serious developments were taking place. On March 3/16, the metalworkers union passed a resolution demanding power be transferred to a Workers' and Peasants' Soviet, and called for a general trade union conference to discuss the question. When the latter assembled, they endorsed the call for a soviet government by a margin of 68 to 42. They also demanded the withdrawal of the Volunteers, and the release of all political prisoners.[91] The cabinet responded with new measures of its own, forbidding public demonstrations or meetings. But the strike was effective, particularly in Sevastopol.[92] Taking matters into their own hands in a desperate effort to preserve the situation, the French command itself arrested the strike leaders and established martial law. But even these measures were only partially effective.[93]

The general strike proved the last straw for Denikin. With Bolsheviks now penetrating well into the Perekop isthmus, easily pushing aside the outnumbered Volunteers, he issued an ultimatum: unless the government itself declared martial law throughout the region, and transferred power to the army, Volunteer troops would be withdrawn.[94]

Without an army of their own, which they could hardly raise without precipitating open conflict with the Volunteers, there was little the Crimeans could do besides capitulate. Their experiment was failing, subverted alike by allies and enemies. On March 21/April 3, five days after Denikin's ultimatum, the Reds broke through Volunteer defenses at Perekop, and entered the Crimea proper. In another few days, Simferopol was lost. The ministers, now in Sevastopol, frantically sought ways to resist the onslaught. Obeying Denikin indirectly, they transferred their power to a Special Committee for Defense, which included representatives from the army.[95] But this hardly stopped the

[90] *Ibid.*, pp. 18-20.

[91] Telegram Vinaver to Krym, Mar. 20, 1919, No. 1445, in the Vinaver Papers, Yivo Institute; Declaration of the Trade Union Conference, Mar. 14, 1919, in the Crimean Government Archive, file 12.

[92] *Bulletin* [of the Crimean Ministry of Foreign Affairs], Mar. 22, 1919.

[93] *Ibid.*   [94] Denikin, *Ocherki*, v, 61.

[95] Decree No. 1270 of the Crimean Government, Apr. 6, 1919 (N.S.), in the Crimean Government Archive, file 17.

Bolshevik advance; and neither did the use of Allied troops, an additional contingent of which had disembarked to protect the routes to Sevastopol. On March 28/April 10, 1919, with Bolshevik guns sounding in the distance, the Council of Ministers realized the end had come. With perfunctory adherences to legal procedures, they formally transferred all civil administration to municipal councils and zemstvos, and prepared for evacuation. On April 15 they left Sevastopol on a ship named *Hope*, ending their experiment with appropriate irony.[96]

IDEALS AND REALITIES: THE CAUSES OF FAILURE

In the most obvious sense, the Kadets' experiment in the Crimea was wiped out by the Bolshevik advance. But if the Bolsheviks alone had overturned the Crimean government, Kadets might still have achieved their goal of presenting a model for future Russian administrations. An invading Red Army might simply have revealed that democratic forms had to be established in conjunction with a strong, loyal military force. And in the sense of a political apparatus capable of restoring order and winning local support in the midst of the civil war, the liberal government might still have been a "success."

Yet the Kadets' defeat took place instead in conjunction with the collapse of public confidence. And once its moral authority had given way, its liberal policies proving unable to contain social friction, Kadets could no longer claim to have created an exemplary political form. One might argue that the government's authority was undermined solely by the behavior of the Volunteer command. But in fact, the regime's position was weakened not so much by the army's excesses themselves as by its own identification with these excesses in the public eye. And this, ironically, was the result of both the Ekaterinodar and the Simferopol governments being staffed by Kadets, who presumably cooperated together and coordinated their activities, and had come through past politics to represent clear class interests.

Thus once again Kadet attitudes and behavior, and particularly the party's own internal diversity had important practical significance. At

[96] *Zhurnal zasedaniia soveta ministrov krymskogo kraevogo pravitel'stva 16 aprelia 1919 goda na sudne "Nadezhda,"* in Gukovskii, "Krymskoe," 139-47. As this document reveals, even the evacuation was not without its problems. A dispute arose between the government and the French command over the disposition of the government's treasury, and the fate of a large sum of money assigned to "expedite the defense and evacuation of Sevastopol." At one point, the French command refused to let the ministers depart, claiming they had not received the funds promised them. The dispute was finally settled after long, rancorous negotiations, and the ministers sailed as the Bolsheviks entered the city. See the discussion in G. Brinkley, *The Volunteer Army and Allied Intervention in South Russia, 1917-1921*, Notre Dame, Ind., 1966, pp. 135-38.

Denikin's headquarters it was the Kadets themselves who insisted along with the army's field commanders on the danger of Bolshevik insurgency, and who demanded the postponement of the Sejm, the curb on criticism in the press, and the institution of martial law. And it was Stepanov and Astrov who leveled the charges of passivity and political blindness against the Crimean party colleagues, and who backed up the army's commanders when the latter insisted on a change in Crimean policies. There was, moreover, no personal love lost between the two camps. Despite their long-time party comradeship, Astrov now thought Nabokov falsely elegant, egocentric, ambitious, and somewhat insincere.[97] He held similar views about Vinaver.[98] Rodichev thought the Crimean Kadets had been taken over completely by the socialists in the zemstvo group; and Novgorodtsev apparently shared his views.[99] Vinaver, on the other hand, was so incensed by Astrov's refusal to press his government's case in Denikin's Special Council that he asked Peter Iurenev to represent it instead.[100] But Teslenko, Pasmanik, and other members of the Central Committee who frequented Simferopol tended to agree with their colleagues in Ekaterinodar. There was thus no unity of viewpoint even within Crimean Kadet circles; and on these grounds alone the experiment was hardly an auspicious model for the future.

There were other difficulties too. The Crimean government was officially a coalition; by Vinaver's own admission its composition was constructed "with utmost care" to assure cooperation between parties.[101] But the SRs, who had commanded the overwhelming support of the population here as elsewhere in the Constituent Assembly elections, had but one minor representative. The more militant Tatar group had none. Steven and Bobrovskii, the two SDs, were active in most of the government's activities but represented the political group least inclined to support their "bourgeois colleagues" in a moment of crisis. And the Kadets themselves thought of the government as "their" regime. They lived together in the old Governor's Mansion at Simferopol, and made decisions as a closed party group, with little involvement of outside interests. Even here, consequently, traditional Kadet elitism effectively shielded the ministers from their "constituents."[102]

As a consequence, the regime soon lost its rapport with both zemstvo groups and moderate parties on the left. *Priboi* mounted a policy of open opposition; the SRs threatened to withdraw Nikonov; and the Tatars remained persistently antagonistic. Had the cabinet retained

---

[97] Astrov, "Grazhdanskaia voina," p. 116.   [98] *Ibid.*

[99] *Ibid.*, p. 126; Margolies, *God interventsii,* I, 173.

[100] Astrov, "Grazhdanskaia voina," p. 126.

[101] Vinaver, *Nashe pravitel'stvo,* p. 63.   [102] Vinavera, "Vospominaniia," p. 113.

socialist support, it may possibly have been able to blunt the force of hostile propaganda. As matters stood, the latter eventually came to represent a very real danger.

The Volunteers, of course, maintained throughout that Bolshevism was rife in the Crimea. This was probably not the case. According to M. Bunegin, himself an active party member, Lenin's *apparat* was exceedingly weak in this region, unable to function effectively even in the period preceding the German occupation.[103] There was, however, a strong anarchistic current in Sevastopol; and as we have seen, unemployment in some industries was as high as 80 percent by the spring of 1919.[104] When worker unrest culminated in the general strike, it seems doubtful that the government could have overcome this crisis even had the Bolsheviks not been able to drive past the Volunteers. Obolenskii maintains that Denikin's soldiers precipitated the disorder themselves, through their many blatant abuses and particularly their noxious behavior in the three northern Crimean districts.[105] But the problem itself was cyclical: the more the population showed its hostile feelings, the more the army treated Crimeans harshly; and the harsher the army's policies, the greater the resistance to their presence. It is impossible to determine how much the Bolsheviks themselves actually contributed to civil unrest in the region. But even without their conscious effort, the Crimean ministers were obviously faced with an extremely serious internal problem.

In the final analysis, three features stand out from the history of the Crimean Regional Government which bear directly on the general history of the Kadets in the revolution and civil war. The first is the fact that party leaders did attempt to translate conciliationist tendencies into political realities. For all their acquiescence to demands from Ekaterinodar, Vinaver, Nabokov, Krym, Bogdanov, and their supporters still made a game attempt to work with other political and social groups, and build a viable coalition in which the Crimean population could find confidence. Their program was liberal in the best sense of the word, in that the Crimean people were their primary concern, rather than the abstract interests of the Russian state. And despite the sharp opposition of Tatars and radicals, the Crimean ministers never yielded to the temptation to crush their opponents by force. Their ultimate weapon remained persuasion; and in this they contrasted sharply with their colleagues in Kiev, Ekaterinodar, Odessa, and other parts of Russia, who now abandoned any sense of compromise for strict military rule in a vague hope of eventually realizing liberal ideals.

[103] Bunegin, *Revoliutsiia*, p. 126.   [104] Gukovskii, p. 79.
[105] Obolenskii, "Krym," *NCS*, No. 7, 1924, pp. 81-83.

Second, the Crimean experiment showed once again the practical consequences of Kadet disunity. When Astrov, Pepeliaev, Vinaver, Krol, and the other Kadets left Moscow in the summer of 1918 to mobilize the party, they never dreamed that Kadets themselves would disagree so thoroughly on questions of tactics; and despite repeated opportunities, Kadets here and in Ekaterinodar again failed to develop a unified course of action. Again one might argue that such unity would have had little effect on Volunteer policies in the Crimean region; but it is also possible that it could have made the experiment work, prompting a reevaluation or at least a rethinking of general White outlooks.

Finally, the fact that the Crimean government failed to survive and the "laboratory experiment" proved unsuccessful generally foreclosed the possibility of making similar attempts in other parts of Russia. From the moment Krym surrendered his powers, the opponents of political and social democracy could point to the Crimean regime as a perfect example of how not to win the civil war. The politics of military dictatorship—or of state revolution, as it was coming to be known in Siberia—which many in the party had regarded as a dubious means to "resurrect" the nation if not accompanied by a clear commitment to liberal principles, now became the only administrative form to survive the Bolshevik onslaught.

2. SIBERIA

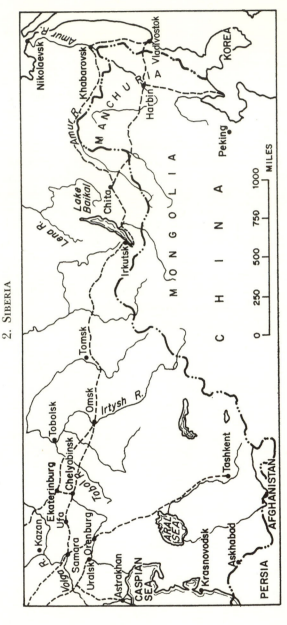

RAILROADS
NATIONAL FRONTIERS

Kadets in Siberia: The Tactics of "State Revolution"

Several weeks after the collapse of the Crimean regime, General Denikin officially subordinated his forces to the "Supreme Russian Ruler" in Siberia, Admiral Alexander Vasilevich Kolchak. The two events were not specifically related, since Denikin was largely responding to pressure from London and Paris, rather than fears about his own political or military situation. But the move reflected the real configuration of forces in the late spring of 1919. While Denikin had lost Odessa and the Crimea, and was once again consolidating his armies in the Don and Kuban regions, Kolchak appeared to be leading a massive force toward Samara and Kazan on the Volga, and northward toward Viatka. A link to the British in Archangel was expected, and some even thought the Siberians were only weeks from marching on Moscow. In these circumstances, Russian representatives abroad were worried about the fragmentation of the Whites, and felt the possibility for strong Allied assistance would be vastly increased by a formal act of union.[1]

Both Denikin and the Ekaterinodar Kadets viewed the act with an inflated sense of self-sacrifice. They were annoyed that it implied a secondary status for the South Russian front, and strange as it seems in retrospect, worried that they might be surrendering too much in the way of their own postwar powers.[2] They were comforted, however, by two considerations. One was that the union meant little in practical terms, since the geographical separation of the two forces preserved full authority for each in its own theater of operation. The other was that Kolchak was known to be guided by a large contingent of Siberian

[1] Both Vasili Maklakov and K. D. Nabokov (Russia's "official" representatives in Paris and London) telegraphed Kolchak and Denikin in the spring of 1919 that Allied support was contingent on Denikin's recognizing Kolchak's primacy. The telegrams are in the Lastours Papers, Hoover Institution, files 1 and 2. See also the extensive discussion in John Thompson, *Russia, Bolshevism and the Versailles Peace*, Princeton, 1966, pp. 268-308; and A. I. Denikin, *Ocherki russkoi smuty*, 5 vols., Paris-Berlin, 1921-25, v, 98.

[2] N. Astrov, "Priznanie Gen. Denikinym Admirala Kolchaka," *GMNCS*, No. 1 (14), 1926, pp. 201-22; K. D. Partiia, "Protokol zasedaniia tsentral'nogo komiteta," May 21, 1919 (O.S.), in the Panina Archive, pack. 3, suppl. 1 (henceforth Central Committee Protocol).

Kadets, who, with one or two exceptions, were less important figures nationally than their colleagues in the south, and would presumably be willing to yield to "greater" party authority should Kolchak actually beat Denikin to Moscow.[3]

The Siberian situation thus represented yet another dimension to Kadet politics during the civil war, and an especially complicated one. Here the Kadet tendency toward conciliation had an opportunity to develop into a government with national competence, based at least indirectly on the Constituent Assembly; and here, too, the party's statist instincts had their final full expression. In both cases, despite all of their weaknesses in 1917, Kadets once again found themselves in a position to influence the course of civil struggle, and hence Russia's future.

THE SIBERIAN POLITICAL BACKGROUND

Just as in the Ukraine, the Kadet party's new-found prominence in the vast areas east of the Urals was somewhat anomalous, since the party had no deep roots in local soil. Before 1917, only three or four major towns had on-going local party committees; and while new groups were organized during the revolution, Kadets bore the stigma of being *navoznye liudi* in the eyes of the local population, unwelcome interlopers who had "carted" themselves into the territory. (The term derived from *voz* meaning "cart" and *navoz* meaning "dung"; it was a slang expression derisively applied in Siberia to new settlers.)[4] Even in Omsk, where the party's largest and best organized committee functioned under V. A. Zhardetskii, a well-to-do lawyer, and where Kadets published a daily newspaper, *Sibirskaia Rech'*, the party secured only a handful of seats in the 1917 city duma elections, and finished fourth in the Constituent Assembly elections behind Mensheviks, Bolsheviks, and Siberian autonomists.[5]

The autonomists were one of the principal reasons for liberal weakness in Siberia. They drew their support from the same intellectual and professional strata as did the Kadets, but were not regarded as *navoznye liudi*. Led by the venerable G. N. Potanin, who had helped create the first major autonomist organization, the Siberian Regional Union, in 1905, the autonomists wanted legislative power in the region exercised by a Siberian Regional Duma, and executive

[3] Central Committee Protocol, May 27, 1919 (O.S.).

[4] Interview with George Gins (Guins), former administrative director of Kolchak's Council of Ministers and member of the Kadet party in 1917, Jan. 1965, Berkeley, Calif.

[5] *Sibirskaia Rech'*, July 17, 1917; L. M. Spirin, *Klassy i partii v grazhdanskoi voine v Rossii*, Moscow, 1968, pp. 420-21.

authority exercised by a responsible cabinet of ministers. Only in questions of genuinely national interest was the territory to remain under central Russian control.[6]

While some local Kadet groups supported both autonomy for Siberia and a Russian federation, a regional Kadet party conference in May 1917 formally rejected these ideas, and Kadets remained officially committed to the concept of Russian unity here as elsewhere.[7] Their opposition to the autonomists increased over the summer of 1917, moreover, as Potanin's group moved in the direction of greater regional independence.[8] In August, the autonomists held a major conference in Tomsk. They elected a Central Siberian Organizational Committee, and then announced plans for an all-Siberian Regional Congress.[9] Though many Siberian Kadets, like their provincial party colleagues in other parts of Russia, were less rigid in their views of state centralism than party leaders like Rodichev and Miliukov, these actions seemed very much to undermine the authority of the Provisional Government.

Events in Siberia thus ran parallel to those in the Ukraine in 1917: the principal political issue was regional autonomy, and like their party comrades in Kiev, Siberian Kadets were forced out of local politics because of their party's determined state centralism. The antagonism between liberals and autonomists continued, moreover, after the Bolshevik coup. In October 1917, Potanin's group formed a provisional Siberian Council. After Lenin's seizure of power, this group moved to assume local authority, convening first an "Extraordinary" Siberian Regional Conference, and then making preparations for a Provisional Siberian Duma to meet in Tomsk.[10] Kadets opposed these efforts, just as they resisted the Ukrainian Rada, but not effectively.[11]

Little came of the autonomists' plans, however, since the Bolsheviks seized Tomsk shortly before the Duma opened, and arrested most of its

[6] I. I. Serebrennikov, "The Siberian Autonomous Movement and Its Future," MS in the Hoover Institution, n.d., p. 2.

[7] *VPNS*, Nos. 8-10, July 20, 1917, p. 33.

[8] See, e.g., *Sibirskaia Rech'*, June 24 and 25, 1917.

[9] Serebrennikov, pp. 2ff; V. Vegman, "Oblastnicheskie illiuzii, rasseiannye revoliutsiei," *Sibirskie Ogni*, No. 3, 1923, pp. 96-100.

[10] Vegman, p. 99; K. I. Morozov, untitled memorandum on the organization of Siberian local government, in the S. P. Melgunov Collection on the Civil War, file B-4a.

[11] Among some Siberian party committees, such as the one in Tobolsk, there was at first a feeling that a regional conference might serve to organize an anti-Bolshevik movement in Siberia, provided it was based on coalition principles. The Siberian Council determined, however, that delegates to the conference should come entirely from local soviets, thus excluding the liberals; and as a consequence, the Kadets turned sharply against the effort. *VPNS*, No. 4, Mar. 21, 1918, pp. 127-28.

leaders. With a desperate effort, the Duma's executive committee did manage to hold a secret session on the night of January 25-26, 1918, and elected a new Provisional Siberian Government under the presidency of a little known socialist, P. I. Derber.[12] And while this group quickly dispersed, unable to exercise any real authority, it did represent the considerable autonomist sentiment in the region, and was a force Kadets themselves would eventually have to recognize if they hoped to organize an effective anti-Bolshevik movement.

In the spring of 1918, however, Siberian Kadets were moving in quite a different direction. The Bolshevik coup and Lenin's subsequent decision to close the Constituent Assembly convinced them the time had passed for democratic niceties. In fact, authoritarian tendencies had been growing for quite some time in the region. Zhardetskii and other Omsk Kadets had been among the party's staunchest supporters of General Kornilov in August 1917; and at times, *Sibirskaia Rech'*, the party's regional newspaper, sounded very much as if it desired the overthrow of the provisional regime.[13] Here, as elsewhere, therefore, events seemed to have "proved" the validity of old perspectives; and like Dolgorukov, Novgorodtsev, and other national Kadet leaders in Moscow, Siberian Kadets now sought to establish a strong regional military dictatorship.

The logical candidate in Siberia for such a post was General Dmitri Khorvat, general manager and virtual tsar of the Chinese Eastern Railroad, and Provisional Government commissar for the Kharbin region. A reactionary monarchist who considered the revolution a national catastrophe, Khorvat was also an ambitious man, anxious to enhance his own power. Consequently, when Kadets arrived at his headquarters in Kharbin in the spring of 1918, insisting he form a new regional government (and arguing, incidentally, that he was the only remaining holder of "legitimate" authority in Russia since he was the sole Provisional Government commissar still actively performing his duties!), he readily consented. With Kadet help, he organized what he called a *Delovoi Kabinet*, or "Businesslike Government."[14]

The *Delovoi Kabinet* was a thoroughly right-wing body, composed largely of obscure Kadets who were convinced "the time for all discussions" had passed, and who unequivocally supported military rule.[15] For a time, Khorvat had also flirted with P. I. Derber and the

[12] Morozov memorandum, pp. 2-4. G. K. Gins, *Sibir', soiuzniki i Kolchak*, 2 vols., Peking, 1921, I, 75-79.

[13] E.g., *Sibirskaia Rech'*, Aug. 20, 1917.

[14] D. L. Khorvat, "Memoirs," MS in the Hoover Institution, n.d., chap. IX, pp. 17-18.

[15] *Ibid.*, chap. XII, p. 4.

autonomists on the chance that they, too, might support his dictatorship, but the Kadets staunchly opposed such efforts, and they were quickly abandoned. Instead, local Kadet organizations in Vladivostok, Irkutsk, and other eastern Siberian cities championed *their* new government, and pressed for its extension.[16]

In fact, Khorvat's domain was quite limited. The vast Siberian expanse was now almost entirely under the control of local soviets and city dumas, mostly Bolshevik-dominated. This was the situation, moreover, as the next important stage of the civil war began in the east in May 1918. A strong band of Czech soldiers—formerly a brigade in the tsarist army but now making its way toward Vladivostok in an effort to join the Allies in France—clashed with the Bolsheviks over the status of their safe conduct, and wound up liberating Omsk, Samara, Ufa, Cheliabinsk, and other major eastern towns from Bolshevik control.[17]

Anxious to avoid undue involvement in Russian affairs, the Czechs yielded local authority to anti-Bolshevik Siberian figures, some of whom had led clandestine movements of their own before the Czechs arrived. It was hoped in Kharbin that these new groups would subordinate themselves to Khorvat's *Delovoi Kabinet*, which provided some of them with funds.[18] And throughout the region, Kadets not only reemerged as forceful opponents both of socialism and of regional autonomy, but sought statements of loyalty to their would-be autocrat, condemning any alliances whatsoever with Siberian socialist-autonomists. ("The time has come to begin an active anti-Bolshevik struggle," one official Kadet statement declared; "agreement with socialist-autonomists at the present political moment . . . is completely inadmissible. . . . All power must be in the hands of one person.")[19]

In most cases, however, the new local governments were not loyal to Khorvat, but composed of Siberian regionalists. In Omsk, several members of Derber's group took control, announcing the formation

[16] A. G., "Komy doverit' vlast'," N. M., "Edinolichnaia vlast'," and N. M., "Kabinet vremennago pravitelia," all on a Kadet party broadside entitled *Vremennyi pravitel' Khorvat' i ego delovoi kabinet*, published in Vladivostok in 1918. Because of local pressure, however, Khorvat soon added two right-wing socialists to his cabinet to preserve the principle of coalition.

[17] On the Czechs in Russia, see in particular: E. Beneš, "Chekhoslovatskaia interventsiia v Rossii," *Volia Rossii*, X-XI, June, 1924, pp. 45-56; J. Kratochvil, *Cesta revoluce*, Prague, 1922; V. Dragomiretskii, *Chekhoslovaki v Rossii, 1914-1920*, Paris-Prague, 1928; R. Gaida, *Moje paměti*, Prague, 1920; J. Bradley, *La Légion tchécoslovaque en Russie, 1914-1920*, Paris, 1965; and I. Vesely, *Chekhi i slovaki v revoliutsionnoi Rossii, 1917-1920 gg.*, trans. F. Chumalo, Moscow, 1965. On the Siberian situation and the Allies in general see esp. George Kennan, *The Decision to Intervene*, Princeton, 1958, pp. 277ff.

[18] Khorvat, "Memoirs," chap. X, p. 3.   [19] *Ibid.*, chap. XII, p. 4.

of a Western Siberian Commissariat. And in Tomsk, power passed to members of the Siberian Regional Duma.[20] One notable exception was in Samara, where a small group of SRs assumed authority. Led by the Kadets' old nemesis, Victor Chernov, they declared themselves the Committee of Members from the All-Russian Constituent Assembly (Komuch), and set up an anti-Bolshevik regime with all-Russian pretensions.[21]

In these circumstances, Kadets once again became a legal opposition, attempting to make the new local governments more conservative and authoritarian, if not actually subordinate to General Khorvat. In Omsk, for example, local party figures expressly rejected the authority of the Western Siberian Commissariat, insisting it was too radical (despite the fact that for a time, it was actually a solid bulwark against Bolshevik rule).[22] And even when a new Council of Ministers under a popular and moderate regionalist, Peter Vologodskii, replaced the Commissariat at the beginning of July 1918, the Omsk Kadet party chairman Victor Zhardetskii insisted with several of his Kadet colleagues that the autonomists' authority was tenuous. However dangerous the Bolsheviks, Siberian Kadets were still completely unwilling to make concessions.[23] As Zhardetskii told a public gathering, "The time for charming myths and illusions" had passed:

> Public opinion has come to the conclusion that in a country invaded full force by the enemy, where the passions of civil war are now boiling, there must inevitably be established a firm, one-man authority, capable of saving the state.[24]

TENTATIVE EFFORTS AT COMPROMISE AND COALITION

Such was the political terrain in the early summer of 1918 on which the two major Moscow centers, the Union of Regeneration and the National Center, linked by the Kadets, hoped to coordinate anti-Bolshevik forces and build a new all-Russian government. In Omsk, a center of autonomist sentiment, Kadets assailed "charming myths" while insisting their goal was to "save the state" through second-rate military dictators like General Khorvat. In Samara, the SRs based the authority of their Komuch regime on the now defunct Constituent

[20] On the formation of these local governments, see esp. J. Bunyan, ed., *Intervention, Civil War and Communism in Russia*, Baltimore, 1936, pp. 277-373.

[21] See esp. Gins, I, 132-33.

[22] L. Krol', *Za tri goda*, Vladivostok, 1922, p. 67-69.

[23] P. Vologodskii, "Dnevnik," MS in the Hoover Institution, notebook I, 26-27, 51.

[24] *Zaria* (Omsk), No. 29, July 18, 1918, in V. Maksakov and A. Turunov, eds., *Khronika grazhdanskoi voiny v Sibiri, 1917-1918*, Moscow, 1926, pp. 207-08.

Assembly, and insisted that body was still in existence. And in cities controlled by members of the Siberian Regional Duma, a split was developing between militant socialists who thought in terms of accommodation with Lenin, and staunch anti-Bolsheviks, who looked somewhat favorably on the idea of military rule.[25]

Between all of these groups, moreover, new disputes were developing over local competency and jurisdiction, and even military objectives. Troops from Omsk refused to aid socialists fighting the Bolsheviks near Kazan. On the Trans-Siberian railroad, the region's vital lifeline, a customs barrier was set up between Omsk and Samara, virtually halting shipments of food. When Astrov, Lev Krol, Victor Pepeliaev, and the Moscow centers' other emissaries left the capital in the early summer of 1918, expecting a national state conference to meet and establish an all-Russian coalition directorate, they hardly foresaw the political labyrinth which lay ahead.

The trail of the young Kadet engineer from Ekaterinodar, Lev Krol, proved particularly discouraging. Representing both the Union of Regeneration and the Kadet Central Committee, Krol hoped to prepare the ground for national unification in Samara, Cheliabinsk, and Kazan (just as it was Astrov's task to go to Kiev, the Crimea, and Ekaterinodar, and Victor Pepeliaev's to go to Omsk). In each city Krol visited, however, he found antagonism and conflict, rather than any desire at broad anti-Bolshevik cooperation. Kadet groups favored military dictatorship, opposing in most cases any cooperation whatsoever with the socialists. In Samara and Kazan, local party groups leaned toward restoration of the monarchy. Elsewhere they sympathized with the German orientation of party colleagues in Kiev, and talked in favor of a similar occupation by the Japanese.[26] The SRs, meanwhile, viewed Kadets with far more hostility than even during the latter months of the Provisional Government. In Samara, the Komuch went so far as to arrest a prominent Kadet publicist, A. I. Korobov, for publicly criticizing its program.[27]

The only success Lev Krol had, in fact, was not so much a result of his efforts as those of Allied representatives in Siberia, particularly the Czechs, who were anxious for anti-Bolshevik unity on the assumption that a forceful second front could still be opened against the Germans. In July 1918, therefore, the Allies encouraged a number of

[25] M. A. Krol', "Sibirskoe pravitel'stvo i avgustovskaia sessiia sibirskoi oblastnoi dumy," *Vol'naia Sibir'* (Prague), IV, 1928, pp. 72-73; Gins, I, pp. 132-33.

[26] Krol', *Za tri goda*, pp. 55-61.

[27] *Ibid.*, pp. 59-60. Argunov and Pavlov, the two SR members of the Union of Regeneration traveling with Krol, were as agitated as the Kadets, feeling their own Central Committee was sabotaging the Union's efforts. See A. Argunov, "Omskie dni v 1918 godu," *Sibirskii Arkhiv*, No. 5, 1935, pp. 191-92.

Siberian groups to meet together in Cheliabinsk. With pressure of this sort behind him, Krol finally received an attentive, if not altogether sympathetic hearing.[28] Thereafter he visited Omsk, where again with the help of Allied representatives, he was finally able to persuade a number of local figures to accept the Moscow plans. Krol also managed to organize a local branch of the Union of Regeneration in Omsk, which even the rightist Zhardetskii agreed to join.[29]

Shortly afterward, while Krol went on to Ekaterinburg, other Moscow center emissaries began having similar success. In Samara, they managed to bring Kadets, SRs, SDs, and even the autonomists together in an Interparty Conference; and again organized a local branch of the Union of Regeneration, which accepted the idea of unification and a national coalition directorate.[30]

Consequently, by the middle of August 1918, as a result both of Allied pressure and diligent work by men like Krol, a tentative ground-work for interparty cooperation was finally laid in Siberia, despite the continuation of local rivalries. And toward the end of the month, as Krol and others waited anxiously for news from Astrov and the south (hoping their colleague had persuaded Denikin to turn his forces eastward), they laid final plans for an All-Russian State Conference to be held in Ufa, just as the Union of Regeneration and the National Center had earlier agreed. Thus the region seemed about to become the base for a new, unified anti-Bolshevik effort, fortified by Allied assistance and perhaps even headed by an all-Russian coalition government.

Toward the end of August 1918, however, these efforts were suddenly undercut; and not by the socialists, but by the Siberian Kadets them-selves. The reason was not a new move by General Khorvat or even the development of any new local conflicts, but ironically, the arrival in Omsk of another Moscow emissary, Victor Pepeliaev. Pepeliaev, like Krol, was a member of the Union of Regeneration and "officially" charged with coordinating local military groups in preparation for their merger with the South Russian Volunteers. But unlike his colleague, Pepeliaev had changed his mind about the desirability of a coalition effort after beginning his travels east (and particularly after discussing the Siberian situation with his brother Anatol, a former tsarist colonel and now a leader of the military forces near Omsk). Instead of pursuing the tactics of interparty cooperation, Pepeliaev

[28] Krol', *Za tri goda*, pp. 63-79.   [29] *Zaria* (Omsk), No. 46, Aug. 8, 1918.
[30] "Mezhdupartiinoe soveshchanie po voprosu ob organizatsii tsentral'noi vlasti vozrozhdaiushcheisia Rossii," unpubl. doc. in the G. K. Gins Papers, Hoover Institution.

came to believe instead that liberals should work for the extension of Khorvat's military dictatorship, and that the role of both autonomists and SRs should be minimized or eliminated. He changed his views, moreover, despite the limited nature of the *Delovoi Kabinet*, and the fact that it still concentrated its power almost entirely around distant Kharbin.[31]

Unlike Krol, Pepeliaev was a national Kadet figure. In 1917 he had gained considerable prominence as commissar of Kronstadt, and had also become well known as one of the party's most consistent defenders of General Kornilov. Pepeliaev could also argue correctly that many prominent Kadets in Moscow shared his views. And as a consequence, meeting with Omsk Kadets in August 1918, he destroyed the tenuous attitude of conciliation Krol had so assiduously developed.[32]

Thus Kadet disunity once again made itself felt. From a long historical perspective, and with the knowledge that General Denikin would not turn the Volunteers eastward, one is tempted to argue that interparty cooperation at this stage of the civil war in Siberia would have made little significant difference. Yet at precisely this moment, Russian political leaders were about to meet in a new state conference in Ufa, a session hoped to be the crowning achievement of the Moscow centers.[33] It was the conference's task to organize the new, all-Russian regime. If all parties could have carried a conciliatory attitude into the sessions, a new regime could conceivably have been organized with wide local popularity, something no other White administration had yet been able to accomplish. And this, in turn, might possibly have rallied both Siberians and the Allies into precisely the type of national crusade Miliukov, Stepanov, and other Kadets so desperately wanted.

As things turned out, however, Kadet recalcitrance not only wrecked the Ufa conference from the start, but led to conditions which would later very much weaken Admiral Kolchak. After intensive discussions, the conference vested provisional all-Russian authority in a five-man coalition Directorate, and assigned it unlimited power until January 1, 1919 (when its activities would be examined by a new conference of Constituent Assembly members). The Directorate's goal was to organize the anti-Bolsheviks, unite all areas under its "all-Russian provisional power," and continue the war against Germany in close

---

[31] Azbuka Report (n.d. but Sept. 1918) in the Wrangel Military Archives, file 141; Krol', *Za tri goda*, p. 80.

[32] *Ibid.*, pp. 80-85.

[33] Some members even maintained in retrospect that this was so. See, e.g., V. Boldyrev, *Direktoriia, Kolchak, interventsy*, Novonikolaevsk, 1925, p. 40.

conjunction with the Allies, a provision designed primarily to stimulate foreign support.[34] But with the exception of Lev Krol and one or two others, Siberian Kadets boycotted the Conference. As a result, no one had confidence that the party's national leadership would join the government simply because a minor functionary like Krol had pledged their support; and no one could seriously believe that the powerful group of Kadets in Kharbin or Omsk would support a compromise to which they personally had not subscribed. Yet without Kadet backing, coalition was impossible, and military unification extremely unlikely.

Thus the new All-Russian Directorate took power in September 1918 under conditions which virtually doomed it to collapse. Its Kadet member was officially Nicholas Astrov, though his place was taken temporarily by Vladimir Vinogradov, a well-known Siberian lawyer and former vice-minister of communications under Nekrasov; and it also included a prominent military figure, General Boldyrev, who stood in for General Alekseev, and two SR moderates, Nicholas Avksentiev, the minister of interior in Kerensky's second coalition, and Vladimir Zenzinov. The Directorate's temporary president, finally, was the well-known Siberian regionalist Peter Vologodskii. But the new regime had no substantial administrative base; and it lacked backing from Kadets in Omsk and Kharbin, whose support was crucial if it was to function effectively. In a word, the new "All-Russian" government was an effort at compromise in a context where divisions among the Kadets themselves had helped make compromise unpopular, and where local antagonisms ran deep. Krol and the other harassed apostles of conciliation had only found as many problems in the east as they had hoped to resolve.

KADETS BECOME THE "PARTY OF 18 NOVEMBER"

Indeed, it was soon apparent that the new Directorate's days were numbered. From all sides came criticism and expressions of nonsupport. In Samara, radical SRs felt the arrangement sacrificed democracy for political expediency, and urged socialists not to obey its directives; the autonomists thought it was they and not *navoznye liudi* who should administer Siberia, and reconvened their own Regional Duma; and Pepeliaev, Zhardetskii, and the Kadets in Omsk and Kharbin considered Lev Krol a "traitor" for supporting such an "absolutely unacceptable" political arrangement.[35]

[34] "Ufimskoe gosudarstvennoe soveshchanie," *Russkii istoricheskii arkhiv*, sbor. 1, Prague, 1929, pp. 247-51.

[35] V. M. Chernov, " 'Chernovskaia gramota' i Ufimskaia direktoriia," MS in the Hoover Institution, n.d., pp. 4-5; Vologodskii, "Dnevnik," Notebook 1, 143; Krol',

The coolness of Allied and Czech representatives also weakened the Directorate's stability, as did the decisions of Astrov, Denikin, and the Volunteers not to turn east. And the Volunteers' decision, in turn, only facilitated the advance of the Bolsheviks, who were now marching on Samara. Ironically, the Directorate's supporters felt the Reds might actually force an improvement in its position by prompting different groups to suspend their bickering. Instead, the would-be ministers soon found themselves under attack by the Kadets, who accused them with little justification of "intolerable vacillation."[36] Within weeks, in fact, as the new government sat in railroad cars near Omsk trying to organize its ministries, Pepeliaev went east to discuss a new program of "mutual action" with General Khorvat and the Kadets in Kharbin.[37] Both he and Zhardetskii intimated to a correspondent of the London *Times* that the new regime would soon be replaced.[38] Meanwhile, real power in the Omsk area remained in the hands of the regional regime.

What the Directorate's replacement would be was obvious from daily conversation in Omsk, where almost everyone was again talking about a military coup, just as in August 1917. American, French, and Czech representatives now openly supported a change of this sort, and so did the so-called Omsk Bloc, an informal group of important military and commercial figures, largely Kadets, who now began to meet together to discuss the situation, and whose views began to appear frequently in the Siberian press.[39] Even Kadet committees like the one in Ekaterinburg, which at first was quite firm in its support for the Directorate, now seriously debated its replacement with military rule.[40]

Early in November 1918 the Omsk Kadets gave more formal party leadership to their cause by organizing a special Eastern Section of the Central Committee (VOTsK). An entirely artificial creation, only one of whose members—Pepeliaev—was actually a member of the official

---

Za tri goda, pp. 150-51. Korobov, the other Kadet delegate at Ufa along with Krol, was so incensed by Zhardetskii's remarks that he sent his seconds around to arrange a duel, but Zhardetskii did not accept the challenge! (Krol', *Za tri goda*, p. 152.)

[36] Report of I. Kliuchnikov to the Russian Political Conference in Paris, June 2, 1919, in the Melgunov Collection, file B-1. See also V. Gurevich, "Real'naia politika v revoliutsii," *Volia Rossii*, No. 14, 1923, pp. 17-19.

[37] Maksakov and Turunov, pp. 92-93, quoting Pepeliaev's diary, which was not available to me.

[38] I. Il'in "Omsk, direktoriia, Kolchak," *NZ*, No. 72, 1963, p. 210.

[39] Telegram from U.S. Consul General Ernest Harris to Vladivostok Consulate, Dec. 13, 1918 (N.S.), in the Harris Papers, cart. 2. Also, Gen. K. V. Sakharov, *Belaia Sibir'*, Munich, 1923, p. 22; S. P. Mel'gunov, *Tragediia admirala Kolchaka*, 3 vols., Belgrade, 1930-31, I, 235-36; Gins, I, 275-84.

[40] Krol', *Za tri goda*, p. 157.

Central Committee elected in 1917, the VOTsK was designed to strengthen the weight of Kadets *as a party* behind military dictatorship, as well as to mobilize public opinion.[41] As a first step, the Committee called a regional conference to meet in Omsk on November 15.[42]

Kadets thus began to move to the forefront of the Siberian political stage, their position enhanced by the support of Allied representatives for "firm authority," and by the weakness of the Directorate, for whose ineffectuality they were much to blame. Omsk was still a city of green and white Siberian banners, rather than Russian ones; and Kadets were still *navoznye liudi* in the eyes of peasants and soldiers. But the more conservative wing of the autonomists had by now moved closer to the liberals on the basis of a forthright anti-socialism; and Kadet leaders were now on much better terms with the local Omsk regime, which they still supported rather than the Directorate. Moreover, just as in South Russia, the Kadets were the only organized nonsocialist party in Siberia which still maintained a network of local committees; and here, too, they also considered themselves bearers of "legitimate" state authority. Following the lead of their colleagues in Kiev and Ekaterinodar, they therefore hoped to take a leadership role in regional politics far greater than they deserved on the basis of popular support.[43]

The opening of the Kadet conference in Omsk on November 15, 1918, consequently attracted great interest—just, in fact, as had the Ekaterinodar conference four weeks before. More than sixty delegates arrived for the sessions, from nine local party committees.[44] What was remarkable about the gathering, however, was not its size, but the unanimity with which Kadets now condemned "unrealizable" democratic slogans, the "illegality" of the Constituent Assembly, and "anti-state socialist elements" like the Komuch leadership in Samara. A clarion call by Pepeliaev for military dictatorship was greeted with enormous enthusiasm, becoming "official" party policy. And the Kadets' well-worn banner of *gosudarstvennost'* now became a touchstone on which the anti-democratic concept of military dictatorship was made ideologically pure. The full energies of local committees, the delegates resolved, were to go toward unifying "national-thinking"

[41] N. S. Trubetskoi, untitled notes on the Kadet party in Siberia, Oct. 22, 1919, in the Panina Archive, pack. 3, fold. 34.

[42] Maksakov and Turunov, pp. 97-98.

[43] A. Klafton, untitled report to the VOTsK, in the Panina Archive, pack. 3, suppl. 2, fold. 4, p. 1.

[44] Materials on the Kadet Conference in the Panina Archive, pack. 3, suppl. 2, fold. 1. Delegates were representing committees in Omsk, Kazan, Samara, Irkutsk, Kharbin, Simbirsk, Vladivostok, Cheliabinsk, and Ufa.

social elements in support of "firm statesmanlike authority," "business-like administration," and "progressive" cultural work. As Zhardetskii explained, this would smooth the transition to military dictatorship on a local level by conditioning social figures and establishing a reservoir of public support. Once a dictatorship was actually created, all of this would also be useful in setting up a new administrative apparatus.[45]

Constitutional Democracy in Siberia thus came out forcefully and "officially" in favor of one-man rule. And after the delegates publicly declared themselves in opposition to the Directorate, they prepared to return for battle to their home committees. In effect, this was the party's final and official response in Siberia to efforts by Lev Krol and other moderates to organize a regional coalition. And just as with the coalition cabinets of the Provisional Government in 1917, the withdrawal of Kadet support was a death blow to Vologodskii's Directorate.

Even before the Kadets dispersed, however, their "victory" was won. At precisely the moment the Conference prepared to adjourn, a small group of cossack officers, acting with the knowledge and approval of Zhardetskii, Pepeliaev, and other party leaders, arrested the socialist members of the Directorate, and presented Kadets with a *fait accompli*. Within hours, local Omsk leaders proclaimed Admiral Alexander Vasilevich Kolchak the "Supreme Ruler" not only of Siberia, but of all Russia. And the Kadets, boasting their full support for the "tactics of state revolution," became "the Party of 18 November."[46]

[45] Resolutions of the Kadet Conference in Omsk, Nov. 1918, in the Panina Archive, pack. 3, suppl. 2, fold. 1.

[46] The exact Kadet role in the coup of November 18 remains obscure. We know the arrests themselves were carried out by cossack officers, and that these men were later defended at their trial by Zhardetskii. (See V. Zenzinov, ed., *Gosudarstvennyi perevorot' Adm. Kolchaka v Omske, 18 noiabria, 1918*, Paris, 1919.) And it is a fair (but unproved) assumption that Zhardetskii, Pepeliaev, and the cossacks worked closely together before November 1918. Pepeliaev, as we have seen, approached Khorvat in October with the suggestion he become dictator; and according to excerpts from Pepeliaev's diary published by Maksakov and Turunov, he not only entered into an agreement with Ivan Mikhailov to work towards overthrowing the Directorate, but discussed these plans with Kolchak himself (Khronika, p. 95). George Telberg, moreover, who later became the Kadet minister of justice in Kolchak's cabinet, refers to Zhardetskii in his unpublished memoirs as "the spirit of the coup." (G. Telberg Papers, Library of Congress, bx. 3.) However, N. I. Rakitnikov, a Left-centrist SR bitterly hostile to the Kadets in Siberia pointedly omits blaming the party for Kolchak's coup, and so does his right SR colleague, A. Argunov. (N. I. Rakitnikov, *Sibirskaia reaktsiia i Kolchak*, Moscow, 1920; A. Argunov, *Mezhdu dvumia bol'shevizmami*, Paris, 1919.) Kolchak himself told the investigating commission at his trial that no political figures came to see him on the question. (E. Varneck and H. H. Fisher, *The Testimony of Kolchak and Other Siberian Materials*, Stanford, 1935, p. 169.)

ADMIRAL KOLCHAK'S KADET ADMINISTRATION

If Admiral Kolchak was to unite the anti-Bolsheviks in Siberia, march on Moscow, overthrow Lenin, and begin the enormously difficult task of Russian reconstruction, he certainly needed all the authority implied in his pretentious title. For military forces he had a legion of ostensibly neutral foreign troops and advisers, and three bickering armies, spread out on a roughly north-south axis from Perm to the Caspian Sea. In the north, near the upper reaches of the Kama River, was the so-called Siberian Army, led by the Czech adventurer Colonel Gaida, and General A. N. Pepeliaev, brother of the Kadet. Near Ufa was the Western Army, some of whose men had earlier fought with the SR leader Colonel Kappel. And in the south were two cossack groups, the Orenburg Cossack Army, and the Ural Cossack Army, both under Ataman Dutov. Numbering almost 130,000 men at the time Kolchak assumed power, these troops were nominally under the command of General Boldyrev and the Directorate. But they faced a Red Army of almost equal size, and were inclined to pursue independent policies. When the Western Army near Ufa badly needed reinforcement, the Siberians in the north advanced instead on Perm, apparently hoping to link up with the British near Archangel.[74]

In addition to these troops in the field, Kolchak also took command of a number of cossack garrisons in Siberian cities, who were uniformly enthusiastic about the overthrow of the Directorate. It was the cossack units, in fact, which effectively prevented the SRs, the autonomists, or any front-line units from resisting the "state revolution." In some places, they followed the lead of their comrades in Omsk and arrested local socialists. Elsewhere they shut city dumas, and occupied municipal offices, usually with the approval of local Kadet committees who considered themselves "first friends" of the new government.[48] For democrats like the Directorate's military commander General Boldyrev, there was thus no mistaking what Kolchak's coup implied for the future of Siberian anti-Bolshevism. When he learned the news at the front, discovering as well that his own foreign advisers were supporting the admiral, Boldyrev tendered his resignation.[49] The question was not whether any force would be mustered in defense of the hapless Directorate, but whether Kolchak himself had the wherewithal to mount an effective and coordinated military dictatorship.

Little in his background suggested he did. The two most important attributes for a successful government in Siberia were personal popu-

[47] G. Stewart, *The White Armies of Russia*, New York, 1933, pp. 253-56; Gins, II, 94ff.

[48] Klafton, Report, pp. 12-13.   [49] Boldyrev, p. 118.

larity and military skill. But Kolchak was a newcomer to the region, having been appointed war minister in the Omsk regime while passing through on his way to South Russia. He was almost an "accidental" choice for "Supreme Ruler," someone conveniently in the right place with more national stature than General Khorvat, and strong backing from the British.[50] Moreover, while his new position demanded sensitivity and a cool head, Kolchak was a nervous and somewhat intemperate man, given to outbursts of sudden rage. He was best known, not for any particular military exploits, but for defiantly throwing his honorary sword of St. George into the Black Sea in the summer of 1917, rather than surrendering it to a sailors' committee, an act symbolic of his views toward the revolution.

Kolchak also had virtually no experience whatsoever in land warfare. His career had been as a fleet officer, and member of the admiralty staff in Petersburg. His only combat assignment on land had been commanding a naval battery during the war with Japan, a position which hardly qualified him for the task of coordinating the movements and strategy of three quarrelsome anti-Bolshevik armies.

From the moment he took power, therefore, the Supreme Ruler was forced to rely heavily on advisers. Among civilians, he chose almost entirely from the Omsk Bloc and the Kadet party, which by now were virtually synonymous. George Telberg, an experienced attorney and prominent Siberian Kadet party member, drew up the "primary statute" for the new regime, just as Stepanov and Sokolov had done for Denikin's Special Council in Ekaterinodar; and the Eastern Section of the Kadet Central Committee provided Kolchak with his administrative secretary (Telberg), the director of his Bureau of Information (N. V. Ustrialov), his minister of interior (Gattenberger), his minister of foreign affairs (Kliuchnikov), and even his director of the militia (Pepeliaev). Through Telberg's "primary statute," Kadets were thus responsible for the "legal" foundations of the new regime, and hence for provisions which endowed the Supreme Ruler with the "right to take extraordinary measures" to establish civil order and legality;[51] and through ministerial appointments, they were also responsible for staffing and supervising Kolchak's state bureaucracy, becoming the leadership core of his administrative apparatus.

[50] Kolchak was actually returning through Siberia from a mission to America, where he had been sent by Kerensky after resigning his naval post in 1917. He intended to join Denikin and Alekseev in South Russia, but was persuaded to join the Omsk regime by Vologodskii and General Gaida after he reached Vladivostok. See Varneck and Fisher, pp. 140ff, and esp. Richard Ullman, *Intervention and the War*, Princeton, 1961, pp. 258-84; and his *Britain and the Russian Civil War*, Princeton, 1968, pp. 33ff.

[51] Maksakov and Turunov, pp. 266-67.

In every department, party members were given positions of influence, much more so, in fact, than in any other anti-Bolshevik government, including Skoropadskii's Ukrainian Hetmanate. The Eastern Section of the Central Committee itself became one of Kolchak's principal advisory bodies, its leadership meeting with the Supreme Ruler on virtually a daily basis.[52]

Thus Kadets themselves finally became the principal force behind a unified anti-Bolshevik regime in Siberia, something of which they were enormously proud. And while *Sibirskaia Rech'* insisted with typical liberal obscuration that the new regime was entirely nonpartisan, acting only in the interests of Russia as a whole,[53] party leaders boasted privately that after months of "playing" with coalition, they had finally taken control of a "firm state authority, destined to resurrect all of Russia."[54]

Kadet boasts would have been more circumspect, however, had Siberian party leaders more fully considered the social and economic conditions of Kolchak's "realm." The new regime ostensibly covered several thousand miles, from Ufa and Perm eastward past Lake Baikal, to Vladivostok. This was sparsely settled territory, inhabited by fiercely independent settlers who generally supported the autonomists and the Socialist Revolutionaries. Its central axis was the Trans-Siberian railroad, which was also its vital military lifeline and political jugular vein. No regime could hope to "resurrect" Russia from Siberia unless it kept the railroad open. And none could keep the railroad open in the winter of 1918-1919 unless it cultivated the loyalty of the Siberian population, and controlled the bands of peasants and cossacks who were already beginning to roam freely through the region, pillaging almost at will.

The wildest of these groups were the ferocious hordes of two self-styled Atamans, Kalmykov and Semenov, who stood astride the railroad east of Lake Baikal. Both were made up largely of ex-convicts and renegade cossacks, and both were responsible for some of the worst barbarism of the entire civil war. Controlling all movement through their territory, they were also armed and supported by the Japanese,

---

[52] A. Klafton, Report, pp. 1-5; N. Ustrialov, "Belyi Omsk," MS in the Ustrialov Archives, n.d., pp. 52-54.

[53] *Sibirskaia Rech'*, No. 99, Dec. 10, 1918; No. 112, Dec. 16, 1918.

[54] G. Telberg, "Notes on Kolchak," misc. MS matls. in the Telberg Papers, bx. 3. S. Elachich, a Kadet from Samara who served in several of Kolchak's ministries, notes in his memoirs how delighted Victor Pepeliaev was to have been offered the directorship of the militia (equivalent to head of Kolchak's special police). In the past, Pepeliaev told the Omsk Kadets, the post was one of the most odious in any administration. With Kolchak's coup, however, it was very important for a Kadet to take the position, from which he could accomplish much. ("Obryvki vospominanii," MS in the Hoover Institution, 1934.)

who hoped in this way to advance their own power and influence in Eastern Russia. Any attempt to control their actions thus had international ramifications.

Officially, the Japanese had disembarked in 1918 as part of the vague and half-hearted plan to reopen a second front. They were soon joined by detachments of Americans and British, who were landed, however, as much to contain their Asian rivals as to keep open the second-front possibility. When the European Armistice was signed shortly before Kolchak's coup d'état, and the ostensible purpose of the intervention collapsed, the Allies shifted to "protecting the railroad." But for whom and from what was unclear. Sending goods through Semenov's greedy fingers was hardly the best way to help Kolchak; and protecting carloads of stolen goods and booty from hungry groups of partisans—whose ideologies at best were hopelessly confused—was sure to undermine whatever meager chances Kolchak still had of becoming a popular leader.

Graft and corruption, furthermore, had already risen to epidemic proportions along the Trans-Siberian even before the Supreme Ruler took power. In part this was simply the inevitable product of harsh wartime conditions, where greed and selfishness emerged as malignant replacements for the lost stabilities of normal times. Kolchak's frost-bitten soldiers went bootless and hungry as profiteers and exploiters sold blankets and clothing to the highest bidder. In part, however, bribery had also become grease for the wheels of a sputtering local commerce, as the few remaining factories and businesses competed for fuel and other scarce resources. To restore "legality," as Kolchak announced was his intention in his first public statement, the new Omsk regime would have to deal with a lawlessness so rampant it had become the only practical means to survive for hundreds of thousands of people.

As in South Russia and the Ukraine, however, there was also a more virulent form of lawlessness: that practiced by local army commanders in rump courts-martial and other formalized brutalities. One of the most hated military men in all Siberia was soon General Ivanov-Rinov, whom Kolchak himself had dispatched to bring order east of Lake Baikal while working briefly for the Directorate. Ivanov-Rinov was a mindless disciplinarian, the worst product of the old tsarist army. Establishing "martial law" but unable to control Semenov or Kalmykov, he eased his frustrations by frequent lynchings of suspected local "Bolsheviks," a category with very broad range. When the Directorate was arrested, this sort of lawless purge extended rapidly. Kolchak pressed his power simply by force of arms. Numerous arrests were made by his cossack supporters in the SR strongholds of Ekaterinburg and Cheliabinsk, and even in the army, among the former SR troops of Colonel Kappel and the Komuch.[55]

All of this created a terrible atmosphere of brutality and horror in the early part of 1919, where death became commonplace. Consider the appeal of a Siberian cooperative organization, which wrote to Kolchak after the assassination of one of its leaders in December 1918:

> When will our long-suffering Russia outlive the nightmare which throttles it? When will the death and violence cease? Does not horror seize you at the sight of an uninterrupted flow of human blood? Does not a horror seize you at the realization that the deepest, most elementary aspects of human existence and society are perishing: the feeling of humanity, the consciousness of the value of life, of human personality, the feeling and awareness of the necessity of legal order in the state?[56]

These, in effect, were the conditions over which the Supreme Ruler and his Kadet advisers were now attempting to establish a firm state authority—one which was to be national in competence, moreover, rather than simply restricted to Siberia.

If the coup of November 18 projected the liberal movement in Siberia into a position of influence and power, it thus pressed on Kadets as well an awesome set of problems and responsibilities. It was true that Kolchak's reliance on the Eastern Central Committee brought Kadets an opportunity to confront these problems directly, by setting government policy. The party leadership's potential here, in fact, was far greater than that of men like Astrov and Fedorov in South Russia. (Kolchak himself devoted almost all of his attention to military problems, even more so than did Denikin.) But Kolchak's dictatorship could only be successful if it acclimated itself carefully to Siberian problems and moods, particularly the tendency toward regional autonomy. This required of Kadets a broad and compassionate vision, an ability to couple military and administrative discipline with a sense of mission, and a recognition of the legitimacy of popular aspirations and grievances. It also required the meshing of legality with justice, some-

---

[55] Some SR leaders, including the socialist members of the deposed Directorate, found protection from Allied advisers, and were escorted safely out of the country. But others were not so lucky. In the middle of December a revolt broke out against Kolchak in Omsk itself. The political complexion of the protesters was not clear, but at one point, they released some 200 prisoners from the city's jails, among whom were a number of Constituent Assembly members. The escapees were all ordered to return immediately, and many did. But hours later, they were taken again from jail by a group of Kolchak's lieutenants, and shot. See Maksakov and Turunov, p. 103.

[56] *Ibid.*, p. 56, and Wm. H. Chamberlin, *The Russian Revolution*, 2 vols., New York, 1935, II, 188.

thing virtually impossible in the midst of civil war, and an effort by Kadets to overcome their well-developed *navoznye liudi* image.

Yet not only were the Siberian Kadets every bit as detached from popular interests and aspirations as most of their Petrograd party colleagues in 1917; they also assumed power in Siberia as a national rather than local authority, and hence had "formal" grounds for minimizing local problems. In rhetoric that is tiresomely familiar, they regarded themselves as defending the interests of the Great Russian State, once again focusing their perspectives in a grandiose, abstract, and conservative way.

From among these perspectives, moreover, they were committed most to what they regarded as the twin notions of order and Russian unity, rather than popular welfare; and they also felt that authority depended on strength, rather than popular support. Thus Pepeliaev not only introduced stern disciplinary measures in the army, but also sharply curtailed the activities of local autonomists, closing their clubs and preventing their meetings from being held; Zhardetskii set out a plan for rigid control over labor in industry; and when George Telberg became minister of justice he created a special committee on "Legality and Order."[57] As Telberg expressed the party's outlook:

> Without a firm sense of legality, without being guided by this sense in every hour of every day, without expressing all of its actions in the clear, universally understood forms of unwavering and consistent legal order, this government . . . cannot unite Russia. For without this basic condition, its cannot preserve the moral conditions . . . which alone will decide the outcome of Civil War. Therefore, the recognition of *legality* as the special mark of our government and armed forces . . . constitutes the first and primary duty of all citizens and patriots.[58]

But what *was* "legality" in the cold, desperate Siberian winter of 1919? By what standards was the seizure of food to be called theft, the payment of inflated fees to be considered bribery, or even shootings of political opponents to be condemned as murder? For their part, the Kadets soon determined to treat illegalities in favor of Kolchak's regime quite differently from those committed by its opponents—a familiar but hopelessly corrupting double standard. They did little about replacing Ivanov-Rinov for example, and worked simply to establish a better *modus vivendi* with Semenov.[59] And when the uprising of workers in Omsk was ruthlessly suppressed by members of

[57] "Notes on Kolchak," bx. 3.
[58] G. Telberg, Speech on becoming minister of justice, Telberg Papers, bx. 2.
[59] *Sibirskaia Rech'*, No. 112, Dec. 26, 1918.

Pepeliaev's militia (who from all accounts took many innocent lives and stuffed the bodies of their victims under the ice on the Irtysh River), the Eastern Section of the Kadet Central Committee greeted this "forcefulness" with applause. Mistakes, no doubt, had been made, the Committee declared; but times were perilous, and the government could only maintain its strength by rooting out those guilty of "anti-state" behavior.[60]

Within Kolchak's administration itself, Kadets also insisted on the strict behavior of government officials, and set up an ad hoc Special Council to root out corruption. The problem here, however, was that Kadets were unwilling to force the issue when they realized how pervasive the problem actually was. Part of the reason for this was the influence on Kadets of other members of the Omsk Bloc, who by now were well established in their own extralegal ways of conducting affairs, and recognized how important the bribe had become to their own survival. Also, many Kadets themselves would most probably have been implicated in any widespread crackdown.[61]

But corruption was also due to the confused administrative structure of Kolchak's regime itself, for which Kadets like Telberg and Pepeliaev were directly responsible. Shortly after it was organized, Kolchak's Special Council of Kadet advisers began expanding its responsibilities, usurping the functions of the regular Council of Ministers. This occurred at first in late December 1918 when Kolchak was ill with pneumonia, but the pattern continued after he recovered, extending to such a degree that by the middle of March, the Special Council was commonly known as the Star Chamber.[62] The result of this was not only a disruption of administrative procedures, rather than their regularization; but a freedom for many officials from effective supervision, which left them receptive to illicit practices. To this was added the distrust of regionalists at lower echelons for many of their Kadet-oriented superiors, a situation which further weakened Kolchak's administrative base.

In late February 1919, one of the more responsible liberal newspapers in Siberia, the transplanted *Russkiia Vedomosti* (now published under the name *Otechestvennye Vedomosti*), began a campaign against the Special Council and the problems it was abetting by calling for a popularly elected representative assembly. The paper argued that such a body would catalyze public sentiment against corruption,

[60] Klafton, Report, p. 13.

[61] "Notes on Kolchak," bx. 3. Telberg himself lamented this on becoming minister of justice.

[62] Interview with G. Gins. Pepeliaev himself later referred to the "Special Council" as a "Star Chamber." See his "Razval Kolchakovshchiny," *KA*, No. 31, 1928, p. 55.

and act as an important but non-coercive instrument of control. The need for a Star Chamber would then be removed, while the population at large developed a greater sense of involvement in the Whites' movement and cause. This, in turn, might channel autonomist and socialist sentiment more in favor of Kolchak.[63]

Otechestvennye Vedomosti's campaign made Kadets uncomfortable. Dismissing the idea of a representative assembly would fuel the fires of Siberian radicalism; but accepting it would admit that the party's own performance was deficient. The actual response of party leaders, however, hardly enhanced their government's popularity, and tells much about the Kadets' reluctance to face existing realities. The Eastern Section of the Central Committee set up a special commission to study the question which met and debated the issues for a number of weeks before deciding that any assembly at all—whether given legislative or executive competence, or restricted to merely consultative functions—would be both "inexpedient" and "untimely."[64] Zhardetskii, meanwhile, offered a counterproposal in *Sibirskaia Rech'*, suggesting Kolchak satisfy the demand for representative government by creating a Technical-Service Bureau, which would appoint "prominent citizens" to "discuss" various issues.[65] But even this was resisted by his fellow Kadets, who felt *any* additional government organ would only weaken Kolchak's power. And Zhardetskii himself soon dropped the idea as well.[66]

Not only was all this reminiscent of right-wing attitudes toward the Constituent Assembly in 1917; it was also symptomatic of Kadet policies toward local dumas and the zemstvos, the principal organs of Siberian self-government. In dealing with these bodies, party leaders worried not so much about political stability, as about the domination of SRs and autonomists. The Ministry of Internal Affairs, for example, when working out plans for zemstvo and city duma elections in early 1919, asked the Kadet Central Committee to select a commission to review its proposals. After looking at the plans, the Kadets decided zemstvo and city organs had effectively been taken over by "revolutionary demagogues," and insisted that if local elections were held at all, they be carefully supervised, and run on the basis of tighter electoral requirements. "The establishment of too broad an electoral corpus," according to the Kadet Central Committee, "will again surrender the country to the rule of those same anti-state, irresponsible elements who have produced the destruction of all local economic life." Siberia

---

[63] Ustrialov, "Belyi Omsk," pp. 146-47.   [64] *Ibid.*

[65] *Sibirskaia Rech'*, No. 56, Mar. 15, 1919; *Nasha Zaria*, No. 61, Mar. 21, 1919 and No. 73, Apr. 4, 1919.

[66] Ustrialov, "Belyi Omsk," p. 147.

needed "good" dumas, ones whose members were "experienced in social affairs."[67]

But experienced members did not include zemstvo personnel or autonomists, whose activities Kadets wanted under the direct control and supervision of the Interior Ministry. Nor did it mean that Kadets thought "experienced" dumas might handle for themselves the problems of peasant unrest, or even local labor disputes. On both these issues, Kadets insisted on directives from Omsk.[68] At the same time, the directives Kadets wanted were not ones designed to implement reforms, or otherwise win mass support. "We were ready to accept any form of authority," the chairman of the Eastern Central Committee wrote later, "if only it satisfied our basic idea of national resurrection and unification."[69]

But Kadets were also quite unwilling to advance social and political reforms which might have served the same end. On the agrarian question, for example, some in the government were urging Kolchak unilaterally to increase peasant holdings. The question was perhaps not as important here as elsewhere in Russia, since many Siberians owned and worked their own land, particularly in the east. But the peasant mood was still sufficiently uneasy for many to feel that peasant ownership rights should be guaranteed and expanded.[70] According to S. N. Melgunov, author of a comprehensive work on Kolchak's regime, the Supreme Ruler himself supported this idea.[71] But the Star Chamber argued that steps in this direction would cost the support of gentry landholders, many of whom played important roles in the army.[72]

The Eastern Central Committee agreed, announcing it stood for strengthening peasant holdings, but creating a special "Agrarian Commission" to meet with Kolchak and urge the question be postponed until some future Constituent Assembly.[73] And while one should not attribute special influence to Kadets for a view which by now was widely shared among officials in Omsk, Kolchak accepted the party's position. Early in April he issued a general declaration on the "land problem" stressing his support for peasant interests, but also announcing postponement of the question until after the war. In the interim, agrarian disorders would not be "tolerated."[74]

The Kadets also pressed to postpone the crucial problem of regional

[67] MS report of Eastern Kadet Central Committee sessions in the Panina Archive, pack. 3, suppl. 2, fold. 2. Also, Klafton, Report, p. 13.

[68] *Ibid.*

[69] N. Ustrialov, *V bor'be za Rossiiu*, Kharbin, 1920, p. 4.

[70] Gins, II, 151.   [71] Mel'gunov, *Tragediia*, III, 255.

[72] Gins, II, 152.   [73] Klafton, Report, p. 23.

[74] S. A. Piontkovskii, ed., *Grazhdanskaia voina v Rossii (1918-1921)*, Moscow, 1925, pp. 301-02.

autonomy.[75] Within the Special Council and the Council of Ministers, Pepeliaev, Klafton, Zhardetskii, and Telberg all insisted that this question could only be decided after Russia was united, since decisions pertaining to one area might not be applicable to another.[76] This, of course, was by now a familiar liberal argument; but it had special importance in Siberia as a result of the local autonomists. Kadets seemed to take pleasure in thinking Kolchak's administration was finally suppressing a disunifying (and long-time rival) political movement. But in effect, the party was simply helping to prevent an "outside" administration from securing the full support of the indigenous Siberian population. By insisting that victory precede reform, and postponing the resolution of crucial social and political issues, Kadets were assuring that Kolchak and his liberal advisers remained *navoznye liudi.*

Moreover, this and other problems were not ones Kolchak and his Kadet advisers could postpone. A resolution of the agrarian and regional problems was a *requisite* to military success in Siberia, just as in South Russia. Nor did graft, corruption, banditry, desertion, or mass unrest decrease because Kolchak declared they would not be "tolerated." Brute force sowed its own resistance, and in many ways contributed to the anti-Bolsheviks' problems.

By the spring of 1919, in fact, at the very moment Kolchak's regime was recognized in South Russia as the principal anti-Bolshevik government, virtually all of the problems affecting Siberia at the time of the November coup had grown worse. In March, General Gaida told an American official that corruption in Kolchak's administration would probably guarantee the Bolsheviks' victory. (Shortly afterward, a Red commander wired facetiously to General Knox, the commander of the British military mission, thanking him for clothing and other supplies.)[77] And Justice Minister Telberg, one of the more competent Kadets in Kolchak's government, was now forced to accept an armed escort in Omsk to protect him from those he wanted to prosecute.[78]

The only bright spot in the Spring of 1919 was at the front. Largely as a result of the Bolsheviks' own weakness, Kolchak's armies had managed to push forward and were now advancing westward along a broad front. In the north, the Siberian Army freed the Kama basin and pressed in the direction of Viatka. The Western Army took Ufa

[75] E.g., *Sibirskaia Rech'*, No. 166, Aug. 2, 1919.

[76] "Notes on Kolchak," bx. 3.

[77] U.S. Dept. of State, *Papers Relating to the Foreign Relations of the United States. Russia, 1919*, Washington, 1937, p. 204; W. Graves, *America's Siberian Adventure*, New York, 1931, p. 301.

[78] "Notes on Kolchak," bx. 3.

on March 12, and advanced even further in early April. Samara, Orenburg, and Saratov thus seemed within striking distance.

It was this, in fact, which encouraged Maklakov and other Russian emissaries in Paris and London, and which largely prompted Denikin's "subordination." But what few realized either inside Siberia or out was that Kolchak's administration was rapidly withering internally. It was only a matter of weeks before the tide against the Supreme Ruler and his Kadet advisers would turn irreversibly.

CHAPTER FOURTEEN

The End of Party Efforts in
Siberia and South Russia

D ESPITE these many signs of weakness in the late spring of 1919, most anti-Bolshevik leaders remained remarkably optimistic. A favorable military situation blurred the dangers of social chaos and political disaffection, and the corrosive influence of reactionary commanders. Also, the problems of a rebellious peasantry, of graft and economic corruption, of military supply, and even of troop discipline seemed to be affecting the Bolsheviks as severely as the Whites. And while many were appalled at the growing brutalization of Russian existence, most men in high places in Omsk and Ekaterinodar were still convinced the war would be won entirely by military power.

This was a fatal miscalculation. The important truth was not that the Bolsheviks were having similar problems to the Whites, but that growing disaffection from the stringencies of war communism brought exceptional opportunities for Kolchak and Denikin to increase their support. In the fall and winter of 1917-1918, after boldly endorsing the Socialist Revolutionaries' land program, Lenin had followed a permissive policy toward the countryside, encouraging land seizures and expropriations. Many peasants looked hopefully to the new regime in these circumstances, fearing above all the return of the gentry *barin*. But Lenin and his followers remained enormously distrustful of Russia's rural proletarians, and hardly enjoyed a firm hold on their loyalties. By the early summer of 1918, a decision was made in the face of serious new grain and food shortages to end the "honeymoon" in favor of strict new controls; and as Red detachments began to confiscate grain and livestock, taking even the supplies which peasants held for their personal needs, resistance grew sharply. Pitched battles broke out in a number of places, weakening the Red offensive in the south and even threatening areas close to Moscow and Petrograd.

To take advantage of these conditions—of what was becoming, in effect, the most massive social and political dislocation in Russia since the end of the sixteenth century—the White governments had to pursue several closely related objectives. They had to translate their verbal commitments to "legality" and "order" into practical reality within the ranks of their own armies; they had to establish careful and orderly administrations in territories they controlled; and they had to cultivate a strong popular backing, reordering their own social and political priorities so that the satisfaction of mass demands became a goal of crucial importance. At the very least, White leaders had to develop an agrarian policy which gave land to the peasants, rather than protecting gentry estates, and work out some generally acceptable form of regional autonomy.

It is hard in restrospect to imagine the White movements abandoning their defense of privileged interests and the welfare of the "state" in 1918 and 1919, but had Kadets in Omsk and Ekaterinodar mustered the full weight of their party organizations behind these tasks, they conceivably could have been accomplished. The considerable personal authority of Denikin and Kolchak should have contained any serious military opposition to such a new course, particularly if White troops were moving forward, and if Denikin and Kolchak were as forceful with right-wing dissenters as they were with those on the left. It might even have been possible to overcome the peasants' conception of the Whites as an army of gentry. Though the massive horror of civil war often involved acts of class brutality, where Whites were slaughtered as "tsarist landlords," and peasants and workers were shot as "supporters of Lenin," it also minimized the importance of past social or political associations. For most, survival was more important than property and party. On occasion, whole army units changed from one camp to the other. Deserters were drafted and redrafted, tsarist officers fought on both sides, Reds and Whites alike "enlisted" their prisoners of war. The real question was whether the leaders of the White movement—and especially the Kadets, who by now constituted the only active major political group in both South Russia and Siberia—could see beyond military goals.

Some clearly could. In the spring of 1919, Lev Krol in Siberia, Nicholas Shchepkin in Moscow, and Nicholas Astrov in Ekaterinodar, among others, all pressed for a change in White perspectives. They wanted progressive policies in crucial areas like land reform, urged the separation of military and civil authority, and desired some form of representative council as a means of developing responsive policies and broadening popular support. Astrov and his supporters were not naive democrats. The former Moscow attorney in particular felt that unrestricted civil liberties could lead to problems like those which had developed in the Crimea, and thought many socialist groups were bent on undermining all anti-Bolshevik authority. A dictatorship was needed. But he, Fedorov, Shchepkin and others now believed that Denikin and Kolchak had to begin supporting progressive social policies and be willing to apply force against their own reactionary elements.

These were goals, moreover, behind which Astrov and others insisted Kadets had to be mobilized *as a party*:

We find ourselves, members of the Kadet Central Committee, scattered to various ends of Russia . . . going off in different directions, unable to give ourselves mutual council or arrange a unified course of action. . . . We present the pitiful spectacle of a madman rushing about in all directions . . . acting and assuming responsibilities sharply contradicting one another. . . . I will not linger on the question of whether or not the party is still needed. Facts show it is essential to Russia, perhaps more now than any other time in the past. . . .[1]

To give substance to these views, Astrov, Iurenev, and others arranged in March 1919 to reconvene the party's official Central Committee in South Russia, first in the Crimea (before it was overrun), and then, regularly, in Ekaterinodar. Meanwhile, Lev Krol in Omsk communicated similar ideas to the Eastern Branch of the Central Committee, and enlisted support from the liberal *Otechestvennyia Vedomosti*. And Nicholas Shchepkin wrote to both camps on behalf of Central Committee members still in Moscow urging the end of reliance on "old persons" and "outmoded policies," and demanding "new, radical steps."[2]

But most Kadets had no intention whatsoever of taking "new radical steps" in the spring of 1919. To Novgorodtsev, Zhardetskii, Sokolov, Stepanov, Pepeliaev, and even Miliukov, writing from abroad, what Russia needed was not a revitalization of the Kadet party, democratic persons, or liberal programs, but "Victory!" The "application of force, naked force," was now "inevitable" in Miliukov's view.[3] And to the rightist Sokolov, writing in the party's official Ekaterinodar journal, *Svobodnaia Rech'*, cooperation with populist groups and the adoption of "socialist measures" were unthinkable. "It would now be fitting for the socialists simply to stand aside," he wrote with shocking arrogance, "and try simply to forget they exist!"[4] Paul Novgorodtsev put the matter this way:

[1] Astrov to Iurenev, Dec. 27, 1918, in the Panina Archive, pack. 5, suppl. 4, fold. 1.
[2] Shchepkin to Pepeliaev, n.d. but prior to July 1919, in the Panina Archive, pack. 3, fold. 16; K. D. Partiia, "Protokol zasedaniia tsentral'nogo komiteta," Apr. 14, 1919 (O.S.), in the Panina Archive, pack. 3, suppl. 1 (henceforth Central Committee Protocols).
[3] Miliukov to Petrunkevich, Nov. 21/Dec. 4, 1918, Wrangel Military Archives, file 135.
[4] *Svobodnaia Rech'*, Apr. 21, 1919 (O.S.).

If nothing remains of our democratism, then that is an excellent thing, since what is needed now is dictatorship, a force for creating authority. . . . There is now no "Kadetism" or "democratism," there is only the task of national unification. The party's own responsibilities derive from this. [Astrov] says the job of the party is to mitigate the excesses of dictatorship. But that is a trivial thing. . . . It is a question of the Nation and the Russian State, and not of the party. . . . Established party dogmas must be done away with; free thinking on these matters is absolutely essential.[5]

Thus Kadets like Astrov and Krol failed to change the views of their colleagues. In the late spring of 1919 the time was not far away when cries for a "new course" would suddenly get receptive hearings in both Omsk and Ekaterinodar, as White troops began to fall back. But with armies advancing on both fronts, with Denikin, Kolchak, and their advisers flushed with the cocky self-assurance of "success," with most Kadets convinced more than ever that "national" rather than "class" or *partiinye* policies were the only appropriate means for Russia's "resurrection," Krol, Astrov, Fedorov, Shchepkin, and those who thought in terms of change were pressured into silence. In Siberia, Lev Krol retired to Ekaterinburg, abashed at the futility of his labors and determined to view subsequent events from a distance. In the south, Astrov made one more determined plea to the Kadet Central Committee, declaring on May 12 that "the time has come when either the Right must throw us off, or we must liberate ourselves from them," and then decided to join a special delegation to discuss Russian problems in Paris.[6]

Shortly afterward, both the Eastern Branch of the Kadet Central Committee and the South Russian group in Ekaterinodar convened new regional party conferences to consolidate their support for the dictatorships. The Siberian sessions opened in Omsk on May 15, sounding the strongest note yet in support of Kolchak's policies. There was no question but that civil liberties, popular government, and even the *discussion* of major social reforms would only weaken the army and hamper its efforts. First the Bolsheviks had to be defeated. Then a "National" Assembly could convene—the Siberian Kadets pointedly dropped the word "Constituent"—and address itself to the problems of a new social order. Party spokesmen made it clear they favored the *eventual* creation of a representative democracy, but only as a long-range goal. For the time being, they would continue supporting the appointment of officials in liberated regions, rather than their

[5] Central Committee Protocol, May 5, 1919) (O.S.).
[6] *Ibid.*, May 12, 1919 (O.S.).

selection in some way by local populations, and the forcible dissolution of local parliamentary organizations, like the city dumas and zemstvos. Groups of this sort were not only inclined toward Siberian regionalism, but also overly concerned with constitutional niceties at the expense of the war effort. Kadets had to recognize that "only extraordinary measures will serve to resurrect the Russian state in this period of unprecedented disorder."[7]

In the South, where a Kadet conference also convened in Ekaterinodar, "unprecedented disorder" was the main concern as well. And here, too, party leaders like Novgorodtsev and Dolgorukov spoke out every bit as forcefully as their Siberian colleagues in favor of "extraordinary measures." No one denied the pervasiveness of administrative abuses or the absence of clear policies on important social issues. But here as in Omsk there was little effort to argue that these factors would have an important bearing on the outcome of the White struggle.

Instead, Denikin was applauded for his "valor, wisdom, lofty patriotism, and nobility"; and Kadets reminded themselves that "criticism and opposition at the present time must have a responsible and statesmanlike character . . . and must be directed toward strengthening the foundations of authority."[8] Even the question of how committed Kadets should be to the gains of the revolution, or conversely, how concerned they should be with the growth of reaction, were dealt with uncritically. Denikin's administration was urged both to "overcome revolutionary tendencies" and "act as a check on the revolutionary mood," while also "standing aside from restoration" and "acting as a check on the reactionary mood." The conference purposely refused to endorse any specific policies toward these ends, recognizing simply that they required "the authority of one-man dictatorship."[9]

As Paul Dolgorukov insisted, the deliberate generality of the Kadets' resolutions helped preserve party unity.[10] But just as during other critical periods in the party's history, unity was again obtained at the cost of political effectiveness. The moment was quite important in the history of the anti-Bolshevik movement: a change in the social and political orientation of the White leadership might conceivably have extended its popularity and support in dramatic fashion. But Kadets failed to press this course of action, or even try seriously to use their

[7] Resolutions of the Kadet Conference in Omsk, May 1919 in the Panina Archive, pack. 3, suppl. 2, fold. 4.

[8] Reports on the Ekaterinodar Conference, June 1919, in the Panina Archive, pack. 3, fold. 18.

[9] Statement of Greetings to General Denikin, and Resolution on Tactics, Panina Archive, pack. 3, fold. 18.

[10] P. Dolgorukov, *Natsional'naia politika i partiia narodnoi svobody*, Rostov, 1919, pp. 14-15.

own party as a force for moderation. Again, nonpartisanship was the justification for inaction, and an excuse for the defense of conservative interests, particularly those of the gentry, just as in 1917; and again, the net effect of inaction was to endorse the prevailing state of affairs, with all its fatal weaknesses. "We stand in the leading ranks of a great struggle—a humanitarian struggle—for the salvation of civilization, for the salvation of law, of the rights of man, the foundations of a true democracy," the Samara Kadet, Alexander Klafton, preached to his party colleagues in May.[11] But so vague were the party's own official directives on waging this struggle, that in the south, Astrov's small group of supporters felt compelled to add two special statements of their own to the resolutions of the Ekaterinodar conference, simply informing local Kadets they should continue their efforts at reestablishing local party groups, and should indeed enter local governments in support of Denikin or Kolchak. Even so, the Central Committee in South Russia was soon being queried by local groups for more specific instructions.[12]

One might well argue that nothing could have greatly increased the popular support of the Whites in the summer of 1919, that mass social prejudices and political hostilities were by now too deeply ingrained, that the Whites' reactionary image was indelible. One might also maintain that even had the Kadets done what Astrov, Fedorov, Krol, and their moderate supporters insisted, and struck out forcefully for radical new policies, it would have made little impression on the anti-Bolshevik military leadership. But however these questions may be answered, and whether or not a "new course" by Kadets would have altered the civil war, the early summer of 1919 was again a time one should have been tried. Unqualified support for the existing dictatorships, with all of their patent disabilities, only hastened the Whites' eventual collapse.

THE END OF PARTY EFFORTS IN THE EAST

In Siberia, in fact, Kadets at the May party conference in Omsk were lashing themselves to a ship that was already sinking. While Denikin's troops were just beginning to gather the momentum of a sustained advance, Kolchak's armies were halting, stopped by tenacious Bolshevik shock detachments and malignant White corruption.

Ufa fell in the first week of June. The Siberian and Western Armies began to stream back toward Omsk, while Kolchak's southern forces

[11] A. F. Klafton, Remarks at the Kadet Conference in Omsk, May 1919, in Panina Archive, pack. 3, suppl. 3, fold. 5.
[12] Panina Archive, pack. 3, fold. 18, 25, and 31.

struggled to regroup. By early July 1919, Kolchak's capital itself was swelled with retreating troops and refugees. Yet while highways and railheads were packed with the starving and wounded, whole train-loads of goods, were still openly diverted by Kolchak's ostensible lieutenants. When the Americans landed a shipment of rifles in mid-summer, General Graves was so sure they would never arrive at the front that he halted their delivery. The shipment went through only when the Americans themselves convoyed it to Irkutsk. "From Tiumen west," an Allied officer cabled General Graves, "all is disorder and panic. Officers and men are leaving the front by hundreds and there is no control. . . ."[13]

Relations with the Czechs and Allies were also growing more bitter. Increasingly, the Czechs sympathized with Russian moderate socialists, many of whom still dominated local dumas and zemstvos. They also resented Kolchak's efforts to extend his dictatorial authority. Often Kolchak interfered with the Czech's own progress eastward, since Czech detachments frequently relied on local authorities for supplies. Kolchak, in turn, resented the fact that the Czechs still controlled important stretches of the Trans-Siberian railroad, and blamed the Allies for failing in their promises of help. Despite professions of neutrality, Czech forces often blocked the tracks, either by accident or design, and hindered White movements.[14]

Growing bands of partisans added to the chaos. Siberian peasants were now openly contemptuous of Kolchak's *navoznyi* administration, and increasingly took matters into their own hands. As "Greens," they fought with equal ferocity against both Reds and Whites; and as an indication of the mass social dislocation affecting Siberia, they symbolized both the poverty of Kolchak's own social policies, and the complete disintegration of normal patterns of existence.

Indeed, it is almost absurd to speak of normal patterns of existence in Siberia during the summer and fall of 1919. Perhaps nowhere else in the civil war was there such extended pain and suffering. And perhaps nowhere else was the breakdown of ordinary government practices so complete:

> In the army, decay; at headquarters, ignorance and incompetence; in the government, moral rot, disagreement, the intrigues of ambitious egoists; in the country, uprisings, anarchy; in society at large, panic, selfishness, bribery, and all sorts of scandalous behavior.[15]

---

[13] U.S. Dept. of State, *Papers Relating to the Foreign Relations of the United States, 1919*, Washington, 1937, p. 206.

[14] *Sibirskaia Rech'*, No. 192, Sept. 4, 1919.

[15] Baron A. P. Budberg, "Dnevnik," *ARR*, xv, 1924, p. 269.

Against this background—the description of its horror abbreviated here only because it has been portrayed so fully elsewhere[16]—the remaining chapter of Kadet history in the east requires little telling. For most of the summer and early fall, most Kadets still considered themselves "first friends of the government."[17] They not only continued to serve in Kolchak's regime, but welcomed new responsibilities.[18] In the Eastern Branch of the Kadet Central Committee, discussion focused not on the weaknesses of the regime, but on the "foreign" causes of difficulty: refugees were "ungrateful" for not being willing to bear arms; the Bolsheviks were everywhere, infiltrating ministries and army units, spreading "venomous propaganda"; the SRs were "political cretins," who "desired uninterrupted mutiny and pillage"; the autonomists dominating local zemstvos and dumas were "traitors" to their motherland.[19]

Inevitably, however, as the Bolshevik drive moved relentlessly toward Omsk, and this and other Siberian cities saw the ever more horrible suffering of soldiers and civilians, some pressure for change did emerge from within the party's ranks, coming from the same group of moderate Kadets who had earlier worked for compromise and coalition with the left. At the end of July 1919, Lev Krol came out of "retirement." Finding himself in Omsk as a result of the Bolshevik's advance, he began to meet with various socialists and autonomists, and again press the cause of social reform and representative government.[20] In June, Kolchak had convened a public conference to deal with Siberia's economic problems, the so-called State Economic Conference.[21] Krol and his comrades urged that this group be transformed into a representative assembly, invested with responsibility for forming a new administration.[22]

[16] See, e.g., W. H. Chamberlin, *The Russian Revolution*, 2 vols., New York, 1935, II, esp. 173-205.

[17] A. Klafton, untitled Report to the VOTsK, in the Panina Archive, pack. 3, suppl. 2, fold. 4, p. 1.

[18] In the middle of July, for example, Telberg accepted a promotion to the post of vice president in the Council of Ministers, while Zhardetskii accepted Kolchak's request that the two begin meeting together on a daily basis to discuss administrative problems. See *Pravitel'stvennyi Vestnik*, No. 184, July 15, 1919; L. Krol', *Za tri goda*, Vladivostok, 1922, p. 179.

[19] E.g., *Sibirskaia Rech'*, No. 192, Sept. 4, 1919; No. 210, Sept. 26, 1919; No. 216, Oct. 4, 1919; No. 221, Oct. 10, 1919; No. 223, Oct. 12, 1919.

[20] Krol', *Za tri goda*, p. 189.

[21] The State Economic Conference was composed partly of members of the government, partly of representatives from public associations like the Omsk bloc. It was charged with pointing out to the government the various financial, industrial, agricultural, labor, and transport measures needed for Siberian economic health. It could also raise questions concerning the supply of the army, and debate government proposals. (Russian Liberation Committee, *Bulletin*, No. 29, n.d., in the A. V. Tyrkova Archive, sect. 3, cart. 11, gp. 3.)

[22] Krol', *Za tri goda*, pp. 189-90.

Most Kadets continued to oppose this idea, repeating arguments made in the spring when the issue was raised by *Otechestvennyia Vedomosti.* But Krol now received support from N. K. Volkov and A. A. Cherven-Vodali, two prominent liberals from South Russia who arrived in Omsk for "liaison" at the end of July. While publicly re-affirming the party's commitment to "equality and cooperation among all population groups," rather than the hegemony of special social interests, the two newcomers argued in private that Kolchak should take immediate steps to improve his popularity among soldiers and peasants.[23] To Kolchak's Cabinet of Ministers for example, Cherven-Vodali urged the convocation of a national representative assembly, as well as strict rules to prevent military interference in civil affairs.[24]

Krol also gained new backing from the small Central Committee group still in Moscow. According to a communication from N. N. Shchepkin to Pepeliaev, the Moscow Kadets were now convinced that only a popular government could effectively resurrect a free and liberal Russia:

> The Central Committee looks unfavorably on the policies of Kadets in the South for their present narrow point of view, and their un-compromising and isolated outlook. It is necessary, on the contrary, to unite all social sectors for a cooperative effort, even if only passively.[25]

Urging the Kadets, as we have seen, not to rely either on "old persons" or "outmoded policies," but to take "new, radical steps,"[26] the Moscow Kadets very much reinforced those of their Siberian colleagues who now demanded sweeping reforms.[27] In Irkutsk, Kadets even formed a special Irkutsk Bloc to combat the influence of the party's leadership in Omsk, and to turn Kolchak's dictatorship in the direction the Moscow Kadets suggested.[28]

At first, Kolchak refused entirely to discuss these issues. Shockingly enough, he even considered arresting the moderate Kadet leadership.[29] But Volkov and Cherven-Vodali carried considerable weight. Volkov in particular was a former assistant minister of food supply in the Provisional Government, a longtime State Duma member from Siberia and prominent party figure in the Central Committee; and he finally managed after a series of meetings with Victor Pepeliaev to win the latter to the moderate's cause. Kolchak was then persuaded to make a

23 *Pravitel'stvennyi Vestnik*, No. 199, Aug. 1, 1919.
24 "Razval Kolchakovshchiny," *KA*, No. 31, 1928, p. 60. (Diary of V. N. Pepeliaev.)
25 N. N. Shchepkin [Koka] to Pepeliaev, n.d. but prior to July 1919, in the Panina Archive, pack. 3, fold. 16.
26 *Ibid.*
27 N. V. Ustrialov, "Belyi Omsk," MS in the Ustrialov Archive, 1919, file 7, p. 141.
28 *Ibid.*, pp. 142-43.   29 "Razval Kolchakovshchiny," p. 60.

modest concession. On September 16 he announced the convocation of a National Zemstvo Congress with the power to advise the regime and challenge its ministers.[30]

The irony of this concession was not that it was so little so late, but that the Eastern Central Committee itself now rose up to object! Siberian regionalists had long demanded precisely such a congress and the prominent separatist Iakushev had even organized a committee in Vladivostok to work for its convocation.[31] Kadets thus saw the decision as a sop to the "separatists," a weakening of "firm dictatorship" in an effort to secure what would prove to be meaningless support:

> The Party of People's Freedom opposes the idea of a legislative or consultative organ, for this will weaken, not strengthen, the dictatorship. Our viewpoint is that it is necessary only to increase the powers of the Supreme Ruler. Our slogan is not only "Dictator," but "Liberator"—a creative dictator. . . . And as for the Cabinet of Ministers, we look on it not as a political cabinet, but as a businesslike council [delovyi sovet] for the implementation of the Supreme Ruler's program. We can only hope that the National Zemstvo Conference will bring the government closer to the people, and make it and its measures more popular. We must try to make it as useful a body as possible.[32]

But even a conference of saints could not make Kolchak more popular in the autumn of 1919. The party's declaration, in fact, appeared just as the government was entering its final days. At the end of October, the Bolsheviks closed in on Omsk. Kolchak and his ministers fled in panicky disorder. The Supreme Ruler, who never effectively ruled and was certainly not supreme, vainly tried to reestablish his administration in Irkutsk, where he turned to Victor Pepeliaev to head his last cabinet. Ironically the former chairman of the Kadets' Eastern Central Committee was thus left to preside over the regime he had worked so hard to create at the moment of its final collapse.

Moreover, with the desperation of a patriot in charge of a hopeless effort, Pepeliaev now underwent a sharp change in his own political thinking—in marked contrast, in fact, to his party colleagues in Omsk. As Kolchak was evacuating his capital, the Kadet group there publicly evoked "God," "historical destiny," and the "spirit of Russian

---

[30] George Gins (Guins), Sibir', soiuzniki, i Kolchak, 2 vols., Peking, 1921, II, 299-300; I. A. Iakushev, "Komitet sodeistviia sozyvu zemskogo sobora," Sibirskii Arkhiv, II, 1929, pp. 74-77.

[31] Ibid.   [32] Russkoe Delo, No. 3, Oct. 8, 1919.

culture" to "prove" the worthiness of their cause.[33] But Pepeliaev now attempted to reform the government by transferring power from military commanders to civilians, and enlisting representatives from the left in his cabinet.[34] But these were frantic and futile gestures, almost a year too late. Within weeks, for all intents and purposes, Kolchak's army had ceased to exist. The Siberian struggle had come to an end.

THE STRUGGLE CONTINUES IN SOUTH RUSSIA
JULY TO SEPTEMBER 1919

Meanwhile, the summer of 1919 brought new hopes to the capital of the Kuban, still the center of political and military activities for the Armed Forces of South Russia (AFSR). None of the major problems of the spring had been settled here either, but they somehow seemed less ominous as Denikin's armies took the offensive. They also occupied less attention in the Special Council. Astrov and other leading Council members were abroad, and Denikin's "subordination" to Admiral Kolchak at the end of May left a definite feeling that the locus of political affairs had shifted.[35] In June a new set of rules was issued to govern the harvest in territories under AFSR control, incidentally reaffirming the property rights of landlords and lessors.[36] Shortly afterward, the cossacks convened a new South Russian Conference, hoping finally to build the foundations of a Don, Kuban, and Terek union, and also to work out recurring problems of local administration.[37] And there was also legislation setting new and harsher penalties for persons "cooperating with Soviet authorities," as well as a new commission to reexamine the whole problem of agrarian reform.[38] But none of these measures touched closely on the Whites' major problems—peasant unrest, regional separatism, the abuses of field commanders—and what is more, no one seemed to care. What mattered was the army's military success. Even the Special Council now met less frequently than earlier in the year, its members generally convinced that major social questions would now be settled in Moscow. More

---

[33] *Ibid.*, Nos. 1-5, Oct. 5-10, 1919.

[34] N., "Poslednie dni Kolchakovshchiny," *Sibirskie Ogni*, No. 2, 1922, pp. 83-84.

[35] See e.g., *Kubanskaia Zhizn'*, No. 25, June 11, 1919.

[36] *Zhurnal Osobago Soveshchaniia pri Glavnokomanduiushchem Dobrovol'cheskoi Armiei*, No. 73, June 25, 1919, in the Wrangel Personal Archives, file 2. The rules provided that one-third of the harvest from any estate was to be reserved for the owner or lessor of the land, even in his absence. If the landlords' portion was not claimed by January 1, 1920, it was to be sold at public auction, and the receipts held for him in permanent trust.

[37] *Svobodnaia Rech'*, No. 142, July 2, 1919.

[38] *Zhurnal Osobago Soveshchaniia*, No. 78, Jul. 12, 1919, and No. 81, Jul. 23, 1919.

often than not, it concerned itself simply with distributing funds. There were even rumors it would soon be dissolved.[39]

The summer of 1919 was a period of relative inactivity for the Kadets as well. The decisions of the June Ekaterinodar Conference meant the party would not develop into a more activist political force, as Astrov had wanted; and many prominent party spokesmen, particularly Dolgorukov and Novgorodtsev, stressed simply the need for "businesslike support" for Denikin and Kolchak's "national dictatorships."[40] From July to September, the Central Committee met a scant three times. Only a handful of members attended and no important matters were discussed. (The absence of direction among Kadets was so great that at one session, when Paul Dolgorukov asked whether the party might support a monarchy in future elections, he received no definite reply.)[41] Party members busied themselves instead with "nonpartisan national public activities," to use Dolgorukov's own awkward expression, writing propaganda for Osvag, working on various pieces of legislation in the National Center, and participating in the different commissions of the Special Council.[42]

Meanwhile, the administration of territories under AFSR control remained chaotic. Peasants complained that landlords returned with the troops; workers protested that their elementary rights were consistently abused:

> Elementary civil liberties are violated all over the territory occupied by the Volunteer Army. Among the occurrences which take place are: murders and arrests of trade-union workers, as in Taganrog; confiscation of union funds, as in Armavir, Maikop, and Alexandrovsk; prohibition of the labor press (the Don territory), closing of labor newspapers, which may be seen everywhere; the forbidding of strikes.[43]

At the same time, relations between Denikin and the government of the Kuban continued to deteriorate. Early in July, Nicholas Riabovol, a leader of the Kuban separatists, was mysteriously assassinated. Shortly afterward the Kuban cossacks quit the South Russian Conference, and a special Rada delegation under Denikin's old antagonist, L. L. Bych, set off for Paris to plead the separatists' case abroad.[44]

[39] *Velikaia Rossiia*, No. 248, Jul. 5, 1919.

[40] Astrov to Denikin, Oct. 23-26, 1924, in the Panina Archive, pack. 5, suppl. 6, fold. 1.

[41] Central Committee Protocol, July 6, 1919 (O.S.).

[42] P. Dolgorukov, *Velikaia razrukha*, Madrid, 1964, p. 124.

[43] Resolution of a Rostov trade union conference, August 1919, as quoted in Chamberlin, II, 257.

[44] G. Pokrovskii, *Denikinshchina*, Berlin, 1923, pp. 146ff. Riabovol was assassinated

But rather than confront these problems, Denikin instead transferred the army's headquarters out of Ekaterinodar, to Taganrog on the Sea of Azov, while the Special Council and the Kadet Central Committee moved to Rostov, thus reducing even further any possibility of effective military and civilian coordination. Quiescence set in so pervasively, in fact, that Denikin himself complained to Dolgorukov that he could find few signs of constructive activity.[45]

There was little "constructive activity" because attention focused on military affairs. By the middle of July, the AFSR numbered almost 150,000 men. Tsaritsyn, Balashov, Kharkov, and Belgorod were all under White control. The advancing front, though precariously thin in places, extended from the Dnepr to the Volga; the capture of Odessa and Kiev seemed imminent.

Flushed with apparent success, Denikin issued his famous "Moscow Instruction," a spirited call for complete military victory. In three general groups, under Wrangel, Sidorin, and Mai-Maevskii, the army was to strike at once for Moscow. Converging lines were to lead from Denikin's left, center, and right flanks to the city of "forty times forty cathedrals," and the "resurrection" of "Russia, One and Indivisible."[46]

The Moscow Instruction was later sharply criticized on strategic grounds, for concentrating forces toward a symbolic rather than substantive victory, and for disregarding a last chance to link up with Kolchak's troops in Siberia. Denikin was also reproached for substituting a headlong race for "honor" and "glory" for a carefully planned offensive.[47] Yet its real weakness lay not in military terms, where the merit of different strategies can be debated, but in the way it obscured critical internal problems of the South Russian administration, whose solution was essential to any military victory. In leaving the cossack strongholds of the south, Denikin's troops were moving into the turbulent black earth plains of central Russia and the Ukraine, where hostile peasants viewed them as landlord-restorationists, workers considered them plutocrats, and the separatist-minded saw them crushing dreams for autonomy. The cauldronlike Ukraine seethed with clashing armies and partisan groups. Petliura's Ukrainians sought freedom from Russian domination, Red or White; Makhno's "Greens" sought anarchist independence; Ukrainian Bolsheviks

---

shortly after making a speech highly critical of the AFSR for behaving as if it represented all-Russian authority.

[45] Central Committee Protocol, July 6, 1919.

[46] A. I. Denikin, *Ocherki russkoi smuty*, 5 vols., Paris-Berlin, 1921-25, v, 108-09.

[47] Astrov to Denikin, Oct. 23-26, 1924; Baron P. N. Wrangel, *Always with Honour*, New York, 1957, p. 89; Chamberlin, II, 245.

fought for a "proletarian union" with Moscow. Even the Poles were reaching into Eastern Galicia, hoping to expand their frontiers at Ukrainian expense. Denikin and his generals could hardly manage the "loyalist" Don and Kuban. Marching north under nationalist banners, with little intention of accommodating peasant or separatist interests, and with morally bankrupt commanders who thought in terms of "enemy" towns and villages rather than Russian ones, they invited disaster.

Much blame for this must fall on Denikin's civilian advisers, particularly the Kadets. It is possible that demands for new policies might only have further discredited the party in the eyes of already hostile officers, and even provoked a move against Denikin; in the early fall of 1919, right-wing newspapers like *Velikaia Rossiia* were already accusing Kadets of "softness" on questions of authority, while army leaders like Wrangel viewed even the conservative Special Council with contempt.[48] But the liberals' past experience should have made the risk worth taking. Kadets knew better than almost any other political group that miliary strength required more than a bare modicum of popular support, that national authority could not simply be proclaimed.

But despite the protests of "conciliationists" and moderates like Michael Fedorov, Vladimir Obolenskii, and Paul Gronskii, who insisted in Special Council and National Center meetings that reforms were absolutely urgent, the army's advance was still beguiling. With Astrov abroad, and most liberals in Rostov and Ekaterinodar convinced that Russia's crisis was one of "spirit," the party as a whole fell under the domination of right-wing figures like Novgorodtsev, Dolgorukov, and Ariadna Tyrkova, who not only considered administrative reforms untimely, but actually inexpedient. Patriotic conviction was the key to victory; Kadets could do nothing to detract from enthusiasm over the army's success; reforms would cause confusion and dissent. When Dolgorukov received two long letters from Petrunkevich and Vinaver, accusing him and others at the June Ekaterinodar conference of "betraying the program and spirit" of Russian liberalism, which had "achieved so much" in 1917, he insisted in response that this was "no time and no place to speak or worry about the 'conquests of revolution.' "[49]

Svobodnaia Rech' expressed the same view, and so did *Velikaia Rossiia*. Russian society was interested in the "spirit" of victory and the "idea" of national reunification, not the details of this or that statute.

[48] E.g., *Priazovskii Krai*, No. 219, Sept. 27, 1919; Wrangel, p. 176.
[49] Dolgorukov, *Velikaia razrukha*, pp. 149-50; also, Astrov to Denikin, Oct. 23-25. 1924.

Even reports of the army's excesses were no longer especially trouble-some. Of course abuses should end; but wars produced suffering, and civil wars produced more suffering than most.[50] When Sokolov admitted his Department of Information was openly pursuing an anti-Semitic policy, despite the fact that some of the Whites' most heinous crimes were being committed against Jews, *Svobodnaia Rech'* actually sug-gested—shockingly—that, given traditional Russian prejudice, anti-Semitism might be a means of increasing peasant support, "a creative force" for "national reunification"![51] Similar feelings were expressed when this question was discussed in the Kadet Central Committee. Denikin's troops would soon be in Moscow. Russia's "salavation" lay in "patriotism," "military valor," and "self-sacrifice," not in political questions like the civil rights of Jews.[52]

By the early fall of 1919, however, precisely these questions were crucial to White success. The greater Denikin's lines were extended, the more it became obvious that popular support was razor thin. Villages cheering the army one day stole its supplies the next; mer-chants (particularly Jewish merchants) locked their shops and hid their stores; soldiers began to desert in growing numbers and were hidden in "liberated" towns; and by the middle of September, resist-ance *behind* Denikin's lines was almost as serious as Bolshevik opposi-tion at the front.

The advance toward Moscow also seemed to bring out the worst in AFSR administration. Even the reactionary Sokolov began to worry:

Reading carefully through the general information gathered by the propaganda section, and discussing the question with my co-workers and various social and political figures, I became convinced that in regions under the administration of the AFSR, things were not going well. The "good administration" which was to win the sym-pathies of the population for a national dictatorship was virtually nonexistent—in fact, there was practically no government whatso-ever. The "provinces" were cut off from the "center" entirely. The intelligentsia was distrustful, workers sullenly hostile, peasants suspicious. . . . Instead of a land policy, there were endless discus-sions. The central administration was working lazily, and clearly was not coming to grips with the monstrously huge tasks which were pressing life forward. There was no general political leader-ship.[53]

[50] E.g., *Velikaia Rossiia*, No. 286, Sept. 1, 1919.

[51] *Svobodnaia Rech'*, No. 217, Oct. 9, 1919.

[52] Central Committee Protocol, Oct. 5, Nov. 10, 1919. See also Central Committee Protocol, May 19, 1919; Astrov to Denikin, Oct. 23-26, 1924; and Pr. E. N. Trubet-skoi, "Iz putevykh zametok bezhentsa," *ARR*, xviii, 1926, pp. 178-79.

[53] K. N. Sokolov, *Pravlenie generala Denikina*, Sofia, 1921, pp. 162-63.

Thus even Kadets on the far right finally began to realize that social and political problems would have to be faced.

Meanwhile, Fedorov, Iurenev, and several other moderates continued their efforts to deal with social questions, although with little discernible progress. Attempting to draw up some comprehensive program of labor reforms, Fedorov held open hearings among Rostov workers—unsuccessfully, as it turned out, since the labor spokesmen insisted on attacking the AFSR, and then angrily walked out.[54] Iurenev participated in the Special Council's commission on agrarian affairs, hoping at a minimum to secure the immediate approval of the National Center's program, supported earlier by Denikin in his "Letter."[55] There were also new meetings with General Romanovskii, the most liberal military figure on Denikin's staff, exploring possible ways of correcting abuses in the field.[56]

Astrov's return in early September added impetus to these efforts. At his insistence, the Central Committee sent a special delegation to newly occupied regions for a better picture of affairs; and hoping to "prepare the ground" for Miliukov's return as well (as a means of increasing the party's influence), also invited comments and suggestions from local party committees.[57] These soon indicated that some Kadets still favored substantial reforms. The Odessa party group, for example, demanded the separation of all military and civilian administration, reporting incredible abuses by the Whites as they reoccupied the Black Sea littoral.[58] From Yalta Kadets called attention to the army's "rampant" anti-Semitism.[59] And in Kiev several party leaders indicated they would seek an alliance with moderate socialist parties for future city elections.[60]

Even more forceful views came from the local Kadet committee in Rostov itself. On October 8/21 this group submitted a memorandum to party leaders requesting that Kadets in the Special Council be held accountable to the Central Committee for the actions of White administrators. Zeeler, Paramonov, and their Don colleagues either wanted Sokolov and Stepanov out of the party, or forced to support new policies.[61] And to combat what they felt was the gross blindness of *Svobodnaia Rech'*, the Don committee began shortly afterward to

[54] Denikin, *Ocherki*, IV, 221.

[55] D. Kin, *Denikinshchina*, Leningrad, 1927, p. 89.

[56] N. I. Astrov, "Neskol'ko spravok o 'novom politicheskom kurse,'" MS in the Panina Archive, n.d., pack. 3, fold. 40.

[57] Central Committee Protocol, Sept. 1, 1919; Panina to Miliukov, Oct. 10, 1919, in Miliukov Archive, bx. 3141.

[58] Panina Archive, pack. 3, fold. 28.   [59] Panina Archive, pack. 3, fold. 31.

[60] *Velikaia Rossiia*, No. 298, Sept. 17, 1919.

[61] Panina Archive, pack. 3, fold. 30.

publish its own daily journal, *Donskaia Rech'*, with a distinctly left-wing bias. The new paper opposed the dominant liberal view that only military questions were important, arguing that a fundamental and possibly fatal error was being made as civilian and military leaders continued to insist on "society's subordination to authority." Authority could not survive independently of social interests, *Donskaia Rech'* now argued; liberal politicians more than anyone had to shed their views of "rulers and ruled."[62]

More important, the Don Kadets also began to speak out forcefully for the greater development of regional autonomy—a fundamental weakness of all Kadet-oriented administrations. Taking sharp issue with *Svobodnaia Rech'*, which continued arguing in favor of strict governmental centralization and opposed regional autonomy as "inevitably" turning into political separatism, *Donskaia Rech'* spoke out in favor of a zemstvo-type local administrative system, in which civilian and military functions would be strictly separated.[63] The Kadet paper also gave support to the idea of strengthening local autonomy through the Don, Kuban, and Terek cossack union, and what was even more heretical from the Kadet perspective, suggested (albeit in somewhat muted tones) that perhaps a *federal* system would, after all, be the most propitious state structure for Russia in the future.[64]

For a while it also seemed that left Kadets might again coordinate their efforts with the Union of Regeneration, which held its own major conference in Rostov at the end of September 1919. The dilemmas and outlooks of left-liberals and moderate socialists were still very much alike, despite the failure of all efforts to construct a coalition regime. The Union's leaders even recognized at their conference the "necessity" of supporting the AFSR, for all of their deep opposition to specific policies and practices, and still insisted on a unified struggle of all anti-Bolshevik social forces.[65] Provided the AFSR established some form of representative assembly in South Russia, a "High Council," made up of members from zemstvos and city dumas, the Union was even willing to postpone "final" solutions of problems like land reform until the convocation of a new constituent assembly.[66]

But despite these urgent voices, success in South Russia was still being measured exclusively in terms of the army's advance as late as

[62] E.g., *Donskaia Rech'*, No. 24, Dec. 11, 1919; No. 28, Dec. 15, 1919.

[63] The polemic is discussed in some detail by Peter Ryss in *Posledniia Novosti*, No. 429, Sept. 9, 1921.

[64] *Donskaia Rech'*, No. 27, Dec. 14, 1919.

[65] *Priazovskii Krai*, No. 220, Sept. 28, 1919; *Svobodnaia Rech'*, No. 210, Sept. 29, 1919.

[66] *Ibid.*

September and October 1919. The military dynamic was simply too great to overcome. "The whole question here," the English reporter Harold Williams wrote in September, "is 'shall we be in Moscow before winter?' It is as if the Volunteer Army, having stormed a steep hill and almost reached the summit, was preparing simply to drive the enemy down the other side."[67] Within the Kadet Central Committee, meanwhile, conservatives remained dominant. Demands for holding Sokolov and Stepanov accountable to the Committee were rejected. Astrov himself was quite gloomy, but his mood was not widely shared.[68] Even a new effort on his part to reactivate further local party organs was blunted by a Committee directive that all groups stay strictly nonpolitical:

> In view of increasing administrative disorder and civil chaos, all forces must be directed so that persons will be designated for city and zemstvo organizations who do not view organs of self-government as local parliaments for political struggle, or as a means for accommodation with socialists, but as businesslike organizations capable of satisfying the pressing needs of the population and reestablishing the cultural economic life of the country.[69]

Thus a "businesslike" and "nonpartisan" approach—long the party's rhetoric for the defense of privilege—still precluded any "accommodation" with even moderate socialists.

Similar attitudes emerged against the movement for specific reforms. Through constant pressure, the National Center managed to effect several changes in the composition of the Special Council, but major questions like agrarian reform remained deadlocked.[70] For most of the summer, a special commission under V. G. Kolokoltsev worked on a comprehensive land program. Astrov had initially belonged to the group, but he was abroad during most of its deliberations, and most of its other members were distinctly more conservative.[71] When the commission finally reported to Denikin, it accepted the basic right of peasant "property" in land, but felt that for "political reasons," land redistribution should be postponed for a period of at least three years.[72] This so annoyed Denikin that he dissolved the group alto-

[67] Cable from Harold Williams to the London *Times*, Sept. 22, 1919, in the Tyrkova Archive, sect. 3, cart. 7, gp. 1.
[68] Astrov, "Neskol'ko spravok," p. 4.   [69] Panina Archive, pack. 3, fold. 33.
[70] Sokolov, pp. 176-77.
[71] The commission included A. N. Naumov and A. V. Krivoshein (the minister of agriculture from 1908 to 1915), both members of the conservative Council for Russian State Unification (Sovet Gosudarstvennoe Ob'edineniia Rossii), and S. V. Bezobrazov, the conservative secretary of the Special Council.
[72] Kin, pp. 96-98; Denikin, *Ocherki*, IV, 221-22.

gether. It also alienated both left liberals and conservatives, the former because of the time lapse in land redistribution, the latter because the proposal did include a plan for eventual forced expropriation. Early in the fall, a new commission under V. N. Chelishchev began working on the problem again, but few really expected the question could now be resolved.[73]

Nor was "resolution" what most Kadets wanted. In the Central Committee, lip service was paid to certain general propositions: property in land should be preserved; landless peasants should be transformed into owners of small scale holdings; and land holdings above specific regional norms should be forcibly expropriated, provided, of course, due compensation was paid. This, in effect, was the party's standard position on the agrarian question, unaltered by two years of revolution and civil war. But the Central Committee also clung to the weary old notion of postponing reforms until the convocation of a constituent assembly, precisely what Astrov and the left Kadets opposed.[74]

Similarly, most Kadets in South Russia, like their colleagues in Omsk, also opposed creating any sort of representative body in the region, or relieving the Special Council of any of its basic tasks. Such a body was not only urged by the Union of Regeneration and zemstvo groups, but was a special concern of Don and Kuban loyalists, fighting with Denikin. It was also supported by the Don Kadet committee, and particularly its most prominent cossack member, V. A. Kharlamov.[75] But the Special Council and the Kadet Central Committee both rejected the proposals as "separatist." The commander-in-chief himself was willing to allow a "consultative organ," something Nicholas Astrov had also been supporting since the spring, but the majority of the Council and most Kadets felt even this was too great a concession— an "unwarranted weakening of military dictatorship."[76]

THE KHARKOV CONFERENCE

Against this background, Kadets gathered in Kharkov in early November 1919 their last sorry conference on Russian soil, "sorry," because it revealed the complete dominance of right-wing elements

---

[73] Kin, pp. 98-110; Sokolov, pp. 186-89; Denikin, *Ocherki*, IV, 221-24.

[74] E.g., Central Committee Protocol, Oct. 20, 1919.

[75] Kin, pp. 239-40; V. Miakotin, "Iz nedalekago proshlago," *NCS*, No. 11, 1925, p. 219.

[76] Astrov to Denikin, Apr. 5, 1919, in the Panina Archive, pack. 3, fold. 40; Denikin, *Ocherki*, IV, 205; Central Committee Protocol, Oct. 5, 1919; Sokolov, pp. 200-208, esp. p. 200.

within the Constitutional Democratic movement at a moment when even the most progressive policies would have come too late to save the liberal cause. Led by Paul Dolgorukov, Vasili Stepanov, and Ariadna Tyrkova—three leaders of conservative liberalism since the very first days of the party's formation—the Kadets focused on the tasks of extending military dictatorship, and reconstructing Russia *after* the Bolsheviks were defeated. Tyrkova told her colleagues:

> Our needs are practical, commonplace, and apparent. We must support the army first, and place democratic programs in the background. We must create a ruling class, and not a dictatorship of the majority. The universal hegemony of Western democracy is a fraud, which politicians have foisted upon us. *We must have the courage to look directly into the eye of the wild beast—which is called the people.*[77]

Thus, in the last months of the civil war in Kharkov, Tyrkova herself had finally found the courage to say publicly what many conservative Kadets had believed deeply since 1905; and in so doing, she epitomized for many liberals Russia's whole revolutionary experience. Given the country's grave political, social, and economic backwardness, Tyrkova and her ultraright-wing colleagues believed it had been their task to make a revolution *for* their countrymen, to become a "ruling class," not to be swept up in uncontrollable popular currents of social change. Now she and others were absolutely certain it was too late for anything but a final effort to reestablish order; and that, too, was probably impossible.

What this meant in practical terms was soon apparent. Resolutions demanded universal support for military dictatorship untrammeled by any restrictions ("the basic guarantee that *gosudarstvennye* principles will triumph over anarchistic, mutinous, and separatist ones . . .") and the end of all "illegality and disorder in the countryside."[78] Even the Jews themselves were indirectly blamed for prevailing anti-Semitism: pogroms were "intolerable," but not without explanation in the conditions of the time; and "leading Jewish circles" should themselves take steps to fight those "elements of Jewry" which were actively participating in the Bolshevik movement.[79]

There was also no doubt that despite their rather pathetic optimism, which envisioned the party meeting next in Moscow, the Kadets at Kharkov saw a long period of dictatorship ahead. As Dolgorukov told the delegates:

[77] Protocols of the Kadet Conference in Kharkov, November 3-6, 1919, Panina Archive, pack. 3, fold. 34. My italics.
[78] Panina Archive, pack. 3, fold. 34.   [79] *Ibid.*

The Conference must affirm the necessity of a preliminary period of dictatorship by the same authorities on whom have fallen the historical tasks of national reunification, once the Bolsheviks are beaten. These authorities must restore the apparatus of government which the Bolsheviks have destroyed, overcome mutinous anarchistic elements, and re-create the elementary conditions of society and social peace until the convocation of an *All-Russian Representative Assembly.*[80]

With only a single dissenting voice, the delegates agreed.

Thus the Kadets at Kharkov pledged themselves wholeheartedly to a system which, at the beginning of November 1919, was weeks away from collapse. And while *Priazovskii Krai, Svobodnaia Rech'*, and *Velikaia Rossiia* all applauded the Kadets for their "statesmanlike" refusal to criticize the anti-Bolshevik military, a more accurate appraisal would have seen the party's right-wing leaders blind to Russia's social and political realities.

This, in fact, was the response of those few remaining liberal moderates and leftists, now grouped around Astrov, Fedorov, Iurenev, and the Don Regional Committee. *Donskaia Rech'* had nothing but disdain for most of the Kharkov resolutions, particularly the one concerning the Jews.[81] Most of these figures had stayed away from the conference, rightly believing their voices would be futile, and preferring instead to continue with their various official duties. Now they were sure the sessions marked the bitter end of their long struggle to balance different viewpoints within one broad liberal structure, and make the party an active force for preserving liberal democratic traditions.[82] Eighteen months remained before the party as a whole would formally break apart. But Astrov and the others were now convinced the process was irreversible.

ASTROV'S "NEW COURSE" AND THE END OF THE PARTY'S EFFORTS IN THE SOUTH

The Kadets at Kharkov did not know it, but winter would bring the same nightmare to anti-Bolsheviks in the south as fall had brought to Siberia. As late as the end of September 1919, optimism in Rostov was still virtually unrestrained. Word had it that General Iudenich and his Northwestern Army were only miles from Petrograd, and moving forward with British help; in Siberia, Kolchak was "advancing after

[80] *Ibid.*   [81] Williams cable, Dec. 6, 1919.

[82] *Ibid.* Also, Central Committee Protocol, Dec. 1, 1919; and Astrov's Letter to Denikin, Oct. 23-26, 1924.

setbacks," even causing some to worry whether he or Denikin would be first in Moscow.[83] On September 23, a new journal made its appearance in Rostov, triumphantly titled *To Moscow!* (*K Moskvu!*).[84] Most felt victory was simply a matter of time. Few conceived of how suddenly and completely Denikin's forces would collapse.

The turning point came early in October. With Iudenich closing in on Petrograd (but the Siberian front now almost entirely under Lenin's control—the Bolsheviks at this time were just about to take Omsk), the Red command threw a new shock detachment against Denikin's troops near Orel, the farthest major town on their northern advance. On October 7/20, the Whites were forced to retreat. Voronezh was evacuated four days later, and Chernigov on October 23/November 5, just three weeks after the Whites' triumphant entry. Simultaneously, Trotsky himself rallied Red troops outside Petrograd, turning back Iudenich. The retreat that followed on both fronts was remarkably rapid. When Kursk fell on November 4/17, a visible collapse occurred in White morale. Thereafter, while Iudenich's troops were routed, Denikin's forces also retreated hastily, the Reds advancing without serious resistance.[85]

These developments deprived the resolutions of the Kadet conference at Kharkov of any practical significance, but also prompted party moderates to press more insistently for immediate reforms. Perhaps the most scathing indictment of the whole South Russian effort came, in fact, in the second week of November 1919, when Nicholas Astrov presented a comprehensive report to Denikin and the Special Council on his "tour" of White-occupied areas.[86]

The product of many weeks' thought and investigation, the report argued in the first instance that Denikin's regime was hopelessly alien to vast sectors of the Russian population. Astrov saw seven main areas of abuse: (1) excesses by military authorities themselves, including requisitions without compensation, and open pillage of occupied areas; (2) punitive expeditions by the army in response to partisan attacks, involving the shooting of innocent civilians; (3) the extreme tardiness with which civil administrators assumed their posts; (4) the use of known criminals in counterintelligence activities; (5) arbitrary solutions to administrative problems; (6) assistance by the army to

---

[83] *Priazovskii Krai*, No. 222, Oct. 1, 1919. Iudenich led a group of some 20,000 White troops from the Baltic region, and was encouraged and advised (but not militarily assisted in any degree) by the British. See the discussion in V. Gorn, *Grazhdanskaia voina v severozapadnoi Rossii*, Berlin, 1923.

[84] *V Moskvu!*, No. 1, Sept. 23, 1919. This was a rabidly anti-Semitic sheet, which contained in its first edition an article describing the "satanic role" played by Jews in fomenting the revolution.

[85] Denikin, *Ocherki*, v, 230-38.   [86] Astrov, "Neskol'ko spravok."

landlords seeking to regain possession of their former holdings; (7) pogroms against the Jews. In effect, these abuses created conditions which made White authority absolutely untenable:

> The unrestrained pillage of the rural population by military detachments, the debauchery of the troops in the countryside, the propensity of representatives of authority to take bribes, the uncontrolled speculation, venality, brigandage, the overt criminality of counterintelligence agents in areas occupied by Bolsheviks—all this compels the population on whom our army is supposed to be based to say: No! This is not a government which is capable of saving the country or resurrecting Russia, for the same conditions existed under the Hetman's regime in the Ukraine, and all other governments which have already been deposed. A genuine government will conduct itself with firmness, but not by means of force.[87]

All this led Astrov to conclude that Denikin had to take urgent measures to reduce popular hostility, and create a firm, authoritative administrative order in which the masses of Russian people might find some true representation of their interests. Yet the Moscow Kadet could not help fearing that his report tolled the death knell of anti-Bolshevism in the south. "We must immediately change our course" he concluded "if it is not already too late."[88]

But how? Astrov's right-wing party colleagues were scandalized by his views, considering them completely harmful and unpatriotic. For them it was still "dangerous and harmful" to think of reform. The army's failure was largely the result of anti-White agitation directed by Germans, Bolsheviks, separatists, and "other enemies of the Russian state." Reform would add to the confusion, further weakening the White's resolve.[89] But the real fault of Astrov's report was not in its call for reform, but in its lack of specific proposals. When the moderate Kadet leader met with Denikin several days later, having been told by the Special Council to develop a concrete plan of action, his best advice was that the army "take decisive measures to define a moderate position . . . articulate aims and tasks clearly, and insist all branches of government—central and regional, military, and civilian—precisely fulfill the tasks assigned to them."[90] But this was hardly helpful. At best, it seemed to aim for a few new men in old positions. Yet not only were very few competent men to be found; Astrov himself was concerned that in the process of shifting personnel, those like

---

[87] *Ibid.* [88] *Ibid.*

[89] Statement by Novgorodtsev, included with Astrov's "Neskol'ko spravok" in the Panina Archive, pack. 3, fold. 40.

[90] Astrov, "Neskol'ko spravok"; see also Denikin, *Ocherki*, v, 277-78.

General Wrangel, who by now were anxious to see Denikin himself replaced, would only consolidate their own personal power.[91] (Astrov even objected to replacing the notorious General Mai-Maevskii on these grounds, despite shocking abuses he had committed as governor-general of Kharkov.)[92]

Meanwhile, Denikin's armies continued to retreat, and Kadets and other civilians in the Don and Kuban regions grew more anxious. Local newspapers like *Svobodnaia Rech'* and *Vechernee Vremia* became increasingly anti-Semitic, a sure sign of tension; and just as in Petrograd during August and September 1917, long columns of available housing began to appear. Suddenly the news from the east was also quite bad; and in the beginning of December, word arrived as well of Trotsky's victory over General Iudenich.[93]

There was also depressing information that the National Center in Moscow had collapsed. For months there had been almost no information from the capital, but Kadets had expected the army to advance rapidly, and fears were suppressed. Now it was learned that all of the Center's leading members, including several Kadet Central Committee colleagues and two of Astrov's brothers, had been captured. Even the liberals' opponents in the south were dismayed, while the party leadership as a whole felt a sudden and profound shock of grief.[94]

Finally, there were also new problems in Ekaterinodar—or rather old problems, long since simmering on the coals of regional self-determination. In November 1919 the Kuban Rada reconvened, shortly after the local press reported its delegation in Paris had signed an independent peace treaty with several "states" of the Northern Caucasus. At the Rada's first meeting, one of the delegation's members, Kalabukhov, made a long report on its work, simultaneously attacking Denikin and the Volunteers for breaching Kuban sovereignty. The following morning, General Wrangel, who was in Ekaterinodar with a detachment of White troops, ordered Kalabukhov's arrest. He and General Pokrovskii then dispersed the Rada with force, while at the same time disarming the Kuban's own Taman division. Kalabukhov, Makarenko, and other leading separatists were arrested. The following morning, Kalabukhov was tried and hanged.[95]

The consequences of this action are easy to imagine. Overnight, the very heart of anti-Bolshevik South Russia lay seething in new discontent. Having never recognized the legitimacy of separatist aspirations

91 Williams cable, Dec. 20, 1919.   92 *Ibid.*
93 *Donskaia Rech'*, No. 23, Dec. 10, 1919.
94 N. Astrov, "Moskovskaia katastrofa i smert'moikh brat'ev," MS in the Panina Archive, n.d., pack. 5, fold. 7.
95 Denikin, *Ocherki*, v, 206-16. Wrangel, pp. 100-107.

in his drive for "Russia, One and Indivisible," Denikin suddenly found the hostilities of the independent-minded Kuban welling up at a moment he could least afford them. At the front, Kuban troops began deserting in large numbers.[96]

Back in Rostov, meanwhile, Denikin issued a public declaration calling for the precise fulfillment of administrative responsibilities, and restating the army's basic goals.[97] But Astrov himself admitted this mild measure would make no impression, and that something more drastic would have to be done. On December 15/28, the Kadet called a group of Special Council members to his own apartment. Discussing the army's situation, the group concluded that the Special Council itself would have to be replaced. Astrov then secured the consent of General Lukomskii, and thus armed, wired Denikin, urging that this step be taken.[98] The following morning Denikin himself consented, and terminated the Council's activities. The "New Course" had borne its single positive reform. Denikin made plans to consolidate his administrative apparatus, and appoint new directors to govern its programs.[99]

The prorogation of the Special Council effectively ended the role of Kadets in the south. Astrov hoped Denikin would replace the Council with a liberal regime, headed by Romanovskii and including himself.[100] But this the White commander could not bring himself to do. His lieutenants hated the moderate politicians and Denikin himself felt their appointment would bring wholesale disaffection.[101] The only alternative seemed to be the reappointment of a few respected former Council members. Thus the new administration, with seven "ministers," rather than the Special Council's eighteen, turned out to be little more than a consolidation and reshuffling of the old. Moreover, when the new administration was forced to evacuate Rostov in the face of the Bolshevik drive, a number of Kuban leaders objected to its returning to Ekaterinodar. The new government was consequently forced to spread out, Denikin and his closest aids going to the Kuban capital, most of the administration itself moving to Novorossiisk and the Crimea.[102]

And for all the concern surrounding its creation, the new "government" lasted only a matter of weeks. In January, the cossacks finally took matters into their own hands, and created a new South Russian Government in Ekaterinodar with V. F. Zeeler, the moderate Kadet

96 Williams cable, Dec. 27, 1919.   97 Denikin, *Ocherki*, v, 280-81.
98 Astrov, "Neskol'ko spravok."   99 Denikin, *Ocherki*, v, 284-85.
100 Astrov to Denikin, Oct. 23-26, 1924.   101 Denikin, *Ocherki*, v, 278.
102 Williams cable, Dec. 27, 1919.

from Rostov, as minister of internal affairs. The new regime was openly leftist and, while supporting the concept of Russian indivisibility, promised a representative assembly to the inhabitants of the Don, Kuban and Terek regions, security for workers, land to the peasants, a new Constituent Assembly, and cossack autonomy.[103] Forced out of Rostov by the advancing Bolsheviks, Denikin entered a series of discussions with the new administration, and finally made his peace. Retaining only command of the army, he yielded all political authority, and in a last desperate effort to hold the Red advance, became simply a soldier again.[104]

The course of events thus outstripped the Kadets, moderates, leftists, and conservatives alike. Faced with the Bolshevik onslaught, the Central Committee held its last short session on December 15/28, after which its members left Rostov. Regrouping briefly in Novorossiisk, the Kadet leaders held only a handful of "unofficial" private meetings in January and February 1920, concerned entirely with the tasks of evacuation.[105] "We tried to work conscientiously in the atmosphere of impending disaster," Sokolov wrote later, but "life had flown from political associations."[106] When Denikin finally realized he no longer enjoyed the confidence even of his own field commanders, he transferred his command to General Wrangel, and left for Constantinople. Only a handful of Kadets were left behind, and the Kadet party as a whole in Russia—Astrov's "living fabric" for the unification of all anti-Bolshevik movements—was totally destroyed. Its only future was abroad.

[103] N. M. Melnikov, "Grazhdanskaia voina na iuge Rossii," MS in the Columbia Russian Archive, n.d., pp. 155-57.

[104] *Ibid.*, pp. 158-61.

[105] N. Astrov, "Grazhdanskaia voina (vospominaniia)" MS in the Panina Archive, n.d., pack. 3, suppl. 3, p. 102.

[106] Sokolov, pp. 254-55.

PART FOUR

EPILOGUE: THE EMIGRATION

CHAPTER FIFTEEN

Kadets in Emigration, 1920-1921

Ironically, Kadets played out their role in Russian history in the same circumstances in which their chief competitors for the mantle of tsarist authority, the Social Democrats, began their successful climb to power: in small, isolated émigré committees, with few contacts in Russia and almost no public support. But while Lenin, Plekhanov, and the early Bolsheviks sustained themselves with an optimistic determinism, Kadets faced only the despairing realization that history was passing them by. They were becoming "superfluous men," as Anton Kartashev, one of their former provisional government ministers, hesitatingly admitted;[1] and the pain of emigration was hardly eased by the gnawing realization that they themselves bore a share of responsibility for the Whites' political collapse. The ironic satisfaction of even a left-wing Kadet like Peter Ryss, who exulted to a party gathering in November 1920 that "at last there is no dictator upon whom the Kadets might sacrifice their principles," was laden with remorse.[2]

From the spring of 1920, when most Kadet leaders straggled out of Russia with General Denikin, until July of the following year, when the party finally split apart, Kadets struggled to maintain themselves in the vanguard of a still-flickering anti-Bolshevik movement. They established committees in various émigré centers, met together on a regular basis, communicated with other groups, and even reactivated their Central Committee. In Paris they worked both with émigré SRs and former State Duma leaders, trying first to re-create the Constituent Assembly abroad, and then subordinating themselves to the much more conservative Russian National Committee. In Constantinople they worked closely with General Wrangel, and the battered remnants of the Volunteer Army. But with Lenin secure in Moscow, and Russians staggered with fatigue after six solid years of war; with European governments deeply involved in the problems of their own reconstruction, and finally ready to consider the possibility of coexistence with the Bolsheviks; and with Kadets themselves still badly divided, their task was hopeless. The activities of emigration had no effect on Russia's political future.

[1] Protocol of the Kadet group in Paris, Nov. 18, 1920, in the Archive of the Constitutional Democratic Party (henceforth KD Archive).
[2] *Ibid.*

Yet, the Kadets' final quest for still another "new tactic" reveals much about their movement. It serves as a fitting epilogue to their struggle with revolution and civil war.

KADETS REGROUP IN PARIS. THEIR
RELATION TO GENERAL WRANGEL

Emigration had an interesting effect on Russia's leading partisans of state authority. For some, distance reinforced past hostilities. Despite the dramatic change in their physical surroundings, they took up old battles, and fought with new intensity. For others, from conciliationist moderates to rigid conservatives, distance bred a new perspective: the cultured European capitals brought an ability to reflect on the limitations and errors of their own past policies, and a willingness to strike out in new directions.

The first sign of change came almost from the moment the exodus began, shortly after the Bolsheviks took power. Émigré efforts centered in Paris in these first hesitant months of the civil war, where Vasili Maklakov, acting on his authority as the Provisional Government's last official representative to France, struggled to organize the so-called Russian Political Conference. This was an ad hoc group of former Russian diplomats and political figures, who Maklakov hoped might represent Russia at the Paris peace talks while also coordinating the anti-Bolshevik movement as a whole.[3]

Maklakov, of course, was one of the Kadet party's most prominent conservatives. Few who met or heard him in the spring of 1917 would forget his anger over the unraveling of state authority, or his own intense conviction, expressed dramatically to the old State Duma conference at the time of the first coalition, that Russia was proving "unworthy of the liberty she has achieved."[4] It was Maklakov's open support for General Kornilov, in fact, in the summer of 1917, that initially brought him to Paris. The French capital was a convenient diplomatic exile in which his considerable brilliance as an orator and parliamentarian could still be used to Russia's advantage.

Once in Paris, however, Maklakov's vision began to broaden. Despite his own deep conservatism, he began to recognize the desirability of presenting a united front to the Allies, and of trying to coordinate all political groups, from socialists to monarchists, in the task of preserving Russian state integrity. He consequently welcomed to the Russian

---

[3] For a detailed description, see John Thompson, *Russia, Bolshevism and the Versailles Peace*, Princeton, 1966, pp. 66-78.

[4] *Rech'*, May 5, 1917.

Political Conference not only well-known former tsarist officials, like S. D. Sazonov, a respected conservative who had served as foreign minister from 1910 until 1916 (and who was soon designated Denikin's foreign minister as well); but also prominent former leftists like the colorful ex-terrorist Boris Savinkov, Kerensky's old lieutenant, and Nicholas Chaikovskii, leader of the Popular Socialist party. He also acted both on his own initiative and as a spokesman for the Political Conference to press social and political reforms on his Kadet party colleagues in Omsk; and he urged a reconciliation of local political differences to Denikin and Kadets in the south.[5] From abroad, it was quite apparent what the effect these differences were having on the anti-Bolshevik movement as a whole.

Maklakov's efforts were undermined, however, by both the ambivalence and the inconsistency of Allied statesmen, some of whom seemed to change their position on the Russian problem almost monthly in the course of 1919 and 1920, and by the activity of less "statesmanlike" Russian émigré groups, particularly the SRs. In the aftermath of the war, as is well known, the Allies found themselves in a web of contradictions. Anxious to extend their own national interests yet timorous about military intervention, they could never really commit themselves to full-scale assistance for the Whites. At the same time, while supplying Denikin and Kolchak with advisers and matériel, they were also attracted by the possibility of peaceful and perhaps profitable relations with Lenin and his comrades, though still fearing the effect of Bolshevism on the development of European radicalism and desperately anxious to contain it.

The émigré SRs, meanwhile, were enormously troublesome to the anti-Bolshevik cause. Just as Kadets had spent so much time in 1917 castigating them for abetting the spread of radicalism, the SRs now spent most of their energies accusing liberals of sabotaging "their" revolution. Writing first in a Paris publication, *Pour La Russie*, and later in the Prague journal, *Volia Rossii*, they struck with full force against the "reactionary Kadet dictatorships" in Siberia and South Russia, insisting the Whites were "hostile to democracy and the interests of the Russian people."[6] More important, they also deplored Allied military assistance to the Whites, which made the task of Maklakov, Sazonov, and the Russian Political Conference extremely difficult. They took as their motto "Neither Kolchak nor Lenin," a slogan they ap-

[5] E.g., Letter to the National Center in Ekaterinodar, June 1919, in the Wrangel Military Archives, file 135; wire to Omsk government, Nov. 1918, in the Maklakov Personal Archive, ser. B, pack. 1, file 2.

[6] *Pour la Russie*, No. 1, Oct. 29, 1919; *Volia Rossii*, No. 1, Sept. 12, 1920.

plied with equal fervor against both Denikin and his successor, General Wrangel.[7] On one occasion, as John Thompson has pointed out in his recent study, they went so far as to address a special letter to the American representative, Colonel House, specifically opposing Allied recognition for Kolchak. Instead, they asked the Allies to set out a broad program of democratic principles, and then support any group which pledged its acceptance.[8]

In countering these attacks, Maklakov got little help from the arrival in Paris in early 1919 of Paul Miliukov, whose reputed "German orientation" caused such a furor that he soon moved on to London; or from Ariadna Tyrkova's Russian Liberation Committee, whose early propaganda in favor of the White dictatorships in 1919 was so antagonistic to the revolution that it seemed to substantiate the SRs' charges. For most of 1919, moreover, even after Tyrkova herself returned to Russia in July, the Kadets in London spent as much time attacking the SRs as they did defending Kolchak and Denikin, which hardly encouraged the Allies to deepen their involvement in Russian affairs.

Gradually, however, these Kadets also began to undergo a change in outlook. The émigré climate was a tempering one, and the futility of continued political rivalries became increasingly apparent as the likelihood of White success began to diminish. There were also a growing number of critical reports from Ekaterinodar and Omsk, indicating the unpopularity of White policies and the increasing hostility of local populations. Some of the most informative and critical commentary, in fact, came from Tyrkova's own husband, Harold Williams, who wrote from Ekaterinodar and Rostov for the London *Times* and *Daily Chronicle*.

Williams' reports were soon supplemented by the arrival in Paris and London of refugees from the "model laboratory experiment" in the Crimea, and from Nicholas Astrov, who visited the French capital in the summer of 1919 before returning to work out his "new course" with General Denikin. By the end of 1919, as the magnitude of the South Russian and Siberian catastrophes became apparent (and as the Allies' own disinterest became clear), even Miliukov began to realize that White policies would have to be closely reexamined.[9] Early in 1920, when the London Kadets began publishing a new weekly journal, *The New Russia*, its pages were opened to a "frank investigation" of the causes of White mistakes, and to "exponents of

[7] *Pour la Russie*, No. 8, Dec. 20, 1919; No. 30, May 22, 1920.
[8] Thompson, pp. 291-92.
[9] Miliukov to Petrunkevich, March 16, 1921, in the Panina Archive, pack. 8.

opinions other than our own." In "free polemics," "newly arising questions" were to be "more fully illuminated. . . ."[10]

Thus began one of the most searching self-evaluations in Kadet history. And unlike earlier analyses, when party leaders focused on such questions as the nature of Russia's cultural development and the historical meaning of the revolutionary intelligentsia, the Kadets concentrated now on reexamining past policies, and attempting to determine what had been wrong in their own political orientation. The discussions began in the spring of 1920, when the most pressing "newly arising question" was the transfer of White authority in South Russia from Denikin to General Wrangel. They ended sixteen months later when the party formally split in two, and for all practical purposes was dissolved.

General Baron Peter Wrangel was an imposing military figure, haughty, self-confident, brutal, insufferably vain, and undoubtedly fearless. (Once, with little ado, he ordered some 370 suspected Bolsheviks to be shot on the spot, a feat he later boasted about in his memoirs.)[11] But Wrangel was also openly hostile to the Kadets. He attributed most of the Whites' political failures to their "malicious" influence; and he considered them generally "incapable of any creative work."[12] And as he now established a new White beachhead in the Crimea, having evacuated the remnants of Denikin's army from the Kuban, he gathered around him a coterie of right-wing nationalists including V. S. Nalbandov, the former minister of trade under the German puppet Sulkevich; Count Apraksin, an old-time tsarist governor in the region; and G. V. Glinka, an arch-conservative former senator. Kadets thus had to decide exactly what their posture was to be toward this last-ditch anti-Bolshevik effort.

A number of party leaders remained deeply committed to continuing support, whatever Wrangel's policies or attitudes. To Vasili Stepanov, a diligent state servant under Lvov and Denikin, and a Kadet for whom the slogan "Russia, One and Indivisible!" was now an article of unshakable faith, Kadets had no alternative but to back Wrangel as fully as they could. The remaining White troops in the Crimea were Russia's last best hope.[13] Konstantin Sokolov, the "songbird" of military dictatorship, also felt this way; and so did Paul Dolgorukov, Paul Novgorodtsev, and a number of other leading Kadets in Berlin and Con-

[10] *The New Russia*, No. 1, Feb. 5, 1920, p. 3.
[11] Baron P. N. Wrangel, *Always with Honour*, New York, 1957, p. 59.
[12] *Ibid.*, pp. 171-72.
[13] Protocol, Paris Kadet Committee, May 17, 1920, in the KD Archive.

stantinople, who seemed psychologically incapable of accepting the notion that past liberal politics had failed.[14]

But for many other party leaders, particularly those grouped around Miliukov and Vinaver in Paris and London, the spring of 1920 finally brought the realization that right-wing dictatorships could not succeed. For some, like Michael Fedorov, the question was academic. Wrangel could not take Moscow without British and French assistance; and far from being willing to offer new vigorous aide to the Whites, the Allies were interested in a negotiated settlement. Since Wrangel's own intransigence made peace negotiations a remote possibility, even under Allied auspices, the future belonged to Lenin.[15]

For others, however, like Sergei Shtern, for fourteen years the Kadet committee chairman in Odessa, Paul Gronskii, who had served on Denikin's Special Council, and Alexander Konovalov and Ivan Demidov, who had helped solidify the party's conciliationist faction in late 1917, the question now turned on the basic issue of anti-Bolshevik policies. Gronskii put the matter succinctly: "I for one am decided," he told a Paris Kadet gathering in April 1920; "I cannot serve Wrangel. He is an enemy of the nation, following the path of the Black Hundreds. He is a man of the past. Not a single Kadet ought to work directly or indirectly in his support!"[16] What was necessary was a fundamentally new approach. Kadets had finally to recognize that state authority was intimately related to the question of popular support. And popular support meant Kadets had to abandon their own past conservatism on critical issues like land reform, regional autonomy, and the postponement of "constitutional" questions until the Constituent Assembly. They had instead to strike out finally as a voice *of* as well as for the Russian people. Only if Wrangel himself adopted this viewpoint was there a chance he might succeed.[17]

Thus the question of direct or indirect Kadet support for Wrangel in Paris was tied by Gronskii to the whole manner in which Kadets had approached the revolution and civil war, an issue which now became the focus of intensive party discussions. Gathering in Paris in late April and May 1920, Astrov, Vinaver, Adzhemov, Miliukov, Konovalov, Pasmanik, Demidov, Nolde, Panina, Stepanov, Fedorov, and several others—all party figures of the highest rank—explored the

14 *Ibid.*, Protocol, Constantinople Kadet Committee, Nov. 20, 1920, Feb. 11, 1921, in the KD Archive.

15 Protocol, Paris Kadet Group, May 6 and 7, 1920, Paris Kadet Committee, May 17 and 20, 1920; P. Miliukov, "Dnevnik," unpubl. MS in the Columbia Russian Archives, pp. 692-94.

16 Miliukov, "Dnevnik," p. 709.

17 Protocol, Paris Kadet Group, May 6 and 7, 1920; Paris Kadet Committee, May 17 and 20, 1920.

alternative political opportunities to a new dictatorship. At first they considered joining a Russian "government-in-exile," which the Provisional Government's first minister-president, George Lvov, was attempting to organize in conjunction with Maklakov's Russian Political Conference, largely as a barrier to an Allied-Bolshevik détente. But it soon became clear that the Allies would reject such a group unless it included a broad cross section of political opinion; and Gronskii and Peter Ryss, having both met with SR leaders in Paris, could report a "100 percent probability" that the socialists would not participate.[18] The Kadets then considered restricting themselves to cultural and social activities, such as émigré relief and education. Zemstvo and city unions were regrouping abroad, and there was much work to be done through the émigré Russian Red Cross. But this seemed tangential, far too removed from what many still assumed was their political obligation to the motherland. Finally, they determined the best course was to move in a bold new fashion on their own, sketching their own basic commitments, and more important, laying out in clear detail the "grave mistakes" which they considered primarily responsible for their own lack of past success and the failure of the anti-Bolsheviks as a whole.[19]

To begin with, they declared themselves firmly against any type of accommodation with Lenin:

> No reconciliation whatsoever is possible with the Bolshevik regime, which is destroying the Russian state, its economic life, and its culture. The struggle against Bolshevism must be continued by force of arms, and by all other means available.[20]

Thus General Wrangel would get the party's "support," for whatever it was worth, though by grouping his army with "all other Russian military organizations," the Paris Kadets made it clear they did not regard him as the "sole bearer of state authority."

Then, more significantly in terms of the party's own internal evolution, the Paris Kadets set out their specific list of "grave mistakes":

a) The refusal of certain classes to reconcile themselves to the passing of land to the peasants;

b) The disregard displayed by authorities toward local interests in dealing with local forces, and the return to former methods of administration;

c) Hindering the reconstruction of Russian economic life . . . ;

[18] Miliukov, "Dnevnik," pp. 690-92.
[19] *Ibid.*, Protocols of the Paris Kadet Committee and Group, May 6, 7, 17, and 20, 1920.
[20] Protocol, Paris Kadet Group, May 20, 1920.

    d) The refusal to meet the legitimate demands of autonomy, free-
       dom, and national self-determination;

    e) . . . The distintegration of discipline within the army, leading
       to acts of violence and anti-Jewish pogroms. . . .[21]

Here, for all to see, was an open censure of many of their own past
attitudes, particularly on land reform, national self-determination,
and anti-Semitism—all of which had been endorsed by party leaders
at the Kharkov Kadet conference seven months earlier in precisely
the way the Paris Kadets now condemned.

Finally, the Kadet group in Paris offered five specific proposals, the
first of which represented perhaps the sharpest break yet with past
traditions:

    1) The lands which have passed into peasant hands must be recog-
       nized as their own property, and *this must immediately receive*
       legal sanction without awaiting the convocation of an elected
       Constituent Assembly.

    2) The local populations, as represented by municipal organs, the
       zemstvos, and such private persons who possess the confidence of
       the population, must be called upon immediately to collaborate
       actively with the authorities.

    3) The freedom of private initiative and popular freedom of move-
       ment . . . must be considered the only true path toward rehabilita-
       ing the entire commercial, industrial, and transportation ap-
       paratus [of Russia].

    4) The State must keep constantly in touch with local organizations
       for the purpose of preparing the ground for a new decentralized
       governmental administration. At the same time, the aspirations
       for independence of certain regions as well as certain nationalities
       must be satisfied in a measure compatible with the reconstitution
       of Russia as a whole.

    5) While reestablishing order in liberated territories, the adminis-
       tration must conform its actions rigorously to the elementary
       principles of liberty acquired by the revolution.[22]

Thus Kadets in Paris finally abandoned their commitment to postponing social reforms until a Constituent Assembly. They also accepted the need to establish popular decentralized local governments,
and admitted in a clear and unequivocal way the need to recognize
the achievements of revolution, even in the midst of civil war. And it
was on these terms—terms more radical than any adopted by the party

---

[21] *Ibid.*   [22] *Ibid.* (my italics)

since the tsar's abdication—that they reluctantly agreed to support General Wrangel.

Ironically, however, the Paris Kadets were finally shifting their perspectives at a moment when they lacked any influence whatsoever among the White military leadership. Progressive policies were less capable of being successfully implemented now than at any other time in the party's history.

It was soon apparent, moreover, that the strictures of Kadets in Paris were quite academic to Wrangel's regime. Despite his own conservatism (and that of his advisers), the new White leader had actually come to many of the same conclusions about the anti-Bolshevik struggle as had the Paris Kadets. In particular, he had also begun to recognize the army's dependence on popular support. And his general administrative program involved the implementation of what was described as "left policies with right hands," precisely what the Paris Kadets were urging.

The most important of these policies involved transferring land to the peasants. On April 8, 1920, just four days after assuming command from Denikin, Wrangel ordered the preparation of new land regulations. These were to be based on the principle of broad peasant land ownership, and the mediation by state authorities of any disputes between peasants and former landlords. At precisely the moment the Kadets were meeting in Paris, the new regulations were being prepared. And in their most important provisions they guaranteed the peasants' right to tenure over all land actually in their possession, irrespective of legal title or whether or not the land had been illegally seized.[23]

This had quick results, suggesting, incidentally, what might have been the effect for Denikin or Kolchak had Kadets persuaded them to adopt the same course in 1919. While most Crimean peasants did not actually see the regulations, rumor rapidly spread that the land was theirs. According to one account, Wrangel became something of a popular hero almost over night.[24] Coupled with an imposition of strict military discipline and a cautious policy of fortifying the Crimea itself, rather than moving out to engage the Reds, this initially gave his regime considerable local stability.

Meanwhile, the Kadets greeted these developments in Western Europe with much enthusiasm. "Liberal reforms are proving completely realizable in the operation of Wrangel's conservative ministry,"

---

[23] P. P. Gronsky [Gronskii], "The Agrarian Question and General Wrangel," *The New Russia*, No. 29, Aug. 19, 1920, pp. 493-97.

[24] V. Obolenskii, "Krym pri Vrangele," *NCS*, No. 9, 1925, p. 16.

Astrov wrote in *Obshchee Delo* for example.[25] And in *Golos Rossii*, Miliukov maintained that Wrangel had "learned the lessons of the past," recognizing that "another, far different, road is necessary from that taken by other generals who have stood at the head of the anti-Bolshevik military forces."[26] *The New Russia* in particular reflected this approach, reporting as late as September 16 that General Wrangel was sure Bolshevik resistance had been almost completely overcome.[27]

But much of Wrangel's apparent military success was due not so much to his own administrative policies, which were now much too late to change the overall course of events, but to the Bolsheviks' own preoccupation with the war with Poland, one of the last and most complicated episodes of the civil war. Feeling the tugs of their own deep-rooted nationalism, the Poles had attempted in the late spring of 1920 to take advantage of Russia's weakness, and had launched an attack toward Kiev. In response, the Bolsheviks decided to ignore Wrangel for the moment, and rushed most of their South Russian forces to the Ukraine's defense. This proved successful in stopping the Poles, and by midsummer, the Reds themselves were driving toward Warsaw.

Thereupon, Wrangel tried to take advantage of the situation, sending his own troops northward out of the Crimea. Within weeks, they secured most of the Northern Tauride. They then began a descent into the Kuban, but by this time, the Bolsheviks had stabilized their front with Poland, and the Whites soon met stiff resistance. By the end of September 1920, they were again withdrawing through the Perekop isthmus into the Crimea. And soon they began preparing for what was destined to be their last defense.[28]

In the process of retreat, moreover, a reactionary spirit crept back into Wrangel's political administration, despite the lofty hopes of the spring. Orders of the general's competent minister of civil affairs, A. V. Krivoshein (a former tsarist minister of agriculture), were no longer being obeyed.[29] Right-wing pressures were everywhere; and serious friction developed between the army and local public organizations, like the zemstvos. Wrangel's chief of militia, meanwhile, the old Okhrana functionary General Klimovich, began to take senseless "anti-radical" measures. By early September 1920, children going off to school in Sevastopol and Simferopol had to accustom themselves to

[25] *Obshchee Delo*, No. 81, July 31, 1920.
[26] *Golos Rossii*, No. 114, May 28, 1920.
[27] *The New Russia*, No. 33, Sept. 16, 1920, p. 95.
[28] See the discussion in Wm. H. Chamberlin, *The Russian Revolution*, 2 vols., New York, 1935, II, 318-35.
[29] Stepanov to Konovalov, June 15, 1920, in the Miliukov Archive, bx. 8141, fold. 19a.

the sight of "suspected Bolsheviks" hanging from streetposts, a horror even the army's supporters protested as exceeding any these cities had seen in the entire civil war.[30] Learning of these developments in Paris, the Kadets again set out their earlier critique, this time in a special "Note" which they hoped to convey to Wrangel directly. But before the committee could find a courier to Sevastopol, the White commander was already ordering his troops to prepare their final evacuation.[31]

The "New Tactic"

It was inevitable that the final defeat of the anti-Bolshevik armies should come as a profound shock to the émigré Kadets. What political figure can easily adjust to the notion that he has become, as Kartashev suggested, a "superfluous man"? And how could Kadets accept the idea that their long, difficult struggle for a free and liberal Russia had finally come to an end? Just weeks before, the Russian émigré press had adopted a new tone of optimism in reporting developments from South Russia. Wrangel's troops were said to be making "good progress"; conditions for success were considered "generally favorable."[32] As late as the end of October 1920, Wrangel himself was insisting that the Bolsheviks would never see the Crimean shores; and in expectation of new French military assistance, the value of the Wrangel ruble was rising on the Paris exchange.[33] For all the Kadets' presentiments and critical perspectives, the actual *fact* of Wrangel's total collapse thus brought sudden confusion. On November 22, Kadets sent urgent telegrams to party representatives all over Europe, calling them to Paris.[34]

Superficially, there still seemed a range of strategic possibilities for the Kadets. From Vladimir Burtsev and the émigré daily *Obshchee Delo* came an urgent plea for help in saving Wrangel's army, still thousands strong and now preparing to set up camp near Constantinople. Burtsev wanted the entire anti-Bolshevik emigration to organize now into one great coalition, forgetting past differences and laying the ground with Allied assistance for a new, more powerful armed struggle.[35] The SRs, meanwhile, were reiterating their longstanding "third-force" strategy, hoping émigré efforts would be coordi-

---

[30] Obolenskii to Tyrkova, Sept. 14/27, 1920, in the Panina Archive, pack. 3, fold. 29.

[31] Protocol, Paris Kadet Committee, Oct. 28, 1920.

[32] *Obshchee Delo*, No. 89, Sept. 24, 1920.

[33] *Posledniia Novosti*, No. 160, Oct. 30, 1920; No. 162, Nov. 2, 1920; No. 164, Nov. 4, 1920.

[34] Protocols, Paris Kadet Committee, Nov. 18-23, 1920.

[35] *Obshchee Delo*, No. 125, Nov. 17, 1920; No. 145, Dec. 7, 1920.

nated not in support of "bankrupt" military dictators or armed invasion, but of an internal uprising of anti-Bolshevik workers and peasants.[36] Also, Alexander Guchkov and several other members of the old State Duma committee were planning a new Russian National Conference, which they hoped might finally secure recognition from the Allies for a government-in-exile.[37] And finally, a group of émigré zemstvo figures renewed their plea for humanitarian work, rather than any effort to continue the political or military struggle.[38]

But in effect, the only real choice for Kadets was whether to continue with policies leading to a new armed invasion against Lenin, using the remnants of Wrangel's army; or to seek some totally new approach, such as the policy of encouraging mass internal resistance advocated by the SRs and *Volia Rossii.* Neither course held much promise of success. Armed invasion was almost totally impractical, even if Kadets desired it; and the hostility of SRs toward Miliukov and his colleagues was now so caustic as to make cooperation in support of an internal uprising virtually impossible. "What has changed from yesterday, and where does the notion come from that Kadets might finally turn to the left?" *Volia Rossii* inquired rhetorically in November 1920. "It comes from the fact that the dictators have disappeared . . . and the Kadets, their fate linked to the doom of reaction . . . now want desperately to remain in the forefront of political life."[39] The best liberal leaders could hope, consequently, as they gathered once again to plot their future, was that their own organizational strength and political experience might still provide some effective way out.

This was particularly the goal of Paul Miliukov himself, the one man who had come best to personify both the strengths and weaknesses of the Kadet party over the years, and who arrived from London on December 1, 1920, determined finally to reestablish a firm personal hand over whatever was left of the party's future destinies. With a stunning lack of perceptivity, Miliukov was convinced his party stood at one of the most important thresholds of its long and variegated career. It was crucial that the right decisions be made now, before all was lost! And with his characteristic hard-headedness—a trait which now, as always, infuriated friends and enemies alike—the former foreign minister was also convinced the Kadets could still lead

[36] *Volia Rossii,* No. 66, Nov. 30, 1920; No. 67, Dec. 1, 1920.

[37] "Informatsionnoe soobshchenie prezidiuma parizhskago komiteta partii narodnoi svobody po voprosu o 'russkom parlamentskom komitete zagranitsei,'" KD Archive.

[38] Material on the zemstvo and municipal organizations abroad, Maklakov Archive, ser. B, pack. 1, file 13; and pack. 5, file 6h.

[39] *Volia Rossii,* No. 66, Nov. 30, 1920.

a successful anti-Bolshevik effort. What was needed was an even more thoroughgoing reorientation of the party's approach to Russian problems than the Paris Kadets had set out at the time Wrangel assumed command from Denikin, a totally "new tactic."

According to Miliukov, the strategy of organizing military dictatorships now had to be scrapped entirely. So, too, did the "military-civil servant" [voenno-chinovnye] bureaucracies which had sustained them. In criticizing the anti-Bolshevik leadership, Miliukov and those who supported these new views were careful not to lay blame directly. Personal inadequacies, they argued, were not as much at fault as the whole military-gentry milieu in which the Whites had found themselves. But precisely because of this milieu, they now insisted, the remaining anti-Bolshevik effort had to be separated from both its former leaders and the "narrow nationalistic traditions" which had set their policies.

In particular, the Whites had to abandon any approach to nationality or agrarian issues which differed from that of most Russian people themselves. Despite the fact that Miliukov himself had done so much to establish "narrow traditions" on these questions, he, Vinaver and others now decided that the Russian masses were not, in fact, responsive to the traditional state authority they represented. A critical error of both the Kadet party and the White movement as a whole was in ignoring popular aspirations: withholding land from the peasants, repressing the general desires of regional nationalities, relying on the old bureaucracy, and generally ignoring true popular interests. If Lenin *was* eventually to be displaced, the Kadets would have to try like the Bolsheviks to win the support of the people on their own terms.

This not only meant that peasants would have to be given land without waiting for a new Constituent Assembly, a course Paris Kadets had earlier urged on Wrangel; but also that the idea of "Russia, One and Indivisible" would have to be replaced by support for the concept of a national federation of autonomous minorities, organized on a geographical basis. Russia in the future would become a federal democratic parliamentary republic. The Kadets' only course was to "turn the party to the left." Its effort had to be the creation of a massive insurrection inside Russia on the basis of popular policies.

This meant, finally, a firm tactical coalition with the socialists. According to Vinaver, Miliukov, and other Paris leaders, the Kadets' only remaining course was to work through a conference of former Constituent Assembly members which the SRs had decided to convene in Paris, and organize an "all-Russian" political coalition. Only such a group could eventually lead the anti-Bolsheviks to Petrograd and Moscow.[40]

Needless to say, this was indeed a startling departure from Miliukov's own past policies. Almost four years from the moment when such a change in perspective might have altered the course of revolution and civil war, Paris Kadets were abandoning their desire to impose liberalism "from above," and in effect, declaring invalid a basic premise of liberal politics during the entire preceding fifteen years; the idea that Russia's masses were "insufficiently developed" to know their own interests or Russia's, and had to be guided in an authoritarian (but liberal and constitutional) manner by the Kadets. Party leaders now intended to work with SRs in Paris in a way they could never bring themselves to work with the Petrograd Soviet: in developing mass allegiance and support, particularly from the peasants—Tyrkova's "wild beast"; and in contrast to past positions, there was little concern for the formalities of liberal legalism in Miliukov's argument, and even less for the interests of privileged Russia or the welfare of the "state," particularly in international terms. The implementation of reforms was to be supported without waiting for a Constituent Assembly; and even the question of a Russian federation was no longer beyond the range of possibility, despite the dangers of "Balkanization." Bitter experience had proved the power of popular aspiration; and emigration had made the desire to defend liberal social welfare irrelevant.

The ideas Miliukov was expressing had been heard before—from Michael Mandelshtam at the time of the first two Dumas, from Nicholas Nekrasov in the period before and during the war, from Nekrasov, Adzhemov, Frenkel, and other conciliationists in 1917, and finally, from Vinaver, Krol, Nicholas Shchepkin, and even Nicholas Astrov, to some extent, in the course of the civil war. But at no time could these Kadets secure substantial party backing; and one of the reasons for their failure was the opposition of Miliukov, perhaps the party's most prominent and self-assured leader.

Now, however, in the desperation of involuntary exile, Miliukov himself was paving the way for the Kadets' reorientation, trying to wrest the party from the political cocoon of *nadklassnost'* and *nadpartiinost'*, that untranslatable aloofness from mass concerns and demands which had constantly hindered efforts to gain a broad base of popular support. Meeting and arguing with some fifteen of his long-time party colleagues—including Maklakov, Vinaver, Demidov, Fedorov, Grimm,

40 Protocols, Paris Kadet Committee, Dec. 2, 3, and 4, 1920; *Obshchee Delo*, No. 143, Dec. 5, 1920; M. M. Vinaver, "Popytki obedineniia," *Posledniia Novosti*, No. 314, Apr. 28, 1921; *Volia Rossii*, No. 79, Dec. 15, 1920; No. 86, Dec. 23, 1920.

Gronskii, and Kharlamov—the historian-cum-politician persuaded most of them both to accept his views, and repeat them in a comprehensive new party statement, unofficially titled "Notes on a New Tactic." This, in turn, set the stage for the final dramatic sequence in the history of the Constitutional Democratic movement, in which the tenuous bonds holding the party whole for fifteen difficult years would finally be broken.[41]

OPPOSITION TO THE NEW TACTIC; NEW DIVISIONS AND GROWING BITTERNESS

The shift in Paris Kadet perspectives was so dramatic it could not help but generate serious new animosities among the Kadets. Some were already developing even before the final collapse of Wrangel's forces. Throughout most of the summer of 1920, small party groups in Berlin, Sofia, Prague, and especially Constantinople were enthusiastically applauding Wrangel's efforts, and resenting the criticism from Kadets in liberal journals like *The New Russia*. Even at the time of the Crimean evacuation, Paul Dolgorukov was telling his colleagues that "a creative one-man dictatorship is now needed more than ever"; while the Constantinople party committee as a whole stood "resolutely" in favor of perpetuating "united authority and creative one-man rule."[42] More important, Kadets in most émigré centers continued to recognize Wrangel personally as the only bearer of "legitimate" Russian state authority; and after the Bolsheviks' final victory in the Crimea, they continued to regard his exiled administration as the only "legal" power around which to organize further anti-Bolshevik efforts. In Constantinople, Kadets were even working with former State Duma and Senate members in a self-styled "Political Unification Committee," organizing a new administration for the émigré army.[43]

It is hardly surprising, therefore, that Kadet groups outside of Paris had a shocked and indignant response to Miliukov's "new tactic." In Berlin, where a small committee under Joseph Gessen, Paul Novgorodtsev and Vladimir Nabokov had just begun publishing their own

[41] Protocols, Paris Kadet Committee, Dec. 9 and 10, 1920. The final vote in favor of cooperating with the SRs was 12 to 3. Supporting Miliukov were Gronskii, Konovalov, Ryss, Shtern, Vinaver, Demidov, Eliashev, Kharlamov, Mikhelson, Svechin and Kartashev. Volkov, Fedorov, and Kliuchnikov were opposed. The "Notes on the New Tactic" appeared later in print as "Chto delat' posle krymskoi katastrofy," *Posledniia Novosti*, No. 374, July 7, 1921.

[42] Protocols, Constantinople Kadet Group, Nov. 20 and 25, 1920.

[43] "Politicheskii Ob'edinennyi Komitet (POK)," document in the KD Archive; Protocol, Constantinople Kadet Group, Dec. 16, 1920. After leaving the Crimea, the remnants of Wrangel's army settled in military camps in Turkey. While their leaders decided what to do, they drilled and conducted field maneuvers.

émigré newspaper *Rul'*, Kadets felt the whole idea of a Constituent Assembly conference was "ridiculous," a "regressive bloc" which no "rational" liberal could conceivably join.[44] In Sofia, Kadets accused their Paris colleagues of "capitulating" to the one political group most responsible for the Bolshevik coup.[45] In Belgrade and Constantinople, the new tactic was condemned as "morally indefensible," "utopian," "absurd," and "irreconcilable" with "appropriate" Kadet behavior.[46] Even Nicholas Astrov in London, whose "New Course" in Ekaterinodar had been an early start in this direction, was appalled at yet another "sudden 180 degree turn" on the part of Miliukov. For his part, Astrov realistically insisted that Kadets supporting the new tactic were dooming themselves to absolute ineffectiveness.[47]

As a consequence, when the key organizational instrument of the new tactic, the Constituent Assembly Conference, actually opened on January 8—amid much fanfare and confusion, incidentally: one French paper even announced the Russian Duma was reconvening!— most Kadets regarded it with real consternation. They hoped, simply, that it would not do too much damage to Wrangel and his army. Knowing this, many in the Paris Committee now had misgivings themselves (though Miliukov, according to Fedor Rodichev, still remained "complacent" and "boundlessly self-assured").[48] And their feelings were hardly assuaged by the barrage of anti-liberal editorials which continued appearing in *Volia Rossii*. Despite conciliatory statements by moderates like Nicholas Avksentiev, the more radical SRs clearly intended to keep the Conference strictly under their control.[49]

This they managed to do, in fact, with very little difficulty. The few Kadet delegates were badly outnumbered. And while they agreed with the majority on virtually all substantive issues, SRs like Kerensky, Minor, and Zenzinov lost no opportunity to deride the possibility of any future coalition. Speaking for the SRs Minor told the Conference:

[44] Novgorodtsev to Astrov, Jan. 11, 1921, Panina Archive, pack. 4m, fold. 61; *Rul'*, No. 37, Dec. 30, 1920; No. 40, Jan. 5, 1921; No. 44, Jan. 9, 1921; No. 45, Jan. 11, 1921.

[45] "Zapiska sofiiskoi gruppy o taktike gruppy chlenov partii v soveshchanii chlenov uchreditel'nago sobraniia," n.d., KD Archive.

[46] Makletsov to Konovalov, Jan. 28, 1921, KD Archive; Resolution of the Yugoslav Group of the KD Party, Jan. 28, 1921, in KD Archive; Protocols, Central Committee members in Constantinople, Dec. 13, 1920, and Constantinople Kadet Group, Dec. 16, 1920, in KD Archive.

[47] Astrov to Iurenev, Dec. 26, 1920, in the Panina Archive, pack. 4, fold. 61.

[48] F. I. Rodichev, "Notebooks," unpubl. MS in the Rodichev Papers, bx. 21.1.2.2, gp. 5, sect. 4, entry for Jan. 26, 1921.

[49] Compare *SZ*, No. 1, 1920, pp. vii-viii, where Avksentiev and others subscribe to a political program very similar to the "new tactic," and No. 2, 1921, pp. 298-308, where Avksentiev himself notes that "the resurrection of Russia is on the path of coalition," with *Volia Rossii*, No. 95, Jan. 6, 1921; and No. 96, Jan. 7, 1921.

You must know that in raising our Socialist Revolutionary banners, we have always fought, and will continue to fight, on two fronts: we reject any compromising union or coalition on the right, and also decisively reject any capitulation to the left. We will overthrow the tyrannical dictatorship of the Bolsheviks only in the name of democracy and in the interests of the future destiny of Russian socialism, not for the bourgeoisie, or in alliance with it.[50]

Even Kadet capitulation on the question of a Russian federation did not soften the SR left, despite the dramatic change this represented in the outlook of men like Miliukov. For session after session, Kadets had to sit uncomfortably as an endless stream of speakers denounced them for their past.

When the conference finally ended late in January 1921, the most the new tacticians had been able to accomplish was the creation of an ongoing special committee, charged with pleading the anti-Bolshevik cause to the Allies. Kadets hoped the group might work out detailed plans for a new "Representative Organ", which could coordinate an anti-Bolshevik uprising inside Russia and assume direction for the White movement as a whole. But since most SRs still had no intention of working closely with Kadets—*"cruelly mistaken"* was how *Volia Rossii* described those who tried to see the sessions as the first step toward a coalition of socialist and nonsocialist groups[51]—even Miliukov had to admit that the results of his labors were exceedingly meager.[52]

"Exceedingly meager" in fact, was a generous way of describing them. The anti-Bolshevik movement was shriveling, helpless without an active army and with no conceivable means of returning successfully to Russia. In Constantinople, General Wrangel still bickered with Dolgorukov and others about the composition of his Russian Council; in Sofia, Prague, Berlin, and Belgrade, Kadets and socialists alike still worked on problems of émigré relief; and in Paris, Miliukov and the new tacticians continued to meet with moderate SRs, clinging to their hopes for a coalition. But in fact, the cause was lost; and late in the winter of 1921, three blows struck in rapid succession, sounding the death knell of the anti-Bolshevik movement.

The first was the announcement on March 14 that the French Government intended to stop all support for General Wrangel. The decision had actually been pending for weeks, as French officials grew increasingly concerned about their own domestic economic problems,

---

[50] *Obshchee Delo*, No. 192, Jan. 23, 1921.
[51] *Volia Rossii*, No. 105, Jan. 18, 1921; italics theirs.
[52] Protocols, Paris Kadet Committee, Jan. 18, 20, 1921.

and saw little point now in continuing to subsidize the Russian forces near Gallipoli. With what some regarded as an incredible lack of sensitivity, Wrangel's troops were given the choice of either returning to Russia with French assistance, or accepting an offer of asylum in Brazil![53]

Two days later, the British signed a trade accord with the Bolsheviks in London. This, too, was not altogether unexpected. A Soviet trade delegation had been in Britain since the summer of 1920, seeking to extend economic contacts and perhaps secure assistance for the staggering tasks of Russian reconstruction. As the accord was initialed, however, the émigrés were given to understand that it effectively signaled de facto recognition of Lenin's regime.[54]

But the most bitter blow of all came not from the French or British, but from the Russians themselves. At the beginning of March 1921, sailors at the famous Baltic fortress of Kronstadt broke out in rebellion against the Bolshevik regime. The peasant-sailors of the fortress were known as crack Red guards; and their revolt signified both a profound disillusion with Russian conditions, and deep bitterness over the Bolsheviks' unfulfilled promises. Pressing complaints against food shortages and harsh conditions, they demanded the government take immediate steps to relieve Russia's hardship. On March 2 they elected a Provisional Revolutionary Committee, arrested the commissar of the Baltic Fleet and the chairman of the Kronstadt Soviet Executive Committee, and pushed their demands even further: new elections were to be held throughout Russia; freedom of speech, press, and assembly were to be reestablished; there was to be equality in rationing and full freedom for peasants over the land; and most important, Bolsheviks were to be eliminated from government and military positions. In a word, the rebellious sailors demanded a "free Soviet Russia" without the Bolsheviks.[55]

As Paul Avrich has shown in his recent book, the emigration had little to do with the actual Kronstadt revolt, though plans for such an uprising had been percolating abroad for some time, and an episode such as this was exactly what Kadets anticipated in formulating their new tactic.[56] But the significance of the uprising in terms of the emigration was not so much the émigrés' actual participation, as the way in which for a moment it enormously inflated White hopes that Lenin's regime was about to collapse.

[53] A copy of the telegram to Wrangel is in the KD Archive; April 1 was set as the cut off date for aid.

[54] *Posledniia Novosti*, No. 279, Mar. 18, 1921, and M. V. Glenny, "The Anglo-Soviet Trade Agreement, March 1921," *Journal of Contemporary History*, No. 2, 1970, pp. 63-82.

[55] See the thorough treatment in Paul Avrich, *Kronstadt 1921*, Princeton, 1970.

[56] *Ibid.*, chap. 3.

In Paris, where Miliukov had just taken over the editorship of *Posledniia Novosti*, a leading émigré daily, the new tacticians reacted with unrestrained joy. A thick black headline—almost unheard of in Russian journalism—stretched across the paper's front page to herald the arrival of "Revolutionary Days!" "Glory to the Fighters of Freedom!" it declared; "We do not know when our liberation will be won. No one knows that. But we do know—and everyone knows—that the hour is near!"[57] One could almost hear the liberals packing their trunks as the paper announced "general fighting in the streets of Petrograd," and exalted in the apparent vindication of the Paris Committee's new tactic: "We have known that the liberation of Russia would come from within and not from abroad. . . . Now we see that yesterday's opponents of our tactic also greet the new day with an outburst of enthusiasm as if they too had believed it for centuries."[58] And as Miliukov began to speculate on the type of government that would have to replace the Bolsheviks, Ivan Demidov wrote "with authority" that the wheels had definitely turned: the overthrow of Lenin "could be assumed as an accomplished fact."[59]

Perhaps only those who have themselves experienced the trauma of involuntary emigration can fully understand the desperate anticipation of Miliukov and the Paris Kadets. Surely nothing in the liberals own political experience gave the slightest cause to expect that even if the sailors were successful, the Kadets might regain a place in the mainstream of Russian political life. Nabokov, Gessen, and the Berlin Kadets recognized this, and they covered the event in *Rul'* with little enthusiasm. In Nabokov's view, the "obscure leaders" of the revolt bore "the same marks as the leaders of the Bolshevik coup, four years before."[60]

When the rebellion proved short-lived and was rapidly crushed, *Rul'* and Kadets in Berlin therefore showed little disappointment. But in Paris, where these same "obscure" Kronstadt leaders were regarded as a vindication of the party's alliance with the SRs, the revolt's collapse brought enormous frustration and despair. The new tactic had suddenly proved fruitless, just as it appeared on the verge of success. And almost as if to rub salt in open wounds, a torrent of abuse from all corners of the liberal emigration also began to pour in on Miliukov and the Paris Kadets, castigating them for their "incredible folly."[61] If anything, the flames of Kronstadt only deepened liberal divisions.

[57] *Posledniia Novosti*, No. 270, Mar. 8, 1921.
[58] *Ibid.*, No. 273, Mar. 11, 1921; see also No. 272, Mar. 10, 1921.
[59] *Ibid.*, No. 273, Mar. 11, 1921; No. 276, Mar. 15, 1921.
[60] *Rul'*, No. 93, Mar. 8, 1921.
[61] Protocol, Paris Kadett Committee, Apr. 14 and 21, 1921.

By April 1921, no one in the emigration had much cause for satisfaction. The end of French assistance effectively meant the end of Wrangel's army. In Constantinople, the so-called Russian Council held its first "triumphant" session on April 5, as *Obshchee Delo* described it, and set as its task both the official representation of Russia abroad and the continued maintenance of the much-suffering émigré army.[62] But the group was almost totally without funds. However optimistic Dolgorukov and the Constantinople party committee insisted they still were, it was clear that the army and their hopes were both about to break apart.

In Paris, meanwhile, the Special Committee of the Constituent Assembly Conference began to publish its own *Bulletin*; and Vinaver, Miliukov and their colleagues continued to insist that the new tactic was still perfectly valid.[63] Three working commissions were being organized by the Conference, one to defend the rights of Russian citizens abroad (under Vinaver); a financial-economic commission (under Konovalov and the SR Makeev); and one on international political affairs (under Miliukov, Avksentiev, and—Kerensky).[64] Thus, according to the Paris Kadets, relations with the SRs were proceeding "in an atmosphere of complete agreement and accord"; and despite the total suppression of the Kronstadt uprising, the revolt was still the harbinger of a new anti-Bolshevik upsurge.[65]

But in fact, most émigré liberals finally recognized by the spring of 1921 that events were totally out of their hands. Their efforts could turn instead only to humanitarian relief work, and the struggle somehow to preserve the rudiments of liberal Russian culture. As Vladimir Nabokov wrote from Berlin, cultural concerns were one way in which Russian liberals could still protect Russia's basic heritage, even while Lenin ruled in Moscow.[66] And from the spring of 1921 onward, this became their principal objective.

It was with just these concerns that the party had begun.

[62] *Obshchee Delo*, No. 266, Apr. 7, 1921; "Zhurnal soveshchaniia po voprosu o sozdanii russkago soveta," Mar. 7, 1921, and "Zhurnal russkago soveta," No. 1, Apr. 5, 1921, both in the Wrangel Personal Archives, files 12 and 16.

[63] Protocol, Paris Kadet Group, Mar. 17, 1921.

[64] "Otchet o deiatel'nosti ispolnitel'noi komissii soveshchaniia chlenov vserossiiskogo uchreditel'nogo sobranii," MS in the Miliukov Archive, n.d., bx. 8141, fold. 23.

[65] Protocol, Paris Kadet Group, Mar. 17; Protocol, Paris Kadet Committee, Apr. 14, 21, 1921.

[66] *Rul'*, No. 100, Mar. 16, 1921; see also No. 134, Apr. 27, 1921; No. 162, June 2, 1921.

CHAPTER SIXTEEN

Parting of the Ways

Late in July 1921, as Lenin and the Bolsheviks in Moscow were enjoying their first full summer as undisputed rulers of Soviet Russia, the Kadet party finally split in two. As Peter Ryss described it in *Posledniia Novosti*: "For three years Russia's only liberal party, which derived its strength from internal solidarity and the talent to maintain a middle ground, has failed to find a compromise line. While one party faction drifted more and more to the right, frequently breaking with the party's program, another group . . . turned to the left. Thus Russian liberalism has come to a parting of the ways."[1]

The specific cause of the rupture was Miliukov and his supporters' dogged pursuit of their new tactic, a last desperate effort to turn the party homeward which virtually all sectors of the emigration now recognized had no chance of success. Actually, as Ryss rightly noted, the split had long been developing. "Right" and "left" wings had existed from the very moment of the party's organization in 1905, and had persisted through the early hopeful months of Russia's fledgling Duma, as well as the years of "loyal opposition" and "patriotic anxiety." Divisions had also persisted and grown throughout the revolution, the party as a whole never developing a consistent tactical line, or even a uniform understanding of what the revolution's goals should be.

Yet in all these years, Kadets had always assumed the future would eventually be theirs. Divisions were overcome by a persistent optimism, derivative both of the party's intelligentsia origins, with its Western concept of progress and social development, and an understanding of Russia's own historical evolution which always underestimated the popular attractiveness of radical social transformation. Had Kadets in Paris seriously believed their party still had a future, the schism caused by the new tactic might also have been healed. But as several party leaders themselves now admitted, an "emigrant psychology" had finally gripped their ranks, a feeling that even as a single organization there was little Kadets could do.[2] Since a split now made no practical difference, long-time bitterness finally erupted. Most party leaders seemed quite willing to let the division occur.

[1] *Posledniia Novosti*, No. 348, June 7, 1921.
[2] Protocol of the Kadet Group in Paris, July 15, 1921, in the Archive of the Constitutional Democratic Party, Hoover Institution (henceforth KD Archive).

FINAL SESSIONS OF THE CENTRAL COMMITTEE

The steps leading to this final climactic episode can be quickly traced. They began at a last conference of the party's Central Committee, which convened in Paris at the end of May 1921. The sessions were called to see if even at this late date, Kadets could still preserve some semblance of a unified organization. In Berlin, Nabokov, Nolde, and Novgorodtsev wanted unity as a means of giving coherence to the emigration as a whole and of facilitating cultural work. Iurenev, Dolgorukov, and other Kadets in Constantinople wanted support for the remnants of Wrangel's army. And with his own incurable self-confidence, Miliukov still hoped Kadets could finally be consolidated behind his own "coalition" with the socialists.

The Committee's sessions lasted more than a week. Rather than revealing a willingness to compromise, however, they showed instead how deep divisions now ran in the party's leadership. The only serious effort at bringing Kadets together was made by Nicholas Astrov, who, in effect, took up the role of mediator which Miliukov himself had played in the years before the revolution. In Astrov's view, the essence of Constitutional Democracy had always been its centrism, despite the wide diversity of individual opinions within Kadet ranks. And it was this centrism which was now the key to maintaining leadership in the anti-Bolshevik cause. Speaking with authority as an early supporter of conciliation and as one of Denikin's more responsible and progressive assistants, the Moscow Kadet argued that since previous attempts at associating with the left had consistently failed, no new coalition could possibly be successful now. But neither, on the other hand, could any attempt to maintain the discredited ways of military dictatorship. General Wrangel was a relic. The Russian right had proved its inability to adjust to new conditions.

In Astrov's opinion, what was needed was not the continuation of efforts to ally with any specific right- or left-wing group, but a new "new tactic" [*noveishii taktik*], in which all alliances and coalitions were discarded, and the party reasserted itself as the centrist nucleus of the emigration as a whole. Affirming traditional liberal values, and consolidating various émigré groups, Kadets could emerge in the foreground of all émigré activities, and lead their countrymen abroad in facing whatever lay ahead.[3]

Here, indeed, was the voice of liberal moderation, humanitarian in its outlook, cautious in its tactics, and resigned once again to a long period of evolution before the rudiments of political liberalism could emerge in Russia. But no sooner had Astrov completed his report than

---

[3] Protocol, Central Committee in Paris, May 26, 1921, in the KD Archive.

Paul Miliukov destroyed all prospects of harmony. Miliukov's response, moreover, is worth following in brief detail, for it signified the final turn in the thought of the party's most prominent spokesman and leader.

The problem with Astrov's perspective, Miliukov began somewhat unfairly, considering Astrov's own past insistence on the need for reform and popular support, was that it failed to comprehend the full significance of what had occurred in Russia during the preceding four years. The revolution and civil war had clearly demonstrated that Kadets had little backing from among the mass of Russian people; the polarized elements of Russian society, in other words, were profoundly unequal both in numbers and power; and Kadet policies in the past had proved inadequate to overcome the party's own narrow base of support. While the masses desired far-reaching social reforms and a revolutionary democracy, Kadets had endorsed the postponement of reforms, supporting authoritarian policies and military dictatorships imposed "from above." Most Kadets simply did not understand the extent to which the Russian people had developed politically. They were no longer the passive peasants of tsarist times, but a conscious political mass, infused with the concepts of radical democracy and reaching for leadership. However barbarous their principles, Lenin, Trotsky, and the Bolsheviks at least perceived this fact; the Kadets and their military dictators did not. And it was this, rather than military failure, which was ultimately responsible for the White catastrophe.

The new tactic, Miliukov went on, was not an idle political alliance. It derived expressly from the conviction that there could be no victory without the support of the people. And the people, he affirmed again, were clearly bound to Russia's social transformation, as advocated by parties of the left. He and his supporters had no liking for socialism; they had always opposed it, and would continue to do so, even if the new tactic succeeded. But the SRs had at least remained true to Russia's popular mood. Of all the anti-Bolshevik groups, they alone could still command the support of the broad peasant masses. Liberalism in any guise could never reappear in Russia without their help.

Finally, Miliukov admitted his own personal role in the party's past mistakes. His support for the monarchy in particular had been a grave error. But past faults could hardly be corrected by continuing discredited patterns. Traditional liberal centrism had failed in 1917 and it would fail again. The Russian people would simply not accept it. And however hopeless the future now appeared, the party as a whole still had to conduct itself on the assumption that eventually, its members would return to their homes.[4]

[4] *Ibid.*, May 27, 1921.

Thus Miliukov rejected Astrov's prospective compromise, and set the grounds for a formal division of ranks. He himself protested that a split was not what he desired, and even objected strongly to the Central Committee's adopting any specific resolution. "What will be gained by resolutions?" he asked, revealing the emigration had blunted none of his past hard-headedness. "In opposition to one resolution I will pose another, contradicting its positions." The best possible solution was for the Committee to adjourn, each local party group returning to the specific policies it thought best. When the Bolsheviks eventually collapsed, Miliukov told his colleagues, "we will gather again in Russia, and settle our differences then."[5]

But most Central Committee members were now quite reluctant to leave the question unresolved. "Otherwise," as Nabokov remarked, "why have we met in the first place?"[6] The awesome privations of civil war had sharpened personal feelings; and many Kadets closely identified with anti-Bolshevik administrations could no longer tolerate even an unofficial tactical alliance with the SRs, whose Central Committee equated Denikin, Kolchak, and Wrangel with Lenin and Trotsky, and urged the European powers not to provide the Whites with military assistance. Nabokov, Rodichev, Tyrkova, Dolgorukov, and others also favored taking a definite stand because they hoped to themselves to create a new nonpartisan coalition of émigré social and political organizations, joining in some form of "national committee." This was the course being urged on the emigration by Vladimir Burtsev and his *Obshchee Delo*; and it was the object as well of a special Congress of Russian National Unification, which Burtsev and a number of Miliukov's Kadet opponents had scheduled to open in Paris on June 5. After Miliukov's lengthy response to Astrov, therefore, which occupied the better part of two Committee sessions, four more meetings were held. And once again, while the Bolsheviks in Moscow were busy charting Russia's future, Kadets did verbal battle with themselves.

In the end, a majority of the Committee finally determined to take the step that many recognized would end more than fifteen years of close political associations. Insisting that Kadets should still do all they could to preserve party unity, and that "the party's tactics might be finally determined only when an active relationship can once again be established between Russia and the party in the continuing struggle for democratic government, the establishment of basic freedoms, and a rule of law in the homeland," the Committee nonetheless officially condemned the new tactic. And thus by implication, they also finally rejected the party's long-time titular leader, Paul Miliukov.[7]

[5] *Ibid.*, May 28, 1921.   [6] *Ibid.*, May 31 and June 2, 1921.
[7] *Ibid.*, June 2, 1921. In voting, the Central Committee was almost evenly split.

SCHISM

One day after the Central Committee's official rejection of Miliukov and the new tactic appeared in the émigré press, a Congress of National Unification convened in Paris in the old Hotel Majestic, providing a forum for most Kadets to reaffirm their traditional views. Anton Kartashev, the group's presiding officer, set the keynote with familiar rhetoric: "The aim of this congress," he told some 120 delegates from more than 40 different émigré organizations, "is the unification of Russian anti-Bolshevik forces abroad into a nonpartisan political organization, standing above parties and dedicated to the liberation of Russia from communist slavery."[8] Paul Dolgorukov from the Central Committee, Tyrkova from London, Teslenko from Constantinople, and even Vladimir Nabokov, on behalf of the party's group in Berlin, all echoed these views. Each urged the creation of a nonpartisan Russian National Committee to lead the defense of Russia's national interests, and each insisted the Kadets as a whole maintained their traditional principles. These, moreover, they now sought to implement in cooperation with Russia's "cultured elements," not with political radicals of the left.[9]

As *Obshchee Delo* noted in giving its impression of the sessions on June 6, the Congress of National Unification was strikingly reminiscent of the 1917 State Conference in Moscow, only without the left. One could sense in the shadows the figures of Kornilov, Alekseev, Kaledin, and Kolchak, the paper reported, the fallen "greats" of the anti-Bolshevik cause. There was also a sense of destiny in the air, a reverent dedication to the hopes of the past, and a renewed hope that earlier efforts would not be in vain, just as there had been four years earlier.[10] *Obshchee Delo* applauded these similarities, and the analogy was apt. But what its editors failed to note was that the Moscow Conference was not the start of effective liberal government in 1917, but a symbol of the end of practical authority, a mark of privileged Russia's detachment from the masses.

According to Miliukov in *Posledniia Novosti*, this same cultured detachment now represented a renewal of "Octobrism" in the ranks of

---

The resolution against the new tactic carried by 9 to 7, but Paul Gronskii apparently voted by mistake with the majority. A motion to "reconsider" failed by an 8 to 8 tie (with Gronskii this time voting the right way), and hence the original resolution passed. Although individual votes were not recorded, those most likely supporting it included Dolgorukov, Kartashev, Astrov, Maklakov, Nolde, Panina, Teslenko, and Rodichev, while those opposed were probably Miliukov, Gronskii, Demidov, Volkov, Mandelshtam, Adzhemov, Vinaver, and Konovalov.

[8] *Obshchee Delo*, No. 325, June 6, 1921.

[9] *Ibid.*, No. 326, June 7, and No. 328, June 9, 1921.

[10] *Ibid.*, No. 325, June 6, 1921.

Russian liberalism, a conservative orientation which had little regard for practical politics.[11] In the editorial columns of *Rul'*, as the Congress adjourned, Nabokov himself was not inclined to disagree. If Miliukov meant that the sessions embodied the historical sense of Russia's basic liberal tradition, devoted to the principles of civil liberties and cultural maturation, and opposed to radical change, there was no real difference in their understanding. Despite his own past efforts in the Crimea (or perhaps, in part, because of their failure), the Berlin Kadet leader was "deeply satisfied" that the Congress had taken a proper course.[12]

But such a course was devoid of any practical political application, at least in terms of Russia herself, as Miliukov noted in a subsequent reply; and this was precisely where both the National Congress and the opponents of the new tactic failed. They simply could not understand that radical tactics were now the only possible means left to achieve the party's objectives. Liberals and conservatives alone could never be successful; it was necessary to come to grips with the mood of the Russian people. "We are now clearly divided," Miliukov wrote, "on whether we view the revolution positively or negatively; on whether we want to construct a government to liberate Russia on the basis of authoritarian principles abroad or democratic principles within Russia; and finally, on whether we want to bring the party close to a democratic social base, which up to now it has stood upon only in principle." Nabokov, Dolgorukov, Pasmanik, Kartashev, and others had forced these distinctions in both the Central Committee and the National Congress; the Paris Kadets who supported the new tactic could now disassociate themselves from their comrades along clearly defined lines.[13]

The disassociation officially came three weeks later. At a huge gathering of émigré Kadets in Paris, a larger meeting than at many other times in the party's history in Russia, Miliukov and his supporters made one last effort to convince their colleagues of the necessity for following a new line. The party should strive above all "to defend the interests of democratic elements of Russia's peasant and urban populations . . . ," he argued; it had finally to establish a firm popular base, and categorically abandon its past adherence to the concepts of *nadklassnost'* and *nadpartiinost'*. This required a rewriting of the party's program, to take into consideration the drastic reordering of Russia's social, economic, and political structure that the revolution

---

11 *Posledniia Novosti*, No. 354, June 14, 1921.
12 *Rul'*, No. 175, June 17, 1921.
13 *Posledniia Novosti*, No. 356, June 16, 1921.

had brought; and it necessitated the Kadets' eliminating from their activities abroad "all relationships which could make mutual understanding between various party groups and the broad masses of Russian people more difficult," that is, their participation in the new Russian National Committee.[14]

But once again, just as at the Central Committee sessions, Miliukov failed to gain the support of most of his colleagues. Shortly afterward, on July 28, 1921, Miliukov, Vinaver, and a small coterie of their supporters gathered in a special room in the Café Voltaire, and formed a new political organization, the Paris Democratic Group of the Party of People's Freedom. The basic principles of the Democratic Kadets were those of the "new tactic": a positive attitude toward the revolution; a faith in the creative strength of the Russian people; and a determination to defend the interests of the masses, particularly the peasants. In the meantime, the regular Kadet group elected a new executive committee, and with "great reluctance," officially announced the schism.[15] After sixteen enormously trying years, the Kadet party had finally split apart.

SOME CONCLUSIONS

Always attuned to the judgment of posterity, the Kadets no sooner split apart than the leaders of both factions set out their explanations of what had occurred "for the future historian of the party." "If the historian manages to plow through the sea of words which has flowed around the question of the 'new tactic,' " the editors of *Rul'* wrote on July 26, 1921, ". . . if he studies all the events which have occurred since the end of last year to the present time, we think he will come to very simple and clear conclusions. . . . The authors of the new tactic ran themselves into a blind alley. Having chased after phantoms, they deceived themselves."[16] The phantoms, according to *Rul'*, were the SRs and the revolutionary Russian people; the former, pretending

14 *Ibid.*, No. 386, July 21, 1921.
15 Circular letter of the Paris Democratic Group of the Party of People's Freedom, in *Posledniia Novosti*, No. 412, Aug. 20, 1921; undated (but July 1921) statement of the Paris Kadet Committee, KD Archive. In August 1921 the Paris Democratic Group included Miliukov as president, Vinaver as vice president, Volkov as secretary, and A. M. Mikhelson as treasurer. Other members included: S. I. Bass, A. S. Bezchinskii, M. V. Braikevich, E. M. Vinaver, P. P. Gronskii, I. P. Demidov, I. N. Efremov, P. Iu. Zubov, A. I. Konovalov, A. V. Kossikovskaia, A. S. Miliukova, N. M. Mogilianskii, M. A. Ryss, P. I. Ryss, A. A. Svechin, V. A. Kharlamov, I. S. Shneerson, and L. E. Eliashev. Prominent in the new "regular" Kadet committee were Obolenskii, Rodichev, Teslenko, Pasmanik, and Fedorov.
16 *Rul'*, No. 208, July 26, 1921.

to have the power to lead Russia to a viable democracy; the latter, appearing ready to rise up against the Bolsheviks and willing to support the establishment of a moderate non-Bolshevik regime. In neither case did the image fit reality. The SRs were no more capable of political administration now than in 1917; and the Russian people, no more responsive than ever to statesmanlike leadership. The split in the party derived, therefore, from the sheer intransigence of the party's new tacticians, especially Miliukov. Unwilling to learn the lessons of the past and blindly self-confident, he and his followers simply refused all rational proposals for keeping the party together. They pretended instead that "profound differences of principle" existed between various party members.[17]

Quick to respond in *Posledniia Novosti*, Miliukov for his part warned the future historian of the party against accepting *Rul'*'s simplistic explanation. Profound differences of principle *did* exist, and it was they, not the capriciousness of individual party leaders, which underlay the *raskol*. There was, first, a fundamental difference in the way the Kadets now viewed the revolution. Whatever their feelings in the past, those desiring an alliance with the SRs saw the events of 1917 as a positive aspect of Russia's historical development, a crucial turning point in the process of democratizing Russia's social and political structure. Those supporting the Congress of National Unification and opposing the new tactic saw the revolution as a retrogression, the unleashing of chaotic forces whose control was necessary to the orderly transformation of the state. There was also a profound difference on the question of how authority had to be constructed in order to liberate Russia in the future: in an authoritarian manner from without; or democratically, from within, based on the popular will. Finally, Kadets were fundamentally divided on the question of the party's proper social base. The new tacticians believed Kadets had to politicize Russian liberalism by reconstructing its program and principles to conform to mass aspirations. The tactic's opponents still believed in *nadklassnost'* and *nadpartiinost'*, defending the interests of Russia's cultured elite, who were most capable of determining the nation's "real" needs.[18]

There was, of course, a measure of truth in both points of view. The new tacticians had, in fact, run themselves into a blind alley. A new revolutionary upsurge inside Russia was unlikely after Kronstadt, and particularly after the inception of NEP, despite continued peasant agitation. There was even less likelihood that such an uprising could ever be captured or controlled by liberals should it actually occur.

[17] *Ibid.*
[18] *Posledniia Novosti*, No. 393, July 29, 1921.

Kadet associations with the SRs were also extremely tenuous. *Volia Rossii*, the organ of SR radicals, had persistently warned Miliukov and his colleagues that there was no possibility of effective interparty coalition. The tactic had failed in 1917, it had failed at Ufa in Siberia, it had failed in the Crimea, and it had even shown its weakness in Moscow organizations like the National Center. Moreover, the new tacticians' cause itself lacked definition. They despised Bolshevism, but gave little thought to what form of government might be established in its stead. In the summer of 1921, Miliukov and his colleagues were still living with the illusion that Russia's future was theirs. It would take many years before their hopes completely faded.

But in supporting the new Russian National Committee, with its continued reverence for General Wrangel and the notion of using organized force to dislodge Lenin, Miliukov's opponents had themselves worked into an insoluble bind. Even if a forceful White army could again assault the Bolsheviks, which it could not, right-wing military dictatorship had proved its weakness; and the new tacticians were perfectly justified in asserting that by reaffirming traditional *nadklassnost'*, their colleagues had not learned the political lessons of the past. Kadet speeches at the Congress of National Unification did indeed reveal a negative attitude toward the revolution, a desire to continue defending old privileged interests, and a profound misunderstanding of the needs and aspirations of Russia's masses. The differences dividing Kadets were hardly superficial and never had been. The schism in the party was not, as the editors of *Rul'* asserted, merely the result of individual hard-headedness.

Perhaps the principal reason why the Kadet party ruptured in July 1921 was because its leadership had never effectively solved the dilemma of how to relate to the principal forces of Russian social change. From the moment it was formed in 1905, the party had struggled to lead the country toward Western constitutionalism, equating modernization with parliamentary government, universal civil liberties, economic growth, and a rule of law. With few exceptions, Kadets never openly represented themselves as partisans of special interests; their goal was to serve the nation "as a whole," avoiding the "harmful and destructive egoism of class conflict" and even the open pursuit of partisan interests. And while Miliukov and the party group in Petrograd eagerly sought power, fully confident in their own abilities and the crucial importance of their program for Russia's future, most party members outside the capital were not political activists at all in the strict sense of the term, but intellectuals and professional people committed first and foremost to social progress through legal reform and civil liberties. How to secure these liberties was a question of practical politics for which they never developed a clear or uniform answer.

Uniformity on this question was difficult partly because as national liberals, ostensibly standing above classes and particularistic interests, Kadets never had a strong natural constituency. Before 1917, left Kadets hoped they could constructively lead a mass movement, channeling popular radicalism "from below" in such a way as to pressure the tsar into granting them power; but they were never really accepted as allies by left-wing parties, partly because of their colleagues' willingness to compromise with the government, partly because their policies in fact, defended Russia's professional middle classes, her "liberal bourgeoisie." Meanwhile, more conservative Kadets remained enormously fearful of social disorder, and worked within the confines of the Fundamental Laws in the hope that Nicholas would appreciate the nationalist loyalty of their constitutionalism, and sooner or later call them to power "from above." Instead, the tsar and his advisers condemned the party as a whole for inciting mass unrest, refusing to recognize the difference between its right and left flanks. Between these two strains, finally, Miliukov and his followers on the Central Committee struggled to hold the movement together, immersing themselves with the Duma delegation in everyday affairs of practical legislative politics, and hoping Russia's natural evolution would eventually bring a liberal government. But rather than "natural" Western evolution, Russia instead became increasingly more polarized.

One might take the position that given this polarization and Russia's general condition of social and economic underdevelopment, and particularly the absence of a well-developed middle class, the ambivalent and diverse politics of Kadets before 1917 were ideally suited to their context. Had the party been given the opportunity to exercise power, its radical wing might well have sapped the strength of revolutionary violence, while its concern for legitimacy smoothed relations with conservative forces and the established bureaucracy. Standing "above classes," Kadets might have overcome the problems of popular support stemming from the numerical insignificance of Russia's liberal bourgeoisie, and allowed peaceful transition to a new liberal order.

But the problem here was that the Kadets could not *obtain* power on their own. Before 1917, therefore, their political task remained either to secure mass support, or persuade the regime itself to acquiesce, neither of which was served by tactical ambivalence. One might also argue that the Kadet failure before 1917 simply reinforces the notion that revolutionary change was inevitable in Russia—that industrial and social underdevelopment left political stresses which liberals like the Kadets could simply not overcome. But while it seems very likely that the various imperatives of industrial modernization did indeed predetermine drastic political and social changes in Russia, this view ignores the fact that Miliukov and his followers did have a range of choices in defining their tactics and policies; and it is in terms of this available range that their tactics and policies must be evaluated.

This range of choices continued, moreover, past the February revolution. One can well maintain that Kadet policies would ultimately have made no difference to Russian development in these turbulent months. Even if the Provisional Government had temporarily repressed the Bolsheviks, as the tsarist regime had done, Lenin and his colleagues were determined to take power. Eventually they would have made the attempt, even if a Constituent Assembly had convened successfully, and even if it established a new regime on legitimate constitutional foundations. Yet the Kadets' role in the revolution must still be understood by comparing the party's actual course with conceivable alternatives, not in considering long range historical possibilities.

In these terms, as Miliukov and the new tacticians themselves eventually recognized, the greatest failing of Petrograd party leaders in the early part of 1917 was in assuming the legitimacy of their own authority, presuming to determine themselves what Russia's national interests and priorities should be. Led by Miliukov, Kadets in the government acted as if they were a "ministry of confidence," appointed by the tsar at the behest of the Progressive Bloc. But while they themselves lacked the traditional instruments of power through which their authority could be sustained, they also haughtily resisted any functional dependence on the far more popular soviets, which conceivably were a means of keeping their policies "responsible." As Shakhovskoi, Nekrasov, and a number of provincial Kadet delegates argued at the seventh and eighth party congresses, governmental authority depended in 1917 on "rapidly implementing the popular will in all of its forms,"[19] that is, on popularity and mass support. While Kadet ministers played a leading role in the first two provisional regimes, their party and its policies lacked both.

One reason for this, as we have seen, was that in two of the major issues facing revolutionary Russia, those of land reform and the war, Kadets maintained positions sharply at variance with mass desires—or to be more exact, Kadets either reaffirmed their own basic outlook on these questions or drifted somewhat to the right, while masses of Russians moved rapidly to the left. As national liberals, bound to statist traditions, most Kadets viewed the war in terms of Russia's competitive

---

[19] *Rech'*, Mar. 29, 1917. The phrase is Nekrasov's.

international posture, rather than her own peoples' immediate welfare. And while in ordinary times, this perspective would have identified Kadet leaders as typical Western statesmen, in 1917 it further divorced the party from the mass of Russian people, undermining any chance of political stability. As Izgoev once phrased it, the important question for many Kadets was whether Russia would be a great world power, democratic, liberal, and free, or a tiny Muscovite principality, subordinate to foreign interests.[20] But the vital questions for workers, peasants, and soldiers in 1917 concerned peace, land, and bread.

In this, the Kadet outlook in 1917 contrasted sharply to what it had been in 1905-1906, although Kadets were never monolithic on any issue, including the appropriate role for Russia as a "great world power." The difference in 1917 lay in the party's belief that all restraints to Russia's evolution as a leading Western power had now been removed with the tsar's abdication, that the goal of struggle was no longer to obtain political freedom, but to preserve and protect it from foreign encroachment. This meant mobilizing all resources in support of the war, even if mobilization required postponing popular reforms and even national elections.

It seems possible in retrospect, however, that the Provisional Government might have survived even if Russia had not withdrawn entirely from the fighting. By the beginning of June 1917, front lines on the eastern front were far more stable than they had been in March and April; and many soldiers who had earlier deserted had returned to their units. An inactive front could conceivably have produced as much tranquillity as peace itself, giving ministers time to implement social reforms, and deepen their popular support. Furthermore, recent evidence suggests that the Germans themselves might have welcomed such a detente;[21] and surely it would have been acceptable to the mass of Russian people. In these circumstances, even if peasant soldiers had streamed home to receive their share of newly divided land (as many Kadets feared they would), the process of reform might still have been accomplished with a minimum amount of violence and social disorder.

But most Kadets, particularly those grouped around Miliukov in Petrograd, saw the revolution not as a means to stop the killing, or as a chance for rapidly improving Russia's social welfare, or even as an opportunity to develop a more popular democratic government. Unlike many on the left, for whom the events of February 1917 were a profound and historic opportunity to alter exploitative social relationships and institutions, the establishment of the provisional regime

[20] *Svobodnyi Narod*, July 11, 1917.
[21] See the discussion in O. S. Fedyshyn, *Germany's Drive to the East and the Ukrainian Revolution, 1917-1918*, New Brunswick, 1971, pp. 42-59.

for liberals was a necessary but potentially dangerous opportunity to rationalize social, economic, and political processes in support of the war. The revolution was to provide for *future* economic, social and political maturation, while its immediate goal was "Victory!", something most workers, peasants and soldiers soon felt had little tangible importance. One can only speculate on what the course of the revolution would have been had Miliukov and others had the wisdom of hindsight, and opposed the June offensive in favor of immediate social reforms. But it seems quite certain that had Kadets been as forceful in pursuing these goals as they were in demanding the war be prosecuted to the fullest, and had they used their considerable argumentative powers to contain any possible right-wing opposition to this course, particularly from within the army, the chance of a successful Bolshevik coup would have been greatly reduced.

A similar argument can be made in terms of the Kadets' "juridical" conception of the Provisional Government, as *Izvestiia* once rightly described it,[22] a conception which also deterred many party leaders from endorsing immediate social change in crucial areas like land reform. Undoubtedly, in 1917, a number of Kadets feared the consequences of radical programs in terms of their own material welfare, particularly in the provinces. Many had country estates, and all shared privileges which derived in some way from Russia's social and economic inequities. Unlike the SDs or SRs, moreover, whose specific goals included the transformation of Russia's social system in the interests of workers and peasants, many Kadets would doubtless have been content with a minimum of economic and social reform. The party's program supported some progressive social legislation, but it was for political rather than social democracy that Kadets had led the fight for "liberation."

Yet to interpret Kadet policies in 1917 primarily in terms of class interest is to misperceive the basic mode of Russian liberal politics, at least in Moscow and Petrograd. Kadets above all were committed to legality and a rule of law, which, as Rodichev described it as far back as 1894, was to govern everyone, and "particularly the representatives of authority."[23] Radical land reforms enacted by the Provisional Government would have been "illegitimate" in the view of most leading Kadets, an arrogant misuse of power which usurped the prerogatives of the Constituent Assembly. Kadets like Miliukov also feared such reforms would further weaken Russian social stability, since those who

[22] *Izvestiia*, Apr. 26, 1917.
[23] F. Rodichev, "Iz vospominaniia," *SZ*, No. 43, 1933, p. 240.

opposed them could claim their own legal rights were being infringed, and fight against them, possibly with force.

This fear of opposition to "illegitimate" reforms should not be underestimated in evaluating the Kadets in 1917, conciliationists, and their more conservative colleagues alike. The specters first of counter-revolution from the right and then of full-fledged civil war were very real as Russia experienced increasing social violence and polarization, much more so at times, in fact, than the actual dangers. The conciliationist tendency within the party largely developed, in fact, in the hope of reducing social antagonism, rather than obtaining the Kadets' own political or social program; while Miliukov, Rodichev, Tyrkova, and others who gradually assumed a "civil war mentality" did so for the most part because they felt a united Russia was no longer possible, that social disruption could only be contained by loyal units of the army.

In their stress on legitimacy, however, there was a great irony in Russian liberal politics. Despite the Kadets' factional diversity, the basic legalism of all party groups was essentially conservative, just as was the party's related emphasis on *gosudarstvennost'* and its concern for the welfare of the state. It is true that by insisting all parties and social organizations confine themselves strictly to legal action, and not preempt the Constituent Assembly, Kadets could justify their own continued exercise of power, especially when it soon became clear that universal elections would lead to a socialist cabinet. More important, however, is that legitimacy was mistakenly perceived as a means of overcoming social unrest, as if law, order, and stability were synonymous. Yet it was precisely the implementation of basic social reforms that might ultimately have allowed a liberal democracy to survive in 1917; and it was opposition to such reforms—based largely on legitimacy arguments—that prompted the majority of Kadet Central Committee members to withdraw their support from both the first and second coalitions. Seeking authoritative and legitimate government, in other words, the Kadet Central Committee itself played a major role in undermining what power the government actually possessed.

Here one can focus clearly on a crucial aspect of the party's political significance in 1917. Of all political organizations after February, Kadets were in a unique position to contain the natural enemies of social and political change. Despite programmatic differences, their ties with leading gentry and bourgeois groups, with Russia's professional elements, and most important, with the officer corps of the army, were quite extensive. This was particularly so after the ninth party congress in July, as we have seen, when Miliukov and other party leaders assumed leading roles in groups like the Union of Public Organizations, which united virtually all of privileged Russia. On this basis, it is not inconceivable (or even overly idealistic) to think that the Kadets could have mobilized their energies not to attack the moderate socialists or the Petrograd Soviet, toward whom the country as a whole was increasingly showing its allegiance, or even to resist the formation of a workable coalition, but to prevent critical non-socialist groups from challenging the revolution.

Such a policy might not have weakened Bolshevik ambitions. But if a majority of the party's Central Committee leadership had followed the course urged by Nekrasov, Astrov, Volkov, Vinaver, and other conciliationists in 1917, had Miliukov and his supporters used their influence at the Congresses of Public Organizations, the Moscow State Conference, and the innumerable discussions they had with the army's commanders to reduce rightist dissidence rather than stimulate it as a means, in part, of pressuring the left, had the Kadets, in other words, become the *loyal* opposition to the first and second coalitions rather than the leading force of right-wing resistance, the least result might have been to avert the Kornilov rebellion. And this, in turn, might have allowed the Provisional Government to limp to a Constituent Assembly, avoiding for the time being at least, a new challenge from Lenin. The very coalition with moderate socialists that Miliukov and the new tacticians strove for so persistently in emigration *was* possible in the summer of 1917. One has only to read the speeches of Avksentiev, Tsereteli, and others at the various soviet congresses and conferences to realize how much these political leaders desired the same authority and political stability demanded by Kadets. Here was an opportunity for Russia's leading liberal party which was vastly disproportionate to its actual strength.

Instead, Kadets officially remained "above politics" and "above classes," which in practice very quickly became an implicit defense of privilege. It might be maintained that a posture of *nadpartiinost'* and *nadklassnost'* was politically adroit for Kadets in 1917, just as before the revolution, given the unlikelihood of attracting massive new electoral support. A "drawing together" (*sblizhenie*) of liberals and moderate socialists might only have weakened what support Kadets did have among their nonsocialist constituents, while also forcing the party as a whole into a position of subordination to the soviets. At the same time, openly assuming the defense of bourgeois interests might only have evoked even greater hostility from the left than Kadets already faced. Thus one might argue that *nadpartiinost'*, though in effect a reaction after February to understandable fears of social chaos, rather than a strategy of optimism, and *nadklassnost'*, which by now was a posture of despair, rather than hope, were the best of meager liberal choices.

Yet by stressing their identification with "healthy state elements," as Miliukov, Rodichev, Izgoev, and others did at the eighth and ninth party congresses, and by taking into their ranks large numbers of so-called March Kadets from the gentry and urban bourgeoisie, Kadets in effect became a magnet for right-wing forces anyway, as the politically conscious Miliukov and others soon recognized. Hence a majority of the party's leadership attenuated the very problems of social polarization they ostensibly wanted to avoid.

In sum, however difficult the war and Russia's general conditions of social and economic underdevelopment had made their political positions, and however much even right-wing Kadets had the national interests of Russia at heart, true liberal statesmanship in the revolution would have consistently recognized the need for compromise and conciliation.

It is in these terms as well that one must ultimately evaluate the party's role in the various anti-Bolshevik governments of the civil war. While one hardly need argue the party's numerical weakness after the Bolsheviks seized power, the party's potential for pressuring the Siberian and South Russia dictatorships into positive social and political policies was still very great. Instead, however, authority itself was often all that mattered to Kadets. In Siberia and the Ukraine, party leaders joined reactionary administrations with little concern for popular support, or even popular welfare. Liberalism lost virtually all its traditional content in a frantic grasp for order, maintained by bayonets. Only in emigration was the need for "left policies through right hands" generally clear.

There were, of course, notable exceptions to this rule—exceptions which prompt tantalizing speculation as to what might have happened if the party had indeed become the "living fabric" of a progressive anti-Bolshevism which men like Astrov, Shchepkin, and Vinaver so urgently desired. In Siberia, Lev Krol and others waged a game struggle to implement the goals of the Union of Regeneration, seeking a coalition directorate empowered with dictatorial authority, but imbued as well with a progressive social outlook. The Crimean regional government was also an admirable "experiment," an attempt to build "from below" and thus create a civil power with firm popular support. And Nicholas Astrov and others struggled (albeit fitfully at times) to sway Denikin to the left. Astrov's "new course," in fact, was very similar to

Miliukov's own "new tactic," though the former Moscow attorney himself eventually broke with Miliukov's democratism.

But at times when it might have counted, in South Russia in the fall of 1918, in Siberia in the spring of 1919, and when Denikin's forces began their final push toward Moscow, most Kadets felt compelled instead to yield to the right. The army was power, and in the civil war, military strength had illusory forcefulness. Moderate, conciliationist Kadets were again undermined by their conservative colleagues, men like Vasili Stepanov, who came to delight in the prerevolutionary aspects of Ekaterinodar, or influential conservatives like Dolgorukov, Sokolov, or Novgorodtsev, who easily shed the party's historical aversion to reactionary rule. Civil war touched the depths of liberal nationalism, which equated regional autonomy with treason, and again insisted on the postponement of even urgent social and economic reforms. "Russia, One and Indivisible!" cast a captivating spell; and brandishing the party's name in support of policies most Russians could not accept, these Kadets associated Constitutional Democracy in the eyes of the Russian people with the war's worst excesses.

Ironically, Miliukov himself eventually split away from most of his colleagues over these issues as we have seen. Rather than insisting on controlling events, the party's titular chairman was once again reconciled to the role of opposition leader, clearly assuming a subordinate role to the socialists in future Russian politics. To him, the revolution and civil war had both finally demonstrated the vacuity of governments or parties "hanging in air," of liberals trying to maintain legitimate authority without clear popular support. And along with other new tacticians, he was no longer willing to accept the Kadets' detachment from workers or peasants, even though the figurative isolation of 1917-1920 had now been replaced by geographical reality.

Here again one might well argue that ultimately the party's posture in this regard made little difference. It was necessary for the party's leaders to cooperate with their generals if Kadets were to have any role at all in the White movement, and perhaps if more liberals had, in fact, pressed for progressive social policies in South Russia and Siberia, the army's leadership would have driven them out, just as they did the Mensheviks and the Socialist Revolutionaries. But again, the question is not so much whether Kadet policies would have been successful, as whether they followed a course consonant with basic party goals.

Finally, perhaps one should observe that Kadets could only have become a strong force in support of coalition government and progressive social policies in the 1917-1921 period had they been a monolithic or tactically uniform political group; and this, in the main, was never their intention or design. During the revolution and even before, as we have stressed, the Central Committee in Petrograd made no effort to control local party organizations, or even to require a uniformity of outlook, saving only a general adherence to the party's program. Local organizations and individual Central Committee members pursued policies of their own choosing, articulating personal philosophies about revolution, authority, and social change which often contradicted those of close party associates. There were even significant divisions, as we have seen, over such crucial issues as whether to join the first coalition, whether to resign in July 1917, and what principles the party would support as the basis for participating in subsequent Kerensky cabinets.

Even greater disorganization developed in the course of the civil war. Central Committee groups in Moscow, Omsk, and Ekaterinodar failed to control the activities of their own members, much less direct the politics of the movement as a whole or pursue a uniform course. Declarations emerging from a number of "official" conferences were never binding, even on issues as important as the "German orientation"; and Kadets who had not participated in the meetings often did not learn of their decisions until months afterward. In such circumstances it was hard to imagine the Kadets becoming the "living fabric" of any kind, much less one in support of progressive social reform.

This looseness, it is worth reemphasizing, was not due to any lack of political consciousness among Kadets, or to any general feeling of political apathy. On the contrary, it resulted from efforts of party leaders to maintain a maximum degree of political effectiveness for Russia's relatively small liberal intelligentsia, whom the party basically represented. Almost all Kadets believed that in the absence of a massive national following, the influence of this group would wither if the Kadet party formally split apart; and division would surely have resulted from any attempt to enforce tactical uniformity. Such a "Leninist" effort would also have been morally repugnant to Russia's "party of professors," who placed great value in individual autonomy, and who consistently hoped their sheer collective prestige could overcome whatever problems tactical diversity provoked. Paradoxically, as we have seen, this diversity only allowed the Kadets' opponents to tar the party as a whole with broad, indiscriminant brushes. Yet most Kadets themselves saw no acceptable alternative.

In the end, therefore, it makes little sense to blame Kadets for not being other than what they were. They themselves paid a staggering price for their weakness; and whether the revolution and civil war could ultimately have been altered by a disciplined and conciliatory liberal party is only speculation. The wisdom of hindsight is always easy; and one must recognize that the revolution and civil war presented staggering tasks to all Russian political groups, even the most progressive.

I. ARCHIVAL MATERIALS AND MANUSCRIPTS

*Collection of the Archive of Russian and East
European History and Culture at Columbia University*

A. ARCHIVES

General A. I. Denikin Papers. Includes letters, speeches, clippings, manuscripts.

Mme. A. I. Denikin Personal Collection. Includes correspondence with various Kadet leaders in emigration.

N. M. Melnikov Collection. 44 dossiers. Manuscripts, letters, materials on the anti-Bolshevik movement in South Russia.

P. N. Miliukov Personal Archive. Letters, notes, largely on the civil war and emigration.

S. V. Panina Archive. Rich collection of Kadet party materials for 1917 through 1921, with most material on the civil war. Contains Central Committee protocols, reports of local party conferences, manuscripts, and the letters and papers of F. F. Kokoshkin, F. I. Rodichev, V. D. Nabokov, M. M. Vinaver, P. N. Miliukov, A. I. Konovalov, P. P. Iurenev, V. A. Maklakov, N. I. Astrov, and others. Includes Astrov's MS "Grazhdanskaia voina."

F. I. Rodichev Papers. Includes memoirs.

A. V. Tyrkova-Williams Archive. Papers, letters, manuscripts, and reports on the political situation in South Russia in 1919 by her husband, Harold Williams, correspondent for the London *Times*.

B. MANUSCRIPTS

Borman, A. "Vospominaniia o strashnykh godakh, 1917-1918," n.d.

Dmitrenko, P. P. "Vospominaniia," n.d. On local Kadet activities, 1905-06.

Dmitriev, N. V. "Deiatel'nost' soiuza gorodov vo vremia grazhdanskoi voiny na iuge Rossii," n.d.

Golitsyn, A. D. "Vospominaniia," n.d.

Gurevich, B. "Krasnyi sfinks. Vospominaniia," n.d. Discusses the Kadet left.

Kefeli, Ia. I. "Oktiabr'skii perevorot," 1953.

Kirilov, I. "Deiatel'nost' vserossiiskago soiuza gorodov v Sibiri vo vremia grazhdanskoi voiny," n.d.

Liubimov, D. N. "Russkaia smuta nachala deviatisotykh godov," n.d.

Melnikov, N. M. "Grazhdanskaia voina na iuge Rossii," n.d.

Mendeleev, P. P. "Vospominaniia," n.d. Recollections of conservative zemstvo figure.

Miliukov, P. N. "Dnevnik." May 1918 until April 1920.

Nikolaev, N. N. "Vospominaniia," n.d.

Poliakov, I. A., "General Kornilov," n.d.

Sannikov, A. S. "Vospominaniia, 1918-1919," Belgrade, 1926. Memoirs of a South Russian government official.

Shavel'skii, P. G. "Vospominaniia: v dobrovol'cheskoi armii," n.d.

Shlippe, F. V. "Vospominaniia," n.d. On the zemstvos.

Svechin, M. A. "Dopolnenie k vospominaniiam," n.d. On Krasnov and Skoropadskii.

Collection of the Hoover Institution
at Stanford University

A. ARCHIVES

Bylevskii Papers. Reports on the Russian army in 1917.

A. V. Cheriachukin Papers. Reports, correspondence.

Constitutional Democratic Party Archive. Letters and protocols of Kadet party groups in emigration.

Crimean Regional Government Archive. 19 files collected largely by M. M. Vinaver.

D. R. Francis Collection. Materials on 1917.

I. V. Gessen Archive. Materials on the Civil War.

G. K. Gins [Guins] Archive. Documents of anti-Bolshevik groups in Siberia.

General N. N. Golovine Papers.

E. L. Harris Papers. Papers of the U.S. Consul in Omsk.

G. Lastours Papers. Materials from the Russian Embassy in Paris, 1919-21.

The V. A. Maklakov Archive of the Russian Embassy in Paris, 1918-23. 4 boxes, largely diplomatic papers.

V. A. Maklakov Personal Archives. 2 series. 17 boxes. Correspondence, memoranda.

The S. P. Melgunov Collection on the Civil War. 11 boxes, largely on the anti-Bolshevik left.

M. V. Rodzianko Documents. 14 files.

Iu. F. Semenov Papers in the Boris Nicolaevsky Archive. Materials on the Kadet party and the National Center in South Russia, 1918-19.

N. V. Ustrialov Personal Archive. Correspondence, diary. Includes the MS "Belyi Omsk," 1919.

General Baron P. N. Wrangel Military Archives. 352 files. The principal archive of the anti-Bolshevik forces in South Russia.

Wrangel Personal Archives. 133 files, partially restricted. Contains the journals of General Denikin's Special Council, letters, and materials on the Russian Council in Constantinople, 1921.

B. MANUSCRIPTS

Anichkov, V. P. "Vospominaniia," 1936. On Siberia.

Aronson, G. "Sud'ba professional'nogo soiuza sluzhashchikh v 1917-1920," n.d.

Balk, Gen. A. "Poslednie piat' dnei tsarskago Petrograda," 1917. Diary.

Bunin, V. M. "Deviatyi val: Vospominaniia uchastnika grazhdanskoi voiny 1918-1920," n.d.

Chernavin, V. "Katastrofa 1920 g. na fronte vooruzhennykh sil iuga Rossii i otkhod protivobolshevitskikh voisk v Krym," n.d.

Chernov, V. M. " 'Chernovskaia gramota' i ufimskaia direktoriia," n.d.

Elachich, S. "Obryvki vospominanii," Peking, 1934. Memoirs of a Samara Kadet.

Khorvat, D. L. "Memoirs," n.d.

Kolobov, M. "Bor'ba s bol'shevikami na dal'nem vostoke," 192?. On the Kadets and General Khorvat.

Miliukov, P. N. "From Nicholas to Stalin," 194?. On Russian and Soviet foreign policy.

Pares, B. "Siberian Log," 1919.

Rodichev, F. I. "Vospominaniia o 1917," 1924.

Serebrennikov, I. I. "Vospominaniia, 1917-1922," n.d. On Siberia and Kolchak.

Vatasi, M. P. "The White Movement, 1917-1920; Memoirs," n.d.

Vinavera, R. G. "Vospominaniia," 1944.

Vologodskii, P. V. "Dnevnik," Omsk-Kharbin, 1918-25.

OTHER COLLECTIONS AND MANUSCRIPTS

German Foreign Office Archives. Microfilm holdings from the U.S. National Archives Series in the Center for Research Libraries, Chicago, Ill.

A. I. Petrunkevich Collection, Yale University. Includes the correspondence of I. I. Petrunkevich.

G. G. Telberg Papers. Collections of the Library of Congress. Materials on Siberia by an official in Kolchak's government.

M. M. Vinaver Papers. Yivo Institute, New York. Correspondence, documents of the Crimean Regional Government.

Obolenskii, V. A. "Vospominaniia," 1937. MS lent by Professor Nathan Smith.

II. Kadet Party Publications and Works Written by Kadets

Aikhenval'd, Iu. *Rein i sena*. Moscow, 1917. Central Committee pamphlet.

———. *Svoboda sovesti*, Moscow, 1917. Central Committee pamphlet.

Alekseev, A. A. *Avtonomiia i federatsiia*. Rostov, 1917. Rostov committee pamphlet.

Ancharova, M. *Zhenshchina i vybory v uchreditel'noe sobranie*. Moscow, 1917. Central Committee pamphlet.

Antsyferov, A. N. *Zemlia*. Moscow, 1917. Moscow committee pamphlet.

Arnol'di, G. M. *Armiia i revoliutsiia*. Petrograd, 1917. Central Committee pamphlet.

Astrov, N. I. "Iasskoe soveshchanie," *Golos Minuvshago Na Chuzhoi Storone*, No. 3, 1926, pp. 39-76.

———, et al., eds. *Pamiati pogibshikh*. Paris, 1929.

———. "Priznanie Gen. Denikinym Adm. Kolchaka," *Golos Minuvshago Na Chuzhoi Storone*, No. 1(14), 1926, pp. 201-22.

———. *Vospominaniia*. Vol. 1. Paris, 1941.

———, et al. *Zakonodatel'nye proekty i predpolozheniia partii narodnoi svobody 1905-07 gody*. St. Petersburg, 1907.

Blokh, A. Iu. *Vybory v uchreditel'noe sobranie*. Petrograd, 1917. Petrograd committee publication.

Bor'ba. Petrograd. Only 3 issues published, November 1917.

Borman, A. *Chto takoe anneksiia i kontributsiia*. Petrograd, 1917. Central Committee pamphlet.

Braikevich, M. V. "Iz revoliutsii nam chto-nibud' . . . ," *Na Chuzhoi Storone*, No. 5, 1924, pp. 217-50.

Bulatov, E. *Monarkhiia i respublika*. Moscow, 1917. Central Committee pamphlet.

Burskii, Gen. P. D. *Armiia svobodnoi Rossii*. Moscow, 1917. Central Committee pamphlet.

Chernenkov, N. N. *Agrarnaia programma partii narodnoi svobody i eia posleduiushchaia razrabotka*. St. Petersburg, 1907.

Cheshikhin, V. E. *Chego khochet partiia narodnoi svobody*. Nizhni-Novgorod, 1917. Nizhni-Novgorod committee pamphlet.

———. *Kak dumaet partiia narodnoi svobody reshit' zemel'nyi vopros*. Moscow, 1917. Central Committee pamphlet.

Dobiash-Rozhdestvenskaia, O. A. *Chto takoe Frantsiia v proshlom i nastoiashchem i za chto ona voiuet.* Petrograd, 1917. Central Committee pamphlet.

Dobrovol'skii, V. I. *Pochemu ia stoiu za partiiu narodnoi svobody.* Petrograd, 1917. Central Committee pamphlet.

Doklad po evreiskomu voprosu ts. komiteta partii K-D. n.p., 1916. Report to June 1915 meetings.

Dolgorukov, P. D. *Natsional'naia politika i partiia narodnoi svobody.* Rostov, 1919. Rostov committee pamphlet.

———. *Velikaia razrukha.* Madrid, 1964. Written 1926.

Donskaia Rech'. Rostov. Nov.-Dec. 1919 only.

Druzhinin, N. P. *Meshchane i zemel'nyi vopros.* Moscow, 1906. Moscow committee pamphlet.

Gerasimov, P. V. *Novyi stroi i prava svobodnykh grazhdan.* Moscow, 1917.

Gertsenshtein, M. Ia. *Konfiskatsiia ili vykup?* Moscow, 1917. Moscow committee pamphlet.

———. *Zemel'naia reforma v programme partii narodnoi svobody.* Moscow, 1906.

Gessen, I. V. *Iskaniia obshchestvennago ideala.* 3rd ed. Berlin, 1922. First published in 1919.

———. *V dvukh vekakh.* Berlin, 1937.

Gessen, V. M. *Russkoe uchreditel'noe sobranie.* Petrograd, 1917. Central Committee publication.

Gredeskul, N. A. *Rossiia prezhde i teper'.* Moscow, 1926.

Gronskii, P. P. "F. I. Rodichev," *Le Monde Slave*, No. 1, 1934, pp. 115-22.

———. *La Chute de la Monarchie en Russie.* Paris, 1923.

———. *Novaia volost'.* Petrograd, 1917. Petrograd committee pamphlet.

Gubskii, N. *Revoliutsiia i vneshniaia politika Rossii.* Moscow, 1917. Documents published by the Moscow committee.

Iablonovskii, S. *Kto zavoeval' svobodu.* Moscow, 1917. Central Committee pamphlet.

———. *Nadklassovaia bor'ba i zadachi momenta.* Moscow, 1917. Moscow committee pamphlet.

Il'in, I. A. *Demagogiia i provokatsiia.* Moscow, 1917. Central Committee pamphlet.

———. *O sroke sozyva uchreditel'nago sobraniia.* Moscow, 1917. Central Committee pamphlet.

———. *Partiinaia programma i maksimalizm.* Moscow, 1917. Central Committee pamphlet.

Il'in, I. A. *Poriadok ili bezporiadok?* Moscow, 1917. Central Committee pamphlet.

Iordanskii, N. M. *Vybory v gorodskiia dumy.* Moscow, 1917. Moscow committee publication.

Izgoev, A. S. *Nashi politicheskiia partii.* Petrograd, 1917. Central Committee pamphlet.

————. "Piat' let v sovetskoi Rossii," *Arkhiv Russkoi Revoliutsii,* x, 1923, pp. 5-55.

————. *Russkoe obshchestvo i revoliutsiia.* Moscow, 1910.

————. *Sotsialisty i krest'iane.* Petrograd, 1917. Central Committee pamphlet.

————. *Sotsialisty vo vtoroi russkoi revoliutsii.* Petrograd, 1917. Central Committee pamphlet.

Izvestiia Khar'kovskago Komiteta Partii Narodnoi Svobody. Kharkov. Apr.-May 1917 only.

Kak predpolagala nadelit' krest'ian zemleiu partiia narodnoi svobody v vtoroi gosudarstvennoi dume. Petrograd, 1917. Central Committee publication taken from report by A. I. Shingarev.

Kaminka, A. and V. Nabokov, eds. *Vtoraia gosudarstvennaia duma.* St. Petersburg, 1907. Kadet self-analysis.

Kareev, N. I. *Chem byla parizhskaia kommuna 1871 goda?* Petrograd, 1917. Central Committee pamphlet.

————. *Otchego okonchilas' neudachei evropeiskaia revoliutsiia 1848 goda?* Petrograd, 1917. Central Committee pamphlet.

Kaufman, A. *Chto govoriat' tsifry o zemel'nom voprose.* Petrograd, 1917. Central Committee pamphlet.

Khrushchov, A. G. *Andrei Ivanovich Shingarev.* Moscow, 1918.

Kizevetter, A. A., "Iz razmyshlenii o revoliutsii," *Sovremennye Zapiski,* No. 42, 1930, pp. 344-73.

————, ed. *Napadki na partiiu narodnoi svobody i vozrazheniia na nikh.* Moscow, 1906.

————. *Na rubezhe dvukh stoletii.* Prague, 1929.

————. *Partiia narodnoi svobody i eia ideologiia.* Moscow, 1917. Central Committee publication.

————. *Prostaia rech' o svobode i svobodnoi zhizni.* Moscow, 1917. Central Committee pamphlet.

————. *S. A. Muromtsev.* 2nd ed. Moscow, 1918.

Kliuchnikov, Iu. V. *Na velikom istoricheskom perepute.* Berlin, 1922.

————. *Revoliutsiia i voina.* Moscow, 1917. Moscow committee publication.

Kokoshkin, F. F. *Angliia, Germaniia, i sud'by Evropy.* Moscow, 1918.

————. *Avtonomiia i federatsiia.* Petrograd, 1917. Central Committee publication.

————. *Oblastnaia avtonomiia i edinstvo Rossii.* Moscow, 1906.

————. *Ob osnovaniiakh zhelatel'noi organizatsii narodnago predstav-vitel'stva v Rossii.* Moscow, 1906.

————. *Respublika.* Petrograd, 1917. Report given at the seventh party congress.

————. *Uchreditel'noe sobranie.* Petrograd, 1917. Report given at the seventh party congress.

Konstitutsionno-Demokraticheskaia Partiia. *Informatsionnye doklady.* Paris, 1921. On current political situation.

————. *Ocherednyia zadachi moskovskoi gorodskoi dumy.* Moscow, 1917. Moscow committee publication.

————. *Otchet tsentral'nago komiteta konstitutsionno-demokratiches-koi partii.* St. Petersburg, 1907. Covers the 1905-07 period.

————. *Postanovleniia II-go s"ezda 5-11 ianvaria 1906 g. i programma.* St. Petersburg, 1906.

————. *Programma partii narodnoi svobody.* Petrograd, 1917.

————. *S"ezd 12-18 oktiabria 1905 g.* St. Petersburg, 1905.

————. *Stenograficheskii protokol zasedanii VII s"ezda partii narodnoi svobody.* Petrograd, 1917.

————. *Tret'ia gosudarstvennaia duma. Materialy dlia otsenki eia deiatel'nosti.* St. Petersburg, 1912.

————. *III gosudarstvennaia duma: Otchet fraktsii narodnoi svobody.* 5 vols. St. Petersburg, 1908-12.

————. *Vremennyi pravitel' Khorvat' i ego delovoi kabinet.* N.p., 1918. Broadside of the Siberian Regional Kadet committee.

Kornilov, A. A. *Parlamentskii blok.* Moscow, 1915.

————. *Partiia narodnoi svobody.* Petrograd, 1917. Central Committee pamphlet.

Korovin, E. *Vneshniaia politika obnovlennoi Rossii.* Moscow, 1917. Moscow committee pamphlet.

Kotliarevskii, S. A. *Voina i demokratiia.* Moscow, 1917. Pamphlet of the Moscow War Industries Committee.

Krest'ianam o konstitutsionno-demokraticheskoi partii. Moscow, 1906.

Krol', L. A. *Za tri goda.* Vladivostok, 1922.

Kursanov, A. *Kak russkii narod upravlialsia v stranu.* Moscow, 1906. Central Committee pamphlet.

Levitskii, V. M. *Chto kazhdyi dolzhen znat' ob Ukraine.* Paris, 1939. Brief memoir by Kadet leader in the Ukraine.

Losskii, N. O. *Chego khochet partiia narodnoi svobody?* Petrograd, 1917. Central Committee pamphlet.

Maklakov, V. A. "Iz proshlago," *Sovremennye Zapiski,* No. 38, 1929, pp. 276-314; No. 40, 1929, pp. 291-334; No. 41, 1930, pp. 232-75; No. 42, 1930, pp. 168-91; No. 43, 1930, pp. 288-310; No. 44, 1930, pp. 423-

47; No. 46, 1931, pp. 263-86; No. 47, 1931, pp. 322-51; No. 48, 1932, pp. 346-77; No. 50, 1932, pp. 271-87; No. 51, 1933, pp. 228-50; No. 53, 1933, pp. 251-77; No. 54, 1934, pp. 317-40; No. 56, 1934, pp. 238-56; No. 58, 1935, pp. 258-73; No. 60, 1936, pp. 263-75.

―――. "On the Fall of Tsardom," *Slavonic and East European Review*, XVIII, 1939, pp. 73-92.

―――. *The First State Duma*. Trans. M. Belkin. Bloomington, Ind., 1964.

―――. *Vlast' i obshchestvennost' na zakate staroi Rossii*. Paris, 1938.

―――. *Vtoraia gosudarstvennaia duma*. Paris, 1949.

Malinovskii, I. A. *F. F. Kokoshkin*. Rostov, 1918. Rostov committee pamphlet.

―――. *Monarkhiia i respublika*. Rostov, 1917. Rostov committee pamphlet.

Mandel'shtam, M. *1905 god v politicheskikh protsessakh*. Moscow, 1931.

Mansyrev, S. P. "Moi vospominaniia o gosudarstvennoi dume," *Istorik i Sovremennik* II, 1922, pp. 5-45; III, 1922, pp. 3-44.

Manuilov, A. A. *Sotsializatsiia zemli*. Moscow, 1917. Central Committee pamphlet.

Miliukov, P. N. *Balkanskii krizis i politika A. P. Izvol'skago*. St. Petersburg, 1910.

―――. *Bolshevism. An International Danger*. London, 1920.

―――. *The Case for Bessarabia*. London, 1919.

―――. "The Case of the Second Duma," *Contemporary Review*, No. 92, 1907, pp. 457-67.

―――. *Constitutional Government for Russia*. New York, 1908.

―――. *God bor'by*. St. Petersburg, 1907.

―――. *Istoriia vtoroi russkoi revoliutsii*. 3 pts. Sofia, 1921-24.

―――. "Konstantinopol' i prolivy," *Vestnik Evropy*, No. 1, 1917, pp. 354-81; No. 2, 1917, pp. 227-59; No. 4-6, 1917, pp. 525-47.

―――. "Le Dixième Anniversaire de la Révolution Russe," *Le Monde Slave*, No. 11-12, 1927, pp. 188-246.

―――. "Liberalizm, radikalizm, i revoliutsiia," *Sovremennye Zapiski*, No. 47, 1935, pp. 285-315.

―――, ed. *M. M. Vinaver i russkaia obshchestvennost' nachala XX v.* Paris, 1937.

―――. *Pochemu i zachem my voiuem?* Petrograd, 1917.

―――. *Rossiia na perelome*. 2 vols. Paris, 1927.

―――. *Rossiia v plenu u tsimmerval'da*. Petrograd, 1917.

―――. *Russia and Its Crisis*. Chicago, 1905.

―――. *Russia Today and Tomorrow*. New York, 1922.

———. "Sud' nad kadetskom 'liberalizmom,'" *Sovremennye Zapiski*, No. 41, 1930, pp. 347-71. Discussion of Maklakov's views on liberalism and revolution.

———. *Taktika fraktsii narodnoi svobody vo vremia voiny*. Petrograd, 1916.

———. "The Influence of English Political Thought in Russia," *Slavonic Review*, XIV, 1926, pp. 258-70.

———. "The Representative System in Russia," in J. Duff, ed. *Russian Realities and Problems*. Cambridge, 1917, pp. 25-46.

———. "The War and Balkan Politics," in J. Duff, ed. *Russian Realities and Problems*. Cambridge, 1917, pp. 1-24.

———. *Tret'ia gosudarstvennaia duma*. St. Petersburg, 1909. Brief report.

———. *Tri platformy respublikansko-demokraticheskikh ob'edinenii*. Paris, 1925.

———. *Tri popytki*. Paris, 1921.

———. *Vooruzhenyi mir i ogranichenie vooruzhenii*. St. Petersburg, 1911.

———. *Vospominaniia, 1859-1917*. 2 vols. New York, 1955. English translation available.

———. *Vtoraia duma*. St. Petersburg, 1908.

Mukhanov, A. A. and V. D. Nabokov, eds. *Pervaia gosudarstvennaia duma*. 2 vols. St. Petersburg, 1907. Essays.

N. N. *Kak sovershilsia velikii perevorot*. Moscow, 1917. Moscow committee pamphlet.

Nabokov, V. D. *Rechi*. St. Petersburg, 1907. From the First Duma.

———. "Vremennoe pravitel'stvo," *Arkhiv Russkoi Revoliutsii*, I, 1922, pp. 9-96. Recent English translation available.

Nash Vek. Petrograd. Successor to *Rech'*. Published Nov. 1917 through Aug. 1918.

Narodnaia Svoboda. Baku. July-Nov. 1917 available only.

Narodnaia Svoboda. Cheliabinsk. Nov. 1917 available only.

Narodnaia Svoboda. Kharkov. July-Aug. 1917 available only.

Narodnaia Svoboda. Nizhni-Novgorod. Apr.-Nov. 1917.

Narodnaia Svoboda. Tiflis. June-Nov. 1917.

Nol'de, B. E. *L'Ancien Régime et la Révolution Russe*. Paris, 1928. Thoughtful.

———. *Dalekoe i blizkoe*. Paris, 1930. Essays.

———. *Natsional'nyi vopros v Rossii*. Petrograd, 1917. Central Committee report to the ninth party congress.

———. "V. D. Nabokov v 1917 g.," *Arkhiv Russkoi Revoliutsii*, VII, 1922, pp. 5-13.

Novgorodskaia Zhizn'. Novgorod. Apr.-Nov. 1917.

Novgorodtsev, P. N. *Idealy partii narodnoi svobody i sotsializm*. Moscow, 1917. Central Committee pamphlet.

Obolenskii, V. A. *Krym pri Vrangele*. Moscow, 1927.

———. "Krym v 1917-20 gg.," *Na Chuzhoi Storone*, No. 5, 1924, pp. 5-40; No. 6, 1924, pp. 53-72; No. 7, 1924, pp. 81-110; No. 8, 1924, pp. 5-54; No. 9, 1925, pp. 5-56.

Pasmanik, D. S. *Revoliutsionnye gody v Krymu*. Paris, 1926. Memoir.

Penzenskaia Rech'. Penza. June-Nov. 1917 available only.

Pepeliaev, V. N. "Razval kolchakovshchiny," *Krasnyi Arkhiv*, No. 31, 1928, pp. 51-80. From his diary.

Petrunkevich, I. I. "Iz zapisok obshchestvennago deiatelia," *Arkhiv Russkoi Revoliutsiia*, xxi, 1934, entire.

Poltavskii Den'. Poltava. 1917.

Posledniia Novosti. Paris. 1920-1940. Edited by Miliukov after Mar. 1, 1921.

———. *Iubileinyi Sbornik. 1920-1930*. Paris, n.d. Essays.

Protopopov, D. D. *Chto sdielala pervaia gosudarstvennaia duma*. Moscow, 1906. Central Committee publication.

———, ed. *Ocherk deiatel'nosti S-Peterburgskoi gruppy partii narodnoi svobody*. St. Petersburg, 1908.

Rech'. Petrograd. 1917. Succeeded briefly by *Nasha Rech'*, *Svobodnaia Rech'*, *Novaia Rech'*, and then *Nash Vek*. Not an "official" party organ, but generally taken as such.

Rodichev, F. I. *Bol'sheviki i evrei*. Lausanne, n.d. Vigorous attack on Russian anti-Semites.

———. "Ivan Petrunkevich," *Slavonic Review*, vii, 1929, pp. 316-26.

———. "Iz vospominanii," *Sovremennye Zapiski*, No. 43, 1933, pp. 285-96.

———. "The Liberal Movement in Russia," *Slavonic Review*, ii, 1923, pp. 1-14, 249-62.

Rostovskaia Rech'. Rostov. 1917.

Rozental', N. N. *Istoricheskii ocherk partii narodnoi svobody*. Petrograd, 1917.

Rul'. Berlin. 1920-31. Edited by Nabokov, Nolde, and others.

Ryss, P. I. *Russkii opyt*. Paris, 1921.

Serafimov, B. S. *Nemtsy v Konstantinopole*. Petrograd, 1917. Central Committee pamphlet.

Shakhovskoi, D. I. "Soiuz osvobozhdeniia," *Zarnitsy*, No. 2, 1909, pp. 81-171.

Shershenevich, G. F. *Programma partii narodnoi svobody*. Moscow, 1906. Popular explication of Kadet program.

Shingarev, A. I. *Finansovoe polozhenie Rossii.* Petrograd, 1917. Central Committee publication.

———. *Kak eto bylo.* Moscow, 1918. Diary for Nov.-Jan. 1917-18.

———. *Kak predpolagala nadelit' krest'iane zemlei partiia narodnoi svobody v vtoroi dume.* St. Petersburg, 1907.

Shtein, V. M. *Nashi ekonomicheskiia i finansovyia zadachi.* Petrograd, 1917. Central Committee pamphlet.

Shtern, S. *Desiatiletie K-D partii v Odesse.* Odessa, 1915.

———. *V ogne grazhdanskoi voiny.* Paris, 1922.

Sibirskaia Rech'. Omsk. May-Dec. 1917; Dec. 1918-Nov. 1919.

Smirnov, S. et al. *P. N. Miliukov.* Paris, 1929. Includes bibliography of Miliukov's publications.

Sokolov, K. N. "Orientatsiia," *Russkie Sborniki,* II, 1921, pp. 3-18.

———. *Pravlenie generala Denikina.* Sofia, 1921. Important "memoir-history."

———. *Uchreditel'noe sobranie.* Petrograd, 1917. Petrograd committee publication.

Soloveichik, A. S. *Bor'ba za vozrozhdenie Rossii na vostoke.* Rostov, 1919. Sketch by a Samara Kadet.

Svobodnaia Rech'. Ekaterinodar. Scattered nos. 1919.

Svobodnyi Narod. Petrograd. June-Oct. 1917. "Official" Kadet newspaper.

Trubetskoi, E. N. *Anarkhiia i kontr-revoliutsiia.* Moscow. 1917. Pamphlet by right Kadet.

———. "Iz putevykh zametok bezhentsa," *Arkhiv Russkoi Revoliutsii,* XVIII, 1926, pp. 137-207.

———. *Natsional'nyi vopros, Konstantinopol' i sviataia sofiia.* Moscow, 1915.

———. *Velikaia revoliutsiia i krizis patriotizma.* Rostov, 1919. Osvag pamphlet.

———. *Zverinoe tsarstvo i griadushchee vozrozhdenie Rossii.* Rostov, 1919. Osvag pamphlet.

Tyrkova-Williams, A. *From Liberty to Brest-Litovsk.* London, 1919. Contains some errors of fact.

———. "The Cadet Party," *The Russian Review,* XII, 1952, 173-86.

Ufimskaia Zhizn'. Ufa. July-Oct. 1917.

Ulanov, V. Ia. *Vsem, kto protiv voiny.* Moscow, 1917. Moscow committee pamphlet.

Ustrialov, N. V. *Pod znakom revoliutsii.* 2nd ed., Kharbin, 1927. Essays.

———. *V bor'be za Rossiiu.* Kharbin, 1920. Essays.

[Vernadskii, G. V.] *Pavel Nikolaevich Miliukov.* Petrograd, 1917. Central Committee pamphlet.

Vestnik Narodnoi Svobody. St. Petersburg. 1906-08. Official organ of the Central Committee.

Vestnik Partii Narodnoi Svobody. Petrograd. May 1917-Aug. 1918. Official organ of the Central Committee.

Vilenskii, I. P. *O zemel'nom voprose.* Ufa, 1917. Ufa committee pamphlet.

Vinaver, M. M. *Istoriia vyborgskago vozzvaniia.* Petrograd, 1917.

———. *Konflikty v pervoi dume.* St. Petersburg, 1907.

———. *Nashe pravitel'stvo.* Paris, 1928. On the Crimean government.

———. *Nedavnee.* 2nd ed., Paris, 1926. Biographical sketches and memoirs.

———. *Rechi.* St. Petersburg, 1907. From the First Duma.

Vinavera, R. G. "Vozhdi kadetskoi partii," *Novyi Zhurnal,* No. 10, 1945, pp. 250-62.

Voennoi komissii partiia narodnoi svobody. Instruktsiia po organizatsii partiinykh grupp v voiskovykh chastiakh armii i flota. Petrograd, 1917. Central Committee circular.

III. DOCUMENTARY MATERIALS, MEMOIRS, PERSONAL HISTORIES, AND OTHER IMPORTANT NEWSPAPERS

Adamov, E. A., ed. *Constantinople et les détroits.* Trans. S. Volsky et al., 2 vols., Paris, 1930-32.

Akhun, M. I. and V. A. Petrov, eds. *1917 god v Petrograde.* Leningrad, 1933. Chronicle and bibliography.

———. *1917 god v Moskve.* Moscow, 1934. Chronicle and bibliography.

Alekseev, M. V. "Iz dnevnika generala M. V. Alekseeva," *Russkii Istoricheskii Arkhiv.* Sbor. 1, Prague, 1929, pp. 11-56.

Alekseev, N. N. "Iz vospominanii," *Arkhiv Russkoi Revoliutsii,* XVII, 1926, pp. 170-255.

Alekseev, S., ed. *Revoliutsiia na Ukraine po memuaram belykh.* Moscow, 1930.

Andriievskii, V. *Z minulogo (1917 r. na Poltavshchini).* Berlin, 1921.

An—skii, S. "Posle perevorota 25 oktiabria 1917 g.," *Arkhiv Russkoi Revolutsii,* VIII, 1923, pp. 43-55. On the Petrograd City Duma.

Antonov-Saratovskii, V. P. *Pod stiagom proletarskoi bor'by.* Moscow, 1925.

Argunov, A. A. *Mezhdu dvumia bol'shevizmami.* Paris, 1919. Useful on the Union of Regeneration.

———. "Omskie dni v 1918 godu," *Sibirskii Arkhiv,* No. 5, 1935, pp. 191-207.

Avdeev, N. et al. *Revoliutsiia 1917 goda. Khronika sobytii.* 6 vols. Moscow-Leningrad, 1923-30.

Birzhevyia Vedomosti. Petrograd. Liberal daily.

Boldyrev, V. "Vospominaniia byvshego glavkoverkha ufimskoi direktorii," *Sibirskie Ogni,* Nos. 5-6, 1923, pp. 105-26.

———. *Direktoriia, Kolchak, interventy.* Novonikolaevsk, 1925. Largely from his diary.

Bor'ba za Rossiiu. Paris. 1926-31. Organ of the Russian National Committee. Frequent Kadet contributions.

Browder, R. P., and A. F. Kerensky, eds. *The Russian Provisional Government, 1917.* 3 vols. Stanford, 1961. Documents and materials.

Brusilov, A. *Moi vospominaniia.* Moscow-Leningrad, 1929.

Buchanan, G. *My Mission to Russia.* London, 1923.

Budberg, A. P. *Dnevnik belogvardeitsa.* Moscow, 1929. Important source on Siberia by the Chief of Kolchak's General Staff. Published also in *Arkhiv Russkoi Revoliutsii.*

Bukhbinder, N. "Na fronte v predoktiabr'skie dni," *Krasnaia Letopis',* No. 6, 1923, pp. 9-63.

Bunyan, J. *Intervention, Civil War, and Communism in Russia.* Baltimore, 1936. Documents and materials, Apr.-Dec. 1918.

———, and H. H. Fisher. *The Bolshevik Revolution, 1917-1918.* Stanford, 1934. Documents and materials.

Chaadaeva, O. N. "Soiuz zemel'nykh sobstvennikov v 1917 g.," *Krasnyi Arkhiv,* No. 21, 1927, pp. 97-120.

———, ed. *Soldatskie pis'ma 1917 goda.* Moscow-Leningrad, 1927.

Cherevanin, N. "Dvizhenie intelligentsii," *Obshchestvennoe dvizhenie v Rossii v nachale XX-go veka,* ed. L. Martov et al. 4 vols., 1, St. Petersburg, 1909, pp. 259-90.

Chernov, V. M. *Zemel'nyi vopros.* Petrograd, 1917.

———. *The Great Russian Revolution.* Trans. P. Mosely. New Haven, 1936.

Chirikov, E. *Besedy s rabochim chelovekom.* Rostov, 1919. Osvag pamphlet.

Chugaev, D. A., et al., eds. *Revoliutsionnoe dvizhenie v Rossii v avguste 1917. Razgrom kornilovskogo miatezha.* Moscow, 1959. Documents and materials.

———. *Revoliutsionnoe dvizhenie v Rossii nakanune oktiabr'skogo vooruzhennogo vosstaniia.* Moscow, 1962. Documents and materials.

———. *Revoliutsionnoe dvizhenie v Rossii v mae-iiune 1917. Iiun'skaia demonstratsiia.* Moscow, 1959. Documents and materials.

———. *Revoliutsionnoe dvizhenie v Rossii v sentiabre 1917. Obshchenatsional'nyi krizis.* Moscow, 1961. Documents and materials.

———. *Triumfal'noe shestvie sovetskoi vlasti.* 2 vols. Moscow, 1963. Documents and materials.

Dal'istpart, R.K.P. *Sborniki materialov po revoliutsionnomu dvizheniiu na Dalnem Vostoke.* 3 vols. Chita-Vladivostok, 1923-25.

Dan, F. "K istorii poslednikh dnei vremennogo pravitel'stva," *Letopis' Revoliutsii,* No. 1, 1923, pp. 163-75.

Delo Naroda. Petrograd. 1917. SR daily.

Delo o vyborgskom vozzvanii. Otchet o zasedanii osobago prisutstviia S-Peterburgskoi sudebnoi palaty. 12-18 dek. 1907. St. Petersburg, 1908.

Dem'ianov, A. S. "Moia sluzhba pri vremennom pravitel'stve," *Arkhiv Russkoi Revoliutsii,* iv, 1922, pp. 55-129.

———. "Zapiski o podpol'nom vremennom pravitel'stve," *Arkhiv Russkoi Revoliutsii,* vii, 1922, pp. 34-52.

Demkin, D. I. "Petrogradskaia gorodskaia duma v pervye dni smuty," *Russkaia Letopis',* No. 6, 1924, pp. 141-58. Conservative memoir.

Den'. Petrograd, 1917. Socialist daily.

Denikin, A. I. *Ocherki russkoi smuty.* 5 vols. Paris-Berlin, 1921-25. Invaluable. Partially translated.

Die deutsche Okkupation der Ukraine—Geheimdokumente. Strassbourg, 1937.

Dimanshtein, Ia. B. *Torgovo-promyshlennyi klass i uchreditel'noe sobranie.* Kharkov, 1917.

Dimanshtein, S. M., ed. *Revoliutsiia i natsional'nyi vopros.* Moscow, 1930. Documents and materials.

Dobrynin, V. *Bor'ba s bol'shevizmom na iuge Rossii.* Prague, 1921. A colonel's account.

Donskaia Volna. Rostov. Weekly. 1918-19. Scattered nos. available.

Doroshenko, D. "Getmanstvo 1918 g. na Ukraine," *Golos Minuvshago na Chuzhoi Storone,* No. 5, 1927, pp. 133-64.

———. *Istoriia Ukrainy, 1917-1923.* 2 vols. Uzhgorod, 1930-32.

———. *Moi spomyny pro nedavne mynule.* 4 pts. Lvov, 1923-24. Parts 3 and 4 are on the Hetmanate and the Directorate. A second edition (Munich, 1969) has recently appeared.

Drezen, A., ed. *Burzhuaziia i pomeshchiki v 1917 godu.* Moscow-Leningrad, 1932. Transcripts of the State Duma meetings.

Dubreuil, C. *Deux Années en Ukraine, 1917-19.* Paris, 1919. Sympathetic to Petliura.

Edinstvo. Petrograd, 1917. Plekhanovite daily.

Ekonomicheskoe polozhenie Rossii nakanune velikoi oktiabr'skoi sotsialisticheskoi revoliutsii. 3 pts., Moscow-Leningrad, 1957. Documents.

Erde, D. *Gody buri i natiska.* Kharkov, 1923. On 1917.

"Fevral'skaia revoliutsiia i okhrannoe otdelenie," *Byloe,* No. 1, 1918, pp. 158-76. Documents.

"Fevral'skaia revoliutsiia v Petrograde," *Krasnyi Arkhiv*, Nos. 41-42, 1930, pp. 62-102. Reports to the military commission of the State Duma.

Filimonov, A. P. "Kubantsy (1917-1918 gg.)," *Beloe Delo*, II, 1927, pp. 62-107.

Fleer, M. G., ed. "Vremennoe pravitel'stvo posle oktiabria," *Krasnyi Arkhiv*, No. 6, 1924, pp. 195-221.

Galuzo, P., ed. "Iz istorii natsional'noi politiki vremennogo pravitel'-stva," *Krasnyi Arkhiv*, No. 30, 1928, pp. 46-79.

Gaponenko, L. S., et al., eds. *Revoliutsionnoe dvizhenie v Rossii posle sverzheniia samoderzhaviia*. Moscow, 1957. Documents.

――――. *Revoliutsionnoe dvizhenie v Rossii v aprele 1917. Aprel'skii krizis*. Moscow, 1958. Documents.

――――. *Revoliutsionnoe dvizhenie v russkoi armii*. Moscow, 1968. Documents.

Gins, G. K. *Sibir', soiuzniki i Kolchak*. 2 vols. Peking, 1921.

Gol'denveizer, A. A. "Iz kievskikh vospominanii," *Arkhiv Russkoi Revoliutsii*, VI, 1922, pp. 161-303.

Golder, F. A., ed. *Documents of Russian History*. New York, 1927.

Golikov, G. N., et al., eds. *Oktiabr'skoe vooruzhennoe vosstanie v Petrograde*. Moscow, 1957. Documents and materials.

Golos Rossii. Paris-Berlin. 1921-22. Sometime organ of Paris "new tacticians."

Golovin, N. N. *Rossiiskaia kontr-revoliutsiia v 1917-18 gg.* 5 vols. Tallin, 1937. Includes documents.

Gosudarstvennoe soveshchanie. Moscow, 1930. Steno. reports of the August 1917 State Conference.

Grachev, E., ed. *Kazanskii oktiabr'. Materialy i dokumenty*. Kazan, 1926.

Grave, B. B., ed. *Burzhuaziia nakanune fevral'skoi revoliutsii*. Moscow-Leningrad, 1927. Police documents and materials.

――――. *K istorii klassovoi bor'by v Rossii*. Moscow-Leningrad, 1926. Police materials from the 1914-17 period.

――――. "Kadety v 1905-1906 gg.," *Krasnyi Arkhiv*, No. 46, 1931, pp. 38-68; Nos. 47-48, 1931, pp. 111-39. Central Committee protocols and materials.

Grazhdanskaia voina na Volge v 1918 g. Prague, 1930. Essays.

Grenard, F. *La Révolution russe*. Paris, 1933.

Grimm, E. D. *Kak bol'sheviki zakhvatili vlast' na Rusi*. Rostov, 1919. Osvag pamphlet.

Groener, W. *Lebenserinnerungen*. Göttingen, 1957.

Guchkov, A. I. "Iz vospominanii," *Posledniia Novosti*, Aug. 9, 12, 16, 19, 23, 26, and 30, Sept. 2, 6, 9, 13, 16, 20, 23, 27, and 30, 1936.

Gukovskii, A. I., ed. "Agrarnaia politika Vrangelia," *Krasnyi Arkhiv*, No. 26, 1928, pp. 51-96. Documents.

———. "K istorii iasskogo soveshchaniia," *Krasnyi Arkhiv*, No. 18, 1926, pp. 105-18. Documents.

———. "Krymskoe kraevoe pravitel'stvo v 1918-1919," *Krasnyi Arkhiv*, No. 22, 1927, pp. 92-152. Documents.

———. "Krym v 1918-1919 gg.," *Krasnyi Arkhiv*, No. 28, 1928, pp. 142-81; No. 29, 1928, pp. 55-85. Documents.

Gurevich, Ia. Ia. "Delo grafini S. V. Paninoi v revoliutsionnom tribunale," *Russkoe Bogatstvo*, Nos. 11-12, 1917, pp. 283-98.

Gurevich, V. "Real'naia politika v revoliutsii (Kadetskaia taktika)," *Volia Rossii*, No. 12, 1923, pp. 18-34; No. 14, 1923, pp. 17-31.

———. "Vserossiiskii krest'ianskii s''ezd i pervaia koalitsiia," *Letopis' Revoliutsii*, No. 1, 1923, pp. 176-96.

Gurko, V. I. "Iz Petrograda cherez Moskvu, Parizh, i London, v Odessu," *Arkhiv Russkoi Revoliutsii*, xv, 1924, pp. 5-84.

Iakovlev, A. Ia., ed. *1917 god v derevne*. Moscow-Leningrad, 1929.

Iakushev, I. A. *G. N. Potanin*. Prague, 1927. Biography by a co-regionalist.

Ignat'ev, V. I. *Nekotorye fakty i itogi chetyrekh let grazhdanskoi voiny (1917-1921). Lichnye vospominaniia*. Moscow, 1922.

Il'in, I. A. "Gosudarstvennyi smysl beloi armii," *Russkaia Mysl'*, Nos. 9-12, 1923-24, pp. 230-45.

Il'in, I. S. "Omsk. direktoriia. Kolchak," *Novyi Zhurnal*, No. 72, 1963, pp. 198-217; No. 73, 1963, pp. 216-43.

Ivanov-Razumnik, V. *God revoliutsii*. Petrograd, 1918. Thoughtful critique of the Kadets.

Iz glubiny. Moscow-Petrograd, 1918. Essays.

Izvestiia. Organ of the Petrograd Soviet.

Izvestiia glavnago zemel'nago komiteta. Petrograd, 1917. Journal of the Provisional Government Land Committee.

Izvestiia osobago soveshchaniia dlia izgotovleniia proekta polozheniia o vyborakh v uchreditel'noe sobranie. Petrograd, 1917. Daily, May through July 1917.

Izvestiia otdela po delam mestnago upravleniia. Petrograd, 1917. Journal of the Ministry of Internal Affairs in the Provisional Government. Sept.-Oct. 1917.

Izvolskii, A. P. *Recollections of a Foreign Minister*. Trans. C. Seeger. New York, 1921.

Kak sovershilas' velikaia russkaia revoliutsiia. Petrograd, 1917. Detailed account of the first week, focusing on the Kadets.

Kakurin, N. E., comp. *Razlozhenie armii v 1917 godu*. Moscow-Leningrad, 1925. Documents and materials.

Kariakin, V. N. "Moskovskaia okhranka i A. I. Shingarev," *Golos Minuvshago*, Nos. 1-3, 1918, pp. 309-17.

Kazanovich, B. "Poezdka iz dobrovol'cheskoi armii v 'krasnuiu Moskvu,' " *Arkhiv Russkoi Revoliutsii*, VII, 1922, pp. 184-203.

Kel'son, Z. "Padenie vremennogo pravitel'stva. Vospominaniia," *Byloe*, No. 6 (34), 1925, pp. 192-205.

Kerenskii, A. "Gatchina," *Sovremennye Zapiski*, No. 10, 1922, pp. 147-81.

———. *The Catastrophe*. New York, 1927.

———. *The Crucifixion of Liberty*. New York, 1934.

———. "Politika vremennago pravitel'stva," *Sovremennye Zapiski*, No. 50, 1932, pp. 403-24.

———. *Prelude to Bolshevism*. New York, 1919.

———. *Russia and History's Turning Point*. New York, 1965.

Khristiuk, P. *Zamitky i materialy do istorii ukrainskoi revoliutsii 1917-20*. 4 vols. Vienna, 1921-22. Notes and materials.

Kievlianin. Kiev, 1917-19. V. V. Shulgin, ed.

Kievskaia Mysl'. Kiev, 1917-18.

Kim, M. P. et al., eds. "Iz arkhiva organizatorov grazhdanskoi voiny i interventsii v sovetskoi Rossii," *Istoricheskii Arkhiv*, No. 6, 1961, pp. 58-117.

Kokovtsev, V. *Out of My Past*. Stanford, 1935.

Kolosov, E. E. *Sibir' pri Kolchake*. Petrograd, 1923. Documents and notes.

Konstantinov, M. M., ed. *Poslednie dni kolchakovshchiny*. Moscow, 1926. Documents.

Kotliarevskii, S. A. "Natsional'nyi tsentr v Moskve v 1918," *Na Chuzhoi Storone*, No. 8, 1924, pp. 123-42.

Krasnov, V. M. "Iz vospominanii o 1917-20 gg.," *Arkhiv Russkoi Revoliutsii*, VIII, 1923, pp. 110-65; XI, 1923, pp. 106-68.

Krest'ianskoe dvizhenie v 1917 godu. Moscow-Leningrad, 1927. Documents and materials.

Krishevskii, N. "V Krymu (1916-1918 gg.)," *Arkhiv Russkoi Revoliutsii*, XIII, 1924, pp. 71-124.

Krol', M. A. "Sibirskoe pravitel'stvo i avgustovskaia sessiia sibirskoi oblastnoi dumy," *Vol'naia Sibir'*, No. 4, 1928, pp. 69-82.

Kuz'min-Karavaev, V. D. et al. *Obrazovanie severo-zapadnago pravitel'stva*. Helsinki, 1919.

Ladokh, G. *Ocherki grazhdanskoi bor'by na Kubani*. Krasnodar, 1923.

Lampe, A. A., ed. *Beloe Delo*. 7 vols. Berlin, 1926-33. Memoirs, documents.

Lapin, N., ed. "Kadety v dni galitsiiskogo razgroma," *Krasnyi Arkhiv*, No. 59, 1933, pp. 110-44.

492—Bibliography

―――――. "Progressivnyi blok v 1915-1917 gg.," *Krasnyi Arkhiv*, Nos. 50-51, 1932, pp. 117-60; No. 52, 1932, pp. 143-96; No. 56, 1933, pp. 80-135.

Leikhtenbergskii, G. "Kak nachalas' 'iuzhnaia armiia,'" *Arkhiv Russkii Revoliutsii*, VIII, 1923, pp. 166-82.

Levin, K., and A. Blum. *Kadety*, St. Petersburg, 1906.

Liga Agrarnykh Reform. *Organy zemel'noi reformy: Zemel'nye komitety i liga agrarnykh reform*. Moscow, 1917. Pamphlet of the League.

Lisovoi, Ia. M., ed. *Belyi Arkhiv*. 3 vols. Paris, 1926-28.

Lomonossoff, G. V. *Memoirs of the Russian Revolution*. New York, 1918.

Lukomskii, A. S. *Vospominaniia*. 2 vols. Berlin, 1922. Abridged translation available.

Ludendorff, Gen. E. von. *My War Memories, 1914-1918*. 2 vols. 3rd ed. London, 1919.

Maiskii, I. M. *Demokraticheskaia kontr-revoliutsiia*. Moscow-Leningrad, 1923, Memoir of the SRs in Siberia.

Maksakov, V. V. and A. Turunov, eds. *Khronika grazhdanskoi voiny v Sibiri 1917-1918*. Moscow-Leningrad, 1926. Contains excellent bibliography.

―――――. "Vremennoe pravitel'stvo avtonomnoi Sibiri," *Krasnyi Arkhiv*, No. 29, 1928, pp. 86-138.

Maliantovich, P. N. *Revoliutsiia i pravosudie*. Moscow, 1918. Memoir.

Maliarevskii, A. "Na pereekzamenovke—P. P. Skoropadskii i ego vremia," *Arkhiv Grazhdanskoi Voiny*, II, Berlin, 192?

Maliutin, B., ed. "Nakanune oktiabr'skago perevorota," *Byloe*, No. 6, 1918, pp. 4-41.

Manilov, V., ed. *1917 god na kievshchine: Khronika sobytii*. Kiev, 1928.

―――――. *Pid hnitom nimetskoho imperializmu*. Kiev, 1927. Documents.

Margolin, A. *Ukraina i politika antanty*. Berlin, 1921.

Margulies, M. S. *God interventsii*. 3 vols. Berlin, 1923.

―――――. "Iasskaia delegatsiia," *Letopis' Revoliutsii*, I, 1923, pp. 197-214.

Margulies, V. *Ognennye gody*. Berlin, 1923. Odessa in the civil war.

Martynov, A. "Konstitutsionno-demokraticheskaia partiia," *Obshchestvennoe dvizhenie v Rossii v nachale XX-go veka*, ed. L. Martov et al. 4 vols. III, St. Petersburg, 1914, pp. 1-88.

Martynov, M., ed. "Agrarnoe dvizhenie v 1917 g." *Krasnyi Arkhiv*, No. 14, 1926, pp. 182-226.

Mekler, N. *V Denikinskom pod'pole*. Moscow, 1932.

Miakotin, V. "Iz nedalekago proshlago," *Na Chuzhoi Storone*, No. 2, 1923, pp. 178-99; No. 3, 1923, pp. 179-93; No. 5, 1924, pp. 251-68; No. 6, 1924, pp. 73-100; No. 9, 1925, pp. 279-302; No. 11, 1925, pp.

205-36; No. 13, 1925, pp. 193-227. Detailed study on Union of Regeneration and the Popular Socialists.

Miloradovich, K. *Chernaia kritika (o k-dakh i o bol'shevikakh)*. Petrograd, 1918. A right-wing attack.

Ministerstvo vnutrennikh del. *Sbornik tsirkuliarov*. Petrograd, 1917. Mar.-June 1917. Publication of the Provisional Government.

Mints, I. I. and E. N. Gorodetskii, eds. *Dokumenty o razgrome germanskikh okkupantov na Ukraine v 1918 godu*. Moscow, 1942.

Mogilianskii, N. M. "Tragediia Ukrainy," *Arkhiv Russkoi Revoliutsii*, XI, 1925, pp. 74-105.

Morokhovets, E. *Agrarnye programmy rossiiskikh politicheskikh partii v 1917 godu*. Leningrad, 1929.

Mozzhukhin, I. *Agrarnyi vopros (v tsifrakh i faktakh deistvitel'nosti)*. Moscow, 1917. Publication of the League of Agrarian Reform.

Mstislavskii, S. *Piat' dnei*. Berlin, 1922. SR memoir.

N. "Poslednie dni Kolchakovshchiny," *Sibirskie Ogni*, II, 1922, pp. 76-95.

Nabokov, K. D. *Ordeal of a Diplomat*. London, 1921.

"Nakanune oktiabr'skago perevorota," *Byloe*, No. 12, 1918, pp. 4-41. *Otchety* from secret meetings of the pre-parliament.

Narodnoe Slovo. Petrograd, 1917. Daily Organ of the Popular Socialist party.

"'Natsional'nyi tsentr' v Moskve v 1918," *Na Chuzhoi Storone*, No. 8, 1924, pp. 123-42.

Naumenko, V. *Iz nedavnago proshlago Kubani*. Belgrade, n.d., but 193?. Detailed, but brief discussion of Kuban problems in 1918.

Nesterovich-Berg, M. A. *V bor'be s bol'shevikami*. Paris, 1931.

The New Russia. London, 1920. Weekly publication of the Russian Liberation Committee.

Nizhegorodtsev, A. *Pochemu dobrovol'cheskaia armiia voiuet protiv kommunistov Lenina i Trotskago*. Kharkov, 1919. Osvag pamphlet.

Novaia Zhizn'. Petrograd, 1917. Daily, edited by Gorky.

Novoe Vremia. Petrograd, 1917. Important liberal daily.

Novikov, M. M. *Ot Moskvy do N'iu-Iorka*. New York, 1952.

Oberuchev, K. M. *V dni revoliutsii*. New York, 1919.

Obshchee Delo. Paris. 1919-21. Émigré weekly. V. Burtsev, ed.

Odesskii Listok. Odessa, 1919. Liberal Daily.

Odesskaia Pochta. Odessa. Jan.-Mar. 1919.

Oganovskii, N. P. "Dnevnik chlena uchreditel'nago sobraniia," *Golos Minuvshago*, Nos. 4-6, 1918, pp. 143-72.

Oktiabr' na Kubani i Chernomor'i. Krasnodar, 1924. Essays.

Ot fevralia k oktiabriu v Moskve. Moscow, 1923. Essays and documents.

Otchet o moskovskom soveshchanii obshchestvennykh deiatelei 8-10 avgust 1917. Moscow, 1917. Protocols.

Otdel propagandy osobogo soveshchaniia pri glavno-komanduiushchem vooruzhennymi silami iugoi Rossii. Obzor pechati. n.p., 1919.

Otechestvennyia Vedomosti. Omsk. 1919. Successor to *Russkiia Vedomosti.*

Ovsiannikov, N. N., ed. *Moskva v oktiabre 1917 g.* Moscow, 1919. Documents and memoirs.

Paleologue, M. *An Ambassador's Memoirs.* 3 vols. London, 1923-25.

Parfenov, P. S. *Grazhdanskaia voina v Sibiri 1918-20.* 2nd ed., Moscow, 1925.

"Perepiska Miliukova i Tereshchenko s poslami vremennogo pravitel'-stva," *Bor'ba Klassov,* No. 5, 1931, pp. 84-89.

Peretts, G. G. *V tsitadeli russkoi revoliutsii.* Petrograd, 1917. Notes of a military commander, Feb.-Mar. 1917.

Pervyi vserossiiskii s"ezd sovetov rabochikh i soldatskikh deputatov. 2 vols. Moscow-Leningrad, 1930-31. Steno. reports.

Peshekhonov, A. V. "Pervyia nedeli," *Na Chuzhoi Storone,* No. 1, 1923, pp. 253-319.

Petrogradskii sovet rabochikh i soldatskikh deputatov. Moscow-Leningrad, 1925. Protocols of the Ispolkom sessions.

Piontkovskii, S. A. *Grazhdanskaia voina v Rossii (1918-1921 gg.).* Moscow, 1925. Invaluable documentary collection.

Pokrovskii, M. N., ed. "Iz perepiski V. A. Maklakova s natsional'nym tsentrom v 1919," *Krasnyi Arkhiv,* No. 36, 1929, pp. 3-30.

————. "Ekonomicheskoe polozhenie Rossii pered revoliutsiei," *Krasnyi Arkhiv,* No. 10, 1925, pp. 70-97.

————. "Politicheskoe polozhenie Rossii nakanune fevral'skoi revoliutsii v zhandarmskom osveshchenii," *Krasnyi Arkhiv,* No. 17, 1926, pp. 3-35.

Popov, A., "Inostrannye diplomaty o revoliutsii 1917 g.," *Krasnyi Arkhiv,* No. 24, 1927, pp. 108-63.

Pour la Russie. Paris. 1919-20. Organ of the Left SRs.

Pravitel'stvennyi Vestnik. Omsk. Government daily, July-Nov. 1919 available only.

Priazovskii Krai. Rostov. Oct.-Dec. 1919 only.

Proletarii. Moscow, 1917. Radical Social Democratic daily. Contributors included Gorky.

Promyshlennost' i Torgovlia. Petrograd, 1917. Monthly journal of Trade Industrialists.

Rabochaia Gazeta. Petrograd, 1917. Menshevik daily. Scattered issues available only.

Raenko, Ia. N., comp. *Khronika istoricheskikh sobytii na Donu, Kubani, i Chernomor'e.* (*Mar. 1917-Avr. 1920*). Rostov, 1941.

Raivid, N. and V. Bykov, eds. *Kolchakovshchina.* Ekaterinburg, 1924. Articles and documents.

Rakhmetov, V., ed. "Aprel'skie dni 1917 goda v Petrograde," *Krasnyi Arkhiv,* No. 33, 1929, pp. 34-81.

Rakitnikov, N. I. *Sibirskaia reaktsiia i Kolchak.* Moscow, 1920.

Rakov, D. F. *V zastenkakh Kolchaka.* Paris, 1920. Letters from an SR.

Rakovskii, G. N. *V stane belykh.* Constantinople, 1920.

Ransome, A. *Russia in 1919.* New York, 1919.

Razlozhenie armii v 1917 god. Moscow-Leningrad, 1925. Documents.

Revoliutsiia v Krymu. 9 vols. Simferopol, 1922-30. Articles and documents.

Rezanov, A. S. *Shturmovoi signal P. N. Miliukova.* Paris, 1924. On Miliukov's Nov. 1916 Duma speech.

Rodzianko, M. V. "Gosudarstvennaia duma i fevral'skaia 1917 goda revoliutsiia," *Arkhiv Russkoi Revoliutsii,* vi, 1922, pp. 5-80.

———. "Iz vospominanii," *Byloe,* No. 21, 1923, pp. 218-49.

———. *Reign of Rasputin.* London, 1927.

Romanov, N. V. *Oktiabristy i kadety.* St. Petersburg, 1906.

Rossiia (Velikaia Rossiia). Ekaterinodar, 1919. Anti-Bolshevik daily.

Rozenoer, E. *Germanskaia okkupatsiia Kryma.* Feodosiia, 1919.

Rubinshtein, N. L. *K istorii uchreditel'nogo sobraniia.* Moscow, 1931.

Rudnev, S. P. *Pri vechernikh ogniakh.* Kharbin, 1928. Memoirs.

Russkii Sovet. Paris, 1921. On Wrangel's "Russian Council."

Russkiia Vedomosti. Moscow, 1917. Leading liberal daily.

Russkoe Delo. Omsk. Oct. 1919 only.

Sakharov, K. V. *Belaia Sibir'.* Munich, 1923. Military memoir.

Savenko, A. Iu. *Ukraintsy ili malorussy?* Rostov, 1919. Osvag publication.

Savinkov, B. *Bor'ba s bol'shevikami.* Warsaw, 1920.

———. *Delo Borisa Savinkova.* Moscow, 1924. Articles and abridged transcript of Savinkov's trial.

———. *K delu Kornilova.* Paris, 1919.

Sbornik materialov komiteta moskovskikh obshchestvennykh organizatsii. Moscow, 1917.

Sbornik sekretnykh dokumentov iz arkhiva byvshago ministerstva inostrannykh del. Petrograd, 1917-18.

Sef, S. E. *Burzhuaziia v 1905 godu.* Moscow, 1926.

Seidamet, D. *La Crimée.* Lausanne, 1921.

Serebrennikov, I. I. "Iz istorii sibirskogo pravitel'stva," *Sibirskii Arkhiv,* No. 1, 1929, pp. 5-22.

Serebrennikov, I. I. *K istorii sibirskago pravitel'stva.* Tientsin, 1928.

———. *Moi vospominaniia.* 2 vols. Tientsin, 1937-40.

———. "The Siberian Autonomous Movement and Its Future," *Pacific Historical Review,* III, 1934, pp. 400-415.

Sergeev, A., ed. "Pervaia gosudarstvennaia duma v Vyborge," *Krasnyi Arkhiv,* No. 57, 1933, pp. 85-99.

Shakhanov, N. *1917 god vo vladimirskoi gub. Khronika sobytii.* Vladimir, 1927.

Shchegolev, P. E., ed. *Padenie tsarskogo rezhima.* 7 vols. Moscow, 1924-27.

Shchepkin, G. *A. I. Denikin.* Novocherkassk, 1919. Osvag pamphlet.

Shidlovskii, S. I. *Vospominaniia.* 2 pts. Berlin, 1923.

Shipov, D. N. *Vospominaniia i dumy o perezhitom.* Moscow, 1918.

Shliapnikov, A. *Kanun semnadtsatogo goda.* Moscow, 1920.

———. *Semnadtsatyi god.* 3 bks. Moscow, 1923-27.

Shlikhter, A. G., ed. *Chernaia kniga.* Ekaterinoslav, 1925. Articles, essays, materials on the Ukraine.

Shul'gin, A. (Choulguine). *L'Ukraine contre Moscou—1917.* Paris, 1935.

Shteinberg, I. *Ot fevralia po oktiabr' 1917 g.* Berlin, 1919. Thoughtful analysis.

Shteifon, B. A. *Krizis dobrovol'chestva.* Belgrade, 1928. One of the more interesting military memoirs on South Russia.

Skoropadskii, P. "Uryvok iz 'Spomyniv' Hetmana P. Skoropads'koho," *Khliborobs'ka Ukraina,* bk. 4, 1922-23, pp. 1-40; bk. 5, 1924-25, pp. 31-92.

Slonim, M. "Nashi raznoglasiia," *Volia Rossii,* No. 18, 1923, pp. 33-42.

Smena Vekh. Prague, 1921. Essays.

Sobranie uzakonenii i rasporiazhenii pravitel'stva. Rostov, 1919. Publ. of the Special Council in South Russia.

Sorokin, P. *Leaves from a Russian Diary.* New York, 1924.

———. *A Long Journey.* New Haven, 1963.

Soveshchanie chlenov vserossiiskogo uchreditel'nogo sobraniia. Paris, 1921. On the Jan. 1921 conference.

"Sovet obshchestvennykh deiatelei v Moskve 1917-19 g." *Na Chuzhoi Storone,* No. 9, 1925, pp. 91-103.

Stalinskii, E. "Patriotizm i liberalizm v belom dvizhenii," *Volia Rossii,* Nos. 8-9, 1924, pp. 140-58.

Stankevich, V. B. *Vospominaniia 1914-1919.* Berlin, 1920.

Steklov, Iu. *God bor'by za sotsial'nuiu revoliutsiiu.* Petrograd, 1919.

Stenograficheskii otchet osobago soveshchaniia dlia izgotovleniia proekta polozheniia o vyborakh v uchreditel'noe sobranie. Petrograd, 1917. Sessions 1-11, May 25-June 15.

Stenograficheskii otchet zasedaniia ekonomicheskago soveta pri vremennom pravitel'stve. Nos. 1-8, July 21-Aug. 10, 1917.

Stepanov, P. E. "Nemtsy v Moskve v 1918 (Iz dnevnika)," *Golos Minuvshago na Chuzhoi Storone,* No. 1 (14), 1926, pp. 157-88.

Struggling Russia. London-New York. Weekly. 1919-20. Publ. of the Russian Liberation Committee. Kadet essays.

Struve, P. *Patriotica.* St. Petersburg, 1911. Essays.

————. *Razmyshleniia o russkoi revoliutsii.* Sofia, 1921. Lectures given in Rostov in 1919.

Sukhanov, N. N. *Zapiski o revoliutsii.* 7 vols. Berlin, 1922-23. Superb.

Suvorin, B. *Za rodinoi.* Paris, 1922. Journalistic impressions of South Russia.

Sviatitskii, I. V. *K istorii vserossiiskogo uchreditel'nogo sobraniia.* Moscow, 1921. On the Constituent Assembly and SRs in Siberia, 1918.

Svoboda Rossii. Moscow, Mar.-July 1918. Continuation of *Russkiia Vedomosti.* Most important liberal daily published in Bolshevik Moscow.

Svobodnii Krai. Irkutsk, 1919. Scattered issues.

Trotsky, L. *The History of the Russian Revolution.* trans. M. Eastman, Ann Arbor, 1932. (3 vols. in 1.)

Trubetskaia, O. *Kniaz' S. N. Trubetskoi. Vospominaniia sestry.* New York, 1953.

Tsereteli, I. G., "Rossiiskoe krest'ianstvo i V. M. Chernov v 1917 g.," *Novyi Zhurnal,* No. 29, 1952, pp. 215-44.

————. *Vospominaniia o fevral'shoi revoliutsii.* 2 vols. Paris, 1963. Perhaps the most thoughtful and informative memoir on the first two provisional regimes. Written in the 1920s.

1917 god v Saratove. Saratov. 1927. Essays and material.

"Ufimskoe gosudarstvennoe soveshchanie," *Russkii Istoricheskii Arkhiv,* Sbor. 1, Prague, 1929, pp. 57-280. Protocols of the Ufa conference.

Ul'ianov, A. N. *Pervye demokraticheskie vybory v moskovskuiu gorodskuiu dumu.* Moscow, 1917.

Usov, S. A. *Istoriko-ekonomicheskie ocherki Kryma.* Simferopol, 1925.

Ustinov, S. M. *Zapiski nachal'nika kontr-razvedki.* Berlin, 1923.

Utgov, V. L. "Ufimskoe gosudarstvennoe soveshchanie 1918 goda," *Byloe,* No. 16, 1921, pp. 15-41. Detailed account, focusing on the SRs.

Utro Rossii. Moscow, 1917. Leading conservative-liberal daily.

"V ianvare i fevrale 1917 g." *Byloe,* No. 13 (7), 1918, pp. 91-123. Okhrana reports.

V Moskvu! Rostov. Weekly. Sept. 1919 available only. Reactionary, anti-Semitic.

Vakar, N. P. "Igor Platonovich Demidov (Zhizn' i smert')," *Novyi Zhurnal*, XVI, 1947.

Vardin, I. "Raskol partii kadetov," *Krasnaia Nov'*, No. 3, 1921, pp. 272-84.

Varneck, E., and H. H. Fisher, eds. *Testimony of Kolchak and other Siberian Materials*. Stanford, 1935.

Vasil'ev, N. P. *Pravda o kadetakh*. 2nd ed. St. Petersburg, 1912.

Vechernee Vremia. Rostov daily, 1919-20. Scattered issues. Strong supporter of the White military. Anti-Semitic, anti-Kadet.

Vegman, V. "Kak i pochemu pala v 1918 g. sovetskaia vlast' v Tomske," *Sibirskie Ogni*, Nos. 1-2, 1923, pp. 127-47.

———. "Oblasticheskie illiuzii i vozrozhdennie kolchakovshchiny," *Sibirskie Ogni*, Nos. 5-6, 1923, pp. 140-62.

———. "Oblasticheskie illiuzii, rasseiannye revoliutsiei," *Sibirskie Ogni*, No. 3, 1923, pp. 89-116.

Velikaia oktiabr'skaia sotsialisticheskaia revoliutsiia. Khronika sobytii. 4 vols. Moscow, 1957-61.

Verkhovskii, A. I. *Rossiia na golgofe*. Petrograd, 1918.

Vestnik Vremennago Pravitel'stva. Petrograd. 1917. Organ of the Provisional Government.

Vinnichenko, V. *Vidrodzhennia natsii*. 3 vols. Kiev-Vienna, 1920.

Vishniak, M. *Dva puti*. Paris, 1931. Long, critical essay.

Vladimirskii, M. F., ed. "Moskovskaia gorodskaia duma posle oktiabria," *Krasnyi Arkhiv*, No. 27, 1928, pp. 58-109; No. 28, 1928, pp. 59-106.

Vlast' Naroda, Moscow, 1917. Socialist daily.

Volia Naroda. Petrograd, 1917. Journal of the right SRs.

Volia Rossii. Prague, 1920-21. Organ of émigré SRs.

Volkonsky, P. *The Volunteer Army*. London, 1919.

Vooruzhennye Sily na Iuge Rossii. Osoboe Soveshchanie. Otdel Propagandy. *Biulleten'*. Scattered issues. June-Aug., 1919.

Vpered. Moscow. 1917. Menshevik daily.

Wertheimer, F. *Durch Ukraine und Krim*. Stuttgart, 1918.

Williams, H. *The Spirit of the Russian Revolution*. London, 1919. Russian Liberation Committee pamphlet.

Woytinsky, W. S. *Stormy Passage*. New York, 1961.

Wrangel, P. N. *Always with Honor*. New York, 1957. First published in 1930 as *The Memoirs of General Wrangel*.

Zapiski Instituta Izucheniia Rossii. Prague, 1925. Essays by Peshekhonov, Shreider, Chernov, others.

Zeman, Z.A.B., ed. *Germany and the Revolution in Russia 1915-1918*. London, 1958. Documents.

Zemlia i Volia. Moscow. 1917. "Peasant journal" of the SRs. Daily.

Zenzinov, V. "Fevral'skie dni," *Novyi Zhurnal*, No. 34, 1953, pp. 188-211; No. 35, 1953, pp. 208-40.

———, ed. *Gosudarstvennyi perevorot admirala Kolchaka v Omske.* Paris, 1919. Documents and materials.

———. *Iz zhizni revoliutsionera.* Paris, 1919.

Zhurnal Petrogradskoi Gorodskoi Dumy. Petrograd, 1917.

Zhurnaly Zasedanii Vremennago Pravitel'stva. Petrograd, 1917.

IV. SECONDARY STUDIES

Adamovich, G. V. *Vasilii Alekseevich Maklakov.* Paris, 1959. Sympathetic.

Alekseev, V. N. *Grazhdanskaia voina v TsChO.* Voronezh, 1930.

Andreev, A. M. *Sovety rabochikh i soldatskikh deputatov nakanune oktiabria.* Moscow, 1967. English translation, 1971.

Angarskii, N. *Moskovskii sovet v dvukh revoliutsiiakh.* Moscow, 1928.

Ascher, A. "The Kornilov Affair," *Russian Review*, XII, 1953, pp. 235-52.

Asher, H. "The Kornilov Affair: A Reinterpretation," *Russian Review*, XXIX, 1970, pp. 286-300.

Avrekh, A. Ia. *Stolypin i tret'ia duma.* Moscow, 1968.

———. *Tsarizm i tret'eiiun'skaia sistema.* Moscow, 1966.

Avrich, P. *Kronstadt, 1921.* Princeton, 1970.

———. "Russian Factory Committees in 1917," *Jahrbücher für Geschichte Osteuropas*, XI, 1953, pp. 161-82.

Baumgart, W. *Deutsche Ost-politik 1918.* Munich, 1966.

Belokonskii, I. P. *Zemstvo i konstitutsiia.* Moscow, 1910.

———. *Zemskoe dvizhenie.* 2nd ed. Moscow, 1914.

Benjamin, A. "The Great Dilemma: The Foreign Policy of the Russian Provisional Government. March-May 1917," Dissertation, Columbia University, 1950.

Berlin, P. A. *Russkaia burzhuaziia v staroe i novoe vremia.* Moscow, 1922.

Borman, A. *A. V. Tyrkova-Vil'iams.* Washington, 1964. By her son.

Bosh, E. G. *God bor'by.* Moscow-Leningrad, 1925. On the Ukraine.

Boyd, J. R. "The Origins of Order No. 1," *Soviet Studies*, XIX, 1968, pp. 359-72.

Bradley, J.F.N. *La Légion tchécoslovaque en Russie, 1914-20.* Paris, 1965.

Brinkley, G. A. *The Volunteer Army and Allied Intervention in South Russia, 1917-1921.* Notre Dame, 1966.

Bunegin, M. F. *Revoliutsiia i grazhdanskaia voina v Krymu 1917-20.* Simferopol, 1927.

Burdzhalov, E. N. *Vtoraia russkaia revoliutsiia. (Moskva, front, peri-feriia).* Moscow, 1971.

————. *Vtoraia russkaia revoliutsiia. (Vosstanie v Petrograde).* Moscow, 1967.

Buryshkin, P. A. *Moskva kupecheskaia.* New York, 1954.

Carr, E. H. *The Bolshevik Revolution, 1917-1923.* 3 vols. New York, 1951-53.

Chaadaeva, O. N. *Pomeshchiki i ikh organizatsii v 1917 godu.* Moscow-Leningrad, 1928. Informative.

Chamberlin, W. H. *The Russian Revolution.* 2 vols. New York, 1935. Still the best general account.

Chermenskii, E. D. *Burzhuaziia i tsarizm v revoliutsii 1905-07 gg.* Leningrad-Moscow, 1939. Superior in some ways to recent 2nd ed.

————. "Kadety nakanune fevral'skoi burzhuazno-demokraticheskoi revoliutsii 1917 goda," *Istoricheskii Zhurnal,* No. 3, 1941, pp. 35-45.

Crisp, O. "The Russian Liberals and the Anglo-French Loan to Russia," *Slavonic and East European Review,* xxix, 1961, pp. 497-511.

Curtiss, J. S. *The Russian Revolutions of 1917.* Princeton, 1957.

Daniels, R. V. *Red October.* New York, 1967.

Diakin, V. S. *Russkaia burzhuaziia i tsarizm v gody pervoi mirovoi voiny. 1914-1917.* Leningrad, 1967.

Dolenga, S. *Skoropadshchyna.* Warsaw, 1934. Critical.

Dubrowski, S. *Die Bauernbewegung in der russischen Revolution 1917.* Berlin, 1929.

Dumova, A. "Maloizvestnye materialy po istorii kornilovshchiny," *Voprosy Istorii,* No. 11, 1968, pp. 69-93.

Egorov, A. I. *Razgrom Denikina.* Moscow, 1931. Good military history.

Fedyshyn, O. S. *Germany's Drive to the East and the Ukrainian Revolution.* New Brunswick, N.J., 1971.

Feldman, R. "Between War and Revolution. The Russian General Staff, February-July, 1917," Dissertation, Indiana University, 1967.

Ferro, M. *La Révolution de 1917.* Paris, 1967.

————. "The Russian Soldier in 1917: Undisciplined, Patriotic, and Revolutionary," *Slavic Review,* xxx, 1971, pp. 483-512.

Figurovskaia, N. K. "Bankrotstvo 'agrarnoi reformy' burzhuaznogo vremennogo pravitel'stva," *Istoricheskie Zapiski,* No. 81, 1968, pp. 23-67.

Fischer, G. *Russian Liberalism.* Cambridge, Mass., 1958.

Galai, S. *The Liberation Movement in Russia 1900-1905.* Cambridge, 1973.

Gaponenko, L. S. "Rabochii klass Rossii nakanune velikogo oktiabria," *Istoricheskie Zapiski,* No. 73, 1963, pp. 35-89.

————. *Rabochii klass Rossii v 1917 godu.* Moscow, 1970.

Garmiza, V. V. "Bankrotstvo politiki 'tret'ego puti' v revoliutsii (Ufim-skoe gosudarstvennoe soveshchanie)," *Istoriia SSSR*, No. 6, 1965, pp. 3-25.

Gindin, I. F. "Russkaia burzhuaziia v period kapitalizma," *Istoriia SSSR*, No. 2, 1963, pp. 57-80; No. 3, 1963, pp. 37-60.

Glenny, M. V. "The Anglo-Soviet Trade Agreement, March 1921," *Journal of Contemporary History*, v, 1970, pp. 63-82.

Golikov, G. N. and Iu. S. Tokarev. "Aprel'skii krizis 1917 g.," *Istoriche-skie Zapiski*, No. 57, 1956, pp. 35-79.

Gukovskii, A. I. *Frantsuzskaia interventsiia na iuge Rossii, 1918-19*. Moscow, 1928.

Gusev, K., *Krakh partii levykh eserov*. Moscow, 1963.

Haimson, L. "The Problem of Social Stability in Urban Russia, 1905-1917," *Slavic Review*, xxiii, 1964, pp. 619-42; xxiv, 1965, pp. 1-22.

Hasegawa, T. "The February Revolution," Dissertation, University of Washington, 1969.

Ignat'ev, A. V. *Russko-angliiskie otnosheniia nakanune oktiabr'skoi revoliutsii*. Moscow, 1966.

Ivanov, N. Ia. *Kornilovshchina i ee razgrom*. Leningrad, 1965.

Kakurin, N. E. *Kak srazhalas' revoliutsiia*. 2 vols. Moscow, 1925-26.

Kapustin, M. I. *Zagovor generalov*. Moscow, 1968. On Kornilov.

Katkov, G. *Russia 1917. The February Revolution*. New York, 1966.

Kenez, P. *Civil War in South Russia, 1918*. Berkeley, 1971.

Kennan, G. F. *Soviet-American Relations, 1917-1920*. 2 vols. Princeton, 1956-58.

Kin, D. *Denikinshchina*. Leningrad, 1927. The best Soviet account.

Kirimal, E. *Der nationale Kampf der Krimtürken*. Emsdetten, W. Germany, 1952.

Kochan, L. "Kadet Policy in 1917 and the Constituent Assembly," *Slavonic and East European Review*, xlv, 1967, pp. 183-92.

Komin, V. V. *Bankrotstvo burzhuaznykh i melkoburzhuaznykh partii Rossii v period podgotovki i pobedy velikoi oktiabr'skoi sotsialisti-cheskoi revoliutsii*. Moscow, 1965.

Krivosheina, E. P. *Dve demonstratsii Iiun' 1917*. Moscow-Leningrad, 1931.

Laverychev, V. Ia. "Antirabochie soiuzy kapitalistov v 1917 g.," *Vestnik Moskovskogo Universiteta. Ser. IX. Istoriia*. No. 5, 1960, pp. 26-41.

———. *Po tu storony barrikad*. Moscow, 1967.

———. "Russkie monopolisty i zagovor Kornilova," *Voprosy Istorii*, No. 4, 1964, pp. 32-44.

———. "Vserossiiskii soiuz torgovli i promyshlennosti," *Istoricheskie Zapiski*, No. 70, 1961, pp. 35-60.

Lavygin, B. M. *1917 god v voronezhskoi gubernii*. Voronezh, 1928.

Lednitskii, V. "Vokrug V. A. Maklakova," *Novyi Zhurnal*, No. 56, 1959, pp. 222-50.

Leontovitsch, V. *Geschichte des Liberalismus in Russland*. Frankfurt, 1957.

Levin, A. *The Second Duma*. New Haven, 1940.

Longley, D. A. "Divisions in the Bolshevik Party in March 1917," *Soviet Studies*, xxiv, 1972, pp. 61-76.

Lozinski, Z. *Ekonomicheskaia politika vremennogo pravitel'stva*. Leningrad, 1929.

Mal't, M. "Denikinshchina i krest'ianstvo," *Proletarskaia Revoliutsiia*, No. 1 (24), 1924, pp. 140-57; No. 4 (27), 1924, pp. 144-77.

———. Denikinshchina i rabochie," *Proletarskaia Revoliutsiia*, No. 5 (28), 1924, pp. 64-85.

Martynov, E. I. *Kornilov*. Leningrad, 1927. Thorough.

McNeail, R. H. "The Conference of Jassy: An Early Fiasco of the Anti-Bolshevik Movement," in J. S. Curtiss, ed. *Essays in Russian and Soviet History in Honor of G. T. Robinson*. New York, 1963, pp. 221-36.

Mech, V. et al. *Bor'ba obshchestvennykh sil v russkoi revoliutsii. Vyp. IV. Liberal'naia i demokraticheskaia burzhuaziia*. Moscow, 1907.

Mehlinger, H., and J. M. Thompson. *Count Witte And the Tsarist Government in the 1905 Revolution*. Bloomington, Ind., 1972.

Mel'gunov, S. P. *Grazhdanskaia voina v osveshchenii P. N. Miliukova*. Paris, 1929. Critical essay.

———. *Kak bol'sheviki zakhvatili vlast'*. Paris, 1953.

———. *Martovskie dni 1917 goda*. Paris, 1961.

———. *Na putiakh k dvortsovomu perevorotu*. Paris,1931.

———. *N. V. Chaikovskii v gody grazhdanskoi voiny*. Paris, 1929.

———. "Sud istorii nad intelligentsiei," *Na Chuzhoi Storone*, No. 3, 1923, pp. 137-63.

———. *Tragediia admirala Kolchaka*. 3 vols. Belgrade, 1930-31. Detailed.

Miller, V. I. "Nachalo demokratizatsii staroi armii v dni fevral'skoi revoliutsii," *Istoriia SSSR*, No. 6, 1966, pp. 26-43.

Moiseeva, O. N. *Sovety krest'ianskikh deputatov v 1917 godu*. Moscow, 1967.

Nadinskii, P. N. *Ocherki po istorii Kryma*. Simferopol, 1957.

Oldenburg, S. *Tsarstvovanie imperator Nikolaia II*. 2 vols. Munich, 1939-49.

Pares, B. *The Fall of the Russian Monarchy*. New York, 1939.

Pavlovsky, G. *Agricultural Russia on the Eve of the Revolution*. New York, 1968. Originally published in 1930.

Pershin, P. N. *Agrarnaia revoliutsiia v Rossii*. 2 vols. Moscow, 1966.

Pethybridge, R. *The Spread of the Russian Revolution*. London, 1972.

Pichon, Colonel. "Le coup d'état de l'amiral Kolchak," *Le Monde Slave*, No. 1, 1925, pp. 1-26; No. 2, 1925, pp. 248-70.

Pipes, R. *The Formation of the Soviet Union*. Cambridge, Mass., 1954.

Pogrebinskii, A. P. "Voenno-promyshlennye komitety," *Istoricheskie Zapiski*, No. 11, 1941, pp. 160-200.

Pokrovskii, G. *Denikinshchina*. Berlin, 1923.

Polner, T. I. *Zhizhnennyi put' kniazia G. E. L'vova*. Paris, 1922.

Rabinowitch, Alexander. *Prelude to Revolution*. Bloomington, Ind., 1968.

Radkey, Oliver H. *Agrarian Foes of Bolshevism*. New York, 1958.

———. *The Elections to the Russian Constituent Assembly of 1917*. Cambridge, Mass. 1950.

———. *Sickle Under the Hammer*. New York, 1963.

Ratgauzer, Ia. A. *Revoliutsiia i grazhdanskaia voina v Baku*. Baku, 1927.

Reikhardt, V. V. "Russkaia burzhuaziia v bor'be za sokhranenie ekonomicheskogo gospodstva." *Krasnaia Letopis'*, No. 1 (34), 1930, pp. 4-41.

Reshetar, J. S., Jr. *The Ukrainian Revolution, 1917-1920*. Princeton, 1952.

Riha, T. "Miliukov and the Progressive Bloc in 1915," *Journal of Modern History*, XXXII, 1960, pp. 16-24.

———. *A Russian European. Paul Miliukov in Russian Politics*. Notre Dame, 1967.

Rimscha, H. *Der russische Burgerkrieg und die russische Emigration, 1917-1921*. Jena, 1924.

———. *Russland jenseits der Grenzen*. Jena, 1927.

Roosa, R. A. "Russian Industrialists and 'State Socialism,' 1906-17," *Soviet Studies*, XXIII, 1972, pp. 395-417.

Rosenberg, W. G. "Les Libéraux russes et le changement du pouvoir en mars, 1917," *Cahiers du Monde Russe et Soviétique*, IX, 1968, pp. 46-57.

———. "Russian Liberals and the Bolshevik Coup," *Journal of Modern History*, XL, 1968, pp. 328-47.

———. "Russian Municipal Duma Elections of 1917: A Preliminary Computation of Returns," *Soviet Studies*, XXI, 1969, pp. 131-63.

Schapiro, L. *The Origin of the Communist Autocracy*. Cambridge, Mass., 1956.

———. "The *Vekhi* Group and the Mystique of Revolution," *Slavonic and East European Review*, XXXIV, 1955-56, pp. 56-76.

Serge, V. *Year One of the Russian Revolution*. New York, 1972. First published in 1930.

Shatilova, T. "Petrogradskaia krupnaia burzhuaziia mezhdu dvumia revoliutsiiami 1917," *Krasnaia Letopis'*, No. 6, 1926.

Shchestakov, A. V., ed. *Sovety krest'ianskikh deputatov i drugie krest'ianskie organizatsii.* Moscow, 1929.

Slavin, N. F. "Krizis vlasti v sentiabre 1917 g. i obrazovanie vremennogo soveta respubliki (predparlament)," *Istoricheskie Zapiski*, No. 61, 1957, pp. 31-65.

Smith, C. J. *The Russian Struggle for Power, 1914-1917.* New York, 1956.

Smith, N. "The Constitutional Democratic Movement in Russia, 1902-1906," Dissertation, University of Illinois, 1958.

Solov'ev, O. F. *Velikii oktiabr' i ego protivniki.* Moscow, 1968.

Sovety v pervyi god proletarskoi diktatury. Moscow, 1967.

Spirin, L. M. *Klassy i partii v grazhdanskoi voine v Rossii.* Moscow, 1966.

———. *Razgrom armii Kolchaka.* Moscow, 1957. Good bibliography.

Stal'nyi V. *Kadety.* Kharkov, 1929.

Stewart, G. *The White Armies of Russia.* New York, 1933.

Strakhovsky, L. I. "Was there a Kornilov Rebellion?" *The Slavonic and East European Review*, XXXIII, 1955, pp. 372-95.

Suny, R. G. *The Baku Commune, 1917-1918.* Princeton, 1973.

Suprunenko, N. I. *Ocherki istorii grazhdanskoi voiny i inostrannoi voennoi interventsii na Ukraine.* Moscow, 1966.

Thompson, J. M. *Russia, Bolshevism and the Versailles Peace.* Princeton, 1966.

Timberlake, C., ed. *Essays on Russian Liberalism.* Columbia, Mo., 1972.

Tuck, R. "Paul Miliukov and Negotiations for a Duma Ministry," *American Slavic and East European Review*, X, 1951, pp. 117-29.

Treadgold, D. W. "The Constitutional Democrats and the Russian Liberal Tradition," *Slavic Review*, X, 1951, pp. 85-94.

———. "Ideology of the White Movement: Wrangel's Leftist Policy from Rightist Hands,'" *Harvard Slavic Studies*, Vol. 4, 1957, pp. 481-98.

———. *Lenin and His Rivals.* New York, 1955.

Ullman, R. H. *Britain and the Russian Civil War.* Princeton, 1968.

———. *Intervention and the War.* Princeton, 1961.

Vasil'ev, A. "Pervaia sovetskaia vlast' v Krymu i ee padenie," *Proletarskaia Revoliutsiia*, No. 7, 1922, pp. 3-58.

Vasiukov, V. S. *Vneshniaia politika vremennogo pravitel'stva.* Moscow, 1966.

Veselovskii, B. *Istoriia zemstva.* 4 vols. St. Petersburg, 1909-11.

Vladimirov, A. "Burzhuaziia mezhdu dvumia revoliutsiiami," *Problemy Marksizma*, Nos. 8-9, 1931, pp. 136-60.

Vladimirova, V. *God sluzhby 'sotsialistov' kapitalistam*. Moscow-Leningrad, 1927.

———. *Kontr-revoliutsiia v 1917*. Moscow, 1924. On Kornilov.

Vladimirskii, M. "Moskovskie raionnye dumy i sovet raionnykh dum v 1917-1918 gg.," *Proletarskaia Revoliutsiia*, No. 8 (20), 1923, pp. 79-94.

Volobuev, P. V. *Ekonomicheskaia politika vremennogo pravitel'stva*. Moscow, 1962.

———. "Ekonomicheskaia programma burzhuazii v vremennogo pravitel'stva," *Istoricheskie Zapiski*, No. 67, 1960, pp. 19-76.

———. "Monopolisticheskaia burzhuaziia i vremennoe pravitel'stvo," *Monopoli i inostrannyi kapital v Rossii*. Moscow-Leningrad, 1962, pp. 240-73.

———. "Politika burzhuazii i vremennogo pravitel'stva v rabochem voprose," *Istoricheskie Zapiski*, No. 73, 1963, pp. 127-55.

———. "Predprinimatel'skie organizatsii russkoi burzhuazii v dni Oktiabria," *Istoricheskii Arkhiv*, No. 3, 1959, pp. 205-08.

———. *Proletariat i burzhuaziia Rossii v 1917 g*. Moscow, 1964.

Von Laue, T. "Westernization, Revolution and the Search for a Basis of Authority—Russia in 1917," *Soviet Studies*, XIX, 1967, pp. 156-80.

Wade, R. A. "Irakli Tsereteli and Siberian Zimmerwaldism," *Journal of Modern History*, XXXIX, 1967, pp. 425-31.

———. *The Russian Search for Peace. February-October, 1917*. Stanford, 1969.

Warth, R. D. *Allies and the Russian Revolution*. Durham, N.C. 1954.

Wettig, G. "Die Rolle der russischen Armee im revolutionären Machtkampf 1917," *Forschungen zur osteuropäischen Geschichte*, XII, 1967, pp. 46-389.

White, J. D. "The Kornilov Affair: A Study in Counter-Revolution," *Soviet Studies*, XX, 1968, pp. 187-205.

Wildman, A. "The February Revolution in the Russian Army," *Soviet Studies*, XXII, 1970, pp. 3-21.

Zimmerman, J. E. "Between Revolution and Reaction. The Constitutional Democratic Party, October 1905 to June 1907," Diss., Columbia University, 1967.

STUDIES OF THE RUSSIAN INSTITUTE

PUBLISHED BY COLUMBIA UNIVERSITY PRESS

THAD PAUL ALTON, *Polish Postwar Economy*

JOHN A. ARMSTRONG, *Ukrainian Nationalism*

ABRAM BERGSON, *Soviet National Income and Product in 1937*

EDWARD J. BROWN, *The Proletarian Episode in Russian Literature*

HARVEY L. DYCK, *Weimar Germany and Soviet Russia, 1926-1933: A Study in Diplomatic Instability*

RALPH TALCOTT FISHER, JR., *Pattern for Soviet Youth: A Study of the Congresses of the Komsomol, 1918-1954*

MAURICE FRIEDBERG, *Russian Classics in Soviet Jackets*

ELLIOT R. GOODMAN, *The Soviet Design for a World State*

DAVID GRANICK, *Management of the Industrial Firm in the USSR: A Study in Soviet Economic Planning*

THOMAS TAYLOR HAMMOND, *Lenin on Trade Unions and Revolution, 1893-1917*

JOHN N. HAZARD, *Settling Disputes in Soviet Society: The Formative Years of Legal Institutions*

DAVID JORAVSKY, *Soviet Marxism and Natural Science, 1917-1932*

DAVID MARSHALL LANG, *The Last Years of the Georgian Monarchy, 1658-1832*

GEORGE S.N. LUCKYJ, *Literary Politics in the Soviet Ukraine, 1917-1934*

HERBERT MARCUSE, *Soviet Marxism: A Critical Analysis*

KERMIT E. MC KENZIE, *Comintern and World Revolution, 1928-1943: The Shaping of Doctrine*

CHARLES B. MC LANE, *Soviet Policy and the Chinese Communists, 1931-1946*

JAMES WILLIAM MORLEY, *The Japanese Thrust into Siberia, 1918*

ALEXANDER G. PARK, *Bolshevism in Turkestan, 1917-1927*

MICHAEL BORO PETROVICH, *The Emergence of Russian Panslavism, 1856-1870*

OLIVER H. RADKEY, *The Agrarian Foes of Bolshevism: Promise and Default of the Russian Socialist Revolutionaries, February to October, 1917*

OLIVER H. RADKEY, *The Sickle Under the Hammer: The Russian Socialist Revolutionaries in the Early Months of Soviet Rule*

ALFRED J. RIEBER, *Stalin and the French Communist Party, 1941-1947*

ALFRED ERICH SENN, *The Emergence of Modern Lithuania*

ERNEST J. SIMMONS, editor, *Through the Glass of Soviet Literature: Views of Russian Society*

THEODORE K. VON LAUE, *Sergei Witte and the Industrialization of Russia*

ALLEN S. WHITING, *Soviet Policies in China, 1917-1924*

PUBLISHED BY TEACHERS COLLEGE PRESS

HAROLD J. NOAH, *Financing Soviet Schools*

PUBLISHED BY PRINCETON UNIVERSITY PRESS

PAUL AVRICH, *The Russian Anarchists*
PAUL AVRICH, *Kronstadt 1921*
EDWARD J. BROWN, *Mayakovsky: A Poet in the Revolution*
LOREN R. GRAHAM, *The Soviet Academy of Sciences and the Communist Party, 1927-1932*
PATRICIA K. GRIMSTED, *Archives and Manuscript Repositories in the USSR: Moscow and Leningrad*
ROBERT A. MAGUIRE, *Red Virgin Soil: Soviet Literature in the 1920's*
T. H. RIGBY, *Communist Party Membership in the U.S.S.R., 1917-1918*
RONALD G. SUNY, *The Baku Commune, 1917-1918*
JOHN M. THOMPSON, *Russia, Bolshevism, and the Versailles Peace*
WILLIAM ZIMMERMAN, *Soviet Perspectives on International Relations, 1956-1967*

PUBLISHED BY CAMBRIDGE UNIVERSITY PRESS

JONATHAN FRANKEL, *Vladimir Akimov on the Dilemmas of Russian Marxism, 1895-1903*
EZRA MENDELSOHN, *Class Struggle in the Pale: The Formative Years of the Jewish Workers' Movement in Tsarist Russia*

PUBLISHED BY THE UNIVERSITY OF MICHIGAN PRESS

RICHARD T. DE GEORGE, *Soviet Ethics and Morality*

Library of Congress Cataloging in Publication Data

Rosenberg, William G
  Liberals in the Russian Revolution; the Constitutional Democratic Party, 1917-
1921.

  (Studies of the Russian Institute, Columbia University)
  Bibliography: p.
  1. Konstitutsionno-demokraticheskaia partiia. 2. Russia—History—Revolution,
1917-1921. I. Title. II. Series: Columbia University. Russian Institute.
Studies.
JN6598.K95R67   329.9'47   73-21931
ISBN 0-691-05221-2
ISBN 0-691-10023-3 (pbk)